I0715419

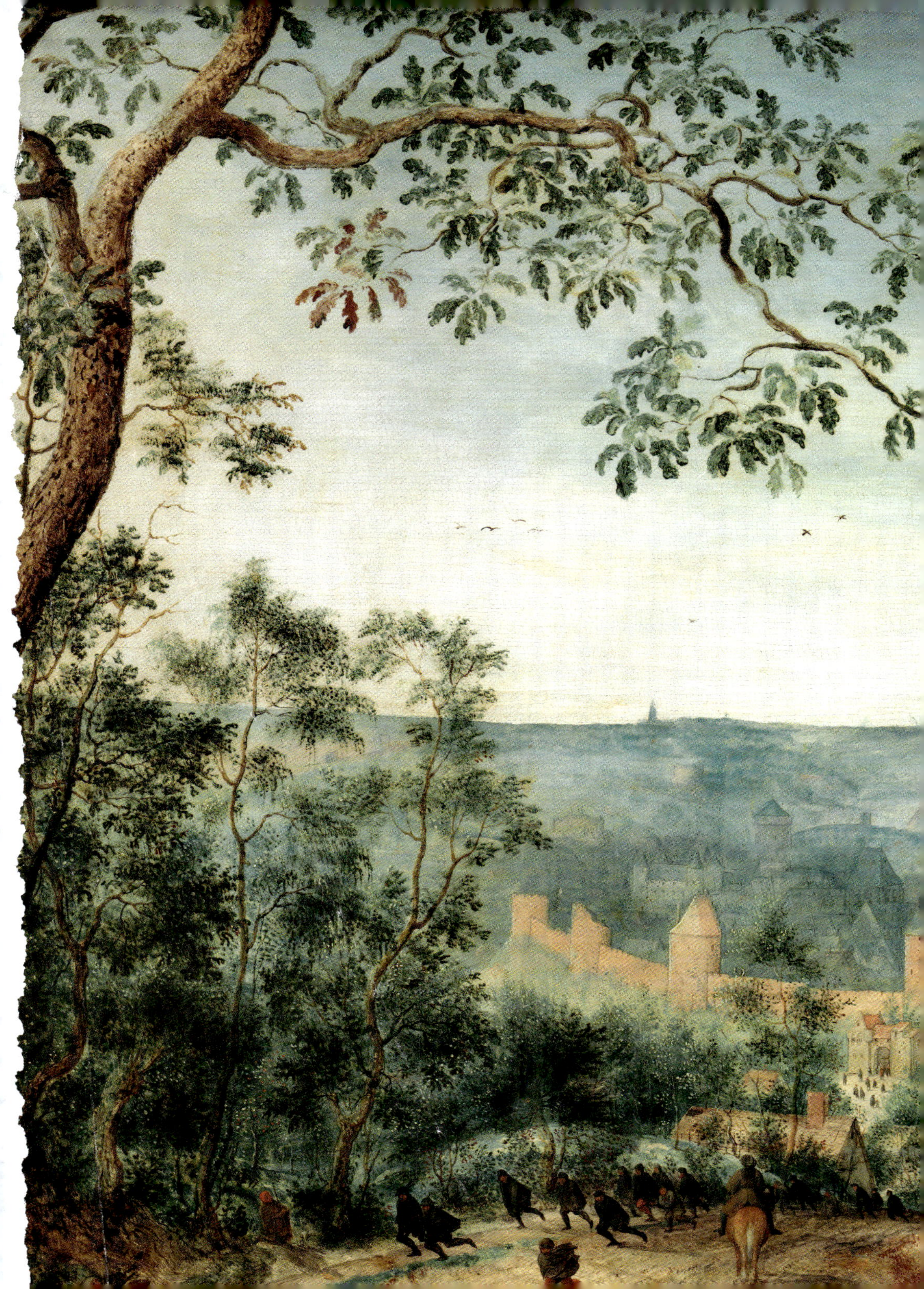

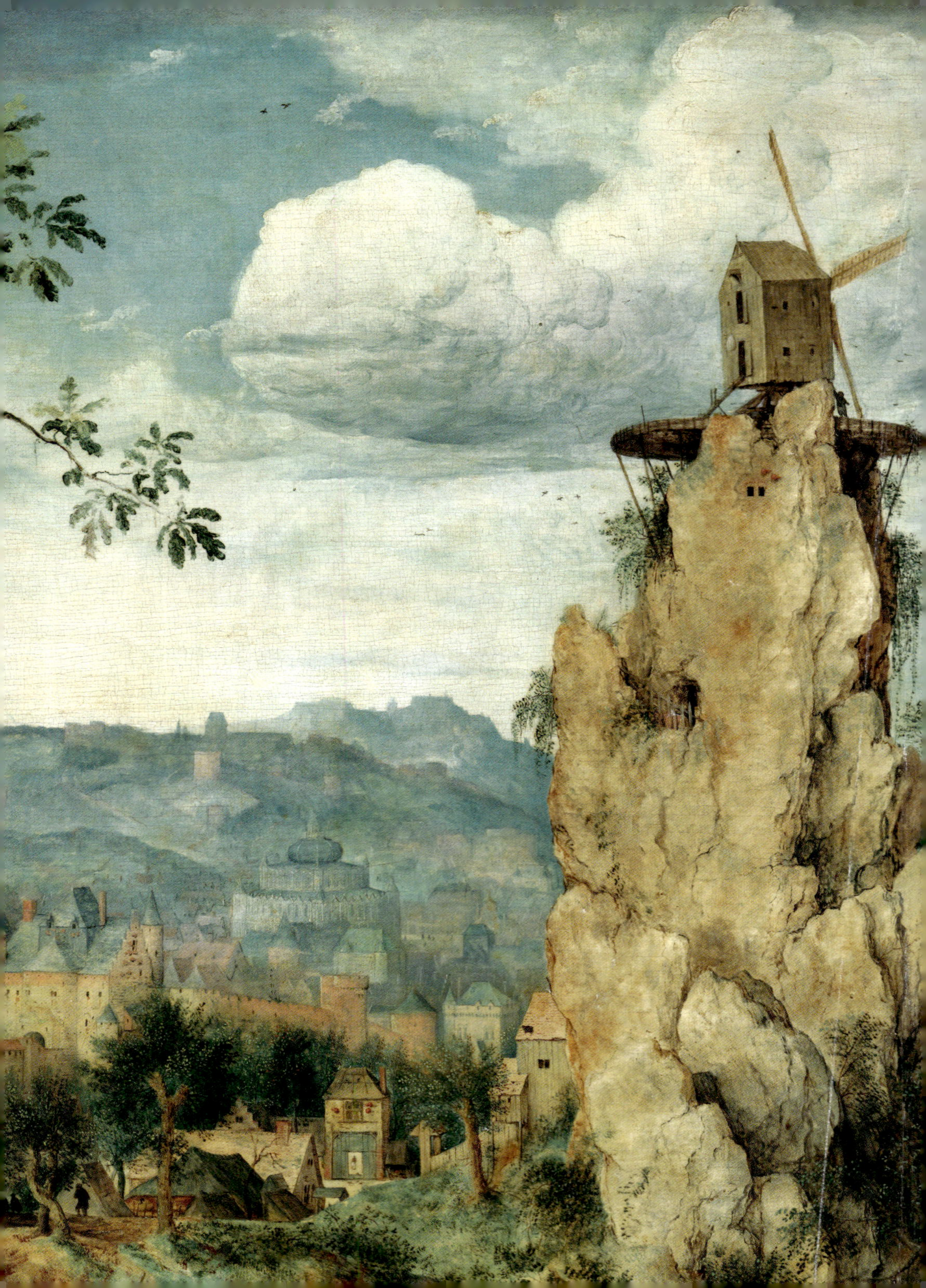

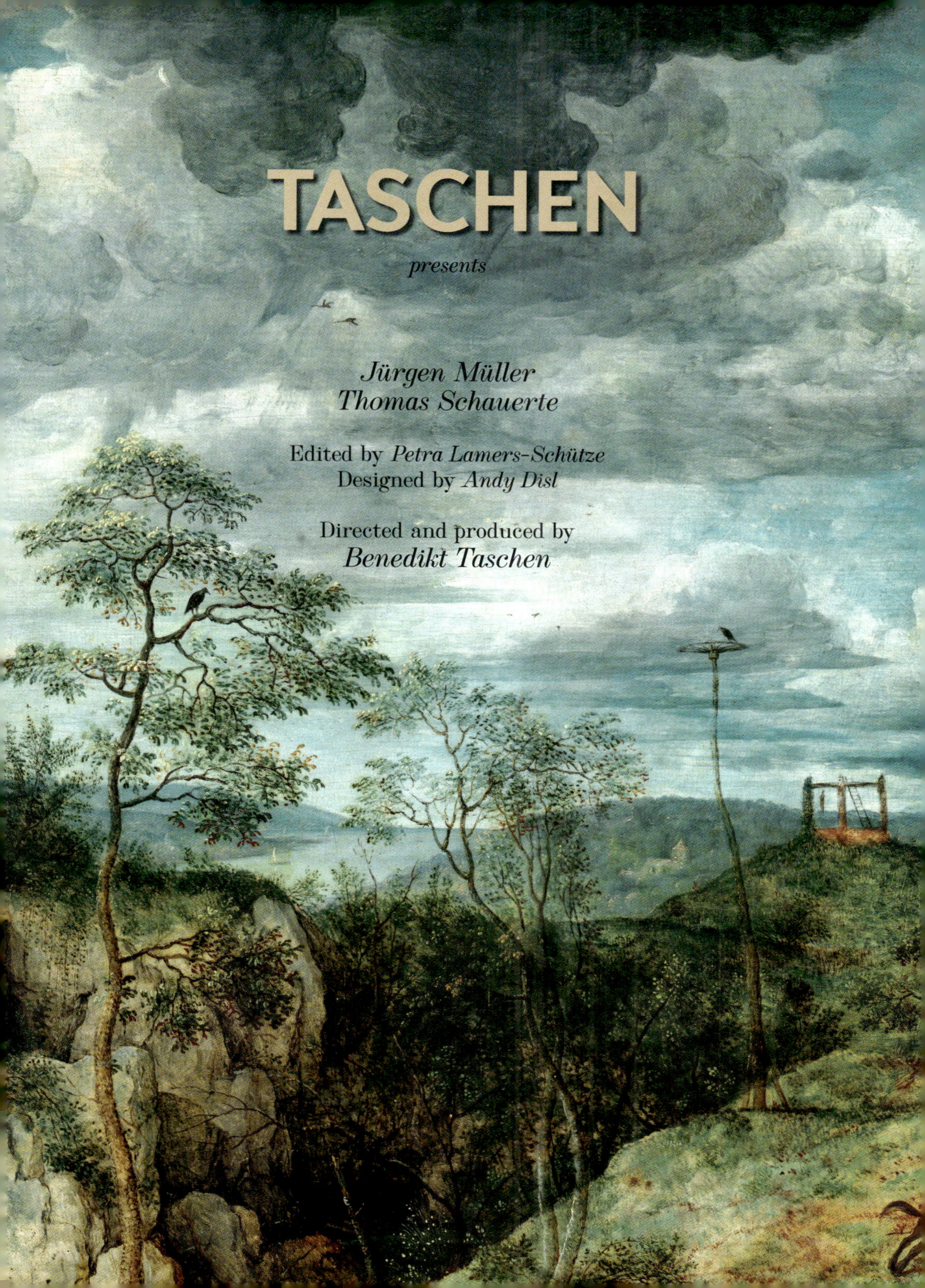

TASCHEN
presents

Jürgen Müller
Thomas Schauerte

Edited by Petra Lamers-Schütze
Designed by Andy Disl

Directed and produced by
Benedikt Taschen

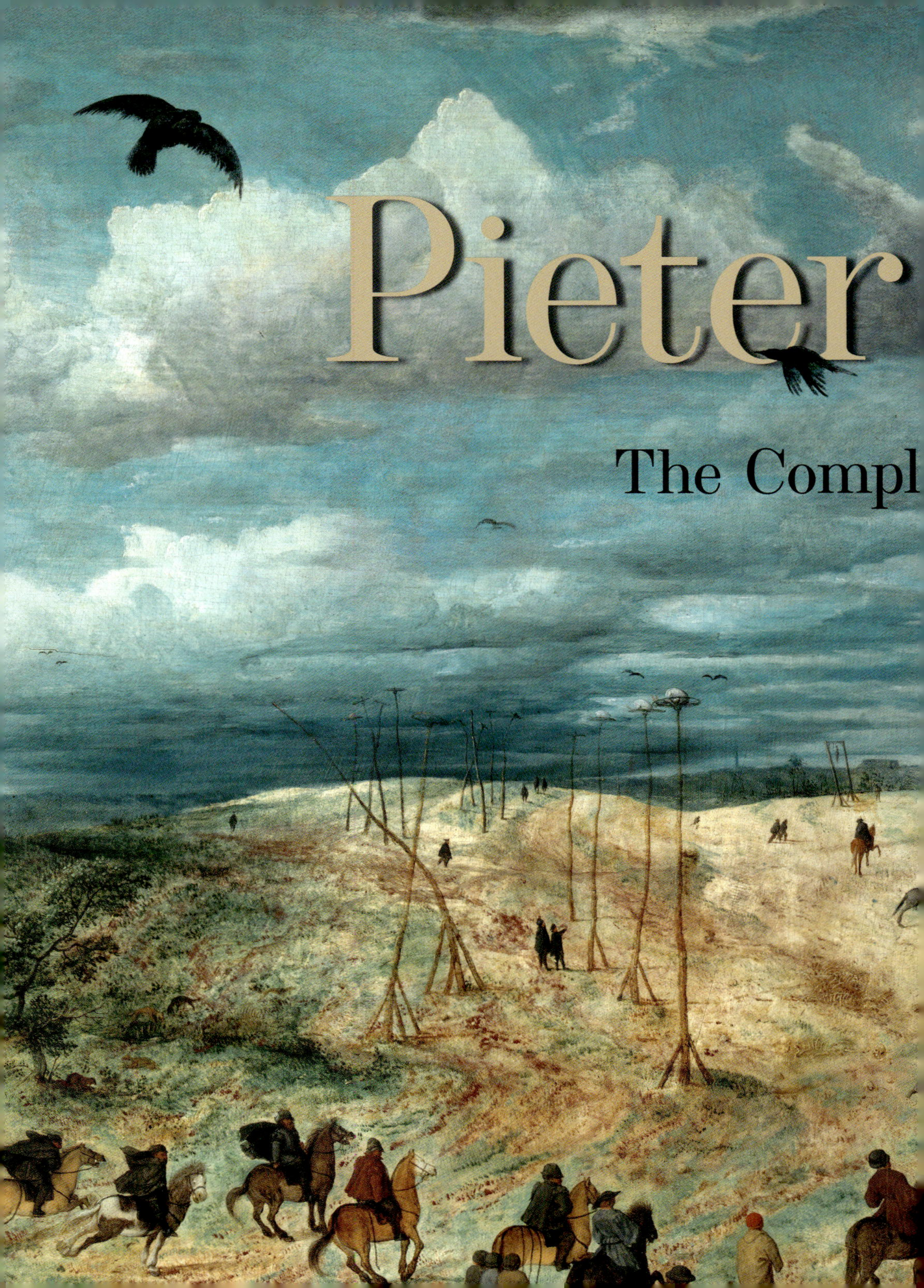

Pieter
The Compl

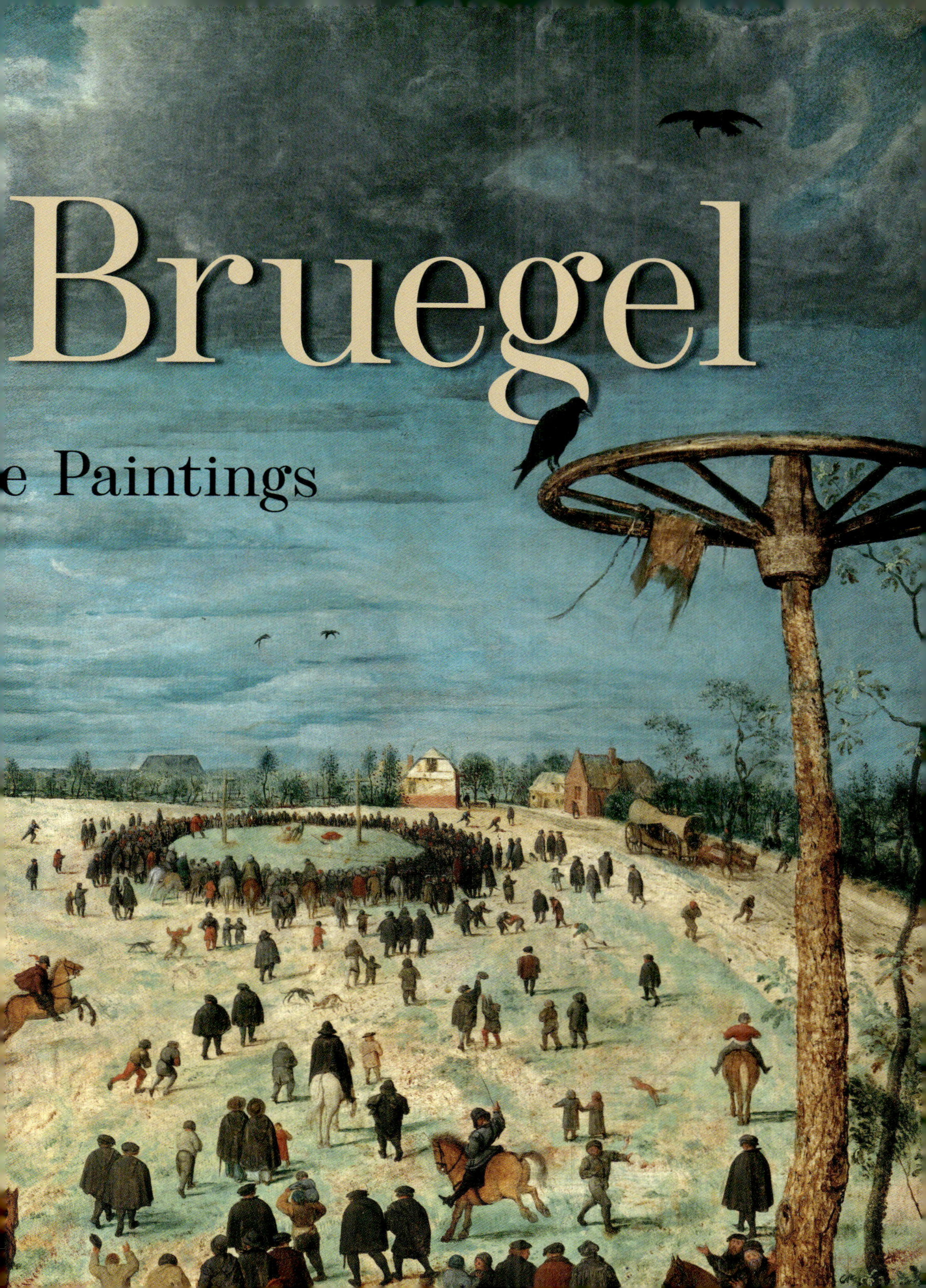

Bruegel
e Paintings

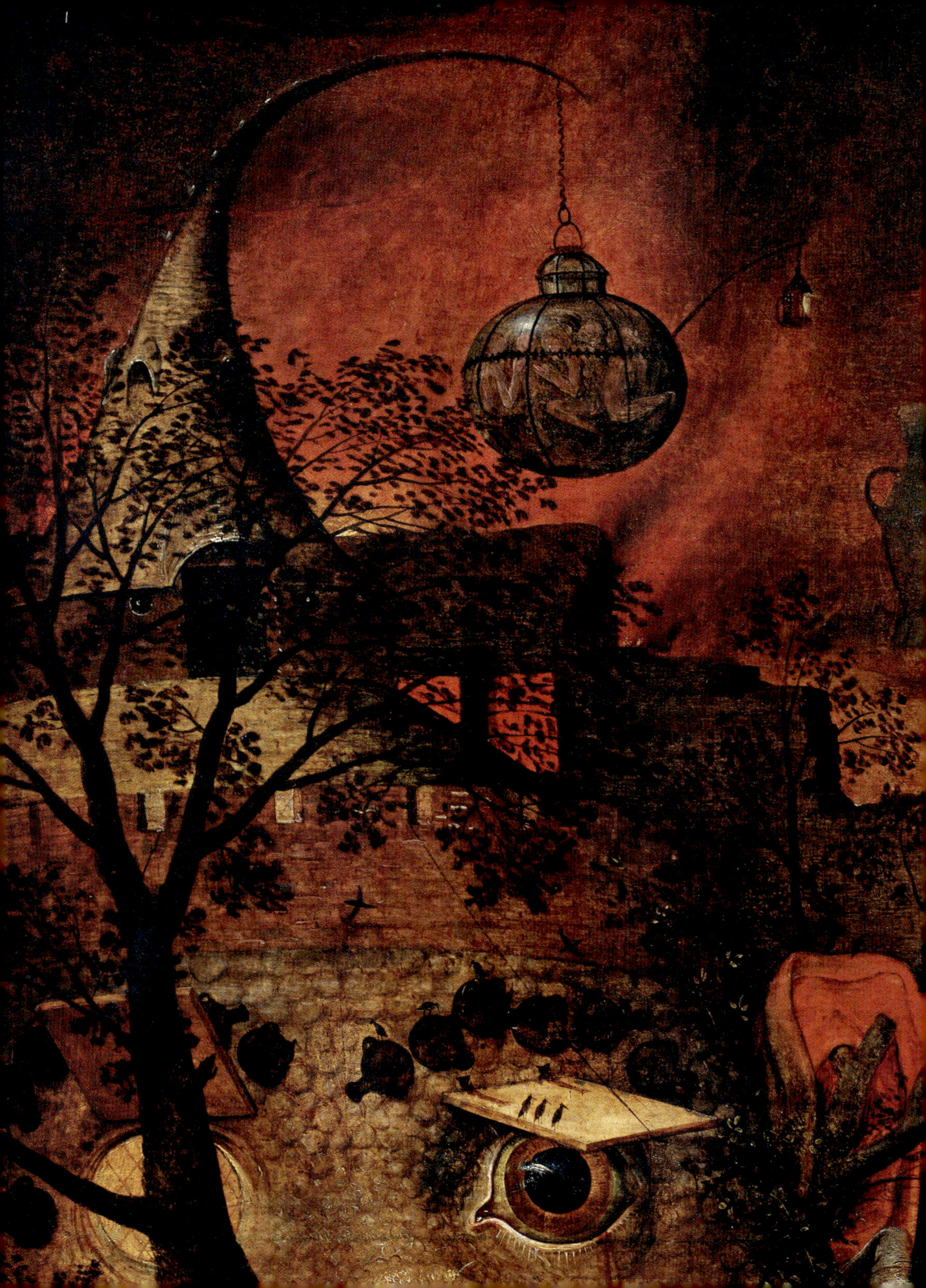

Contents

Pages 6, 8, 13
Dulle Griet (Dull Gret; details), 1563
(see ill. pp. 204/205)

Contents

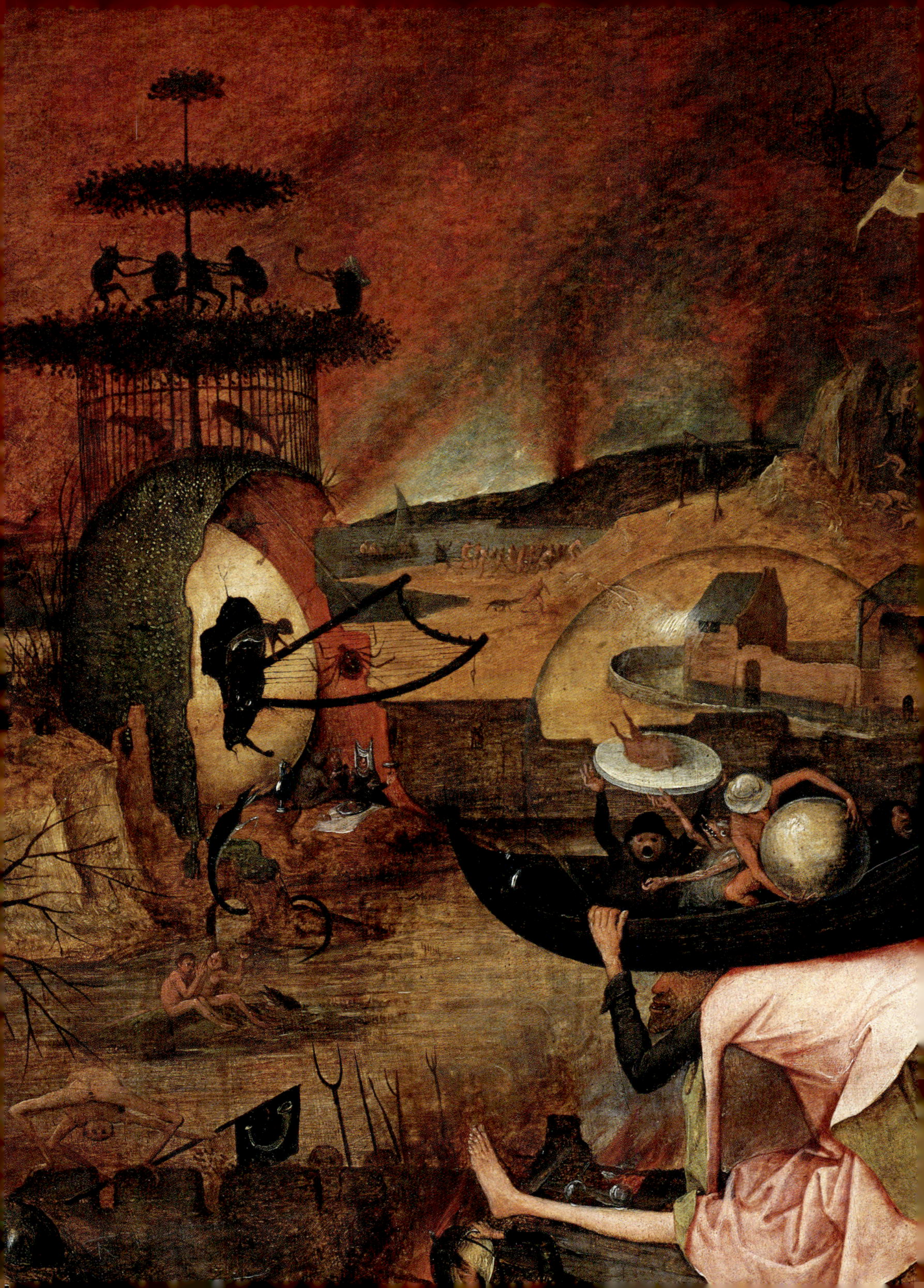

Bruegel Perspectives

The fame of Pieter Bruegel the Elder spread throughout Europe very soon after his death in 1569. This is proven by a posthumous portrait (p. 41) drawn by Bartholomeus Spranger (1546–1611), later painter to the Imperial Court of Rudolf II, and engraved in 1606 by Egidius Sadeler (*c.* 1570–1629).[1] It shows the artist as a humanist with an imposing beard and wearing patrician garb. He is portrayed frontally and gazes self-confidently into the eyes of the viewer. His oval portrait is framed by an allegorical programme. We see the divinities Athene and Hermes united, symbolising wisdom and eloquence and characterising Bruegel's art as classical. Meanwhile Fame, with her trumpet, fanfares the painter's immortal renown, which, as signified in the globe at her feet, is spread throughout the world. Next to her, a genius is shown in mourning, holding the extinguished torch of life and drawing a cloak over his head in grief.

The portrait demonstrates the pride the artist Spranger felt for his countryman.[2] The veneration of Italian artists as heroes by the artists' biographer Giorgio Vasari (1511–1574) is self-confidently confronted with a Flemish identity. Moreover, it stresses how soon Bruegel enjoyed the high esteem of his contemporaries. Alongside Jan van Eyck (*c.* 1390–1441) and Hieronymus Bosch (*c.* 1450–1516) he is regarded as the most important Flemish artist of the early modern age. In contrast to the Italians Michelangelo (1475–1564) and Raphael (1483–1520), he stands for a realistic type of art that does not hesitate to show the ugly and the lowly. We find no nude studies in his oeuvre extolling the beauty of the human body; even the Virgin Mary, Joseph and the Three Kings cannot escape a certain caricature-like exaggeration in Bruegel, not to mention the squat figures populating his pictures, men and women without the slightest hint of beauty.

With regard to Bruegel, realism means not only an illusionistic style of rendering, but also a drastic narrative mode.[3] His pictures are most dynamic when country folk celebrate a wedding or dance. His mockery is legendary, too, for instance when a pompous alchemist makes a family end up in the poor house after cheating the gullible people into thinking he can make gold, or when quacks and mountebanks free deceived patients from a "stone". An ass sings in school, fools dance madly, and misanthropes seem to be lamenting the wretched state of the world. Many of Bruegel's compositions are very famous because they are so extreme. Fat people are not only fat but overwhelmingly gross, while thin people appear as skinny as rakes. His beggar portraits are as grotesque as they are ugly. He tells of an evil world full of terrifying punishments and executions. His pictures make an disproportionately brutal impression on today's viewers, and it was not a rare occurrence that over time some details deemed offensive were painted over.

Today his motifs adorn beer mats, plates and tankards, and appear to celebrate an existence as simple as it is hedonistic. Over the centuries, his work has become part of the collective memory. But in order to become such a household name, the artist has had to give up his real identity. He has become a man of the people, a hedonistic Fleming who knows all about life's snares. This cliché of a popular painter who can identify his countrymen's weaknesses has long dominated Bruegel studies.

Sources elucidating the personal convictions of sixteenth-century artists crop up very rarely. This also applies to Pieter Bruegel the Elder. Neither letters written in his own hand, nor a last will and testament, nor personal documents of any kind inform us of his world view or religious faith. Nor do we know what languages he could speak and what books were therefore available to him. The literature has usually dodged this problem, pointing out the artist's alleged sense of humour as though needing no further explanation.[4] Thus there are basically two approaches in Bruegel studies. While one group sketches him as an educated humanist[5] who was familiar with the debates of his era and also had access to Latin texts, others see him more entrenched in a vernacular tradition and avoid reference to general contexts in the history of ideas.[6] In the following, the painter is regarded uncompromisingly as a humanist who had both feet planted firmly in the philosophical, political and religious debates of his age.[7]

If we look at Bruegel the narrator, it is noticeable that the artist sets the biblical events of the Old and the New Testament in his own time. His pictures lack the decorous use of historical models prescribed by the Italian theory of art of that epoch; they are distinguished far more for their rendering of contemporary life. Thick snowflakes are falling when the Three Kings find their way to the stable in Bethlehem. Clothing and architecture are those of artist's native country. Is Bruegel revealing himself here yet again as a realist?

In explaining this approach, the more discerning interpretations refer to theological contexts, since here the artist keeps to certain pious practices of the Middle Ages.[8] In the prayer books of the time, the faithful are advised to imagine biblical events in their own environment. But the biblical translations of the first half of the sixteenth century might also be just as legitimately mentioned as context. Namely, vernacular texts necessarily involve an updating of biblical events. Be that as it may, this updated narrative style gave the artist the opportunity of adding biting political comments to his pictures. His works are consequently more than simply illustrations of biblical texts, but also richly allusive interpretations.

Yet how should we imagine Bruegel's working practice, or the actual creation of his panels and paintings? He doesn't seem to have run a workshop with assistants and apprentices, as was necessary for producing altarpieces or other ecclesiastical works. Nor did he gain prominence as a portrait painter. The small number of the surviving works suggests that their execution was accomplished with great investment of time and care. So even if we have to presume that patrons must have existed for his artistic production, it doesn't mean that Bruegel should be seen merely as a painter of commissions, illustrating the wishes of his clients, their religious denomination or view of the world. Because even if his painted works also involved commissions, he was already so famous in his own time that people collected his art on account of its uniqueness. People ordered a painting so they could have a Bruegel. This suggests that the painter set out his own view of the world in all his works.

Thus one of the intentions of this book is to come closer to the narrator Bruegel and to seek the common thread that runs through his work.[9] For it is only a monographic study embracing the total range of his oeuvre that can ask what remains through change. The works themselves have to inform us of the artist's worldview and help to clarify his view of his own era.

This book is based on numerous studies of Pieter Bruegel the Elder that I have written over the years. His works have impressed and permanently preoccupied me. One reason for this fascination might be that his pictures always give the impression that despite all the existing literature, we can still discover and more precisely understand something else in them. Every interpretation has something provisional and unfinished about it. And even if we study a picture in detail, every new confrontation with it seems to be the first. His works seem familiar and yet simultaneously alien and enigmatic. I hope that this book is able to communicate something of the aesthetic experience described here.

My thanks go to the publisher, Benedikt Taschen, for our continuous and longlasting collaboration. Likewise to the project manager, Dr. Petra Lamers-Schütze, who incorporated the book into the series and supervised the process. I am extremely grateful to the editor, Brigitte Beier, for our professional work together, and to Frank Schmidt and Florian Kayser for their energetic support. The text is dedicated to my teacher Werner Busch, whose advice has meant so much to me through every stage of my life.

Pages 6, 8, 13
Dulle Griet (Dull Gret; details), 1563
(see ill. pp. 204/205)

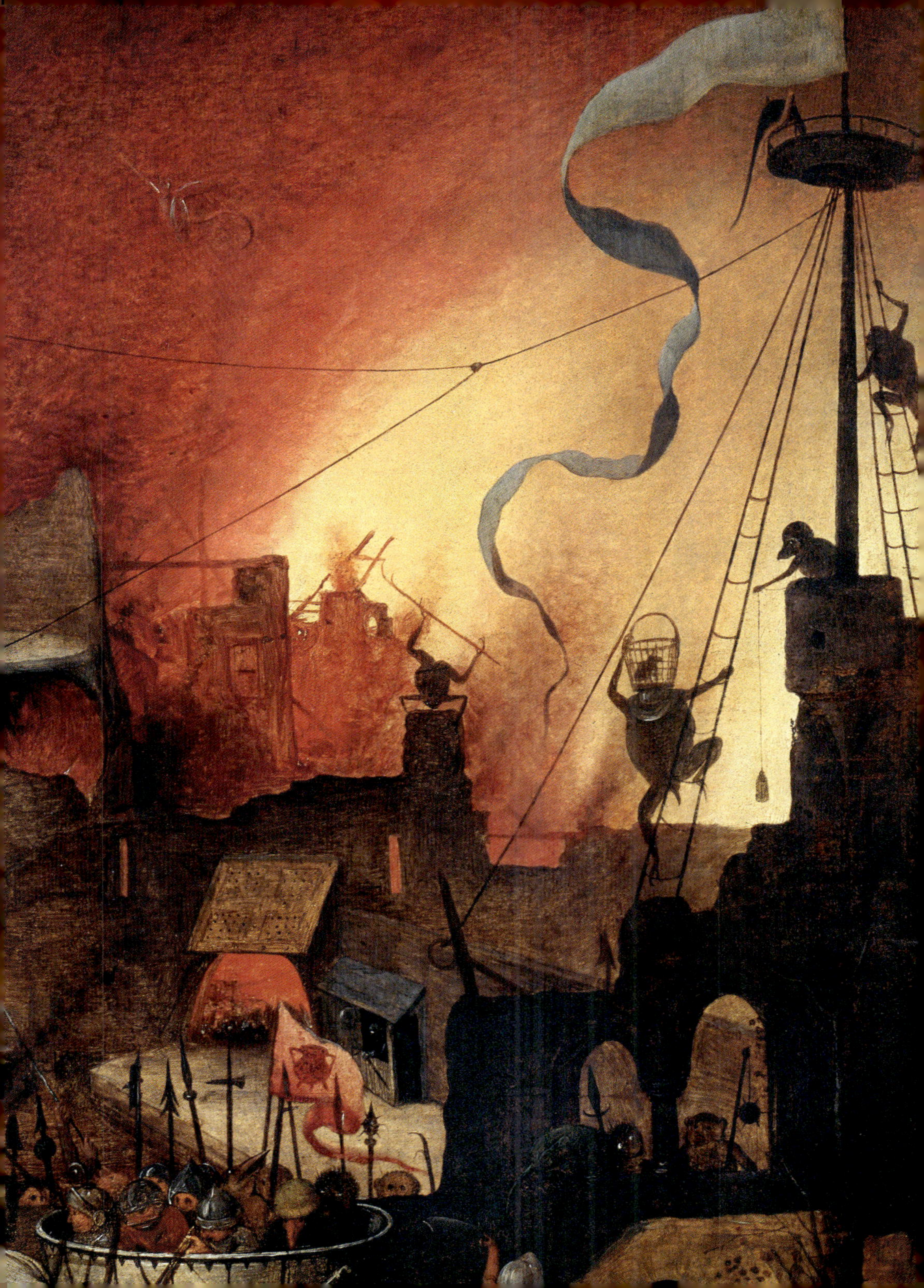

The Life of Pieter Bruegel the Elder

"What artist could compose such monstrously paradoxical works if he were not driven to it, from the very start, by some unknown force?"
— CHARLES BAUDELAIRE, 1845–1859

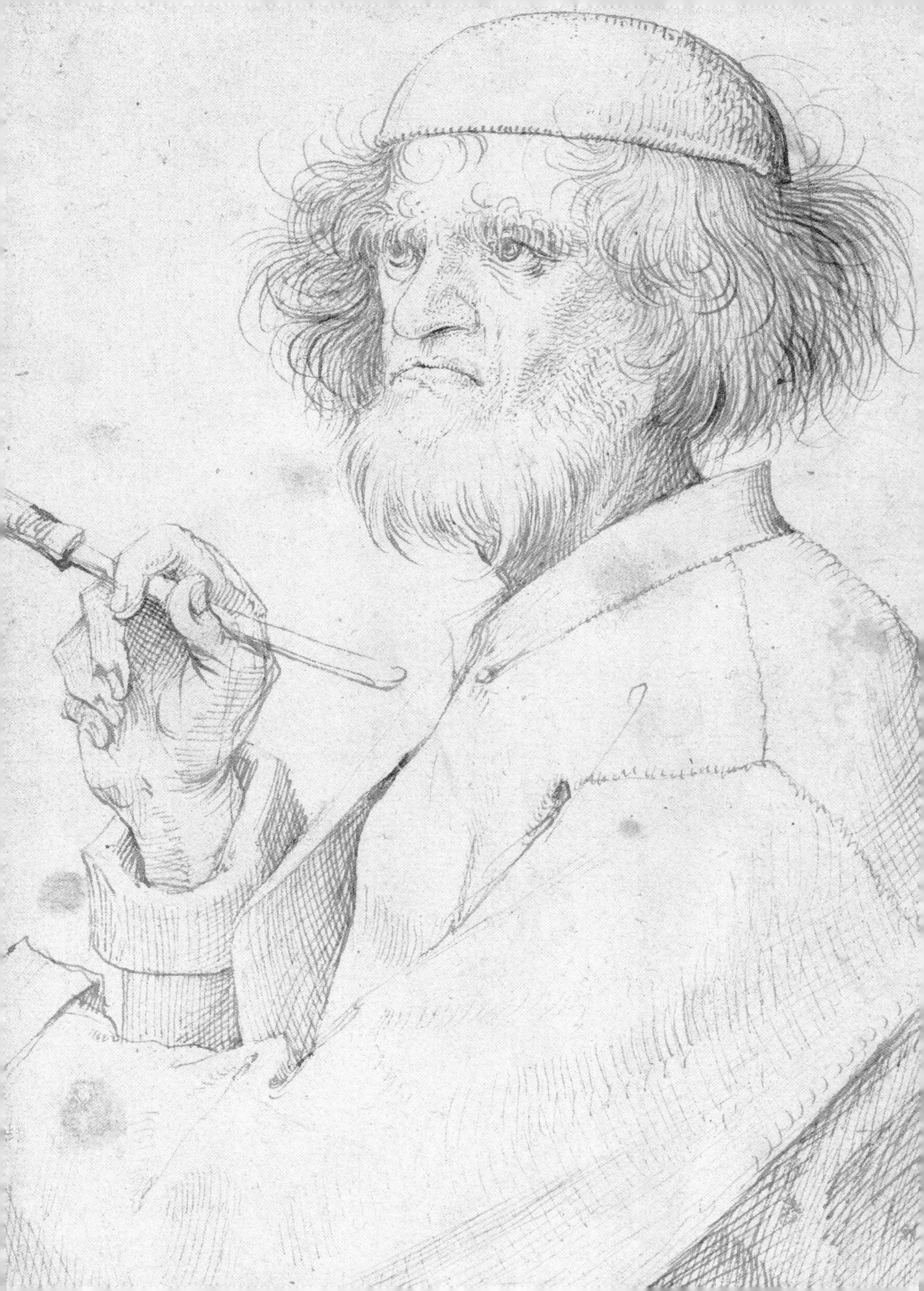

The lost picture

The earliest biography of Pieter Bruegel the Elder is in Karel van Mander's *Schilder-Boeck* of 1604 (p. 17). This scholarly work is nothing less than an encyclopaedia of painting, since it contains not only a theoretical-didactic poem based on the lives of classical, Italian and Flemish-Dutch painters, but also a commentary on Ovid's (43 BC–AD 17) *Metamorphoses* and explanations of allegorical pictures. In keeping with the historiography of that time, it contains not only numerous facts about Bruegel, but also anecdotes intended to cast light on the painter's character.[10] The artist is made out to be an energetic man who made everyone laugh with his bawdy jokes. He is said to have disfigured the perspective paintings of his fellow painter Hans Vredeman de Vries (1527–1609) by adding a peasant with an excrement-smeared shirt and a pair of lovers pleasuring each other. Van Mander reports that Bruegel and his Nuremberg friend Hans Franckert visited country weddings in order to study the boorish character of the festivities and their participants. "With this Franckert, Breughel often went out to the country folk whenever there was a fair or a wedding. They dressed up in traditional rustic clothing and brought presents like the others, pretending they were related to the bride or groom. Breughel had great fun observing the way the peasants ate, drank, danced, jumped around, wooed and otherwise entertained themselves, moments he was able to render very prettily and comically in watercolours […]."[11]

This passage shows Mander evidently wanting to characterise Bruegel's realism: the artist needed reality as his model; his art did not arise from the imagination but required the precise imitation of nature. Thus the biographer, when listing various pictures, finds particular praise for the picture of a peasant wedding, in which, he says, the artist succeeds in capturing the uncouth, sunburnt skin of the country folk. The biographer is evidently most interested in the comical and fun-loving features of Bruegel's art, which even a grumpy person cannot have looked at without at least a smile.

An interesting fact in the quoted passage is the mention of a friend, rare in the biography. The Nuremberger Franckert is entered in the members' list of the Antwerp painters' guild – which naturally cannot be cited to verify his friendship with Pieter Bruegel. In order to complete his portrait as a painter of peasant life, van Mander, for lack of secure information, makes the artist a son of Brabant peasants, whose task was to portray simple country folk: "Nature targeted her man wonderfully well, who in turn was to capture her most felicitously; from the peasants of an unknown village in Brabant she picked out the witty and humorous Pieter Breughel, who has brought such lasting fame to our Netherlands, and made a painter out of him so that he should portray peasants with his brush. He was born not far from Breda in a village called Breughel, whose name he took and left to his descendants."[12] Furthermore, the biographer added a love story to the artist's life by relating that Bruegel married the daughter of his master, Pieter Coecke van Aelst (1502–1550); her mother demanded that because of an affair with another girl, the artist should move from Antwerp to Brussels to free himself from the rival claimant to his affections.

However, not only anecdotes are interspersed in the biography, but many of his works are mentioned as well. Van Mander was particularly impressed by the painter's landscapes. Thus the biography starts by telling of Bruegel's crossing of the Alps on a trip to Italy, from where he brought back numerous landscape drawings. The biographer paints an interesting picture of the artist's procedures: "On his journeys he drew many views after nature, so that it is said that when he was in the Alps he swallowed the mountains and rocks whole and spewed them back out onto his painting panels, so close was he able to approach nature in this respect and others."[13]

Since van Mander frequently used Bruegel's works as biographical sources in his historical narrative, we immediately think of the motif of the vomiting peasant, a constant constituent of the contemporary iconography of peasant vices. Nevertheless, here the intention yet again is to express the realistic character of Bruegel's art, created after nature. But caution is recommended here; this is not necessarily praise from van Mander, since he favoured those artists who oriented themselves on classical antiquity and the great models of the Italian High Renaissance, Raphael and Michelangelo. The biographer uses this metaphor in order to draw attention to the artist's crude realism. It is noticeable

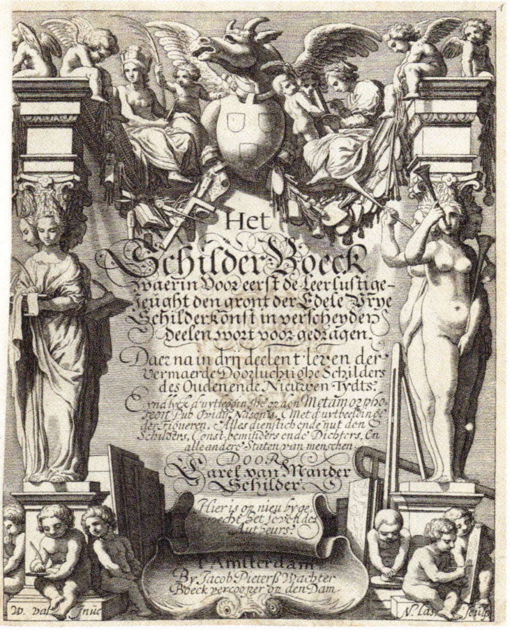

Karel van Mander, **Schilder-Boeck**, [2]1618
Frontispiece Göttingen, Niedersächsische Staats- und Universitätsbibliothek

Page 15
Painter and Buyer (detail), *c.* 1565
(see ill. p. 227)

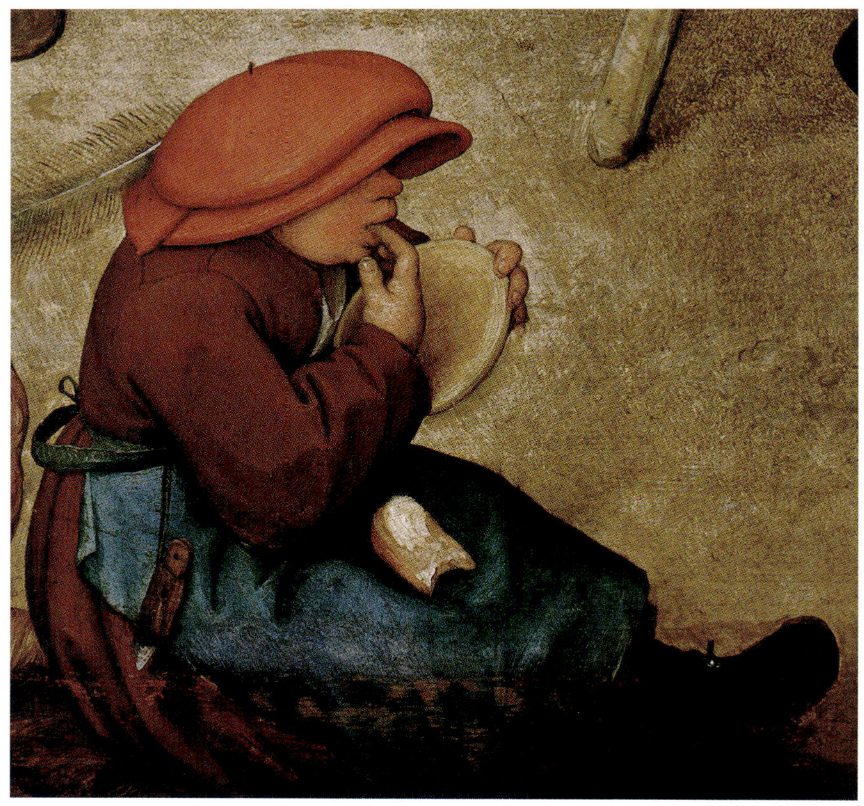

The Peasant Wedding (detail), *c.* 1568
(see ill. pp. 274/275)

The Sermon of St John the Baptist (detail), 1566
(see ill. pp. 166/167)

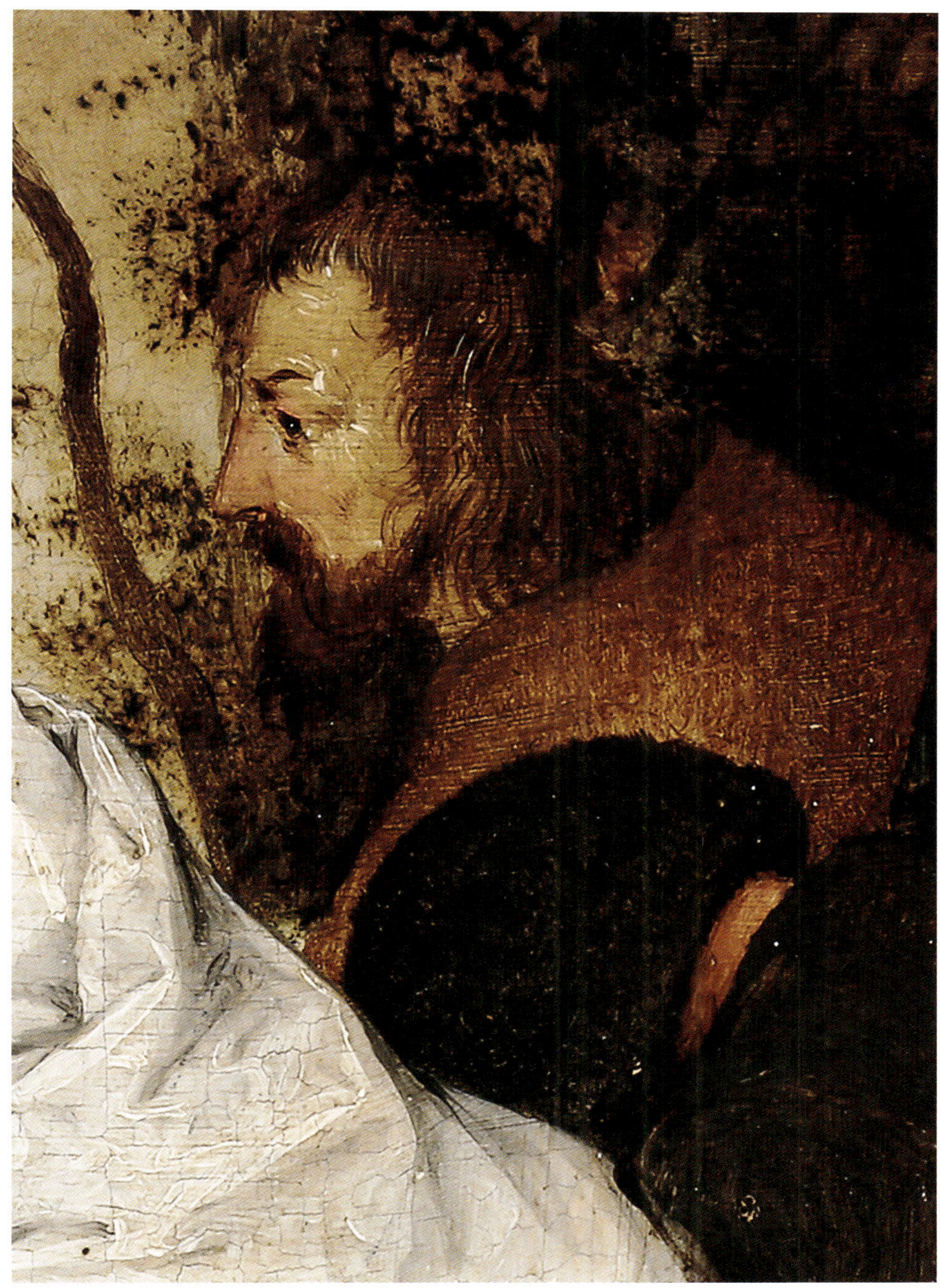

that he relates the ripest lewd stories for the reader. The artist is on a continual quest for droll motifs; he makes fun of his fellow artists and spends his time critically observing the common people.

It is difficult to judge what information was available to the biographer. It has been mooted that he might have based his narrative on information from artists formerly befriended by Bruegel, or from his sons. But the view conveyed of a simple painter of peasant life speaks clearly against this. It must be kept in mind that van Mander, apart from engravings after Bruegel, had no first-hand knowledge whatever of his works, but was familiar merely with the many copies made by Bruegel's older son. The biographer will certainly have compiled all the facts available to him; meanwhile, his judgement of the artist as successor to Bosch is hardly original. Lodovico Guicciardini (1521–1589) in his *Descrittione di tutti i Paesi Bassi* of 1567 and Giorgio Vasari in his *Vite* of 1568 had already opted for this comparison, but in doing so were merely referring to the Flemish painter's engravings, while failing to mention a single panel picture.

The last part of the Life is a list of the works seen by Mander with his own eyes, or those whose whereabouts he knew, among them the panel pictures then owned by Emperor Rudolf II (1552–1612). The biographer tells of the artist's death and informs us that he had two sons to follow him, who were likewise excellent painters. Even so, at the end of his narrative a hint crops up that expresses his sceptical view of Bruegel's work better than all other episodes and anecdotes. He reports how the artist, close to his death, asked his wife to burn all the satirical drawings among his papers, since he feared they could provoke unpleasant consequences: "When he was mortally ill, he ordered his wife to burn a large number of finely and cleanly drawn satires with added inscriptions that were in part too vituperative and imbued with mockery."[14]

Van Mander is obviously alluding to the Catholic Inquisition and the prints that expressed criticism of the Church. Even thirty years after the painter's death the critical content of his work was felt to be extreme. This isn't surprising, because time and again the engravings made after his drawings show attacks on the clerical estate and Catholic religious practices. Nonetheless, the biographer shows some respect for Bruegel's skill in describing the pictures so forcefully and for his portrayal of the emotional content in *The Massacre of the Innocents* (pp. 350/351, Cat. 28).

The description of a now lost panel picture seems particularly successful, which indeed might be imagined as typical of the artist. The Life says: "He furthermore painted a Temptation of Christ. The episode takes place in an alpine landscape, and the viewer looks down through cloud breaks from above onto cities and pastures [...]."[15] Even though this picture has not come down to us, it tells us of the aesthetic possibilities available to Bruegel, and his intentions.

Like no other artist of his time, Bruegel manages to convey an idea of the size and grandeur of the world. Long before the painting of the German Romantics, he was able to capture not only imposing mountain ranges but also the awesome and sublime in natural phenomena. He more than anyone else made it his task to capture the expanse and sublimity of the world. Time and again his landscape graphics and panel paintings take us to exposed locations from where we can cast a glance from high vantage points onto the world stretched out before us.[16] And the artist was able like no other to capture not only size and expanse, but also natural phenomena in the cycle of the seasons. His depiction of winter scenes is of breathtaking beauty and closeness to reality.

We might imagine a picture enabling us to glance through the blanket of the clouds from above, letting us detect cities and landscapes from a great distance. Van Mander perhaps mistakes the picture with another, because an engraving by Bruegel with a Temptation of Christ actually does exist (p. 22). However, this scene takes place in a forest. We are reminded most of all of the painted panel featuring the Conversion of St Paul (pp. 392/393, Cat. 29). Here the eye roams from a high vantage point into a gorge and across a coastal landscape to the horizon. The artist captures the perspective view into the gorge so dramatically that it stimulates a spontaneous feeling of dizziness. Van Mander expressly states that only Bruegel employed the downward perspective in his landscapes.[17]

Be that as it may, the lost picture of the Temptation of Christ has a very emblematic character for Bruegel's art, for it is about the self-empowerment of the human being. No century prior to this had experienced such a prodigious impetus towards modernisation.[18] Book printing brought the main works of ancient authors and the Church Fathers to a more general public. The study of history encouraged the questioning of sources and enabled scholars to determine the authenticity and age of texts. The discovery of America gave a boost to the professional measurement of the globe, cartography showing prodigious progress in the process. Gunpowder and the weapons it needed led to new military strategies and calculation of ballistic trajectories. Moreover, the Reformation was accompanied by a successful rise in literacy, and reading the Bible was no longer the privilege of clerics or a small throng of scholars. Copper engravings and woodcuts enabled the reproduction of new, graphically illustrated knowledge. The discoveries of Copernicus (1473–1543) established a heliocentric world picture that prevailed in academic circles and that led to precise observations of the sky and constellations. The colonisation of America brought great progress in navigational technology and nautics. The knowledge of non-European cultures and their religions demanded new explanations. In anatomy, Andreas Vesalius (1514–1564) wrote his foundational work *De humani corporis fabrica* (1543). All this finds expression in the fact that many scientific works of the time already use the word "new" in their titles.

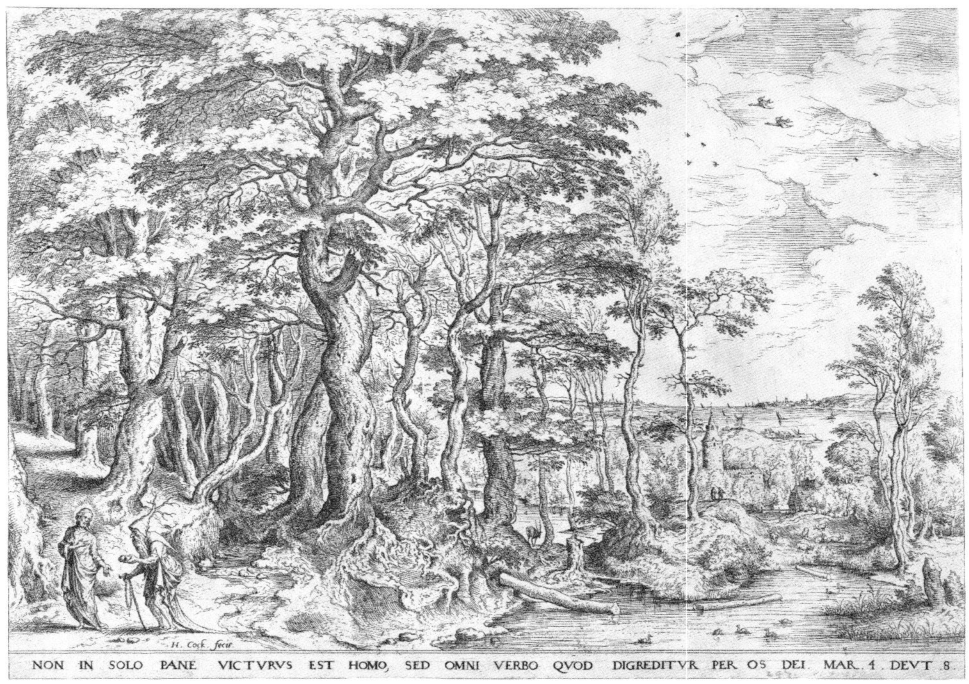

Hieronymus Cock after Pieter Bruegel the Elder,
Landscape with the Temptation of Christ, *c.* 1554
Etching and copper engraving, 31.9 x 43.9 cm (12 ½ x 17 ¼ in.)
New York, The Metropolitan Museum of Art

Yet accompanying these discoveries and inventions we also see doubt; self-empowerment of the human being also has a fearful dimension. Perhaps the lost picture of the Temptation of Christ aimed to express this fear. For since time immemorial the privileged view from above onto the world below has been reserved to the divine sphere. Did God set limits to human knowledge? The story of the Tower of Babel, twice painted by Bruegel, tells of this hubris of mankind (Cat. 12, 13). The human being who comes too close to the divine will be punished – a story likewise and famously depicted by the artist in his painting *Landscape with the Fall of Icarus* (Cat. 42a and 42b). In his works, these scientific developments and achievements are portrayed and critically questioned, for instance when he depicts a series of ships (Müller/Schauerte 2018, Cat. G18–28) or supplements the liberal arts with a representation of cannons (pp. 192/193).[19]

Progress is not an end in itself for Bruegel, and harbours dangers.[20] His pictures contain an impulse towards didactic enlightenment, but also an awareness of its limits.

He makes fun of alchemy and belief in witches, and criticises the self-righteousness of the religious denominations just as much as false erudition and quackery.

Faith in progress and science may have been a permanent constituent of humanist culture, yet this included no doubt whatever as regards belief in a beginning and an end of the world. According to Christian belief, the world would last no more than 6,000 years. The Last Judgement awaits the end. Martin Luther (1483–1546) forecast the Apocalypse three times, and it seems to have irritated him that it failed to happen every time. But this is no wonder. Because if we believe in God's creation, its end seems certain. The idea had lost none of its persuasive powers in Bruegel's time. Even more, the vices he exposes are first given their actual explosive force only with the threat of the Last Judgement. Thus he dealt with this subject in multiple and different ways in his works (e. g. Cat. 7; drawing pp. 186/187).[21]

Abraham Ortelius and his circle

Who was Pieter Bruegel the Elder? We know neither when nor where he was born. Van Mander tells us, following information provided by Guicciardini, that he was born near Breda. However, three places bear this name. Nor is the apprenticeship he is supposed to have had with Coecke van Aelst recorded in any verifiable archival material.[22] If we note that van Aelst was accepted into the Antwerp painters guild in 1527 and took over his teacher's workshop in Brussels in 1544, this means that Bruegel finished his apprenticeship either before 1544 in Antwerp or afterwards in Brussels, although there is no concrete evidence of this. Moreover, Bruegel's art is much more strongly oriented on the works of Matthijs Cock (*c.* 1505–1548) and Jan van Amstel (*c.* 1500–*c.* 1542), who should be seen as his actual predecessors from the artistic point of view. Even the cliché of Peasant Bruegel doesn't stand up to question, since no more than three panel paintings and a few engravings are devoted to the rustic genre (Cat. 25, 31, 32; Müller/Schauerte 2018, Cat. G9, 35, 36, 56). Nevertheless, this stereotype dominated the scholarly critical treatment of Bruegel until far into the twentieth century. Scholars saw in his work the undistorted expression of a Flemish popular spirit. It was only after publication of Karl Tolnai's research that they become increasingly aware of the humanist content in Bruegel's art.[23]

The year of Bruegel's death in Brussels in 1569 is securely recorded.[24] The artist is entombed in Notre-Dame-de-la-Chapelle. In addition, his enrolment as "master artist" in the Antwerp painters' guild in 1551 is verified in the archives. The entry in the members' list names him as "Pieter Breughels". Since the average age of those enrolled in the guild was twenty to twenty-five, the year of his birth has been conjectured to have been in the period between 1526 and 1530. A document also verifies that Bruegel was active between 1550 and 1551 in the workshop of a certain Claude Dorisi (*c.* 1517–1565) in Mechelen.[25] Along

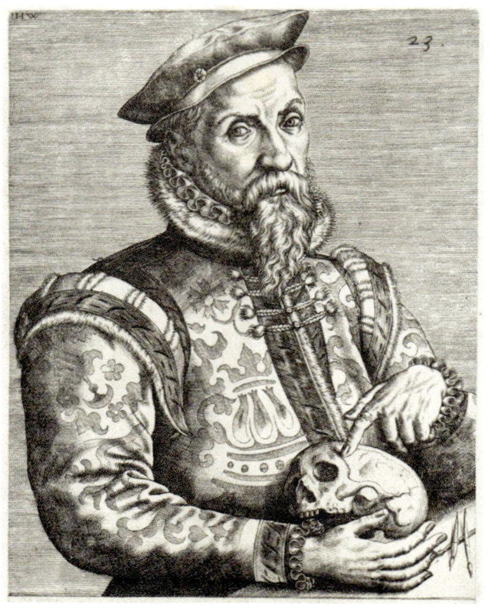

with other artists directed by Pieter Baltens (*c.* 1527–1584), Dorisi was working on an altarpiece for the local glovemakers' guild. Sadly, this work has not come down to us, so we have no idea of Bruegel's contribution. It was the only work produced by the artist in the context of church decoration.

If we look at the quantity and themes of the preserved works, though most are devoted to Christian iconography, Bruegel doesn't seem to have taken on any other commission for an altarpiece or to have collaborated on any such work. Apart from compositions based on the New Testament, his painting revolves around genre subjects and landscapes; portraits and still lifes cannot be found among his works. The earliest drawing dates from 1552, the last painting from 1568. Within this period, he developed from being a draughtsman designing prints to being a painter who worked only for a social élite.

Numerous high-ranking patrons of his art are known to us. First and foremost is the tax official and banker Niclaes Jonghelinck (1517–1570), who owned no fewer than sixteen paintings by Bruegel.[26] An inventory he ordered in the context of a security pledge informs us about many of the pictures in his collection. Among them, besides the series of months (Cat. 18–22), are works such as *The Procession to Calvary* (Cat. 15) and the *Tower of Babel* today in Vienna (Cat. 12). Another collector was the cardinal and personal advisor of Philip II (1527–1598), Antoine Perrenot de Granvelle (1517–1586), who owned pictures by the Flemish artist in his huge art collection.[27] The master of the Antwerp mint, Jean Noiret, was likewise one of Bruegel's patrons. Finally, we need to mention the cartographer Abraham Ortelius (1527–1598), who named a grisaille painting of the *Death of the Virgin* as his own (Cat. 16). Even these few names are sufficient to give us an idea of the class of people buying this art. Bruegel's pictures presume a cultural élite who possessed the necessary discernment and education to understand the rich allusiveness of his art.

Jan Wierix, **Portrait of Hieronymus Cock**, 1572
Copper engraving, 20.3 x 12.1 cm (7 ⅞ x 4 ¾ in.). Amsterdam, Rijksmuseum, Rijksprentenkabinet

This can be endorsed to a certain extent by the most important and simultaneously earliest preserved portrait of the artist. It is dated 1572 and was executed by Jan Wierix (1549–*c.* 1620). The engraving (p. 27) is one of a larger series of artists' portraits devoted to the North-European painters of the early modern age and begins with Jan van Eyck as founder of this tradition. The engraved portraits are supplemented with Latin poems by the humanist Dominicus Lampsonius (1532–1599), who quite often enhanced an artist's specific achievements by comparisons with a painter of antiquity.

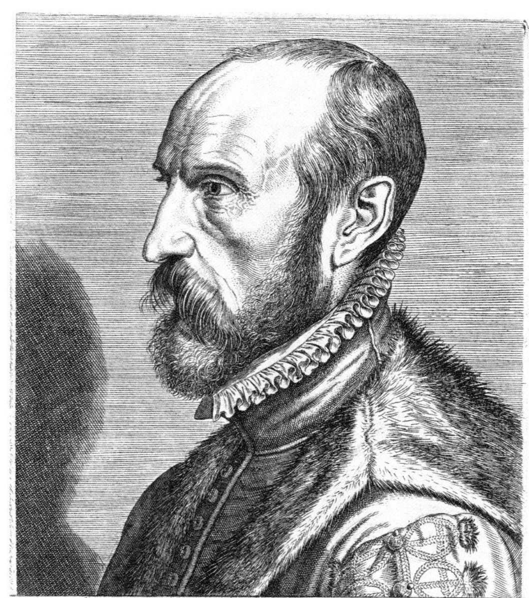

The portrait of Bruegel is certainly very impressive and shows him with a dignified appearance; by no means are we confronted here with the painter of peasant life described by van Mander. He is shown in profile, wearing a velvet beret and sporting an imposing beard. Here we have a portrait of a humanist. Wierix was far more interested in the dignity and seriousness of his portrait than the practical occupation involving brush and paint. As the engraving first appeared three years after Bruegel's death, the question arises as to which pictorial source the engraver relied on. Often pointed out is Bruegel's supposed self-portrait in his panel painting *The Procession to Calvary* (pp. 142/143, Cat. 15), a plausible identification, since Bruegel is portrayed here with the typical painter's beret. This crypto-portrait shows the artist in the midst of the crowd watching the events of the Passion.

The same applies to a figure in *The Sermon of St John the Baptist* who has been named as source for the Wierix portrait; here the painter appears in the crowd on the right edge of the picture (p. 19; pp. 166/167, Cat. 27). Although these are not commissioned works, both portrayals accentuate the close relationship between patron and artist. Thus in the *Sermon of St John the Baptist* there is another portrait besides that of the artist, showing a patrician whose hand is being read by a gypsy and whom we may

Philipp Galle, **Abraham Ortelius**, *c.* 1572
Copper engraving, 17.4 x 12 cm (6 ⅞ x 4 ¾ in.). London, The British Museum

identify as the owner of the picture (p. 169). Did such a close relationship between artist and patron not offer the opportunity to reach an agreement on the contents and special features of the painting, even permitting the artist to accentuate important details in his composition? Anyone who commissioned a picture from Bruegel opted not only for a style but also for his special mode of narrative.

Written sources verify that Bruegel travelled across France and to the far south of Italy.[28] The preserved works lend credence to his journeying through Lyons, Rome, Naples and Reggio di Calabria all the way to Messina. He was probably accompanied on these trips by the cartographer Abraham Ortelius (p. 25) and the painter Maerten de Vos (1532–1603). Around 1553, Bruegel sojourned in Rome and was in contact with a painter of miniatures there, Giulio Clovio (1498–1578), in whose estate inventory a watercolour landscape by Bruegel is documented, though now lost. Many engravings and drawings testify to this trip (Müller/Schauerte 2018, Cat. G2, 5, 13; D1, 2, 10, 11, 20, 21, 28), which will have made the artist familiar with the great works of antiquity and the High Renaissance. In two letters to Abraham Ortelius from the 1560s, the Italian cartographer Scipio Fabius sends greetings to Bruegel, evidence that the artist must have impressed the humanist.[29]

The journey took place between 1552 and 1554. The return to Antwerp, where the artist presumably stayed from 1555 on, will have taken him across the Alps, as documented in many studies of mountains (pp. 28/29; Müller/Schauerte 2018, Cat. G5, D10, 20). The long period of travel is significant in that it suggests the intensive exchange and friendship with the cartographer Ortelius, who dedicated an obituary to Bruegel after his death. This information cannot be valued highly enough, since Ortelius is the only person documented as having a close relationship with Bruegel.

The artist married Maycken Coecke in 1563.[30] The marriage certificate verifies that he had moved in the meantime from Antwerp to Brussels. One year later his son Pieter the Younger (1564–1638) was born and four years later Jan (1568–1625). Both followed in their father's footsteps and became successful painters. Later, Pieter the Younger produced many copies and variations on his father's works. It is difficult to judge whether the move to Brussels was linked to the hope of more commissions for painted panels from the circle of the Court of the Governor (Stadtholder) of the Netherlands, Margaret of Parma (1522–1586).

Be that as it may, the artist now focused on painting. By the early 1560s, he had created numerous design drawings for engravings, appearing in Hieronymus Cock's (c. 1510–1570; p. 24) publishing house "To the Four Winds".[31] Quite often these involve whole series of landscapes, or of virtues and vices (pp. 32/33, 55, 64/65, 190/191, 192/193; Müller/Schauerte 2018, Cat. D20, 21, 34–40, 44–50; G2–13, 63–69, 72–78). Here Bruegel reveals that he is particularly critical of his age, which he sees increasingly

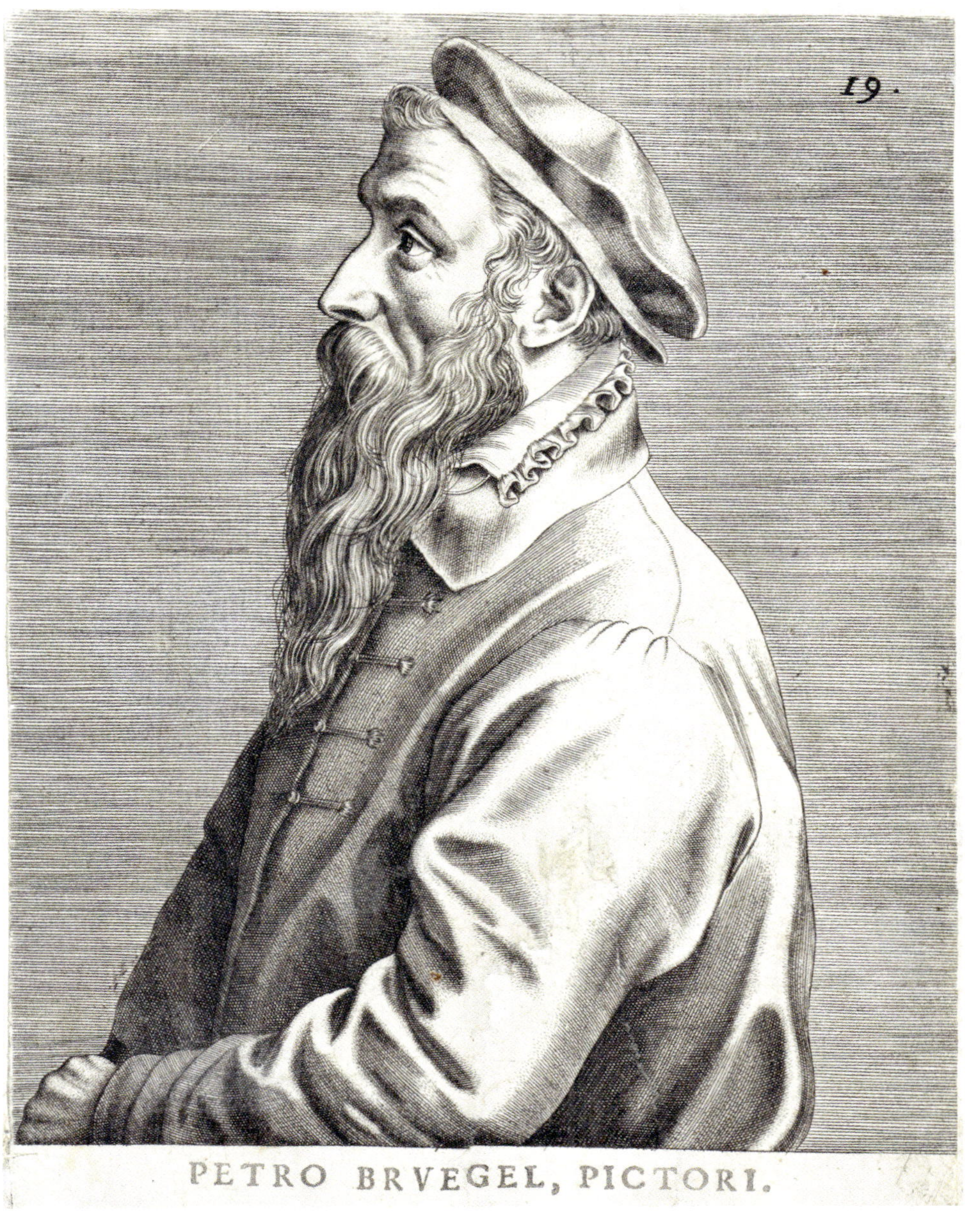

Jan Wierix, **Portrait of Pieter Bruegel** (detail), 1572
Copper engraving, 19.9 x 12 cm (7 ⅞ x 4 ¾ in.). Amsterdam, Rijksmuseum, Rijksprentenkabinet

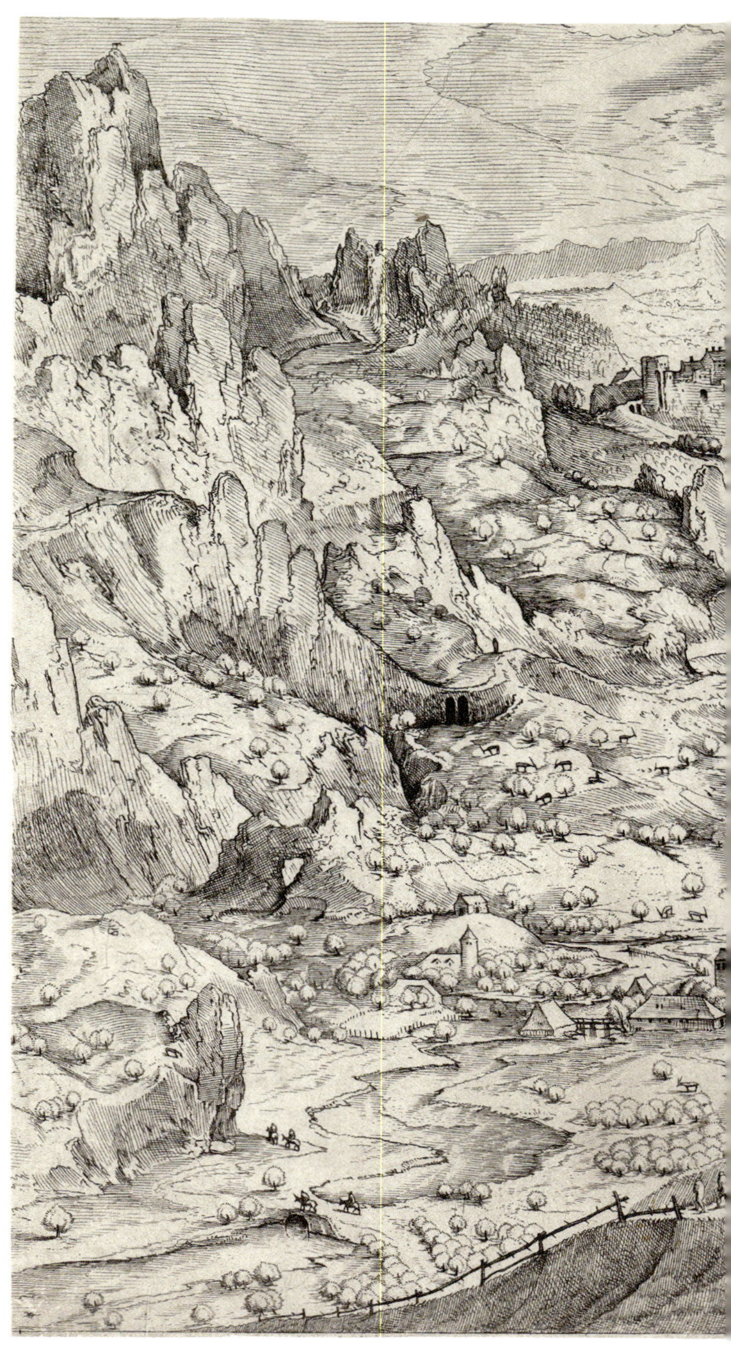

Jan and Lucas
van Doetecum after Pieter
Bruegel the Elder
Large Alpine Landscape,
c. 1555/56
Etching and copper engraving,
36.6 x 47 cm (14 ⅜ x 18 ½ in.)
New York, The Metropolitan
Museum of Art

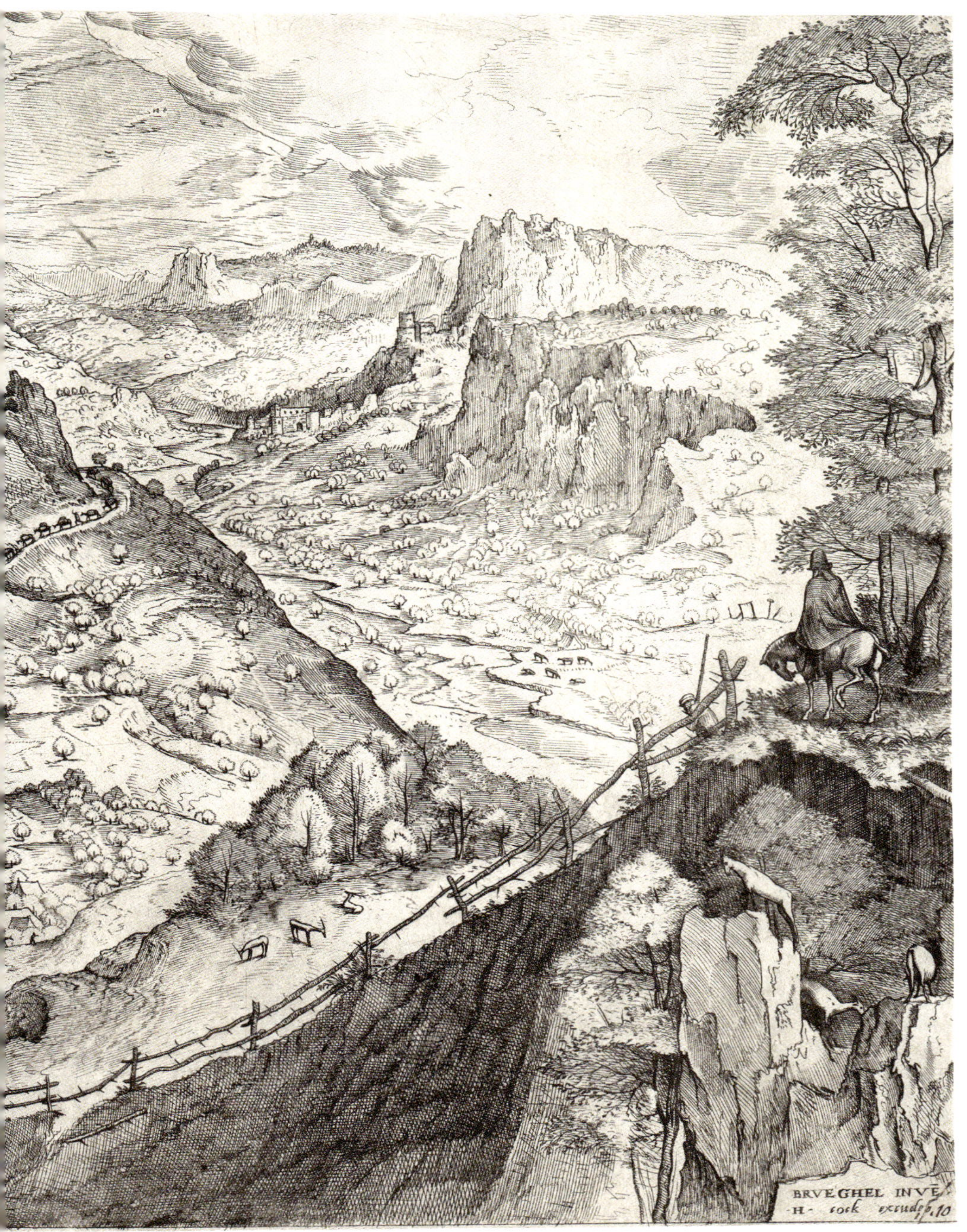
BRVEGHEL INVE
·H· cock excudeb 10

dominated by religious fanaticism. Using the medium of pictorial satire, he harks back to the works of Hieronymus Bosch.

Bruegel seems to have been a Catholic; at least he was buried in the Catholic rite and worked for representatives of the Habsburg Court.[32] On the other hand, given the age in which he lived, this says nothing conclusive about his religious convictions. This is why it is necessary to search for traces in Bruegel's immediate environment that might indicate where he stood in terms of the debates of that epoch. It was not a rare occurrence at the time for people to keep their Catholic identity so as not to be suspected of heresy, and in reality practise a contemplative, mystical form of piety not based on the sacraments. This hidden religious practice, called Nicodemism, was very much a subject of controversy; reform theologians like Martin Luther and John Calvin (1509–1564) rejected it and demanded an open commitment to the Reformation.[33]

We can deduce a first hint in this direction in van Mander's biography, where he speaks of the dangers to which Bruegel's widow might have been exposed by certain drawings of his she inherited. But first and foremost we must look at Bruegel's probable friend Abraham Ortelius, whose *Album Amicorum* (Friendship Album) also contains entries of many artists and scholars Bruegel might have known through the publisher Cock and through Ortelius himself.[34] The album names many illustrious personalities. It mentions the geographer Gerhard Mercator (1512–1594), the poet Lucas de Heere (1534–1584) and the antiquary Hubert Goltzius (1526–1583). But artists have been immortalised here, too. Cornelis Cort (1533–1578), Frans Hogenberg (1535–1590), Georg Hoefnagel (1542–1600) and Lambert Lombard (1505/06–1566) can be found, also theologians and humanists: Benito Arias Montano (1527–1598), Dirck Volkertsz. Coornhert (1522–1590), Marnix van St. Aldegonde (1540–1598) and Christoph Plantin (*c.* 1520–1589). Because of their religious convictions, not a few of them had to leave the Southern Netherlands or were charged with heresy after the arrival of the Duke of Alba (Fernando Álvarez de Toledo, 3rd Duke of Alba, 1507–1582).[35] Plantin sympathised with to a religious sect known as Huis der liefde (House of Love).[36] It seems natural that Bruegel was acquainted with some and even many of the named persons and their religious convictions.

Christianus or Ciceronianus?

As regards the artist's religious identity and denomination, practically all conjectures have been proposed. While earlier studies of Bruegel merely reveal a simple man of the people, today we can opt for Bruegel as Anabaptist, Catholic, reformed or heretic. Since Carl Gustaf Stridbeck's research, the most plausible hypothesis is that Bruegel was familiar with the writings of Sebastian Franck (1499–1542/43) and to an extent motivated by them.[37] This would, however, imply a Nicodemian practice.[38] Which means that publicly he behaved like a Catholic, but in secret thought the rituals and sacraments associated with Catholicism to be worthless.

Whoever thinks it possible that Sebastian Franck influenced Bruegel's art is referring to an author who had already been dead for more than ten years before the start of Bruegel's artistic career. But this does not mean that he was forgotten. For instance, in the mid-1560s the Dutch Anabaptist Dirk Philips (1504–1568) wrote a pamphlet against the German theologian. Two letters written by Franck as early as the 1530s and 1540s to befriended heretics had been translated into Dutch a short time before and compiled into a small pamphlet.[39] This goaded Philips to produce his polemical paper complaining about the German theologian's success. Philips stated that Franck had so many "devotees, readers and apprentices" because he supported the Nicodemian practice.[40] The Anabaptist regarded the concealment of one's actual Christian convictions as hypocrisy.[41] There should be no practice at all of "false divine service". This, he stated, was wrong and a "root of idolatry".[42] The Dutch Anabaptist's vexation is understandable, since Franck had written in one of the letters that even as a dissenter one could participate in the Mass and other rituals of the Catholic Church.

What concerned all Christians after the Reformation was the question of how the denominations should treat one another. The Peace of Augsburg of 1555 marked the Reformation in the Holy Roman Empire of the German Nation as an irrevocable fact of life. This looked different in the sovereign lands of the Habsburgs. In Bruegel's era, the conflict between the reformers and Catholics reached an extreme pitch. The Lutheran breakaway was only the start. The Anglican Church became established in England under Henry VIII (1491–1547). Calvin founded his own Church in Switzerland, and in France the community of the Huguenots was set up in connection with the Geneva reformer – to name only a few of the new denominations, quite independent of groupings such as the Anabaptists. The project of founding a Church from the grass roots up foundered dramatically with the Peasants' Wars (1524/25). And yet all denominations and Christian splinter groups were linked by belief in the salvation of Christ.

Hence it is understandable that there were theologians who identified the problem in the denominations and their institutional characteristics, and endeavoured to look more for the things shared by all the denominations, and even all religions. However, tolerance was indispensable for such an attitude, as was a devaluation of external rituals. Such problems must have been discussed in the circles surrounding Bruegel and Ortelius. Yet again it is Abraham Ortelius whose letters supply us with information in this regard. The cartographer may have remained a Catholic all his life, but he expresses himself quite unambiguously when he describes his personal convictions to his nephew Ortelianus. In a letter written in 1592, he reveals himself to be a follower of Sebastian Franck, whose

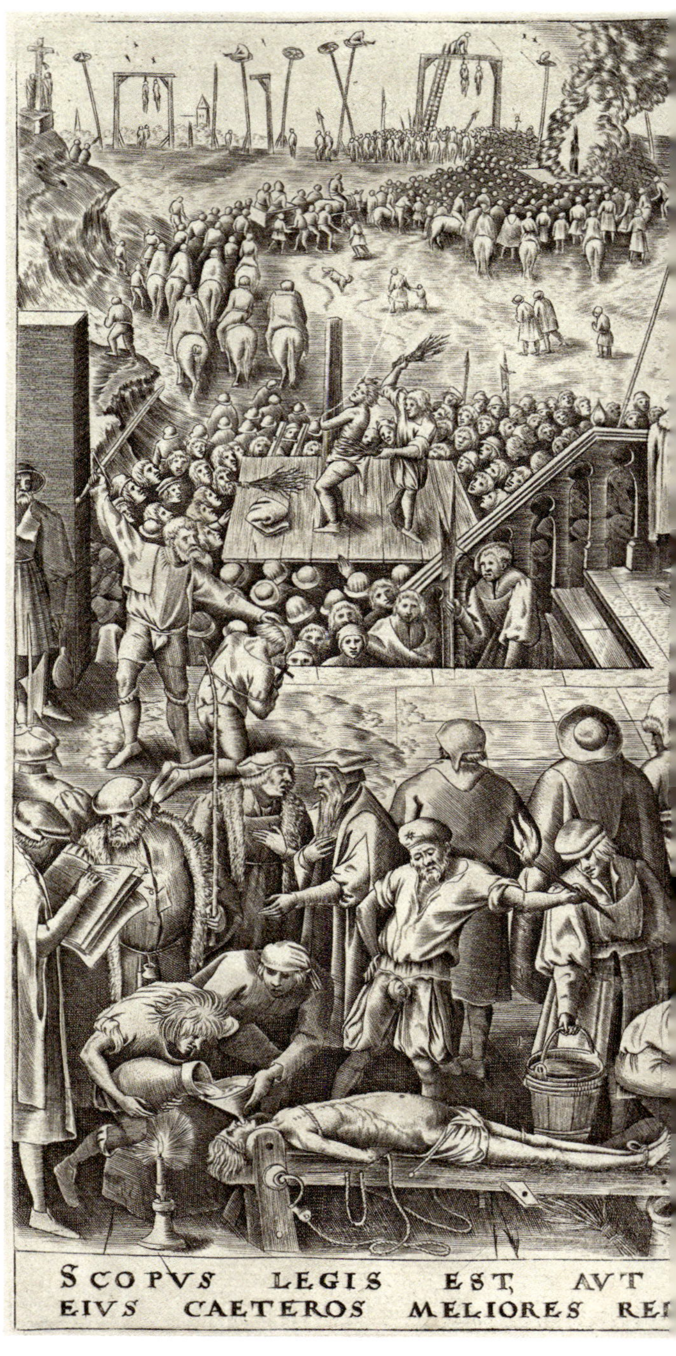

Philipp Galle (attributed)
after Pieter Bruegel the Elder
Justitia (Justice), *c.* 1559
Copper engraving, 22.5 x 29 cm
(8 ⅞ x 11 ⅜ in.)
New York, The Metropolitan
Museum of Art

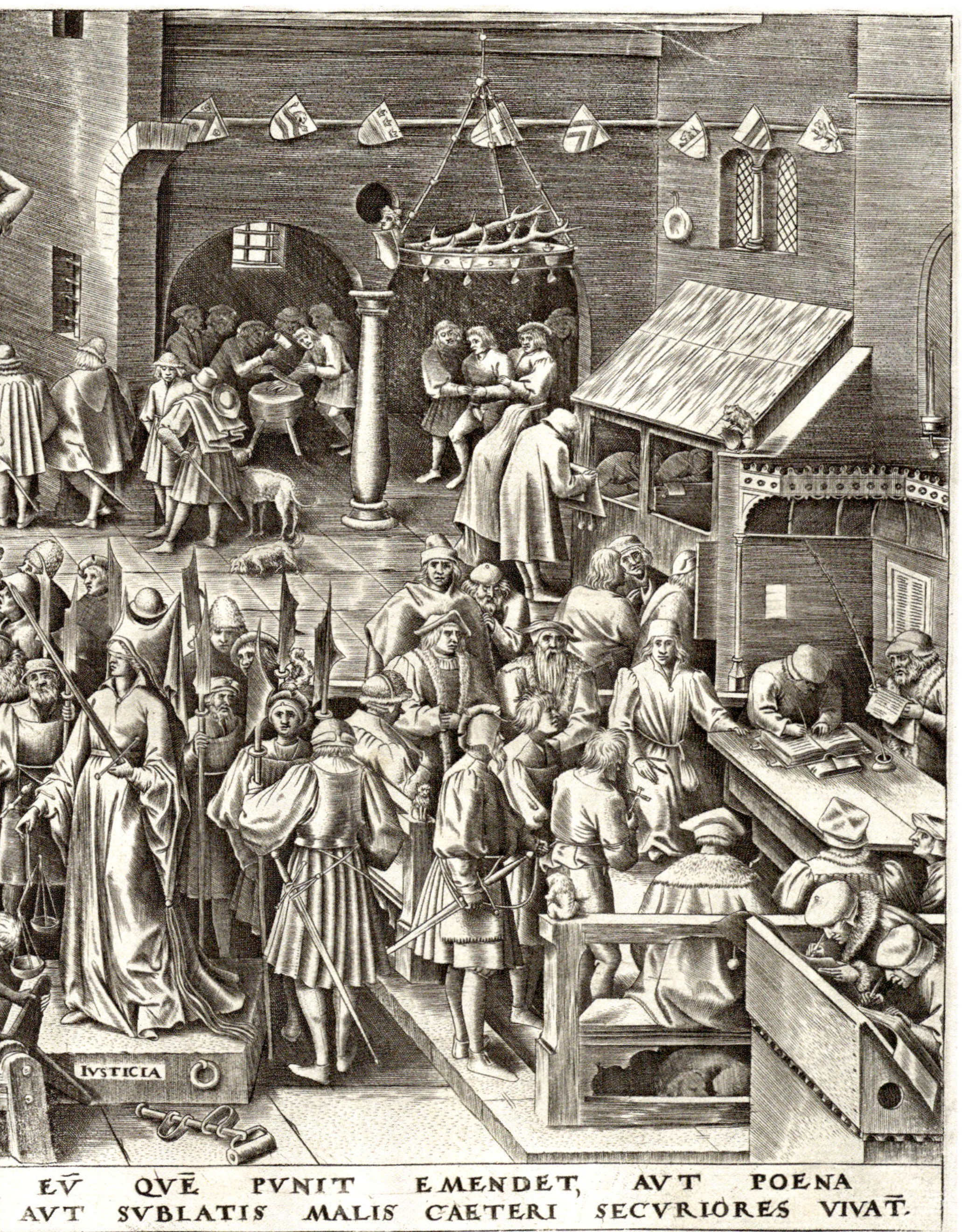

EꝰQVÆ PVNIT EMENDET, AVT POENA
AVT SVBLATIS MALIS CAETERI SECVRIORES VIVAꝉ.

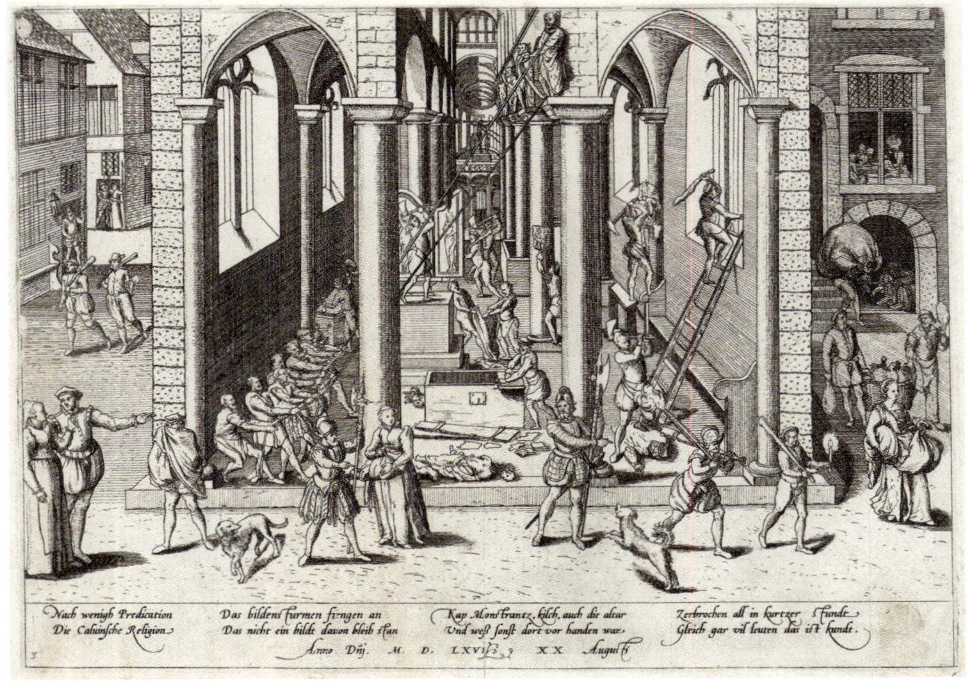

Frans Hogenberg, **The Calvinist Iconoclastic Riot of 20 August 1566,** 1588
Copper engraving, 34 x 26 cm (13 ⅜ x 10 ¼ in.)
Amsterdam, Rijksmuseum, Rijksprentenkabinet

text *Paradoxa* of 1534 he warmly recommends to his pupil.[43] This piece of writing, he avers, exists in Dutch and contains more wisdom than those by other theologians.

As early as the 1560s, thus in Bruegel's lifetime, the cartographer complained about the confusions spawned by the quarrels between the denominations; he compares the Southern Netherlands to an invalid stricken with the "Catholic plague, Protestant fever, Huguenot sickness and other torments brought by black knights and soldiers". What might have interested Ortelius in Franck's writings seems to have been his irenic, trans-denominational point of view. Franck, aligning himself to Erasmus of Rotterdam (1466/67/69–1536), represents a mystical form of Christianity, less interested in ritual and sacraments than in spiritual truths. His many writings were soon translated into Dutch and were widely circulated.[44] He saw the reason for all that had gone wrong particularly in the institutional character of religion, which is why he advocated an "invisible church".[45] God, he averred, reveals himself to all religions and may in no way be seen as the property of one denomination; in this, Franck was following the ideas of Erasmus, but simultaneously radicalising them.

The following text will frequently refer to the writings of Sebastian Franck as a source for Bruegel, and in doing so postulate the artist's irenic attitude towards the peaceful co-existence of the various denominations, since we have to be aware of the high status of religion in people's lives in those days, and also of the special situation in the Southern Netherlands.[46] Religious conflicts inexorably came to a head during the sixteenth century. When Philip II ascended the throne in 1556 after his father Charles V (1500–1558), he made it his mission to persecute heresy even more energetically than before. Professing a denomination other than Catholicism was heresy and was punished with burning at the stake. Antwerp, Bruegel's city of residence, was deemed to be the stronghold of heresy.[47] Archive material from around 1559 makes this quite clear and verifies that heretical contents in any form, whether image, text or theatre performance led to persecution.

As early as 1550, an edict was issued under Charles V for the "Protection of the People", with the aim of exterminating heretical teachings and of prosecuting anyone mocking the Virgin Mary or the saints.[48] Members of the Dutch aristocracy sent a petition to the Governor, Margaret of Parma, asking for the abolition of the Inquisition; her arrogant refusal gave rise to violent unrest. Churches and monasteries were destroyed and in 1566 an outbreak of iconoclasm spread like wildfire throughout the Netherlands (p. 34). A year later, Duke Alba was appointed Captain General (p. 37), his task to re-establish law and order with Spanish élite troops. The revolt was crushed, and subsequently a "Council of Troubles" was introduced that would eventually condemn almost 20,000 people to death. All these events were frequently and precisely described, but where do we see them in Bruegel's art? How could one criticise such a reign of violence without risking the danger of persecution from the Inquisition?

The most harrowing description within this context is seen in Bruegel's Virtues series, produced in 1559/60 (pp. 190/191, 192/193; Müller/Schauerte 2018, Cat. D44–50; G72–78). His portrayal of *Justitia* (pp. 32/33) can be related to the critical situation in the Southern Netherlands. In the foreground we recognise the personification of Justice, with the obligatory attributes of blindfold, sword and scales. She is standing slightly aloft on a stone pedestal, leg irons lying in front. Interrogations are taking place all around her, in part with the use of torture, showing the cruelty of the judicial system in that era. At the left edge of the picture, a man is being beheaded, another in the centre ground is being whipped with the birch. But the crucial scene is the one in the background, where an auto-da-fé is taking place.[49] Death by burning was traditionally the punishment meted out to heretics. Bruegel uses a compositional scheme in this part of the engraving that he used in *The Procession to Calvary*, so that the injustice of the execution hits the eye. This interpretation is supported by the cross on the opposite side to the heretics' fires; the Virgin Mary and St John seem to be standing in front of it.

In addition, the entire horizon is crowded with gallows and wheels, giving the beholder an impression of a multitude of victims.

Above the scene in the bottom-left corner, in which a condemned man is being given prodigious amounts of water through a funnel, we see two scholars in conversation. The man in profile has been identified as very like John Calvin, who had the humanist and religious freethinker Michel Servet (1509/11–1553) executed in 1553, Bruegel perhaps showing here that religious intolerance was not the sole prerogative of Catholics. What is so harrowing is not only the sadism of the henchmen, one of whom is pouring hot pitch from his torch onto the legs of the man on the rack, but also the bureaucratic apparatus, exposed in all its smooth and business-like functioning.

But how can Bruegel express his criticism without himself becoming suspect? First of all through the caption, which speaks of just punishment and of a world made safer by the removal of evildoers. In this way, he integrates his critical design into the larger context of a series of Virtue pictures. The artist thus created the opportunity for himself of presenting his scene as just punishment, and that the critical content was not intentional. Nevertheless, it is not without a certain sarcasm that the blindfold of Justice acts as a malicious comment on the injustice happening all around. Moreover, such types of indirect critique were not new and indeed had enjoyed a boom since the Reformation.

With the *devotio moderna*, a pious practice began in the Late Middle Ages that increasingly personalised faith and sought an experience of God less in church rituals and sacraments and far more in prayer and inner contemplation. The theology of Erasmus of Rotterdam was strongly influenced by this, and his texts were particularly influential in both the Southern and Northern Netherlands until far into the seventeenth century.[50] Erasmus pleaded for an enlightened Christianity and was critical of monasticism, indulgences and the false veneration of saints. His *Manual of a Christian Knight* (1503) challenges the reader to turn his eyes into his own soul in order to see with the heart: he should take heed that he does not turn the eyes of his heart away from the image of Christ. "I admonish you only this: see the essence of piety in neither bread nor ritual nor in anything visible, but in what we have described. Bind yourself to everything in which you recognise the true image of Christ."[51]

At the same time, the theologian places limits on the human capacity to know God, for in the end God remains beyond understanding. All talk of him remains metaphorical and approximate. Even the Bible evades complete understanding and remains enigmatic in the end.[52] The Dutch theologian was known for translating the New Testament from Greek into Latin, and for supporting secular literacy and translation of the Bible into the vernacular.[53] He also wrote numerous books that became genuine bestsellers and also influenced the visual arts. His *Praise of Folly* (1509) presents a sagacious critique of human vanities, but also of the Church and its institutions. In doing so, the author protects himself by making Folly the narrator, thus purporting that her arguments are not to be taken seriously.[54] Nevertheless, the book, like many other of his writings, landed on the Index after his death in 1545.[55] The first German translation we owe to Sebastian Franck, published in 1534. Erasmus' *Colloquia Familiaria* (Colloquies) of 1518 were equally successful, and likewise translated into German a few years later. In two dialogues, the theologian explicitly criticises monasticism and the avarice of the Catholic Church. Once again the author camouflages his critical intent and declares the book to be a school textbook for Latin lessons.

Erasmus is significant for our painter from many points of view. Namely, Bruegel also criticised his own era in a form that offered him options for retreat, placing his biting commentaries in his pictures in such a way that viewers have actively to make sense of the depicted details for themselves. Moreover, Erasmus brings up a problem in his last dialogue, *Ciceronianus* of 1528, that preoccupied many painters afterwards.[56] How much may classical antiquity, in other words pagan culture, act as a model for a Christian?

The Italian Renaissance involved an all-embracing movement back to classical antiquity. It affected not only literature but also the visual arts, which became increasingly oriented on the works handed down from antiquity, which eventually took over as models in current theories of art. Although Erasmus at first greatly venerated ancient authors, towards the end of his life he was besieged by doubt. Should not the Bible be more important as a model for a Christian than a text by Cicero (106–43 BC)? Did not this highly esteemed Roman man of letters come from a pagan world? Erasmus becomes

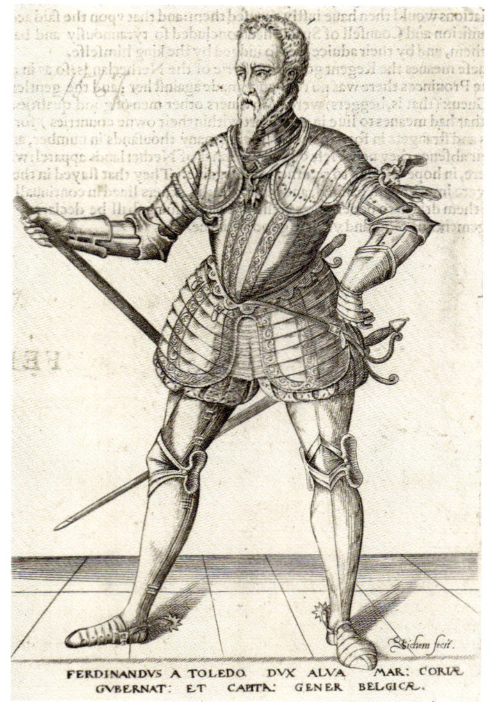

Christoffel van Sichem the Elder after Philipp Galle
Duke Fernando Álvarez de Toledo Alba III, 1601
Etching, 19.2 x 12 cm (7 ½ x 4 ¾ in.). London, The British Museum

unexpectedly polemical in this controversy, declaring that the exaggerated veneration of classical antiquity was a new kind of paganism. But what might pictures look like that are based on the Bible as stylistic ideal? What would a Christian painter do in this respect?

The point of the dialogue *Ciceronianus* is the theological emphasis it gives to the problem of appropriate speech. While ancient rhetoric demanded that the orator should apply figures of speech *(ornatus)* in accordance with the content of what is being said, Erasmus questioned this principle when considering Christian art. Artists and literary figures alike should orient themselves on the Bible, which is written in simple language. The reformer favoured images oriented on real life. Ancient forms, the Dutch theologian considered, were not appropriate for representing their own time, and he rejected them wholesale. He wrote that it was improper to portray Christ as Jupiter and to transpose ancient forms onto Christian contents. If people always based their works on ancient models, it would be like living a lie or masquerading as something else. Art is born of its time and should react appropriately to it.

Erasmus saw the evolution of a new form of art based on the progression of history in general, but also on the achievements of technical progress. Book printing and many other inventions, then called *Nova reperta*, proved the superiority of the present over antiquity.[57] Here we are confronted by the manifesto of a modernist who simultaneously recommends the New Testament as a model. How should we interpret this?

In contrast to the literature of classical antiquity, the language of the New Testament is distinctive for its extreme plainness.[58] Nothing about it is impressive at first sight. The Gospel narration is simple, apparently without any literary ambition. It describes a world of everyday people. It includes tax collectors and the sick, likewise the hard drudgery of those who fish or work on the land. It speaks of the simplest things, like grain or wine. This characteristic of a truly plain and simple language is quite striking in all the evangelists. Ancient literature is completely different. This demands an appropriate command of linguistic skills from the speaker. High language requires adornment in the form of heightened formulations and figures of speech. Ancient art and literature are accordingly distinctive for the relativity of form and content. In contrast, the Evangelists seem positively to indulge in understatement.

Although the New Testament speaks of the Redeemer, this is not reflected linguistically in the Gospels. The New Testament denies the demands of classical "decorum". This is done in order to testify to the fact that the Son of God became Man. The Incarnation of Christ is necessarily a paradox. God humbles himself in becoming Man, in order to redeem mankind. The Messiah cannot be recognised purely from his appearance and is therefore not acknowledged by the masses.

This paradox of Christ's Incarnation is of profound significance, since this concept involves a change of perspective. Artists like Bruegel thus see themselves encouraged to show the world in its humbleness.[59] In his pictures, the Flemish artist does nothing to heighten Christ or the Virgin Mary aesthetically. On the contrary, he portrays them as everyday, prosaic, even almost ugly. His supposed realism has Christian roots.[60] Time and again we see a biblical scene incongruously juxtaposed with a urinating man, or the event of Christ's birth set so far to the edge of the picture we can scarcely detect it. Bruegel also stages in his pictures the lack of recognition spoken of in the Bible. He shifts the most important event not only to the side but also into the picture's depth. The artist is not shy of including ugly and repulsive elements. Many of his figures seem squat and grotesque. Nothing is spared in his paintings and prints. Thus it is no wonder that a key focus of his art lies in genre painting, the depiction of supposedly everyday events.

Egidius Sadeler after Bartholomeus Spranger, **Pieter Bruegel,** 1606
Copper engraving, 30.6 x 20.9 cm (12 ⅛ x 8 ¼ in.). London, The British Museum

Pages 42/43
River Landscape with a Sower, 1557
Oil on wood, 73.7 x 102.9 cm (29 ⅛ x 40 ½ in.)
San Diego, California, Timken Museum of Art

Pages 44/45
Landscape with the Flight into Egypt, 1563
Oil on wood, 37.1 x 55.6 cm (14 ⅝ x 21 ⅞ in.)
London, Courtauld Institute of Art, Count Antoine Seilern Collection

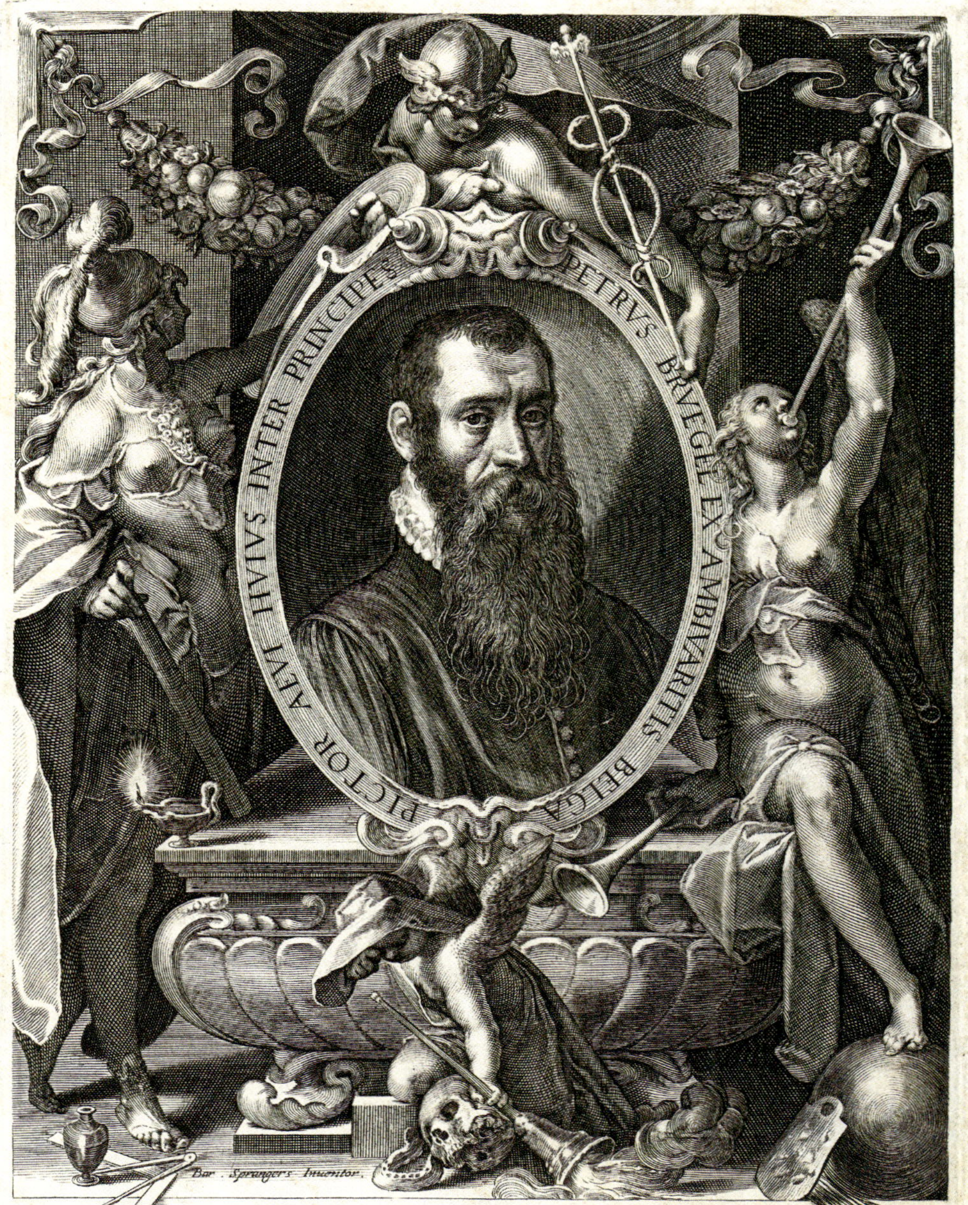

Ars Naturam vicerat, nisi et Ars per Naturam esset: Natura Artem aeternarat, nisi et Naturae nihil aeterni esset. Alumnus Altricem aemulatus, quâ licuit adsecutus est: Altrix Aemulum alumnata, quâ datum prosecuta est. apagè liuor, Artem Naturae, Naturae foedus sociat: apagè dolor, Naturam Arti, Artis foetus sufficit. Viuit in Arte Natura, quam Patris manus expressit: Viuit in Naturâ Ars, quam Fili Genius adsequitur: illam, Naturâ ambiente Virgo Tritonis, Heroum choris inseruit: hunc, Arte prensante Majânatus Olifer, defes flumen reduxit. redâccende facem Lucifuge, inique facis nisi Patrem in Filio nofcis: adtolle tubam Terrigena, nihil agis nisi uterque tibi superstes est.

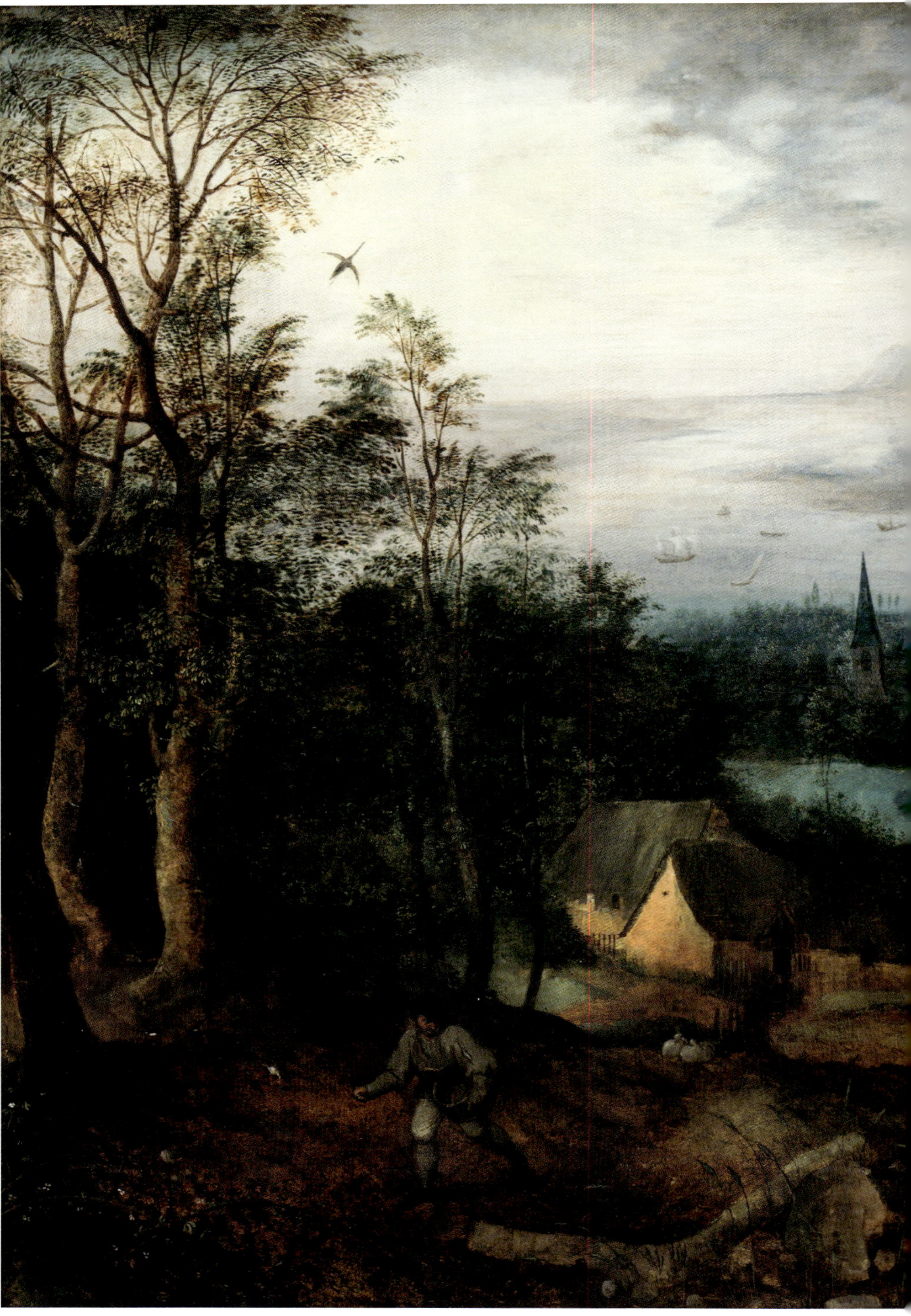

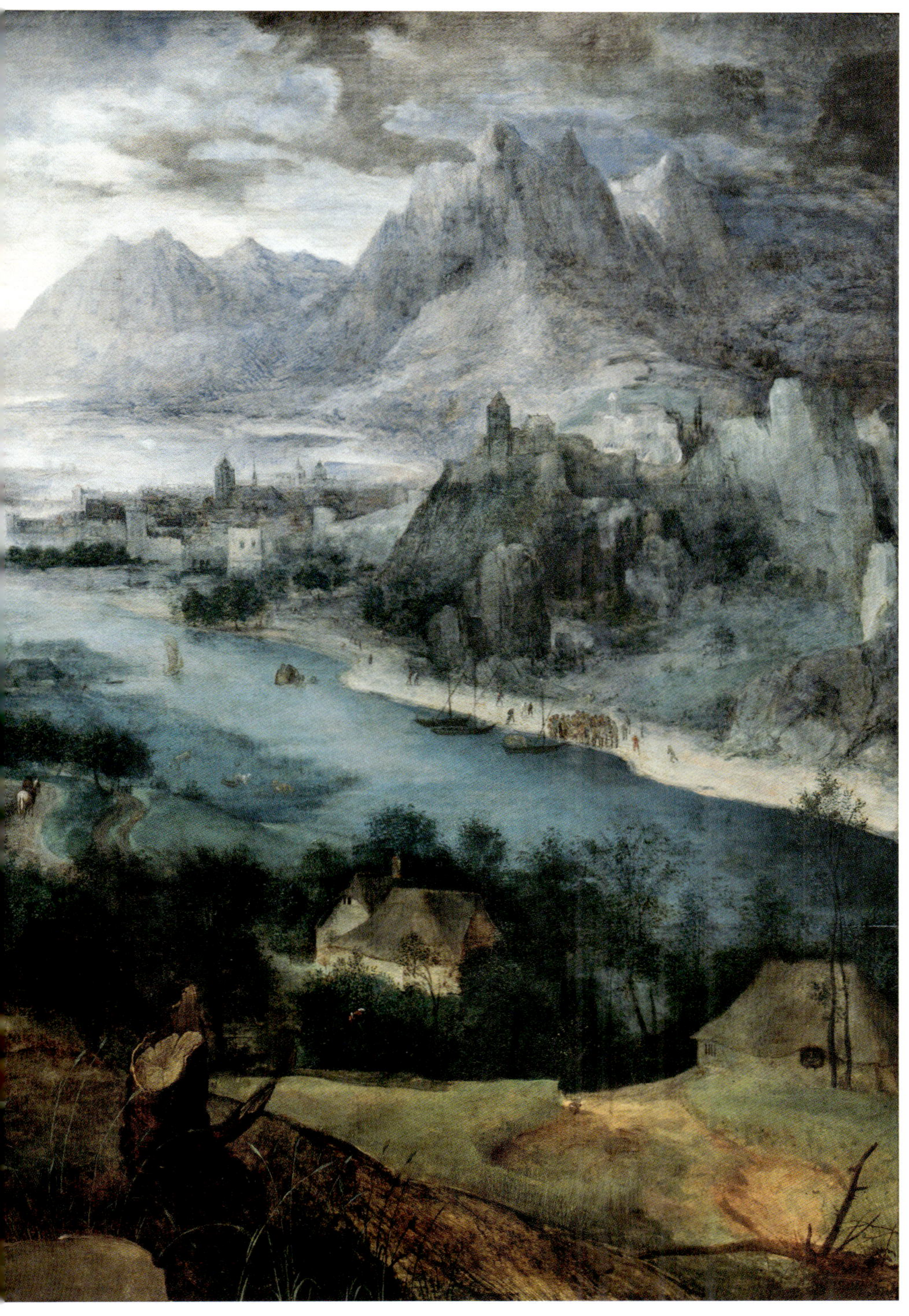

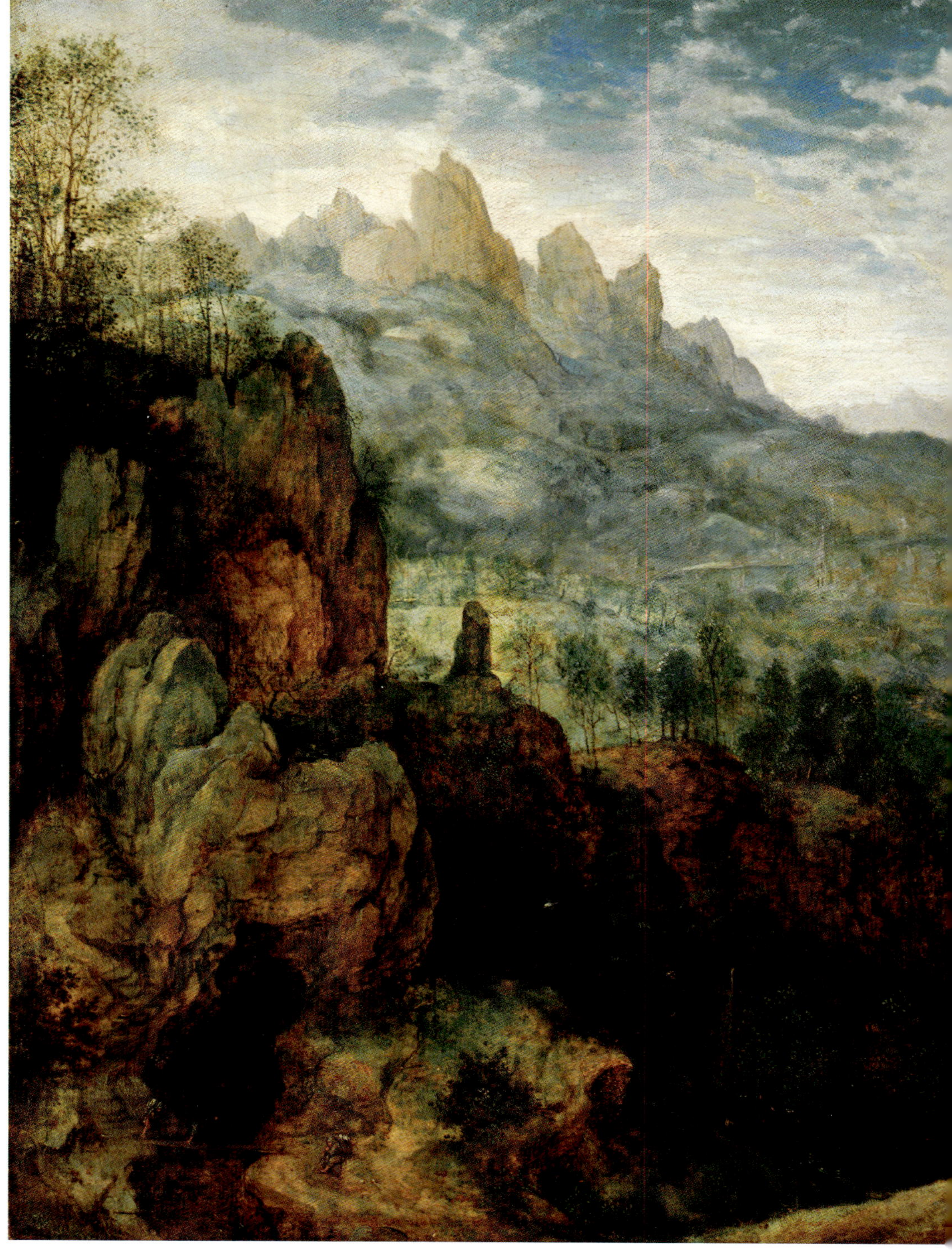

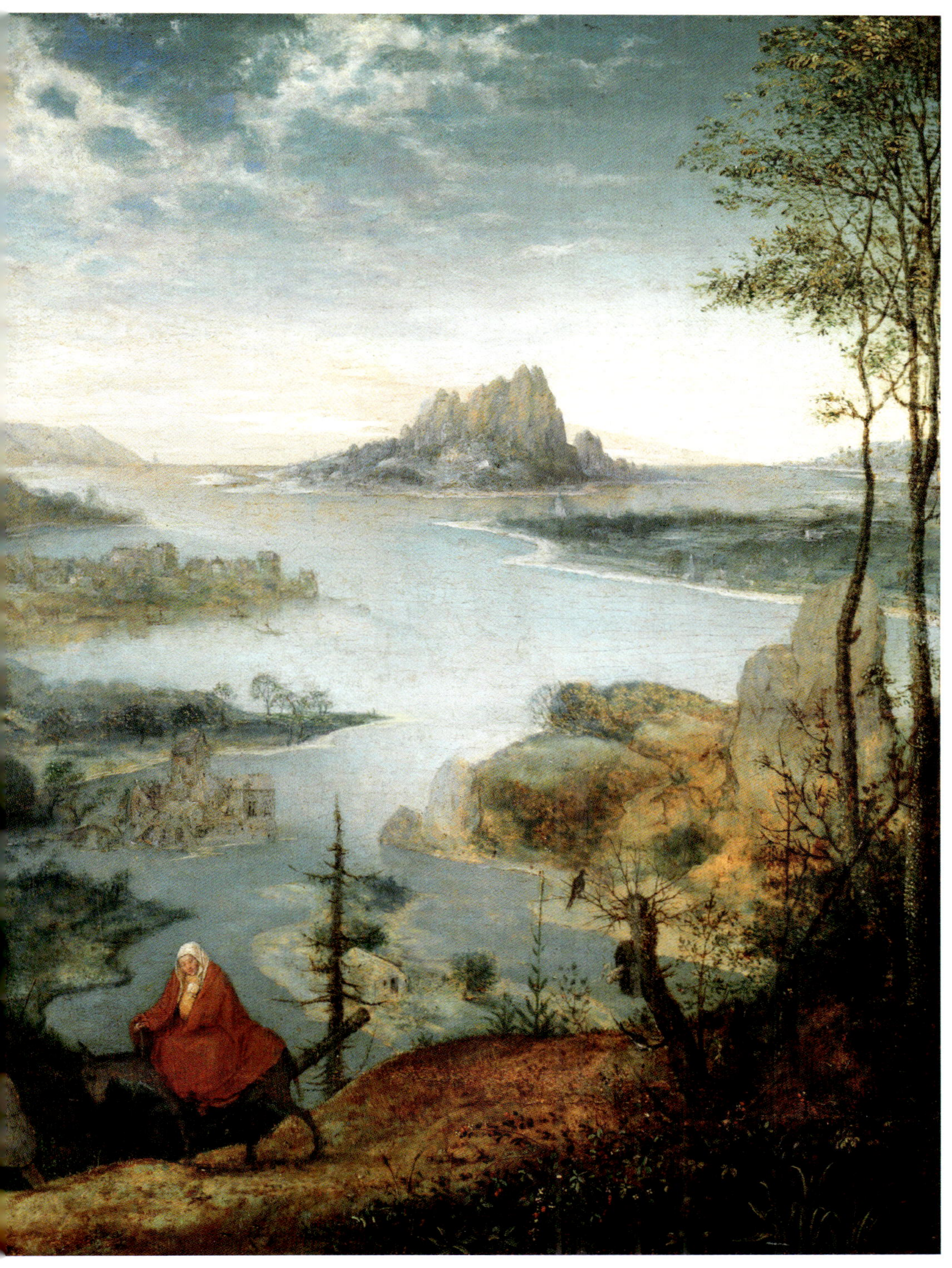

The Labyrinth of Meaning: The Wimmel Pictures

"Things like this make me happy. Bruegel, Hogarth, and Goya, all three have that metaphysical objectivity which is also my goal."

— MAX BECKMANN, 1919

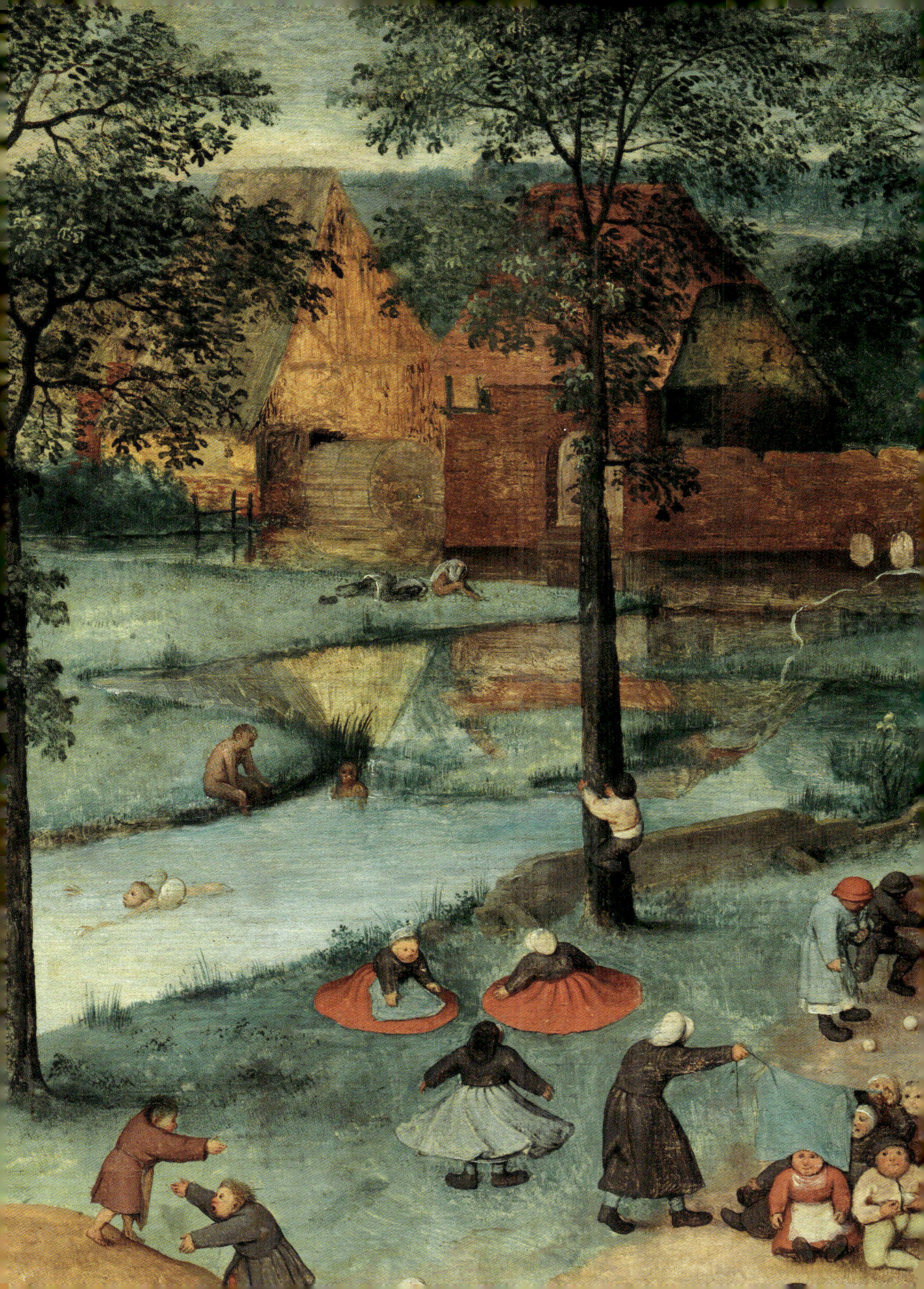

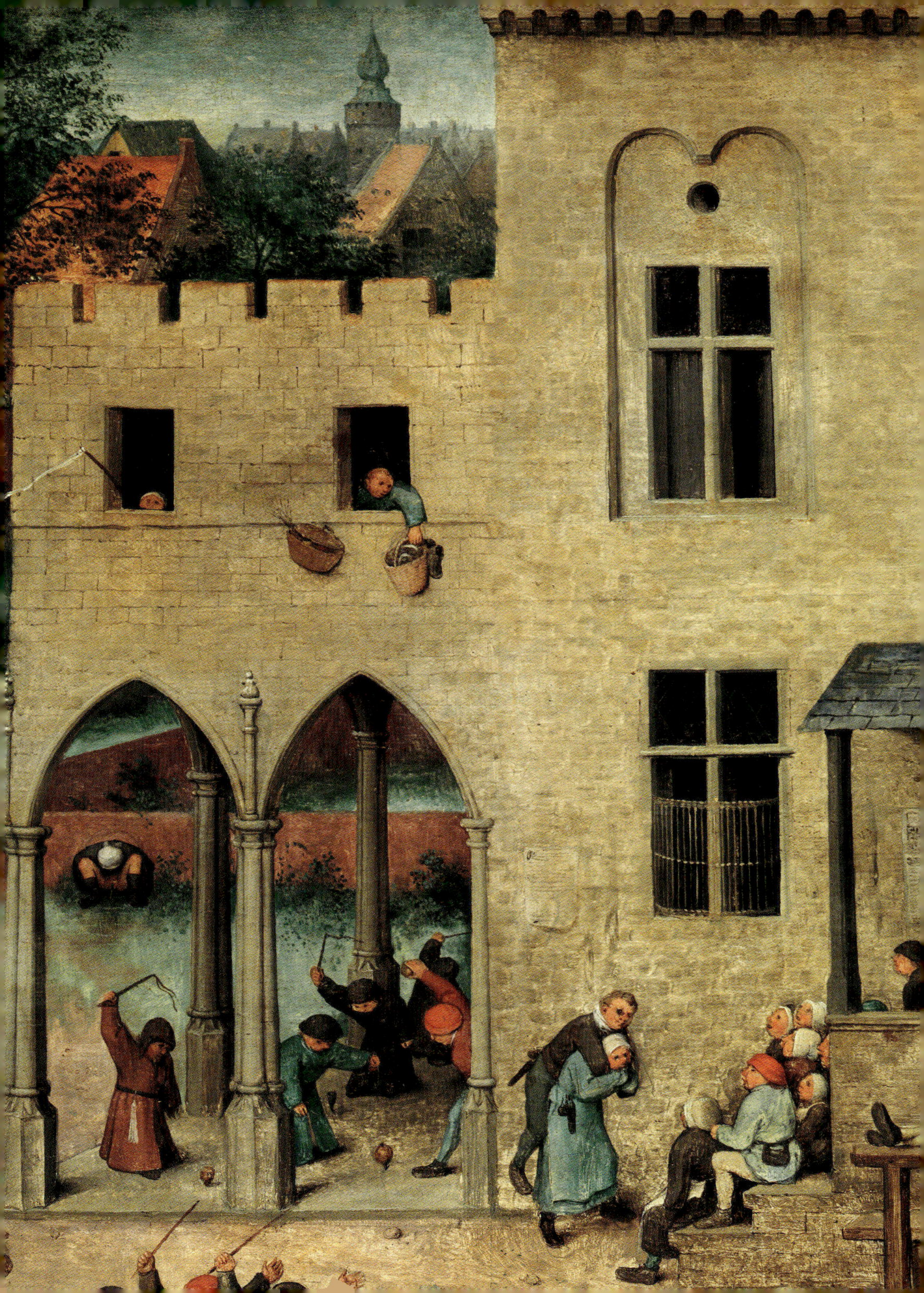

Denominational conflicts

The first panels manifesting Bruegel's characteristic narrative style were produced around 1560. These are three large-format paintings featuring a sharply rising pictorial space and an extraordinarily large number of figures. Often described as "wimmel" pictures – teeming with detail – they belong together not only in their narrative scenes but also in their themes: they tell of the topsy-turvy world. The key picture here is the so-called *Fight between Carnival and Lent* (pp. 76/77, Cat. 4). It is dated 1559 and signed "BRVEGEL". While Bruegel in his early work identifies his authorship in Gothic minuscule, he has now changed to Latin capitals and chooses a Latinised form, a ploy to emphasise his humanist credentials. The signature is on the stone in the bottom left corner. Van Mander mentions the panel in his biography and names its subject, writing: "Breughel also painted a fight between Lent and Carnival."[61]

The pictorial narrative fragments into multiple individual scenes, and the viewer's eye is perpetually tempted to discover something new. In the centre of the lower foreground, a kind of joust is taking place. A fat man bestride a barrel is holding up a skewer on which the head of a suckling pig, a roast chicken and sausages have been impaled, while his rival, a thin woman being pushed on a low cart, is brandishing before her a baking peel like a lance. Two herrings are lying on the flat peel, and behind her chair is a pot of mussels. Also, the thin woman's attire is reminiscent of a Franciscan habit. She is sitting on a small cart carrying all kinds of baked products. The female figure is additionally characterised by rod, book and rosary, attached at her hip. Her processional cart is pulled by two persons also wearing clerical-like clothing. Especially the attire of the man at the front recalls a Dominican habit, underlined by the clearly visible tonsure. Their opponent on the opposite side is being shoved towards them on a kind of sledge.

Here, man is set against woman, fat against thin, meat against fish, the profane against the clerical: Prince Carnival against Mistress Lent (pp. 79–85).[62] The recurring details of empty mussel shells on the right and eggs – prohibited during Lent – on the left also accentuate this opposition. And while all seems to be still on the right, where a sexton is carrying alms of bread and a thurible as in a procession, on the left an infernal din holds sway, expressed in the cacophony and caterwauling of all kinds of peculiar musical instruments.

Even more, in the foreground we see a person in disguise making ribald noises with a jug covered with an animal skin. Carnival is in full swing to drive out winter, and with it the wild carousal that lasts until Ash Wednesday, which is followed by the forty days of

Pages 47, 48
Children's Games (details), 1560
(see ill. pp. 98/99)

fasting in Lent. This is reflected in the many people in fancy dress and the obvious revelry, overriding for a brief time the status quo of law and order. The Carnival celebrates the inverted world that rejects hierarchy of any kind and turns it upside down.

On closer inspection, the panel reveals several critical elements. For instance, the person of Prince Carnival is identified with Luther, who spoke out in his writings against fasting and the abstinence associated with it. For the German reformer, people do not get to heaven through fasting, pilgrimages or good works, but solely through God's mercy. There is a certain plausibility in identifying the man with Luther, when we consider that the two taverns on the left are situated opposite the church on the right. Mass seems to have just finished, because the people leaving the building are being pestered by those begging for alms – another pious practice rejected by Luther, but which was part of everyday life at the time.

While Carnival is still being celebrated on the left half of the picture, at the top edge there are people already walking along a road in the Ash Wednesday procession. The group of people behind the figure of Lent are also worthy of mention in this regard: several of the children have cruciform ashes on their foreheads, which leads us to the inside of the church, where a priest is about to mark the faithful with this sign of transience on their foreheads. Among the people portrayed at the right there are several carrying rosaries, and quite a few nuns are among the people who were at Mass, now leaving the church. There are even two theatre performances in progress. Identifiable at the left edge, just in front of the tavern, is a performance of the play *Mopsus and Nisa*, and in front of the entrance of the second tavern a staging of the *Masquerade of Urson and Valentin* – two popular plays appealing to a wide public, which were reproduced in engravings after Bruegel's death.

It has been suggested that Bruegel oriented his panel on a copper engraving by Frans Hogenberg (p. 51). But comparing the two pictures clearly spotlights their significant differences: while in Hogenberg the church is in the centre, Bruegel shifts it to the right edge and places it opposite the tavern. Furthermore, he presents clearly recognisable forms of Catholic piety not found in the engraving. Among these is the beehive on the head of the figure of Lent, a common symbol of the Catholic Church that also finds a place in other works by Bruegel (p. 55; Müller/Schauerte 2018, Cat. D65, G31, 75). Moreover we can see two kneeling figures underneath a roofed niche at the left of the church portal; they are probably praying in front of a saint's statue, a further reference to Catholic pious practices.

As regards the glutton, Bruegel does not spare his use of caricature. A huge ham is spitted with a knife to the front of the barrel. The glutton's manhood and thus his libido are clearly accentuated, and there is a kind of pasty on his head, while his feet are stuck into large jugs, serving as stirrups. He looks in the direction of the viewer, seemingly

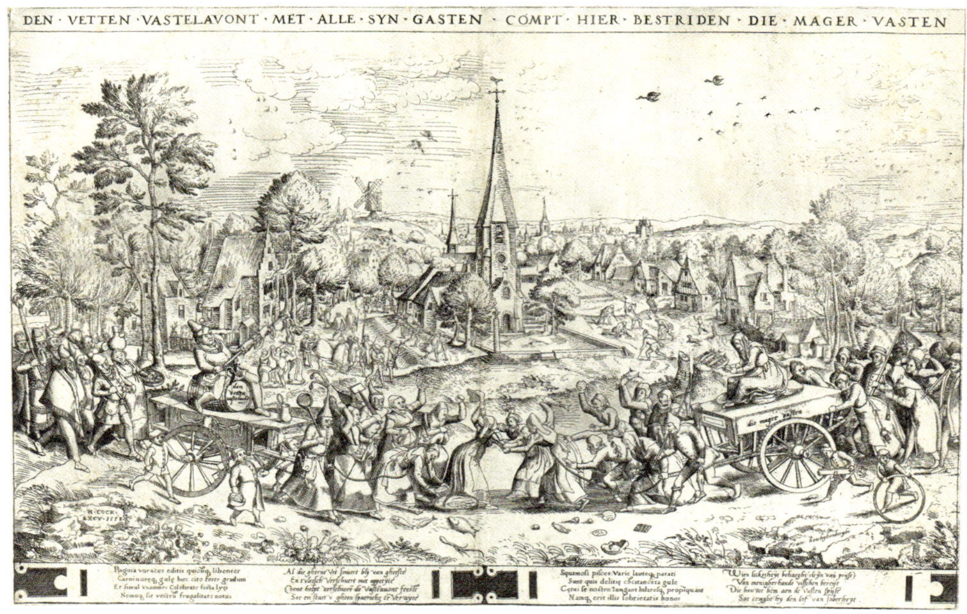

Frans Hogenberg, **The Fight between Carnival and Lent,** 1558
Copper engraving, 33 x 50.7 cm (12 ⅞ x 19 ⅞ in.)
Amsterdam, Rijksmuseum, Rijksprentenkabinet

waving to us with his left hand, thus ironically identifying us as drinking companions. A stark commentary is included above this scene: the pig eating a pile of ordure seems to be a clear parallel to the head of the spitted suckling pig. Bruegel is showing not Lent and Carnival ranged against each, but Catholics and Protestants. Each of the two groups behaves just as foolishly as the other. Bruegel cancels out the differences and exposes both as folly.

Bruegel has devised many scenes showing children playing and dancing, beggars running around and men and women dancing. Especially the scene showing children playing with a spinning top stands for the senseless and ineluctable aspect of Fortuna. There are playing cards underneath Prince Carnival's sledge, likewise indicating a world subject to chance. A key function is given to the person in the geometric centre of the picture. Here a child dressed as a fool is running, paradoxically bearing a torch in the bright light of day, while an elderly couple seem to be following him. Bruegel accentuates this scene conspicuously by brightening the background in this area.

The ways taken by these people cannot go in any reasonable direction, as is evident in the composition's form. Numerous circular and spiral lines extend from this scene, always leading us back to the beginning. For instance, another scene of folly takes place near the people in the procession. While these, led by a bagpipe player, progress as one man, a child has climbed onto a barrel at the corner of the tavern and drinks a tankard of beer in one go, to the delighted applause of the other children. At the same moment, a grown-up empties a chamber pot over him and onto the street. And it is with some sarcasm that a lad in the retinue of the figure of Lent is carrying on his head a basket with clothes for charity in the form of shoes, but the beggar behind him has no feet. We have to learn that "good works" do not always reach their goal.[63]

It is no coincidence that Bruegel depicts the game of dice twice in prominent places. In the bottom left corner, we see two men in fancy dress engrossed in the game, while lads are kneeling on the ground above the torch-bearing child-fool in the centre, just about to throw. A brightly shining lantern directly in front of them accentuates this group conspicuously. This game of dice will have reminded an observer of Bruegel's day of the henchmen's dice thrown for Christ's robe and therefore of the indivisibility of the Church, surely another critique of the conflict between the denominations.

For proof that Bruegel was pursuing a satirical purpose in his panel we need only look at his allegory of *Caritas* (*Charity*; pp. 64/65; see also Müller/Schauerte 2018, Cat. D46), a drawing produced in the year before *The Fight between Carnival and Lent*. Here, too, works of mercy are depicted in satirical form. The act of handing out clothes for charity gives an impression that the beggars are being undressed and not dressed, while the doling out of food has degenerated into a kind of feeding frenzy for predatory animals. A housewife has mixed among the beggars, apparently waiting for charity bread, while the children seem to be fleeing from this scene to seek protection with the female figure of Charity. Moreover, the man marked as a pilgrim being given some bread has a spoon in his hat and not a pilgrim's badge, and so is to be judged here quite negatively as a glutton and good-for-nothing.

Two engravings may be mentioned here, the *Lean Kitchen* and the *Fat Kitchen* (pp. 68/69, 70/71) that yet again have denominational conflict as their subject. The content of these satirical works can easily be grasped, because while the thin Catholics are allotted mussels as Lenten food, the fatty cuisine of the glutton is too much of a good thing. Sausages and hams hang from the ceiling, and everyone present suffers from obesity. Their leader, seated at the head of table, is just about to order a skinny beggar-minstrel out of the house. An interesting figure is the one next to him, his habit perhaps betraying him as the former Augustinian friar Luther. Both denominations are open to ridicule. Namely, while the guest is invited into the *Lean Kitchen*, a way of grasping the opportunity to perform a good work – although there's nothing to eat – the Protestants are exposed to the reproach of gluttony and hardness of heart.

Bruegel's panel *The Fight between Carnival and Lent* is striking in equal measure both for its love of detail as for its prodigal richness of invention. Here he employs a special narrative style. He sets the horizon high, which allows him to accommodate the many scenes in the picture. It is above all the relation of picture format to the size of the figures that forces us close to the picture and robs us of the distance to the portrayed subjects. The panel draws us into a narrative vortex that never ceases to lead the eye breathlessly on to something new. It is decisive that Bruegel condemns intemperate Lutherans as much as he caricatures the pious practices of the Catholics. Both denominations are mocked. Both processions and their participants are equally ridiculed for their folly.

Prisoners of the word

The panel *Netherlandish Proverbs* (pp. 88/89, Cat. 3), dated 1559, is structured according to the same compositional principle as *The Fight between Carnival and Lent*. It is signed in the bottom right-hand corner. But in contrast to the Carnival picture, here Bruegel generates an enormous pull into the picture's depth by leading a diagonal from bottom left along the buildings to the horizon top right. Our eyes leave the town and are guided along a coastal landscape into the distance. The work is without doubt one of the most curious pictorial inventions of the sixteenth century, since it is populated with teeming figures whose peculiar actions we do not immediately grasp. Almost a hundred persons are portrayed on the painting, also animals and numerous objects. A decrepit but stately house stands on the left. Opposite, there is a derelict hut with a brick oven. A path leads between these to a stretch of water close by, where we see the fallen ruins of a small castle. Another house can be seen in the background at the left. The landscape opens up to the right, and the sea is visible on the far horizon. A small ship sails out with hoisted sail. But what is actually being depicted on the multi-figural panel?[64] What are the portrayed people doing? They are given meaning only after we have realised that the scenes are illustrating proverbs. Bruegel has transposed the pictorial element in proverbs into a graphically illustrated action.[65] Naturally, he presents us with Flemish proverbs, though there are frequently English equivalents for them. Studies have discovered no fewer than 119 in the picture, though the identifications are not always completely convincing.[66] They usually refer to moral errors or, putting it in a more positive light, to prudence. Proverbs are easy to remember, because they attach a metaphorical comparison to a problem. If someone defecates onto the world, like the man top left in the window of a house, he is making it quite clear that he doesn't care about anything (p. 90). When big fish eat little fish, as we can see in the water under the castle, we understand that the world functions according to a never-changing power principle. Above this scene, a man throws money into the water, which means he throws his money away on worthless things (p. 93). A little to the right, a man is holding an eel by the tail, thus embarking on a difficult enterprise. All these formulations warn against foolish or dissolute behaviour. Bruegel's achievement here is to give the impression at first that people are serenely going about their normal, everyday business. It takes some time until we realise how meaningless the actions are of the people presented in the picture. Some of the proverbs Bruegel puts into the picture are quite sophisticated; thus he places a scene practically in the centre of the picture that goes back to an ancient fable by Aesop (6th century BC): "The Fox and the Stork". Each animal wanted to deceive the other by serving the food for its guest in dishes that made eating impossible for the other. Thus the fox offers the stork a flat plate, and the latter vice versa serves the fox a dish with an impossibly high rim. Hence superficial courtesy might be hiding covert spitefulness.[67]

Yet again Bruegel uses an etching of 1558 by Frans Hogenberg (p. 58) as his source. Many of the proverbs illustrated by Bruegel can be found here. Moreover, the etching's title at the top edge is significant: *Die Blau Huicke*. It can be translated as *The Blue Cloak* and is a proverbial saying for deception. The title refers to a young woman in the picture placing a cloak over her husband's shoulders, marking her out as a deceiver. A caption explains the scene by saying: "As the blue cloak it has come to fame, but folly of the world would be closer as name."

Besides vernacular axioms, Bruegel's panel also contains some of biblical origin. Close to the horizon we see three blind people making their way – a theme the artist was to handle later in a picture of its own (Cat. 35). The proverb of the blind leading the blind is found in the Gospels and St Paul's Letter to the Romans (Matthew 15: 14; Luke 6: 39; Romans 2: 19) and was a conventional metaphor in Bruegel's time for theological heresies. Another biblical proverb can be seen in the scene in the foreground, where a man feeds roses to pigs; the Flemish "Rosen voor de varkens strooien" can be related to Christ's words "neither cast ye your pearls before swine" (Matthew 7: 6).

Bruegel's encyclopaedic, schematic picture presents a large repertoire of proverbs from which we can glean some important moral insights. If we simply ascribe this intention to the artist we miss the panel's theological content. The objection that it is not plausible to have the few biblical proverbs as criterion for the overall interpretation of the picture does not get to the core of the matter. Here we must note the connection of proverbs and biblical parables.[68] In his Bible forewords, Erasmus of Rotterdam deemed Christ's use of parable-type proverbs to be an exceptional didactic aid. The very fact that the New Testament is addressed to both simple and educated people means that its language has to be graphic. At the same time, he states that Christ wanted to conceal his mysteries from the godless by using illustrative parables, and consequently stresses the opaque character of the New Testament, which communicates its content only to the faithful.

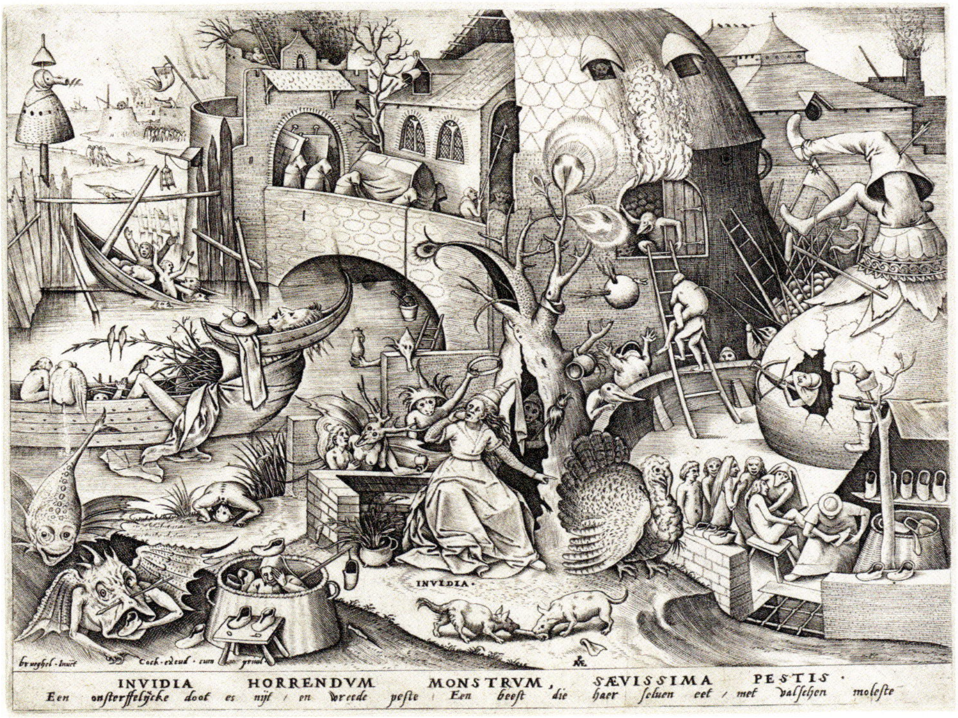

Pieter van der Heyden after Pieter Bruegel the Elder, **Invidia (Envy)**, 1558
Copper engraving, 22.7 x 29.1 cm (8 ⅞ x 11 ½ in.). Kunsthalle Bremen, Kupferstichkabinett

The enthusiasm for proverbs during the Reformation is inseparably linked to the problem of Bible translation and the specific mode of expression in the Scriptures.[69]

We have to note the peculiarly fraught zeal of the people in the picture, its inhabitants caught up almost mechanically – like automatons – in their activities, which are always the same and therefore meaningless. They are prisoners of the word! All vices are mentioned here in the form of proverbs – wrath, intemperance or negligence, deceit and imprudence. Particular attention is given to scenes containing spheres, symbols of the world, among them the aforementioned upside-down or inverted world, which here is being defecated on. A man is seen at the bottom edge of the picture crawling through a sphere, now a glass globe, alluding to the saying that anyone who wants to be an achiever in the world has to stoop low – an image showing that in order to be successful people must have a certain lack of character. Directly next to him we see a nobleman with the world spinning on his thumb, an image of irresponsible behaviour. Another globe features in the scene above. Here, Christ is being given a flaxen beard, a sign for hypocritical

Children's Games (detail), 1560
(see ill. pp. 98/99)

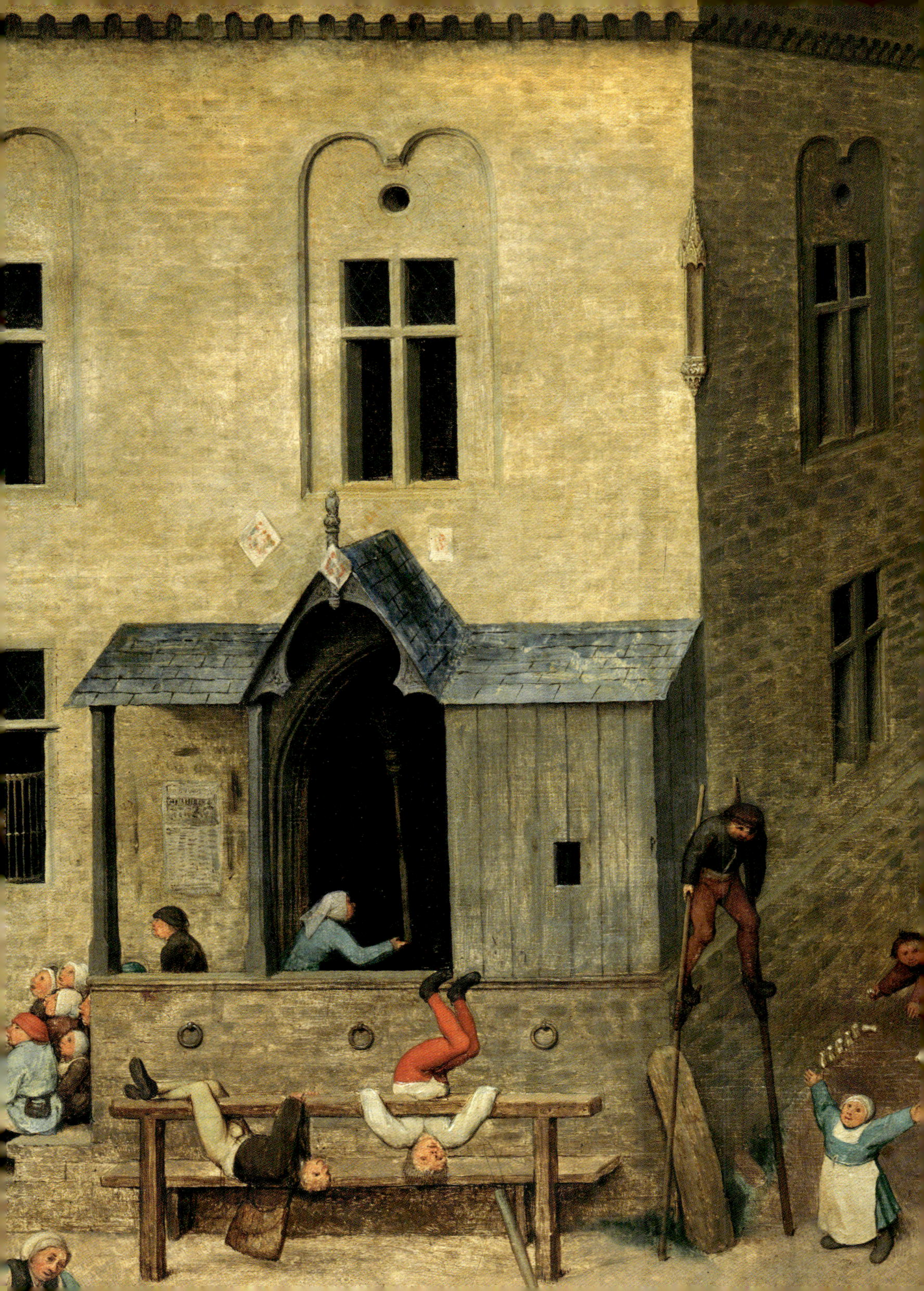

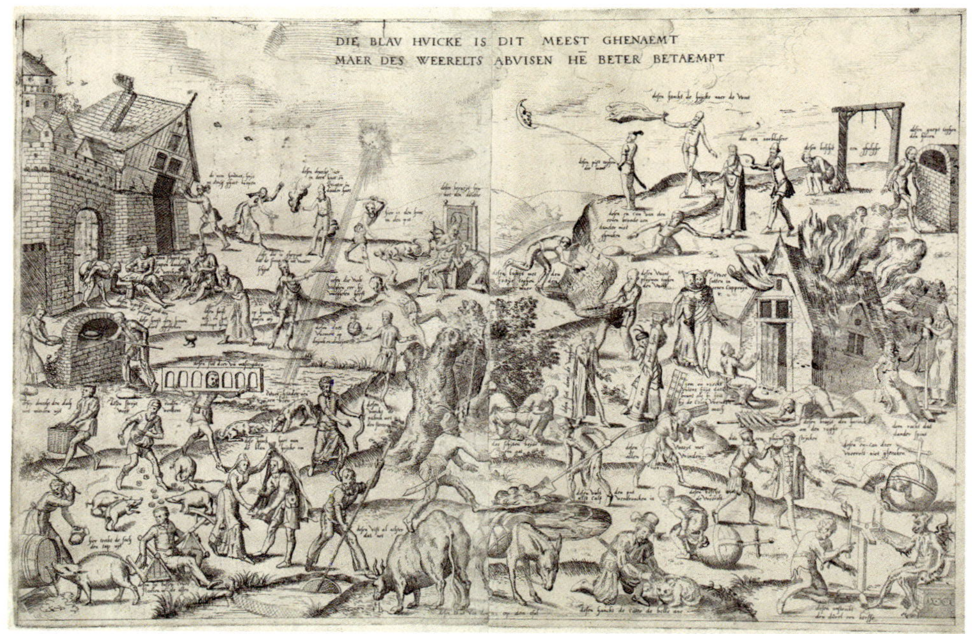

Frans Hogenberg, **Die blau huicke is dit meest ghenaemt …**, *c.* 1558
Etching, 37.8 x 56.8 cm (14 ⅞ x 22 ⅜ in.)
Amsterdam, Rijksmuseum, Rijksprentenkabinet

deception. It is not irrelevant that the culprit here is a monk with a rosary, thus conceived as a supposedly religious person. Bruegel repeats the motif of the globe four times and shows especially in these scenes why we are dealing with an upside-down world, such as Hogenberg intended in the title of his engraving.

This interpretation becomes even more cogent when we look at the visibly attractive persons – two of them, in fact – who are shown mingling with the crowd of ugly people with grotesque visages, and who stand out in their colourful attire. The young woman placing a blue cloak around an old man is standing near the front edge of the picture. She is exceptionally pretty, and Bruegel has designed her red dress with plunging neckline as a decided eye-catcher. She pats the old man's arm amicably; he walks on his bumbling way. To her right is the aforementioned youth spinning the world on his thumb (pp. 96/97). He, too, in contrast to all the other figures, is portrayed as outstandingly attractive and classy, with his pointed shoes, red, well-fitting tights, a costly dagger and a cloak of fine brocade. All this points to a courtly origin and makes him stand out among the crowd of boorishly dressed people. The dashing feather in his hat marks him out in addition to be a real playboy. It is interesting to see how lightly he can bear the Earth's globe on his left thumb and simultaneously point with his right to the man at his feet, who has to stoop low to get through the world. What do these characters mean, picked out conspicuously by their seductive beauty and upright posture among the crowd of crouching, seated and kneeling people? Even before we are aware of whom we might have before us, these two young people have caught our eye. The artist is using them to allude to the allegorical tradition of *Frau Welt* (Madame World) and *Fürst der Welt* (Prince of the World), often found as sculptures on medieval church portals. Observed from the front they are seductive and erotic, but on going past them we see they are rotten at the back. Hence Bruegel, in his portrayal of these figures, has formulated the task of breaking through outer appearance and of exposing the beautiful prince and woman of the world for what they really are.

An interesting feature here is the comparison between the *Fürst der Welt* and the figure of Christ. While the globe spinning effortlessly on the Prince of the World's thumb stands out strikingly from the bright background and seems almost to hover, Christ is holding the world in his hands in such a way that it is only detected at second glance, since it merges in colour and is absorbed by his blue robe behind it. So Christ remains unrecognised, while the man crawling on all fours stoops low, bowing before the prince. And yet it seems no coincidence that Bruegel has arranged the two spheres of Christ and the prince on the same vertical axis.

The actual source of Bruegel's pictorial concept is most probably derived from Sebastian Franck's publication *Paradoxa* of 1534. The literature has pointed out that the Dutch edition does not name a publication year, but theologians were referring to it by around 1560.[70] Much lends credence to the unusual currency of Franck's ideas, comparisons and images in Bruegel's circles, particularly during these years. The German theologian bases his text on the idea that true faith can only be generated by inner enlightenment. Accordingly, the externals of a word conceal the truth even where it originates in the Bible. Franck describes the general reversal ruling the world and observes how perniciously people allow themselves to be blinded. They hold God for the Devil and the actual Devil for God. The Prince of the World is venerated like a god, since he never expects anyone to take up his cross in the spirit of the Imitation of Christ and to follow the Saviour. After the theologian has pointed out the confusion between Christ and the Prince of the World, he turns to the problem of biblical exegesis and explains the function of Christ's parables. In their understanding of the Scriptures, people continually get stuck in the rut of the literal sense, when it is imperative to understand the "eternal allegory". This is exactly what happens in the picture. The insanity and error of human beings consists in taking a metaphorically intended expression literally.

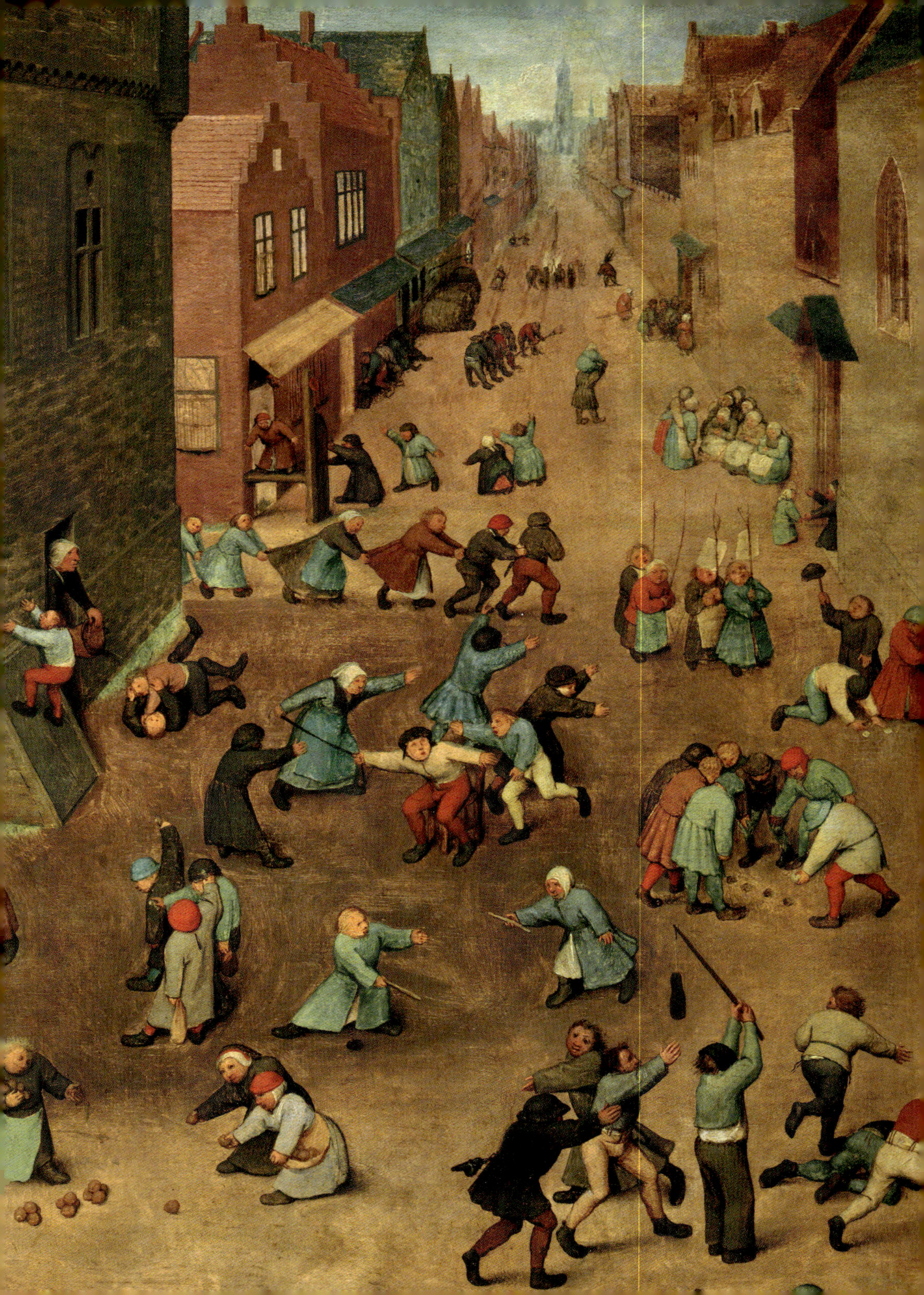

Despite its teeming figures, at first glance Bruegel's *Netherlandish Proverbs* seems to have no one looking directly at the viewer. But did the artist really eschew the opportunity to give the observer a hint? On the vertical axis, we see a man being pilloried as a punishment. This scene is striking because it is placed at the observer's eye level. Within the formal composition, this figure presents the sole opportunity for identification, since we are placed directly opposite. But what is this artless person doing? He's merrily playing a fiddle! It's not enough that the man is exposed to public mockery; he is in fact drawing attention to himself. The saying might be translated as: "He's playing the fool with his head on the block", which means, more or less, "wrongly presuming something". Would it be going too far to detect a warning to the observer in this scene? We are ill advised to make fun of the world and its folly. Anyone doing this makes himself vulnerable – is placed so to speak in the stocks. He had better put his own house in order.

The sacraments as child's play

How can the critique of the denominations we have seen apply to the third encyclopaedic schematic picture, the so-called *Children's Games* (pp. 98/99, Cat. 5)? At first glance, this picture presents a challenge to the theory of denominational critique, for what can be more light-hearted than children's games? The panel is yet again signed and is dated 1560, so it was executed a year before the other two "wimmel" pictures. Here, too, Bruegel uses the familiar overview effect. We see a square in a town where children are joining in all kinds of games. From here a street extends on the right as far as the horizon. Bruegel takes a compositional pattern based on central perspective. In the far distance is a splendid building, its high steeple making it reminiscent of a cathedral (p. 60). On the left, the view leads through to a stream, a meadow with trees, and other houses. Above these we see roofs, dominated yet again by a church tower.

Counting exactly, we find Bruegel has portrayed 168 playing boys and 78 girls.[71] The sheer number defies orientation. Only slowly does the eye come to rest and pick out individual games. At first, games of skill strike the eye; children in the foreground energetically rolling hoops or rocking to and fro on a large barrel. The obligatory leapfrog has to have a place, also a huck-a-pack joust next to it. To the left of this, a group is playing blind man's buff, and gymnastics are being practised in the garden. We see headstand and forward somersault, likewise arms and legs clasped together. Two lads on stilts stalk around in various places in the middle of crowd. Trees and houses have to be climbed and tops spun. One child is hanging upside down on the horizontal bar of a horse tether and

Children's Games (detail), 1560
(see ill. pp. 98/99)

has the sky under his feet. The picture also contains a witty comment by Bruegel – he has put his signature on the front of a little wall in the right-hand corner where a girl is making red pigment out of bricks.

We could spend much time describing other scenes. But what were Bruegel's intentions in depicting around ninety games? Nearly all of them can be identified.[72] It is assumed in the literature that the children are imitating the adult world, if not mocking it.[73] It also suggests that the artist had an ethnological interest, indeed, a documentary intention of making an inventory of all games ever invented. Furthermore, the realistic character of the picture seems to stress Bruegel's intention of portraying the everyday life of peasant children.[74] But why peasant children?

In his picture, Bruegel is thinking far more of the essence of play. We see that this day cannot come to an end; a never-ending new beginning is associated with play. Only those who take the role given to them in play at face value are able to play, those who take fun seriously. This can be most amusing, for instance when the little boy in the foreground riding a hobbyhorse believes he has a fiery charger between his legs, or a girl yelling into a bulbous barrel thinks she is hearing an uncanny noise. Or look at the child in the top window at the left edge of the picture. He or she is wearing a frightening mask and wants to terrify the others. This ability of children to take appearance for reality is Bruegel's subject. A grown-up person crops up only in one place: an elderly woman steps out of a door on the right side of the central house; she has a bucket of water to throw over the lads who won't stop fighting.

The tendency towards ugliness in portraying the children must be cited as an argument against a romanticising vein in the picture. This clearly contradicts the Reformation iconography that puts a positive light on children; for Luther they were nothing less than an ideal image of the faithful. They embody not only innocence but also the necessity of divine mercy. Lukas Cranach the Elder (1472–1553) was the artist whose pictures explored the blessedness of children and made it into a genuine Lutheran theme.

What overriding meaning is the artist pursuing beyond simply listing games and specifying the essence of play? To clarify this question, we are not helped by forming sub-groups and identifying which games are played with and without technical aids, or which are reserved for boys or girls. And indications of the topsy-turvy world or games as *vanitas* symbols require a more precise identification. The most important clue towards a constructive interpretation is provided by Stridbeck, who points out the wedding procession in the centre of the picture.[75] If we follow the two diagonals in the picture, we find at the intersection – thus at the absolute centre of events – the figure of the bride. She is flanked by her bridesmaids, and the procession is led by flower-strewing children. Stridbeck recalls the symbolic significance of the bride in terms of the Church as *sposa Christi*. This reference sensitises us for the depiction of other Church rituals. Thus we should look at the girls playing with dolls in the entrance of the house in the bottom left corner. They are seated directly in front of a cupboard-like piece of furniture rather like an altar. On its top we find other dolls, evocative of a crib scene.[76]

A group of children should also be noted in this context, who are approaching the entrance to this house, one after the other. The child walking ahead is carrying a bundle that looks like a new-born babe. We are reminded of the time when a child must be baptised directly after its birth to prevent its going into Limbo through no fault of its own, should it die suddenly.

There is another group of "pious" children to be noted. At the level of the fighting lads, another procession can be detected to the right; the children are carrying square pieces of cloth like church banners. The tendency towards this playful imitation of pious rituals led Sandra Hindman to an astonishing observation. A fire has been lit on the street on the right, far away from the children. It is St John's Fire, preceding 24 June, St John's Day.[77] Numerous clues support this interpretation. The Sun is high, the shadows behind the people are short. St John's Day is traditionally celebrated as the summer solstice, the beginning of summer. Swimmers and blossoming trees, also the brightly illuminated front of the building, betray the warm season of the year.

Baskets for holding herbs are seen under the windows of the last named building.[78] If gathered on St John's Day, they were thought to have magical properties; attached to houses, they were said to protect against fire and thunderstorms. Further superstitious images associated with this day can be discovered in the picture. For instance, the children swimming and climbing at the left are in great danger (p. 47). The superstition holds that St John claims one swimmer and one climber on this day, therefore these practices are actually forbidden to children on St John's Day. Even the baptism suggested on the left has a special meaning associated with this date, since it promises wealth on this day. But all these scenes just described shift the games into a superstitious context that distorts the Christian message.

Observers sensitised to this problem may detect a group of games that cannot be directly characterised in this way. For Bruegel has included perceptible clues relating to the iconography of the Passion. At the far-right edge, for instance, there is a scene in which children are pulling the hair of one boy in their midst, a "game" called "Haarken plukken" in Flemish. The group's formation, however, clearly recalls the Crowning with Thorns. Under this scene, there is another game alluding to the Passion. A child is being pulled to and fro by his mates, in Flemish "Bofkanten". This immediately makes us think of the laying of Christ's body in the tomb. To the right of this we see two boys crouching on the ground. Behind them is a pile of bricks in semicircular arrangement.

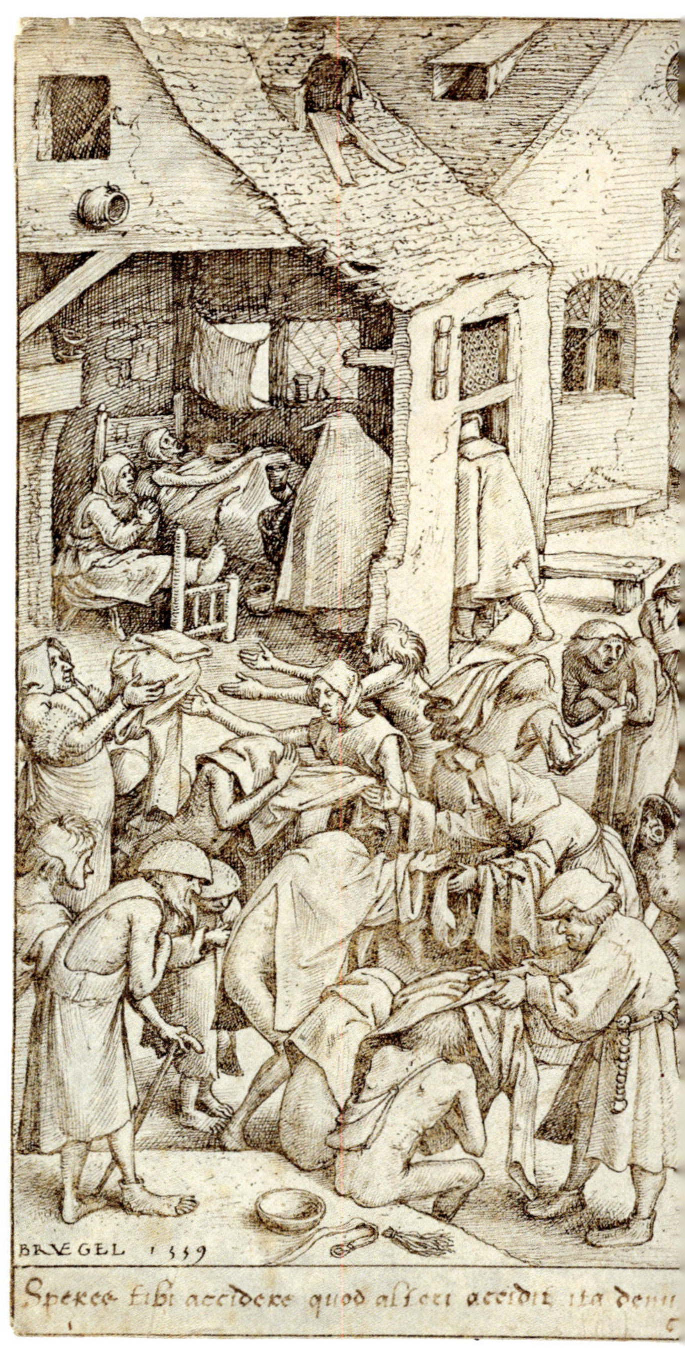

Caritas (Charity), 1559
Pen and blackish-brown ink,
22.4 x 29.9 cm (8 ⅞ x 11 ¾ in.)
Rotterdam, Museum Boijmans
Van Beuningen

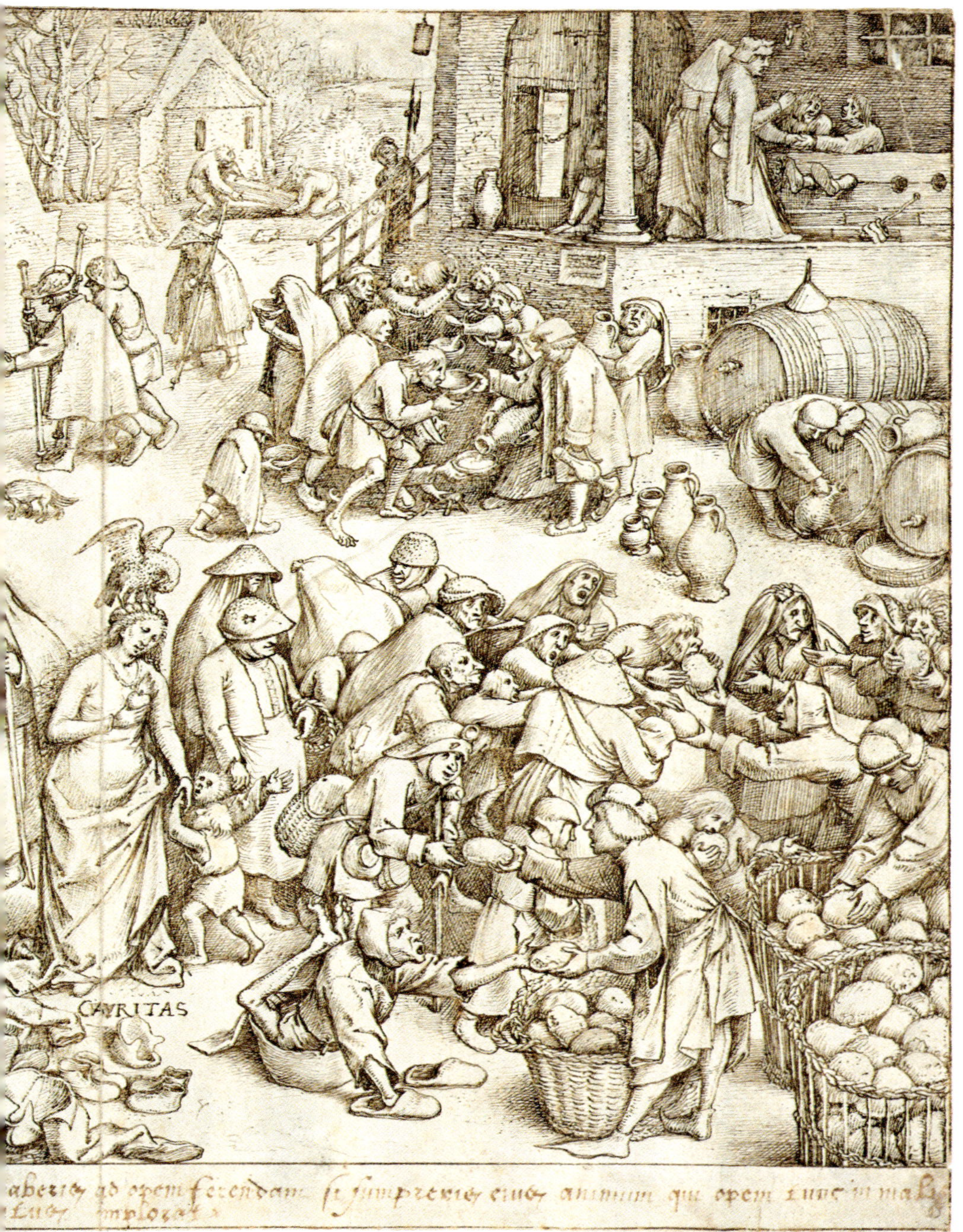
CARITAS

Together with the bricks, the motifs point to the mason's craft "Metselen" or "Huikekes bouwen". Both seem to express surprise or incredulity, reminding us of the soldiers who were supposed to guard Christ's tomb and found it empty. Finally, we see children under the arcades playing spinning top. Several boys raise their whips to hit the tops. One boy stands apart near a column, his posture in connection with the column recalling a henchman from the Scourging at the Pillar.

This and other clues relating to the Passion iconography scattered across the picture form a picture in the spirit of a genuine Imitation of Christ that is counter to the rites and sacraments being mocked here. Bruegel is showing true Christian faith challenging the pursuit of a merely superficial practice of piety. Many of Sebastian Franck's writings are cited in the literature, in which the metaphor of children's games is associated with a negative judgement on ritual. In a letter of 1531 translated into Dutch, the theologian compares the sacraments yet again with children's games.[79] God at first allowed the Church to practise such outer signs, but now it was important to plead for a Church that exists solely according to the spirit, which requires no sacraments. These, he writes, have been debased into "vain children's games".[80]

Bruegel's Silenian poetic imagery

The individual interpretations of the three "wimmel" pictures suggest they were planned as counterparts not only in their almost identical format but also in content. Each draws attention in its own way to the danger of externalising faith. This is most obvious in *The Fight between Carnival and Lent*, with its theme of the conflict between the religious denominations. *Netherlandish Proverbs* reflects the problem of interpretation in terms of a conflict between the literal and the image, and pleads for a metaphorical, allegorical interpretation. *Children's Games*, in conclusion, points out the danger of externalisation through Christian ritual. Bruegel's pictures relate in inverse proportion to one another in that in *Proverbs* everything that should be understood metaphorically is taken literally, whereas in *Children's Games* the playfully enacted reality of the adult world seems real to the children, consequently they understand in the metaphorical sense what actually should be taken literally. It is therefore illuminating to point out the structural correspondence of all "wimmel" pictures in terms of their ironic idiom. Truth lies precisely in the opposite of what we see!

The emphasis on the pictorial programme conveying a critique of the denominations in these panels should not in any way inhibit laughter at individual scenes. On the contrary, Bruegel manages, like Erasmus before him in *Praise of Folly*, to conceal the serious in the frivolous. He makes use of the rhetoric – beloved of humanists – of *serio ludere*, serious play.[81]

If we want to find an explanation for the narrative technique that employs the ironic idiom of inversion, we can be helped by Franck's statement at the end of the 91st paradox in the German theologian's publication of the same name: "This is why appearance must contest with truth and why the world has the appearance, but God retains the truth. This is why truth cannot be to God what it seems to the world, but each thing is reversed, and an inverted Silenus. Furthermore: Inversus Silenus Omnia."[82]

The citation is about the character of the world as one of seeming, which cannot be abrogated for human beings. Alone God can know truth, while humans are caught up in error. The passage relates to a famous text by Erasmus.[83] In his *Adatium Sileni Alcibiadis*, he had described the inverted world as its real state. Everything behaves in inverse proportion to everything else. The Silenus metaphor originated in one of Plato's (428/27–348/47 BC) Dialogues. In the *Symposium*, Alcibiades sets Socrates's ugliness against his inner worth and compares him with small statues of Silenus. These nondescript vessels must be opened in order to reach the treasures within.

Erasmus applies the ironic eulogy on Socrates to Christian teaching and to the world as a whole. Christ's redemptive act sets up a Silenian truth. Jesus rides on an ass into Jerusalem, mixes with the common people, and yet at the end turns out to be the Saviour of humankind. As little as the insignia of power manifest an individual's character, so little can the inside be read on the outside. And this is the same in the everyday world, writes Erasmus. Because precious things are concealed within the low and humble, just as the glory of a grown tree sleeps in a tiny seed.

For Franck, too, the world is subject to the law of reversal. He adopts the Christian philosophy of a Silenian and constantly comes back to this text in the *Paradoxa*, using it as a leitmotif, so to speak. He writes: "In bivio sunt omnia" (Everything is at a crossroads). Already in the introduction to the *Paradoxa* he writes "one must release Silenus" in order to find the Christian treasure. One must deny oneself and seek Christ in one's inner soul and not follow the Churches' claim to power.

The reference to the Silenus metaphor used by Erasmus and Franck allows us to identify Bruegel's inversions as programmatic. His pictures unmask the pretensions of outer beauty and institutional power. Truth is hidden and seen only at second glance. The artist works against appearance. This applies not only to the beautiful and the ugly but also to the visible and the invisible. In Bruegel's art, we must not allow ourselves to be deceived by Silenus' ugly appearance; we must look into his inner being. We ought to consider the *Proverbs* and *Children's Games* again in the light of François Rabelais's (c. 1494–1553) *Gargantua and Pantagruel* from the first half of the sixteenth century.[84] Rabelais already alludes to the Silenus metaphor in the foreword to his text, thus presenting his novel as an expression of the Christian world view according to Erasmus.

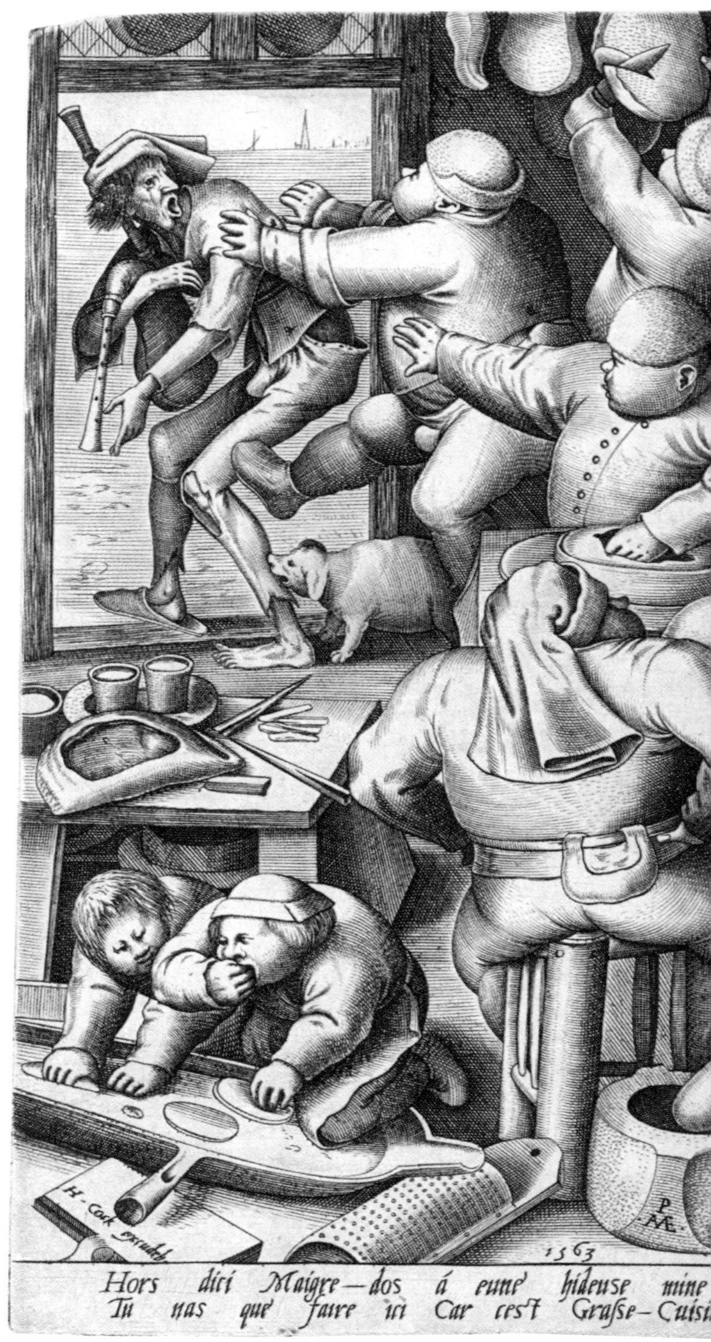

Pieter van der Heyden after
Pieter Bruegel the Elder
The Fat Kitchen, 1563
Copper engraving,
22 x 29.3 cm (8 ⅔ x 11 ½ in.)
Amsterdam, Rijksmuseum,
Rijksprentenkabinet

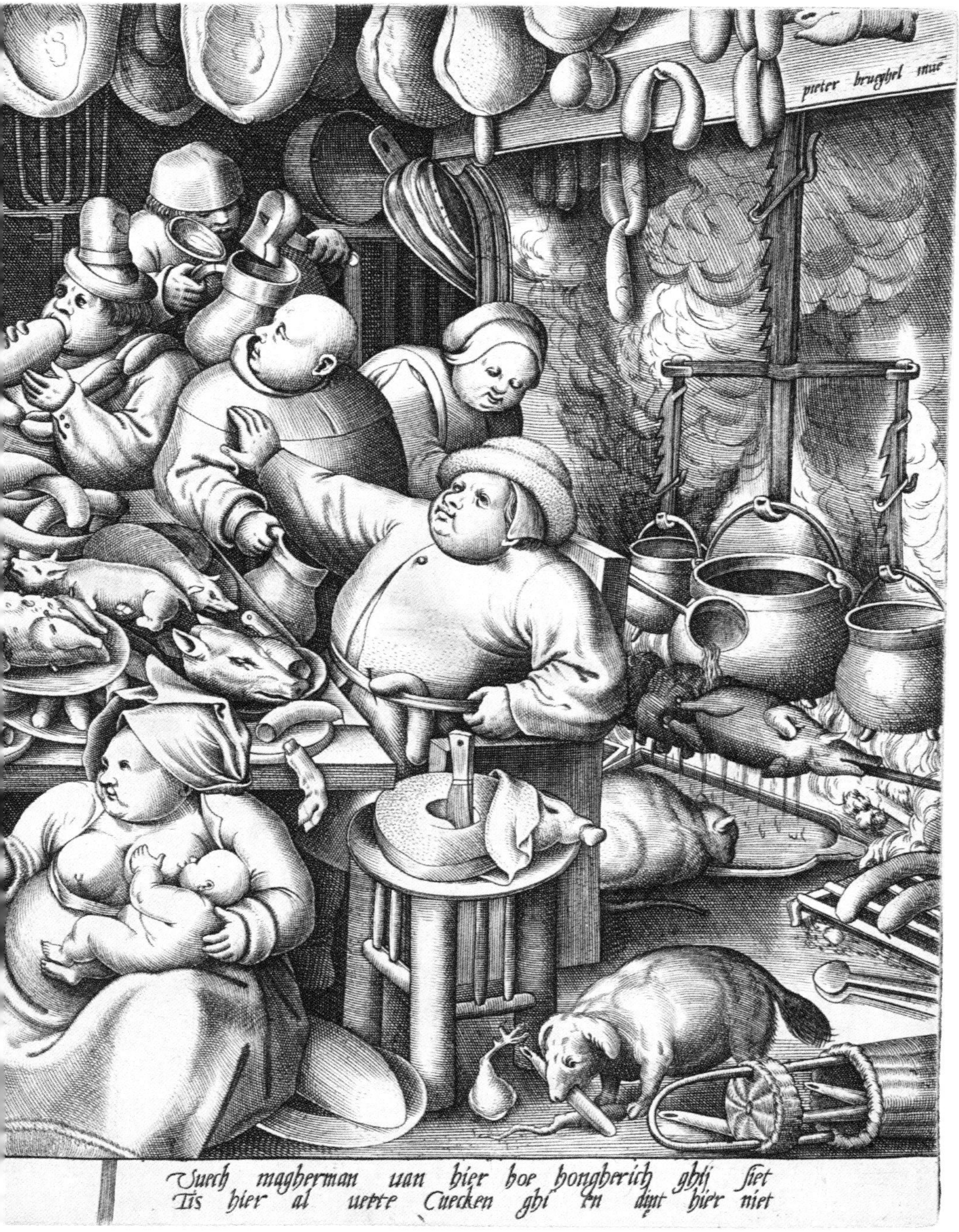
pieter brueghel inue
Uuech magherman uan hier hoe hongherich ghij siet
Tis hier al uette Cuecken ghi en dijnt hier niet

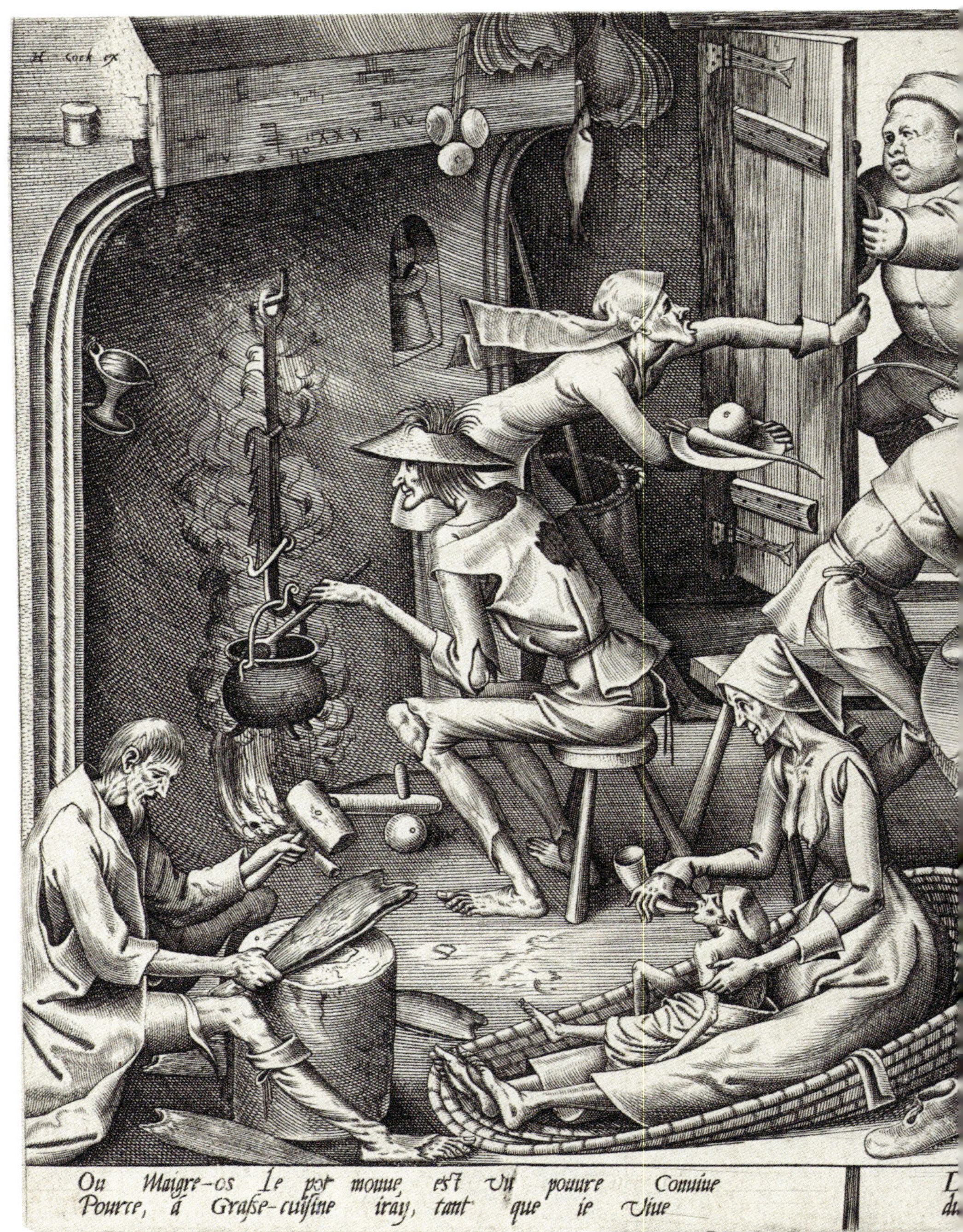
Ou Maigre-os le pot moüe, est vil pouure Conuiue
Pourre, a Grasse-cuisine iray, tant que ie Viue

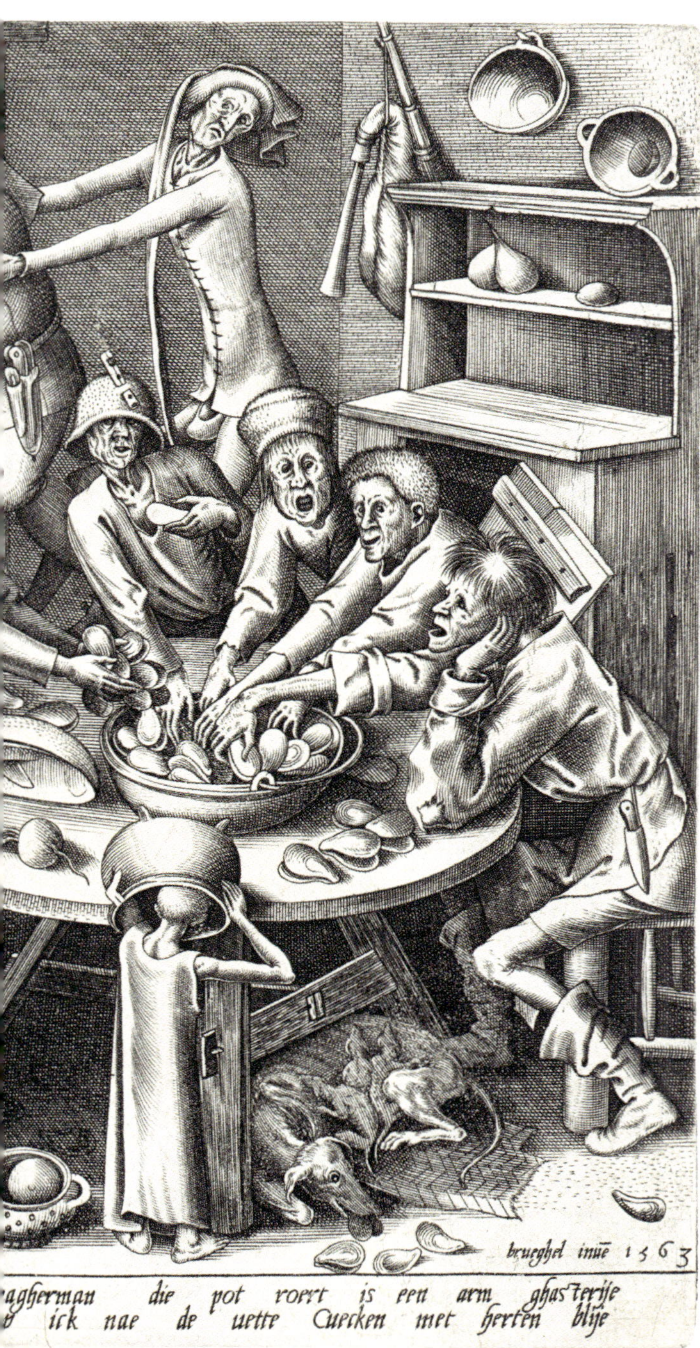

Pieter van der Heyden after
Pieter Bruegel the Elder
The Lean Kitchen, 1563
Copper engraving,
22.4 x 29.1 cm (8 ⅞ x 11 ½ in.)
Amsterdam, Rijksmuseum,
Rijksprentenkabinet

Children's Games (detail), 1560
(see ill. pp. 98/99)

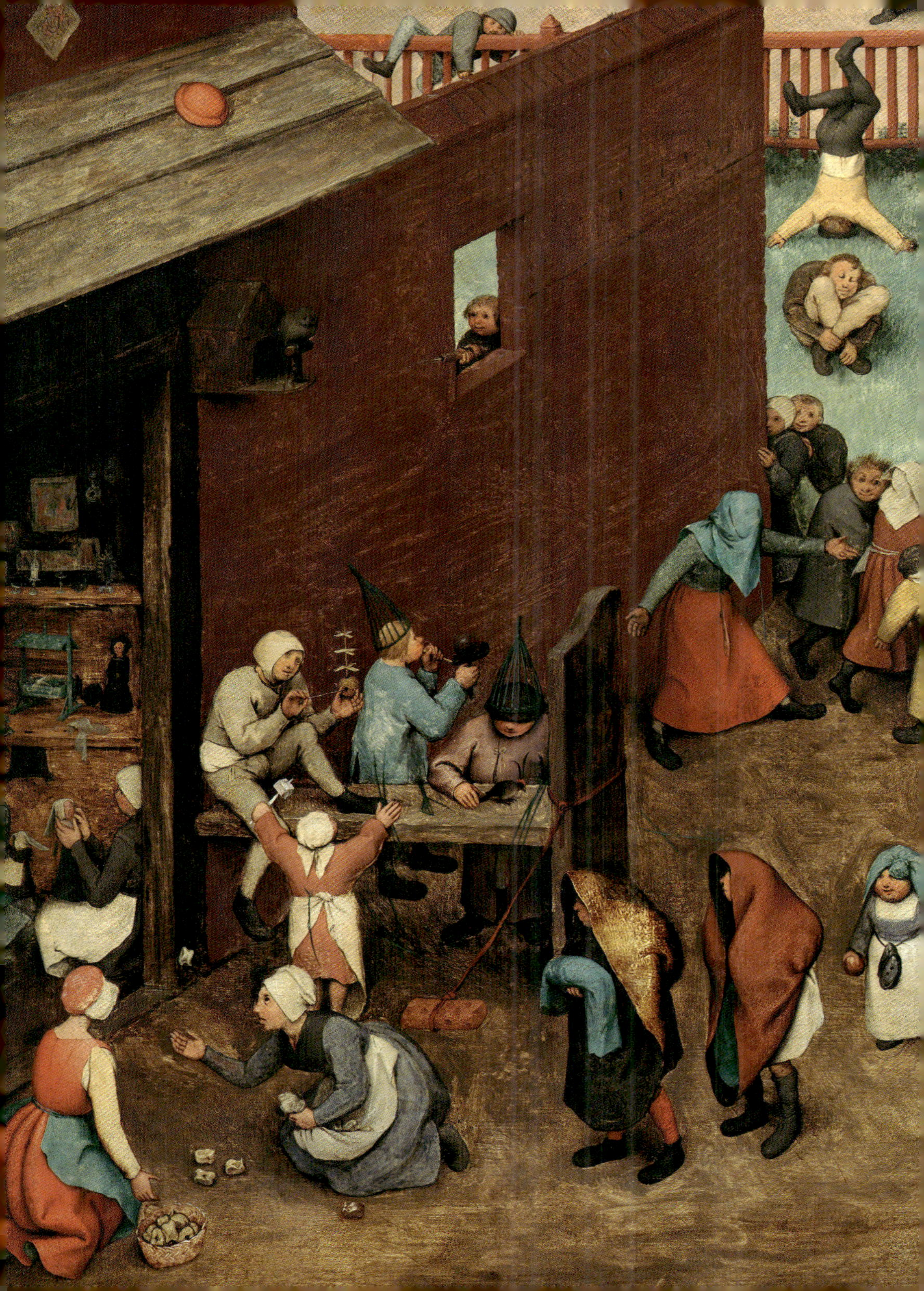

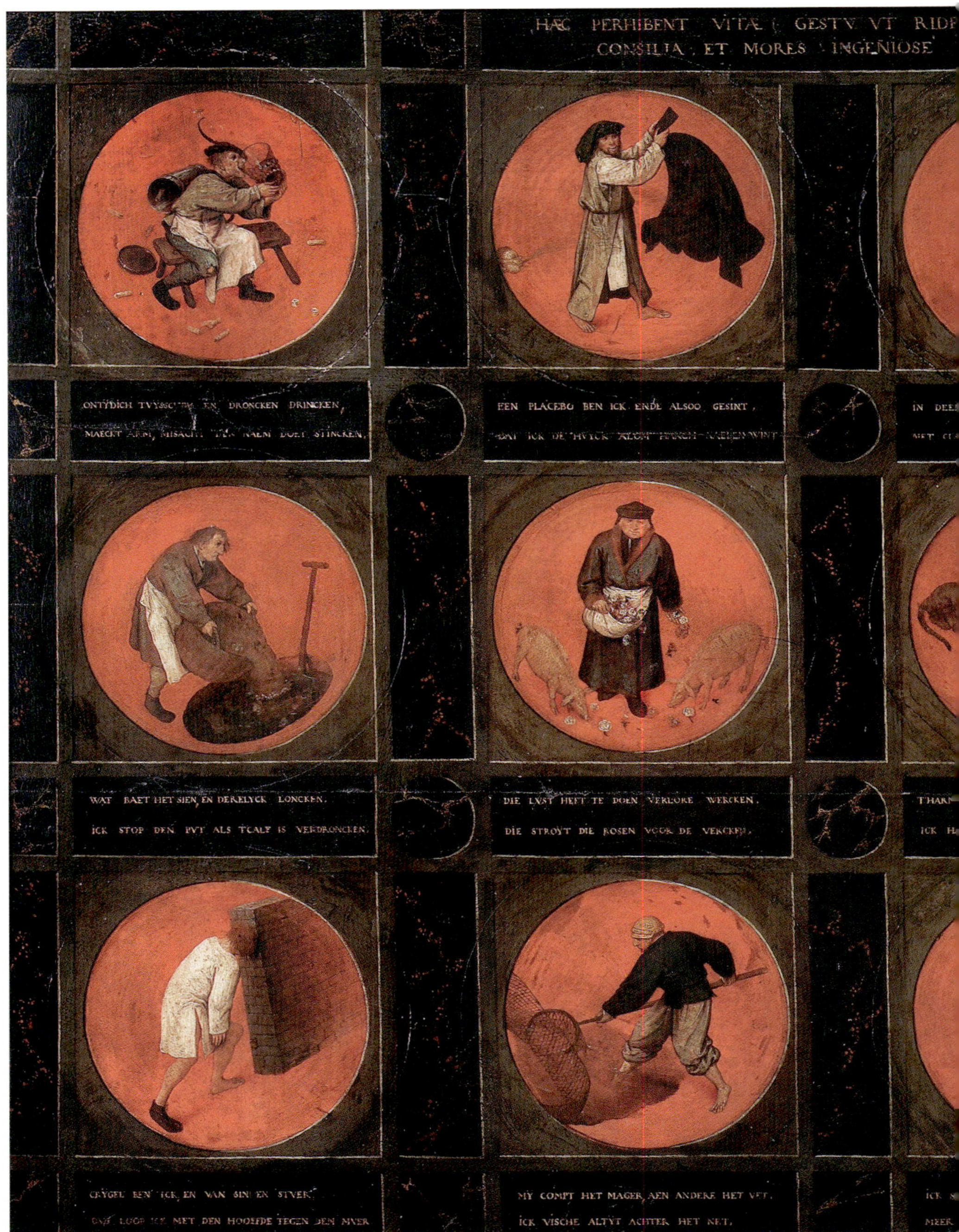

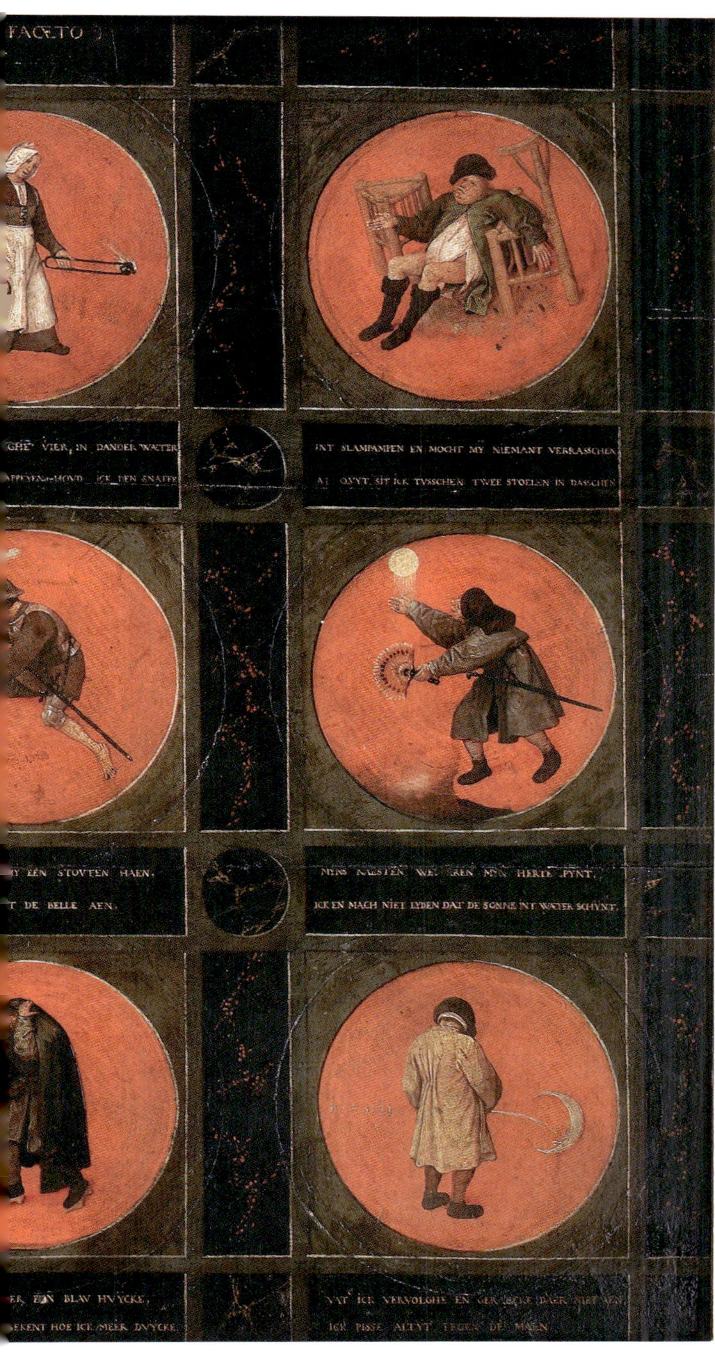

Twelve Proverbs,
c. 1558–1560
Oil on oak, 74.5 x 98.4 cm
(29 ⅓ x 38 ¾ in.)
Antwerp, Museum
Mayer van den Bergh

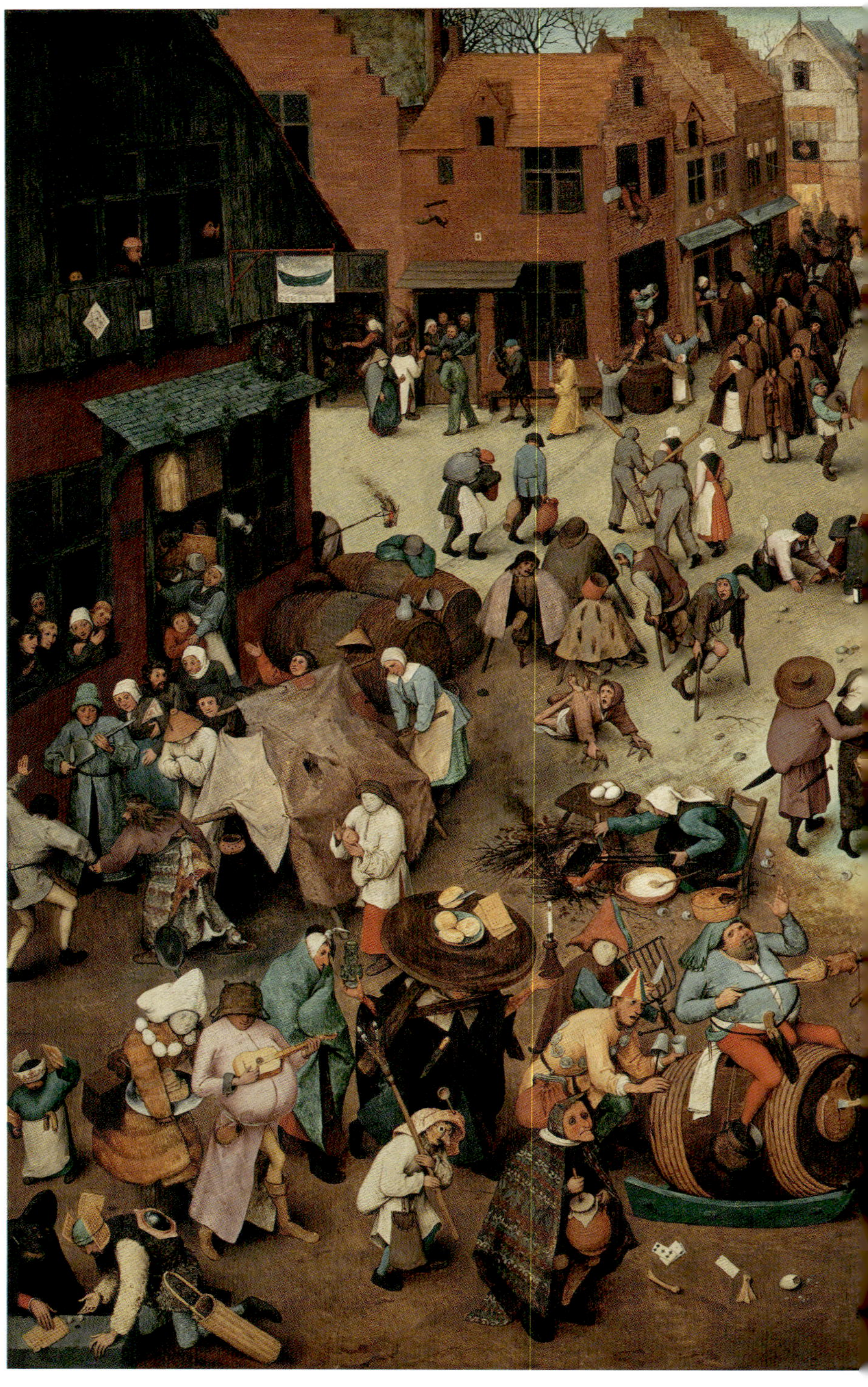

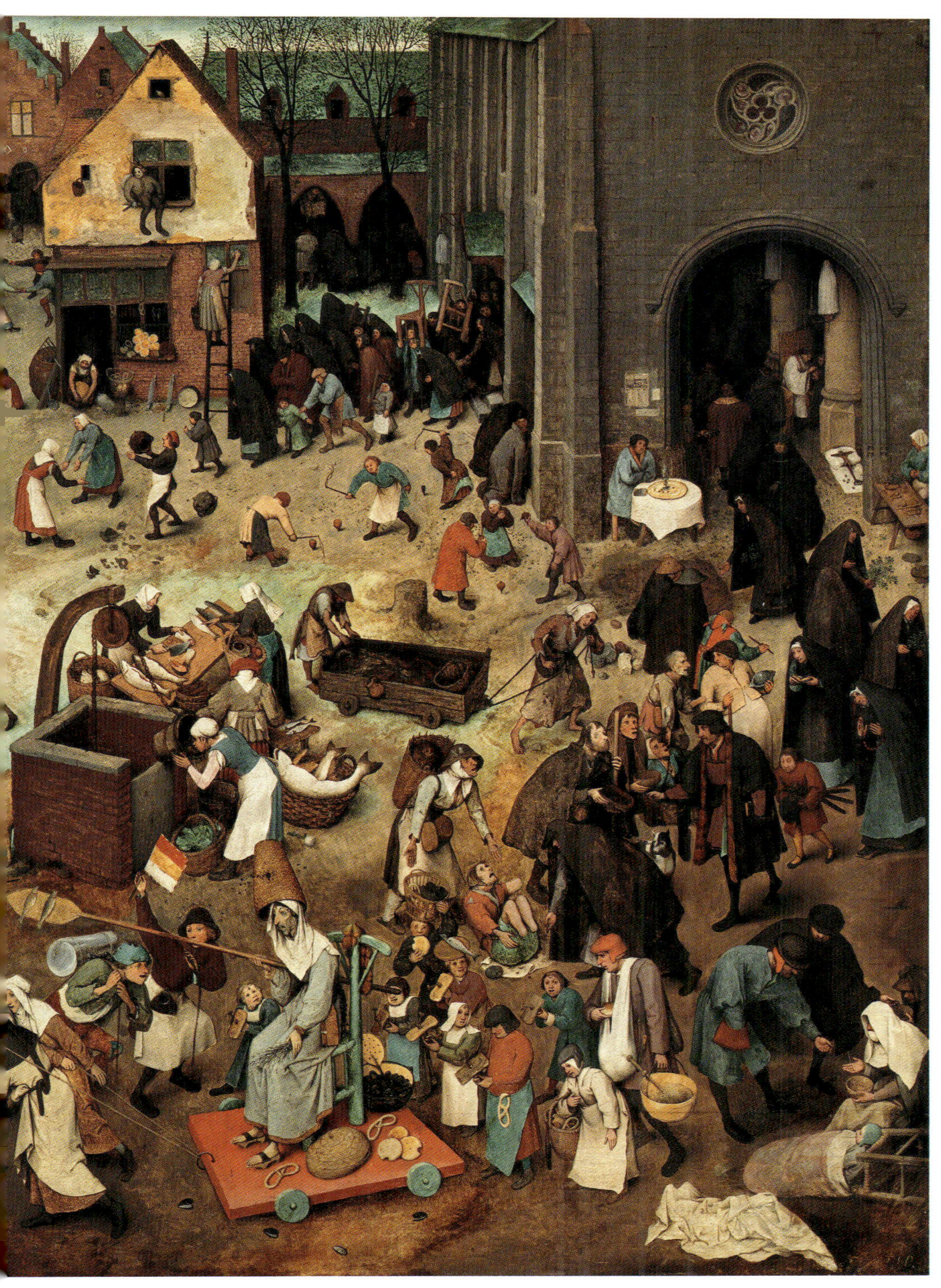

Pages 76/77
The Fight between Carnival and Lent, 1559
Oil cn oak, 118 x 164.5 cm (46 ½ x 64 ¾ in.)
Vienna, Kunsthistorisches Museum, Gemäldegalerie
(details pages 79–86)

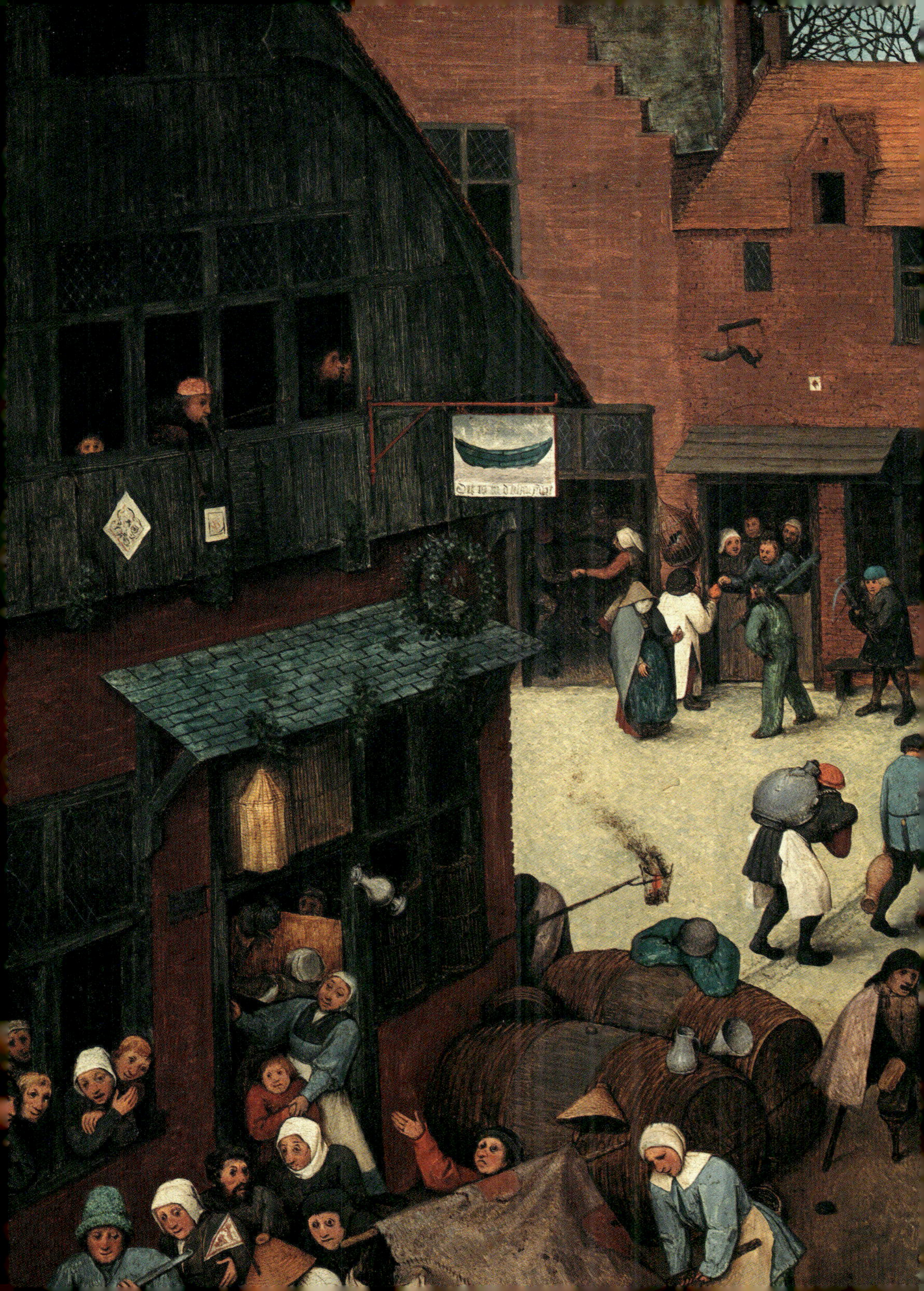

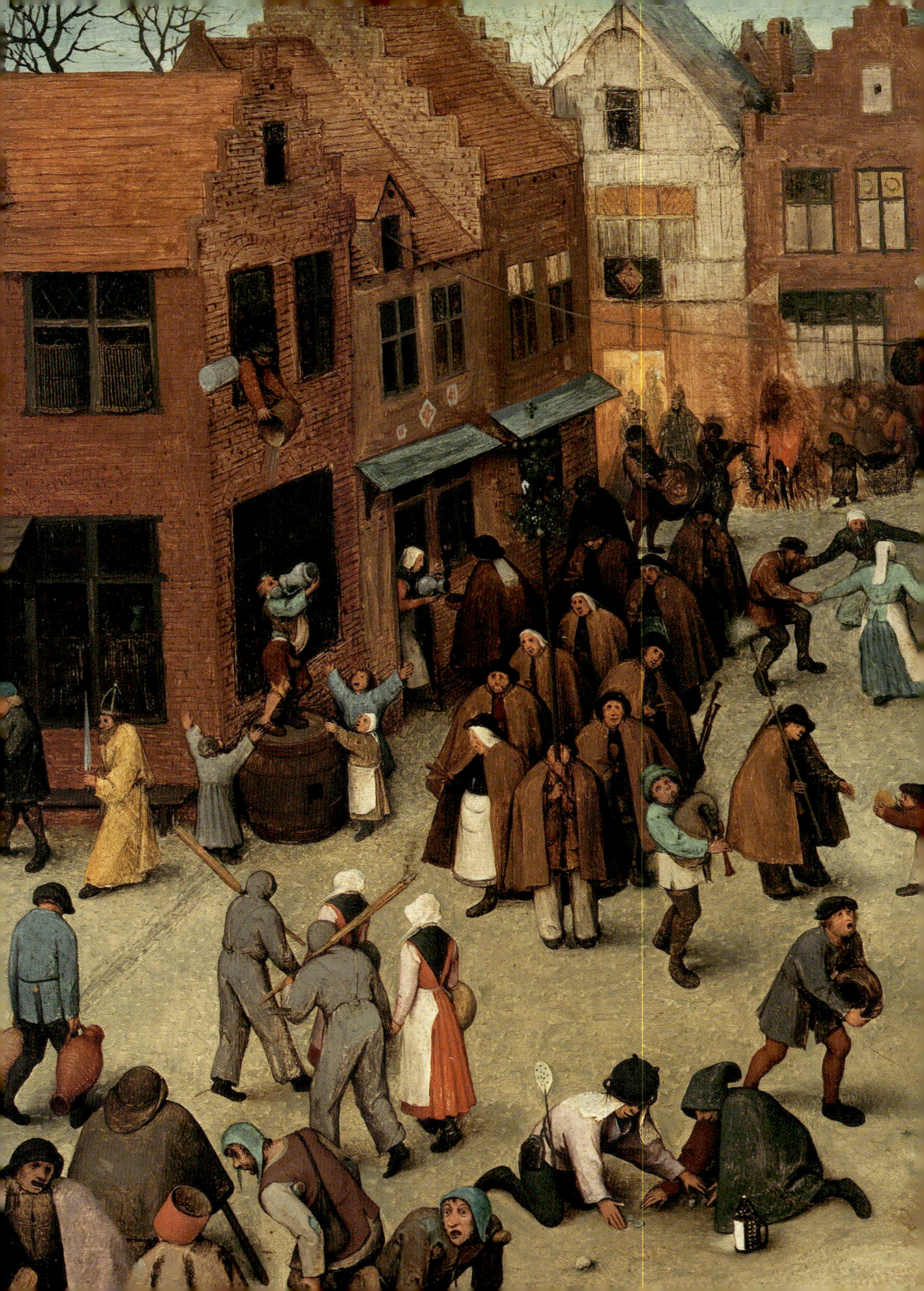

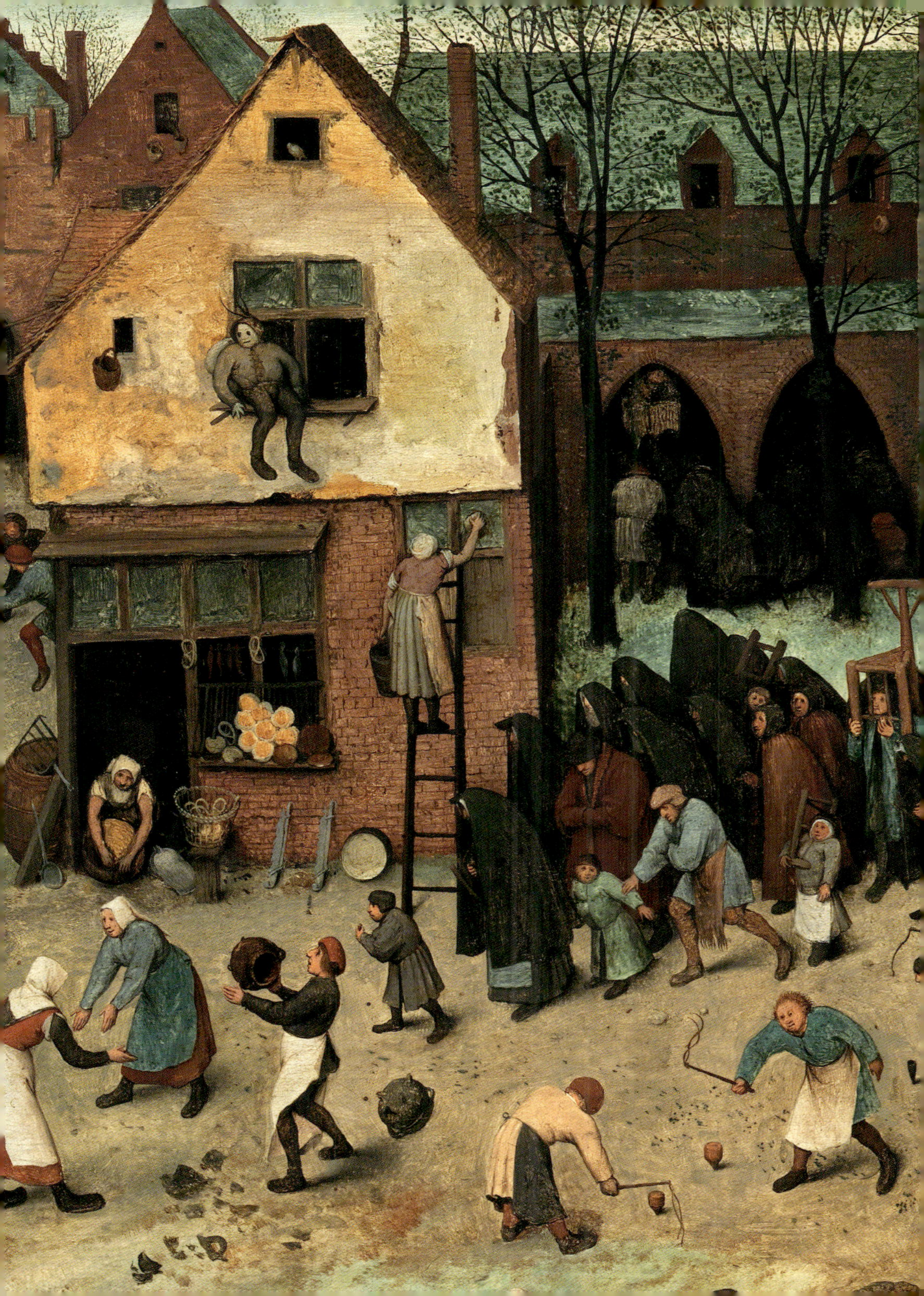

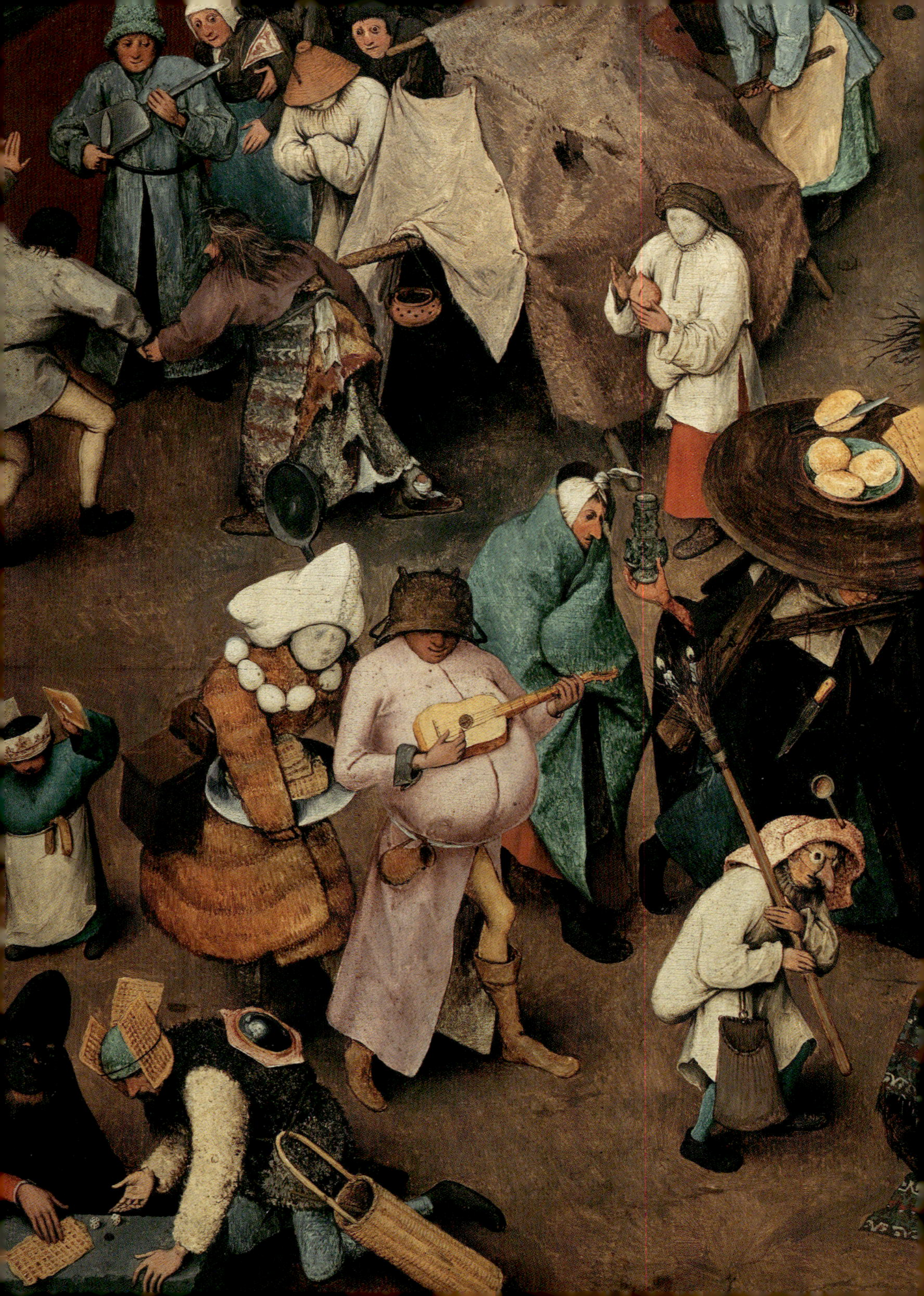

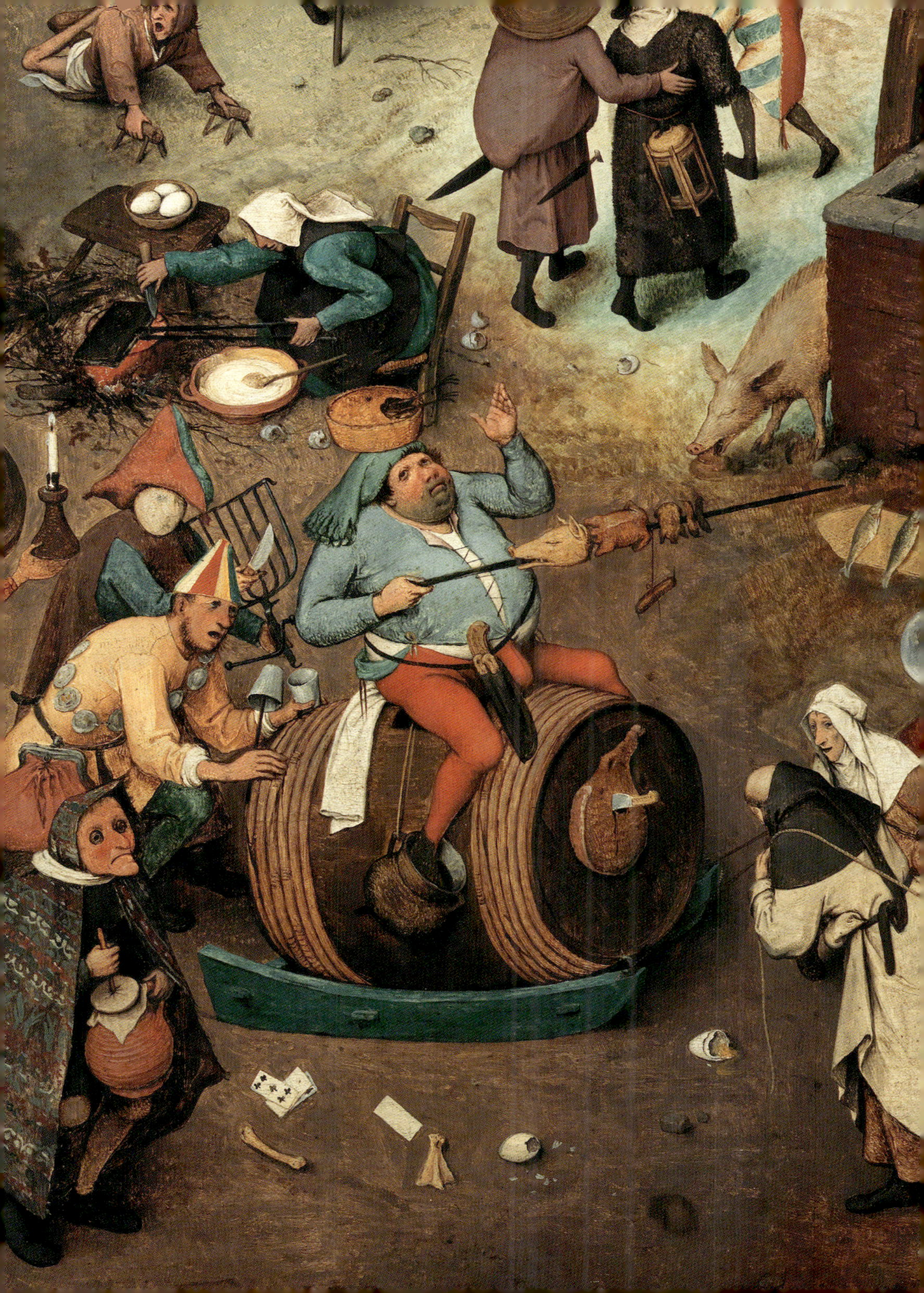

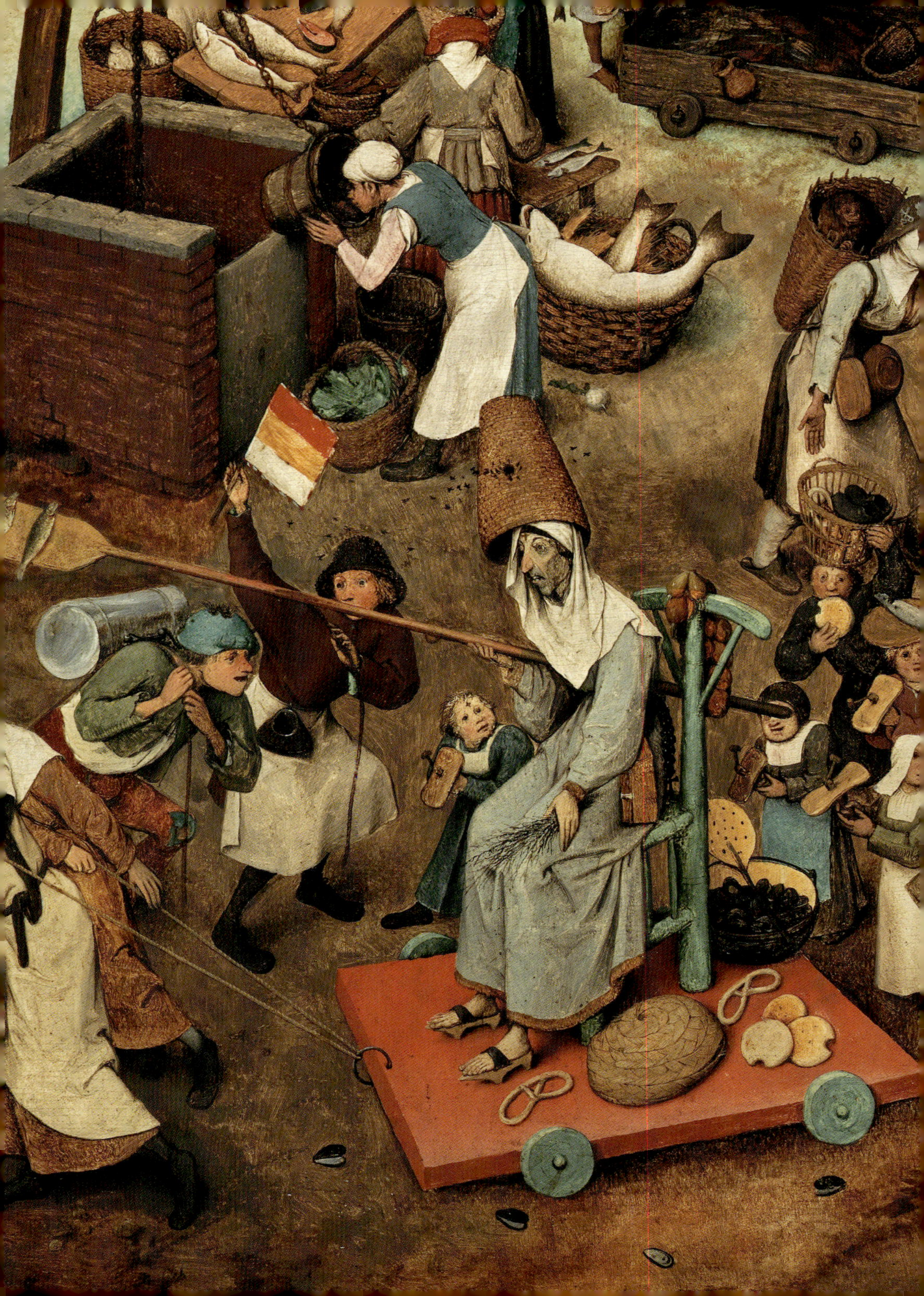

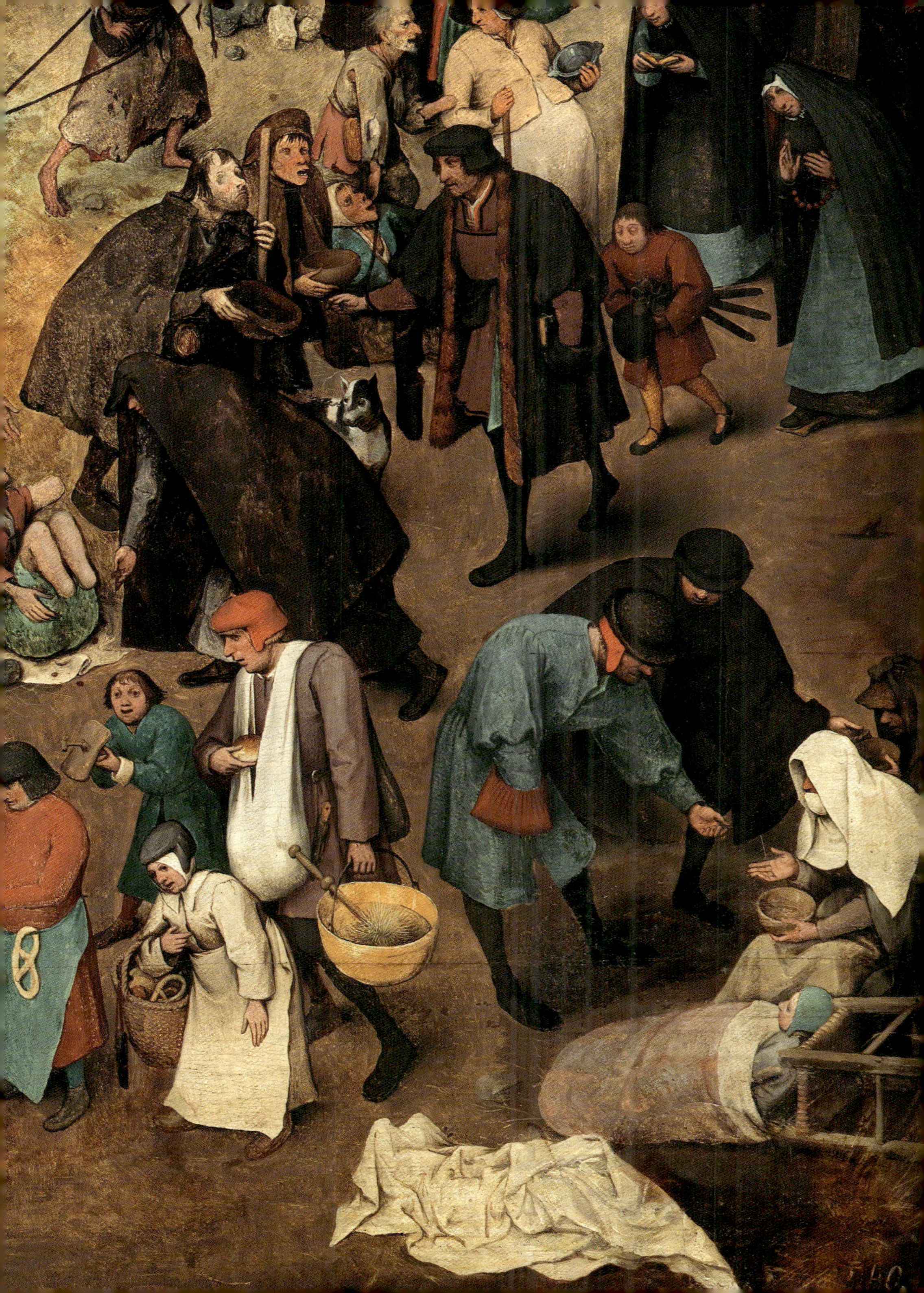

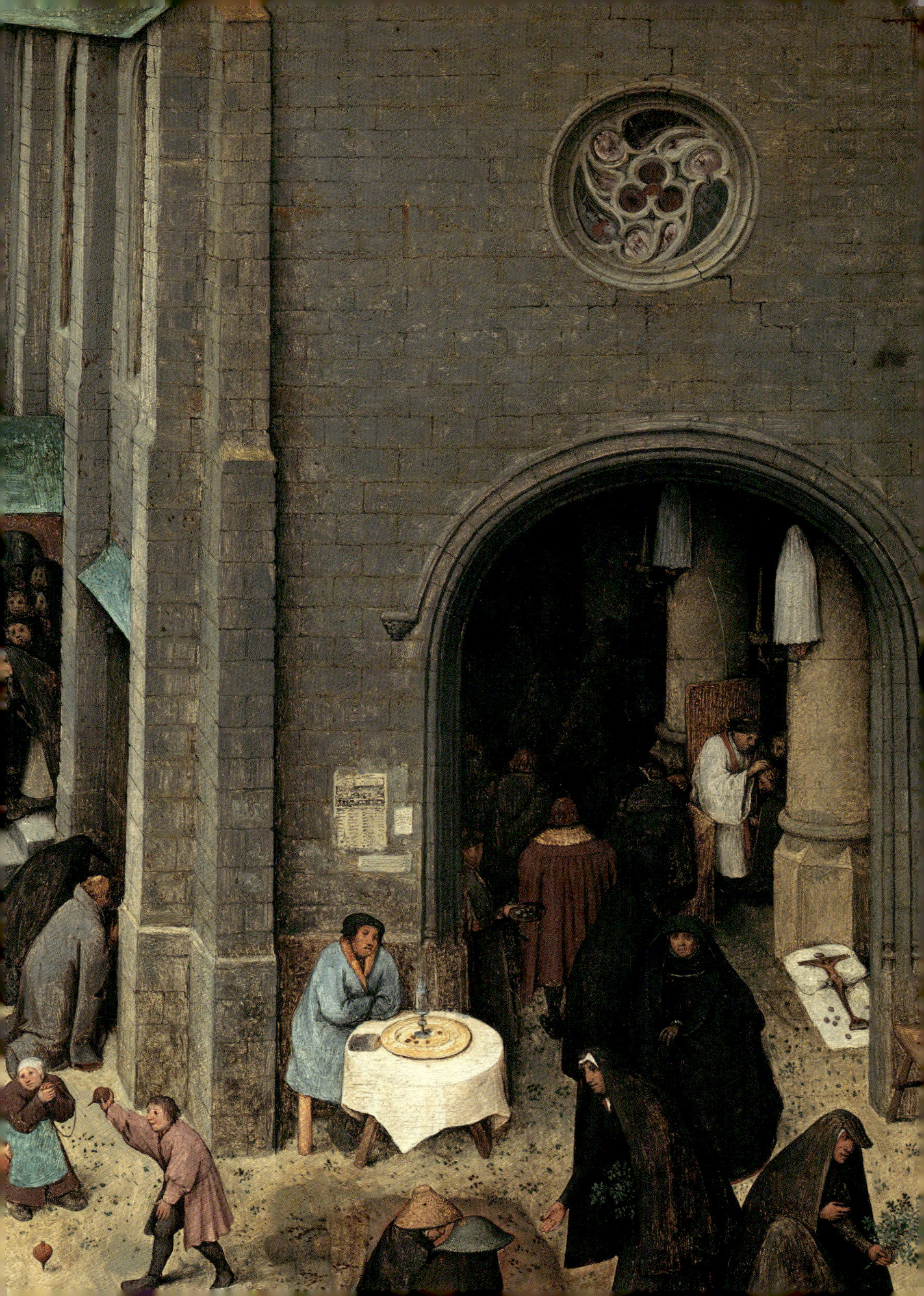

II. THE LABYRINTH OF MEANING: THE WIMMEL PICTURES

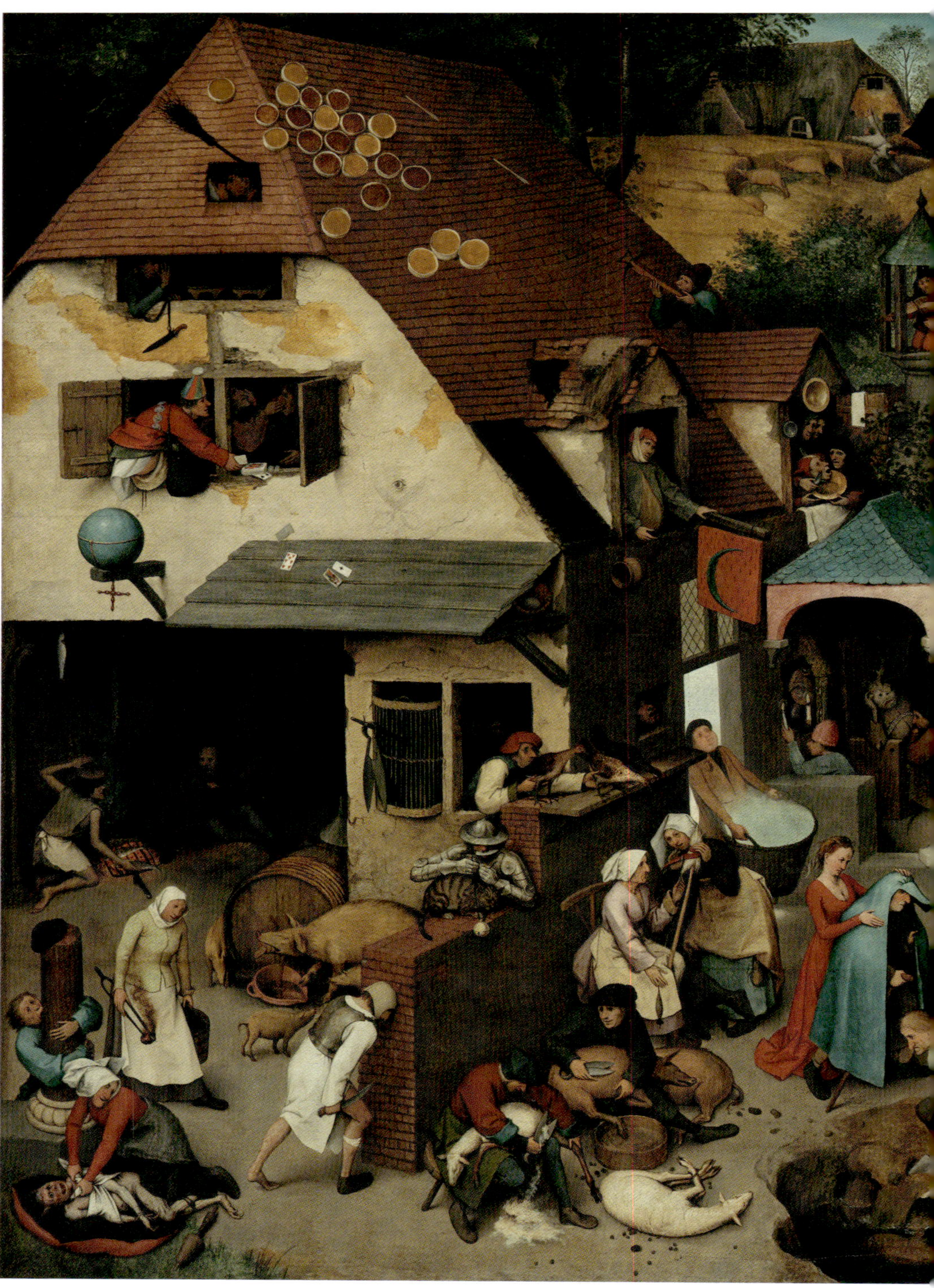

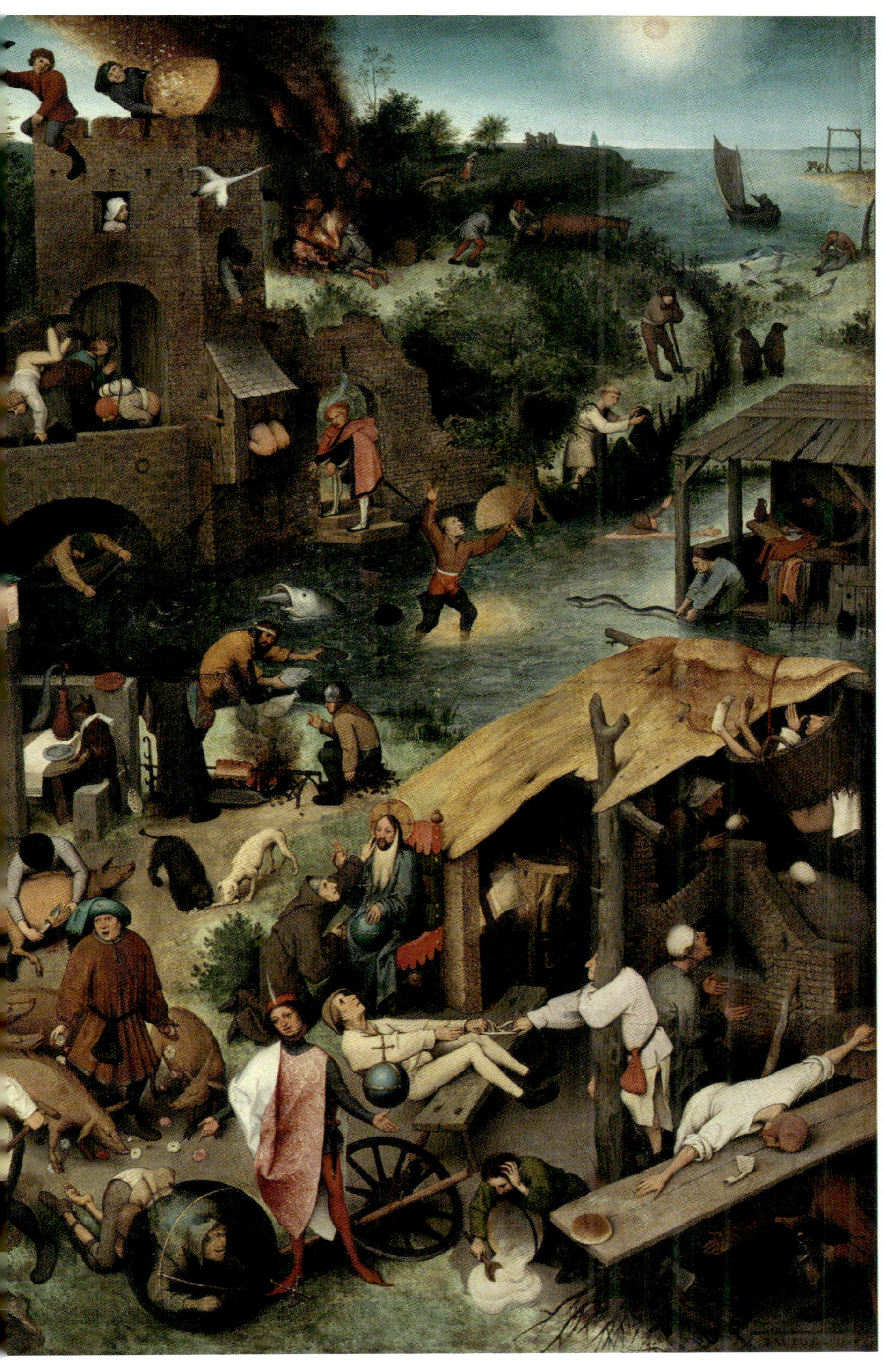

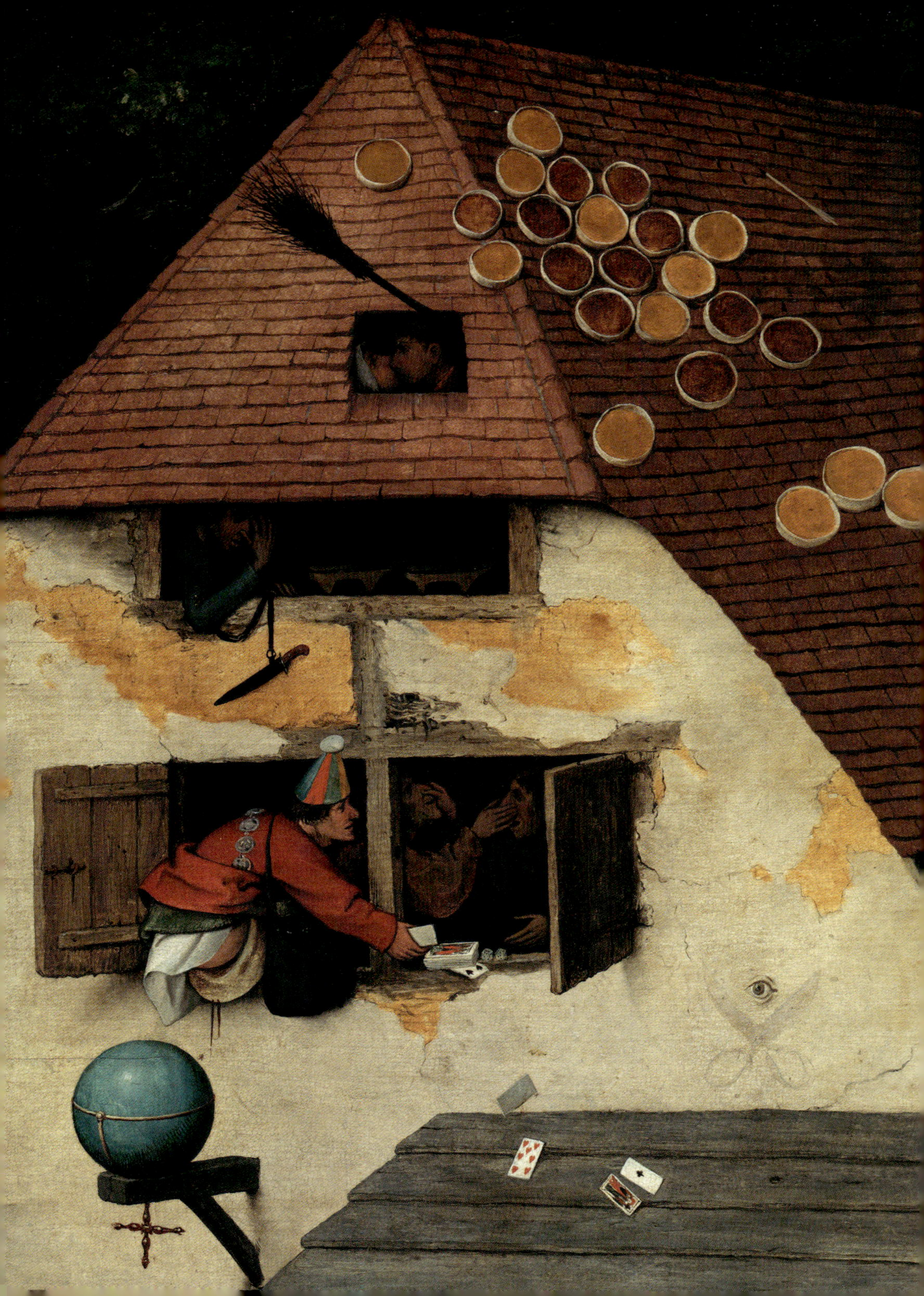

Pages 88/89
Netherlandish Proverbs, 1559
Oil on oak, 117 x 163 cm (46 ⅛ x 64 ⅛ in.)
Staatliche Museen zu Berlin, Gemäldegalerie
(details pages 90, 93, 94, 96/97)

92

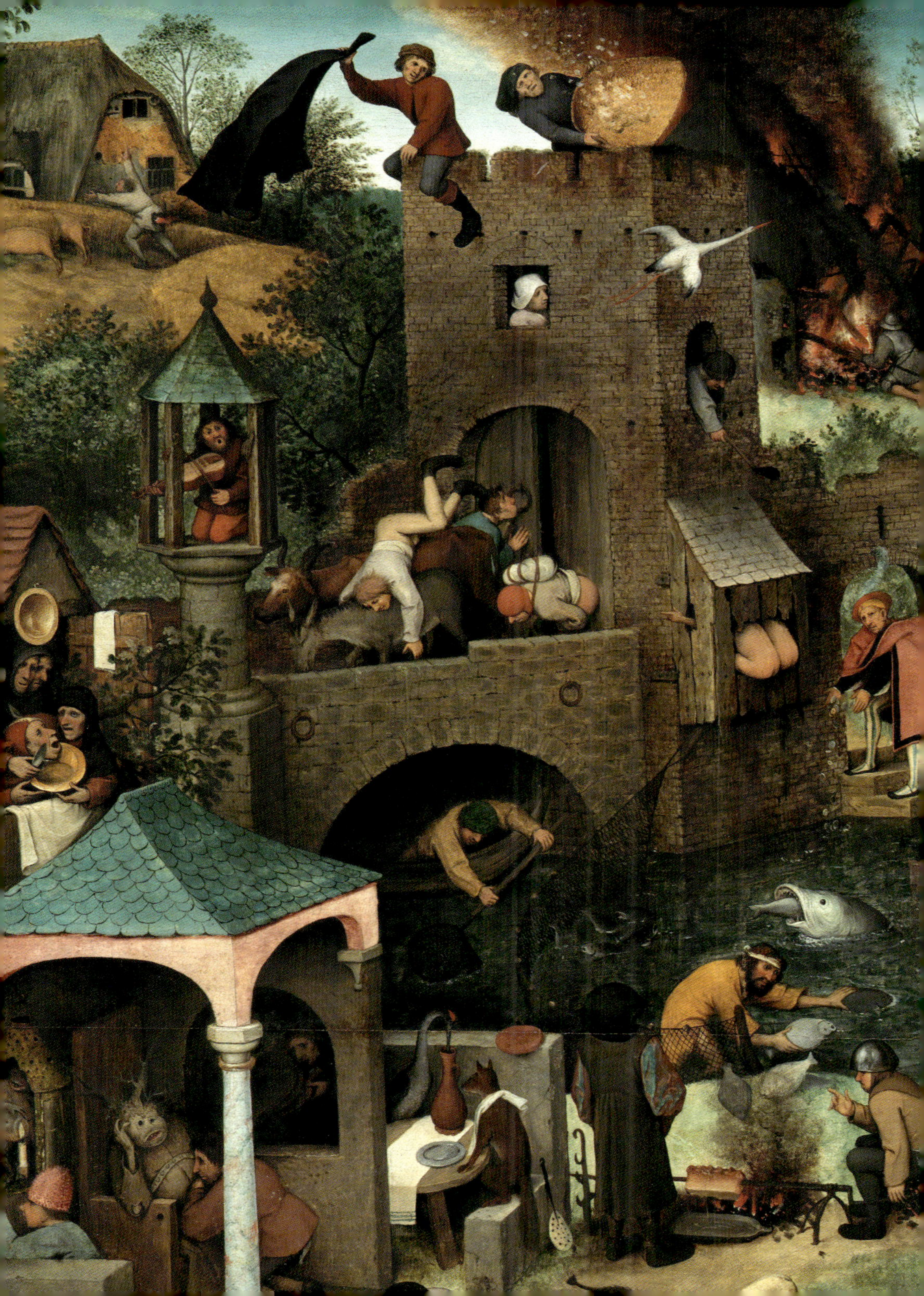

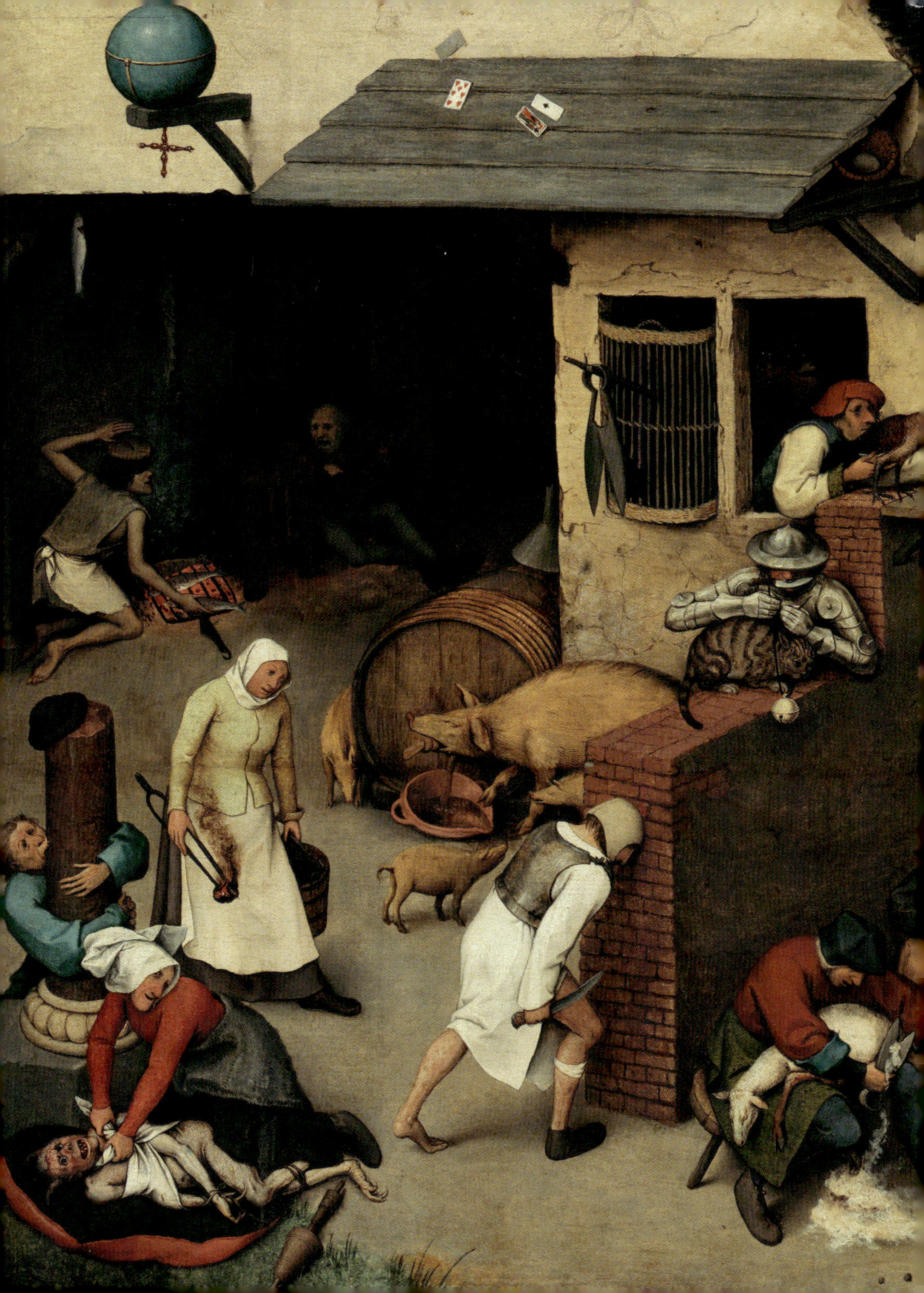

95

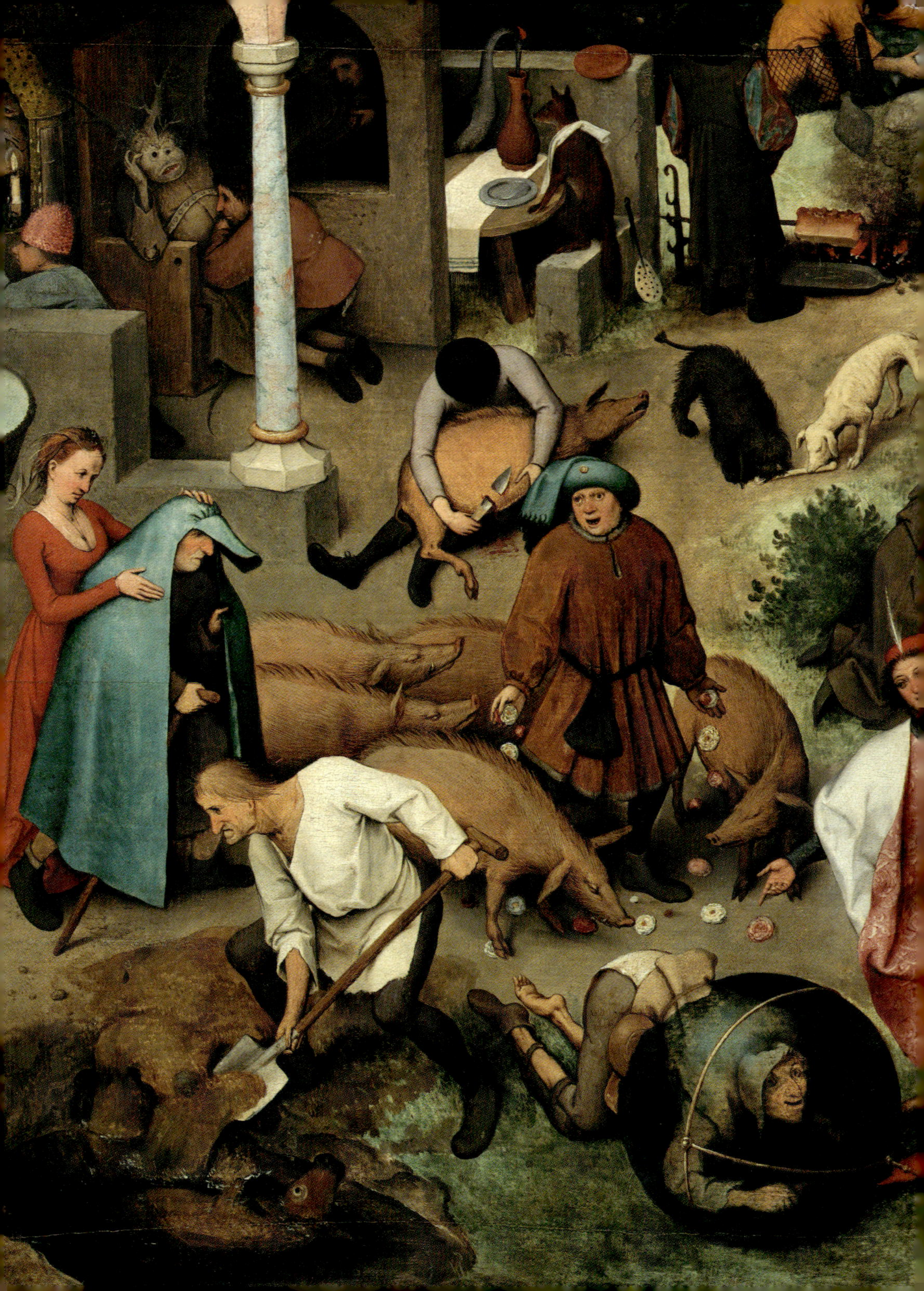

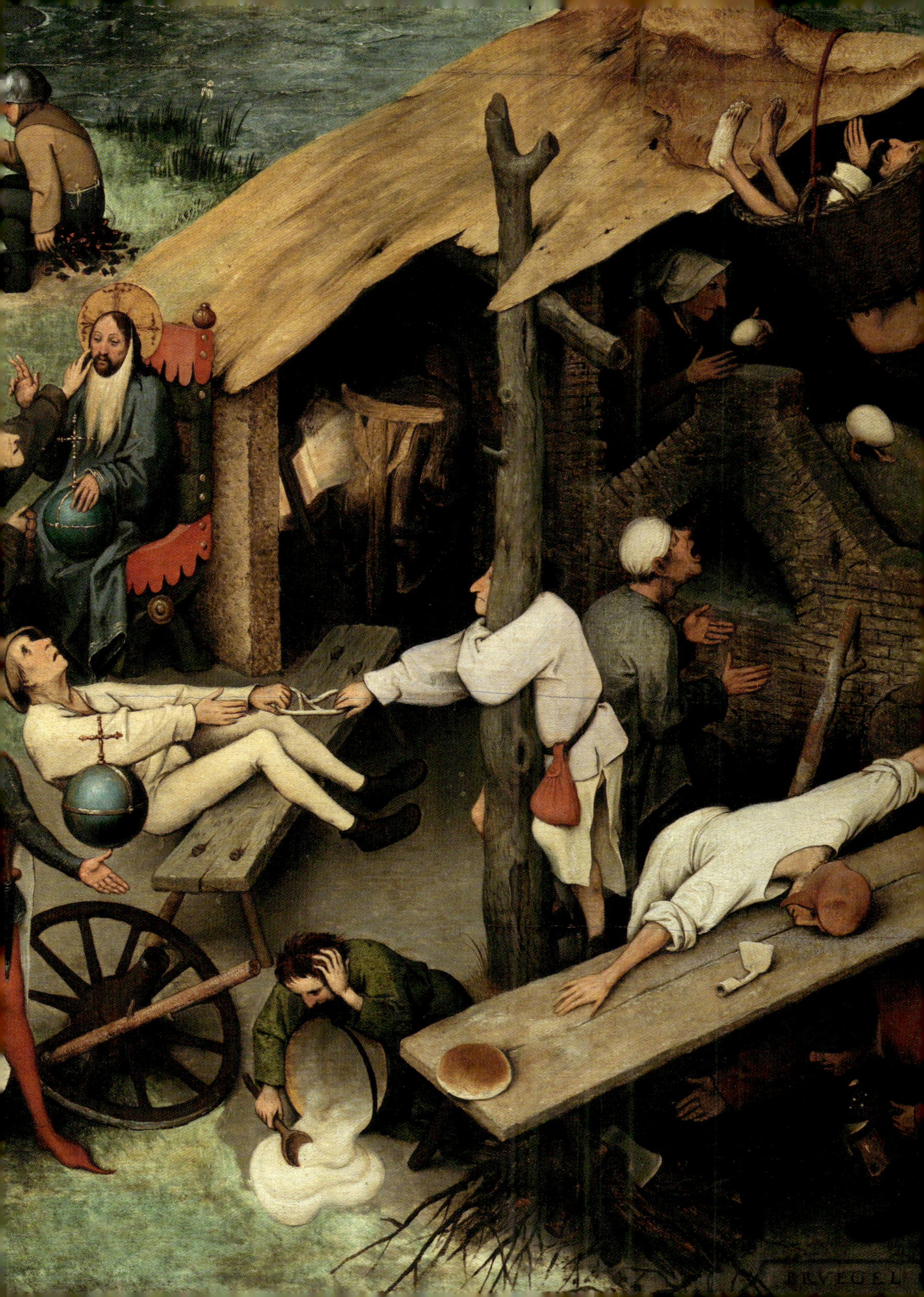

BRVEGEL

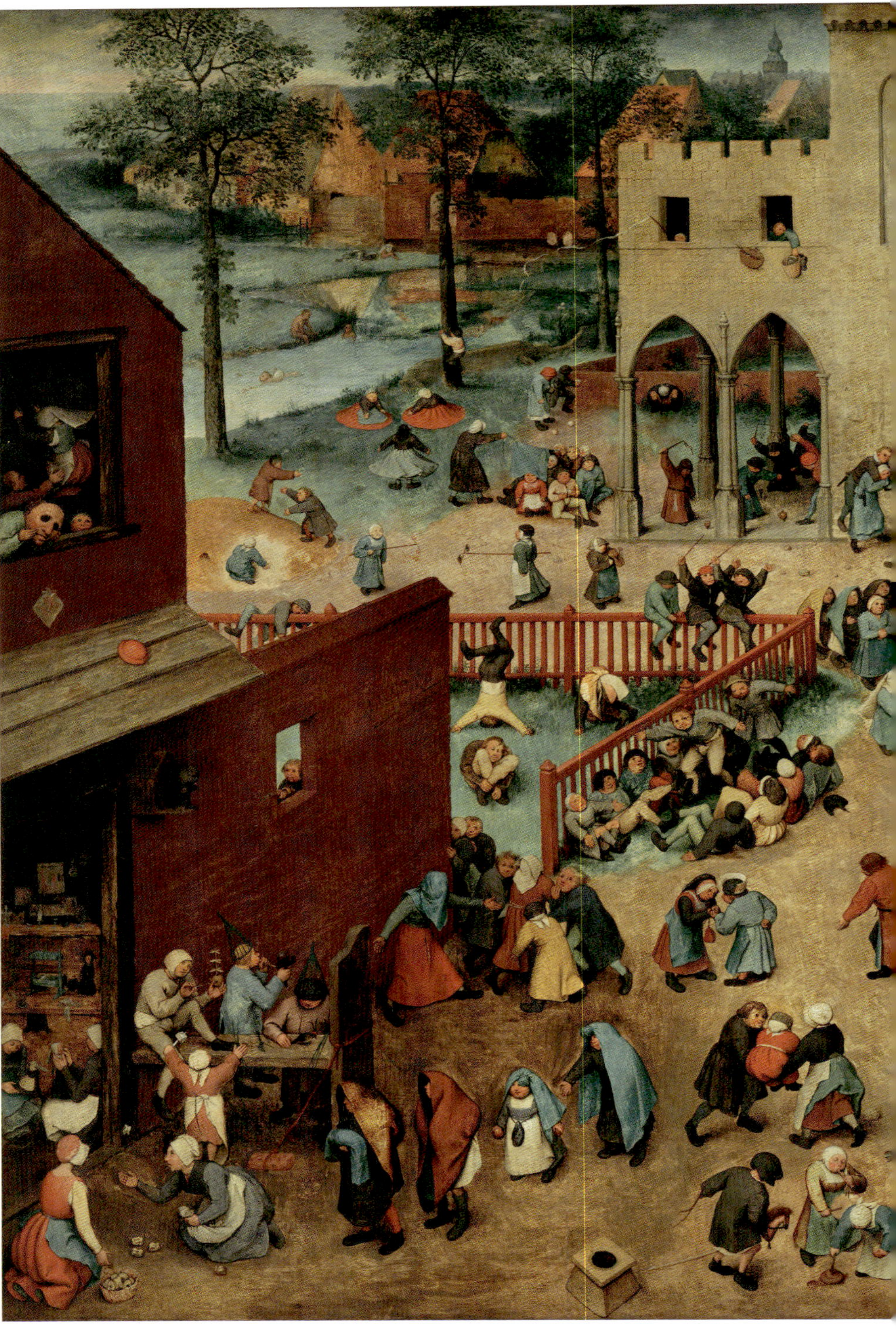

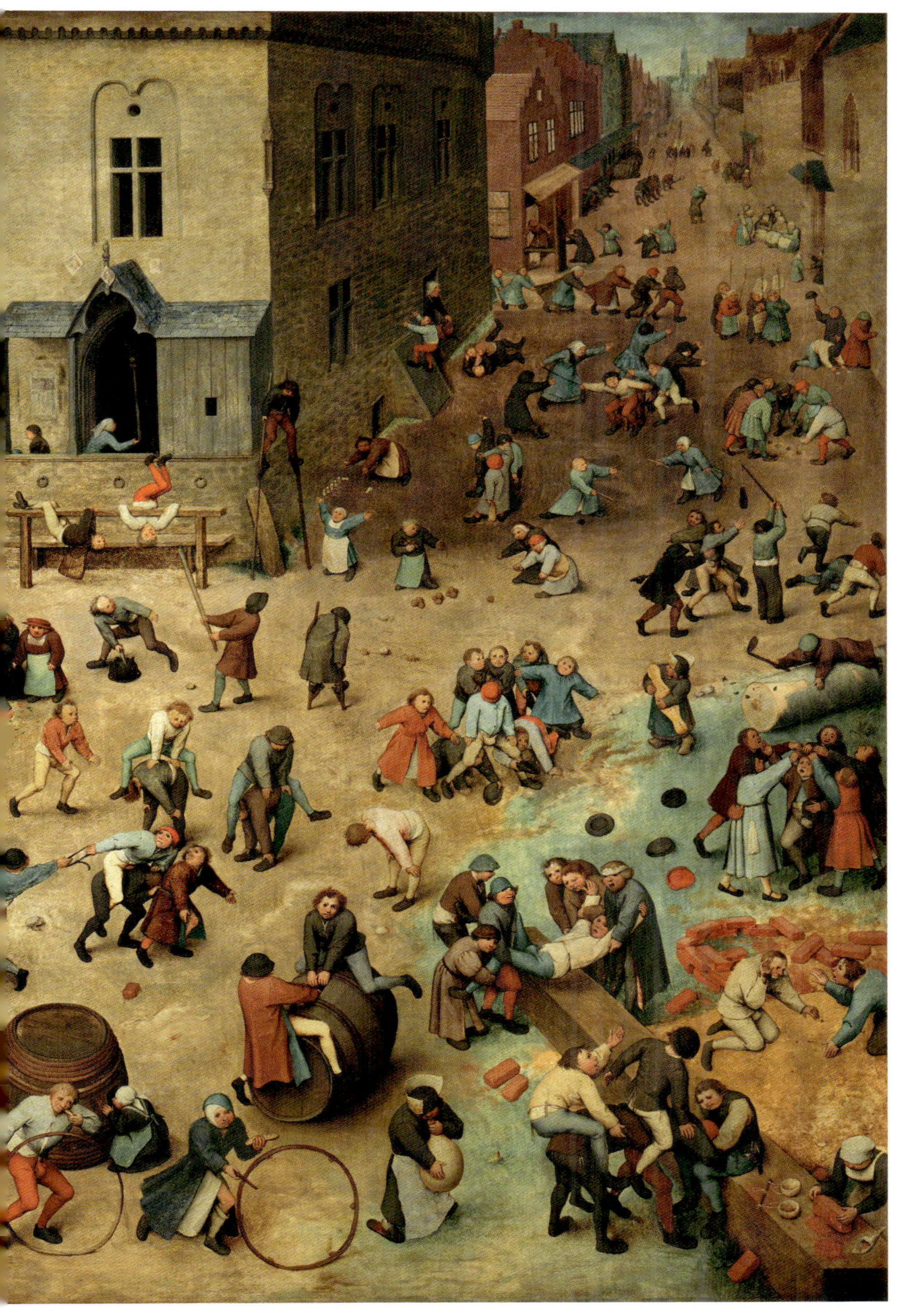

Pages 98/99
Children's Games, 1560
Oil on oak, 118 x 161 cm (46 ½ x 63 ⅜ in.)
Vienna, Kunsthistorisches Museum, Gemäldegalerie
(detail page 101)

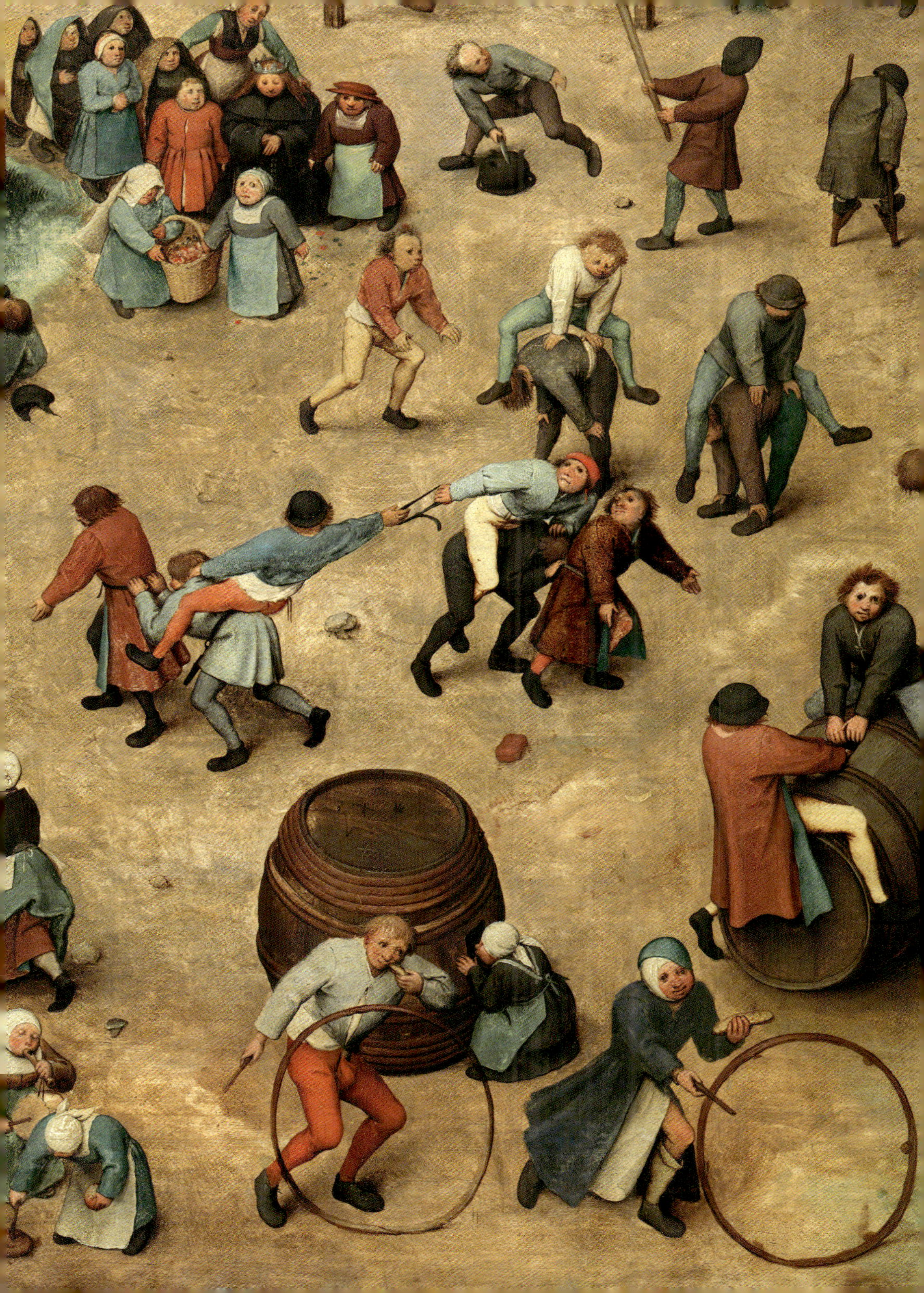

III.

Inner and Outer Vision: Images of the Mistaken Search for God

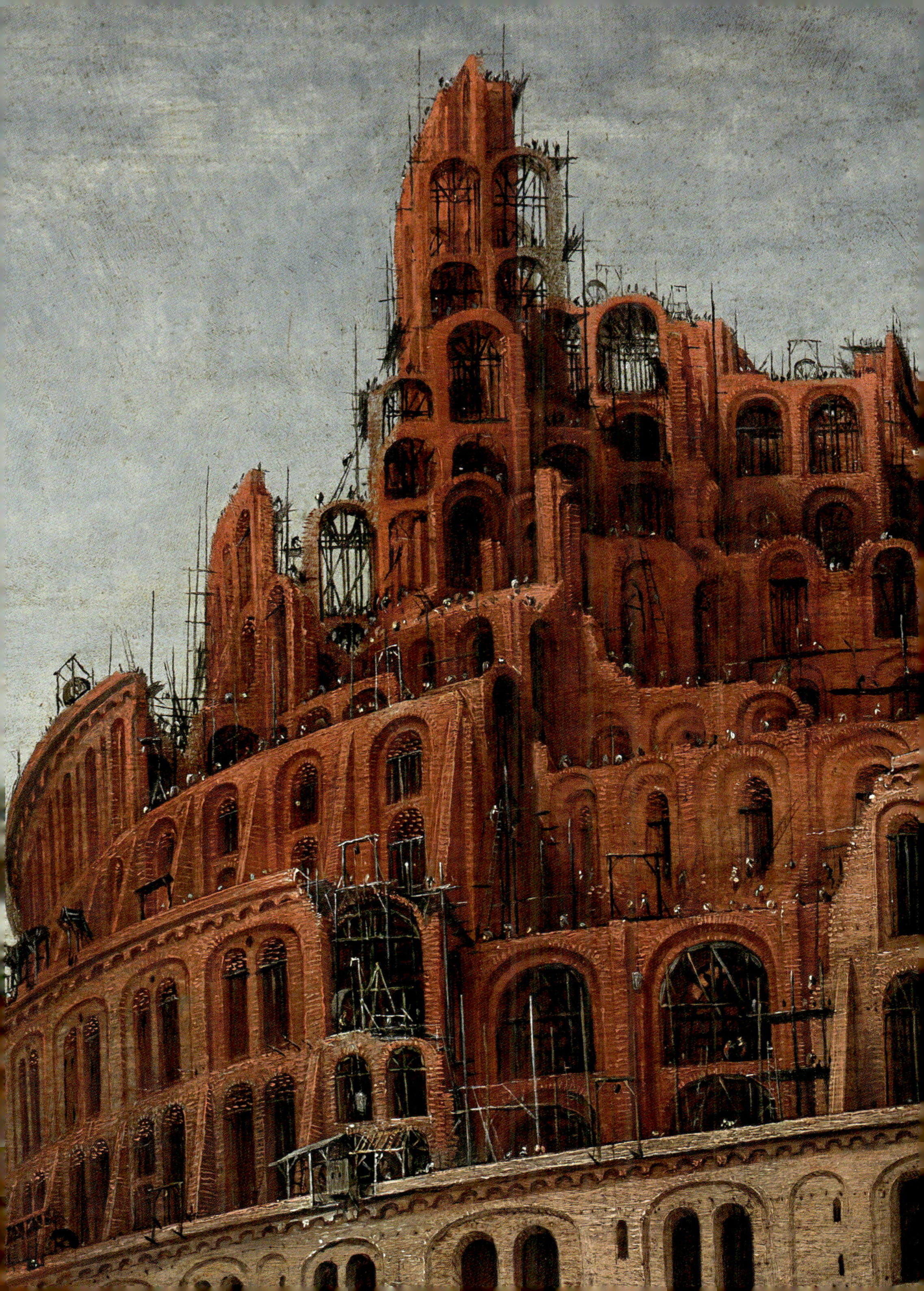

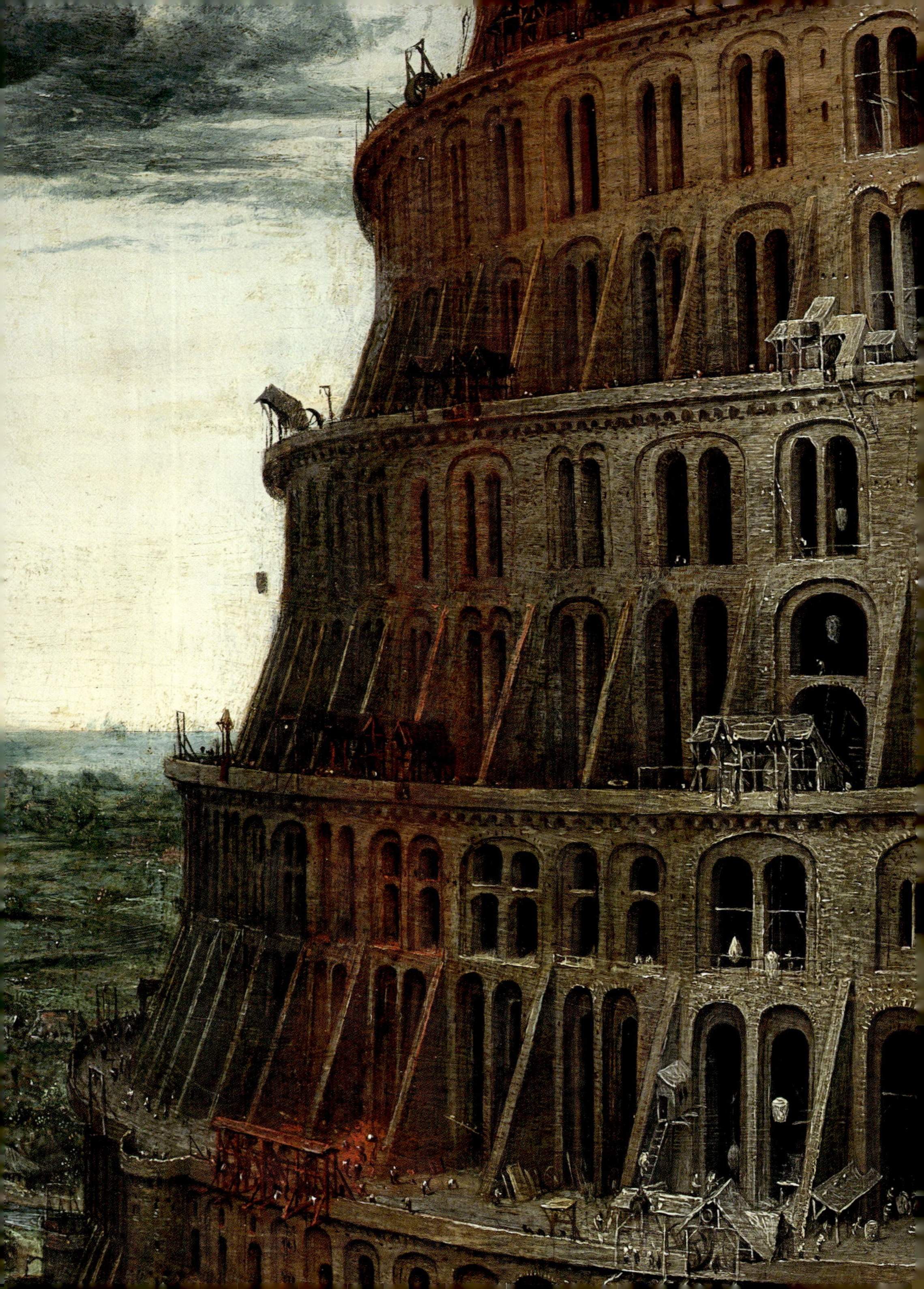

The light under the bushel

Art-historical literature has long established the significance of Sebastian Franck (p. 106) for Pieter Bruegel.[85] But anyone who sees this connection is challenged to explain how it was possible for a painter to relate to this thinker's theology when the latter was a great despiser of painting. How could Bruegel nevertheless make the theologian's scepticism fruitful for his work?

In identifying the divine, Franck principally distrusts the possibilities of seeing and stresses that Christ is only accessible to human beings in spirit and remains hidden to the external eye. In his *Paradoxa*, he programmatically emphasises the impossibility of knowing God and accordingly demands that Christians must eschew all images that embody the divine: "[…] as long as someone relies on images he cannot search his soul for serenity of feeling and for what is inside him. […] Children, you should say farewell to all images, search in the depths of your soul; this is where you should find God, for the Kingdom of God is within you! […] And as Dionysius says, God is not anything that mankind can name or speak about."[86]

Franck is aligned with the tradition of "negative theology", as is apparent from his reference to the Church Father Dionysius Areopagita. For Franck, every image is merely an aid, a shadow that must not be taken as being like the divine in any way, which is why he keeps speaking of the "hidden God". In the 89th paradox, he praises all nations that have abstained from the cult of the image. So how is it possible for a painter to make the non-visualisable visible? He has to take the limits of human knowledge of God as his theme!

Here we can turn to one of Bruegel's early works. *Elck (Everyman)* is one of Bruegel's most complex allegories. A preliminary drawing has survived for the engraving (p. 109), signed and dated 1558 (pp. 110/111). The central protagonist giving his name to the sheet is identifiable as "Everyman", thanks to the Flemish term "Elck" on the hem of his coat.[87] The literary motif referred to here crops up in several vernacular languages and enjoyed great popularity from the fifteenth century. In it, a rich merchant does not realise the vanity of his wealth until he is at death's door, for he can neither take it with him, nor buy a longer life with it.

Bruegel's Everyman is characterised as a merchant by his spectacles, above all, however, by his pen and money belt, his entrepreneurial talents demonstrated as well in his tightly

Pages 103, 104
The Tower of Babel (Rotterdam version;
also: **The "Small" Tower of Babel**; details), *c.* 1565
(see ill. pp. 164/165)

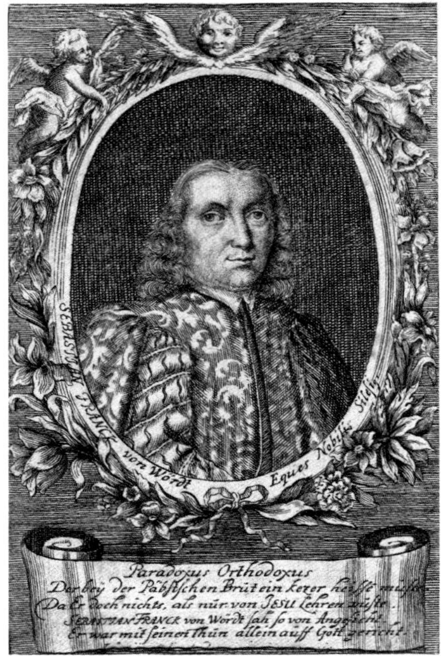

filled pouch. He is surrounded by a teeming confusion of trade goods and tools, and also gaming attributes. The confusing mass of objects at first recalls the "wimmel" pictures produced around the same time. The main actor is about to climb over a globe, without noticing this Christian symbol of the world. The man is far too involved in his quest and is being imitated by doppelgangers all over the picture. These are rummaging in baskets and sacks full of goods or quarrelling about their possessions, like the two men at the left of the engraving, struggling in a tug o' war over a length of fabric. They are all designated as Elcks in inscriptions and are following the sole maxim contained in the picture caption, which says that everyone seeks only his own advantage.

Like several of his companions, Everyman in the foreground is also carrying a lantern. It seems paradoxical that he has lit it, despite the sufficient daylight. Interpreters have with some justification cited Diogenes (*c.* 410–323 BC; p. 113) in conjunction with this motif; tradition has it that in the bright light of noon he searched the marketplace with a lamp to find a wise man.[88] In this context, the Everyman seated in the barrel in the left-hand foreground of the engraving may likewise be seen as an allusion to the proverbial austerity of the Cynic philosopher. But in contrast to Diogenes, Bruegel's figures seem captive in a material world in which their cupidity stands in the way of any self-knowledge. An insightful image here is the one Bruegel has placed conspicuously on the rear wall; namely, the motif of a man regarding himself in a hand-mirror, recalling woodcuts of the Reformation period. It is complemented by a Flemish caption, which – translated – says: "No one knows himself." Directly next to this is a snuffed-out candle in a niche. Those familiar with the biblical allusions will know that Everyman's quest can scarcely bear fruit. It is no coincidence that the motif of searching recalls the place in the Gospel of St Mark where the apostles find Jesus praying and say to him: "Everyone seeks thee" (Mark 1: 37).[89] Furthermore, the candles hidden in a niche and the bushel

Andreas Luppius, **Sebastian Franck**, 16th century
Copper engraving. Private Collection

near the barrel recall the biblical warning that we should not place the light of our faith under a bushel where it cannot light the way for others. Rather, we should place it where everyone can see the light. According to Luke, "the light of thy body is thy eye; if thy eye be healthy, thy body will be full of light. But if it be evil, thy body also will be darksome" (Luke 11: 34).

Bruegel's Everyman nevertheless takes this metaphor all too literally by searching in the material world for something that can be found only in the inner soul: the light of faith, which gives light to mankind. So the engraving can be seen as an allegory of the mistaken search for God. Instead of looking for God in the inner soul, the protagonists lose themselves in externals, in possessions and cupidity. Not least in comparison with other works by Bruegel, Everyman might be seen as representing those Scripture scholars who take the Bible all too literally, cast light on it, and miss its spiritual content.

Moreover, the individuals who believe they are able to reach heaven on their own (John 6: 44) or find the way to Christ following a lantern that lights up earthly goods are not the only ones on the wrong track in Bruegel's engraving. A further level of interpretation is opened up by the scene in the background on the right of the engraving, where a military camp can be seen next to a church, behind which two adversaries are marching in battle array against each other. But a Church that in the denominational conflict sees God's merciful blessings as possession misreads the gift that should be a landmark for the world.

The interpretation has identified in Everyman a false seeker of God and man of the world.[90] He seeks Christ in the world around him, whereas it is imperative to find him in his own soul. Bruegel's allegory is full of allusions to the Bible. Meanwhile, everything is inverted in Silenian terms. At first we think it might be a new Diogenes, who seeks people and is at home in a barrel, then we find he is an avaricious contemporary. Spectacles and burning lantern are inadequate means when searching for God.

The window to the senses

Of all Pieter Bruegel the Elder's works, the panel *Two Fettered Apes* (pp. 146/147, Cat. 10) demonstrates the simplest composition. Two apes sit fettered in a window recess, while stretching behind them is the panorama of a port city. One of the two animals is looking in our direction as though noticing our arrival. The other, which is looking at the ground, turns away from the observer. The wall into which the window is inserted is in parallel alignment to the picture and provides a kind of frame. The silhouette of a great city appears in the distance. Church steeples tower up, and a windmill is hinted at the right edge. Bruegel added his signature directly under the apes, as if identifying with this animal: "BRVEGEL M.D.LXII."

The two apes in the foreground are paralleled by two birds in the background, their flight path leading from right to left. At the front right-hand edge of the niche we see shells of a nut that has evidently been eaten by the animals. Ships lie at anchor in the harbour. Their sails are furled; they seem to be in the process of unloading. These few words suffice to describe the picture's content. A composition that is based on so many contradictions can hardly be more laconic in expression. The proximity of the window niche is juxtaposed to the view onto the remote city, the two apes to the birds in flight, and the panoramic view to the chains in the foreground.

The literature has interpreted the apes in a negative light, alluding for instance to ancient fables about selfish people.[91] The following text, however, aims to interpret the picture rather as an allegory with a significance in the theory of art. We might ask what the opposites included in the picture mean, for instance the two birds in flight in contrast to the fettered apes. They are a symbol of the soul and are flying freely in the skies: "I will let go the souls that you catch", as is written in Ezekiel (13: 20), and likewise in the Psalms: "Our soul is escaped as a bird out of the snare of the fowlers" (Psalm 124: 7). Bruegel uses a Christian image as well in his depiction of the harbour. The only ship under sail in the absolute centre of the picture is symbolically reaching the harbour of "salvation".[92] The apes in contrast are shackled to the "chains of sensuality", which is why the Christian promise of salvation is hidden from them.[93]

In doing this, the painter is presenting a symbol of Christian existence by pointing out the limits of our understanding, and makes us aware of the difference between faith and knowledge. Like the apes, a human being remains captive to his senses and has no direct access to the transcendent. He needs faith. Bruegel has created a symbol of stirring simplicity. We think we are looking at two apes, but what we see is actually an image of ourselves. We should not be permitted in any way to feel superior to the animals. Because just as the apes relate to man, so man relates to God. The consequence is that we have to be humble in relation to the knowledge of God. We cannot leave the place we are in. Human beings are bound by limits.

There is a passage in the 91st paradox of Sebastian Franck that may have inspired Bruegel to his invention. It says: "O, it is a wondrous, hidden God [...], who thus makes all the worldly wise and rich into objects of scandal and those with possessions to beggars, mocking their wealth and seating all erring children of mankind on a bench with the apes."[94]

This "bench with the apes" seen as the existential situation of mankind is the theme of the small panel. The picture is a mirror of the *miseria hominis* (misery of man). With the reference to the "worldly wise and rich", the extract from the *Paradoxa* alludes to the passage in the Letters to the Corinthians in which St Paul speaks of the Silenian inversion

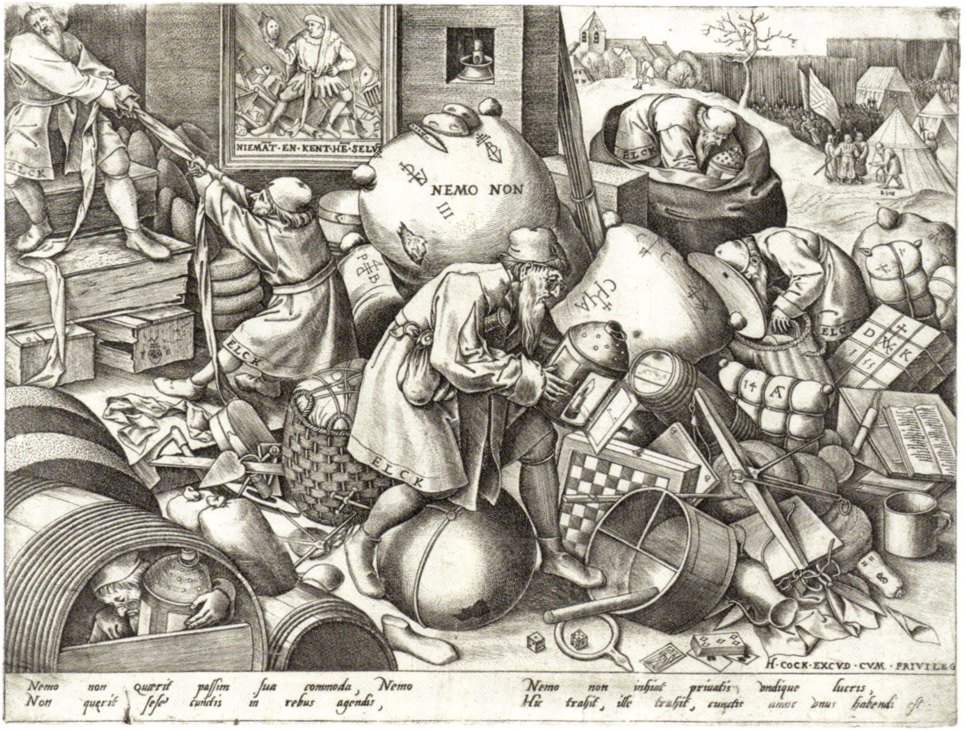

Pieter van der Heyden (attributed) after
Pieter Bruegel the Elder, **Elck (Everyman)**, *c.* 1558
Copper engraving, 22.8 x 29.4 cm (8 ⅞ x 11 ⅝ in.)
Amsterdam, Rijksmuseum, Rijksprentenkabinet

of wisdom and folly when confronted by Christ's self-sacrifice. Wisdom and wealth, signifying so much in this life, fail as a key to salvation in the next world (1 Corinthians 1: 26–27). Also in paradox 64, Franck refers to the Pauline homily on fools and writes that appearance and reality are in constant conflict with each other in this world, and God's Word remains an eternal paradox.

The picture shows the unavoidable situation in the shape of the chains. The artist, too, is subject to this captivity. His potential is limited by his being tied to the senses. We might see this small panel as a "programmatic view", drawing a parallel between human and artistic possibilities and limits. Transcendence cannot be pictured. We always find ourselves this side of the boundary in relation to the divine.

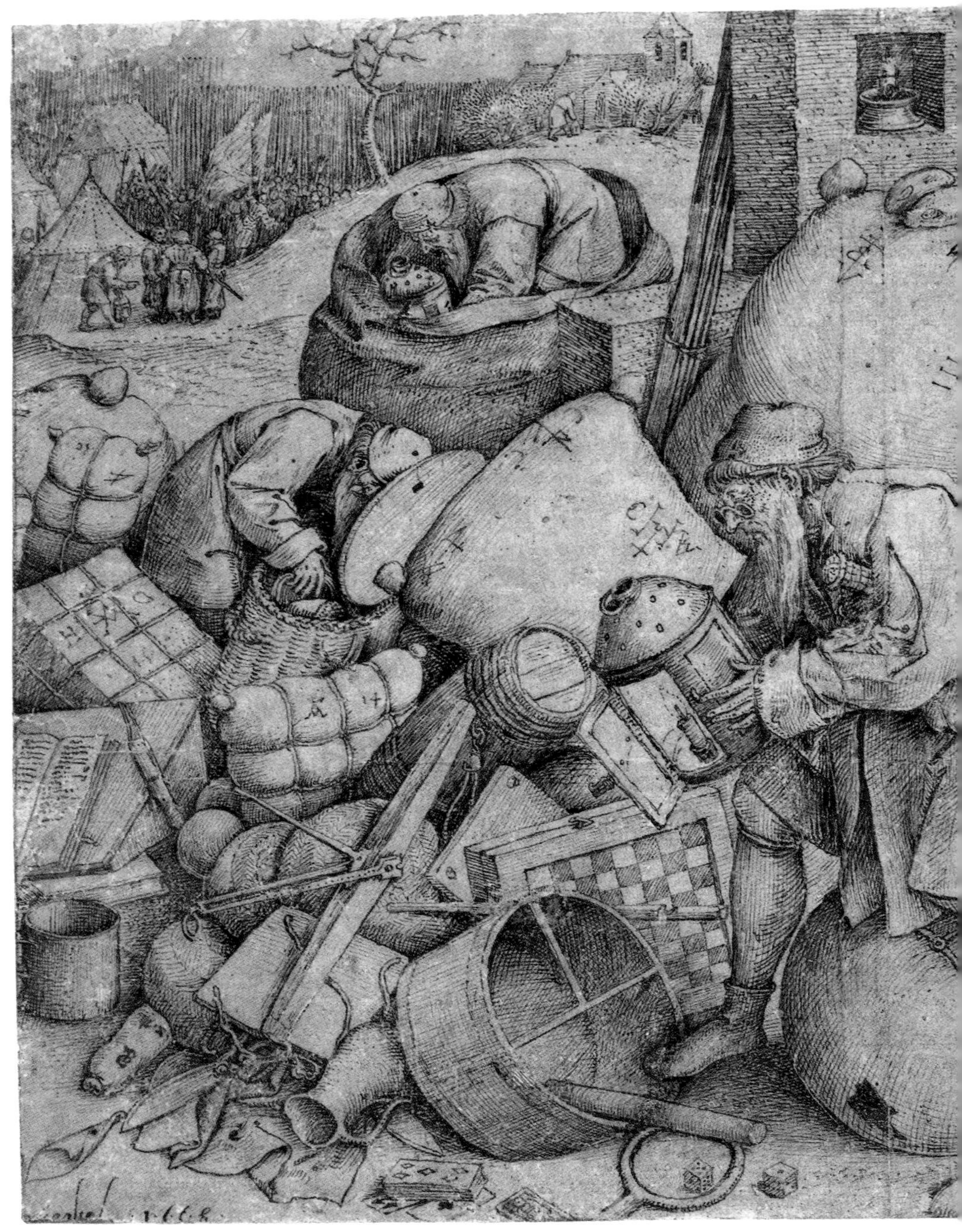

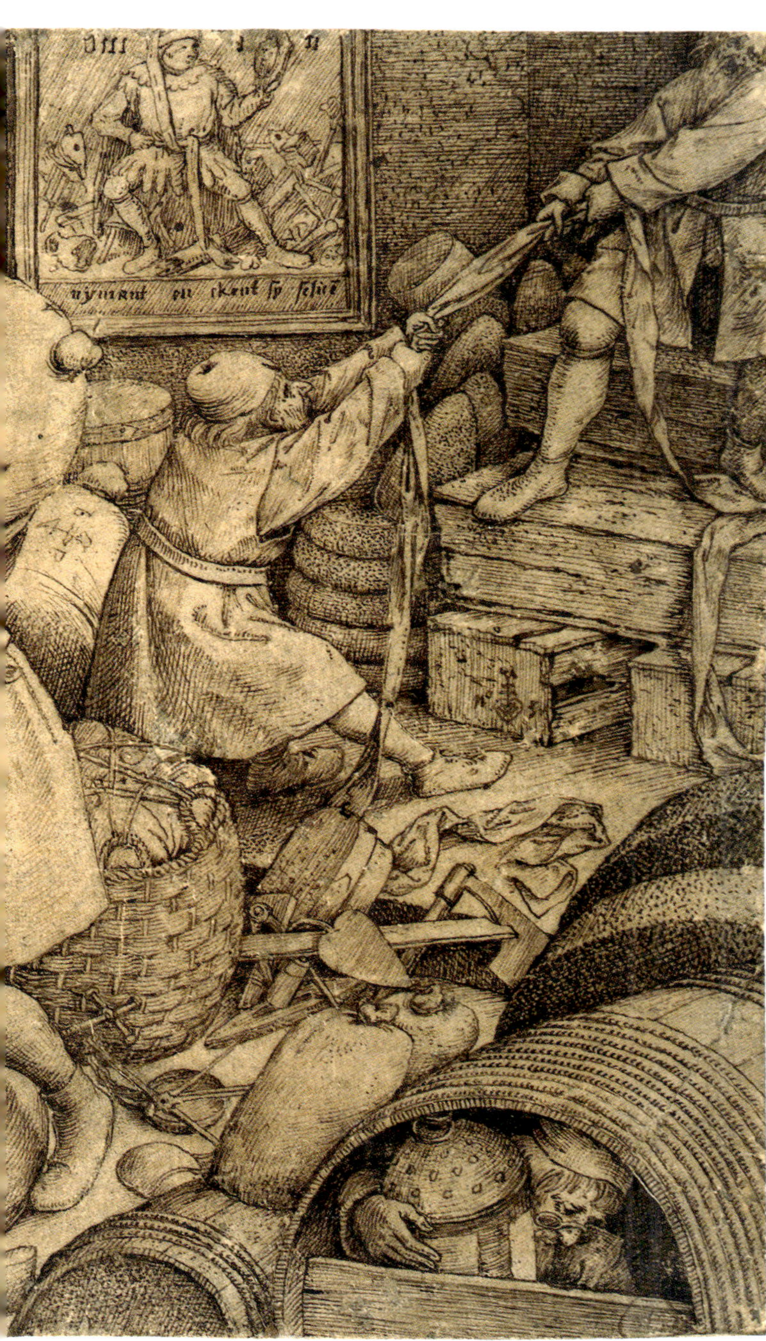

Elck (Everyman), 1558
Pen and dark
reddish-brown ink,
20.8 x 29.3 cm
(8 ¼ x 11 ½ in.)
London, The British
Museum, Department of
Prints and Drawings

Christ in us

In *The Adoration of the Kings* (p. 141, Cat. 17) in London, Bruegel likewise formulates his mistrust of the what seeing is capable of and shows the limits of visual cognition. The artist has chosen an extreme, close-up perspective for his picture. The observer sees himself invited to enter the frontally open semicircle and so behold the Virgin Mary and the Christ Child at close quarters. The figures in the rear are arranged jostling and crowded together. It is one of Bruegel's few pictures in vertical format and his first work with large-scale figures.

How sensitively he portrays the different reactions to the Christ Child! The Epiphany celebrates the manifestation of Christ's Incarnation, the act of seeing it with one's own eyes. The range of reactions in the faces of the kings and their retinue covers everything from amazement and curiosity to sceptical staring. Nor is there a lack of caricature. The scholar at the right edge is wearing spectacles, their thick glass immediately betraying the observer as suffering "mental myopia". The soldier placed near Joseph is staring greedily at the opened goblet held by the king on the left, while the crossbowman seems to be ogling the costly nautilus goblet held by the black king at the right. Seeing in all its variants is the actual theme of the painting.

Bruegel's image of the kings shows traditional forms of veneration and homage. The men are kneeling and bowing. They are also presenting the gifts they have brought. Only the black king on the right is standing upright and not paying any attention to the Christ Child. And, strangely, the Child Jesus is turning away from the elderly king at the left, despite the Virgin Mary's pointing gesture.

In plays about the Three Kings and in their iconography, the Three Kings represent the universal Church arriving from the then known continents, their banners traditionally designating their origins. In the Bruegel, however, only halberds and battle axes reach up to the sky. It is as though the painter wanted to show the secular power of the Church. He also puts on a regular weapons show, for we can also see the crossbow of an archer who has stuck a bolt into his hat and fastened the winch for loading the crossbow on his belt. This figure recalls the crossbowman who in Hieronymus Bosch's *The Crowning with Thorns* (p. 117) in London is placing the crown of thorns onto Christ's head. Bruegel is giving us a clue, helping us to discern the "false" character of the act of adoration, and he points to the future Passion of Christ. This is a unique feature of Bruegel's iconography: he adds elements that anticipate the future.

Bruegel studies have noted that the man next to Joseph seems to be expressing doubt about the Virgin Mary's faithfulness.[95] Bruegel exploits this episode to include a visual joke by aligning the ass's neck parallel to that of the young man in the composition. We can almost see a physiognomic similarity between the two. Moreover, when Joseph covers his manhood with his hat, this can be seen as a sign of his innocence.

Neither do the two kings on the left escape the painter's mockery. As richly as these "saints" are attired, their wrinkled faces are in stark contrast to their resplendent garb and the exquisitely fashioned goblets in their hands. Even though the attire enhances the status of the kneeling rulers, the over-long sleeves look ridiculous.[96] One sleeve is lashed onto the belt, the other drags on the floor. Meanwhile, the costly borders ornamented with zodiac signs and fine ermine trimmings on hem and collar are exceptionally luxurious. Bruegel is evidently aiming at caricature here. We have to imagine the king putting on his headdress, which is much too large for his small head. He has no hope of not looking ridiculous.

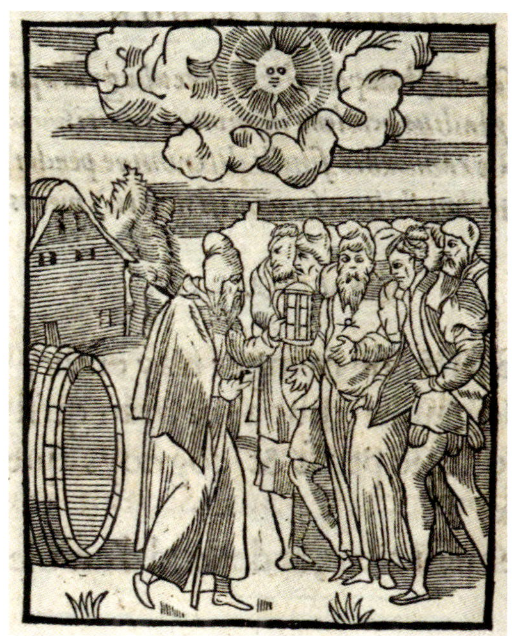

Among all the figures in the picture, the black king at the right assumes a special role. In contrast to the persons looking at the Christ Child, he seems deep in contemplation and clearly lost in reverie, not aware of the scene. He bears his gift for the Christ Child at his chest in a slightly impassive way.[97] To interpret this figure, we may recall Hieronymus Bosch's *The Adoration of the Magi* in Madrid (p. 117). Here, too, the black king is carrying an elaborate gift, a capsule of myrrh, which he offers with stately gesture. As in Madrid, in Bruegel's picture the black king's gift contains a figural scene that has the function of a commentary.[98]

First of all its shape as a ship reminiscent of a cog acts as a signifier. Instead of a sail, the ship carries a nautilus shell. A rock crystal forms the top crown, which in turn has a gemstone in a setting fastened on it, like a crow's nest. A tiny figural scene is perceptible; a figure leans out as if from a snail's shell, arms reaching out to grasp a pearl set in gold. The black king's gift might be a reference to the ship as traditional symbol of the Church.

Diogenes with a Lantern in Search of an Honest Man, 1553
Woodcut, 5.5 x 7.3 cm (2 ⅛ x 2 ⅞ in.). In: Guillaume de la Perrière, *Morosophie*, Lyon 1553, Emblem 31
Munich, Bayerische Staatsbibliothek

The Tower of Babel (Rotterdam version;
also: **The "Small" Tower of Babel**; details), *c.* 1565
(see ill. pp. 164/165)

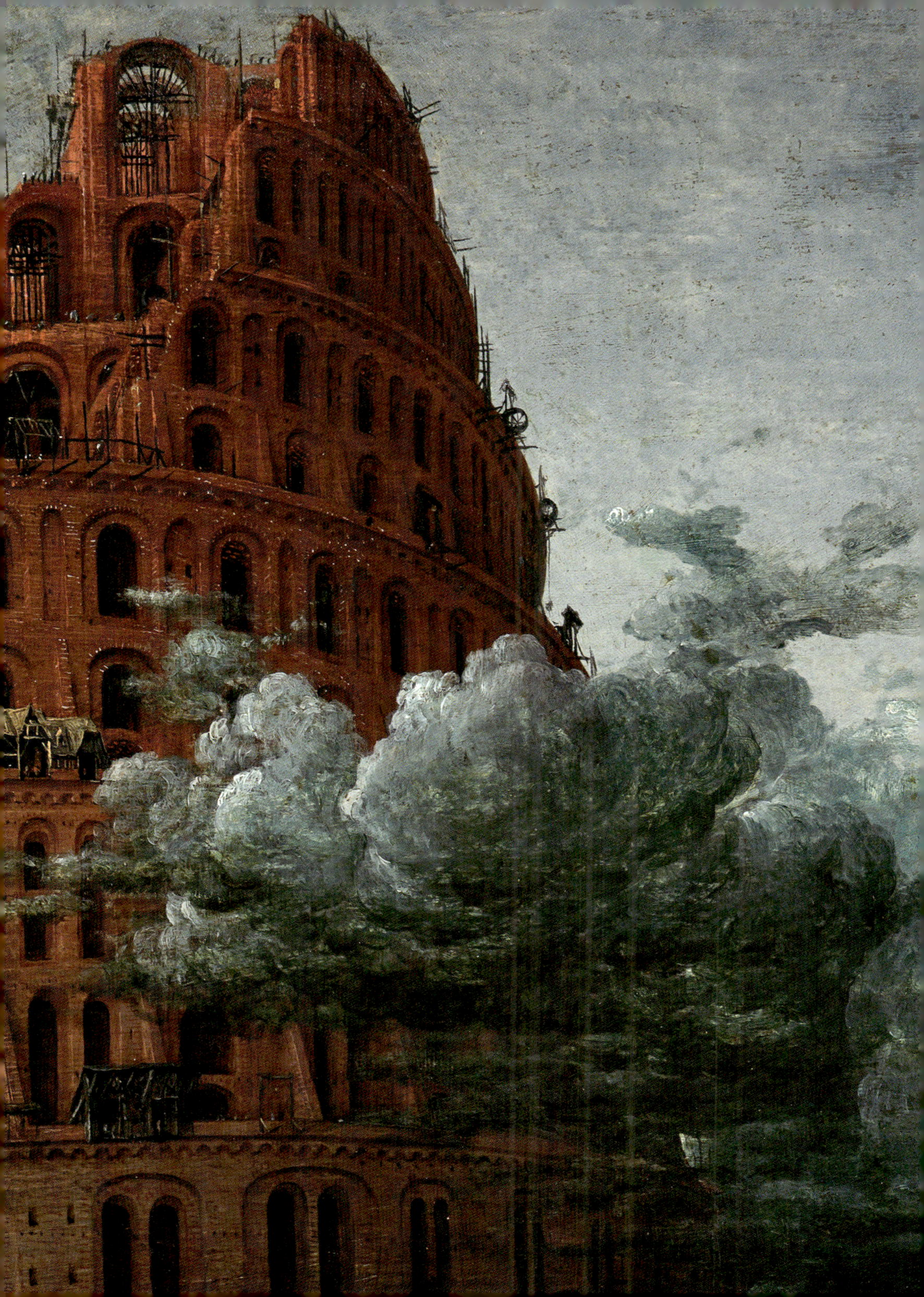

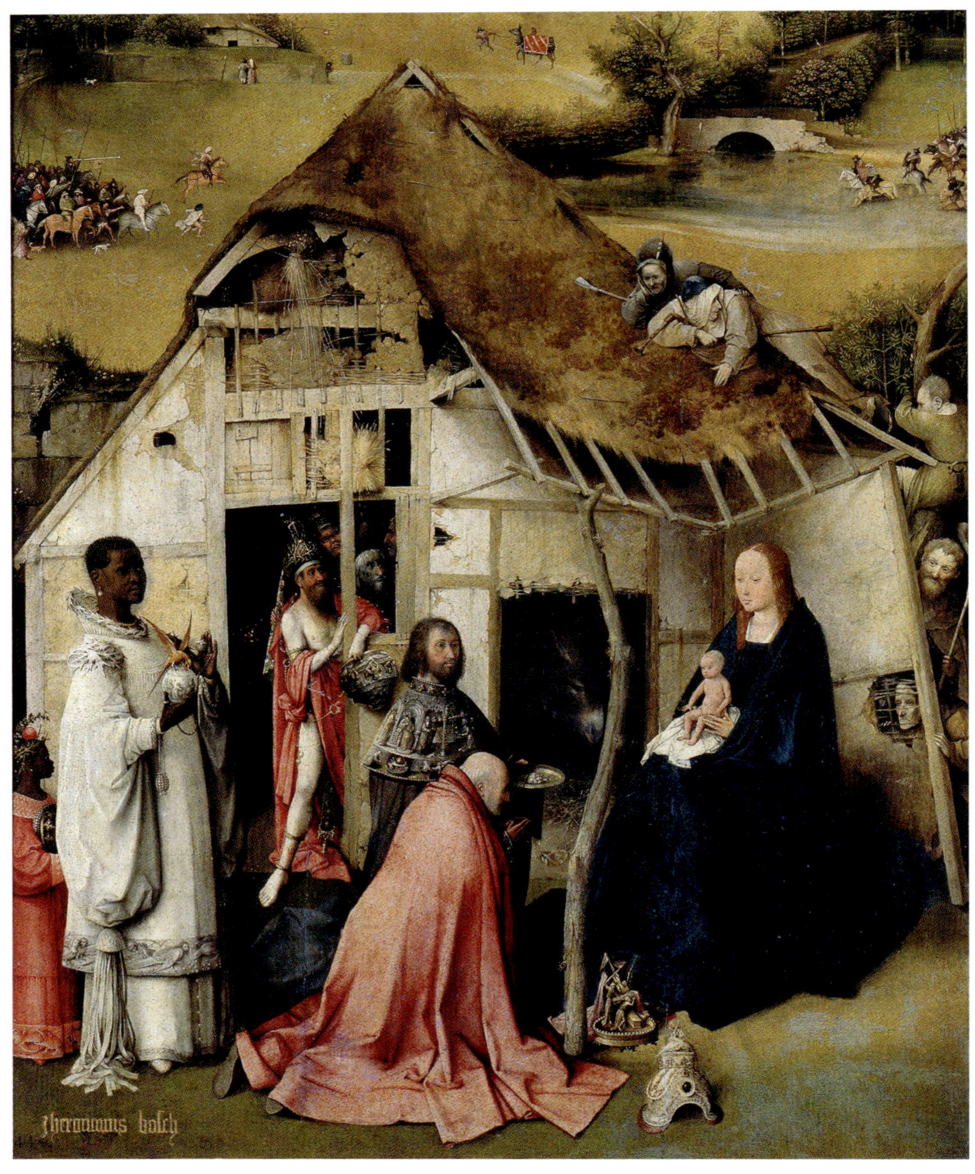

Hieronymus Bosch, **The Adoration of the Magi** (detail), *c.* 1496/97
Oil on oak, central panel: 146.7 x 84 cm (57 ¾ x 33 ⅛ in.). Madrid, Museo Nacional del Prado

Also, the spiral form of the nautilus shell is now given a specific meaning, since it too symbolises inner contemplation and self-knowledge.

The glance of the black king holding the ship in his hands leads out of the picture and is apparently fascinated by something not of this Earth. Christ hovers before his spiritual, inner eye. He is carrying the goblet as a sign. The ship becomes the symbol of a spiritual Church. The true Church of Christ knows the Saviour in its heart and does not need the outer sign in order to venerate him. In *The Adoration of the Kings*, Bruegel stages the opposition of inner and outer knowledge of God. The adoration of the kings on the left and the avaricious stares of the soldiers are in stark contrast to the attitude of the king at the right, who is deep in contemplation.

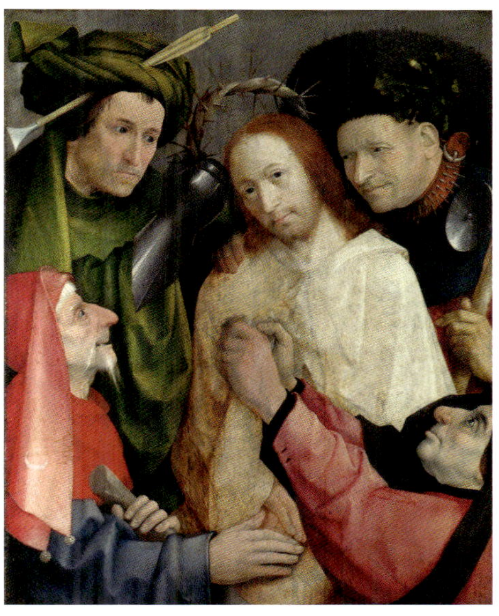

Although the crib is mentioned in the New Testament, the two animals, the ox and the ass, are not, yet they both have a firm place in Christmas iconography. The Old Testament is cited to explain their presence. To quote Isaiah: "The ox knoweth his owner and the ass his master's crib, but Israel doth not know, and my people doth not consider" (Isaiah 1: 3). In Bruegel's version, the ass eats hay out of the crib in which the Infant Jesus has just been laid. There is an interesting passage in Franck's *Paradoxa* in this regard, in which the flesh of Christ is called "food for the soul": "When I see Christ with spiritual eyes and not like the Pharisees only from the outside and I recognise him in spirit [...]. Thus the Body of Christ becomes spiritual and food for the soul."[99] Evidently the German theologian is describing the Eucharist here as the spiritual way to Christ within.

Bruegel in addition stages an opposition of significance between crown and sceptre in the insignia of outer power on the one hand and the supposedly insignificant straw on the other. Christ fortifies man within, just as he eschews externally visible symbols of power for himself. The straw seemingly scattered at random on the ground leads the eye to the crib with the ass feeding from it. At the right to its rear is a saddle resting on a stand.

Hieronymus Bosch, **The Crowning with Thorns**, *c.* 1510
Oil on oak, 73.8 x 59.1 cm (29 ⅛ x 23 ¼ in.). London, The National Gallery

Knowing Christ merely on the outside is not enough. Only when the beholder becomes Christ's humble "beast of burden" and turns his eyes away from the things of this world can he recognise the Saviour. This panel of Bruegel's too shows the limits of external sight. It clearly pleads that in order to know the divine, man needs inner contemplation.

Eternal recurrence

In *The Procession to Calvary* (also: *Christ Carrying the Cross*; pp. 142/143, Cat. 15), the opposition of inner and outer vision plays an important role.[100] Very few pictures by the Flemish painter are as dramatic as this. The calamity is heralded not only on Earth, but also in Heaven. Clouds scud over the land, the wind tugs at people's cloaks and tears the hats from their heads. While the expansive procession of the voyeuristic crowd is making its way to the place of execution, a mighty thunderstorm is gathering overhead. Near the horizon, we can see those people waiting who have already found their way to the two erected crosses.

The picture is distinctly divided up into two zones. A narrow foreground strip screens off the actual picture space. A pedlar among others has taken up his place here in order to view the spectacle. Concentric circles of movement surround the steep rock, a windmill on its peak. The most dynamically effective compositional feature consists in the animation of the picture space. People come from the left and move to the right, while the dark thunderclouds move in the opposite direction. Like the hub of a wheel, the rock stands almost at the fulcrum of movement. Bruegel's pictorial composition incorporates the viewer's imagination: we see more than is actually depicted. Soon, the people who are hastening away from the town will reach the place of execution and will have greatly increased the voyeuristic crowd gathered around the cross. The gathering storm clouds will by then have fully covered the sky. But Bruegel is also able to represent the past as well as the future. A glance at the bright sky on the left of the picture clearly indicates that the weather must still have been benign for the people then leaving Jerusalem. The circular movements in the sky and on the Earth seem like cosmic powers. The sequence of the salvific history is predestined. As fervently as people believe they are following their own wills when making their way to Golgotha, it is obvious to the observer that they are being drawn there. The vortex pulling them to the place of execution is overwhelming and inexorable.

Although Bruegel has placed Christ in the picture centre, the Redeemer, collapsed under the cross (p. 145), is only perceptible at second glance.[101] The picture also gains its power by making the events seem almost prosaic and everyday. People leaving town to proceed to the execution encounter farmers who are going back to town with their produce and livestock. All social levels will take part in this execution. Families are making their way to Golgotha just as much as single persons or small groups. We also see riders in red jerkins, moving out of town in the same direction. Many riders and spectators accompany the cart with the condemned man. It is almost like a fair, crowds of people setting off in anticipation. And Bruegel is quite obviously employing the New Testament theme in order to portray his own environment.

The picture at first fragments into a great number of supposedly incoherent individual scenes, a comment on the calamitous state of the world. The episode of Simon of Cyrene in the foreground at the left is an optimal comment on the behaviour of hypocritical Christians. When he is compelled to carry Christ's cross, his wife holds on to him tightly and struggles with all her might to resist the soldiers. Her distinctly visible rosary is an evident sign of her false piety. The woman is one of those Christians of whom Erasmus writes in *The Manual of a Christian Knight*, those who bear the Gospel not in their hearts but merely round their necks.[102]

One basis for a fruitful interpretation of *The Procession to Calvary* is the realisation that there is an element missing in Bruegel that is a traditional component of this iconography. Usually, this theme includes a portrayal of St Veronica. The lack of this figure is significant in that it eschews an important legitimation for the existence of painting.[103]

To arrive at the actual meaning of the picture, it is necessary to go further than the information provided by sensory perception. We should look at the group of four in the bottom right-hand corner of the picture. Here, St John is supporting the Virgin Mary, who is collapsing in a faint, and it is striking that none of the figures turn directly to the procession, in contrast to the pedlar at the left, who thinks he is watching a theatre performance. In this Lamentation group, which seems like a quote from Old Netherlandish painting, indeed like a "picture within a picture", Bruegel is alluding to another theme: an observer well versed in iconography will have seen the arrangement as reminiscent of a Crucifixion or Descent from the Cross. The literature has referred to a panel by Rogier van der Weyden (1399/1400–1464) as a possible model (p. 121).[104] In any event, the figures are in late-medieval attire and stand out clearly from the other people, who are otherwise wearing contemporary clothes. Bruegel depicts different stylistic phases simultaneously and thus engineers an aesthetic disruption for the viewer.

At first we become aware of the many scenes, then the contradiction in the variously portrayed dramatis personae. Finally, going beyond the people portrayed in the picture, we see that Bruegel has composed an invisible cross. According to this theory, an observer of early modern times would have identified the Crucifixion type in the Lamentation group and would have completed the picture with the cross in their centre. However, such a Lamentation group can be verified in other versions of the Carrying of the Cross, so it might merely be an example of an iconographic set piece. So how can we decide whether an invisible cross is really included here?

Bruegel takes as his subject outer and inner vision, the visible and the spiritual knowledge of God; he demonstrates this in the persons surrounding the Lamentation group. In the small family to the immediate right of the group, the father is pointing with his right hand in the direction of the execution procession, while one of the children pulls impatiently at the mother's skirt to draw her attention to the spectacle. But the woman turns away and puts a cloth in front of her face – virtually an ironic reversal of the Veronica motif. In contrast, the figures directly behind St John and St Mary Magdalene are looking with great perturbation at the visible Christ. In conspicuous contrast to the two Franciscan nuns behind a large rock who have raised their hands melodramatically in prayer, we have to point to the quietly praying pair of mother and child standing at the left a little below St John. Both are looking at something that can only exist in their imagination – they have turned to the invisible cross. Hence, paradoxically, the only persons to be judged positively are those who have turned away from the madding crowd, from the theatre of the world, and from the external Christ, because what matters is the Christ within. A passage from the Erasmus' *Manual* is illuminating in this context, where he speaks of the "Cross within us":

"You think it the most wonderful thing that you possess in your house a piece of the True Cross. But this is nothing in comparison with the mystery of bearing the Cross within you. Otherwise, if these things make a man pious, who would then be more pious than the Jews, the most nefarious among them having in part seen Christ alive in his body, with his own eyes, heard with his own ears, touched him with his own hands? Who, then, is happier than Judas, who touched the divine mouth with his mouth? You stare spellbound at the robe or the sudarium attributed to Christ, and fall asleep while you read the words of Christ's law?"[105]

The devaluation of outer appearance expressed here, for instance regarding Veronica's sudarium, tallies with the concept of Bruegel's work. The reference to the invisible "Cross within us" is decisive, as is the resulting necessity to eschew merely external images. Yet what is so unexpected in the citation is the ire with which Erasmus criticises the external images and thus painting. It can be interpreted as a kind of self-accusation that the painter has portrayed himself at the far right edge of the picture, where he has stopped next to a figure reminiscent of the remorseful Judas.

Contrary to all previous interpretations, we can assume that none of the figures turning in perturbation towards the fallen Christ is to be seen in a positive light, least of all the Franciscan nuns. "Christ outside of us brings no benefits" is the title of the 133rd paradox by Sebastian Franck, "Christ, known only in the flesh, is of no effect", the next. It will never be possible to represent God from the perspective of the world. Accordingly, every attempt to represent the divine is in conflict with itself and must remain an eternal

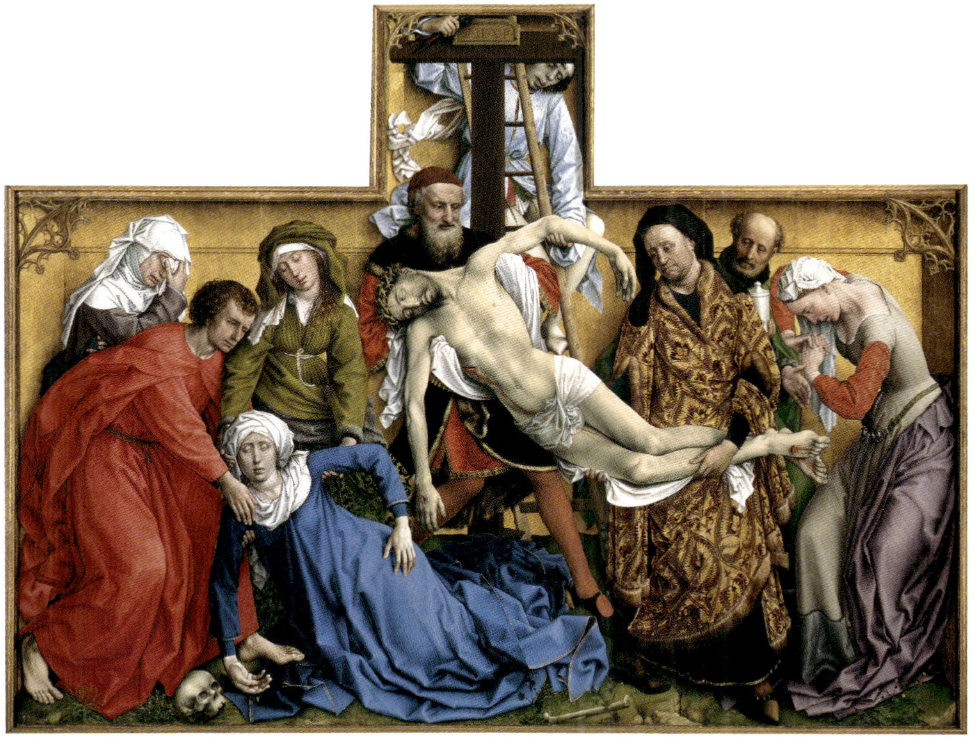

Rogier van der Weyden, **The Descent from the Cross,** before 1443
Oil on wood, 204.5 x 261.5 cm (80 ½ x 102 ⅞ in.). Madrid, Museo Nacional del Prado

paradox. Only now can we clearly discern the meaninglessness of the bustle jostling around the steeply rising rock. It is never-ending, Bruegel seems to be saying; the wheel of time turns, and just as unceasingly Christians are still being killed today for their faith.[106] This never-ending Passion is underlined even more by the windmill on the rock.

Bruegel's *Procession to Calvary* includes a further, previously unnoticed, paradox. Just as the Crucifixion has not yet taken place, as we see in the background at the right where only two crosses have been erected, the Lamentation group in the foreground at the right indicates on the other hand that it has already occurred. It is as if the past had advanced towards us out of the future and the future had already happened! This dizzying idea of an eternal recurrence under the sign of the Passion can be found in Franck's 106th paradox, which can help in understanding the picture:

"One day drives away the last; the world is expedient, and all things are cyclic, like the Sun, there is nothing constant or permanent on Earth. Thus the saying: *Onmium rerum*

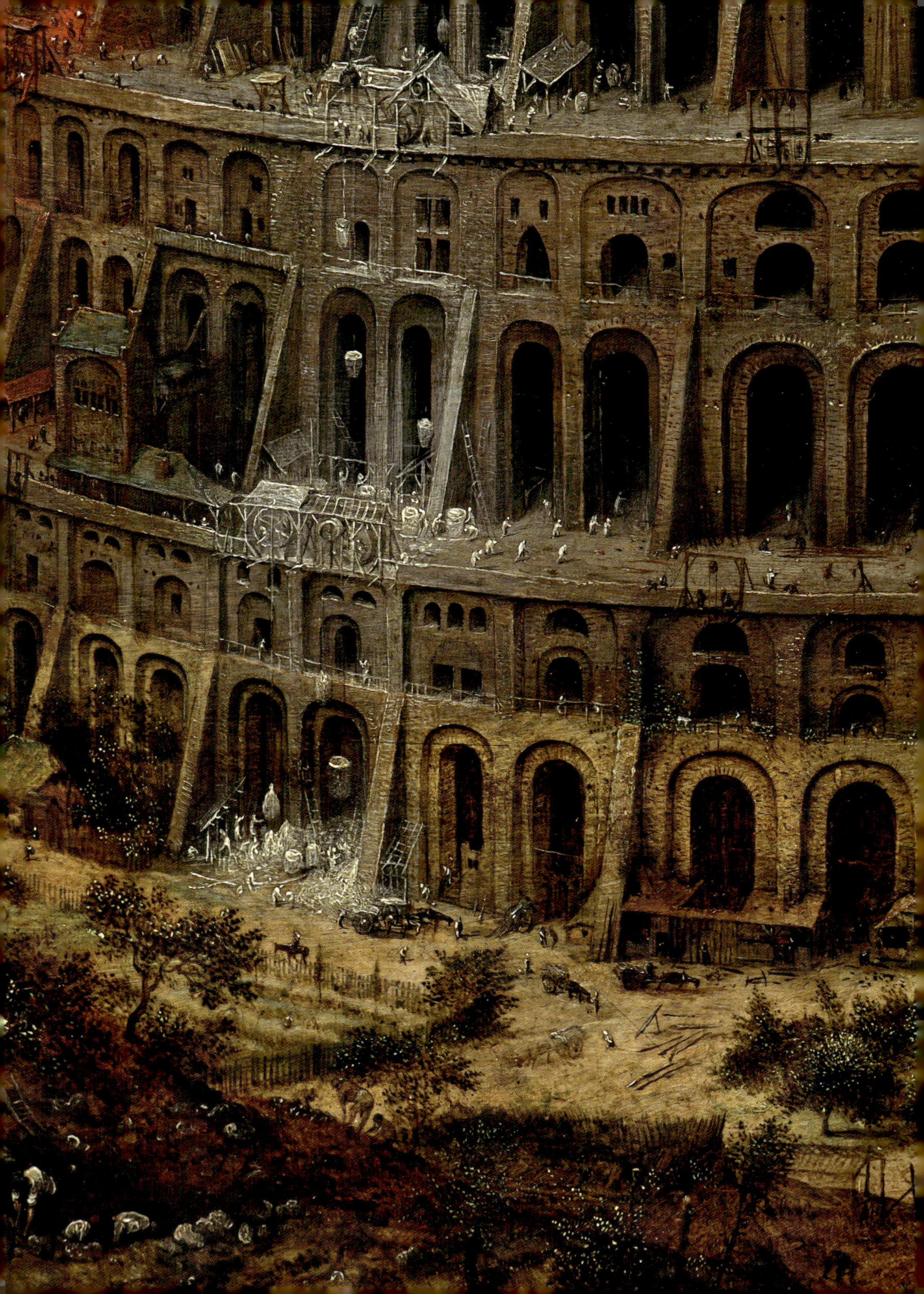

vicissitudo; what has happened is no more, but will come again. Therefore the entire Bible must be repeated again and again and be consubstantiated […]. It all takes place within us; and if Christ happened to come again externally, comes and suffers every day in all his physical attributes, we would crucify him again and again, fulfilling the measure of our ancestors in him. […] World is always world, and the globe of the world must always roll round, so that what was today will not be tomorrow and come again." [107]

This is a truly cosmic vision that Franck elaborates out of the diurnal round of the world, out of the Earth's spherical shape: everything moves in meaningless revolution, styled to never-ending recurrence, which produces the paradoxical figure of time, "so that what was today will not be tomorrow and come again". In Bruegel's unredeemed world, the past is distinctive in that it happens in the future, and the future in that it has always happened, so that past, present and future dissolve as finite dimensions. The as yet unredeemed world is robbed of its present and represents a self-accelerating allegory that speaks ever louder of the absence of God.

Confusions of speech

The supposition that in this period Bruegel continually pondered the problem of the mistaken search for God is supported in his two pictures of the Tower of Babel, dated to the mid-1560s.

In the bottom left-hand corner of the large *Tower of Babel* in Vienna (pp. 150/151, Cat. 12), we see King Nimrod visiting the building site to check the project's status. The ruler is standing in the midst of a group of courtiers, while at his left a man seems to be informing him of something; he might be the architect giving a progress report. The workers at the king's feet have knelt down, and directly in front of him one of the workers is humbly prostrating himself. One glance at the tower is enough to indicate that it requires an incredible effort to build it. Busy workers are perceived in all parts of the building. Their unconditional zeal is impressive, as is the perfect organisation behind everything. The Bible itself testifies to this human zeal: "Come, let us make a city and a tower, the top whereof may reach to heaven: and let us make ourselves a name, lest we be scattered over the face of the whole earth" (Genesis 11: 4).

Bruegel's panels impart a minor role to the Old Testament in comparison to New Testament themes. [108] Apart from *The Suicide of Saul in the Battle on Gilboa Mountain* (Cat. 6), he chose only the narrative of the Tower of Babel, but then in two versions (see

The Tower of Babel (Rotterdam version; also:
The "Small" Tower of Babel; detail), *c.* 1565
(see ill. pp. 164/165)

also Cat. 13). The iconography presents the painter with a demanding task. How can he convincingly convey the immense size of a building, and how can he suggest the failure of this megalomaniac project? Painters have many times settled for depicting large, regularly formed buildings or their collapse. To cope with this task, Bruegel chose a large picture format. The tower fills practically the whole of the panel; the building, and not the surrounding landscape, is the scale to which everything else is subordinated. The artificial mountain of the tower seems overwhelming. Meanwhile, Bruegel manages to integrate a change of perspective into his picture. While we at first look down at the left onto the group around King Nimrod, our eye in turn has to wander upwards in order to include the tower into our field of vision. This seemingly simply compositional strategy makes the tower seem all the bigger and more monumental. It silhouette is set off strikingly against the sky. Behind it stretches a port city, its wall quite distinct. On the left, our eye is led to the horizon, where it discerns a far-away mountain range. To the right, we see stretches of a coast and in the distance an island on the horizon.

The observer is at first overwhelmed by the mighty impact of the building, only to realise the impossibility of its succeeding. In the Vienna version, this overwhelming feeling in the observer corresponds at first to astonishment at the accomplishment. The very fact that the achievement seems so imposing makes the failure all the more dramatic. Experience shows that the lack of moderation probably always means the lack of a proper goal.

Here, Bruegel proves yet again to be an attentive reader of the Bible. It states that God sees the capabilities of human beings when building the tower, but evidently there are no limits set for them, whereupon he confuses their speech. When the Lord comes down from Heaven to inspect the building of the tower and the city, he speaks the following words: "Behold, it is one people, and all have one tongue: and they have begun to do this, neither will they leave off from their designs, till they accomplish them in deed. Come ye, therefore, let us go down, and there confound their tongue, that they may not understand one another's speech!" (Genesis 11: 6–7). In the Old Testament episode, speech and design, understanding and building belong together. These capabilities demand collective endeavour.

The Tower of Babel has been correctly interpreted as symbol of mankind's hubris. We can find a possible basis in Chapter 15 of Sebastian Brant's (1457/58–1521) *Ship of Fools* (1494), with the eloquent title "Of Foolish Planning". The Tower of Babel is also mentioned in the many examples of foolhardy people who become victims of their own delusions of grandeur. The building – obviously inspired by the Colosseum in Rome – was also associated with the papacy. If we agree with this interpretation as a critique of the papacy, we might recall a scene from Vasari's fresco in the Sala dei Cento Giorni, which shows the pope as commissioning patron of St Peter's (p. 125). When perusing Bruegel's city more closely, it is notable that a large number of churches are standing next to each

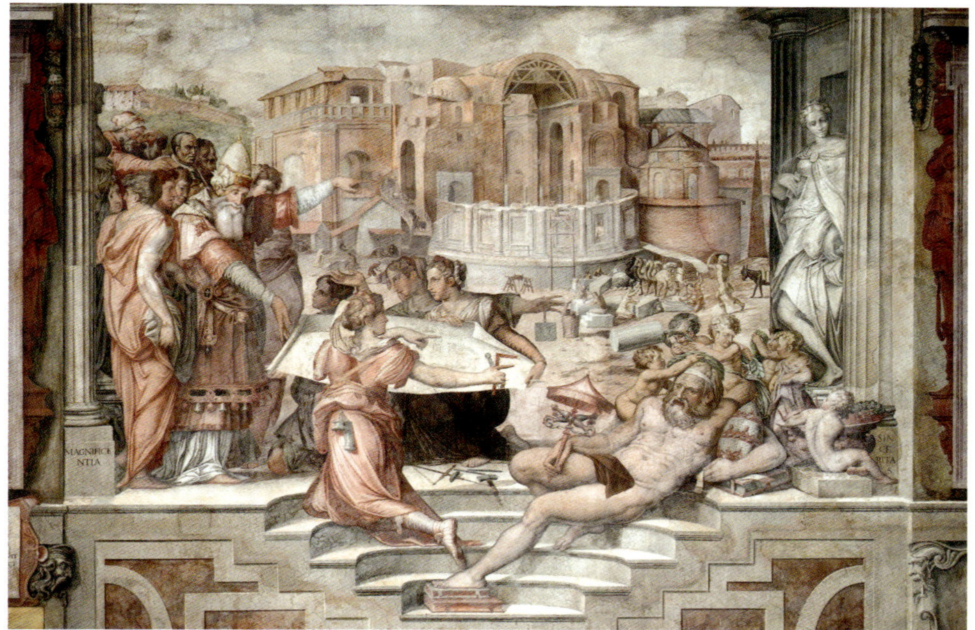

Giorgio Vasari, **Pope Paul III Directing the Continuation of St Peter's**, 1546
Fresco. Rome, Palazzo della Cancellaria, Sala dei Cento Giorni

other in a restricted space. Seven storeys have already been erected for the tower. As with
the Colosseum, the façade shows protruding half-pillars and a double-storey wall
articulation with double arcading. It is difficult to say whether Bruegel was inspired by his
sojourn in Rome or by Hieronymus Cock's engravings (p. 126). Looking at the many
scenes with workers, we might think we are finding images of self-sacrificing industry and
technical expertise. Bruegel suggests the feasibility of the project. He supplies cranes,
winches, ships, and diverse devices indicating human ingenuity. He depicts the potential
of homo faber.

There is no notion here of linguistic confusion. Everyone knows his task, everything
is proceeding in order. While in the inside of the building enormous quantities of bricks
have been built up, to the right of the tower more stones are being delivered, which now
have to be hoisted up the building. Bruegel not only gives us an inside view into the
procedure but also suggests something specific to make us realise that the people in the
city, at the foot of the building, can see only the finished parts. They have no reason to
doubt. On the contrary, they have the impression that the building is as good as ready,

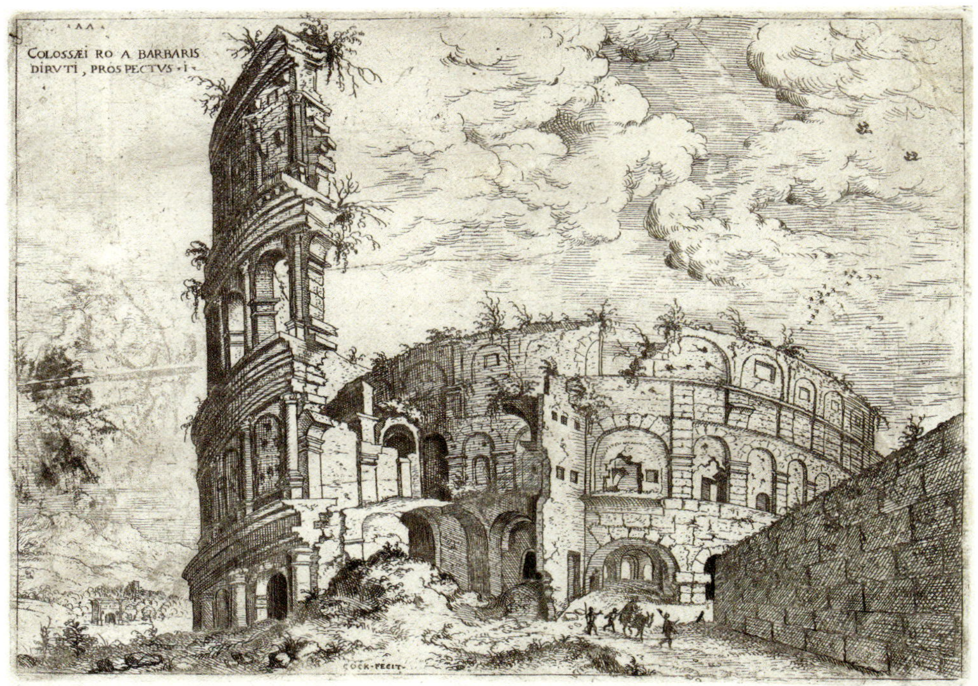

Hieronymus Cock, **Views of the Colosseum**, 1551
Etching, 23.4 x 32.2 cm (9 ¼ x 12 ⅔ in.)
Amsterdam, Rijksmuseum, Rijksprentenkabinet

even though they might regret having to live for ever in the shadow of its bulk. Only when we look closer at the part of the building invisible to the townspeople do we discover an impending catastrophe. As becomes apparent at the top section, the shell and the inner construction do not fit together. It cannot be said with certainty what led to this error. But the picture shows us an enormous rock that has to be integrated, and that possibly led to wrong calculations. We are reminded of Christ's words about the rock upon which he will build his Church (Matthew 16: 18), the famous part of the Bible upon which the Catholic Church was founded with Peter as the first pope – perhaps this, too, is a covert criticism of the papacy.

Bruegel gives us an image for our imagination.[109] On one hand we are meant to discover the difference between the completed façade and the incomplete inner construction, and, on the other, form an idea of the impression the people in the city of Babylon have of the building. They think they are at the goal of their desires, the tower already looming up so high into the sky that it penetrates banks of cloud.

In Bruegel's panel, the problem of time plays a major role. We should note the simultaneity of all activities, and ask how long it would take to get from the harbour at sea level up to the top of the building. In the scene with Nimrod in the bottom left-hand corner, a basic constructional unit is detectable (pp. 158/159). How long does it take to hew such a stone, and how many stones have now been used in the building? How incalculable the achievement seems! But the monster these efforts have produced can no longer be mastered. Even the way up takes so long that by the time a worker reaches the top he is no longer required for the task he was sent to perform. The nightmare is exacerbated when we move inside the building erected around the rock. What kind of gigantic labyrinth is awaiting us here?

The people have not only built a tower: they have set up an idol. They misrepresent the tower. It is no longer a site set aside for the divine, but the focus of their lives. But what does this eidolon stand for? Are the people celebrating their own technical expertise and therefore actually themselves? Is it simply an expression of their hubris and no more? This interpretation does not adequately explain the picture, for here we are dealing with an allegory of a mistaken understanding of God and a wrong interpretation of the Bible.

Writings in classical antiquity already compared texts with buildings. In the context of anamnesis, but also in general, texts represent an ordered system comparable to a building. This comparison even crops up in Bible frontispieces. For Bruegel, we might mention the tradition of the Tower of Grammar as depicted for instance by Heinrich Vogtherr the Elder (1490–1556) in a woodcut dated 1548. Here, too, we see a tower and the apparatus necessary for its erection.

When juxtaposing the pictorial version of the Tower of Grammar to Bruegel's Tower of Babel, the question arises here as to whether the artist is alluding to the problem of adequate scriptural exegesis.[110] In accordance with Sebastian Franck in this context, a complete understanding of Holy Scripture is impossible.[111] It cannot contain the divine, only indicate it, which is why he writes in the *Paradoxa*: "The Gospel is nothing but an eternal oration of miracles. […] The letter of the script, the sword of the Antichrist, kills Christendom. The script without the light, life and interpretation of the spirit is a dead letter and a snuffed-out lantern."[112] In light of the Franck citation, the huge building becomes a mere shell, a form without content. The people have confused the letter for the spirit, the word has become an idol, a "paper pope", as Franck writes. For the spirit is not found in the external forms of script, neither in words nor grammatical forms. People must strive to go beyond the words. The actual challenge lies in leaving them behind.

The Rotterdam *Tower of Babel* (pp. 164/165, Cat. 13) is distinctly smaller than the Vienna version, which simultaneously alters the size of the figures in relation to the building. In this case, the people populating the tower justifiably remind us of ants.

The Tower of Babel (Rotterdam version; also:
The "Small" Tower of Babel; detail), *c.* 1565
(see ill. pp. 164/165)

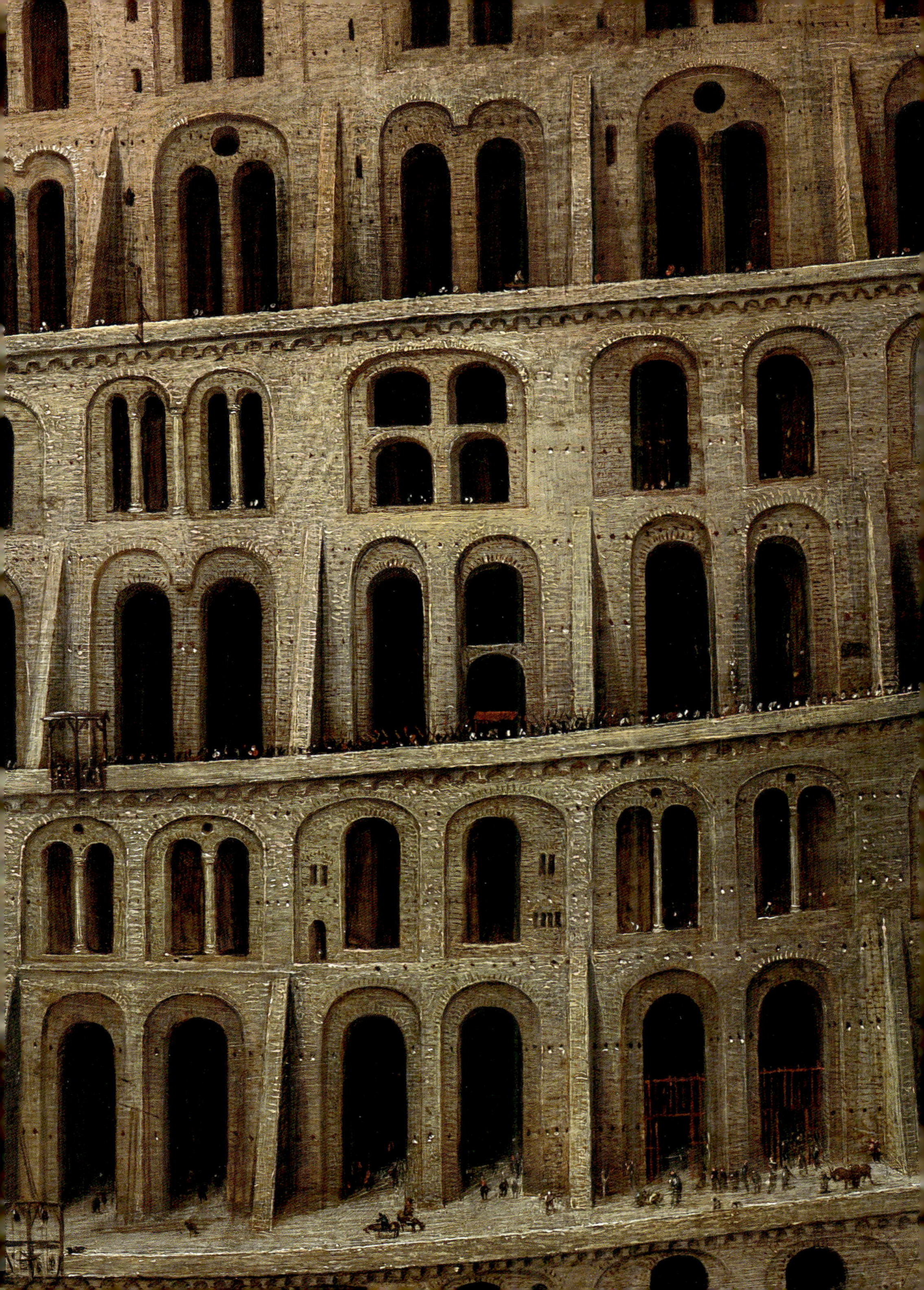

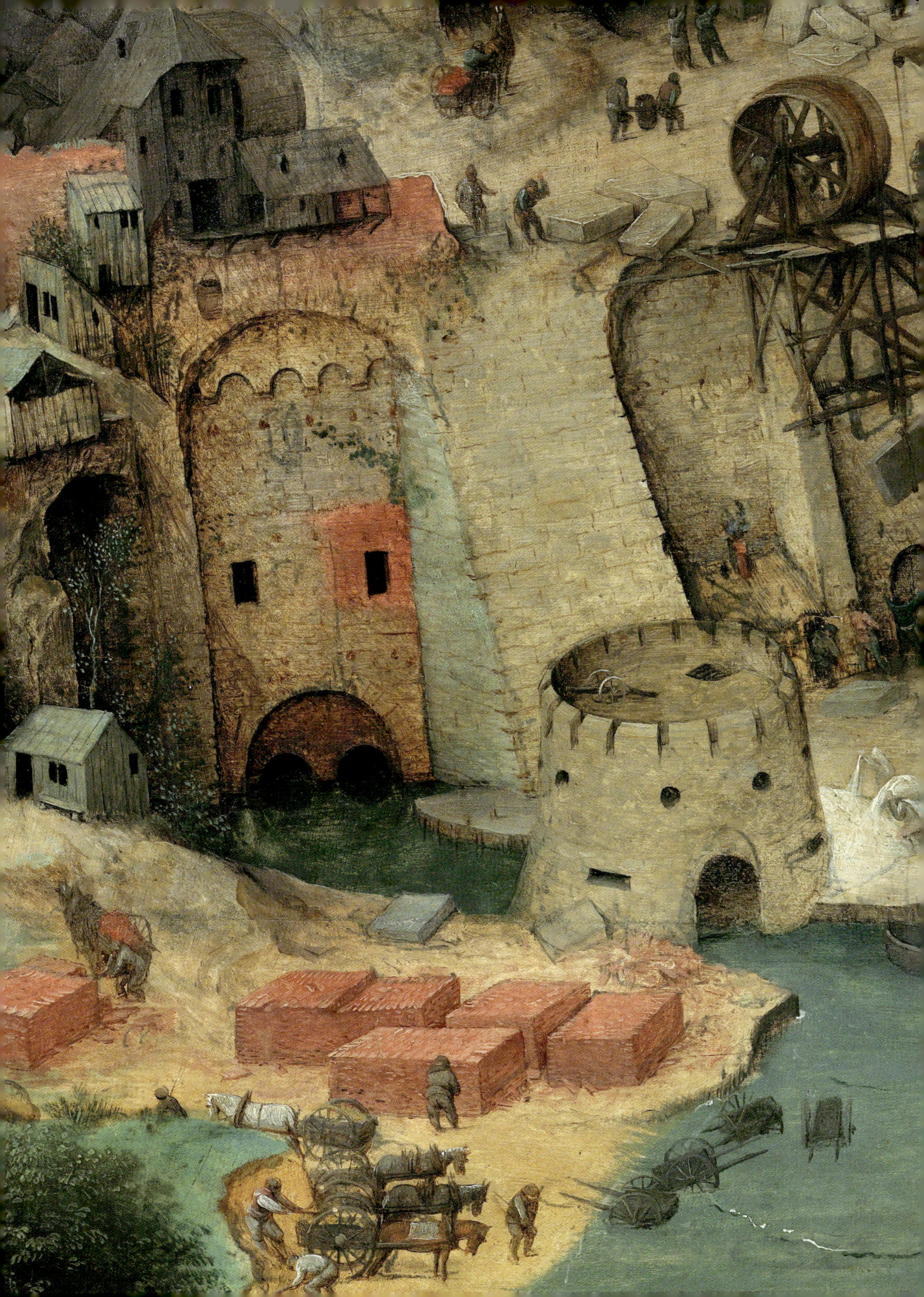

In composition, the Rotterdam differs little from the Vienna version. The huge building stands on the shore of a sea, and while the view at the left opens up onto city and mountains on the horizon, on the right we see the harbour with ships lying at anchor. Yet again, the Colosseum in Rome was the model.

The tower has reached enormous proportions in the Rotterdam version, too, and seems to be close to completion; it is already piercing the clouds. But in contrast to the Vienna version, there are no signs of failure. It seems as stable as it is indomitable. Also, Bruegel dispenses with the Nimrod scene. When examining the architectural elements, we notice that the double-storey arcades are rendered without uniformity, without being able to detect any clear intention.

In his undated and unsigned panel, Bruegel presents us with painting that is striking for its extreme miniaturisation. Meanwhile, his technical virtuosity is such that he monumentalises it at the same time. A magnifying glass is needed in order to detect certain scenes on the surrounding ramps. Another especially successful feature is the play of light and shade. The top of the tower piercing the blanket of cloud glows ruddy in the evening Sun.

Studies have drawn attention to an interesting detail. A procession is depicted on the fourth storey in the absolute centre of the picture, and we notice a red spot, which on closer scrutiny turns out to be a procession baldachin.[113] The procession is progressing towards one of the tower chambers in which a church is installed. One of the arcades in the top part is closed by tracery and a glass window, and in the lower there is a carillon. In his rendering of the scene, Bruegel might have oriented himself here – it has been suggested – on an engraving by Maarten van Heemskerck (1498–1574; p. 133) showing a papal procession.

Nevertheless, we can be spared the question as to whether this is to be deemed as an anti-Catholic statement. For people have established themselves permanently on all floors, and it seems as if there is a depiction of another church portal reminiscent of a cathedral, placed one storey lower directly under the procession. The Babylonian confusion of speech would therefore in reality be a confusion of religion. It spawned many denominations, all claiming to represent true Christianity. Isn't there a certain suggestion inherent in this discovery? Because when all these tiny people enter the great arcades inside the building, it is as if each is entering a different church. Babel is the absolute confusion of religion, as is written in a Ghent chronicle dating to the 1560s.[114]

The Tower of Babel (Vienna version; detail), 1563
(see ill. pp. 150/151)

It must be fairly obvious that Bruegel is pursuing a critical path here. Instead of searching for an invisible, mystical Church, people keep founding one official Church after another, which only alienate them all the more from true Christianity.

Where is Christ?

Bruegel also deals with the limits of knowing God, and with his doubt in what seeing is capable of, in *The Sermon of St John the Baptist* in Budapest (pp. 166/167, Cat. 27), dated 1566. In this composition, Bruegel varies a scheme that we have already seen used in the *The Procession of Calvary*: the main subject is not staged prominently, but shifted to the rear of the picture space. John the Baptist is moved slightly to the left of the vertical axis in the centre ground. His appearance is nondescript, and his brown, hirsute garb does not make him stand out from the crowd. He catches the observer's eye simply through the gesture of his arm pointing to the right – hands and lower arms are seen distinctly in only a few figures in the picture.

On discovering the Baptist relatively quickly, we find we have followed the looks of the people in the picture. At the same time, he towers over the people sitting in front of him. The faithful have gathered at the edge of a forest, and it was supposed that here a forbidden Protestant "hedge service" is being shown, where the reformed Christians met to hold religious meeting outside town.[115] However, it remains difficult to decide whether those assembled on this site are merely seeking shade and a cool place, or whether they wish to hide from the gaze of the curious.

The picture was painted when hedge sermons were at their height. There was apparently a genuine mania from June to September 1566, so that services were even held twice a day, for congregations of many thousands. With regard to an outdoor sermon, it must be said that in Bruegel's work church architecture generally appears as a place remote from God. In the allegory of Faith, for example, engraved after his drawing (Müller/Schauerte 2018, Cat. D44, G74), the sacraments are rendered as compulsive Church ritual.

Trees frame the crowd left and right, the mighty tree trunk at the left acting as a repoussoir. The coarse texture of the bark is so vividly captured that it seems tangible. Close to these trees, figures seen from back curtain off the pictorial space. The audience is seated in serried rows. Only the top third of the picture on the right opens up the picture space to a river, its course and gentle meandering quite distinct. Furthermore a town extends along the bank, above its roofs enthrones a mighty church. A diagonal leads from the left into the picture depth towards the hazy horizon. The pictorial depth thus achieved is enhanced to great effect by the fall of light. It is all the more astounding that Bruegel based his composition on an engraving after Raphael (p. 134).[116]

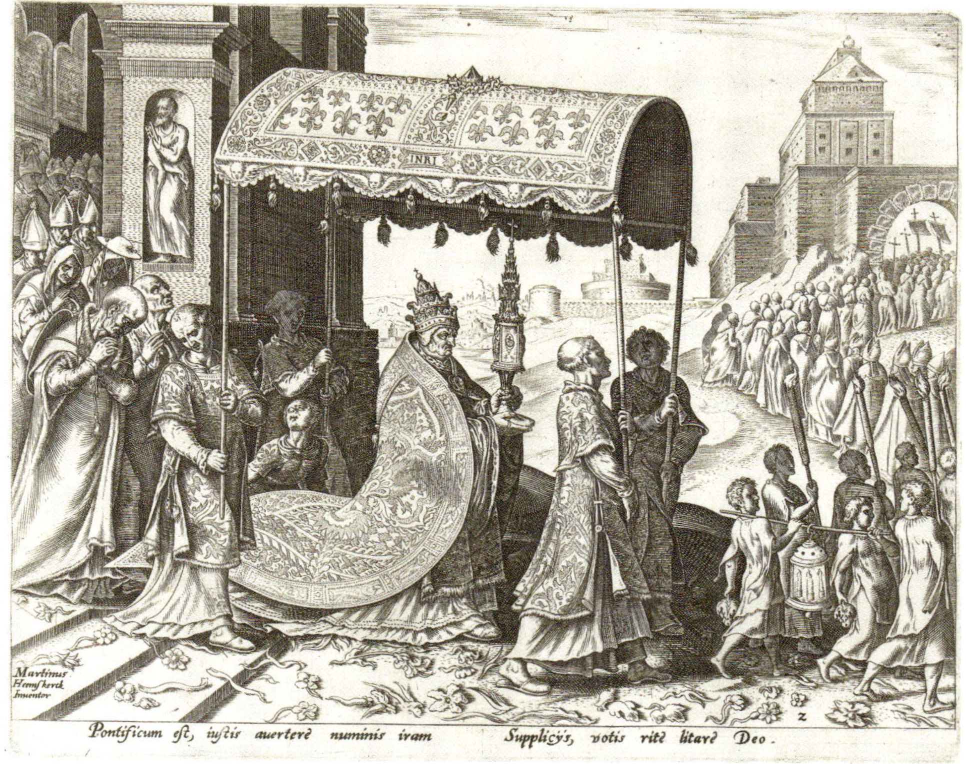

Philipp Galle after Maarten van Heemskerck
The Pope Celebrating a Religious Feast, *c.* 1565–1568
Sheet 2 from the series *The Divine Charge to the Three Estates.* Copper engraving,
20.4 x 24.6 cm (8 ⅛ x 9 ⅔ in.) Amsterdam, Rijksmuseum, Rijksprentenkabinet

Bruegel made it his task to connect close and distant views through the technique of dark moving to light, a technical masterstroke that greatly intensifies the illusion of space. Furthermore, we have the impression that he wanted to show as many religions as possible among the great crowd, as well as various Christian groups. At the left edge of the picture is a man wearing a turban, who, curiously, has his hands clasped in prayer and is being watched balefully by his neighbour. To the right of the tree sits a pilgrim whose headdress is adorned with numerous signs, and next to him are two gypsies in dress typical of these gypsies at that time.[117] Various religious orders are shown as well. In the right-hand corner are two monks, one of whom is pointing in John's direction; the T-cross of the Antonites is attached to the hem of his habit. Further up, two

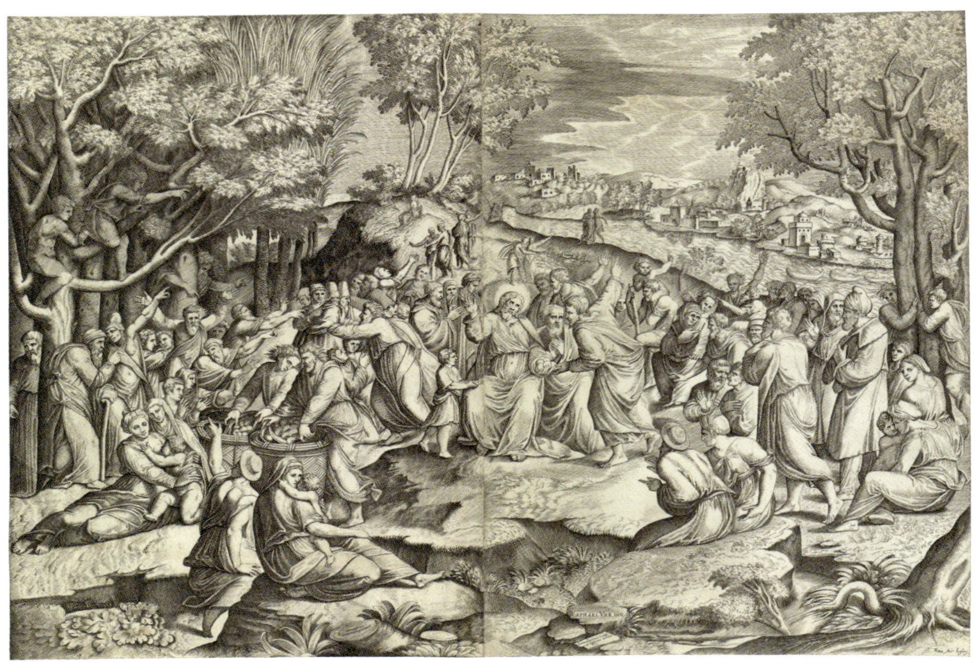

Giovanni Battista de' Cavalieri after Raphael
Miracle of the Bread and the Fishes (Feeding of the Five Thousand), 1535–1601
Etching and copper engraving from two plates, 52.1 x 67.5 cm (20 ½ x 26 ⅝ in.)
Amsterdam, Rijksmuseum, Rijksprentenkabinet

Franciscans are discernable, apparently listening attentively. Bruegel produces a great number of faces without repeating himself once.

Overall, we have the impression that the entire congregation is listening devotedly to the Baptist's words. Only one person is looking in our direction. To the right of the tree on the left, there is a man characterised by his attire as a landsknecht (a mercenary soldier), who seems to have noticed our arrival. Evidently, Bruegel wants to show people from different estates and cultures listening to the sermon. St John's sermon hence applies to all people of all times. John is the intermediary between the Old and the New Testament. With the baptism of the Redeemer, he builds the bridge from the old covenant to the New Testament, resulting in the replacement of the Law by the Gospels. During the Reformation, there were many pictures depicting his sermon simultaneously with his baptism of Christ.

The prophet places his right hand on his breast and points behind with a spacious gesture of his left hand. A figure stands behind him with his arms crossed over his chest, whom we might identify as Christ. Certainly his bright blue robe makes him stand out among the great number of brown tones. The question arises as to whether there is a concrete significance in this gesture. Does it express rejection, or at least cautious expectancy? At least two persons close to the Baptist have adopted this posture, one of them a woman, so to speak the counterpart of Jesus on the opposite side. She also has her arms crossed on her breast and is listening sceptically to the Baptist's words. Likewise, the figure on the left next to the prophet is characterised by such a gesture of scepticism and reserve.

Common to all the Gospels is the gesture of John indicating the immediate arrival of Christ. However, it is difficult to decide if the Baptist in Bruegel's picture has already seen Christ behind him. Sightlines are a practical problem in any case for the audience, and several of them have climbed trees to be able to follow the sermon better. At any rate, Christ appears unnoticed by all.

It has been pointed out that a baptism is taking place exactly on the bend of the river, but miniaturised so extremely by Bruegel that it is hard to see with the naked eye.[118] People in white baptismal robes have gathered at the riverbank. It is impossible to see who is baptising and who is being baptised. If this were depicting the Baptism of Christ, it would make it the only one of Bruegel's panels in which the unity of time and space is not maintained.

In the context of St John's sermon, the problematic of seeing and knowing is specified to a certain extent in the Bible, because it mentions that the people are uncertain as to whether John is already the Messiah or not. Hence in Luke we read: "And as the people were of opinion, and all were thinking in their hearts of John, that perhaps he might be the Christ; John answered, saying unto all: I indeed baptize you with water; but there shall come one mightier than I, the latchet of whose shoes I am not worthy to loose: he shall baptize you with the Holy Ghost, and with fire" (Luke 3: 15–16). In connection with this, it is important to be aware of the difference between water and fire baptisms, as Sebastian Franck formulates in a letter to the theologian and Anabaptist Johannes Campanus (*c.* 1500–*c.* 1574). In rejecting outer ceremonies and signs, Franck names the example of baptism and writes:

"And just as the Church today is a purely spiritual thing, so are law, Father, Spirit, bread, wine, sword, realm, life all in the spirit, and nothing is external any more. Therefore may the one Spirit alone baptise with fire and spirit all the faithful and those who obey the inner word, wherever they are in the world. For God sees not the person, but is for the Greeks as much as the barbarians and Turks as lord to the servant, in so far as they keep the light that is infused into them and that gives their hearts an eternal radiance."[119]

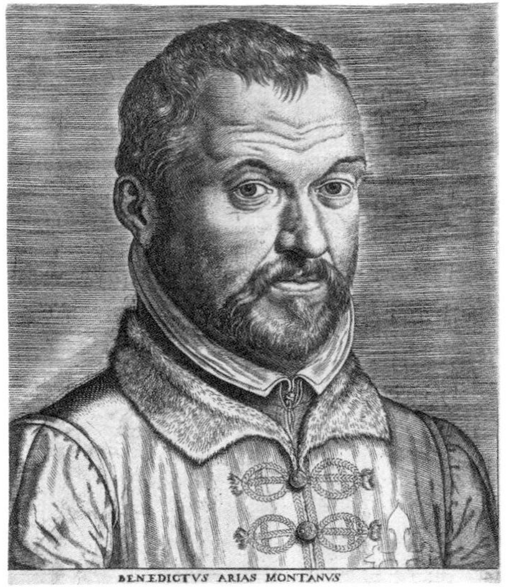

Through his portrayal of the Muslim and the gypsies, thus different religions and classes of people, Bruegel's work obviously agrees with this passage. Thus his picture appeals in an exemplary way to all religions, since Christ also died for all those who were not baptised in his name.

The previous interpretation has left out a scene in the foreground that strikes the viewer's eye. The aforementioned two gypsies reading the palm of an elegantly dressed patrician. It has been supposed that here Bruegel has placed the commissioning patron in his picture (p. 169). But this links the latter to a practice that has been deemed a superstition since the era of St Augustine (354–430). There have been many suggestions as to his identification, which cannot all be listed here. However, one person from the circle of Ortelius shows a certain similarity to the portrayed person: namely, the theologian Benito Arias Montano (p. 136), who at the time was commissioned by the Catholic Church to publish a multilingual edition of the Bible, and was subsequently exposed to the suspicion of heresy. If Montano had himself portrayed here, two questions arise: Why did he do this, and what does this mean for the overall context of the scene? Does it even have a key function in interpreting the picture?

There is a lengthy passage in the Gospel of St John that promises clarification:

"After these things Jesus and his disciples came into the land of Judea: and there he abode with them, and baptized. And John also was baptizing […], and they came and were baptized. […] And there arose a question between some of John's disciples and the Jews concerning purification. And they came to John, and said to him: 'Rabbi, he that was with thee beyond the Jordan, to whom thou gavest testimony, behold he baptizeth, and all men come to him'." (John 3: 22–26).

The irritation of St John's disciples is expressed very clearly. They are in error in their belief that baptism is the privilege of John. But the latter's baptism with water is

Philipp Galle after Frans Pourbus, **Benito Arias Montano**, 1572
Copper engraving, 17.2 x 11.9 cm (6 ¾ x 4 ⅔ in.). Amsterdam, Rijksmuseum, Rijksprentenkabinet

The Tower of Babel (Vienna version; detail), 1563
(see ill. pp. 150/151)

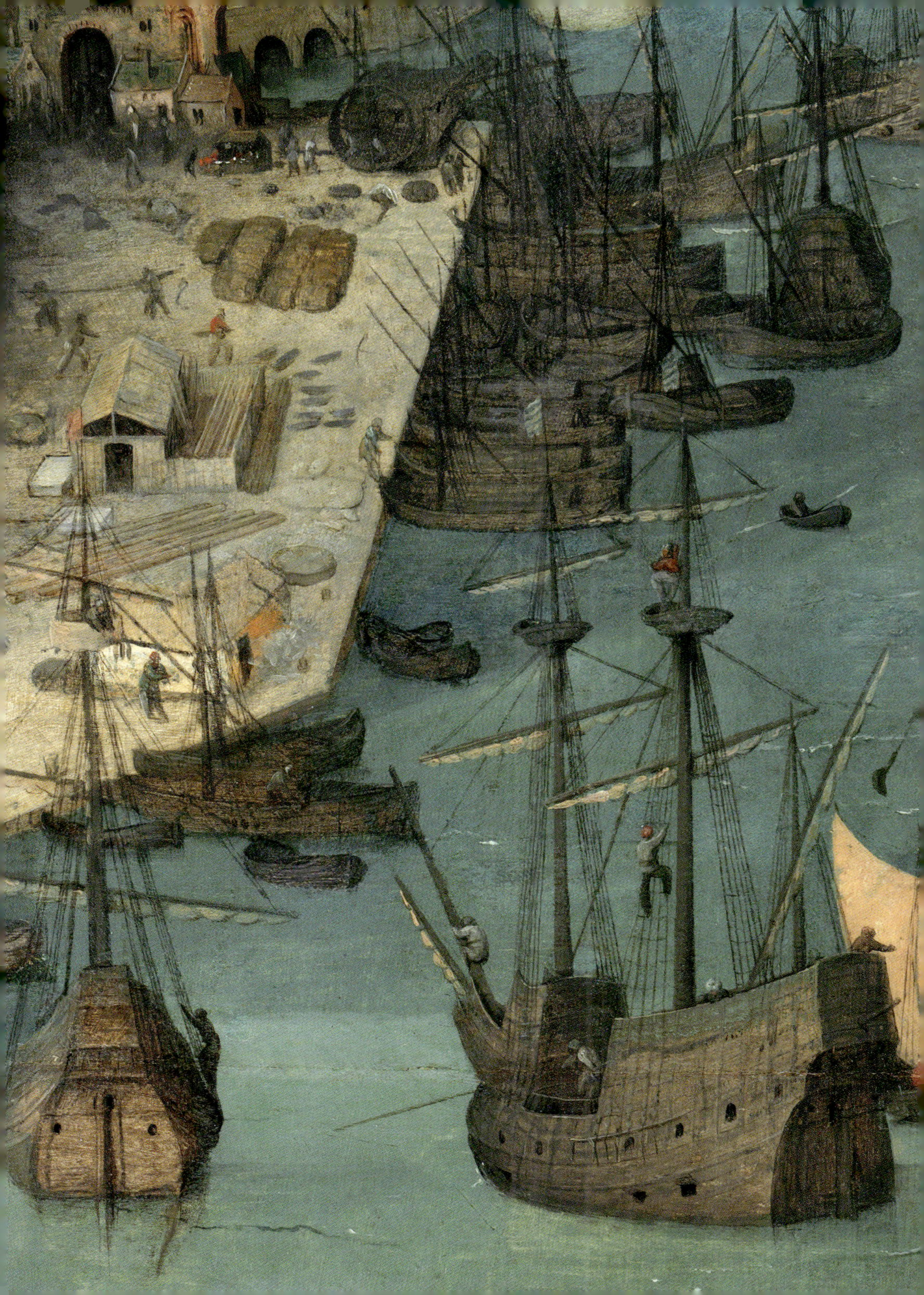

like an outer cleansing, while the spiritual baptism of Christ means an inner purification of mankind. Baptism has no effect if the Holy Ghost is not active within the person. In addition, the passage says that John preaches on this side of the Jordan, while Christ baptises on the other side of the river. But if this is the case, who is the man we thought to identify with Christ? – an Antonite! The Antonite canon portrayed in the foreground at the right is not pointing towards Christ or John, but to another member of the order in a light-blue habit, whom he has discovered in the distance. If we take note of Bruegel's colour composition of *The Sermon of St John the Baptist*, we see that all red, brown and white tones are integrated in the scheme of things, while light blue is separate and stands out.

For the observer, Bruegel's temptation consists in his satisfying the latter's desire for an outer sign helping him to know God. We believe we have identified Jesus, meanwhile he is baptising, undetected by us, on the river Jordan. The person we thought to have identified as Christ is furthermore on the same vertical axis as the palm-reading scene. This is certainly not a coincidence, since an external knowledge of God is manifested as worthless here, as Franck formulated so frequently in his *Paradoxa*.

The necessary inner and therefore unseen purification of mankind by means of baptism through the Holy Ghost provides the reason for shifting its representation into the background and for miniaturising it. It cannot be manifested on the outside, but is accomplished as a spiritual act. Each attempt to render it visually fails and descends into superstitious soothsaying. In the process, the picture presents several contradictions. Firstly, two forms of soothsaying confront each other. Palm reading is juxtaposed to the true prophecy of John. Then we are persuaded, in the spirit of Franck, to distinguish between visible water and invisible spiritual baptism. This is not at all easy to capture in a picture, as is proven by the fact that the painter, too, is among the listeners to the sermon. He sits in the top right-hand corner and listens like all others to the words of the prophet (p. 19).

The Tower of Babel (Vienna version; detail), 1563
(see ill. pp. 150/151)

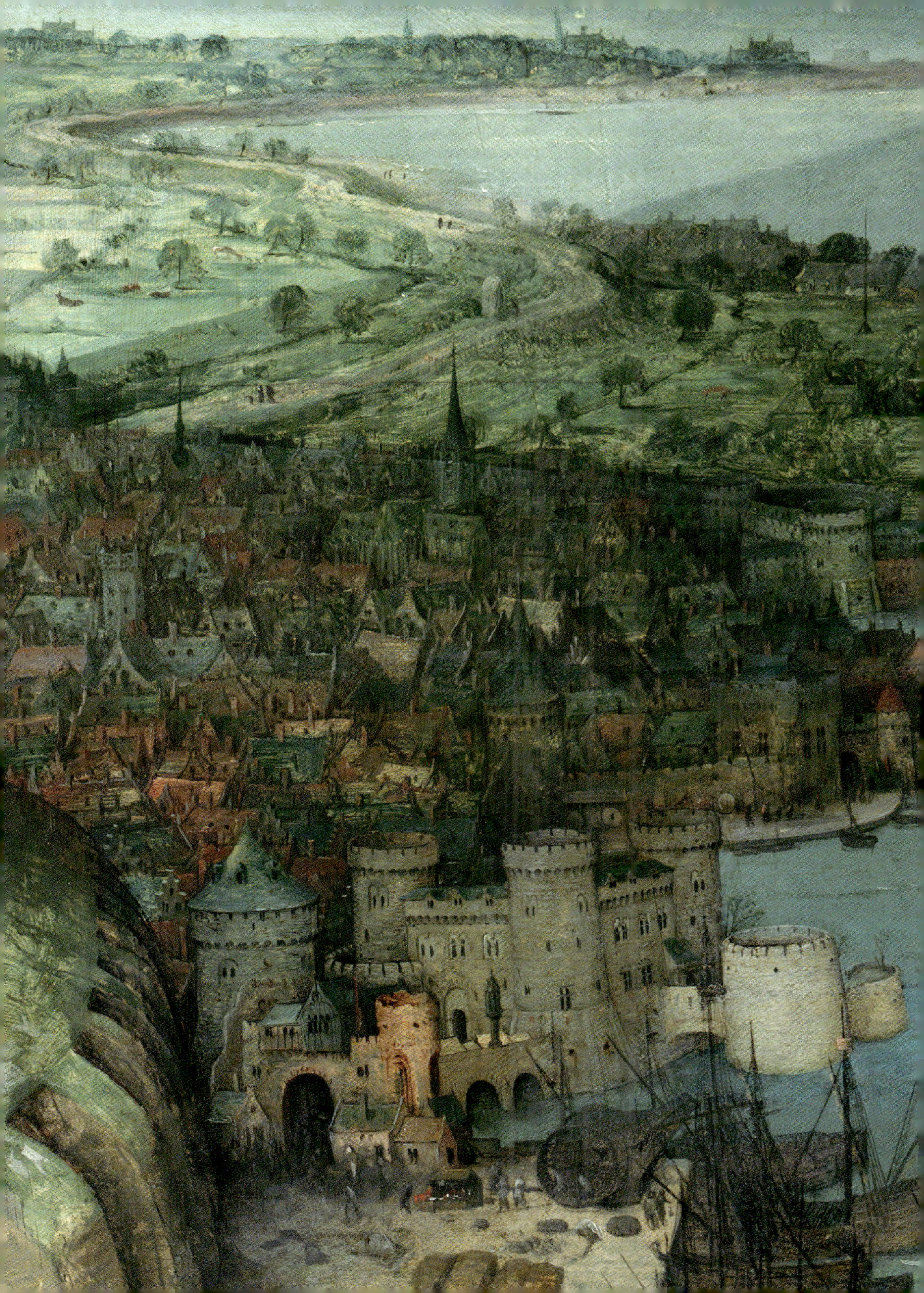

The Adoration of the Kings, 1564
Oil on wood, 111 x 83.5 cm (43 ¾ x 32 ⅞ in.)
London, The National Gallery

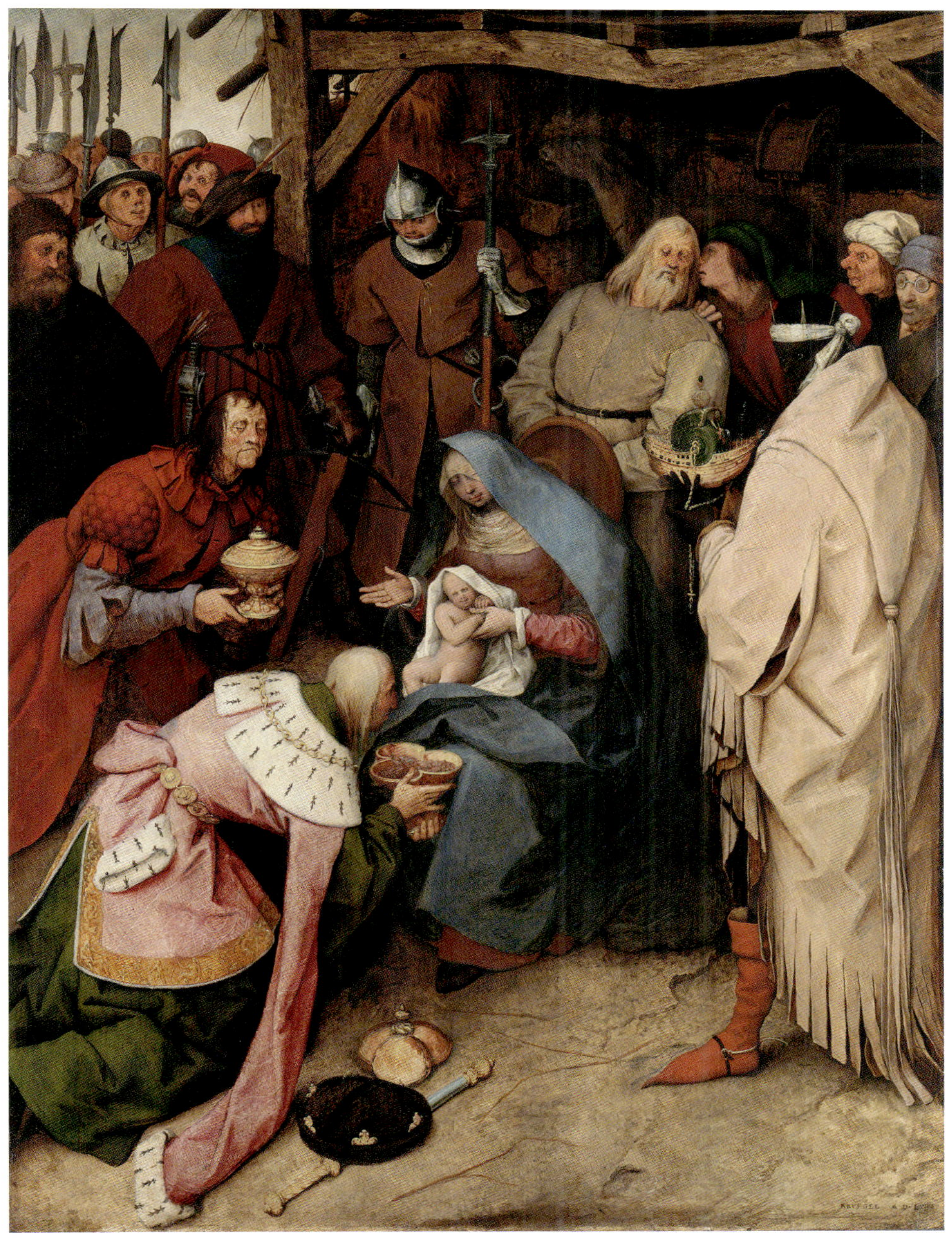

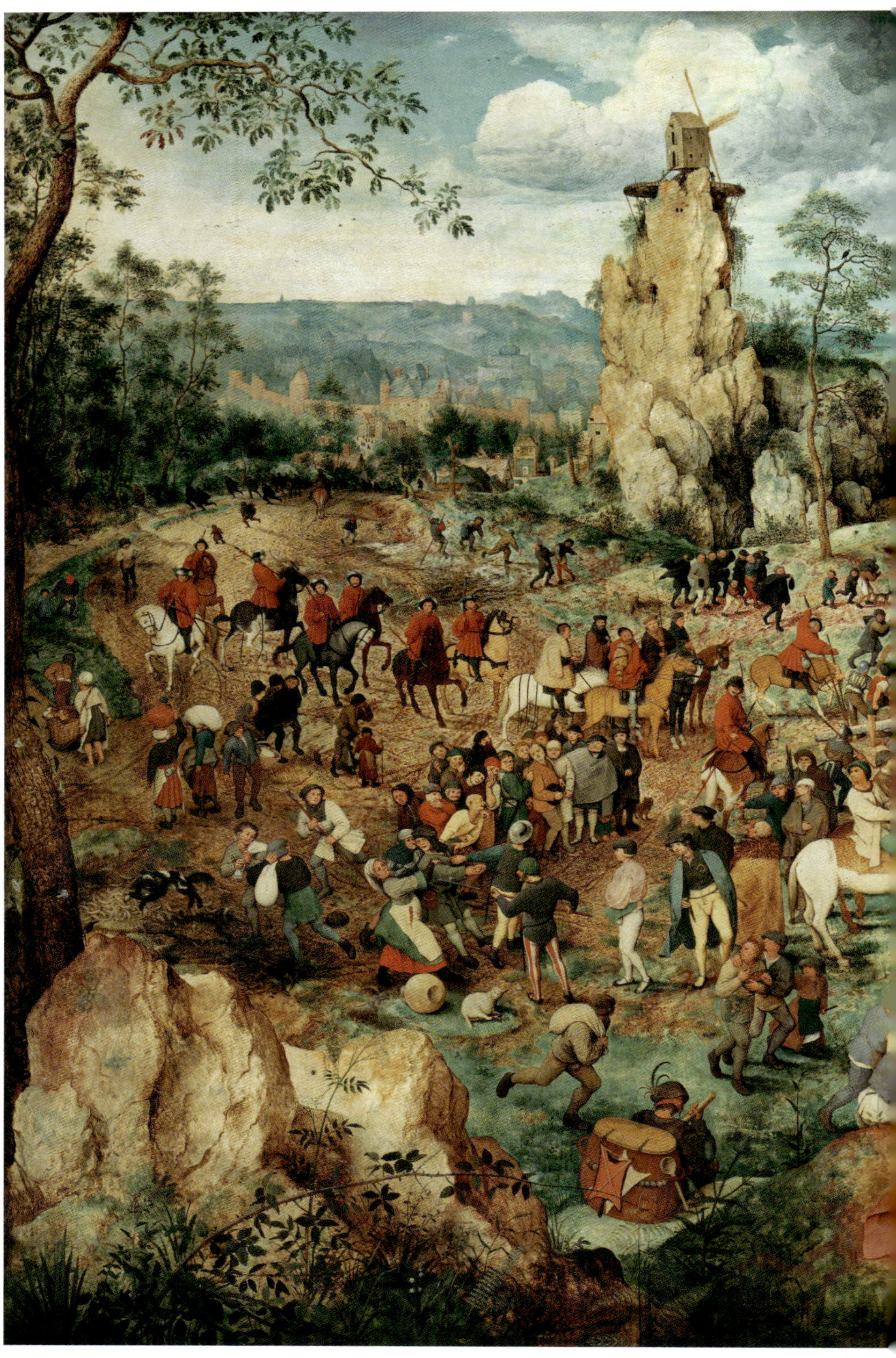

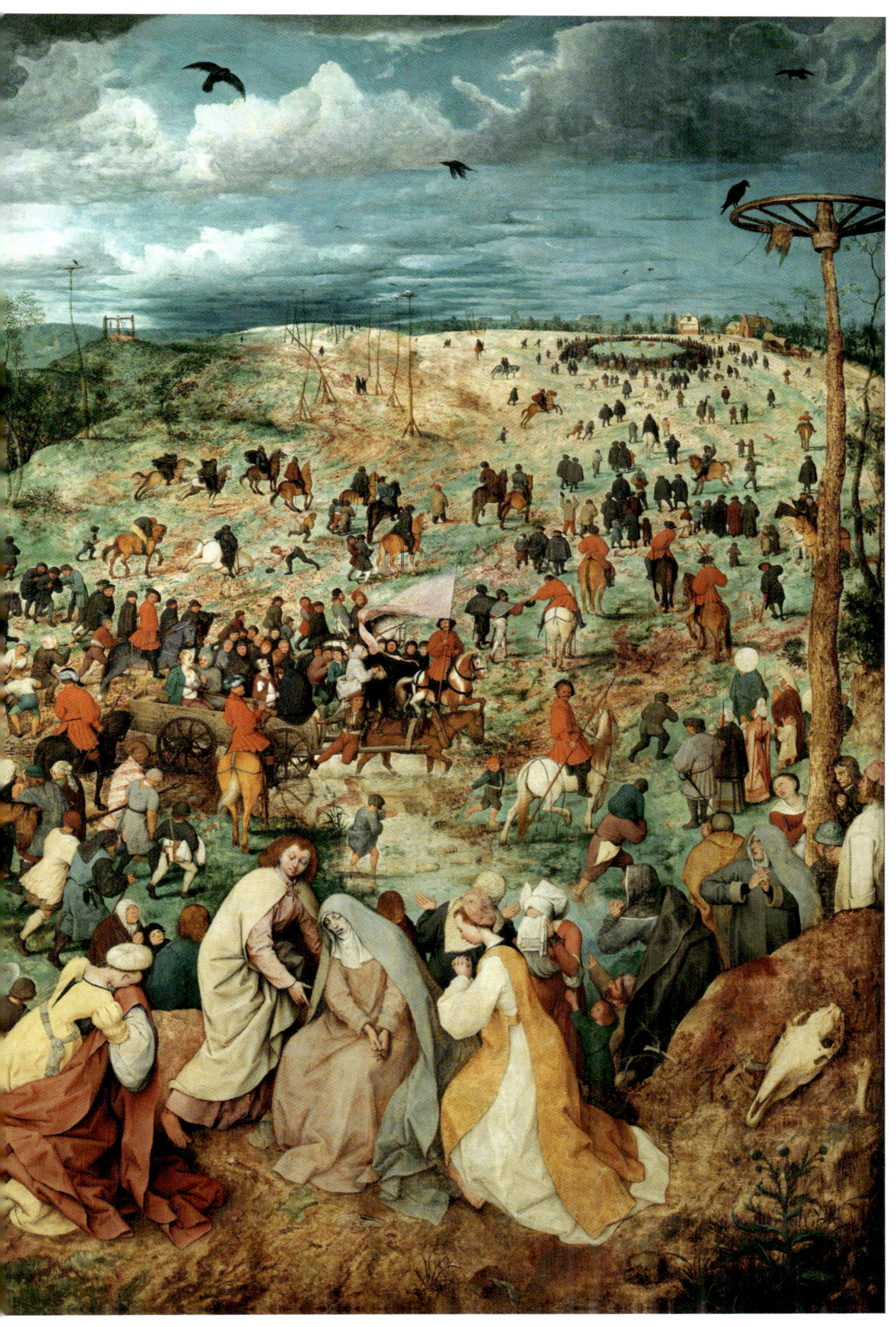

Pages 142/143
The Procession to Calvary (Christ Carrying the Cross), 1564
Oil on oak, 124 x 170 cm (48 ⅞ x 67 in.)
Vienna, Kunsthistorisches Museum, Gemäldegalerie
(detail page 145)

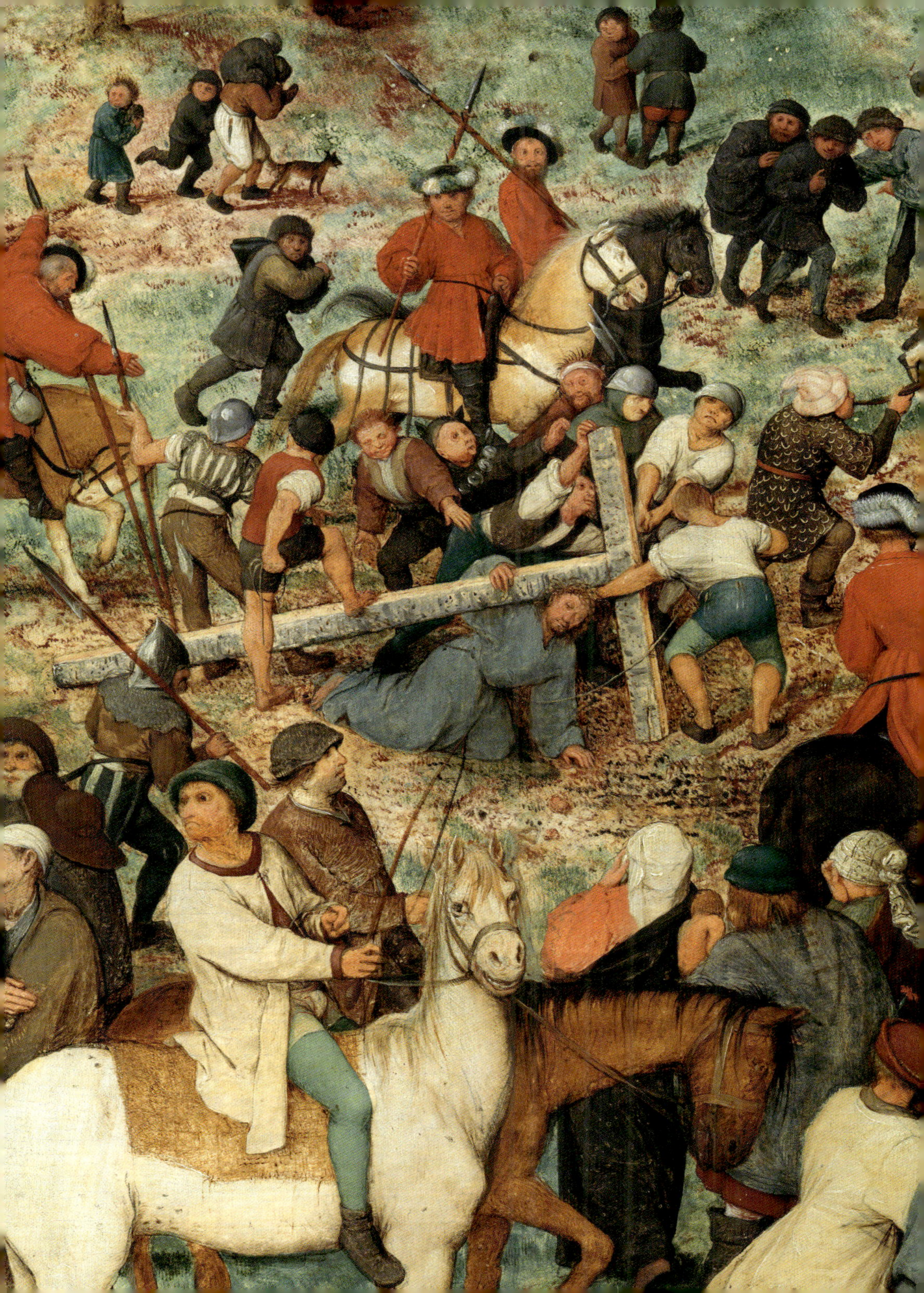

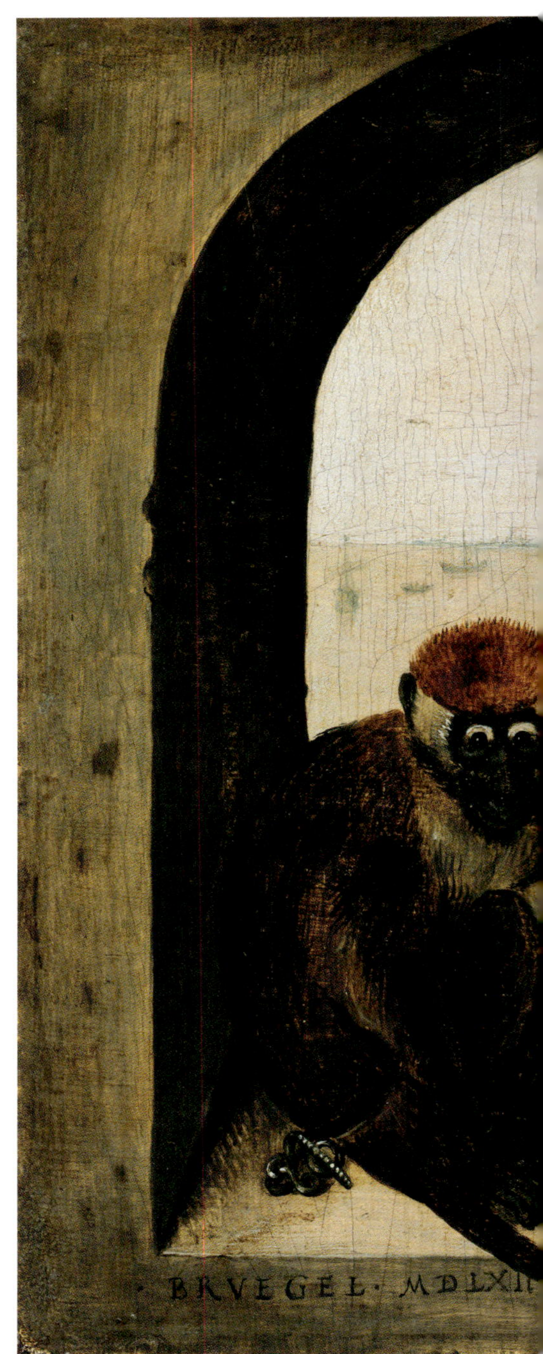

Two Fettered Apes, 1562
Oil on oak, 20 x 23 cm (7 ⅞ x 9 ⅛ in.)
Staatliche Museen zu Berlin, Gemäldegalerie

Pages 148/149
**The Suicide of Saul in the
Battle on Gilboa Mountain**, 1562
Oil on oak, 33.5 x 55.5 cm (13 ¼ x 21 ⅞ in.)
Vienna, Kunsthistorisches Museum,
Gemäldegalerie

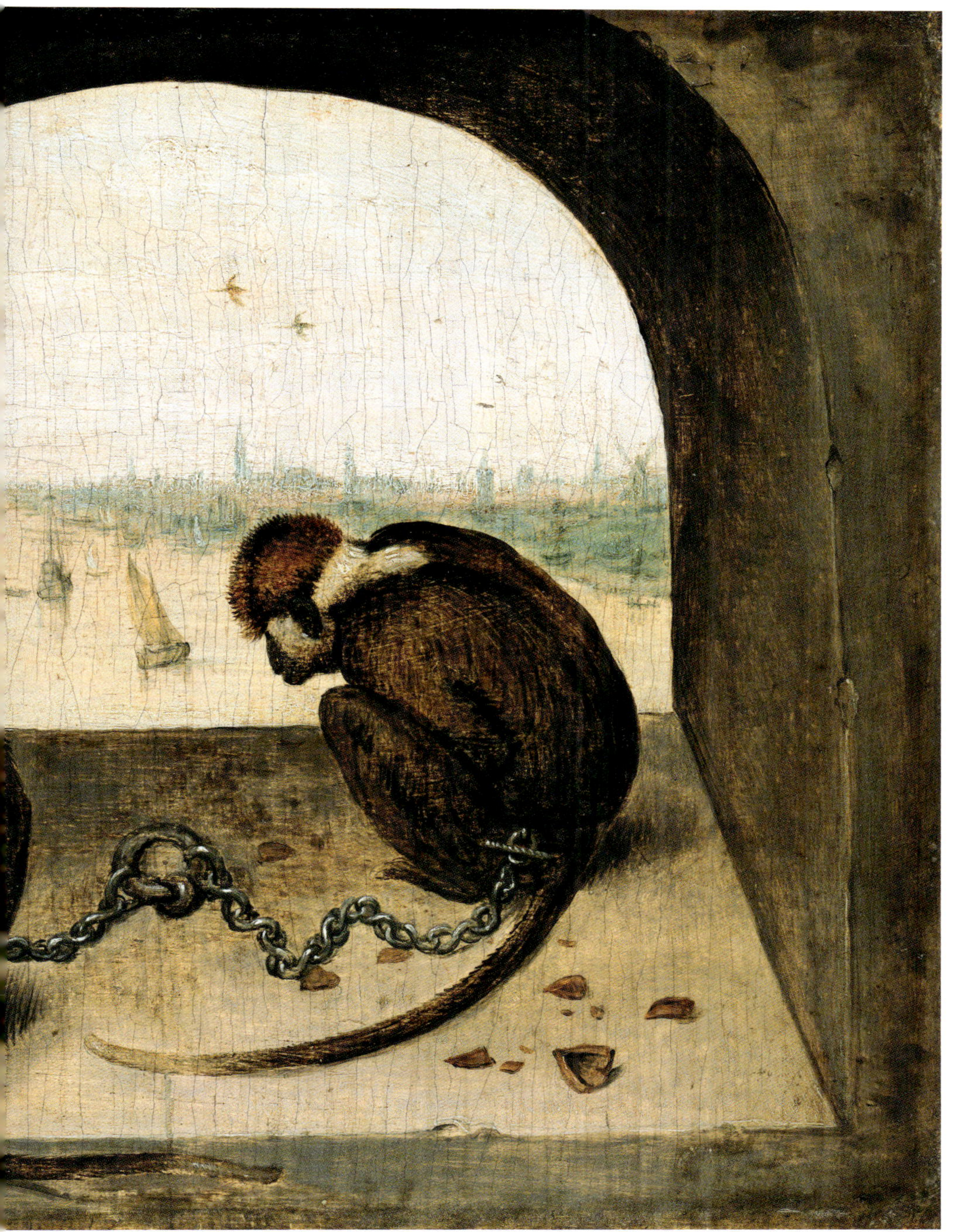

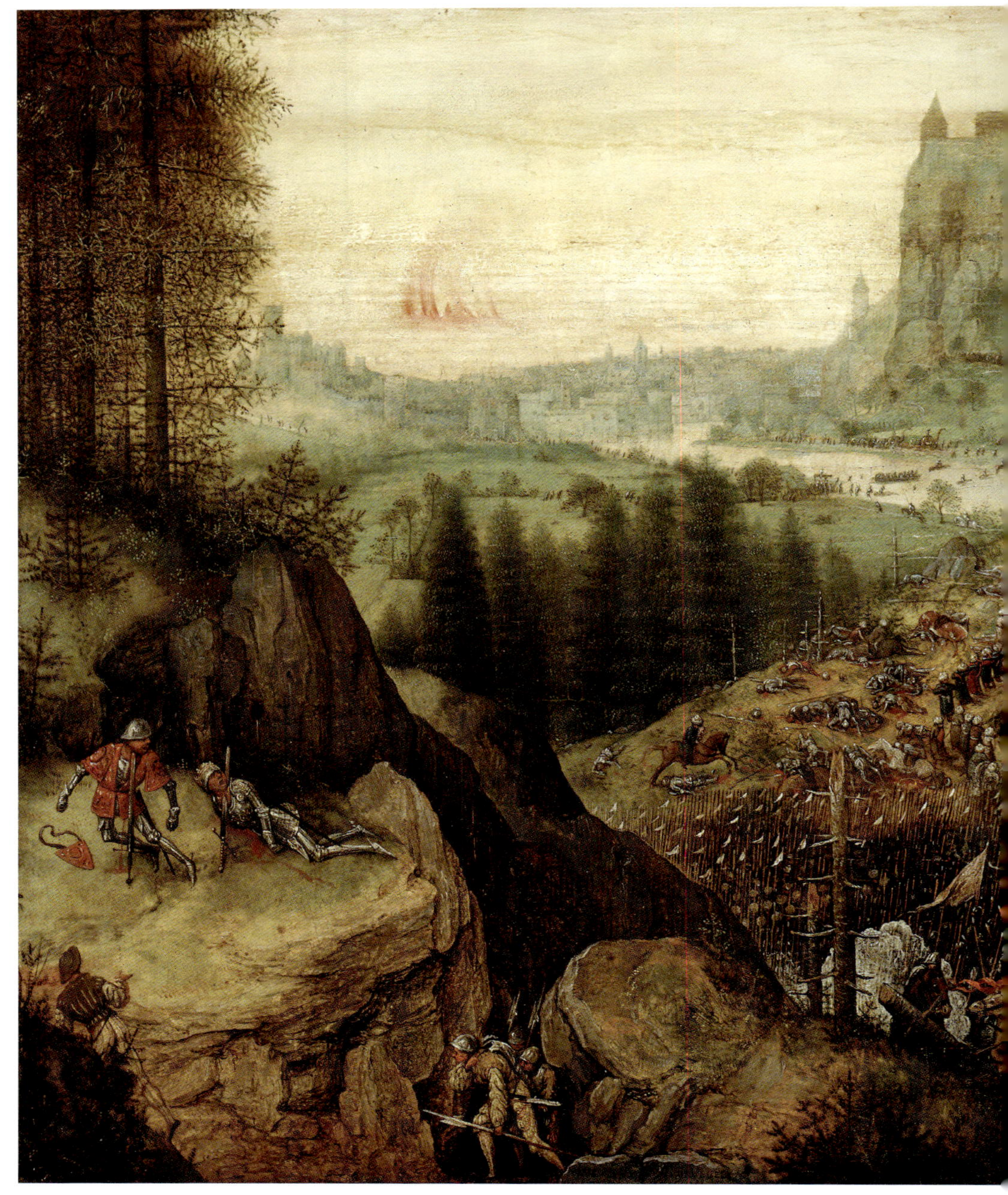

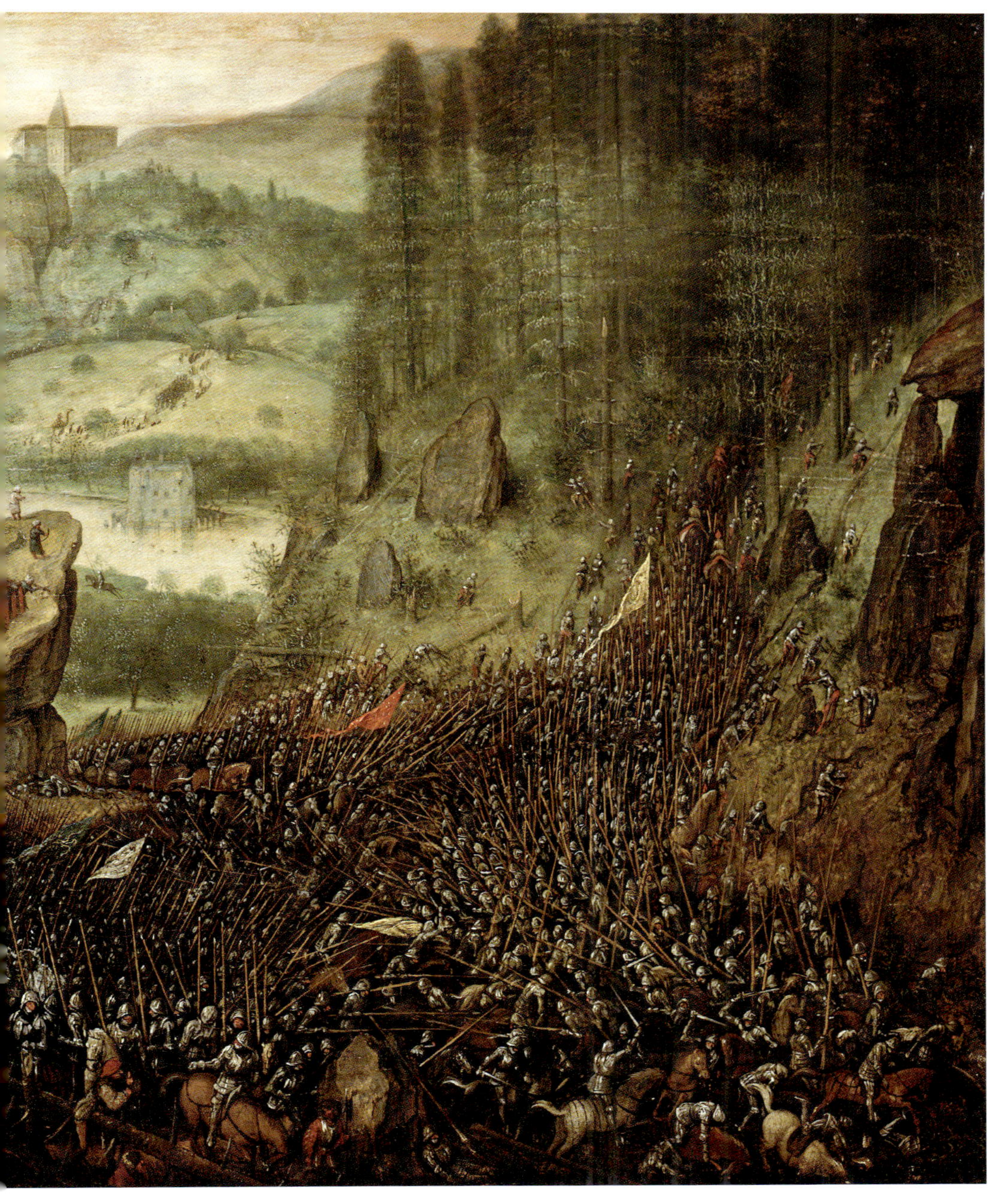

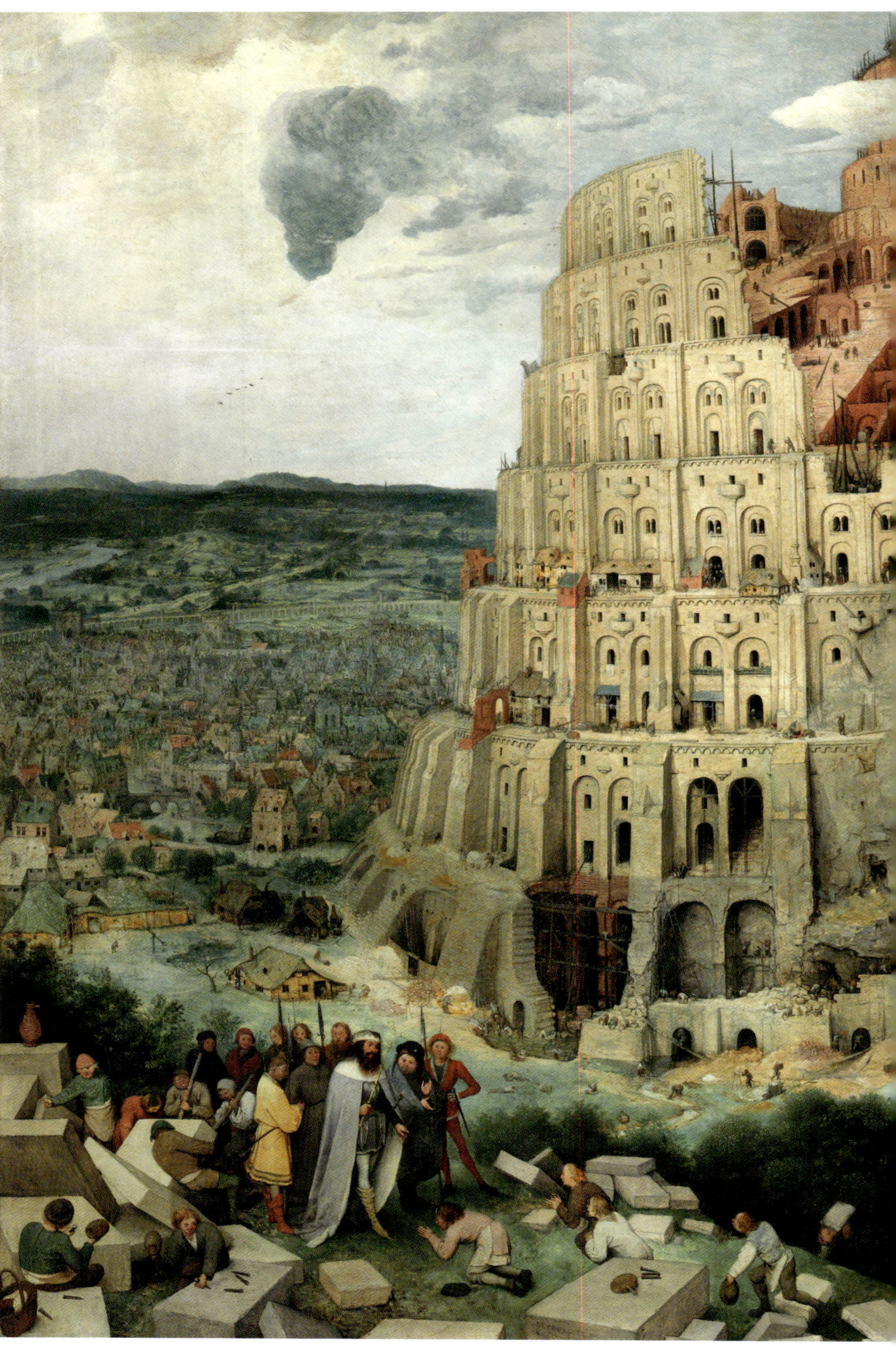

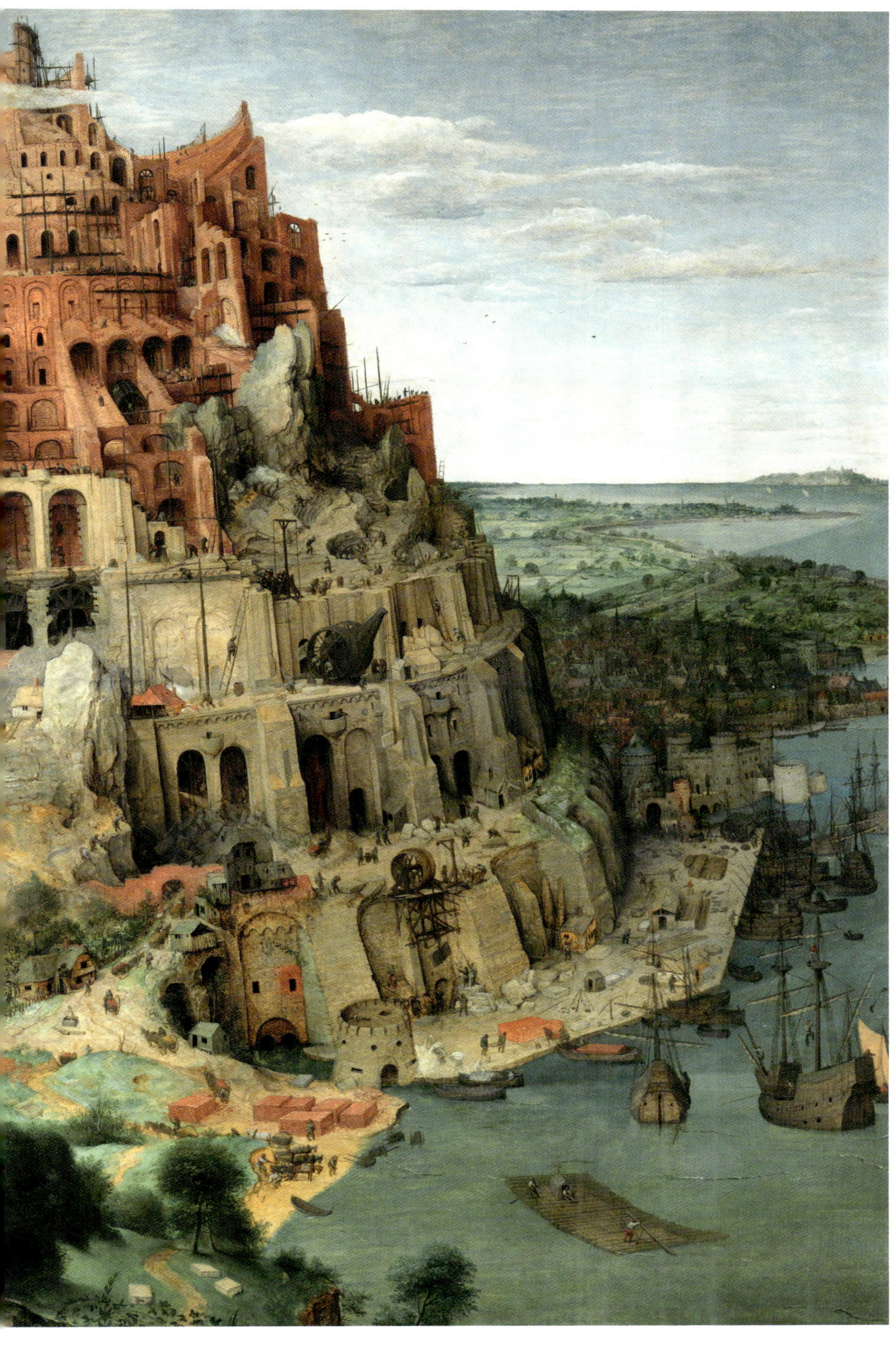

Pages 150/151
The Tower of Babel (Vienna version), 1563
Oil on oak, 114 x 155 cm (44 ⅞ x 61 ⅛ in.)
Vienna, Kunsthistorisches Museum, Gemäldegalerie
(details pages 153–163)

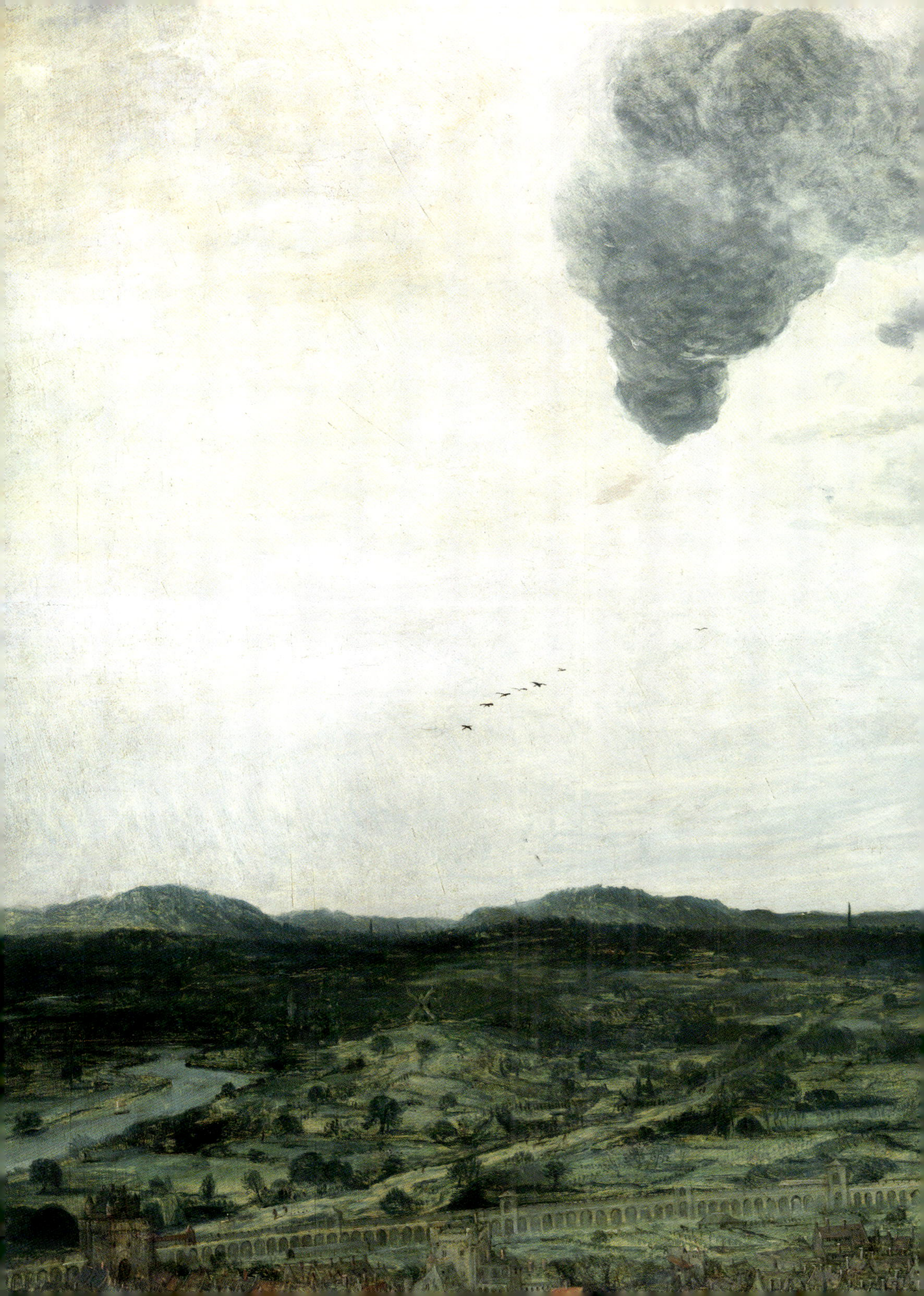

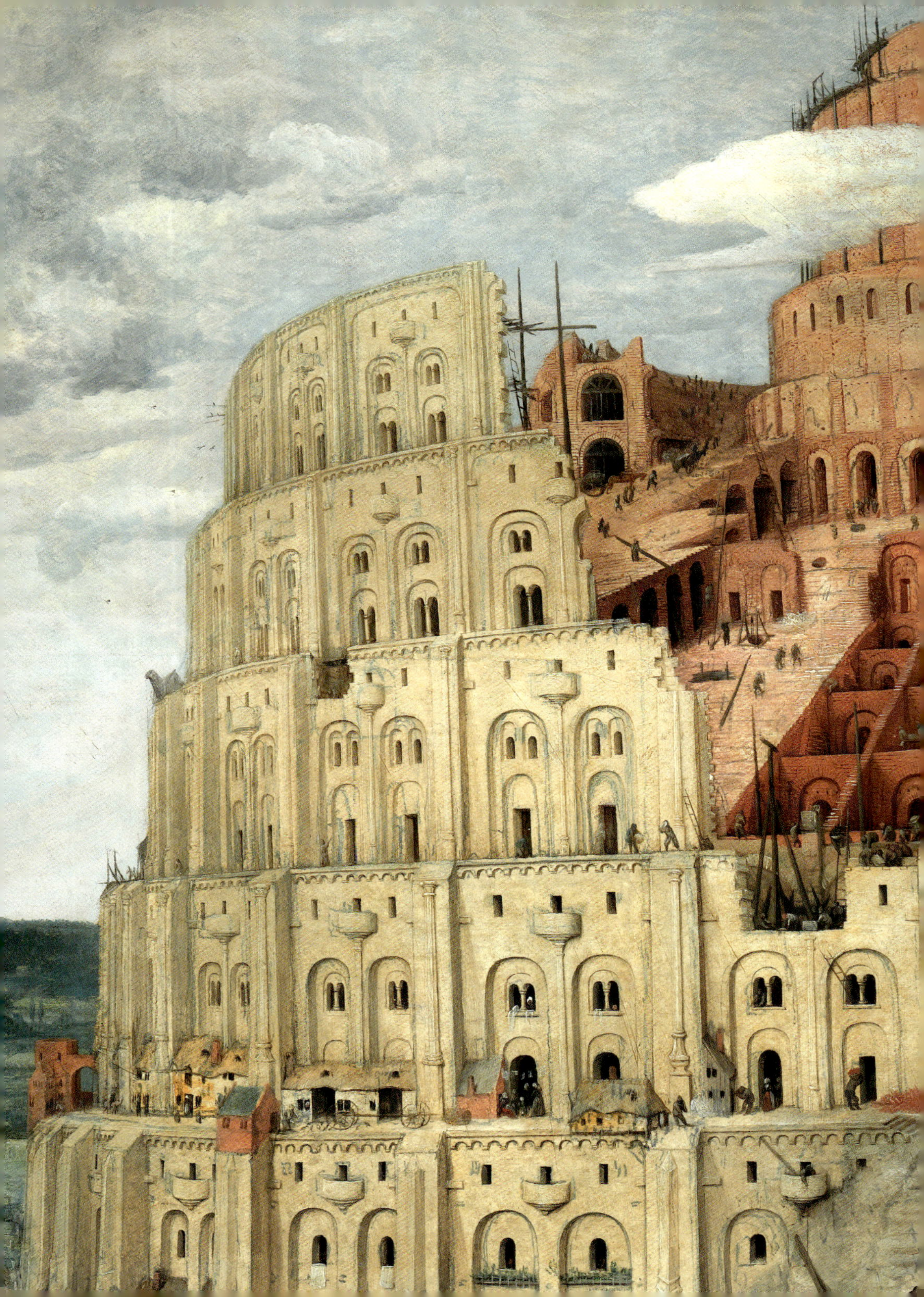

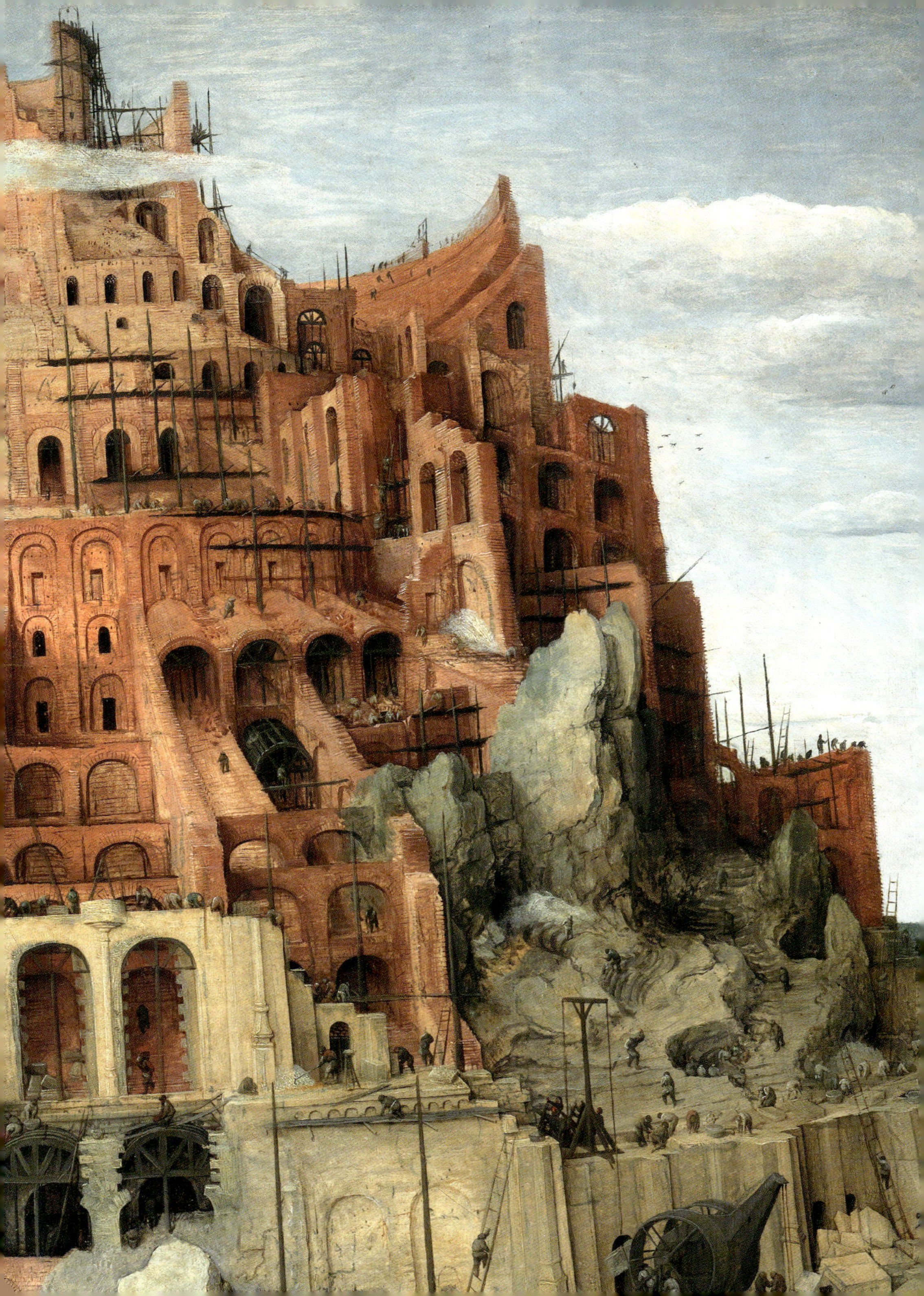

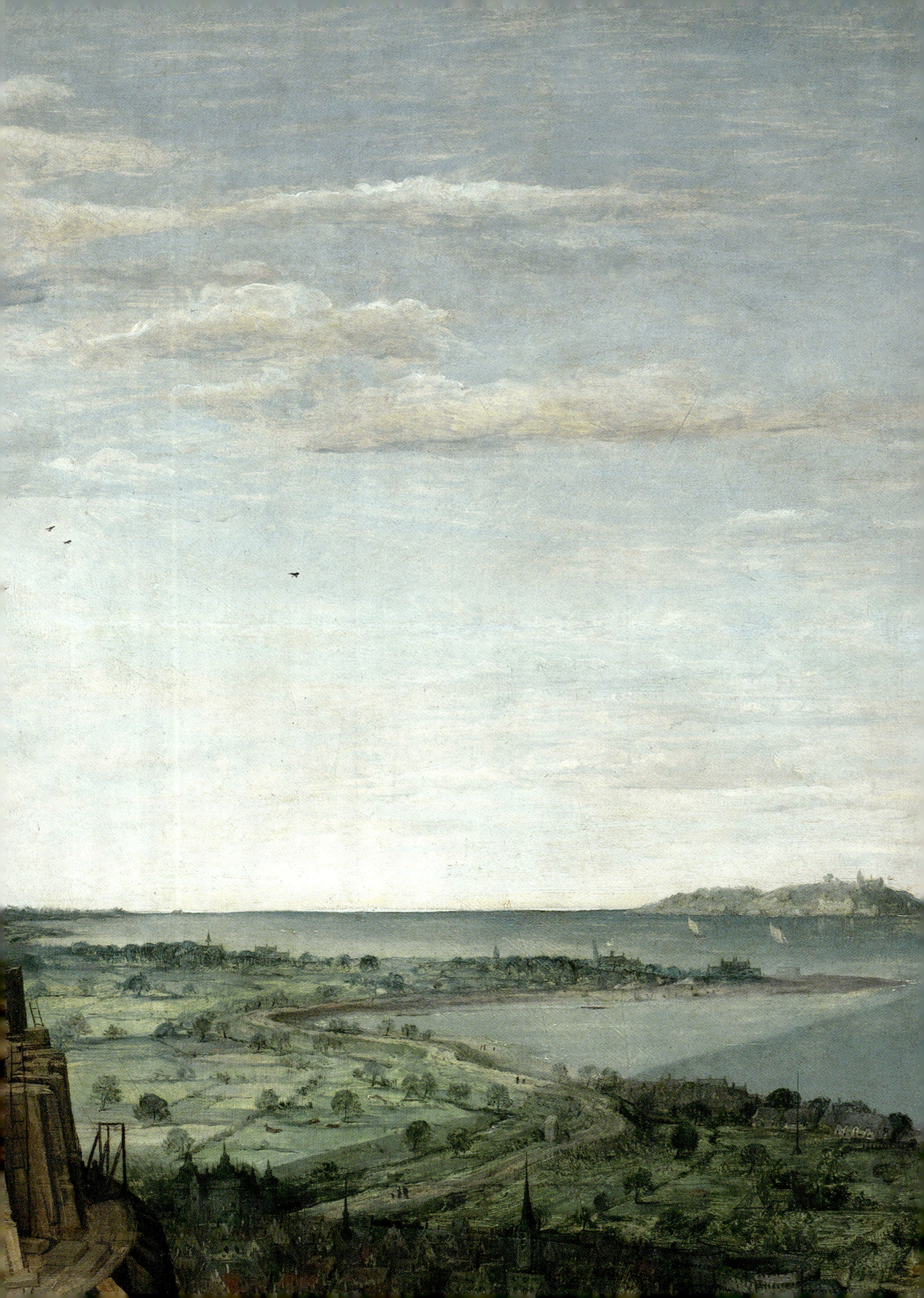

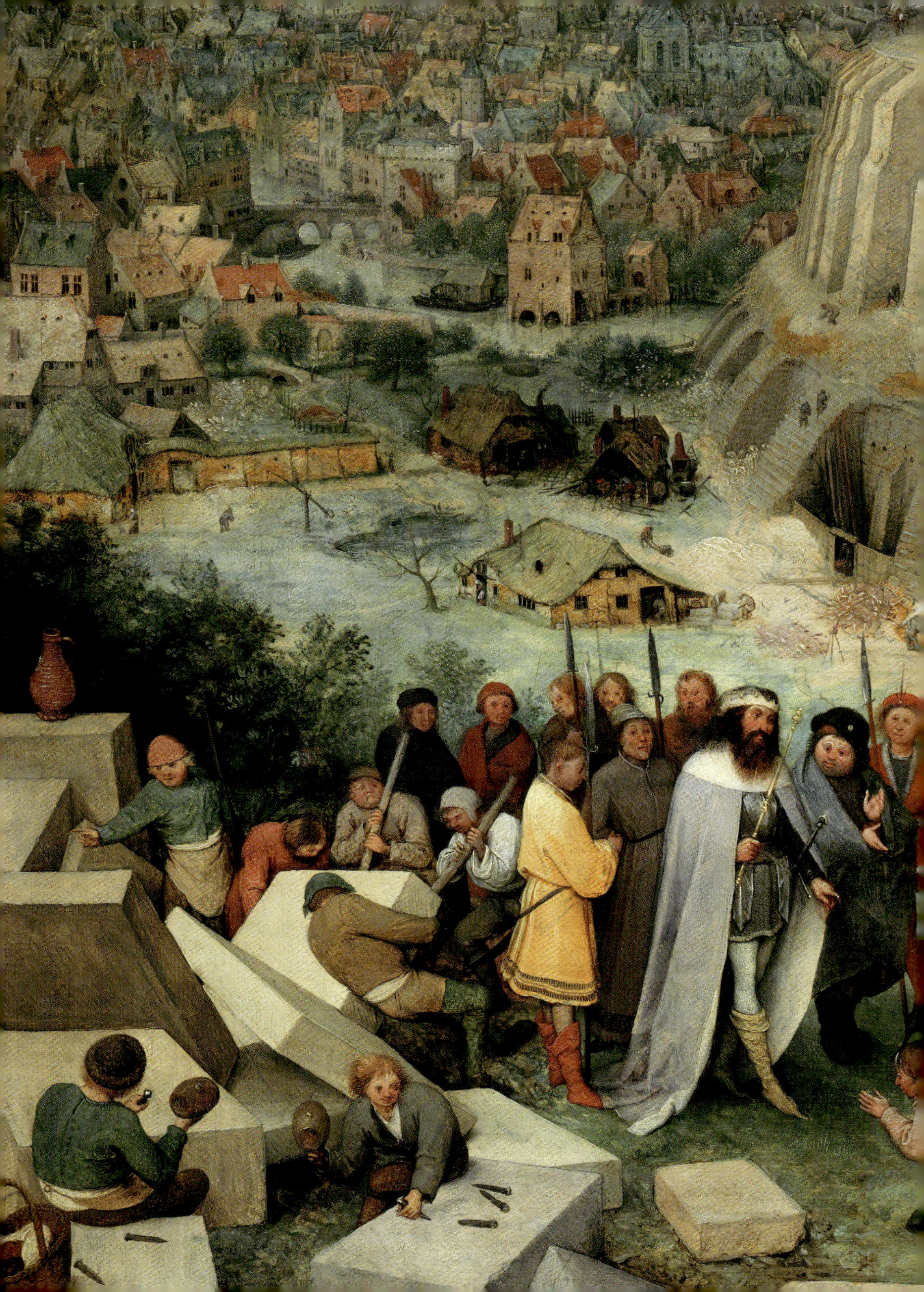

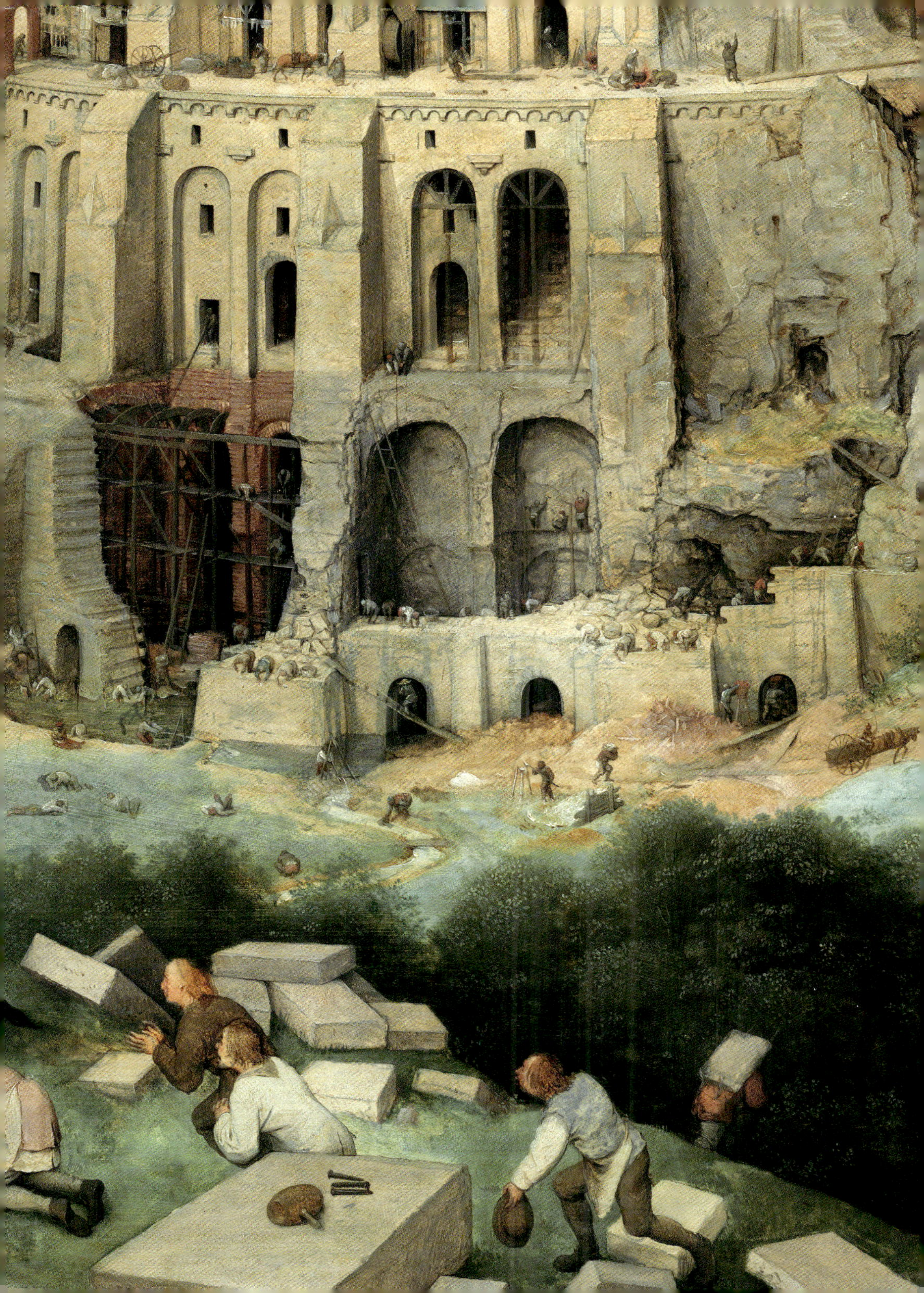

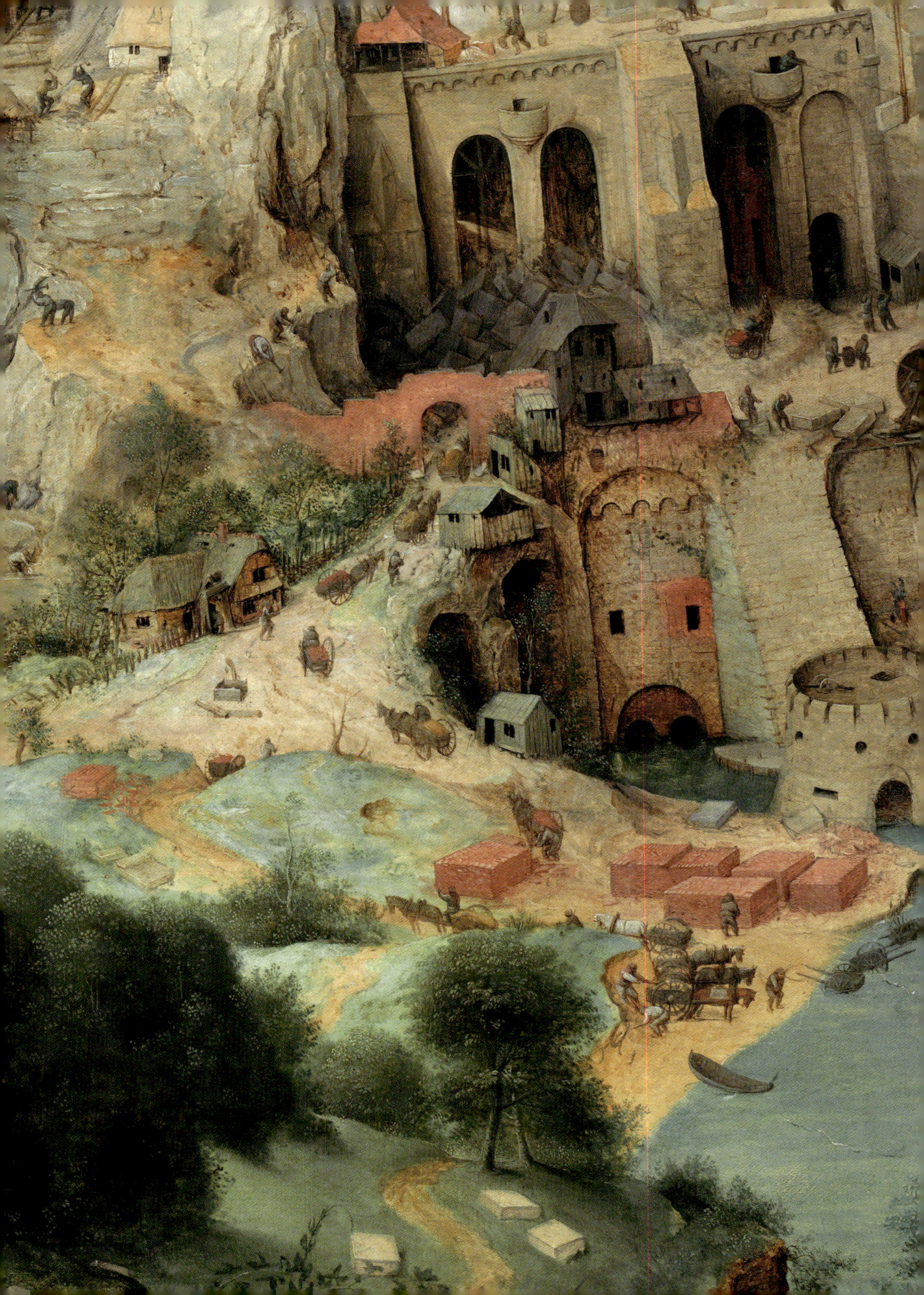

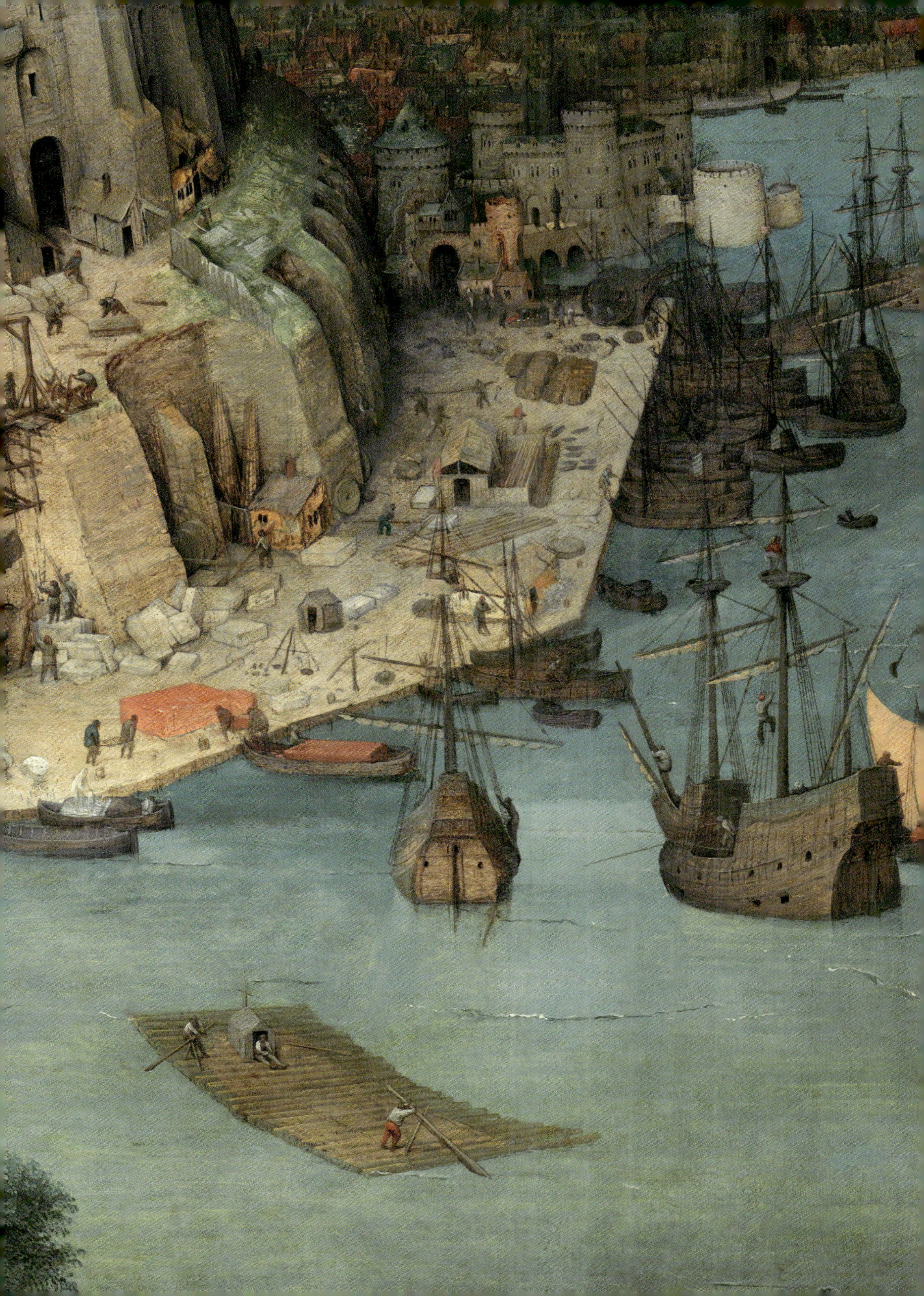

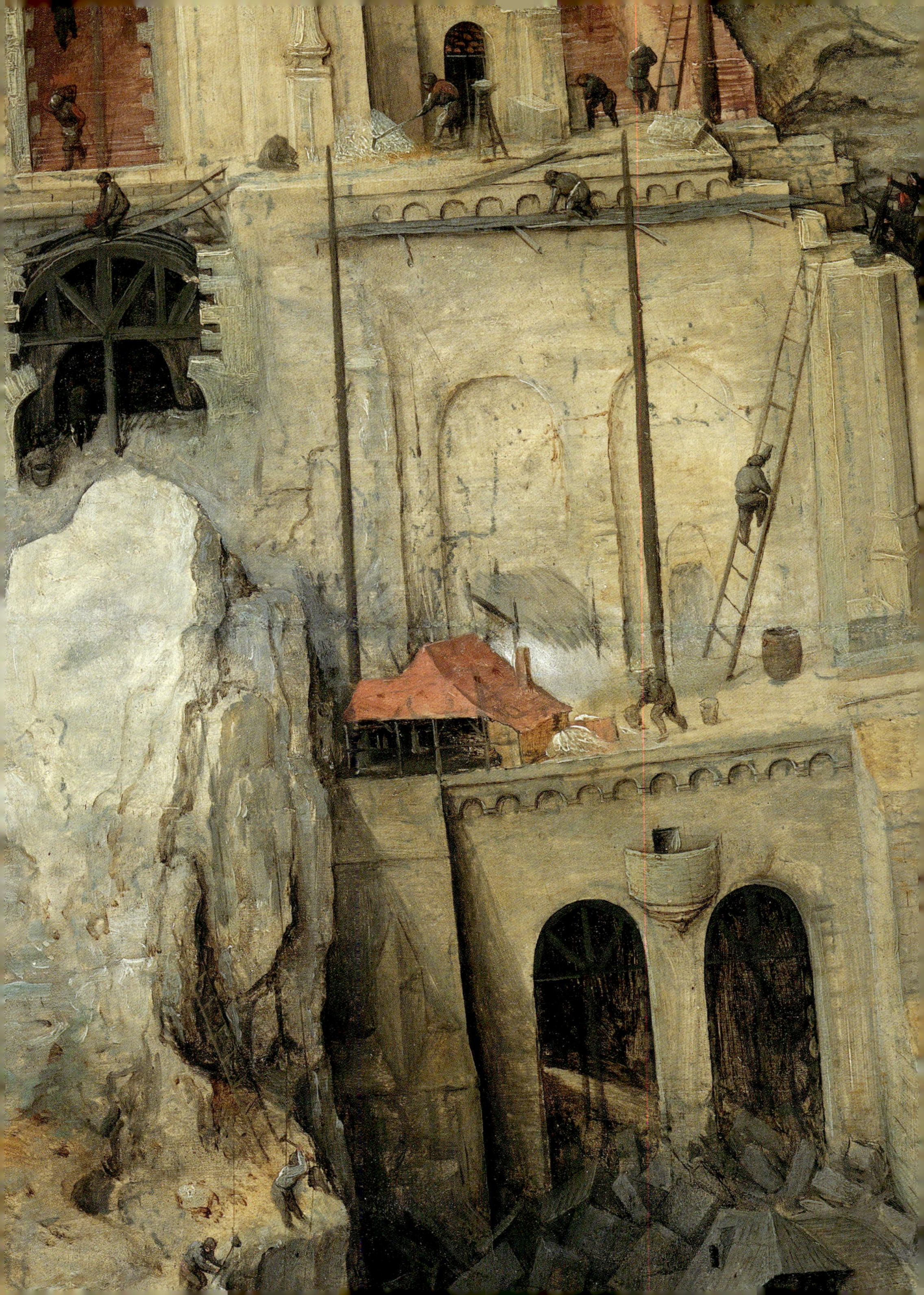

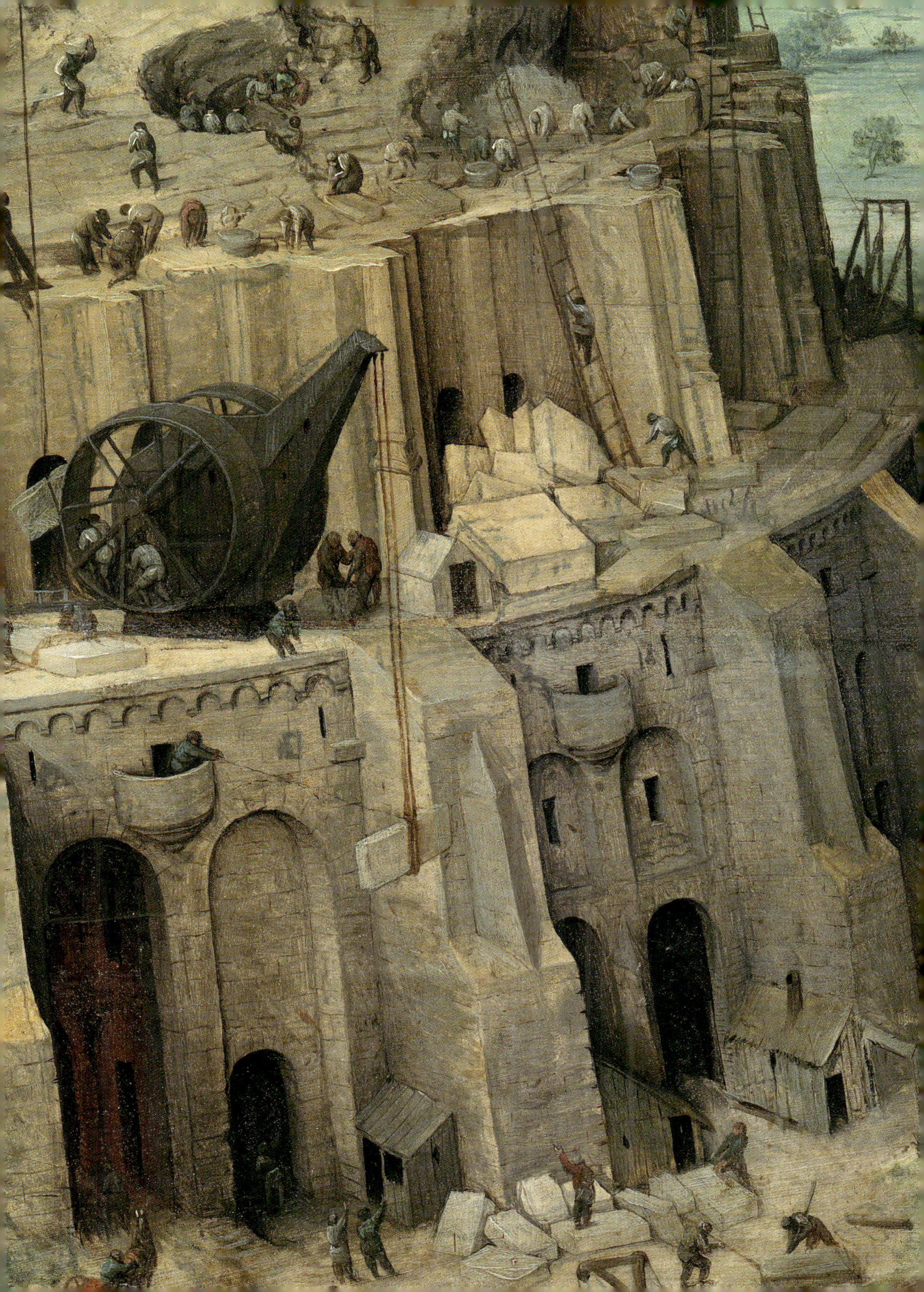

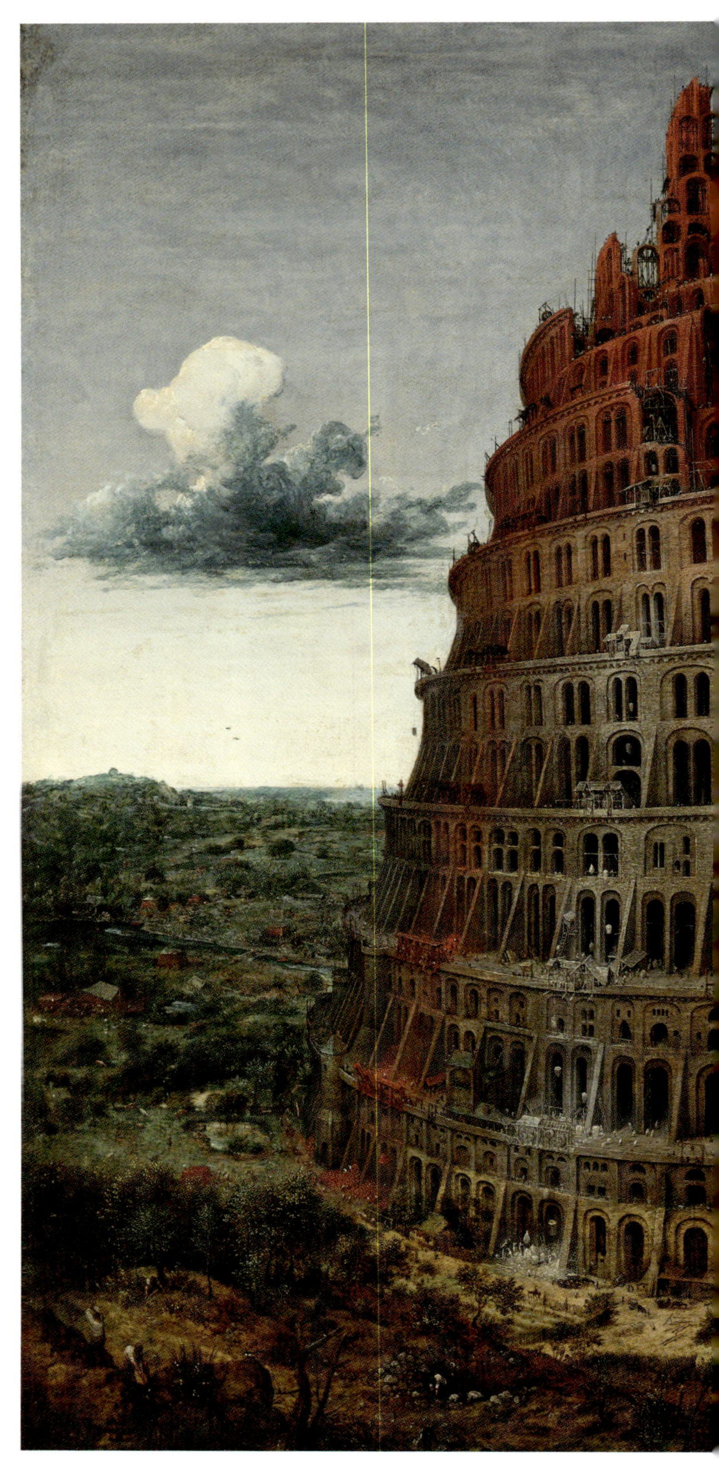

The Tower of Babel
(Rotterdam version;
also: **The "Small" Tower
of Babel**), c. 1565
Oil on wood, 59.9 x 74.6 cm
(23 ⅝ x 29 ⅜ in.). Rotterdam,
Museum Boijmans Van Beuningen

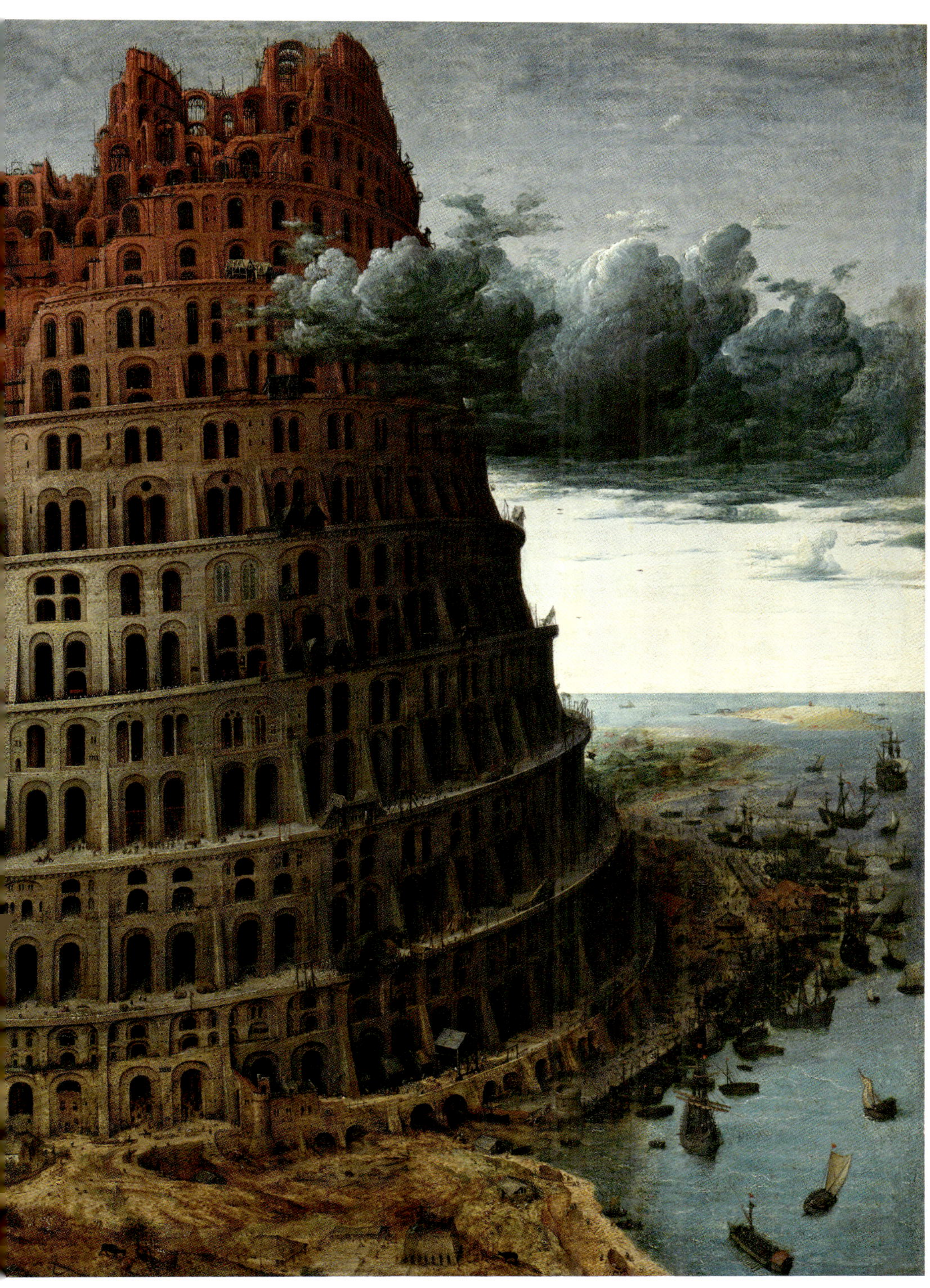

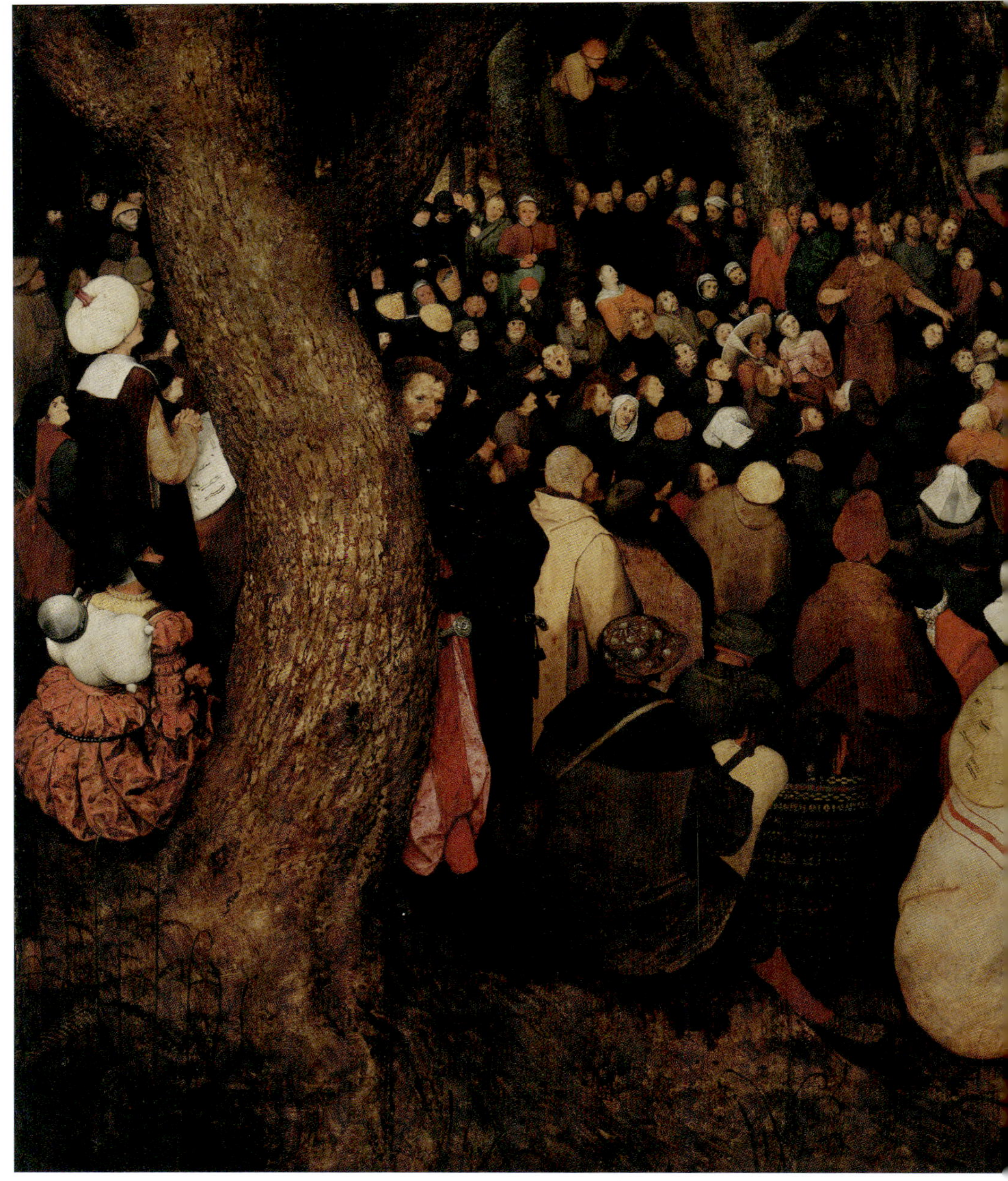

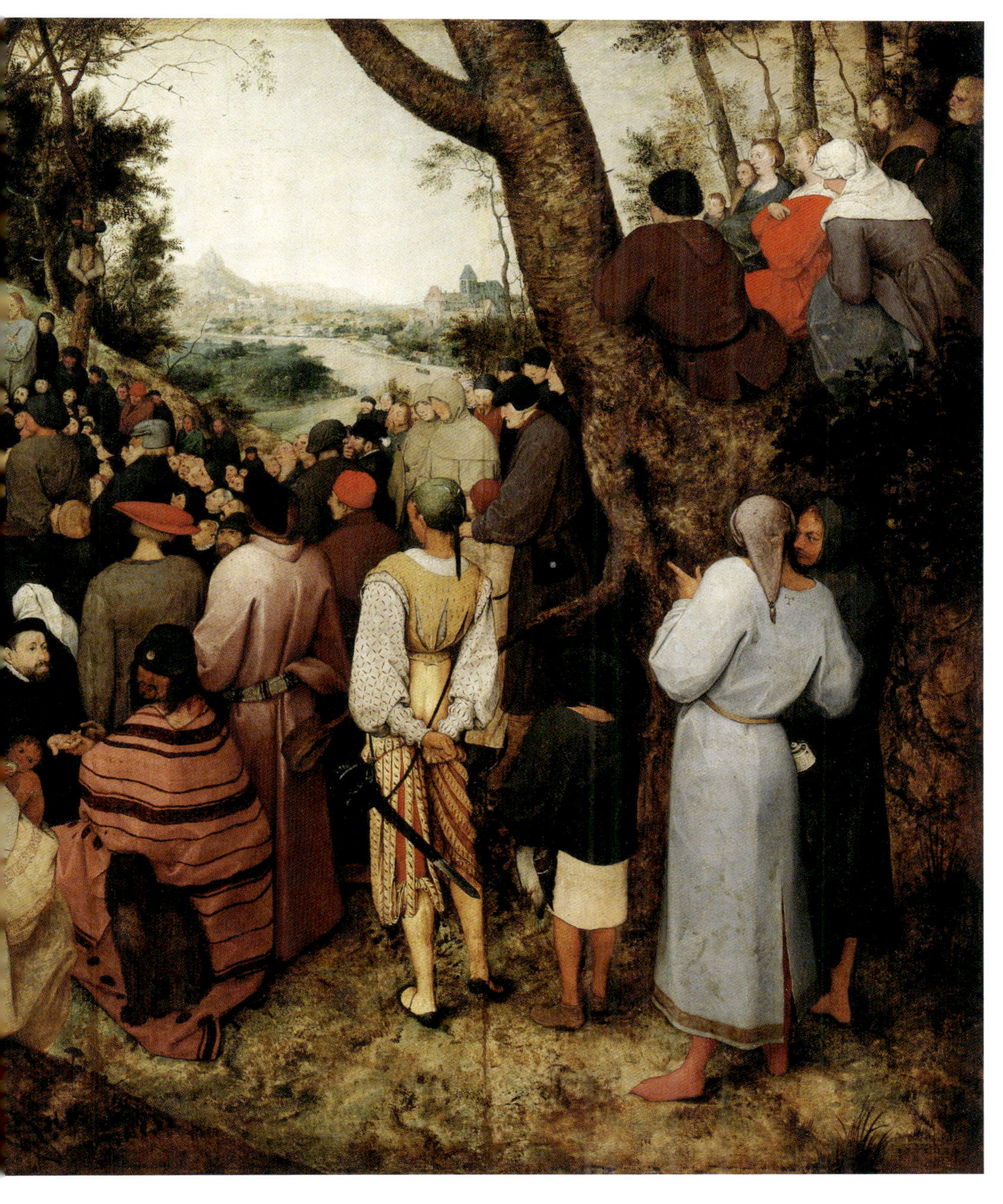

Pages 166/167
The Sermon of St John the Baptist, 1566
Oil on oak, 95 x 160.5 cm (37 ⅜ x 63 ¼ in.)
Budapest, Szépművészeti Múzeum
(detail page 169)

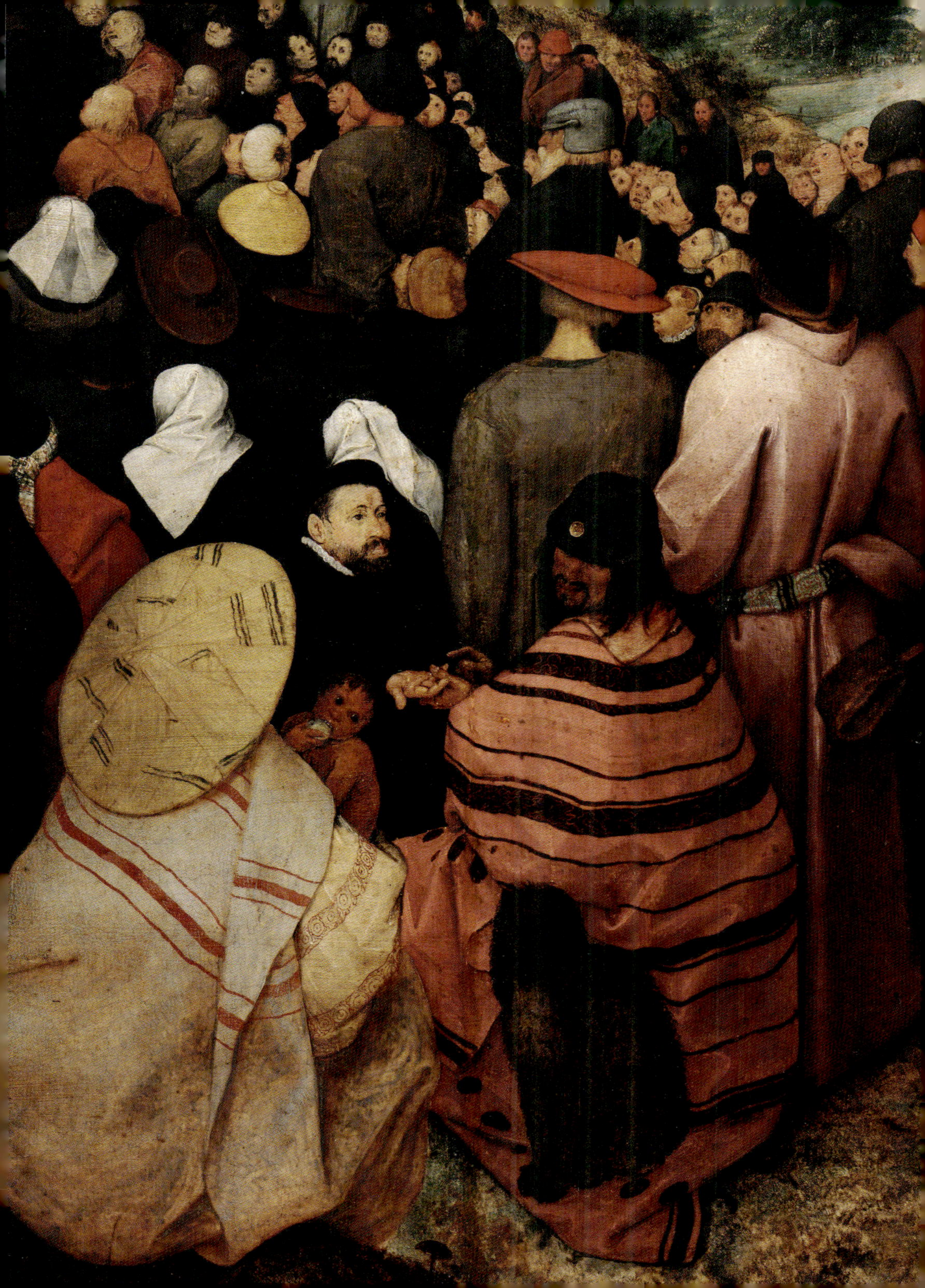

IV.

Hell on Earth: Bosch and Bruegel

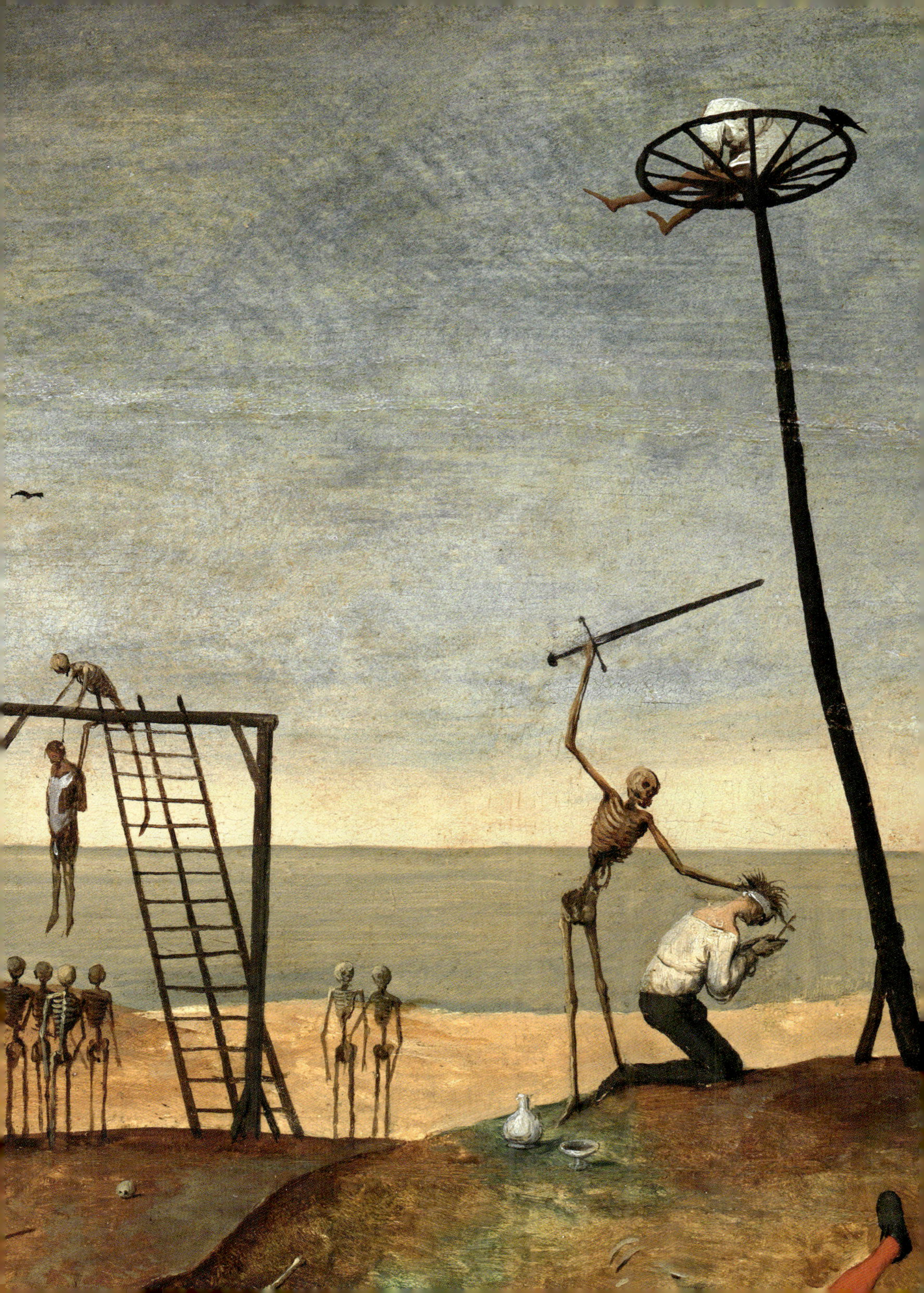

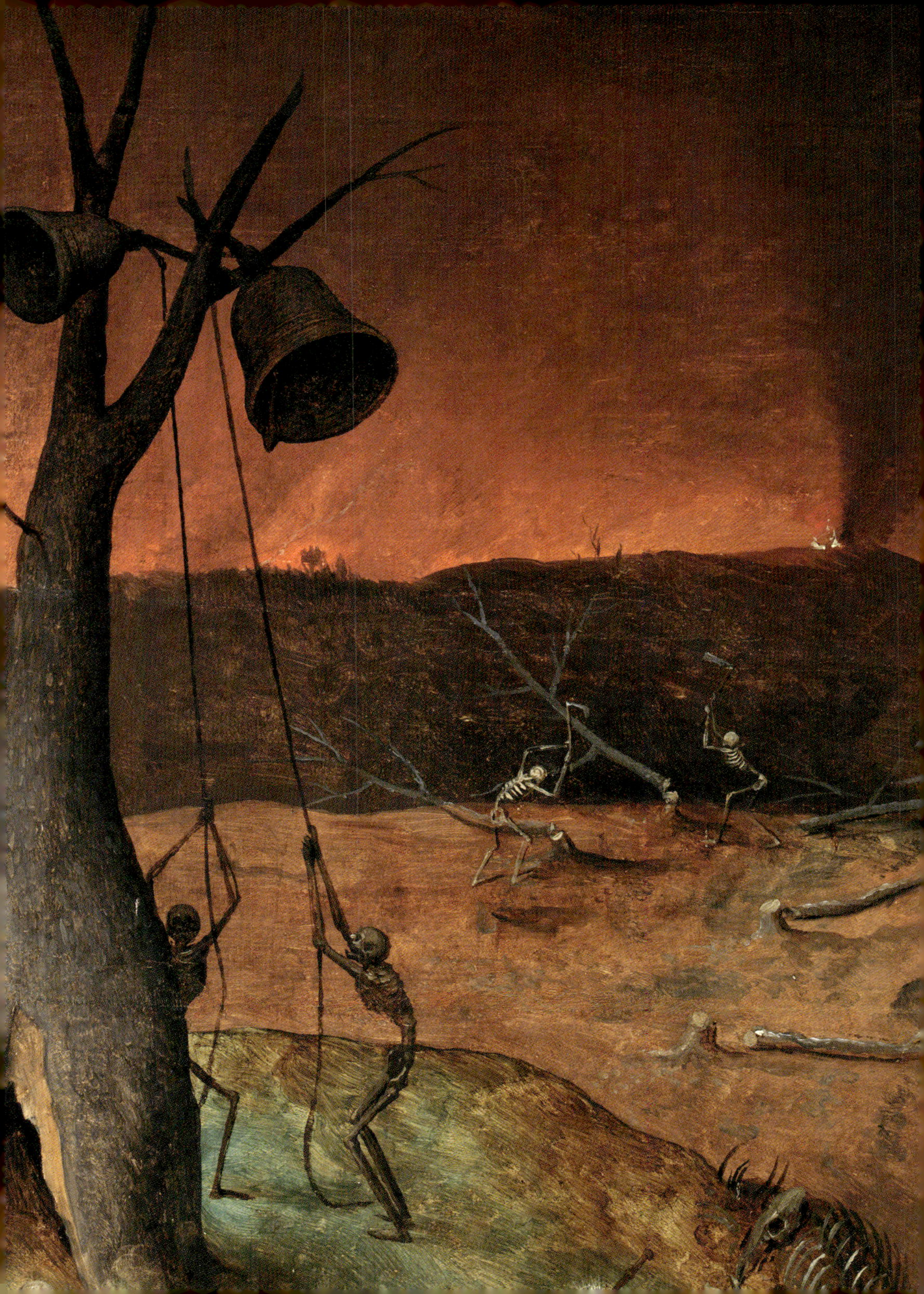

Before a closed door

A group of artworks exists in which Bruegel harks back in theme and composition to medieval sources and thus contradicts the dictates of Italian art as the prime exemplar. A closer look at the engraving *The Parable of the Wise and Foolish Virgins* (pp. 176/177)[120] will demonstrate this. Probably produced around 1560–1563, it shows a similar figural ideal to *The Fall of the Rebel Angels*, dated 1562 (pp. 210/211, Cat. 7). The name of the publisher, Hieronymus Cock, is added on the left, and opposite we see that of the artist, Bruegel. The latter indulged in a joke by setting his signature on the side of the foolish virgins directly under a large jug that is upset on the floor.

St Matthew is the only evangelist to tell the parable of the wise and foolish virgins (Matthew 25). The theological context is the Second Coming of Christ at the Last Judgement. Because the foolish virgins have failed to check the oil in their lamps, their way to Heaven, in contrast to that of the wise virgins, is barred to them. If we compare the engraving with the biblical passage, we are struck by the liberties Bruegel takes in the interpretation. While the Bible makes an abstract mention of Christ's return, Bruegel creates a graphic version of a moral and theological argument. He has divided his composition clearly into two zones; the top shows the entrance into Heaven, while the lower visualises what is happening on Earth.

On the right, we see the foolish virgins, dancing in abandon to the tune of a bagpipe. They have interrupted their work to let their hair down. We see all kinds of objects pointing to the neglect of their domestic duties. With them, their oil lamps take the shape of wine goblets, and the upset jug on the right offers an explanation for the young women's exuberance. In addition, the bagpipe has an erotic connotation, since it can represent the male sex. One of the women sporting slit sleeves is particularly "dressed to kill" and might be a prostitute.

On the opposite side we see the wise virgins, all busy with housework, spinning and darning, to name only a few of their activities. Next to each of them is a burning oil lamp. The polarities of dancing outdoors and a domestic interior – identified by the fireplace – appears important. A broom is standing next to the latter, a metaphor of cleanliness. While on the left side the symbols of the virtuous housewife are suggested, the profligate characters are revealed on the right.

What is interesting is the formal framing of these polarities that makes Bruegel's engraving so unique. In order to separate left and right he has set a mighty tree trunk in

Pages 171, 172
The Triumph of Death (details), *c.* 1562
(see ill. pp. 196/197)

the vertical axis. Above this is a bank of cloud with three angels pointing to the beginning of the Apocalypse. In the middle we see Michael bearing the sentence on a banderole that refers to Christ's Second Coming: "Behold the Bridegroom cometh! Go forth to meet him!" (Matthew 25: 6).

Tree and cloudbank together form a large "Y", effectively visualised by the artist. Behind the bank of cloud we see the ambulatory of a Gothic church and steps, leading to a kind of ciborium. While the virgins at the left hold up their lit lamps to be recognisable to Christ in the darkness, we see the foolish virgins in front of the closed door. The scene is certainly allegorical, as we see in the "naked souls", reminding us of pictures of the Last Judgement.

The setting of Gothic architecture and the extremely elongated portrayal of the persons and angels are richly instructive. In the heyday of the omnipresent enthusiasm for Italian models, the artist deliberately adopted a medieval stylistic idiom. To demonstrate to his contemporaries that he knows the humanist ideas stemming from Italy, he has inscribed a Pythagorean Y into his picture. It points to the tradition of Hercules at the crossroads, who – as is seen in the form of the letter – has to choose between virtue and vice. But Bruegel transposes this humanist image of the two paths – one of which man has to choose – into a Christian allegory, simultaneously referring to a tradition of the Middle Ages. Indeed, the parable of the Wise and Foolish Virgins found its most prominent place in cathedral sculpture, for instance on the portal of Strasbourg Minster.

In the debate initiated by Erasmus of Rotterdam about the relevance of ancient models for Christian art, Bruegel takes a clear position against pagan antiquity. While artists like Frans Floris (1517–1570) or Maarten van Heemskerck follow Italian models inspired by classical antiquity, he takes a provocative path by identifying with the Middle Ages, so scorned by the Romanists.

Killing and dying

A thunderstorm seems to gathering at the left on the horizon, consisting of fire and destruction and soon to destroy the whole world. Gallows and wheels tower up to the sky. In the end, death is always the victor, as Bruegel seems to be saying with his large-format *The Triumph of Death* (pp. 196/197, Cat. 8). The picture is neither signed nor dated, but its authenticity has never been doubted. Several scholars have tried to show a connection to *The Fall of the Rebel Angels* (Cat. 7) and *Dulle Griet* (Cat. 9), because the allusions to Bosch are particularly distinct in these pictures.[121] Despite the identical format, we may indeed doubt this, because there are no perceptible references in content between the pictures, and the artist also used this format for other panels with no detectable relationship to Bosch. So there is no reason to see these works as counterparts.

Iconographic analyses have always provided the main access to *The Triumph of Death*. References were made early on to its dependency on Hans Holbein the Younger's (1497/98–1543) *Imagines mortis*.[122] Moreover, scholars have pointed out Bruegel's enormous skill in exploiting and synthesising further traditional motifs for his picture.[123] He conceives a genuine *Theatrum mortis* and fashions palpably acting beings out of the abstract figure of Death. The latter wreaks havoc as a more or less decomposed skeleton chasing after the living. Here Death goes through all possible variant guises. In this regard, the picture does show real parallels to the encyclopaedic pictures *Children's Games* (Cat. 5) and *Netherlandish Proverbs* (Cat. 3), which have similar dimensions. If this applies, the question arises, however, as to what message is concealed under the cloak of completeness.

Death is at work. Many people whom he's after fight or try to flee. But he is an over-powering opponent, who emerges as victor not only through brute force but also through cunning. Even Nature and her forces have placed themselves in his service, with ships sinking or towns being caught up in conflagrations in the background (pp. 198/199).

Bruegel has incorporated key scenes in the two bottom corners. On the left, a ruler in armour and ermine-trimmed cloak has sunk down and is at the point of death, while another skeleton is about to plunder the state treasury (pp. 200/201). On the opposite side, we see a pair of lovers making music, unaware that Death, playing a viola da gamba, is joining in. The observer must conclude that neither power nor love can stop Death. We can mention further scenes occurring on the foreground edge. A senior cleric is carried away by a skeleton wearing a cardinal's hat, a pilgrim dies while a landsknecht tries to fight off an opponent with a two-handed sword. As a comic element, Bruegel intro-duces a jester, who is yelling in terror and trying to hide under a table (pp. 202/203).

The further the eye penetrates the inner regions of the picture, the more we encounter collective forms of death. Death as an army equipped with scythes slaughters large groups of people or drives them into a coffin-like building. Nor is there any use fleeing to a remote place. Death lurks everywhere to find his victim. Everyone will fall, families, the old and the young, men with turbans. Vice versa, death takes on all guises that are necessary for his business. He is gravedigger, musician, servant or executioner. He is a master of disguise and does everything to outwit his victims.

On the left side in the middle ground, we see a peculiar execution taking place. A mill-stone has been hung around a man's neck. His death has been decided, and a henchman is throwing him over a wall into the water where he is bound to drown. The group of judges who condemned him stand there wrapped in white cloths (p. 183). A blood-red cross towers up in their midst, and not far from this at the right at the edge of the walled basin is another cross, and a third one above the wooden portal leading to this place. We cannot say with certainty whether this peculiar building is a monastery or not.

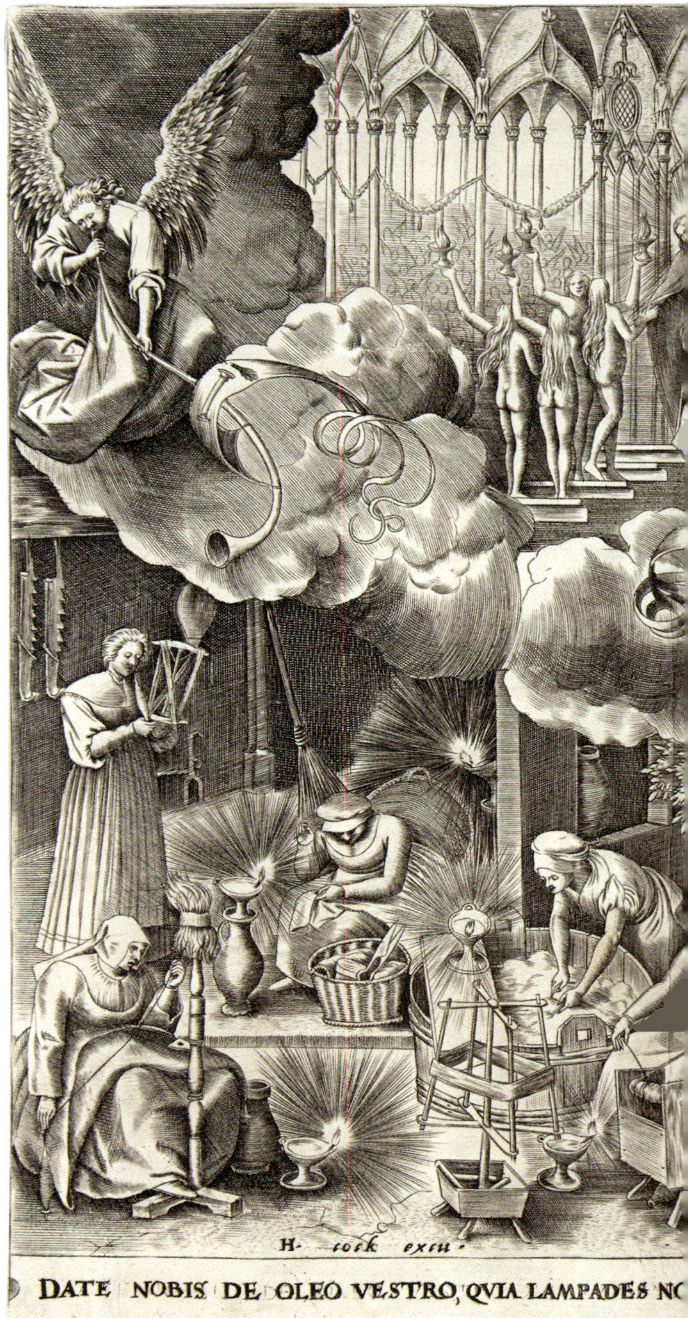

Philipp Galle (attributed) after
Pieter Bruegel the Elder
**The Parable of the Wise and
Foolish Virgins**,
c. 1560–1563
Copper engraving, 22.3 x 29.1 cm
(8 ¾ x 11 ½ in.)
New York, The Metropolitan
Museum of Art

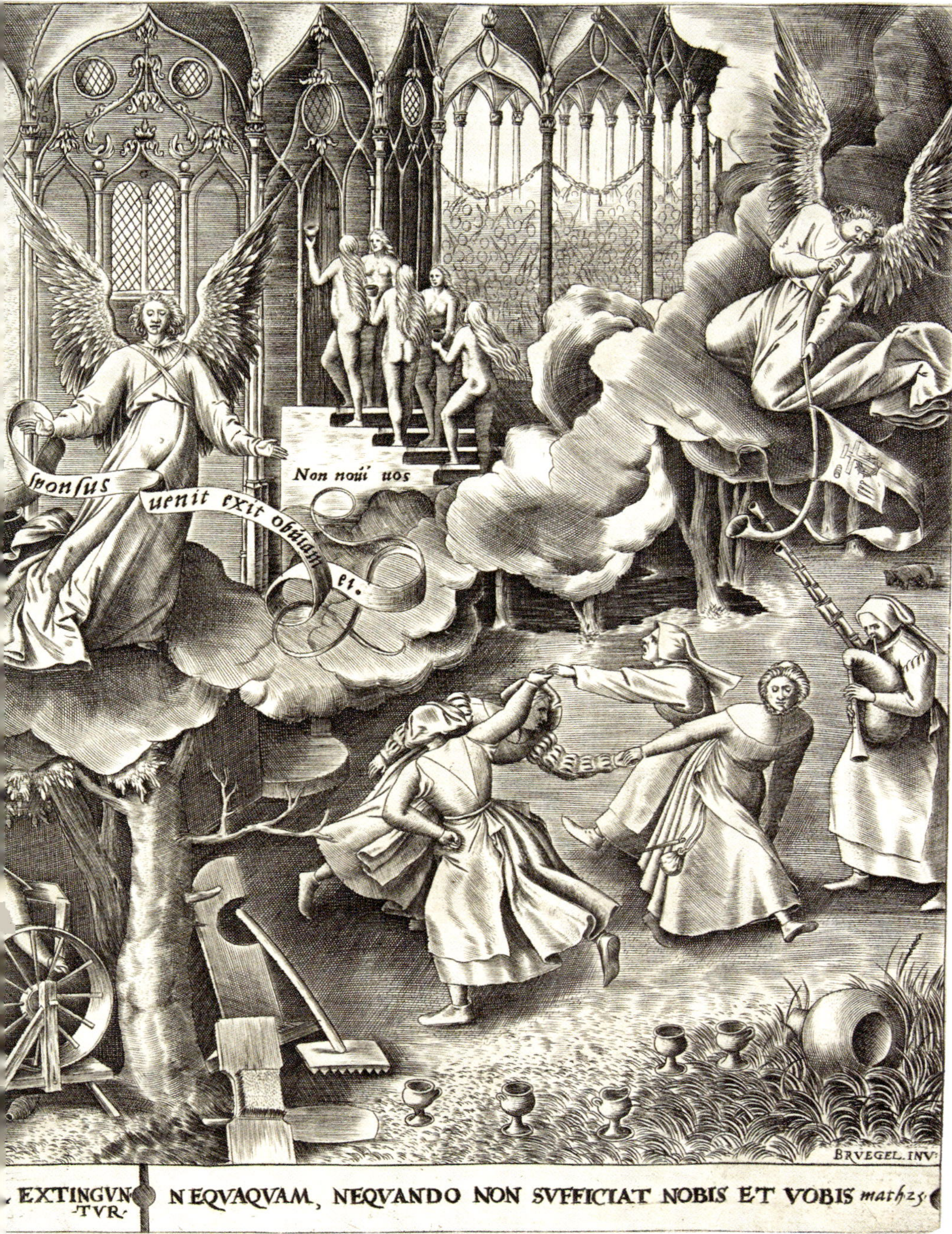
Non noui uos
sponsus uenit exit obuiam et.
BRVEGEL. INV:
EXTINGVN
·TVR·
NEQVAQVAM, NEQVANDO NON SVFFICIAT NOBIS ET VOBIS mathz5

But we can identify all the more clearly the skeletons inside the cloisters wearing black habits. One of them is even holding a candle, its flame weakly lighting the darkness. Finally, we shouldn't miss mentioning the cross on the opposite side in the delinquent's hands, whose head is about to be cut off by Death (p. 171) – a scene almost identical to one seen in Bruegel's allegorical depiction of Justice (pp. 32/33, 180/181).

The familiar symbol now seems alien. It is as if an execution takes place in its name, and as if the execution with the millstone is an act of the Inquisition. This scene is also picked out here because it recalls a sentence from the Gospel of St Mark: "And whosoever shall offend one of these little ones that believe in me, it is better for him that a millstone were hanged about his neck, and he were cast into the sea" (Mark 9: 42). Confronted by this cruel killing, a scene appears at the immediate left that is all the stranger. A dead man has taken his place on a step and is cradling his head in his hands in melancholy despair. In the midst of this melee, the reason for his grief seems absurd and hypocritical: he is looking at a dead bird stretched out in front of him, its decease evidently causing his mourning.

When we have sharpened our eyes to note these details, we can also contextualise the activities of the two skeletons on the opposite side of the water; they have caught people in a net: this is an allusion to the "miraculous catch of fish", when Simon the fisherman becomes a fisher of men, as Mark narrates (1: 16–20). There is an instructive detail in that among the people the "fishers" have caught in the net are two black men, which reminds us of the colonisation and Christianisation of Africa.

There are also other notable episodes. The aforementioned central scene in the middle of the bottom edge shows the killing of a Catholic pilgrim to Santiago de Compostela, recognisable by the badge on his hat. His pilgrim attributes lie scattered around him, and Death bends over him, about to cut his throat. He, too, is perhaps being murdered because of his faith, because on closer scrutiny Death is not portrayed as a highwayman, but is wearing a coat of mail. This makes it clear that killing in the name of religion is not a privilege only of Catholics.

This now makes sense of the presence of the dead Muslim who is lying to the left of the table, his head covered with a turban. It seems no coincidence that above him on the door of the coffin-like building we see a Maltese cross, that of the Knights Hospitallers of St John of Jerusalem, alluding to the Crusades and the fight against the infidel. The personifications of Death whose attire recalls ecclesiastical habits now appear in another light, likewise the mighty invading army at the right of the coffin-like building, ready to kill.

The strategy Bruegel uses to encode his message is familiar to us. He distributes various scenes across the picture plane that per se do not have any critical significance.

Only his juxtapositioning of them gives rise to a sceptical position as regards religion. Many supposedly meaningless details then acquire a deeper meaning. Meanwhile, the cumulative narrative scheme can end our attempts to interpret the picture, for to do this we have to negate the spatial continuum. The man with the millstone is one of several people being drowned. Not the neighbouring scenes, but the ones separated from each other belong together. As long as we discover similarities only in what is placed close together, no overriding pictorial sense comes through. The achievement of the "wimmel" picture consists in concealing the extraordinary in the ordinary, the criticism of the Church in a putative enumeration. In the end, however, the question remains whether it makes any difference to die or be killed. And we must ask further whether Death always acts here in his own name or whether he has a commissioning master. Finding and addressing these cryptic questions seems to be the actual intention of the picture.

Hell as folly

It is clear from a pictorial perspective that we have to see *Dulle Griet* (pp. 204/205, Cat. 9) as an allegory. Larger than all other figures in the picture, the title figure, sometimes known as "Mad Meg", forges onwards, eyes glaring and enraged. Her threatening sword points ahead, and, along with the loot in her basket, proclaims unmistakably that everyone should keep out of her way. Van Mander mentions the picture in his Life of Bruegel, and it seems plausible that it was in Prague in the early seventeenth century.[124] It wasn't until the nineteenth century that it was rediscovered and went to Belgium through the agency of Max Friedländer.

Bruegel plays here with the misogynous motif of "woman power" in the figure of the contentious woman.[125] There is no need to decide if he used one or even several proverbs for this. In any event, there is a scene on the bridge behind Griet in which a woman seems to be tying up a devil, which refers to the saying "she is tying the devil onto a cushion", which is also depicted in *Netherlandish Proverbs* (Cat. 3; p. 94). The fun of the picture lies in its exaggeration. The assertiveness of women is so strong that they can even take on the devil. There's no one here who wants the role of husband. Even the anthropomorphic face of the leviathan is aghast at the terror spread by Griet.

Bruegel distances himself from the traditional image of Hell and the nightmare images of a Hieronymus Bosch by exploiting the supposedly demonic occasion for comic effect. Sebastian Franck, too, criticised the ideas of Hell in his *World Chronicle* and calls statements about Hell folly. The artist mocks such ideas and bans them recognisably to the realm of fable.

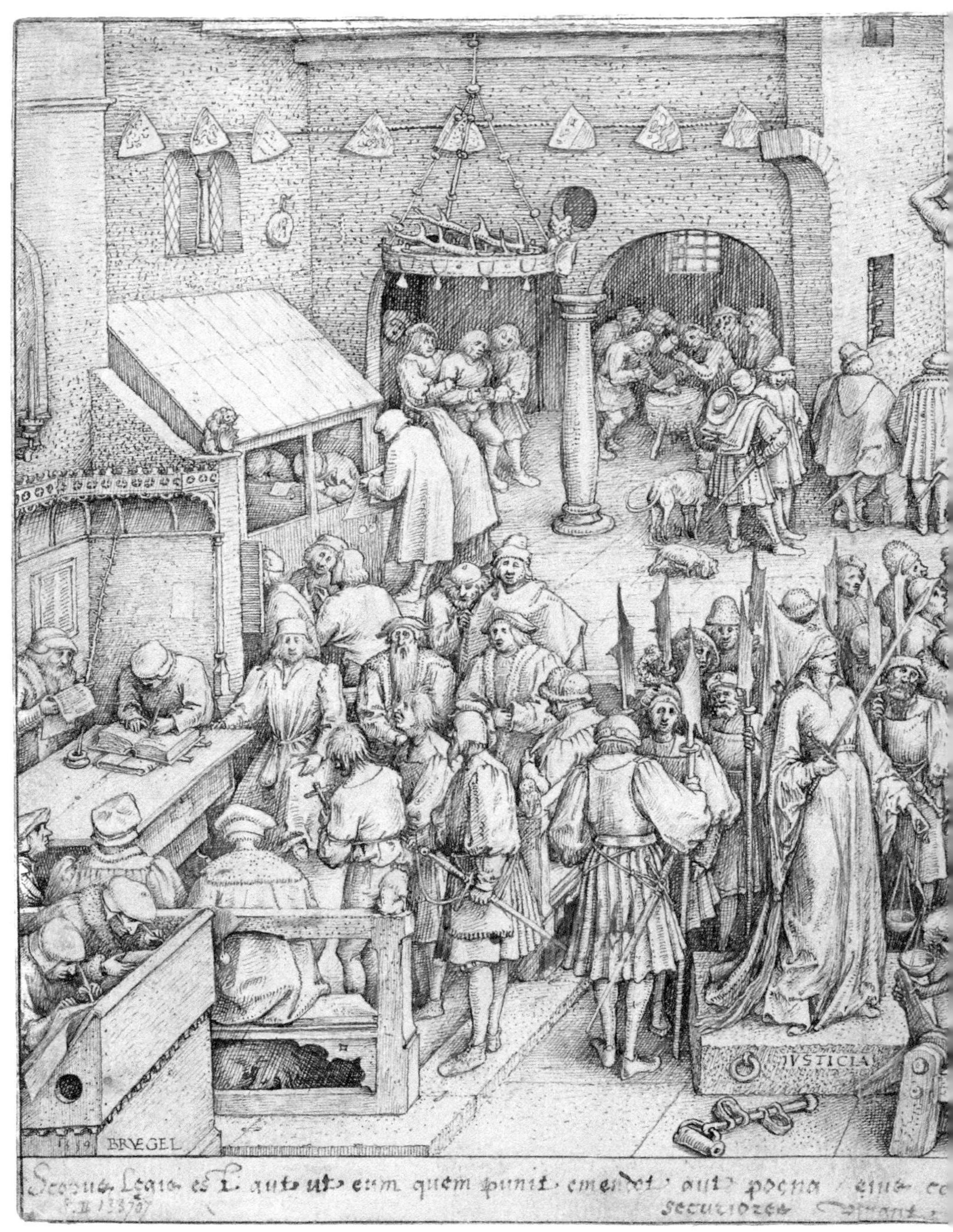
1559 BRVEGEL
IVSTICIA
Scopus Legis est aut ut eum quem punit emendet aut poena eius ceteros
securiores efficiant

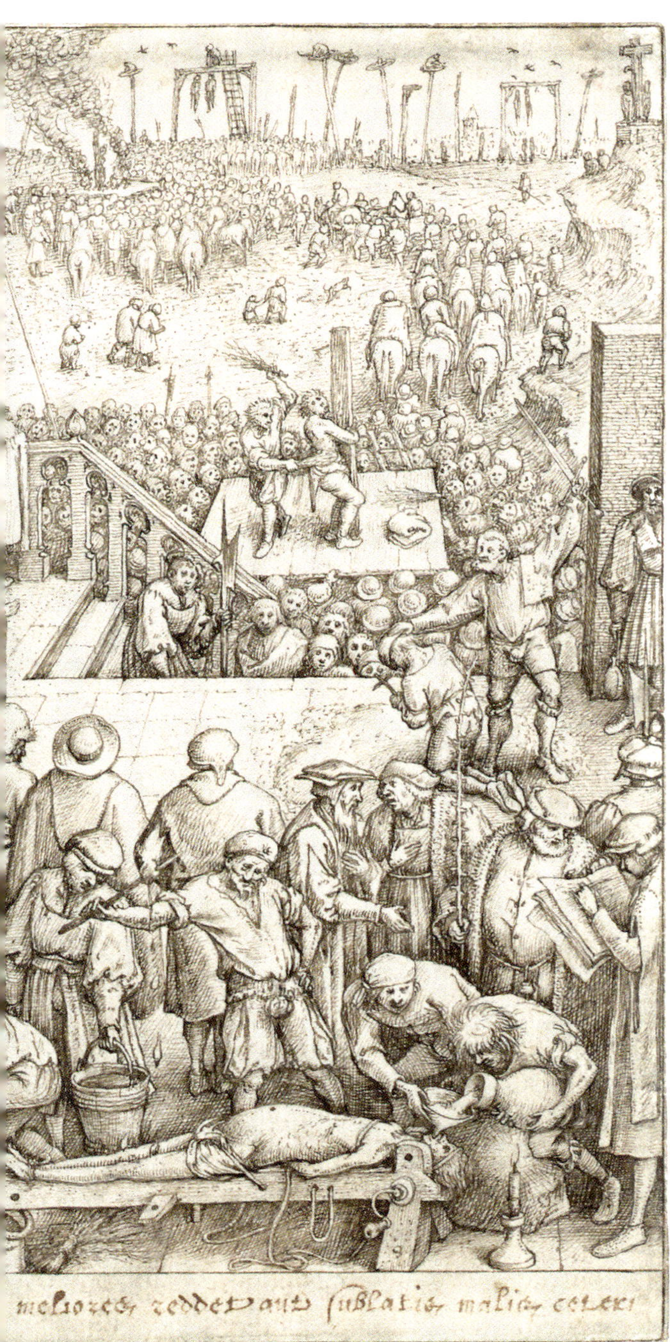

Justitia (Justice), 1559
Pen and brownish-grey ink,
22.4 x 29.5 cm (8 ⅞ x 11 ⅝ in.)
Brussels, Koninklijke Bibliotheek
van België, Prentenkabinet/
Bibliothèque royale de Belgique,
Cabinet des Estampes

The Triumph of Death (detail), *c.* 1562
(see ill. pp. 196/197)

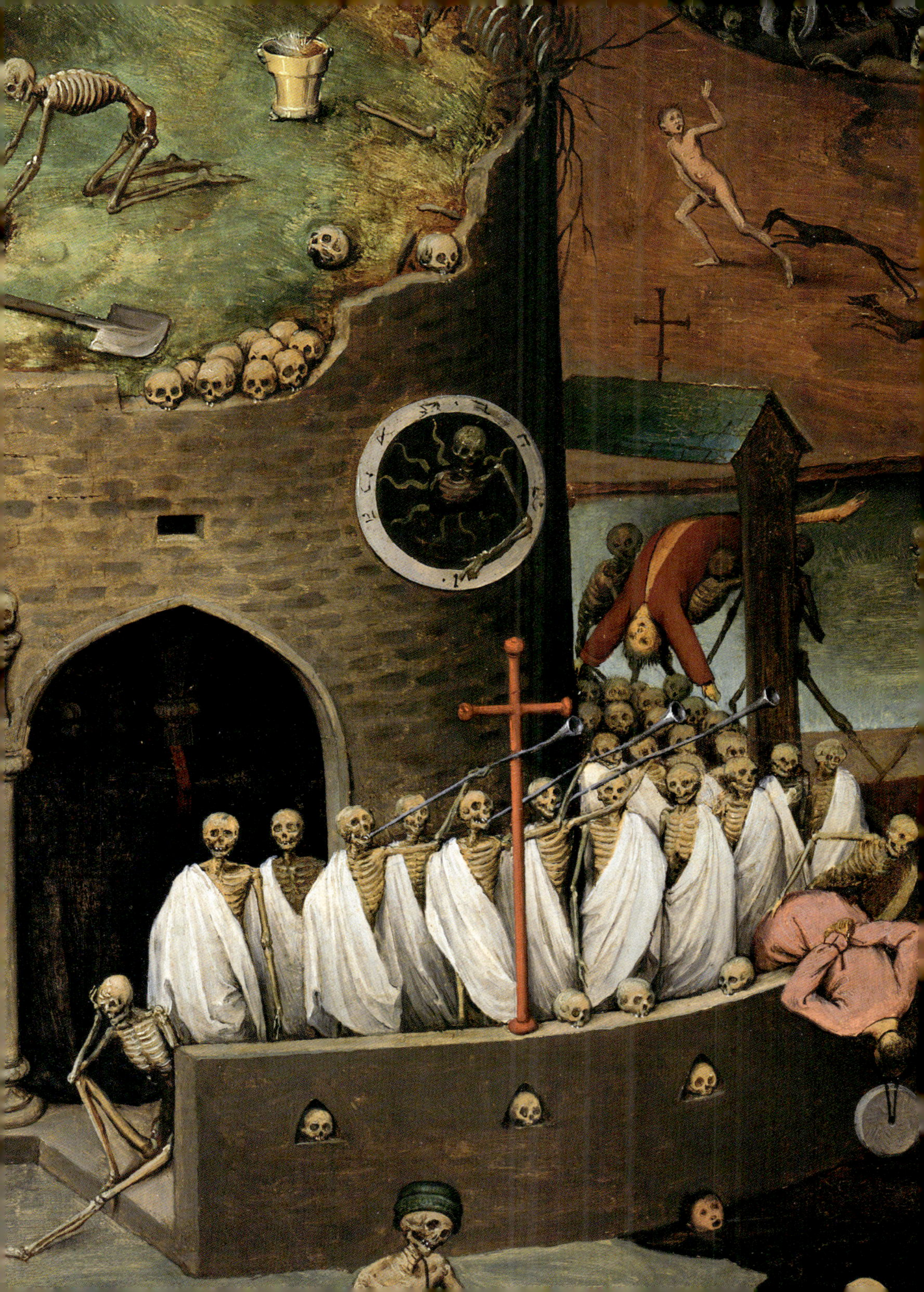

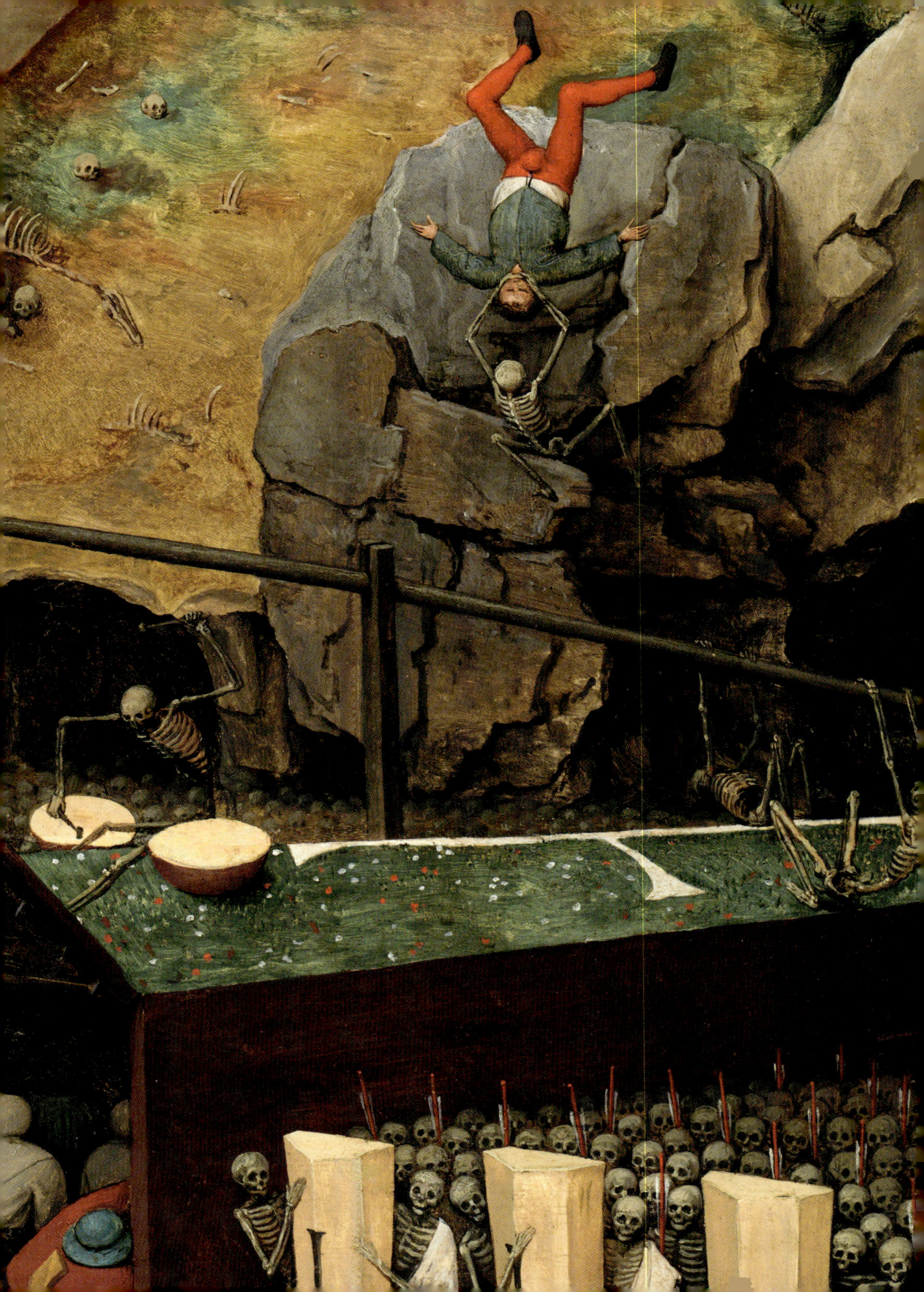

Open Heaven

Once more the maws of Hell have opened dangerously wide. The huge fish jaws of the leviathan are ready to swallow the souls being taken to their fateful destination by demons in a huge barge. Graves open. Souls beg for aid, while bizarre goblins scout after further victims.

The drawing *The Last Judgement* (pp. 186/187), dated 1558, was executed in the same year as an engraving (Müller/Schauerte 2018, Cat. G70). The contrast with the Last Judgement pictures of Hieronymus Bosch could not be greater. While in Bosch no more than a handful of human souls can be saved at the end, Bruegel lets the whole of mankind ascend to Heaven. Besides which, the Virgin Mary and St John are missing as mediators on the Last Day. The souls need no mediation in Bruegel, they turn directly to Christ. Prophets and saints are portrayed left and right of the World Judge, as described in the Apocalypse. Only the prisoners in the ship will have the worst of it, as the observer must perceive.

Scholars have interpreted this concept of Bruegel's as a critical comment on the ministerial Church, but also on Bosch, by expressing his spiritual disposition.[126] It seems no coincidence that the ship, as traditional symbol of the Church, is transporting its occupants to Hell. But Bruegel distances himself also in his artistic approach from the nightmarish concepts of his legendary predecessor. The concept palpable in the picture of saved humanity is nothing less than a fully alternative agenda to the horror of the Last Judgement.

The horror of Medusa

It is helpful to recall this preparatory drawing before attempting to interpret *The Fall of the Rebel Angels* (pp. 210/211, Cat. 7) dated 1562, because here, too, it is about demystification, not only in the religious sense, but also the aesthetic. In the centre of the drawing is St Michael, bearing in his left hand a shield with a Greek cross. The world is in uproar around him. Countless creatures encircle the highest of the archangels but seem helpless in the face of his superior spiritual power. This impression is reinforced by his being depicted full figure.

No demon comes near enough to pose a serious threat. It matters not how many swords are brandished against him, no danger threatens Michael. On the contrary, Bruegel shows rather the rage of the creatures at their own impotence at not being able to tempt him. We are not seeing a real fight, but, far more, outrage.

The Triumph of Death (detail), *c.* 1562

(see ill. pp. 196/197)

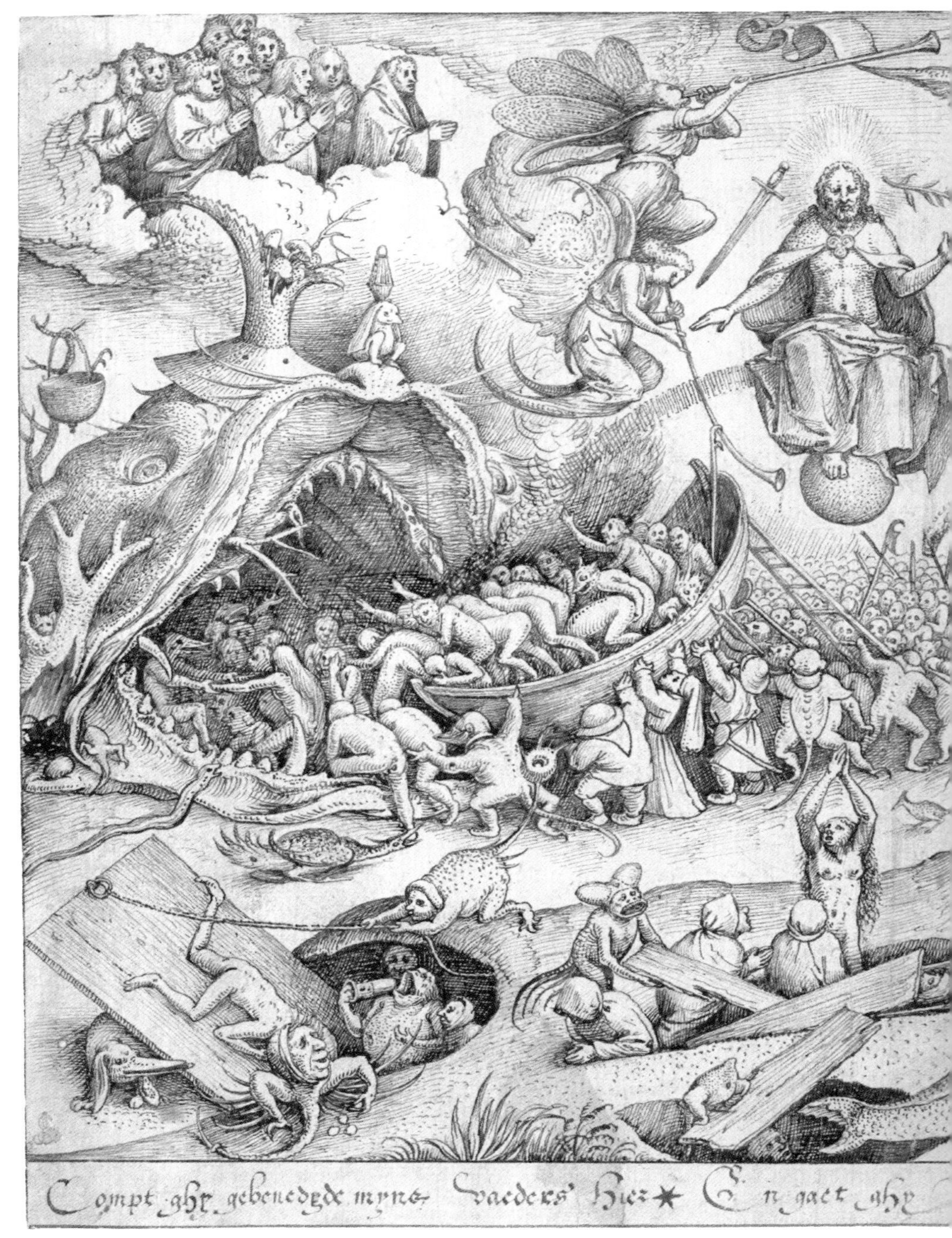
Compt ghy gebenedyde myns vaeders Hier ✶ En gaet ghy

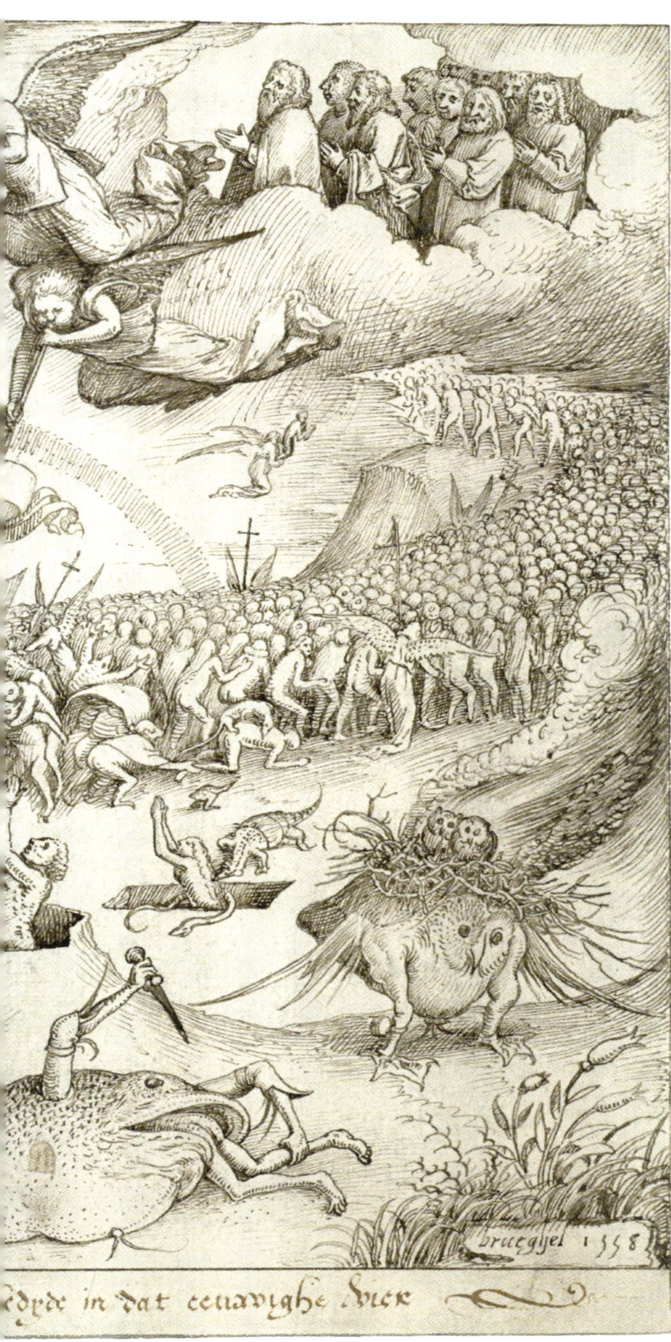

The Last Judgement, 1558
Pen and blackish-brown ink,
23 x 30 cm (9 ⅛ x 11 ¾ in.)
Vienna, Albertina

The literature has identified two passages in the Bible that can be related to the picture: from the Old Testament, the Fall of Lucifer, whom God banishes from heaven because of his pride; and, from St John's Book of Revelation in the New Testament, the Apocalypse.[127] St John's Apocalypse is more relevant, because in the traditional iconography the final struggle of the angels between the powers of darkness is represented alongside the Last Judgement. This is indicated by the angels blowing trumpets (pp. 212/213), as in Albrecht Dürer's (1471–1528) famous woodcut.

Frans Floris (p. 189) had painted the Fall of the Angels only eight years previously as part of an altar for the swordsmen's guild in Antwerp Cathedral, which was partially destroyed during the iconoclastic depredations. Hence it is often suspected that with this picture Bruegel was entering into a conceptual contest with the aforementioned work by his fellow painter. Floris, too, includes a densely packed group of angels and monsters. But in contrast to Bruegel, he uses his picture to demonstrate a superior technique in portraying the nude. The demonic figures have muscular male physiques throughout, while their heads are monstrous. In this way he manages to show bodies from all possible perspectives and to impress us with his mastery in portraying the human anatomy. We see a physical fight: with the utmost force, Michael tramples on the opponent in front of him with his left foot in order, the next moment, to finish him off with his sword.

Things are very different in Bruegel's painting. Here the whole of creation seems to be rebelling. The encyclopaedic pictorial programme dazzles the eye. Animals from all continents have gathered together, fishes and sloths, apes and dragon-like creatures. Not only this, but Bruegel deploys all kinds of movement and the four elements. He has placed several human heads among the many animals, as if they were part of the natural order. Moreover, the picture is nothing less than a lesson in mimetic painting. The painter renders all conceivable textures and surfaces meticulously. Altogether, we find sundials, weapons and musical instruments in his composition. *Literae* and *arma* are equally present, thus the attributes of the liberal arts and the armourer's craft.

This universal show was linked to the mode of collecting, customary at the time, of the cabinet of curiosities, which here, so to speak, is rendered in the form of a picture.[128] But it seems equally plausible that the artists wants to allude with his confusing mass and diversity of images to the world in its totality, Mundus, in all its phenomena. Not evil, but the world with all its abundance of creatures has been put in its place by an overriding principle. Part of this is the way Bruegel produces graphic metaphors of procreation and fertility. An animal shows the inside of its belly, in which numerous progeny are seen in the form of eggs (pp. 218/219). On the opposite side, an angel attacks a monster carrying a wicker basket with fish-like young in it, trying to protect them. Others show their sex obscenely and break wind. The meat of the mussels reminds us as well of the edibility of individual animals.

While Frans Floris shows us the abundance of movements of the human body, Bruegel shows us the indescribable diversity of the world. And it is impressive to see how he manages to lend human emotions even to animals. The rage of the puffer fish or the incredulous faces of the animals confronted by their own impotence strike the eye. Particularly expressive is the female demon underneath Michael, who consists of a body tapering to a point. Outraged, she is about to lift herself up with her arms (pp. 216/217). Underneath is another woman washing her hair in a helmet, recalling a scene from Bruegel's engraving *Superbia* (*Pride*; pp. 190/191). Taken all together, many references can be used to compile a whole iconography of vice.

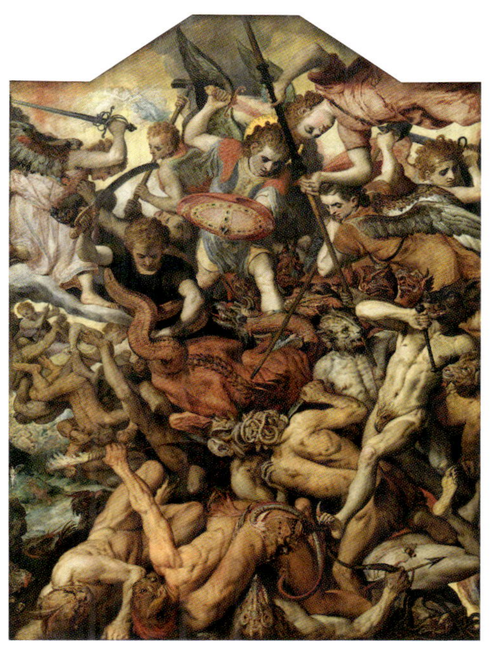

Some creatures fall and hurtle down; they straighten up and seek their opponent, the cause of their pain. Michael and the angels are generally of androgynous form. Their bodies are extremely elongated; their heads appear far too small. Sublime, they hover around as if free of gravity. In modern terms, they move in slow motion. Michael wields his sword to strike, but this happens as a delicate gesture and not with physical force – a dramatic technique that incidentally characterises Raphael's depiction of angels. His golden armour recalls the angelic figures of Hans Memling (1433/40–1494), and, with the head of the crowned dragon at his feet, Bruegel alludes as well to Dürer's version of the Apocalypse.[129] But what does the artist wish to convey to us in his pictorial concept? The complex references to other artists have led to the plausible interpretation that here we can discover an ironic confrontation with tradition.[130] Bruegel, it suggests, has even integrated in cryptic form a portrait of Jan van Eyck, which we might identify in the demon with the pointed headdress. This seems doubtful at first, but is thoroughly convincing if we compare him with van Eyck's alleged self-portrait.

Frans Floris, **The Fall of the Rebel Angels**, 1554
Oil on wood, 308 x 220 cm (121 ¼ x 86 ⅝ in.). Antwerp, Koninklijk Museum voor Schone Kunsten

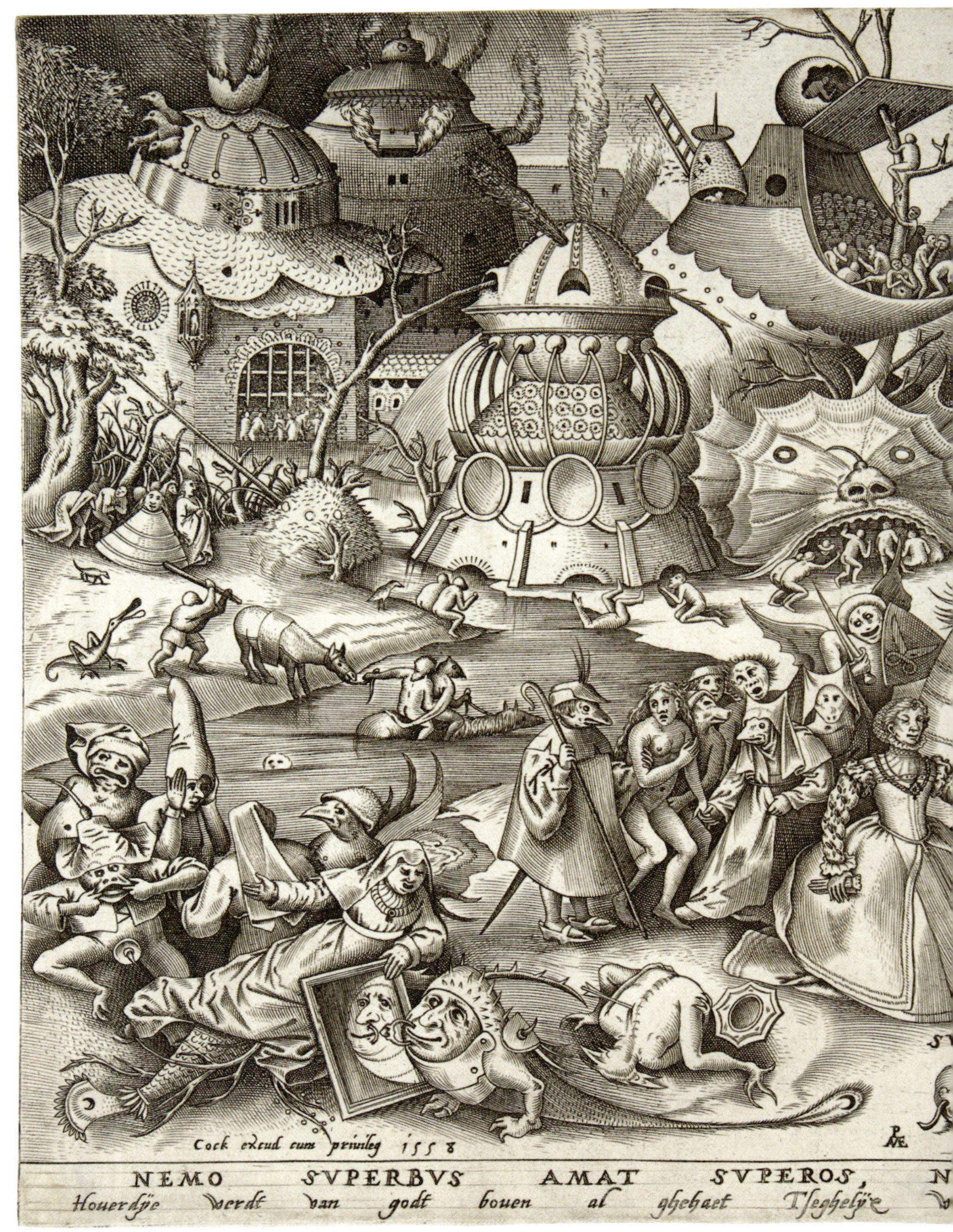

Cock excud cum privileg 1558
NEMO SVPERBVS AMAT SVPEROS,
Houerdye werdt van godt bouen al ghehaet Tseghelye

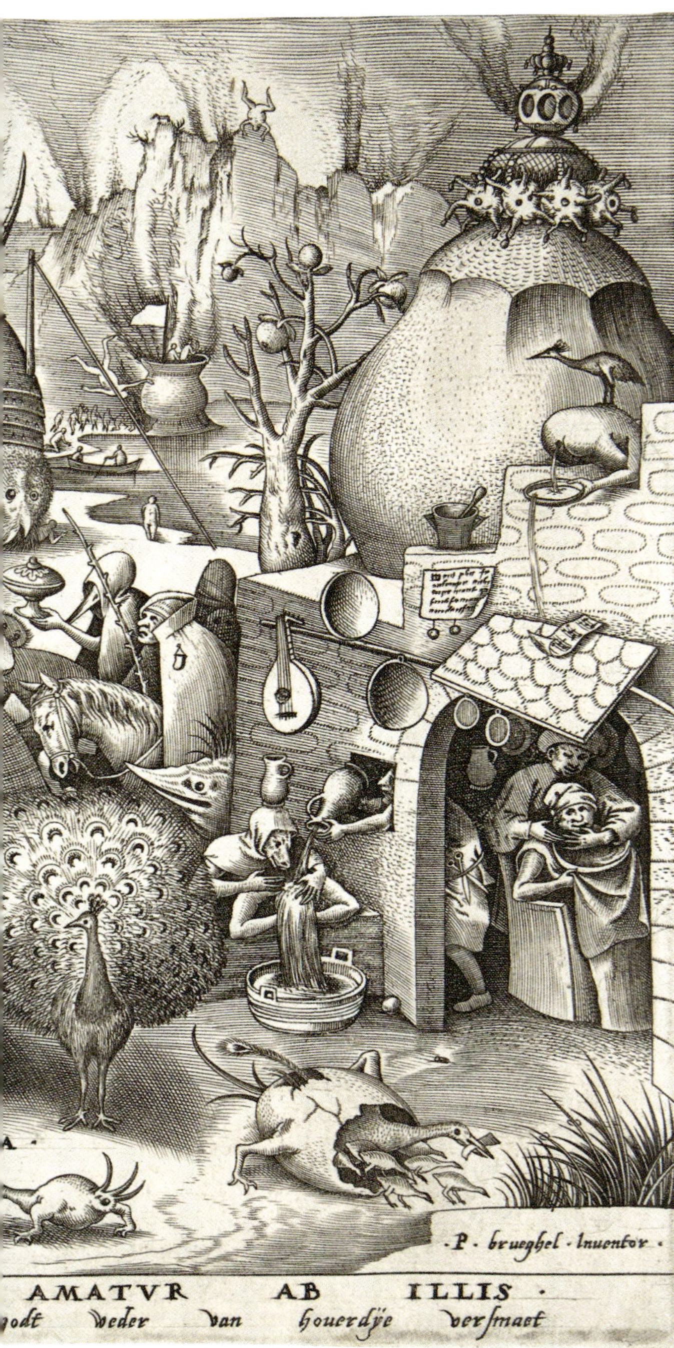

Pieter van der Heyden after
Pieter Bruegel the Elder
Superbia (Pride), 1558
Copper engraving, 22.7 x 29.2 cm
(8 ⅞ x 11 ½ in.)
New York, The Metropolitan
Museum of Art

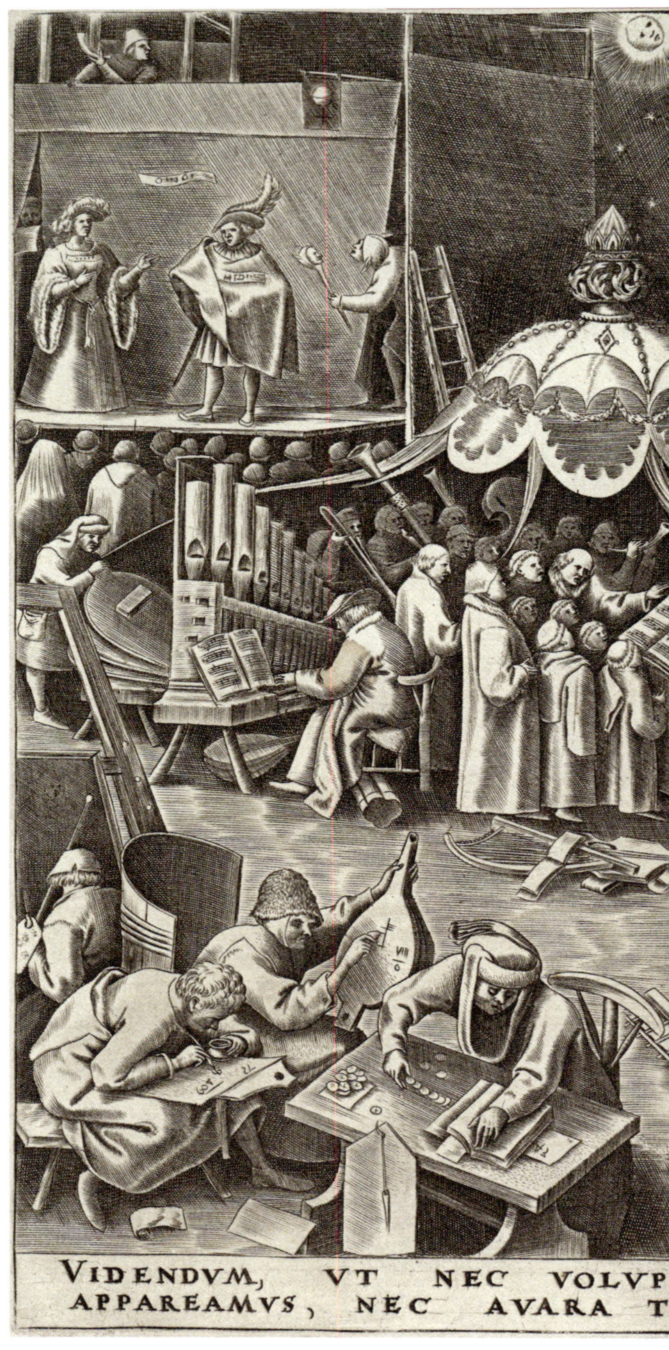

Philipp Galle (attributed) after
Pieter Bruegel the Elder
Temperantia (Temperance),
c. 1559/60
Copper engraving, 22.3 x 29.1 cm
(8 ¾ x 11 ½ in.)
New York, The Metropolitan
Museum of Art

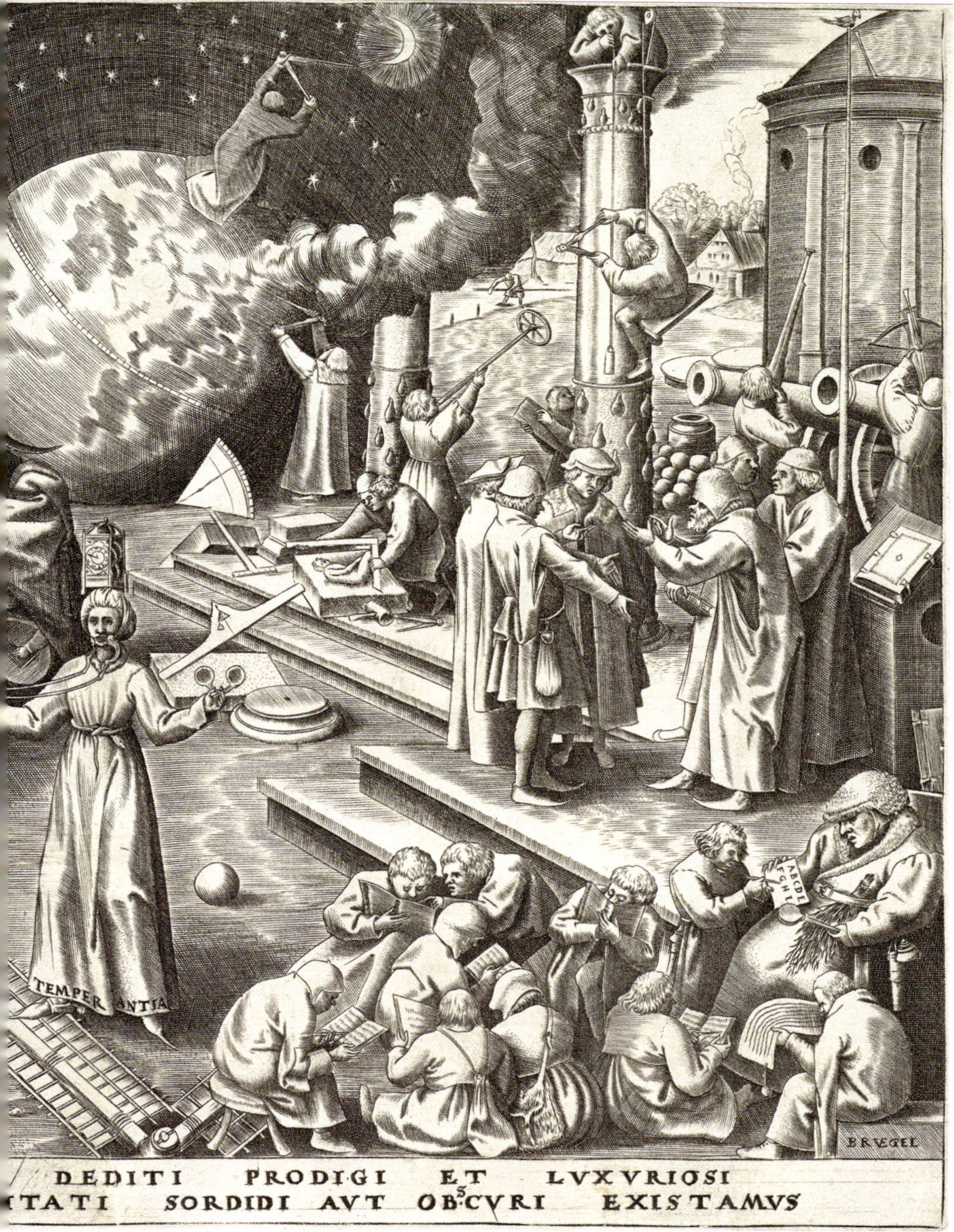
TEMPERANTIA
BRVEGEL
DEDITI   PRODIGI   ET   LVXVRIOSI
TATI   SORDIDI   AVT   OBSCVRI   EXISTAMVS

This interpretation is supported when we look at the grotesque, grimacing face in the bottom right-hand corner resembling the terrifying Gorgon Medusa. This horrific image has her hair writhing like serpents around her head and her glance, inclined downwards, tells of her power to turn men to stone. Like the dragon of the Apocalypse, she too wears a diadem on her head as if she were one of his seven sinful heads. Here Bruegel is giving a warning, criticising the desire to surpass which spurred on his predecessors. Against this mania to surpass, he turns to emulation. Of course he alludes to tradition, but does not enter into competition with it. The originally beautiful Medusa is a distortion of the artist consumed by *Invidia* (p. 55) and *Superbia* (pp. 190/191). Envy and pride ought not to be the driving forces of artistic work. Like Perseus, the conqueror of the Medusa, the artist has to succeed in making himself invisible – which, however, Bruegel seems not to manage.

Pages 196/197
The Triumph of Death, *c.* 1562
Oil on wood, 117 x 162 cm (46 ⅛ x 63 ¾ in.). Madrid, Museo Nacional del Prado
(details pages 195, 198–203)

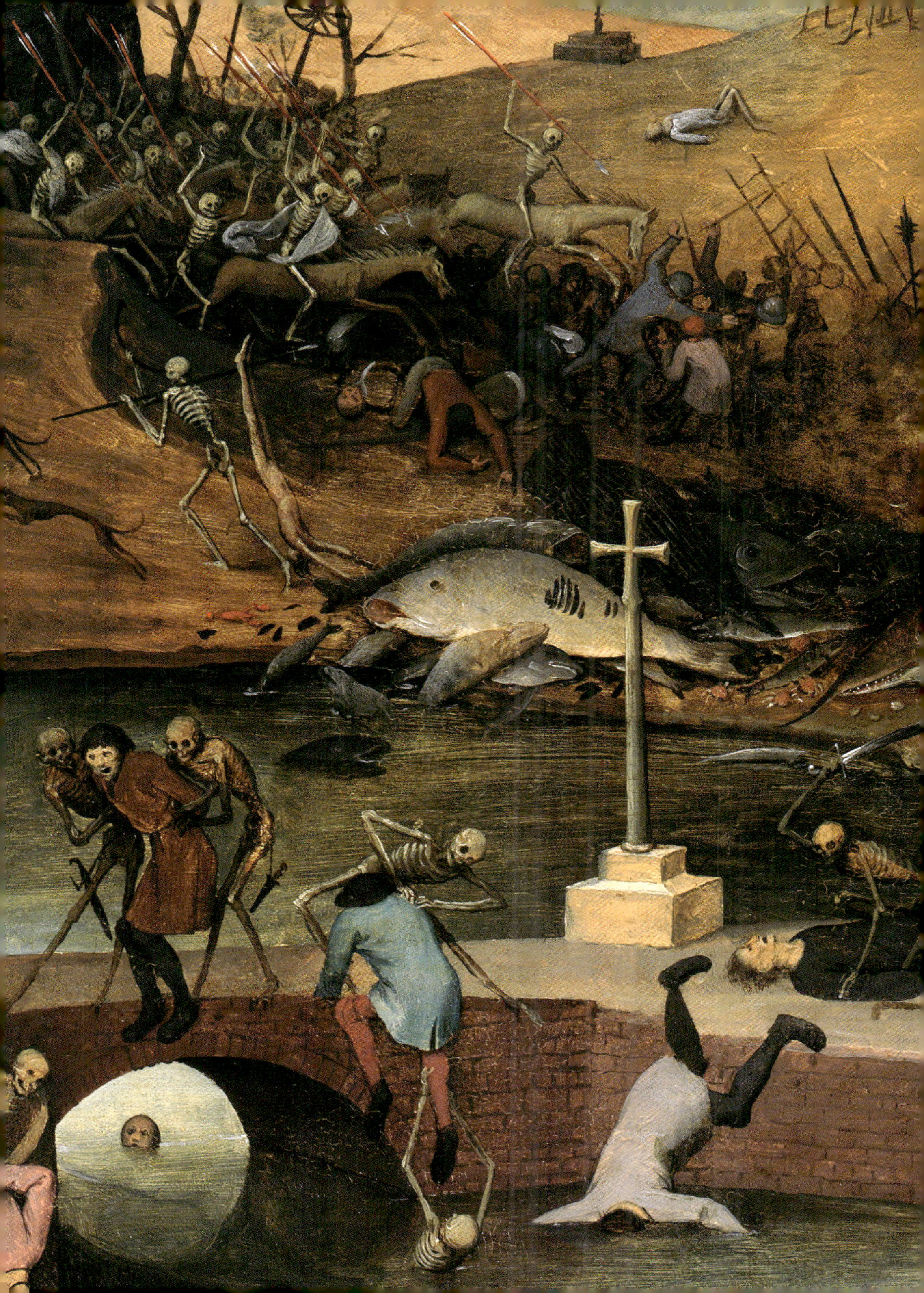

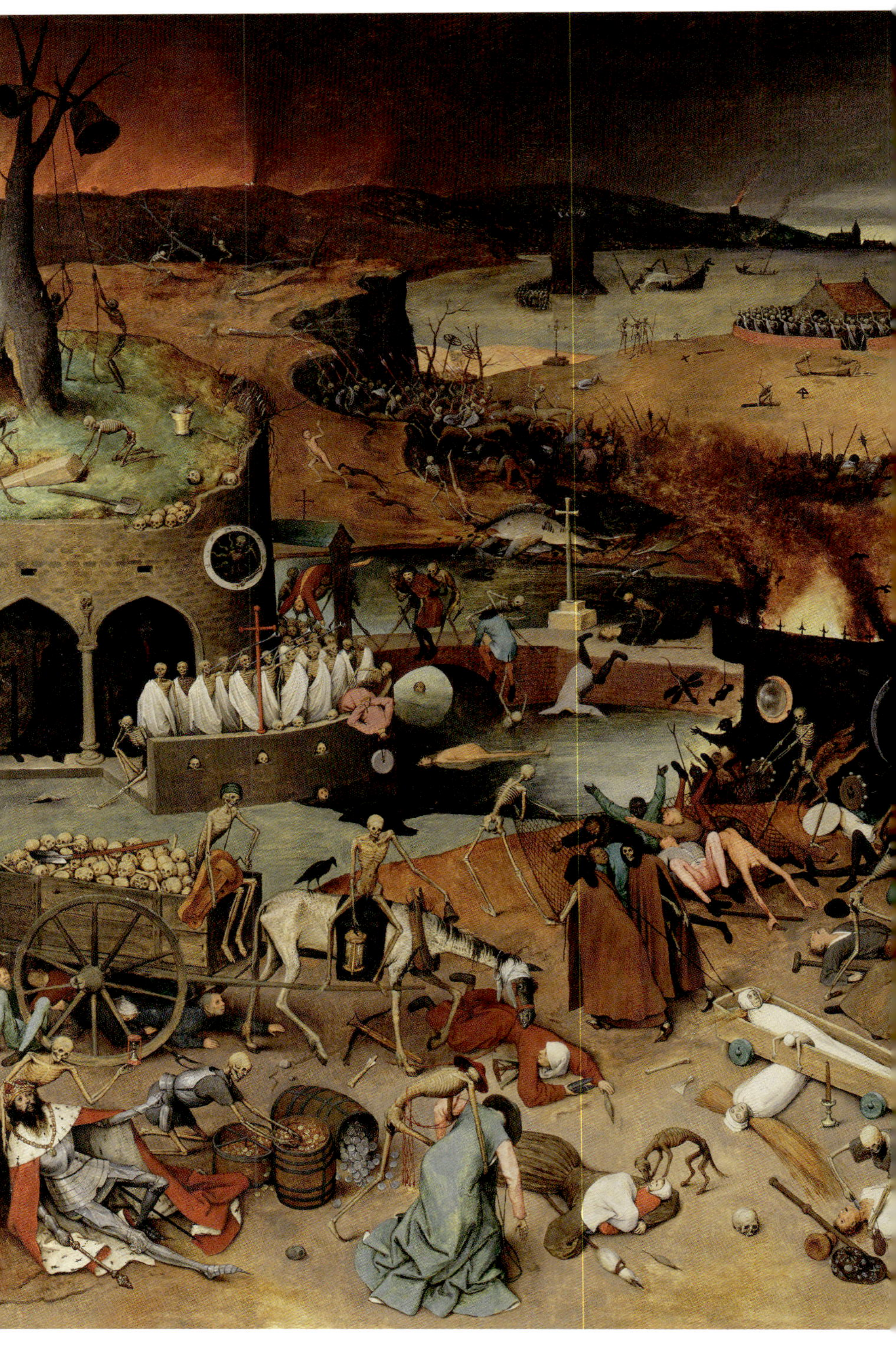

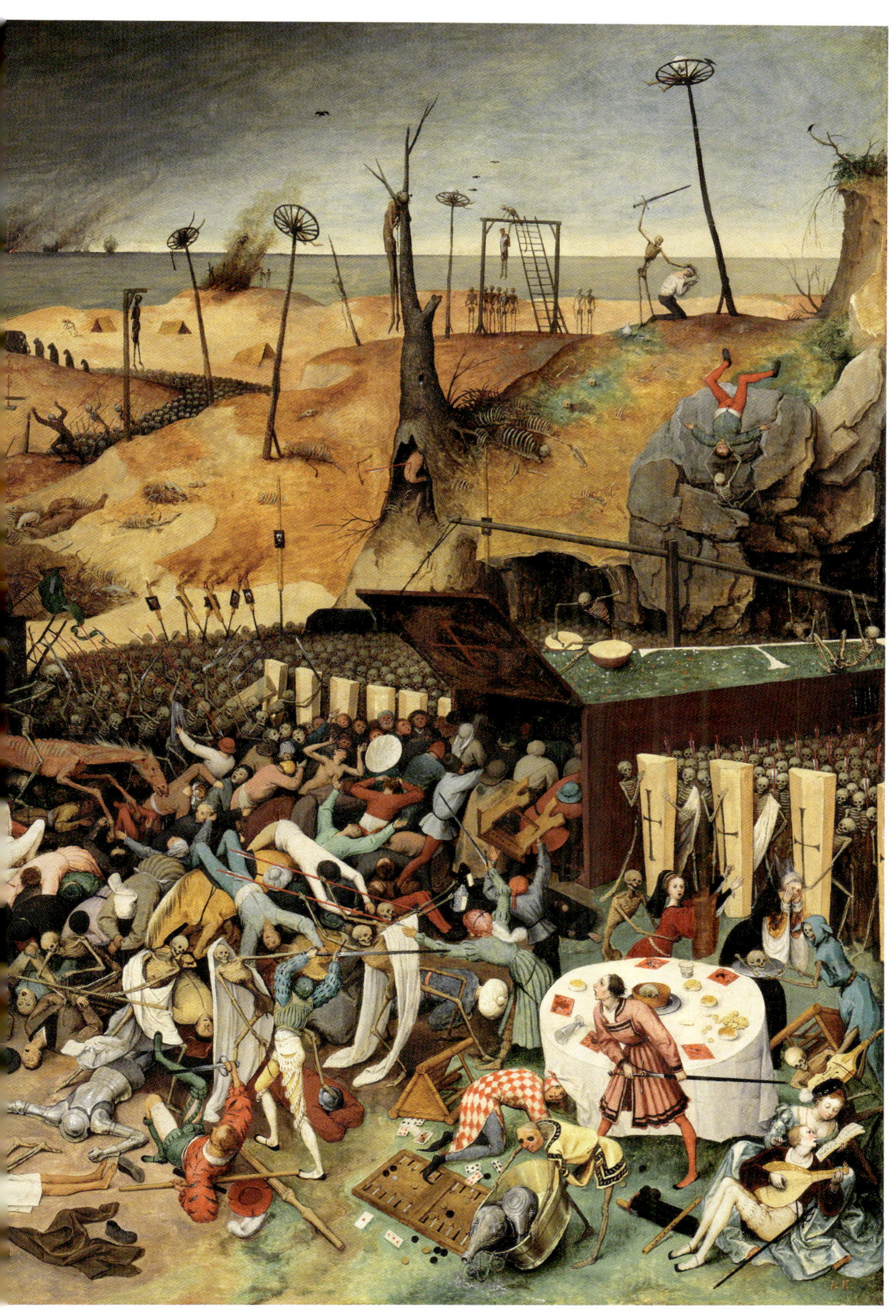

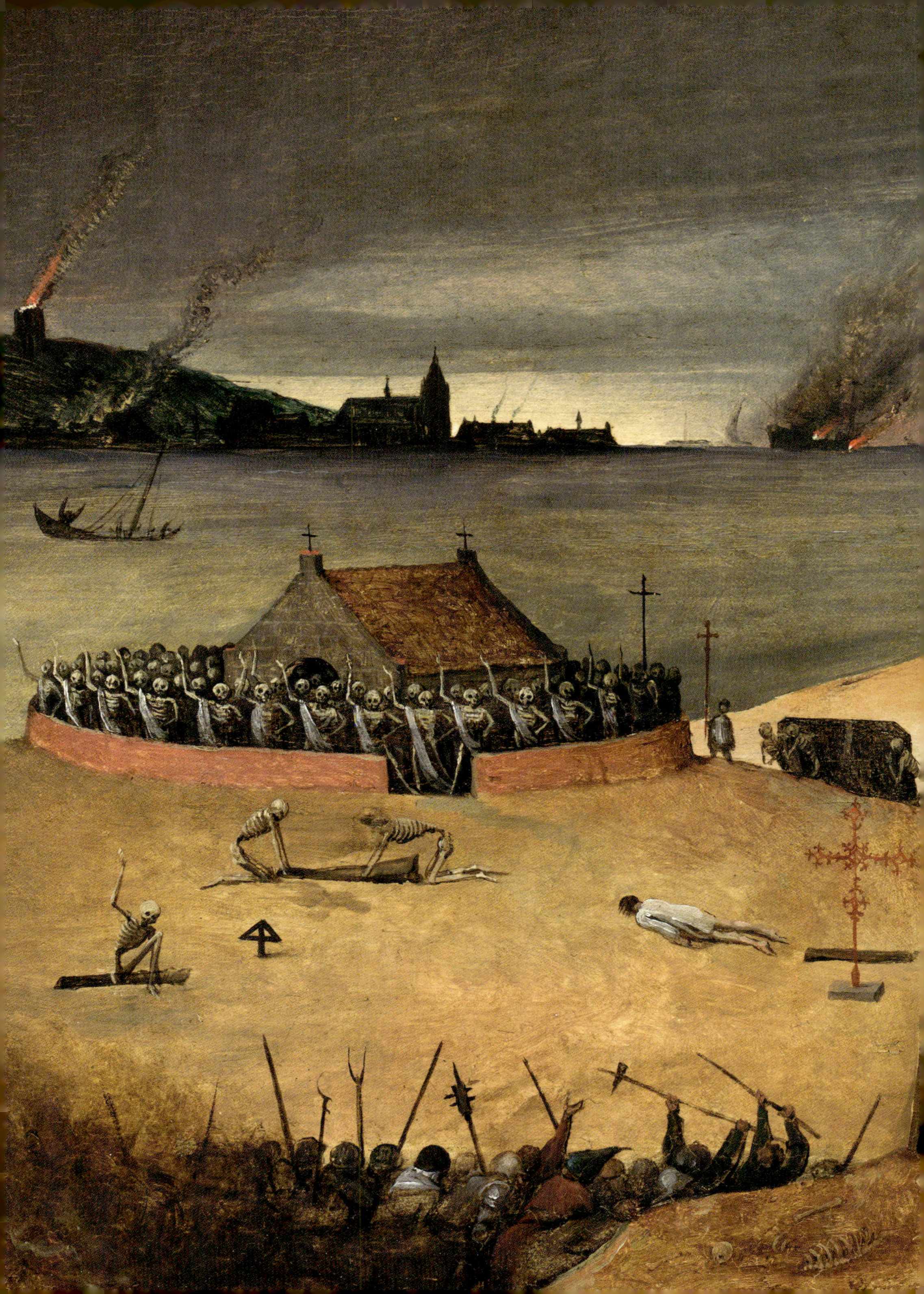

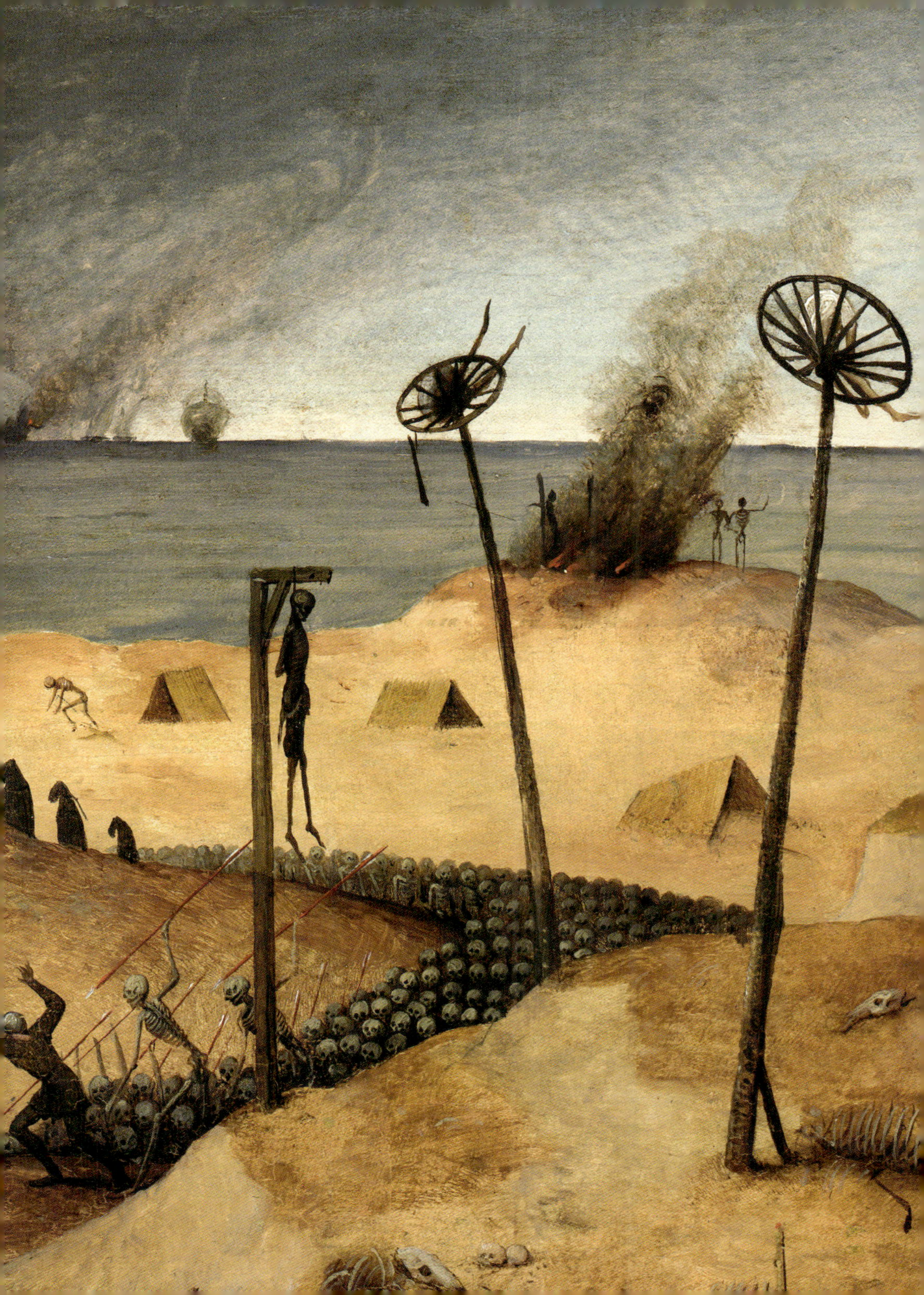

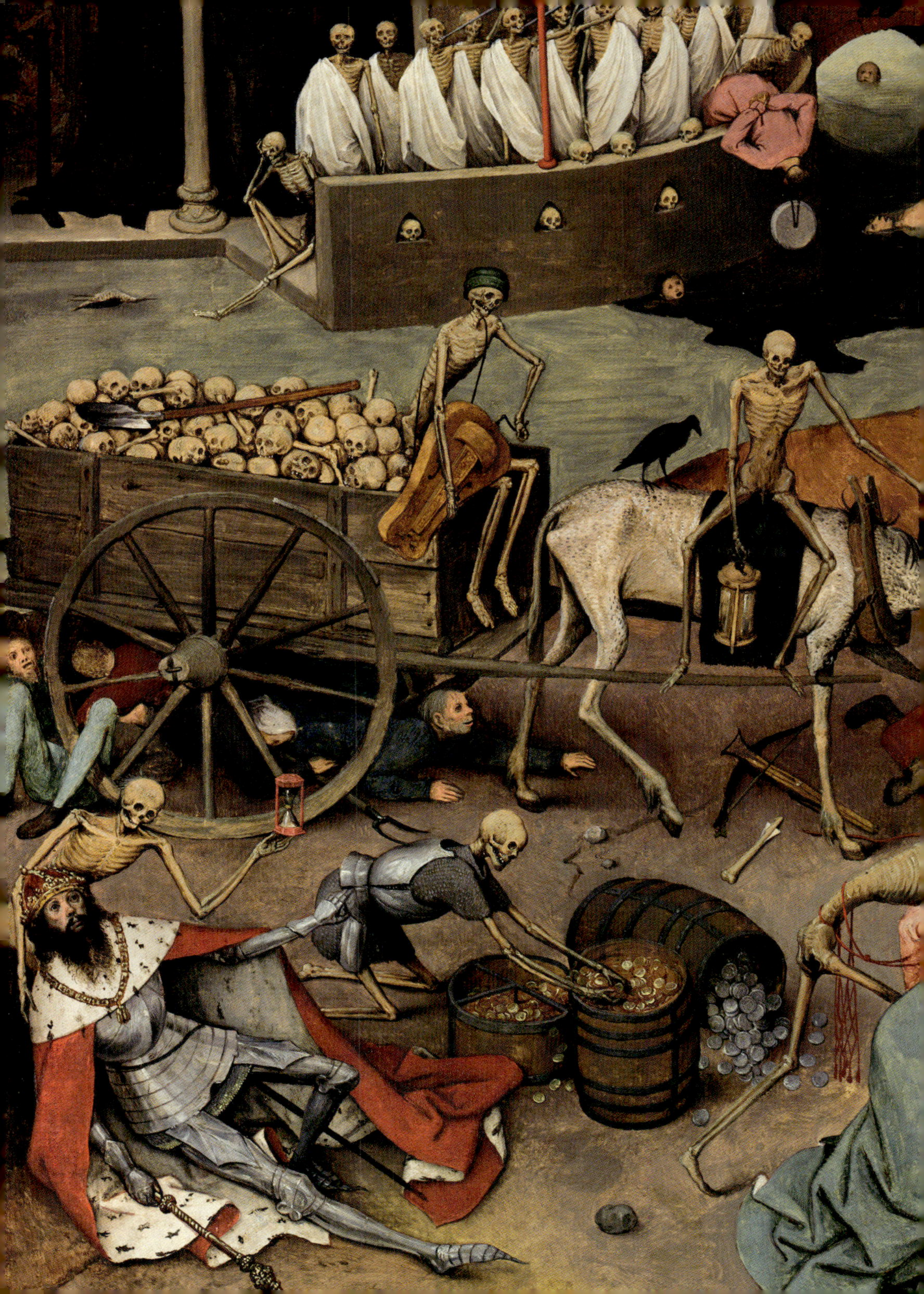

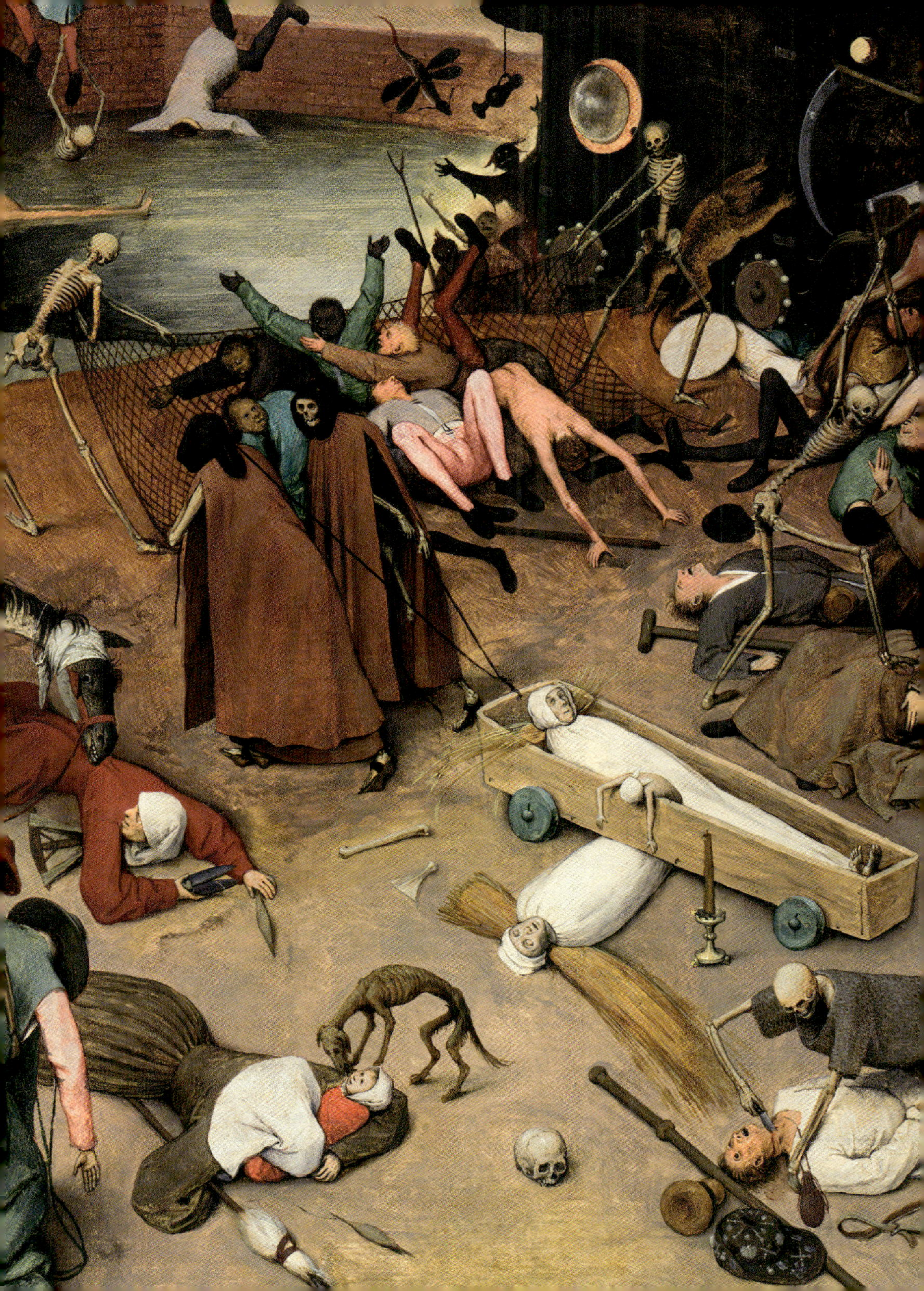

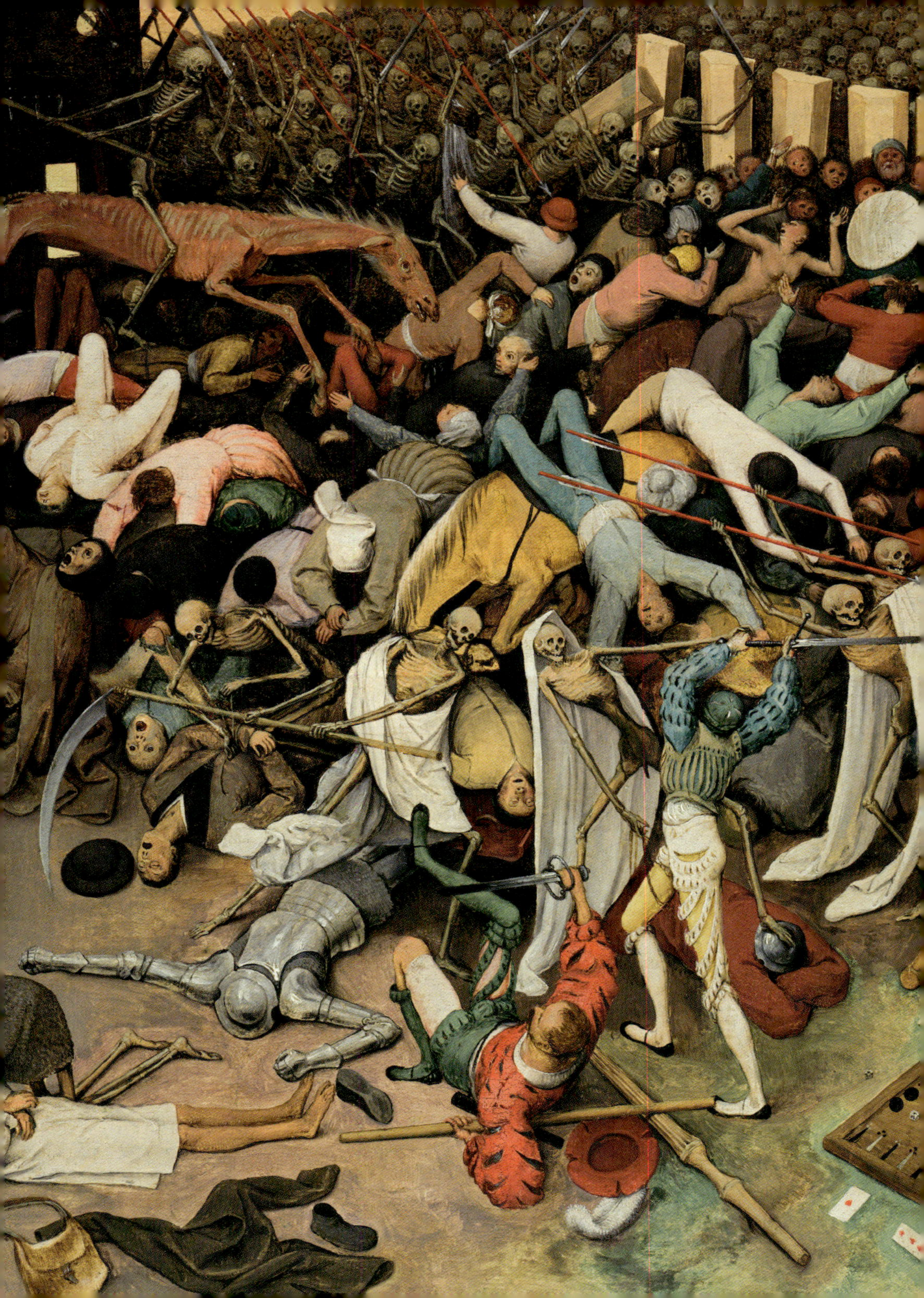

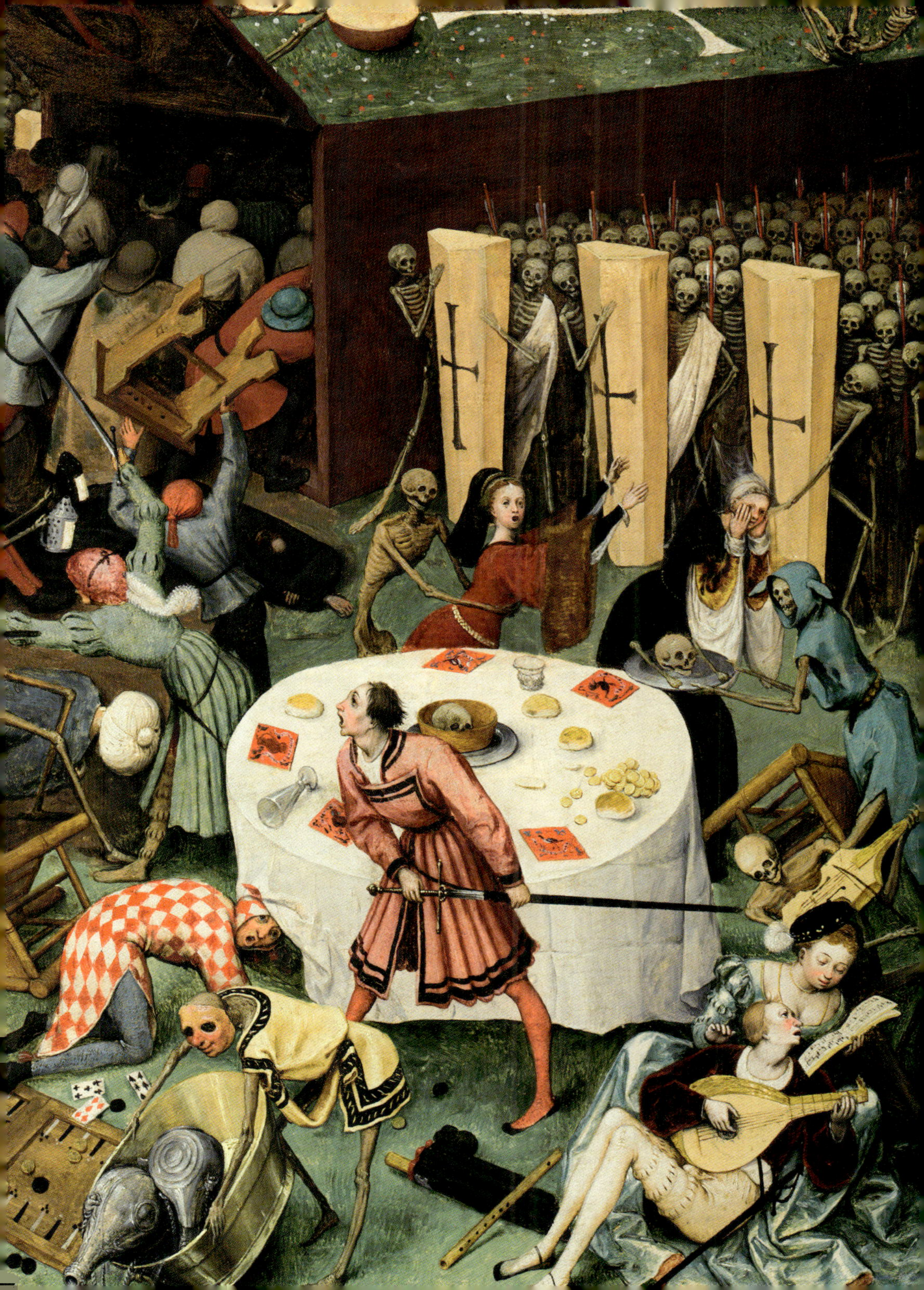

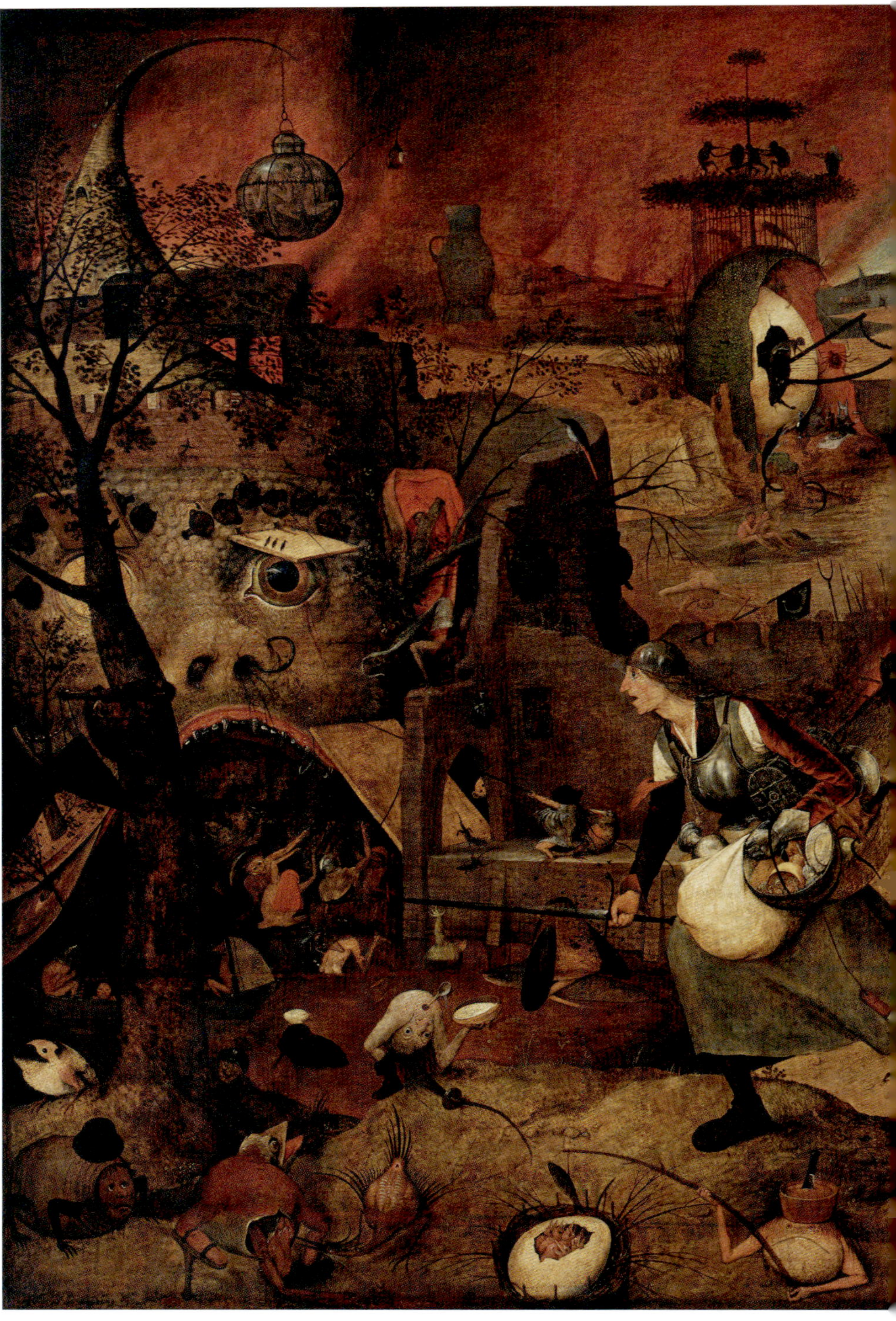

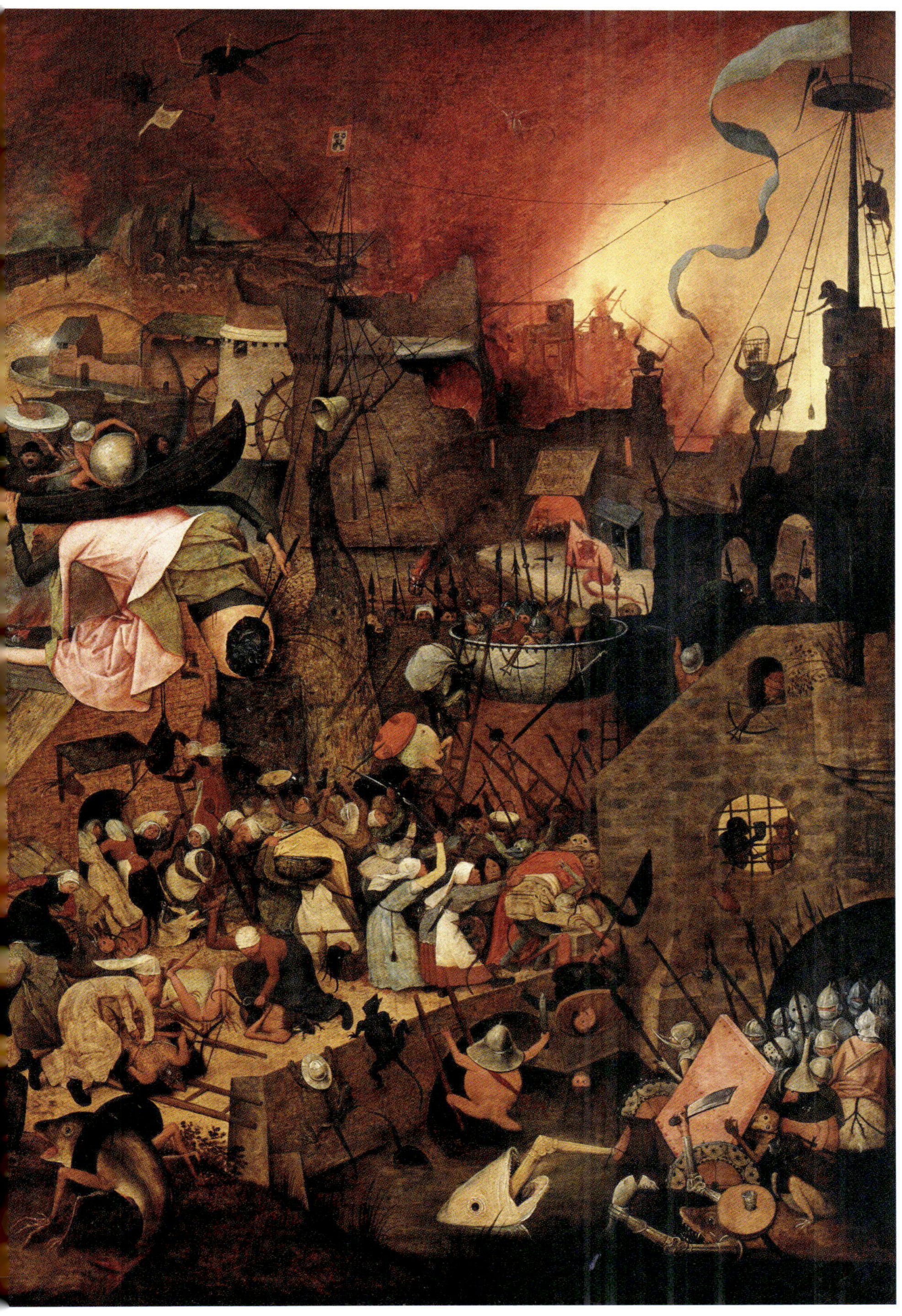

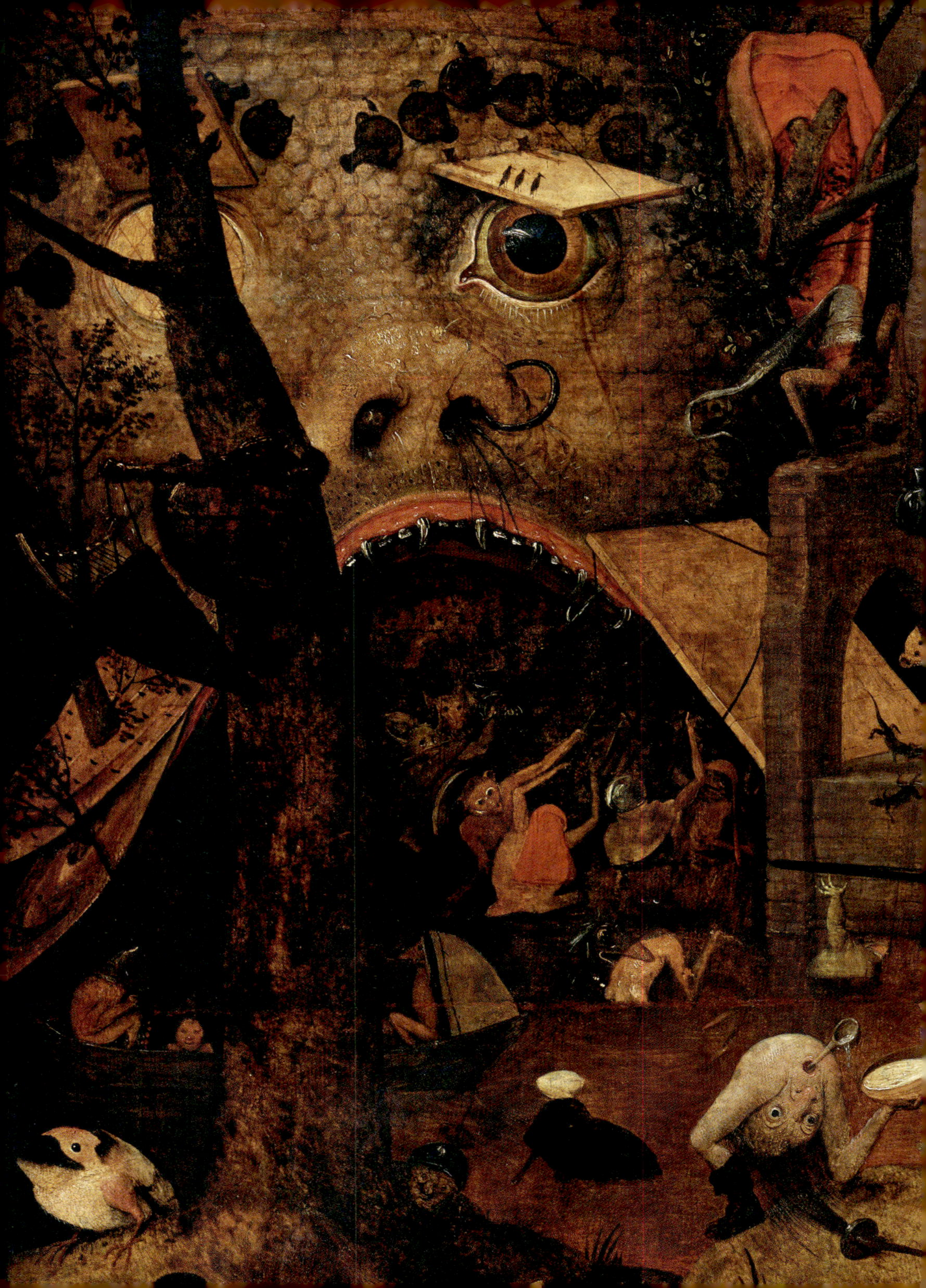

Pages 204/205
Dulle Griet (Dull Gret), 1563
Oil on wood, 117.4 x 162 cm (46 ¼ x 63 ¾ in.)
Antwerp, Museum Mayer van den Bergh
(details pages 206, 209)

Pages 210/211
The Fall of the Rebel Angels, 1562
Oil on oak, 117 x 162 cm (46 ⅛ x 63 ¾ in.)
Brussels, Musées royaux des Beaux-Arts de Belgique/
Koninklijke Musea voor Schone Kunsten van België
(details pages 212–219)

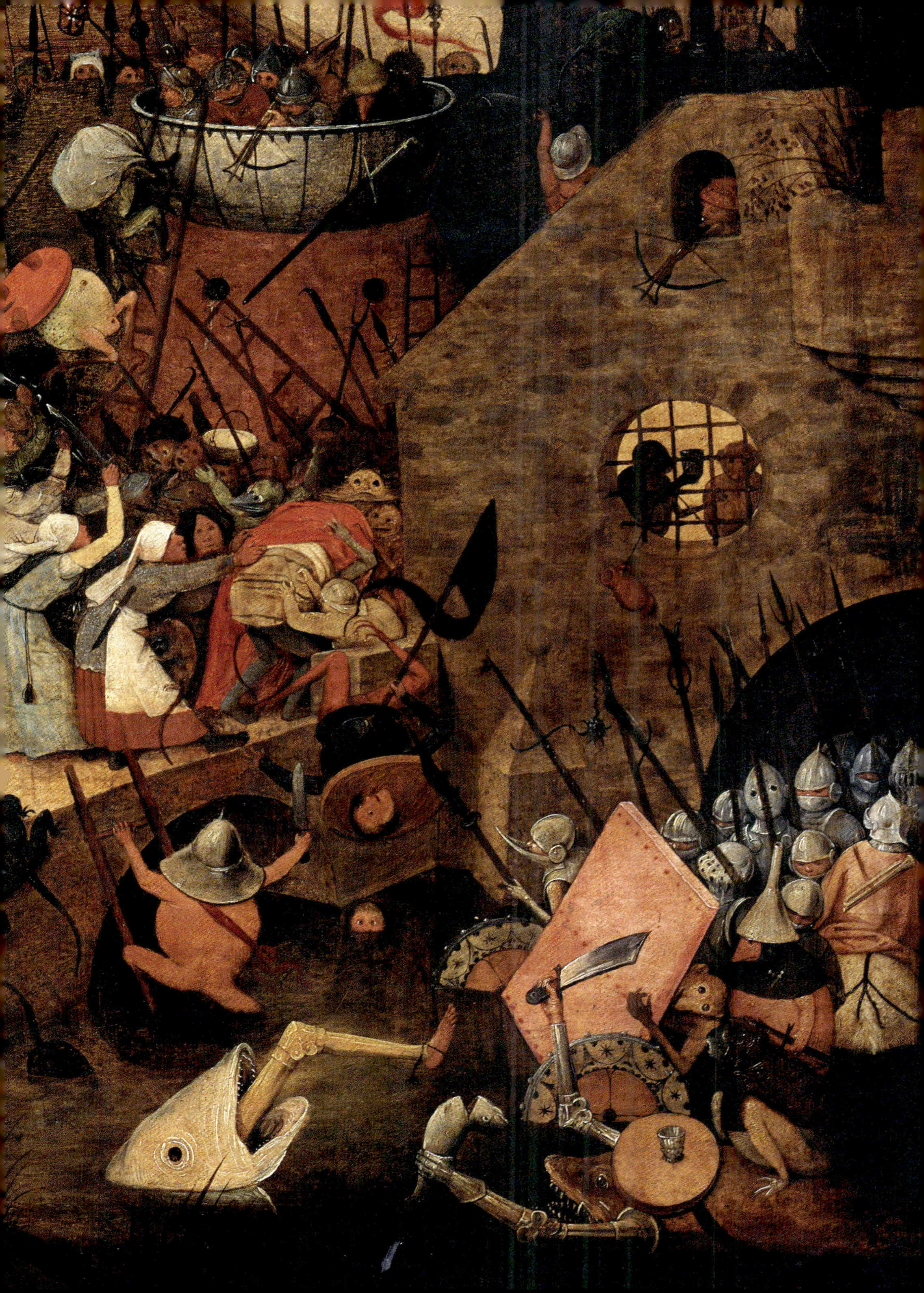

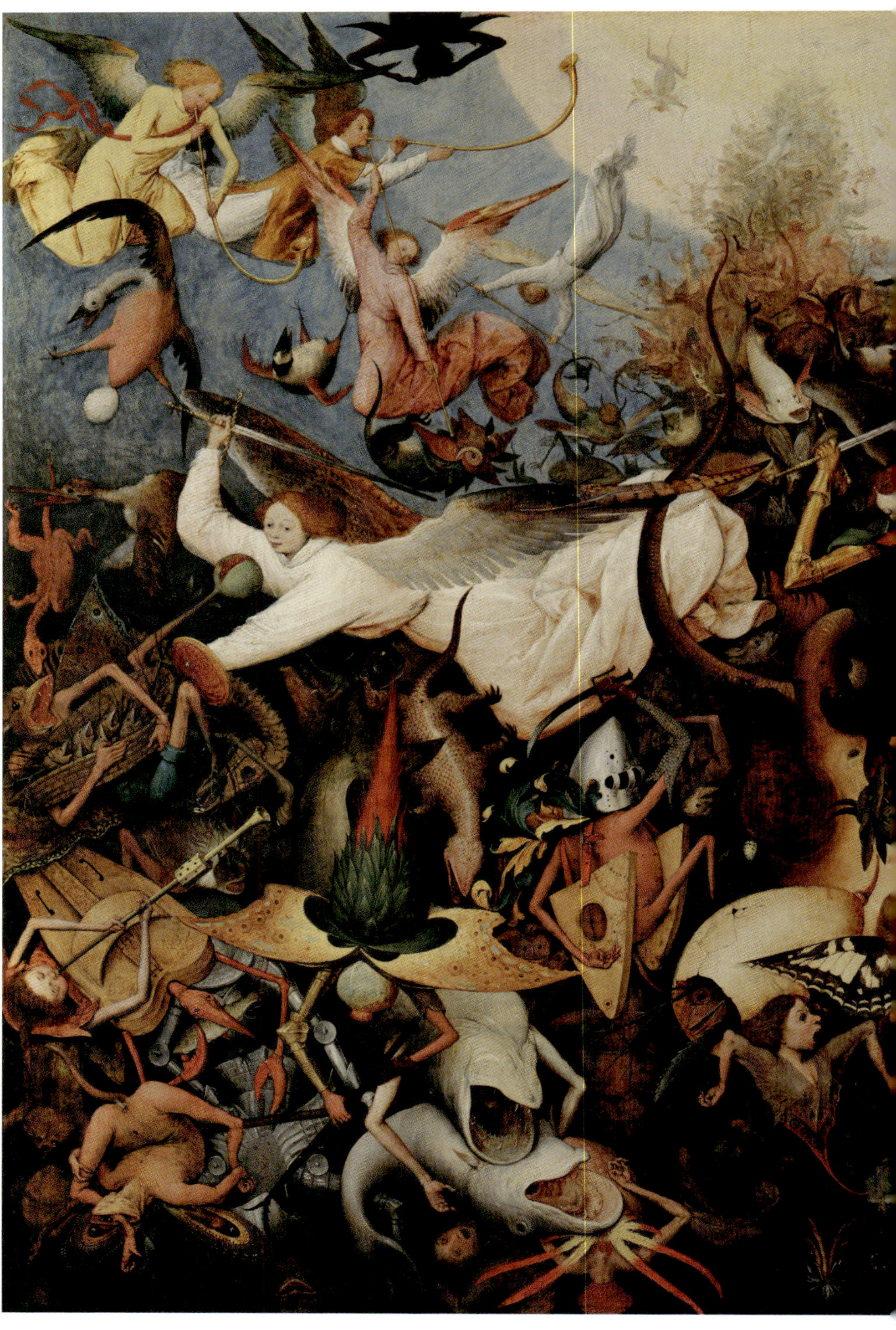

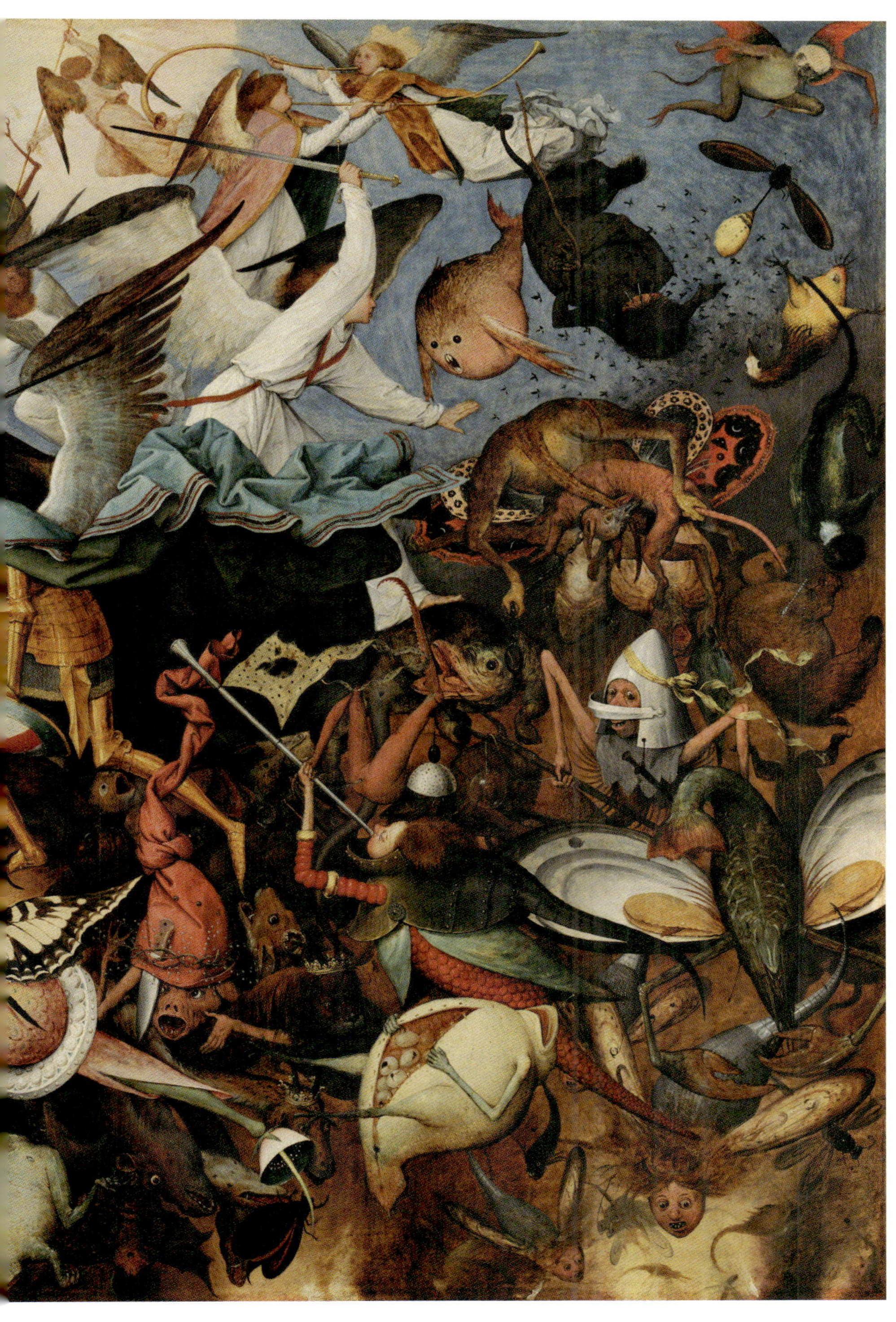

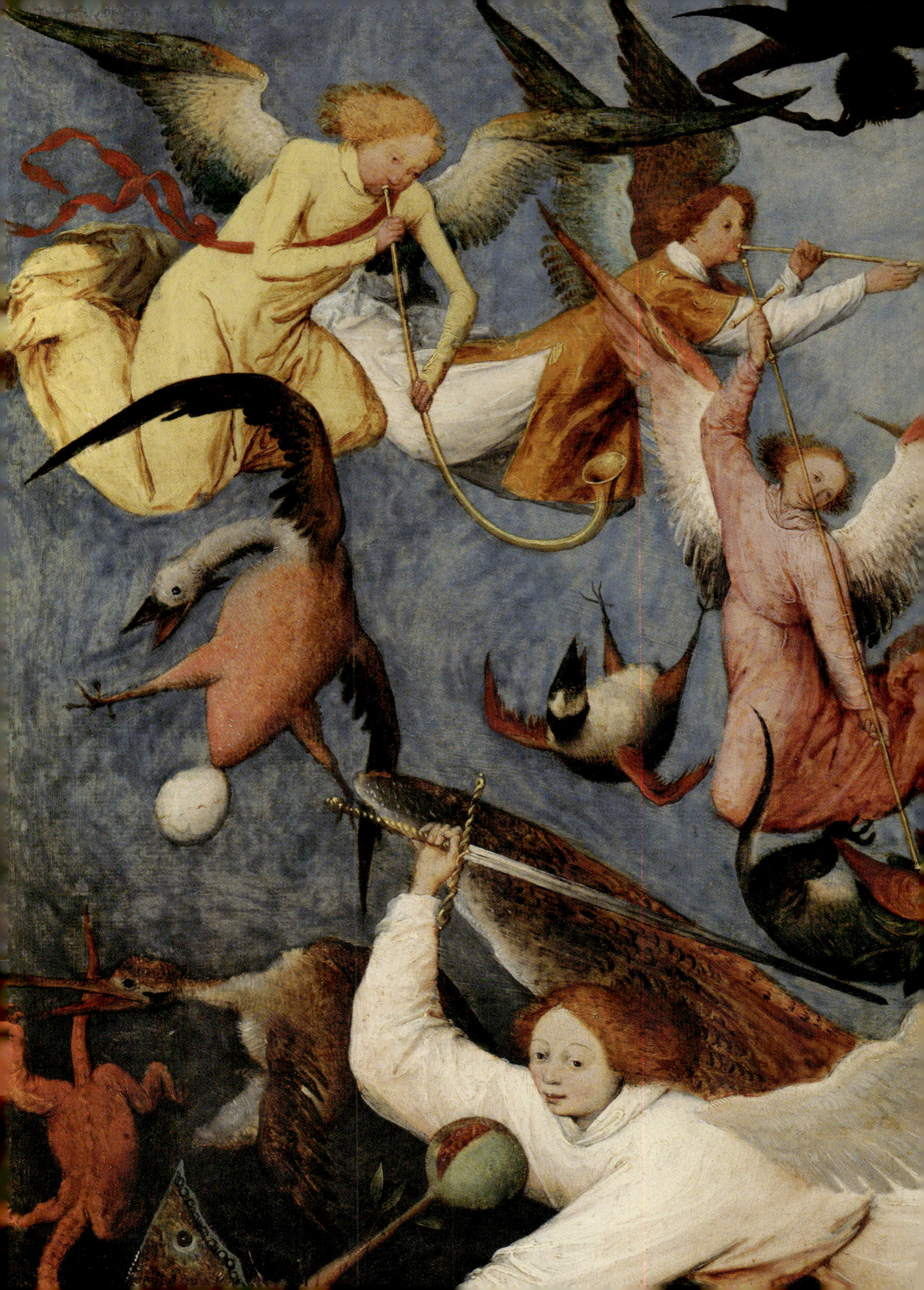

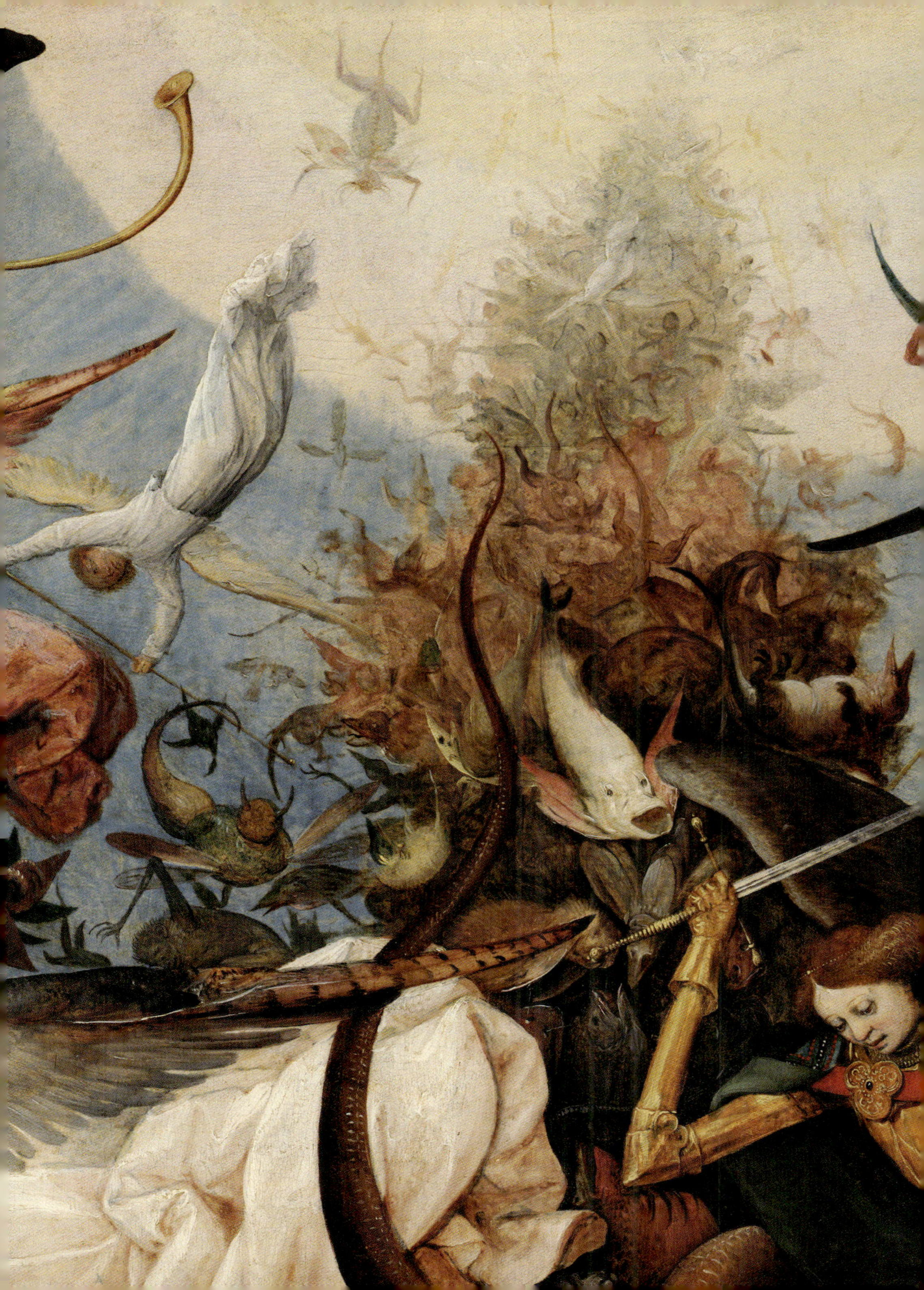

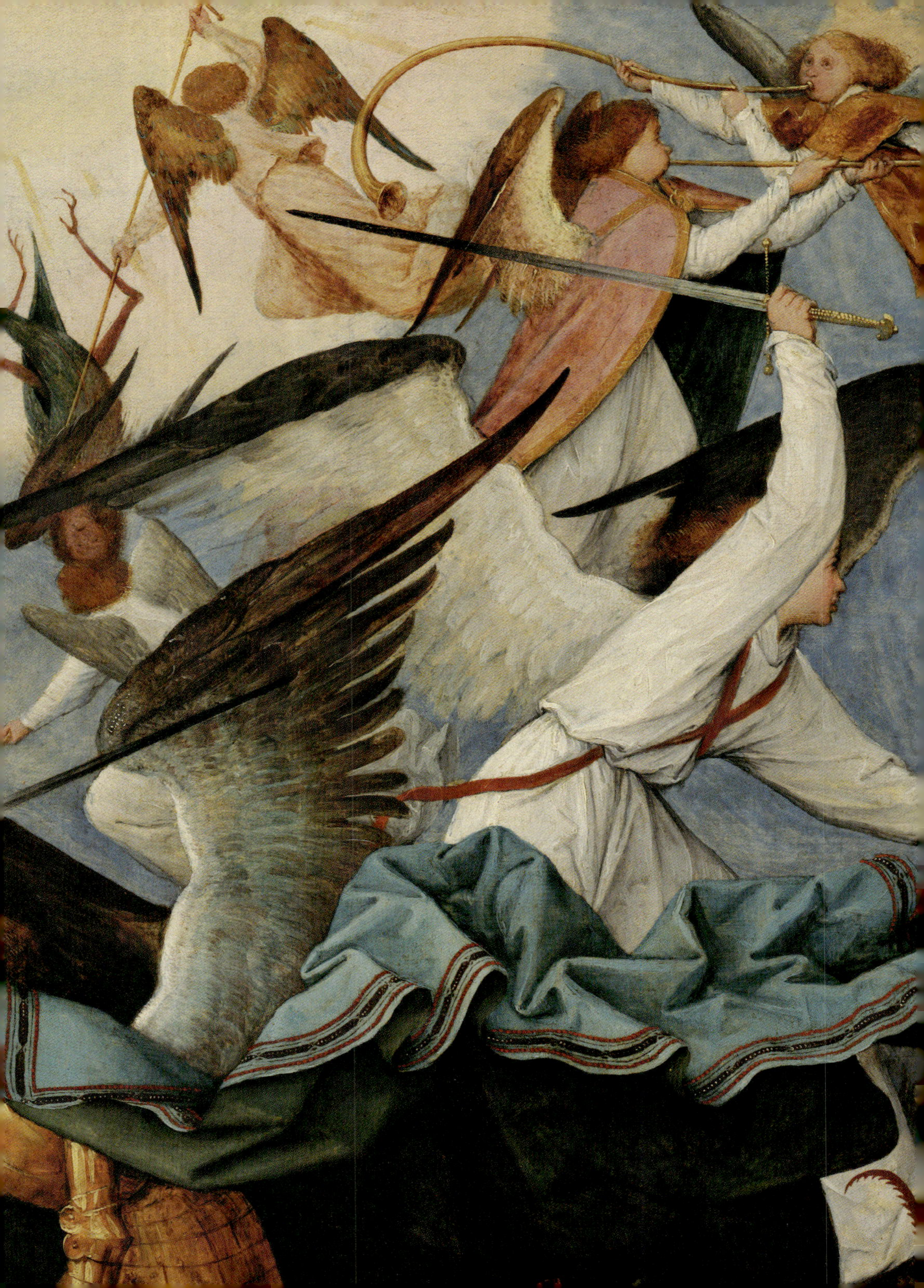

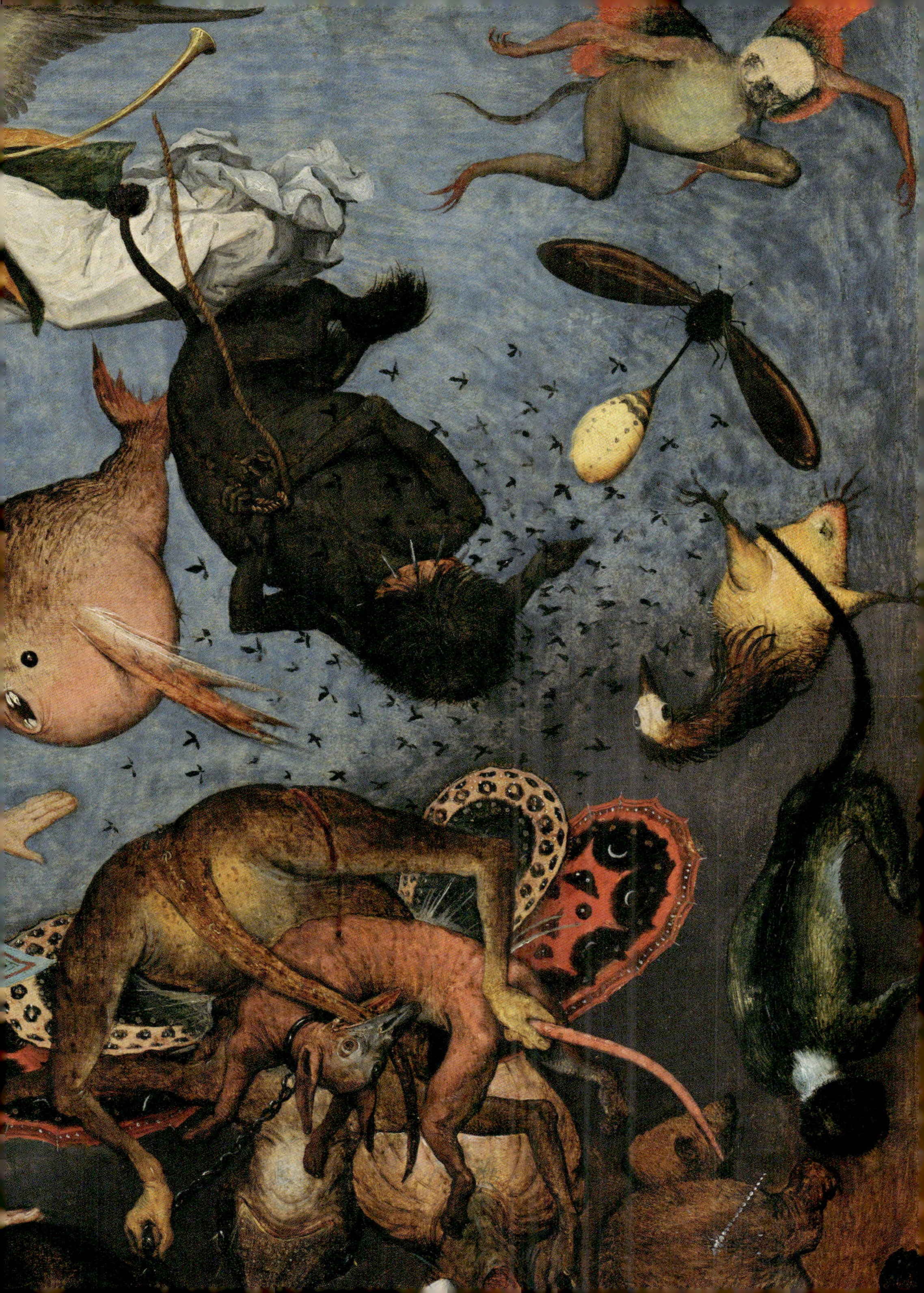

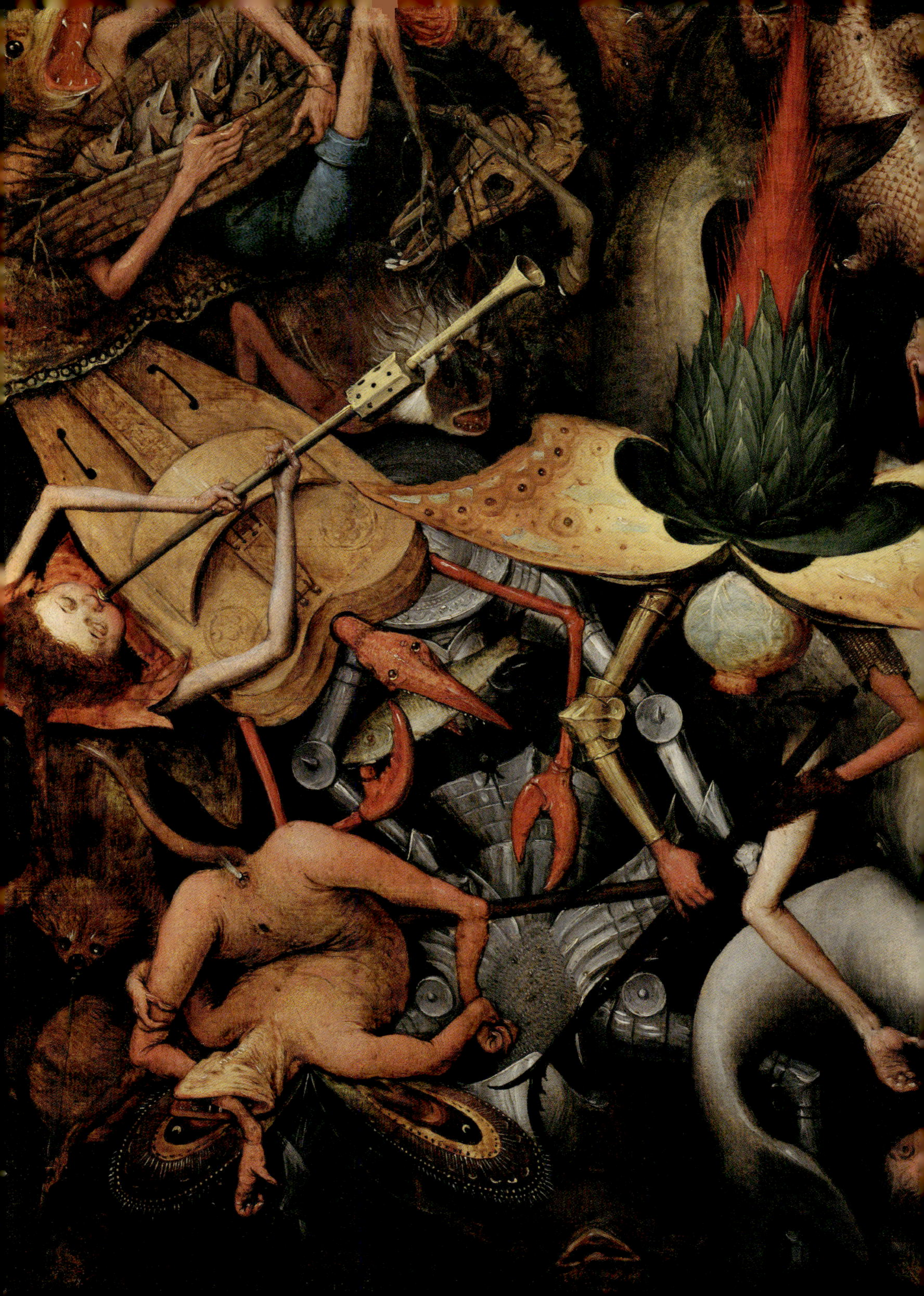

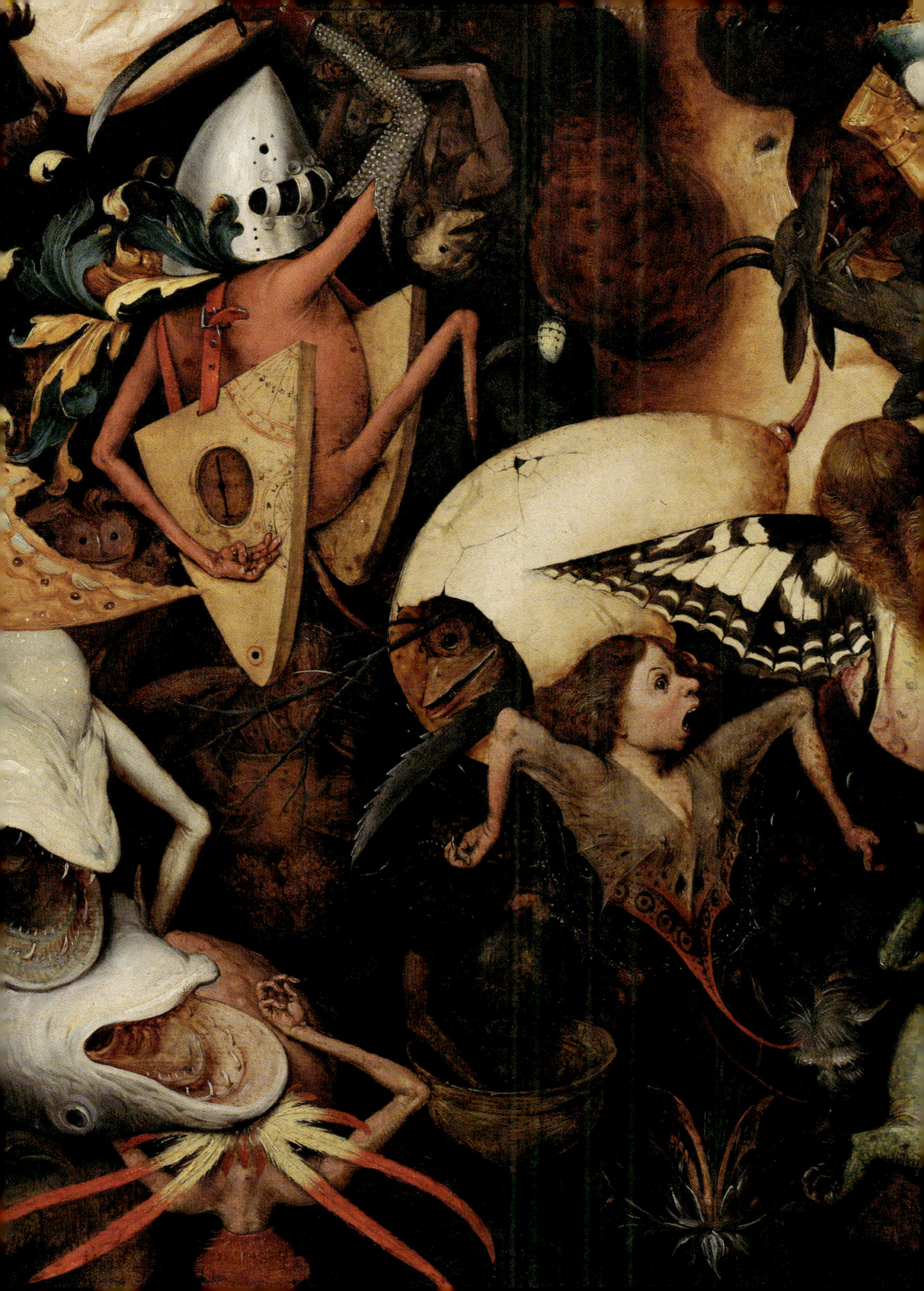

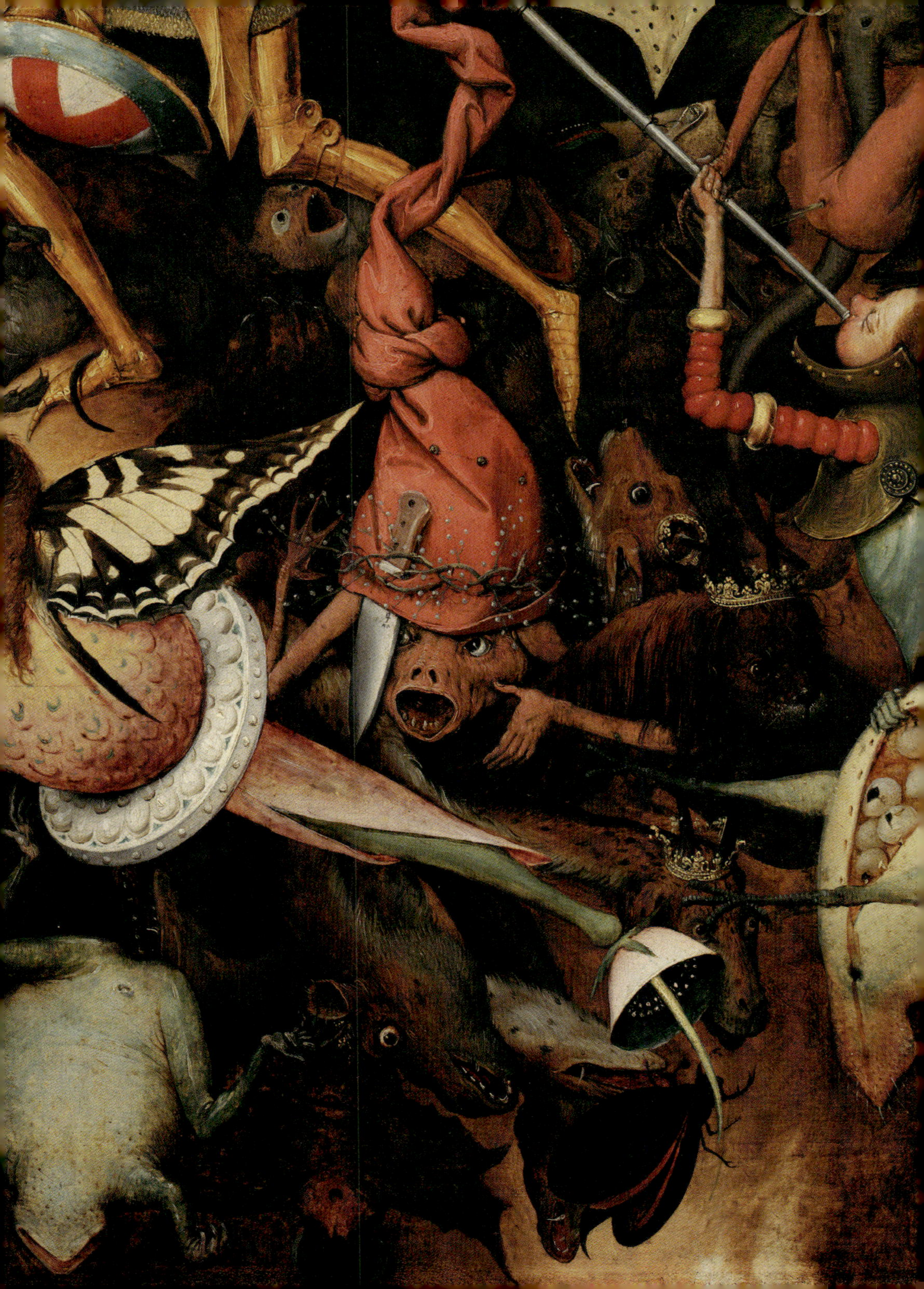

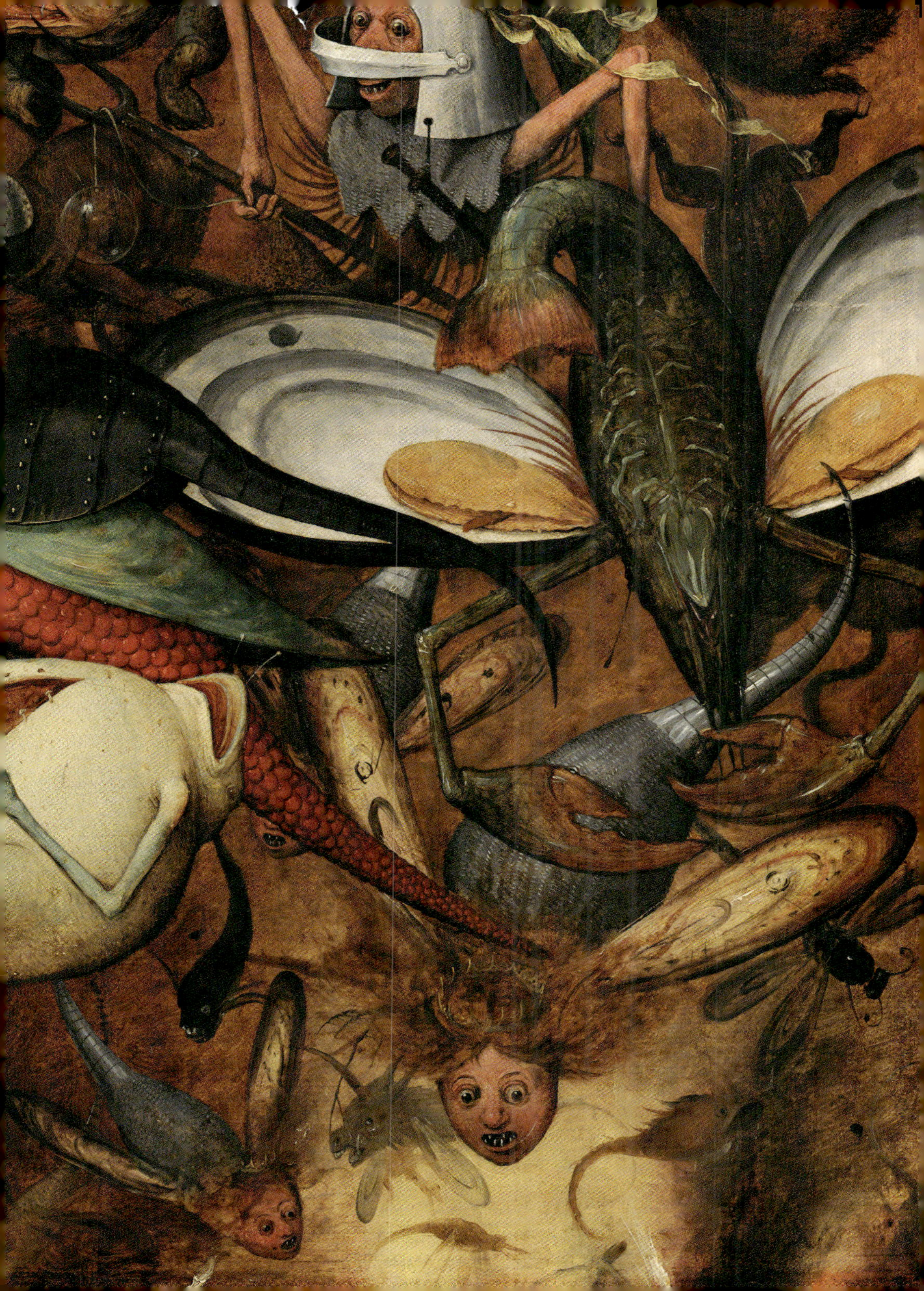

Another Apelles: The Grisailles

"*According to this, everything was better when we had fewer resources. This is because [today] we are worried about material value and not about the spirit.*"

— PLINY THE ELDER, AD 77–79

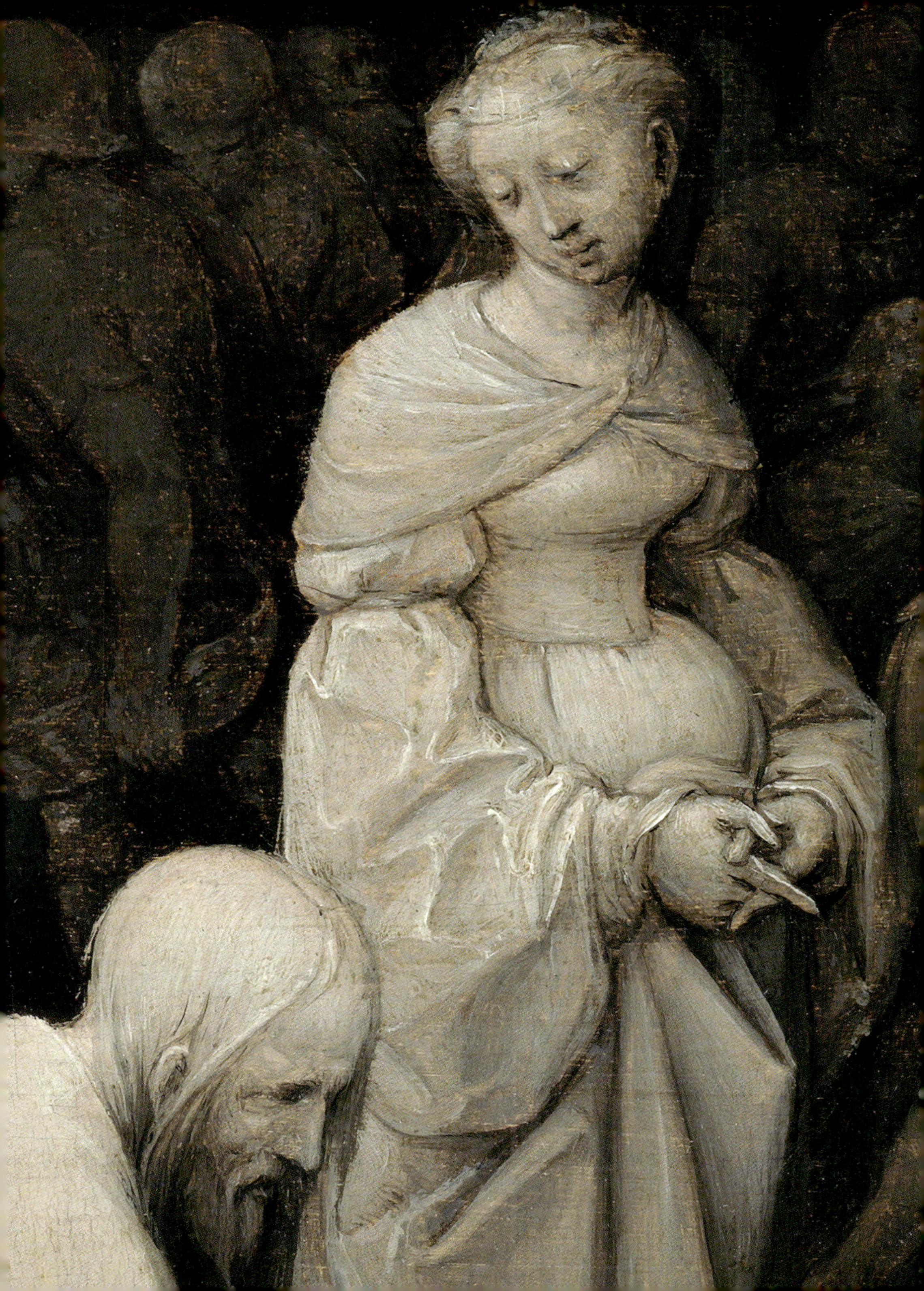

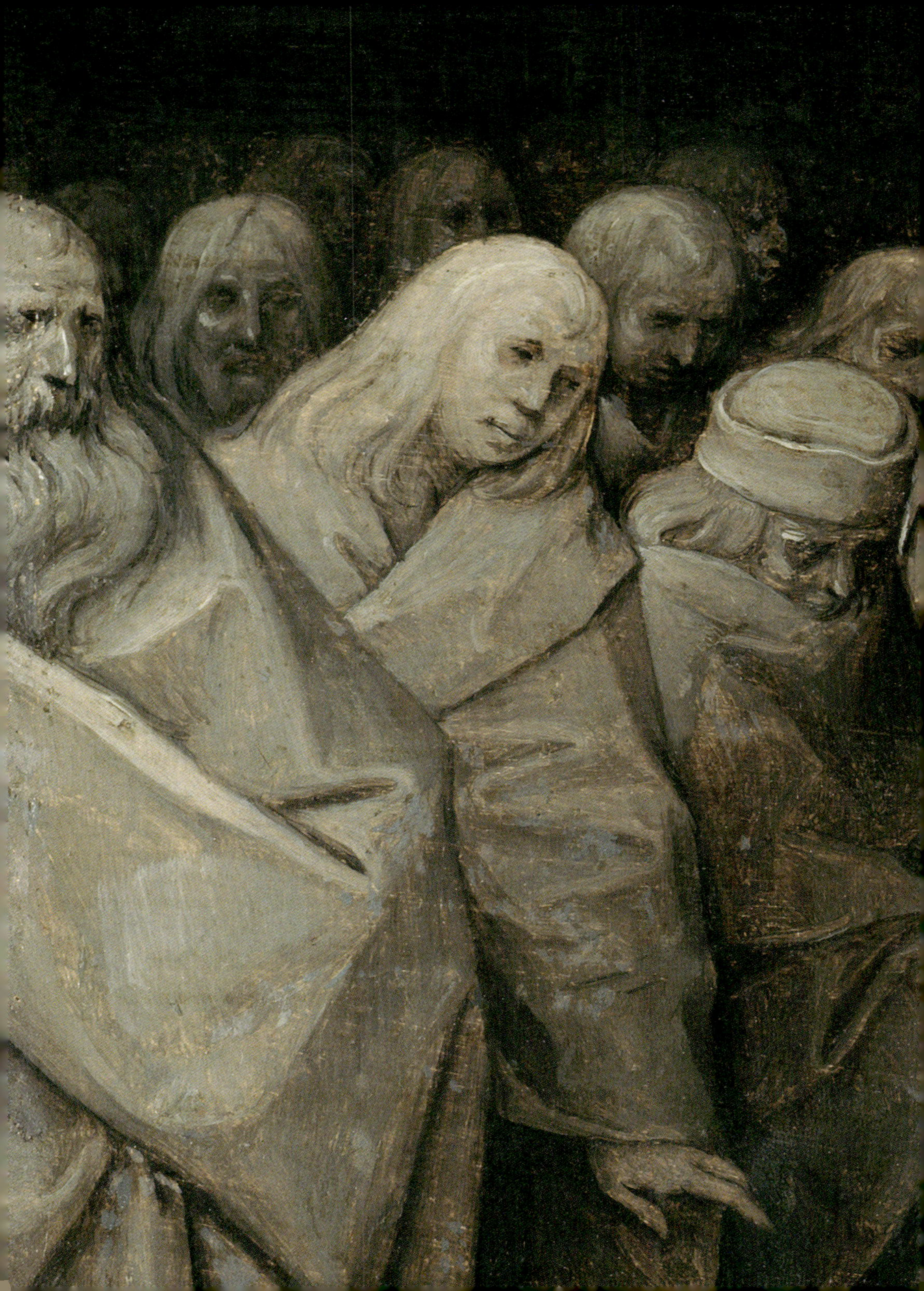

The defamer defamed

In 1565, a lampoon written by the poet and painter Lucas de Heere was published. It targeted an anonymous painter, but Pieter Bruegel the Elder was in all probability the intended subject of the satire. The latter is supposed to have ridiculed Frans Floris and slandered his pictures as "little sugary pictures".[131] So the rage and mockery of the poet are all too understandable; with his response, he wanted to reinstate the honour of his former teacher. He piles one new taunt on top of another in seven verses, denigrating the art of the slanderer. De Heere's invective shows the vehemence of the conflict embroiling Bruegel and the Romanists of his time – the name art-historical studies give to the artists of the period who based their work on the Italian High Renaissance. The poet attempts to weaken the invective of the metaphor "little sugary pictures" by praising what was previously criticised. Floris's works, we can read here, was in accord with classical "decorum" and were appropriately embellished and rich in ornament.

As is generally known, decorum was the organisational principle of classical art that requires the painter to use ornament in proportion to the worth of the object being represented. This procedure of appropriate embellishment was combined with the use of approved motifs by great exemplars of the Italian Renaissance. However, Bruegel seems to be putting this very principle in question with his criticism. This is why de Heere reproaches him in return by saying his figures are mere "folk fair puppets", and he objects that on his trip to Italy Bruegel had learned nothing, either of ancient or Italian art.

In order to rehabilitate himself, Bruegel draws on a classical theme in *The Calumny of Apelles* (pp. 224/225), as artists usually did in order to defend themselves against attacks from colleagues or unjust patrons.[132] The ancient author Lucian (*c*. AD 120–180) reports how Apelles (born 375/70 BC) created an allegorical painting in response to a calumny directed against him. He had been accused of having taken part in a political plot against his ruler, and he narrowly avoided a death sentence when one of the plotters exonerated him at the last minute. The theme of the *Calumny* was very popular during the Renaissance. Already in the fifteenth century, it was described as a standard *istoria* (the narrative of a painting), in particular by Leon Battista Alberti (1404–1472) in his treatise *Della pittura* (On Painting, 1435, 1439–1441).

Bruegel's design, drawn with pen and greyish-brown ink, bears, on the right, a signature and the date, 1565. The composition is remarkable for its frieze-like arrangement of the protagonists, allegorical figures actually named by the artist. Naked Truth sits at the

Pages 221, 222
Christ and the Woman Taken in Adultery (details), 1565
(see ill. pp. 242/243)

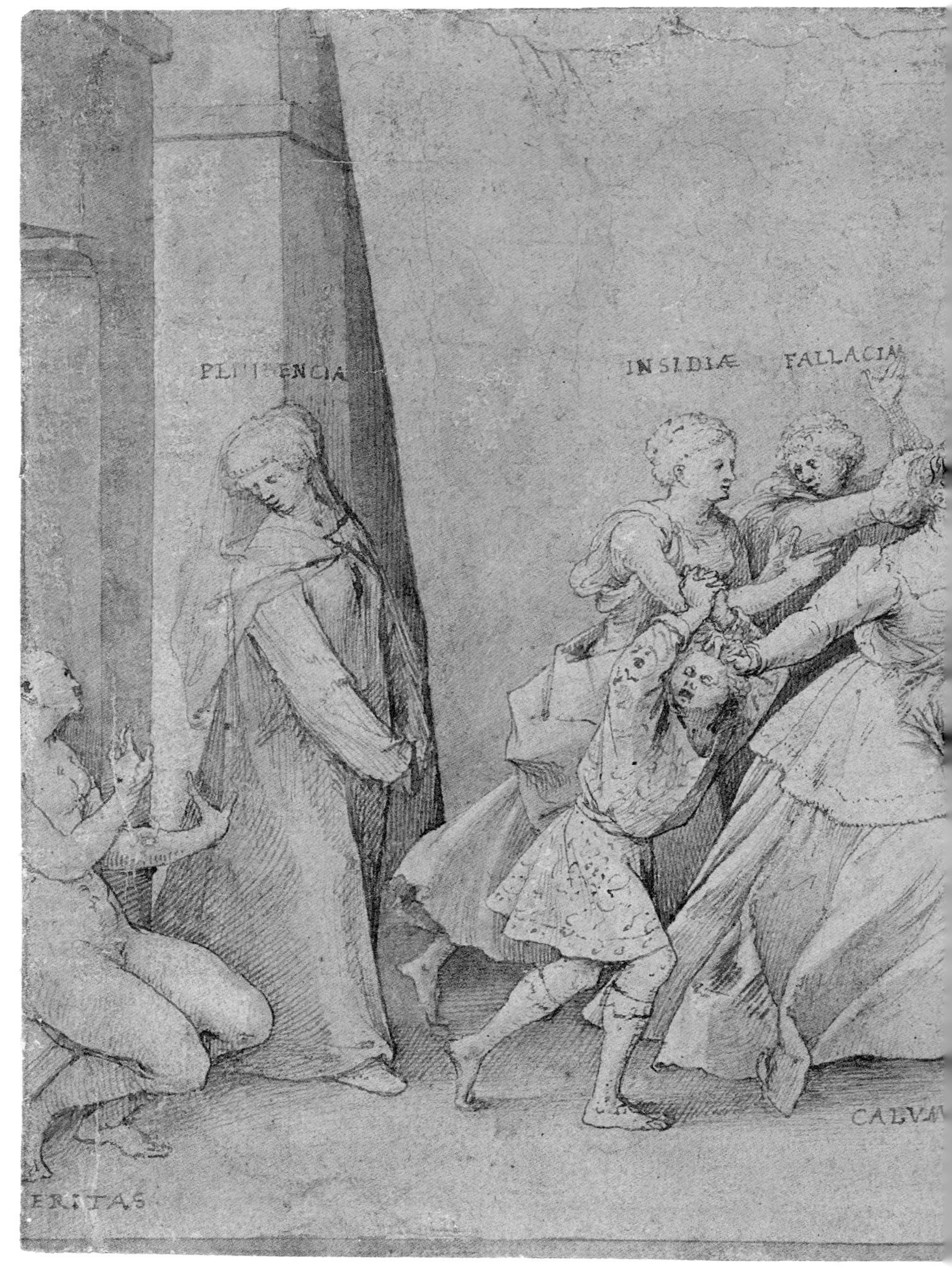
PLENENCIA
INSIDIÆ   FALLACIA
CALVM
ERITAS

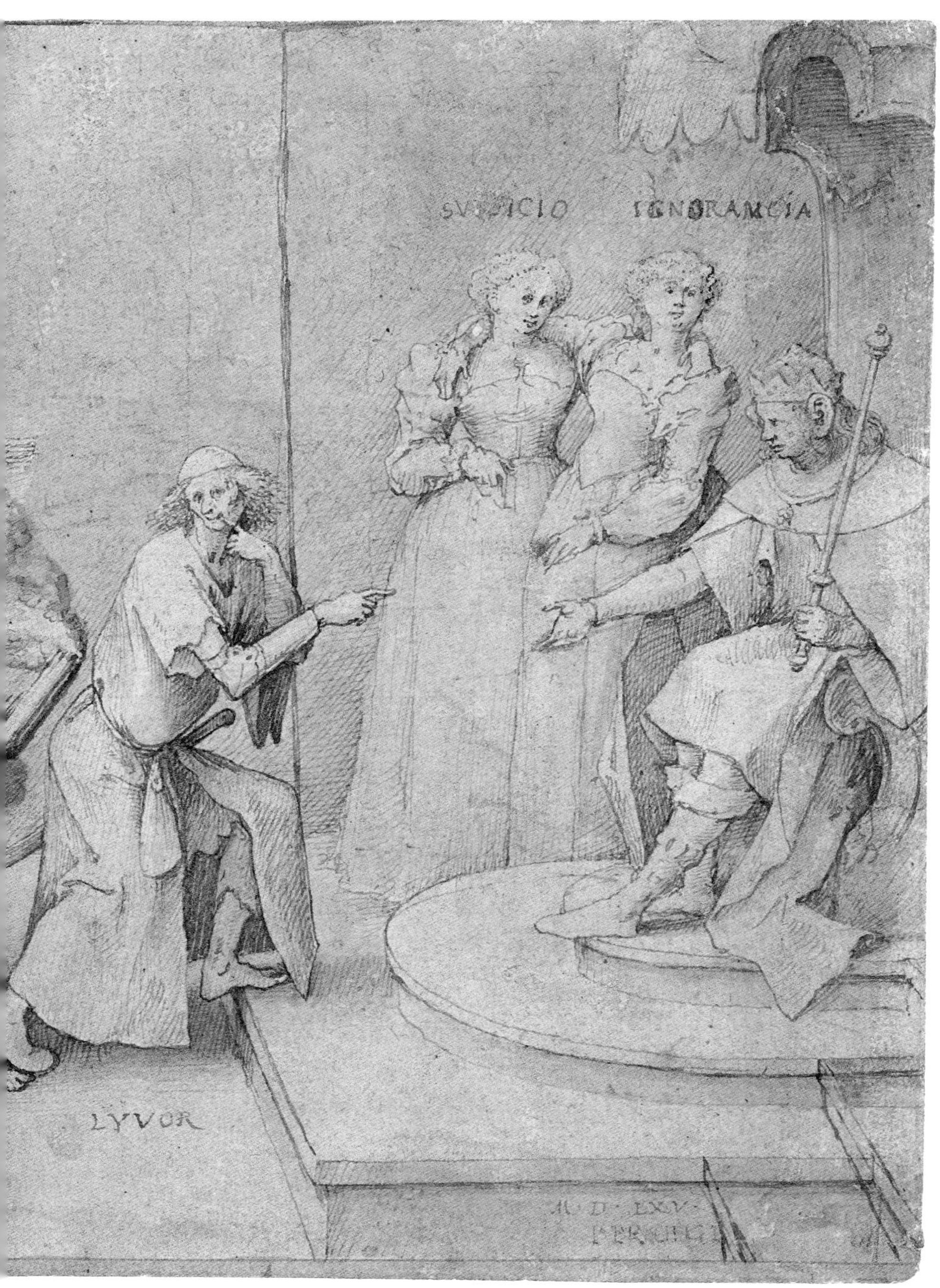

SVSPICIO
IGNORAMCIA
LYVOR
M·D·LXV
PERGIT

left edge, while on the opposite side the ass-eared king has taken his place, false advisors at his side. Bruegel composes his drawing with a spot of irony. He does not, for instance, identify himself with the victim of the calumny, represented as a child, but portrays himself as an inane slanderer with painter's cap, who awkwardly puts his hand on his mouth as though unaware of what he is supposed to have done. The portrayal of Calumnia, the actual slanderer, is especially successful; the artist harks back to ancient models and illustrates her rage as described by the ancient satirist Lucian.

In this way, Bruegel makes a mockery of the quarrel, but at the same time parades his precise knowledge of humanist literature and ancient art. The literature has informed us that the collector Jonghelinck owned panels by Bruegel as well as by Floris and that the rivalry between the two artists became increasingly vehement from the 1560s.[133] Both the lampoon and the *Calumnia* drawing can thus be seen as part of the competition over the patron's favour.

Bruegel characterised himself in a self-ironic way not only in this special case, but in general, as is demonstrated in his drawing *Painter and Buyer* (p. 227), also dated to around 1565. We see painter and "connoisseur" as half-figures in close-up.[134] The painter, with his attributes of cap and brush, is portrayed as grumpy and cantankerous, the buyer marked as short-sighted by his spectacles.[135] Both are staring at an unfinished picture outside the drawing. Although it's not finished, the tight-lipped buyer is holding his purse at the ready to buy it. It is instructive to see that the artist has turned his back to the man, or, more pointedly, is giving him the cold shoulder. Here, too, we are dealing less with a realistic portrait and far more a tongue-in-cheek, staged role play, in which the artist seems to be insisting on his autonomy, while the collector is portrayed as all too impatient.

The Calumny of Apelles is not the only drawing that might have resulted from Bruegel's conflict with the poet de Heere. It is probable that his series of grisaille paintings from around and after 1565 is linked to these accusations, and that he wanted to use these works to deliver a rebuff to the Romanist convictions relating to art history. Bruegel exposes the criticism against him as unjustified by demonstrating his knowledge of Italian models, but at the same time by questioning the canon of the models involved in the dispute. From Bruegel's point of view, the Flemish artists designated as Romanists also represent a very limited perspective, as they ceaselessly oriented themselves on the same works by

Pages 224/225
The Calumny of Apelles, *c.* 1565
Pen and greyish-brown ink, wash, partly worked over by another hand and heightened with white,
20.3 x 30.6 cm (7 ⅞ x 12 ⅛ in.). London, The British Museum, Department of Prints and Drawings

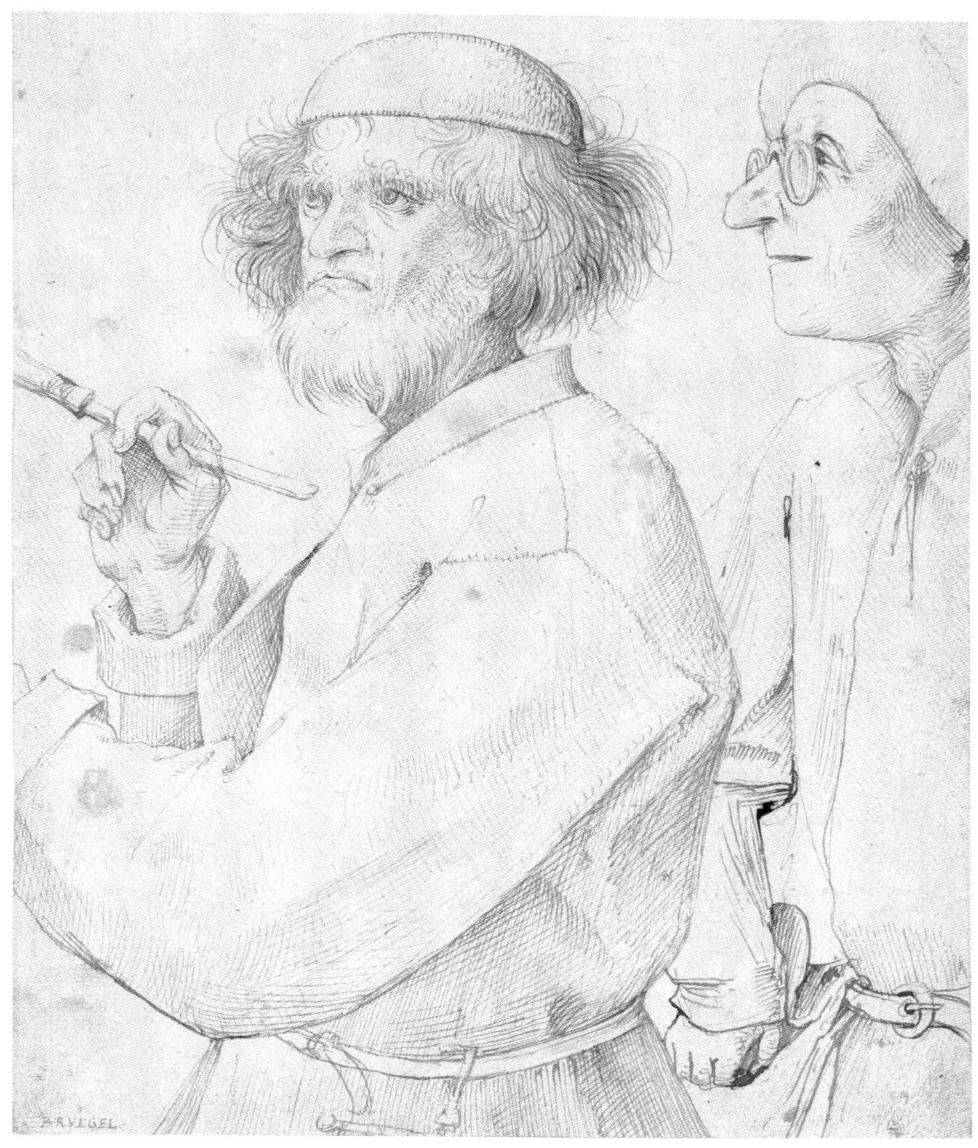

Painter and Buyer, *c.* 1565
Pen and greyish-brown ink, 25.5 x 21.5 cm (10 ⅛ x 8 ½ in.)
Vienna, Albertina

Christ and the Woman Taken in Adultery (detail), 1565
(see ill. pp. 242/243)

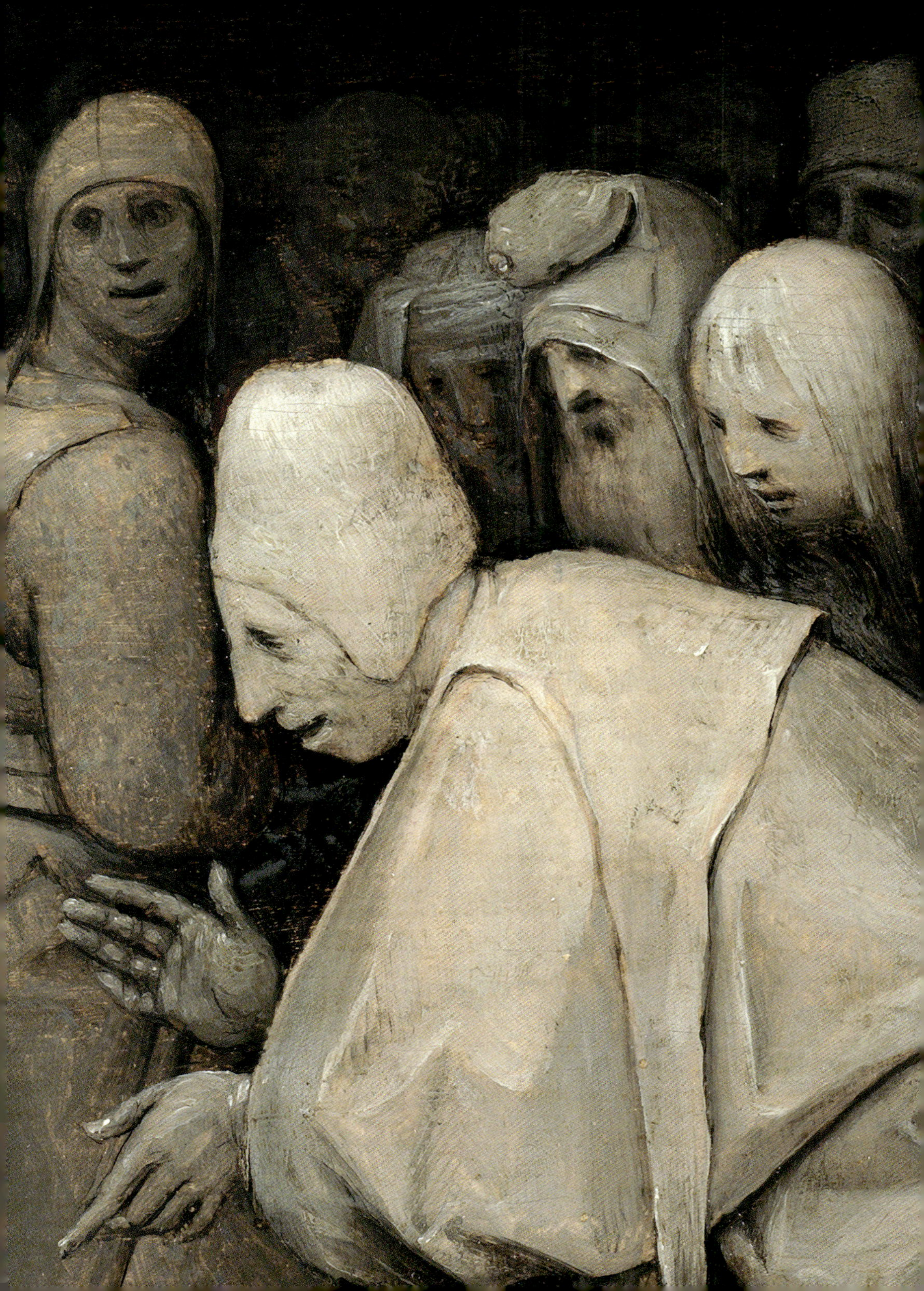

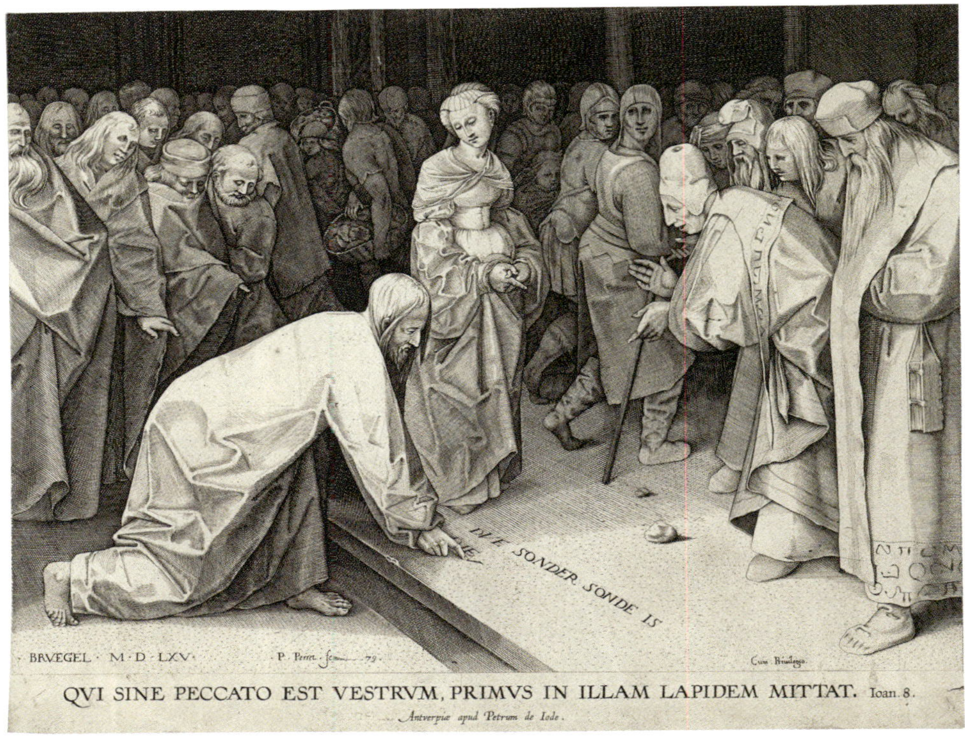

Pieter Perret after Pieter Bruegel the Elder, **Christ and the Woman Taken in Adultery**, 1579
Copper engraving, 26,5 x 34 cm (10 ⅜ x 13 ⅜ in.). Amsterdam, Rijksmuseum, Rijksprentenkabinet

Raphael and Michelangelo or harked back to the famous sculptures of classical antiquity in Rome. It is always the aforementioned ideological canon that the Romanists' pictures unquestioningly reproduced.

The first stone

All of Bruegel's grisaille paintings have a small format and are conceived as extreme chiaroscuro painting, even as night pieces with artificial light. *Christ and the Woman Taken in Adultery* measures little more than 24 x 34 cm (9 ½ x 13 ½ in.; pp. 242/243, Cat. 24). It is signed in the bottom left corner and dated 1565. The small panel was long thought lost and turned up only in 1952. However, Pieter Perret (*c.* 1555–1625) already produced an engraving after Bruegel's composition, which rather precisely reproduces the stock of motifs (p. 230). According to the will of Bruegel's son Jan, the picture was apparently bequeathed to Federico Borromeo (1564–1631), Bishop of Milan, which implies that the panel remained in Pieter's ownership until his death and was then inherited by his son. If this supposition is correct, the father must have held the picture in high esteem, otherwise he would have sold it.[136]

When comparing the grisaille with Perret's engraved copy, we are immediately struck by the dominant artistic characteristic of the former. Firstly, in contrast to the engraving, the smooth transition from light to dark is particularly well rendered here. Secondly, it is virtually a privilege of this technique to capture darkness as a painterly achievement. Our eye compacts the dark areas and tends to anticipate that figures will soon have vanished in the darkness. The grisailles not only depict the present scene, but also its disappearance. It represents an aesthetic of transition.

Bruegel's composition is clearly structured. The standing adulteress sets up an unambiguous emphasis of the vertical central axis. Moreover, the picture shows an isocephalic arrangement, i. e., the heads of those standing around are all at the same level. The young woman seems somewhat statuesque in the midst of the semicircle of men. She is extremely attractive and fitted out with a cloak and waisted dress. This marks her out as a woman of the upper classes. She has inclined her head graciously to the side and is looking at the head of the Saviour (p. 221).

However, the dominant aesthetic vehicle of expression is the dramatic lighting, which gives the picture its effect. Christ is immersed in dazzling side light, making the transition from his robe to his hair seem invisible and dissolving the inside contours of his body. This is conceived as empty space and silhouette, the exact shape of his body no more than intimated. The Redeemer is stylised here as a cipher, and among all Bruegel's pictures this close-up portrayal of Jesus is a rare exception. Meanwhile, the adulteress, with her head inclined, appears humble and, despite her fault, blameless. Bruegel has been influenced in her portrayal by Raphael's Madonnas, as scholarship has frequently pointed out.[137] This relationship to Raphael is particularly evident in the graceful posture of the female figure, but also in the great clarity of the composition. Bruegel managed to render the figures in the background in such a way they are almost entirely swallowed up by darkness, thus creating a gripping pictorial narrative with only few motifs. He was obviously endeavouring to establish a clear opposition. The apostle with the long beard is standing opposite the rabbi at the far right, just as St John directly next to him corresponds to the young man with the long hair who is leaning forwards. Meanwhile, Christ, shown in profile and kneeling, finds, to an equal degree, correspondence and also contrasts in the figure of the gesticulating rabbi. The latter has simultaneously raised his right hand while he points to the Redeemer writing on the ground.

On the left, we can make out the apostles of Christ, the beardless John standing out in particular among them (p. 222). On the right, we see rabbinic scribes and scholars, two of them identified through Hebrew-like script on their long garments. The venerable,

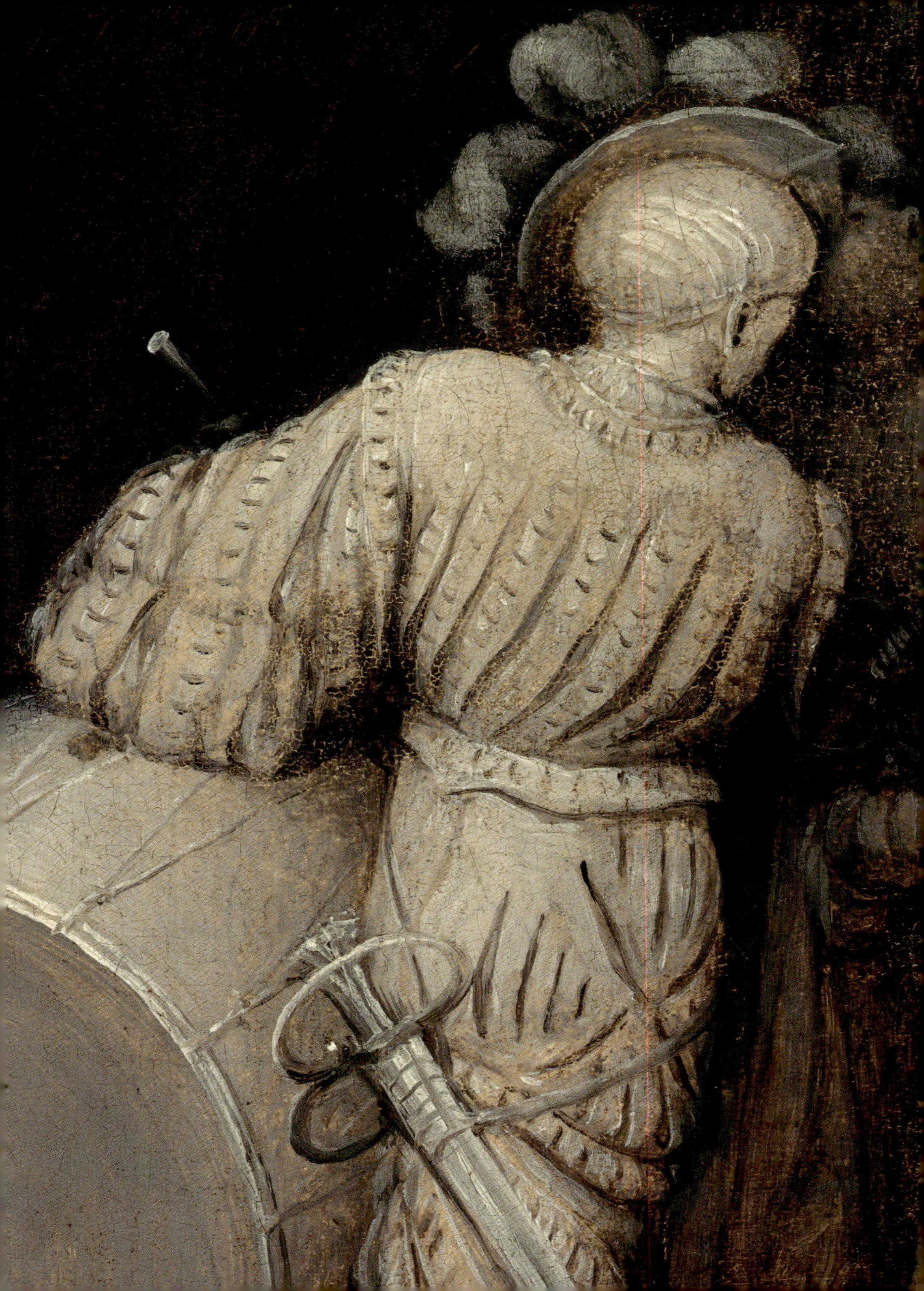

bearded rabbi on the right wears a girdle with a clearly visible girdle book set with locks. He has folded his arms, as though thinking over the sentence Christ has begun. For on the ground we read "Let him who is without sin…"; the sentence breaks off here, but observers will no doubt complete the second half of the sentence for themselves, "… cast the first stone".

We see such a stone on the ground in front of the second rabbi, and the outstretched finger of the adulteress also points in this direction. This unfinished sentence enables Bruegel to shorten the time being represented in the picture. Or, better: we see an action that is about to happen. In linguistic terms, it takes place in a continuous or progressive tense. Bruegel succeeds in dramatising the event. Who will dare to pick up the stone and throw

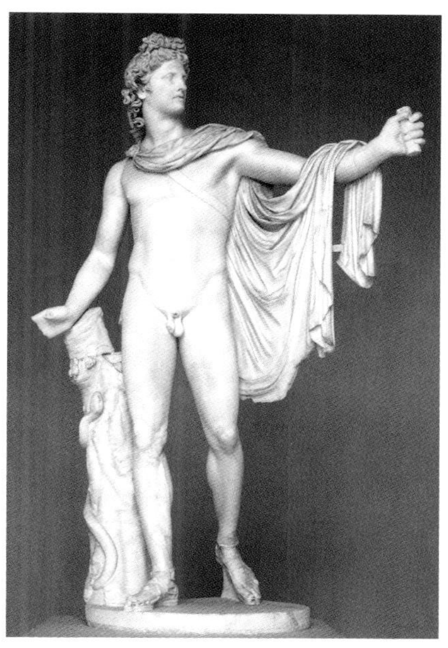

it at the adulteress? It's not yet decided! The light also enables the painter to intensify the dramatic moment – which we perceive as observers – generated by the persons passing by unawares in the middle ground. To be precise, Bruegel manages to make time lapse in the foreground while he makes it pass in the background. To the right of the standing adulteress, the people who are looking round as they pass by are turned into significant figures. While the man on the left of the two seems to be looking at Christ writing on the ground, the man on the right has evidently realised how beautiful the young woman is and is now staring blatantly in her direction. His mouth is agape, graphically expressing his intentions, and thus Bruegel portrays the kind of sinful man who is in no way qualified to throw a stone.

The technique chosen by Bruegel is linked to a specific significance. Erwin Panofsky saw a clue elucidating the contest, the paragone, between sculpture and painting north of the Alps in the painted stone sculptures of Early Netherlandish painting, for instance by Jan van Eyck. The originally liturgically motivated colourlessness of the outside wings of

The Three Soldiers (detail), 1568
(see ill. pp. 244/245)

Anonymous, **Apollo Belvedere**, *c.* 330–320 BC.
Marble, 224 cm (88 ¼ in.) tall. Rome, Musei Vaticani

altars in this context becomes the "touchstone of painting" and acts as a challenge to the painter to surpass the sculptor without the advantage of a wide-ranging palette of colours.

Art-historical studies have pointed to the ancient author Pliny the Elder (AD 23/24–79) in connection with this reduced palette.[138] In the 35th book of his *Natural History*, he writes: "Thus to contemplate all these numbers and great variety of colours prompts us to marvel at former generations. Four colours only were used by the illustrious painters Apelles, Action, Melanthius and Nicomachus to execute their immortal works […] although their pictures each sold for the wealth of a whole town […] Everything in fact was superior in the days when resources were scantier. [139] Thus Pliny concludes his list by commenting that the spiritual and intellectual value of art is not to be confused with the material being used.

The dual line of tradition in grisaille painting mentioned here seems significant for Bruegel because he is indeed capable of connecting supposed opposites. Hence he in no way plays one tradition off against the other, but lets both take the stage. He links the famed tradition of an Apelles with that of Jan van Eyck and Hieronymus Bosch, who was also skilled in exploiting this technique. In terms of art theory, chiaroscuro painting also appears in another light. We might recall Quintillian's (AD *c.* 35–*c.* 96) praise of Zeuxis, who was said to have been the first to have invented "the system of light and shade".[140] It now seems very appropriate to point out the extreme contour in the work, seen in the line of the Saviour's head and back, which stands out strikingly from the dark background. Should we wish to draw on another art-historical source, we might consider Pliny's comment that "Parrhasios won the palm in the drawing of outlines."[141]

In the theory of art, Bruegel aspires towards a system of opposites. But what does the small panel stand for in content? Does it also contain a heterodox message? Why did it mean so much for Bruegel that he didn't want to part with it? If we wish to make a general characterisation of the iconography of *The Woman Taken in Adultery*, his theme takes on a central and equally exemplary role in terms of Christian tradition. Jesus, the renewing force, is confronted with the old religion. Namely, Christ shows how his orthodoxy is weighted on the side of mercy. The Pharisees, however, do not soften and want to stone the woman. In contrast, Christ demands remorse from the adulteress in order to include her as one of his followers again.

But this subject is not only about the theme of sin and forgiveness; far more, the iconography of Christ and the adulteress lets the painter hold a mirror up to the believer.[142] No one may presume to be self-righteous. This narrative is valid for the viewer's own day. It is acted out not in the past, but in the present. *You* are meant! It seems to be pleading: this is all happening here and now, because we are directly drawn into the events depicted through the semicircle opening up to the front. Now, before our very eyes, Christ's incomplete sentence and the stone lying at the ready seem to confront each other.

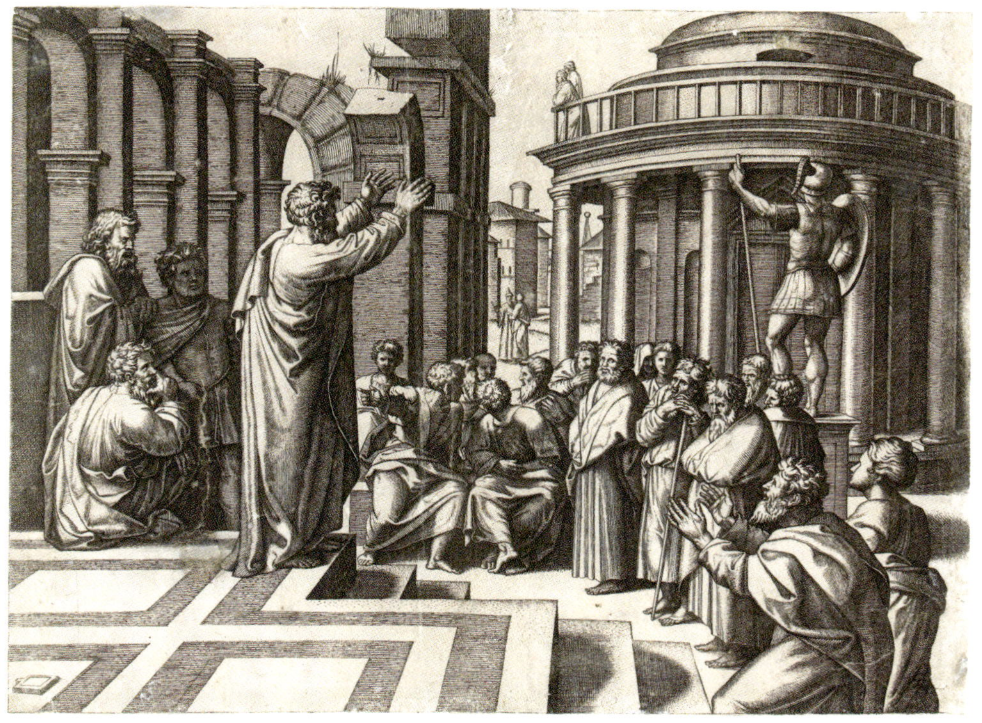

Marcantonio Raimondi after Raphael, **St Paul Preaching at Athens**, *c.* 1520
Copper engraving, 26.4 x 35.1 cm (10 ⅜ x 13 ⅞ in.)
Amsterdam, Rijksmuseum, Rijksprentenkabinet

We have to decide. We see ourselves manoeuvred into the same axis as the adulteress. The addition of the writing moreover proves that it is to be read neither by the apostles, nor by the rabbis. It is directed far more at the viewer. To do this, the painter invents a convincing metaphor for time. With Christ depicted in the act of writing, we find ourselves in precisely that moment before his incomplete sentence is finished off with the words "cast the first stone".

Just as Bruegel is capable of alluding to the ancient four-colour painting of an Apelles and to the Early Netherlandish tradition, so his references to the iconographic tradition are diverse. Fritz Grossmann already determined how much the compact cohesion of the composition is achieved through the contrapposto of the central figure of the adulteress linking the two halves of the picture.[143] No other Flemish artist of that time had a deeper understanding of Raphael's compositional principles. The grisaille most closely resembles a picture by his teacher Pieter Coecke van Aelst, who prior to Bruegel strove after a similar spatial solution and contrasted the tranquil centre, with Christ writing on the ground, with fleeing Pharisees.[144]

The borrowing from Raphael, however, is far more palpable than hitherto recognised. For his portrayal of the contemplating rabbi on the right edge, his hands concealed under his robe, Bruegel combined two figures from Raphael's *St Paul Preaching to the Athenians* into one motif. His sources would have been known to him from the engraving by Marcantonio Raimondi (*c.* 1475–*c.* 1534) after Raphael, dated to around 1520 (p. 235). Among the Athenians, we can see two bearded men who are conspicuously concealing their arms. Both the gestures of the hands concealed under a cloak of the one and the contemplative downward glance of the other have been used by the Flemish artist for his composition.

Yet there is more; another source becomes apparent when observing Christ's posture. We may think in this context of the Saviour falling under the burden of the Cross, as we know the motif from the *Carrying of the Cross* pictures by Hieronymus Bosch. The flat, stencil-like configuration also recalls the works of the great predecessor. Besides Bosch's *Carrying of the Cross* pictures in Madrid and Vienna, we might mention the fallen Christ in an outside panel – also executed in grisaille technique – of *The Temptation of St Anthony* in Lisbon, which shows Christ being taken prisoner (p. 237). Now, however, we have a diagnosis as curious as it is interesting, for while the female figure of the adulteress and that of the rabbi at the right remind us of Raphael, the kneeling Christ resonates with Bosch's works.

A similar element applies to formal principles of composition. While the dialectic form of composition resembles the art of the Italian High Renaissance, which sought to combine significance and vitality, we might on the other hand see the formal problem of increasing darkness inherent in the grisaille as stemming from the art of Bosch. And while the figure of the rabbi standing in clear opposition to Christ reminds us of a Pharisee in Bosch's *Ecce Homo* in Frankfurt, at the same time the key figure of the soldier looking around and striding forward would be inconceivable without Raphael.

In modern terms, Bruegel delivers a "style mix". It must be clear by now that the Flemish artist is formulating an art-historical statement here, that he defines his practice of *imitatio* as a synthesis of various models. In doing so, he is making a plea for a synthesis of examples that are extremely far removed from each other: even if the difference between the two artists could scarcely be greater, Bosch and Raphael are cited to the same extent. During the first half of the sixteenth century, the issue of the *imitatio artis*, the imitation of artistic models, was a matter of controversy.[145] In his practice, Bruegel follows the advice of Erasmus, who in his *Ciceronianus* recommends artists to orient themselves on several models at the same time.

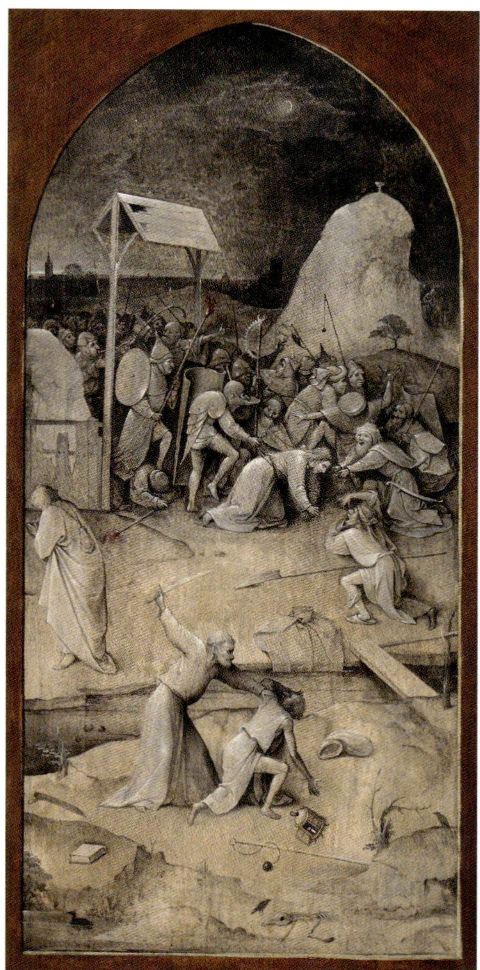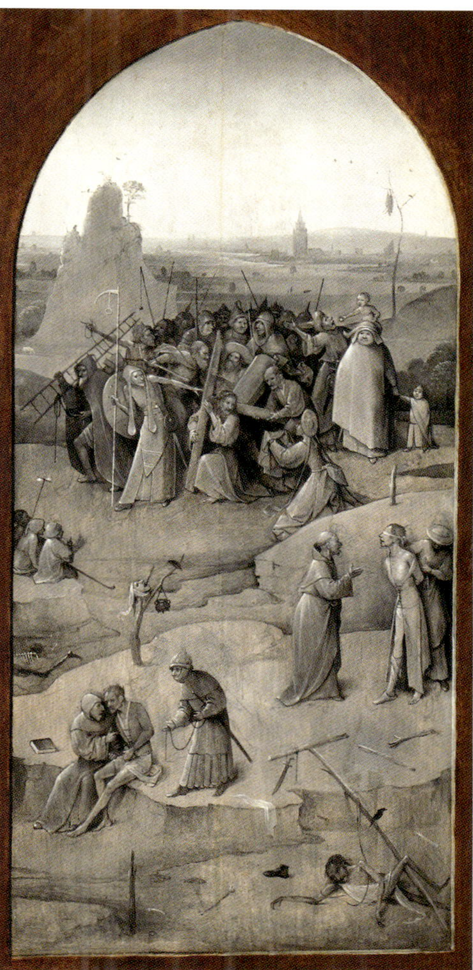

Hieronymus Bosch
Christ Taken Prisoner
(left outer panel of **The Temptation of St Anthony**), 1505/06

Christ Carrying the Cross
(right outer panel of **The Temptation of St Anthony**), 1505/06

Grisaille, oil on oak, 131.5 x 53 cm (51 ¾ x 20 ⅞ in.)
Lisbon, Museu Nacional de Arte Antiga

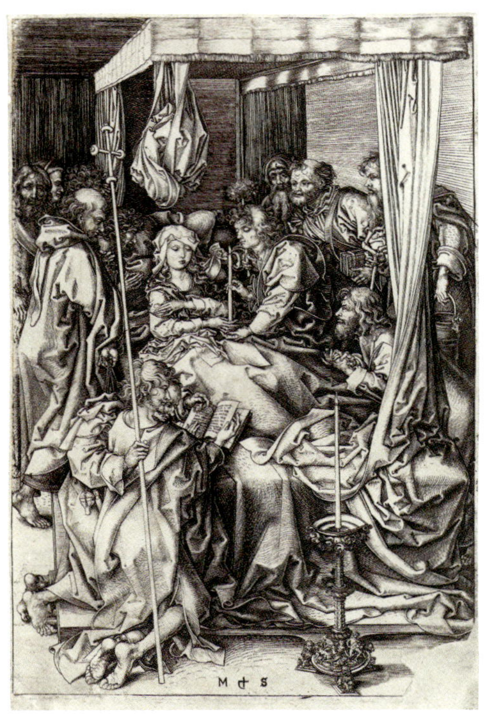

Graceful warriors

Dating from 1568, *The Three Soldiers* (pp. 244/245, Cat. 39) also shows that the artist was familiar with the stylistic idiom of the Romanists. Bruegel again uses the grisaille technique for this panel in cabinet form. This enables him, despite the small size of the picture, to lend a specific monumentality to the figures; his interpretation endows them a statuesque quality. It is virtually an illustration of Pliny's statement that the quality of a work of art has to do neither with the material used nor its dimensions. The panel shows two landsknecht (mercenary soldiers) making music and gracefully moving forwards, while a third soldier holds high a large flag.[146] The panel's theme is aligned to North-European traditions. We owe to such artists as Albrecht Dürer and Lucas van Leyden (1494–1533) engravings that portray these types of early modern mercenaries in self-confident national pose, without connoting any negative values.

For the foreground subjects, Bruegel uses two famous models: the drummer at the left harks back to the ancient sculpture *Apollo Belvedere* (p. 233), and the flautist with an elegant pose to Raphael's *Galatea*. The standard bearer, on the other hand, seems to rely on North-European models, so that here we have ancient, Italian and Flemish art juxtaposed on one panel. Bruegel is here pleading yet again for a plurality of styles, and censures those art theorists who wanted to see only a continual repetition of the same works of Raphael or Michelangelo. He also commingles a typical North European theme with a compositional technique that endeavours to recreate the elegance and grace of Italy.

Meanwhile, he works effectively with the contrast of light and dark. While the figures in the foreground are standing in bright side light and thus seem sculpturally modelled,

Martin Schongauer, **Dormition of the Virgin**, 1470–1474
Copper engraving, 26.5 x 17.1 cm (10 ⅜ x 6 ¾ in.)
Amsterdam, Rijksmuseum, Rijksprentenkabinet

the figure in the background is rendered schematically. Grisaille is deemed to be capable both of making an art-theoretical statement, and of producing a technical showpiece. The transition shown in the light setting is an optical phenomenon that is particularly difficult to capture.

Furthermore, in this context Bruegel plays with the various appearances of planar surface and line. While the outline in the foreground is more dominant owing to the contrast of light and dark, in the background we see softer transitions. Even the white tones can take over the role of an outline. Bruegel was evidently endeavouring to compose nothing less than a classical picture in which he does justice to all the creative means at his disposal.

Thus his signature appears here in a particularly noble and humanist idiom. If we think back again to de Heere's mocking lampoon, this work clearly shows how Bruegel wanted to refute the charges brought against him. He shows off his virtuosity in quoting Italian and ancient models and at the same time demonstrates his consummate skill in integrating these in a new context.

St John's dream

Ultimately, Bruegel's *The Death of the Virgin* (pp. 246/247, Cat. 16) can also be seen as a kind of game in which he plays with the conventions of art theory. This Christian motif has a long tradition, especially in North-European painting, going back to artists like Hugo van der Goes (*c.* 1435/40–1482) and Rogier van der Weyden, and in North-European graphics, with masterpieces by Martin Schongauer (p. 238) and Albrecht Dürer. The subject of the Death or Dormition of the Virgin is not from the Bible but from the *Legenda aurea* (The Golden Legend, a medieval collection of religious stories).[147] It narrates that on the intercession of St John, the Apostles were brought on clouds from all points of the compass to the dying Virgin. And so it is no wonder, considering the veneration of the Virgin Mary, that the Dormition was regarded as the epitome of a programmatic Catholic art and was linked to Jesuitical authors (Müller/Schauerte 2018, Cat. G87).[148]

We see Christ's beloved apostle at the left edge of the picture. He has fallen asleep and yet has his hands folded in prayer. Hence the picture must be regarded as a dream vision of St John, which on the other hand has no corresponding theme in the *Legenda aurea* and is an invention of Bruegel's. Therefore the question as to whether a particularly Catholic position is behind the scene here based on the veneration of the Virgin Mary is more than doubtful. Much supports the argument that Bruegel created the horizontal-format picture for his friend Abraham Ortelius, who, although faithful to the Catholic faith on the outside, was secretly a devotee of the writings of Sebastian Franck.

At any event, in 1574 Ortelius commissioned an engraving by Philipp Galle (1537–1612) after the work. Later the plate was owned by Peter Paul Rubens (1577–1612), deemed to be a great admirer of Bruegel. The artist's prodigious achievement seen in this work becomes clear when we keep in mind that the tradition of the night pieces with artificial light sources burgeoned much later with the art of a Caravaggio (1571–1610).

This picture, too, has Bruegel producing a technical showpiece of chiaroscuro painting. He exploits with the utmost artistry the artificial light sources, creating a scene based on the opposition of light's earthly and celestial origins. While a warm fireplace can be discovered on the left, a cat cosily settled in front of it, behind the head of the dying Madonna we see an aureole that can have no natural source. At the foot of the bed is a pillow with a crucifix on it. In keeping with tradition, the Madonna is holding a long candle. Furthermore, the artists places lamps and other candles around that yet again appear bright in the darkness, but in various intensities. The small-format grisaille from the time around 1564 is also primarily to be seen as an experiment in painting light and shade. But from the iconographic point of view, too, the picture has nothing to do with an orthodox Catholic programme, but with an allegorical motif in the form of a vision. Bruegel has added the framework narrative of the sleeping John; it is not to be found in any of the conventional and well-known versions of the theme. He uses this narrative technique to relativise and fictionalise the story, which is not to be taken literally in any way, as little as the supernatural appearance of the light is capable of representing the divine.

The Three Soldiers (detail), 1568
(see ill. pp. 244/245)

Pages 242/243
Christ and the Woman Taken in Adultery, 1565
Grisaille, oil on wood, 24.1 x 34.4 cm (9 ½ x 13 ½ in.)
London, Courtauld Institute of Art, Count Antoine Seilern Collection

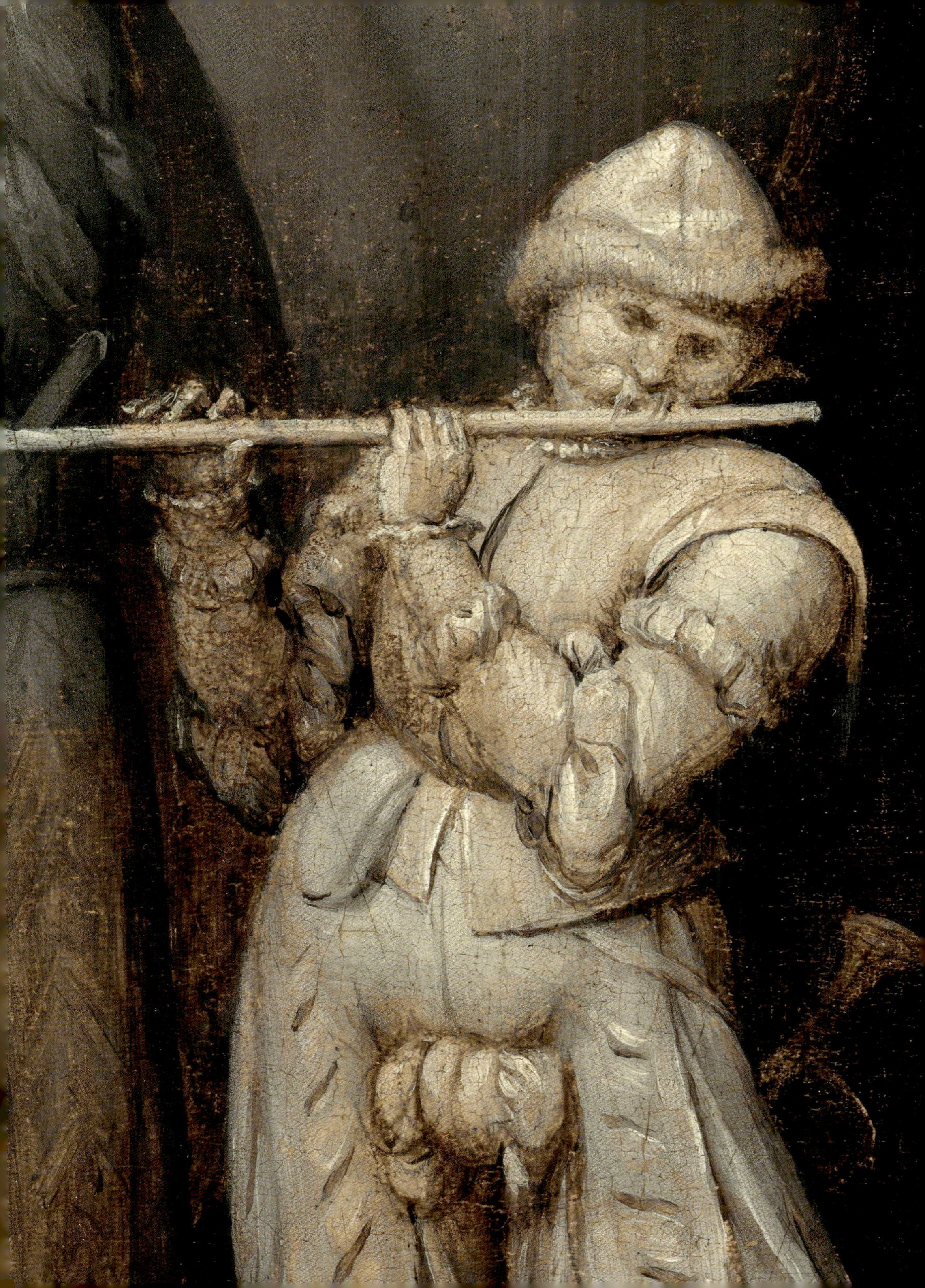

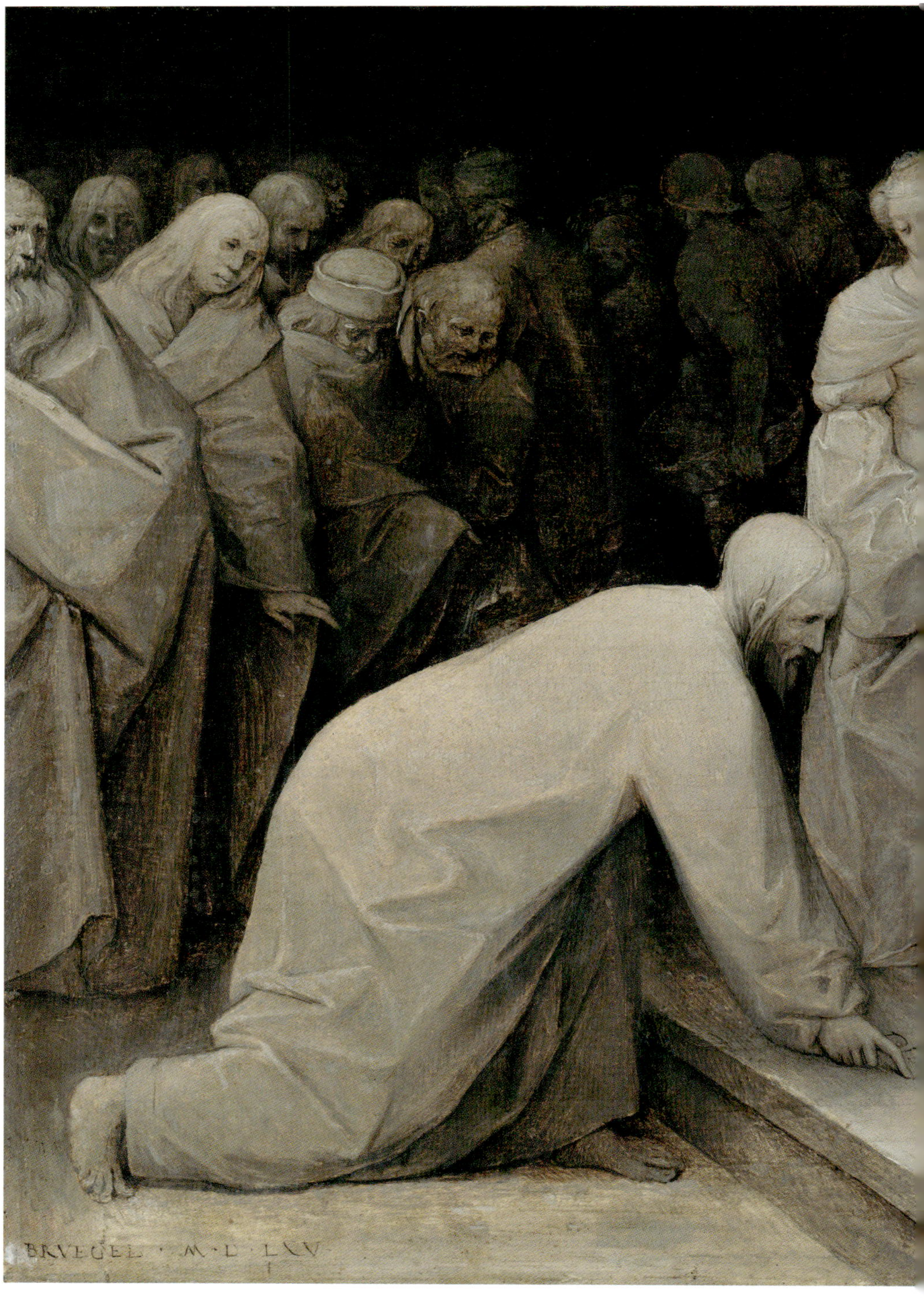
BRVEGEL · M · D · LXV

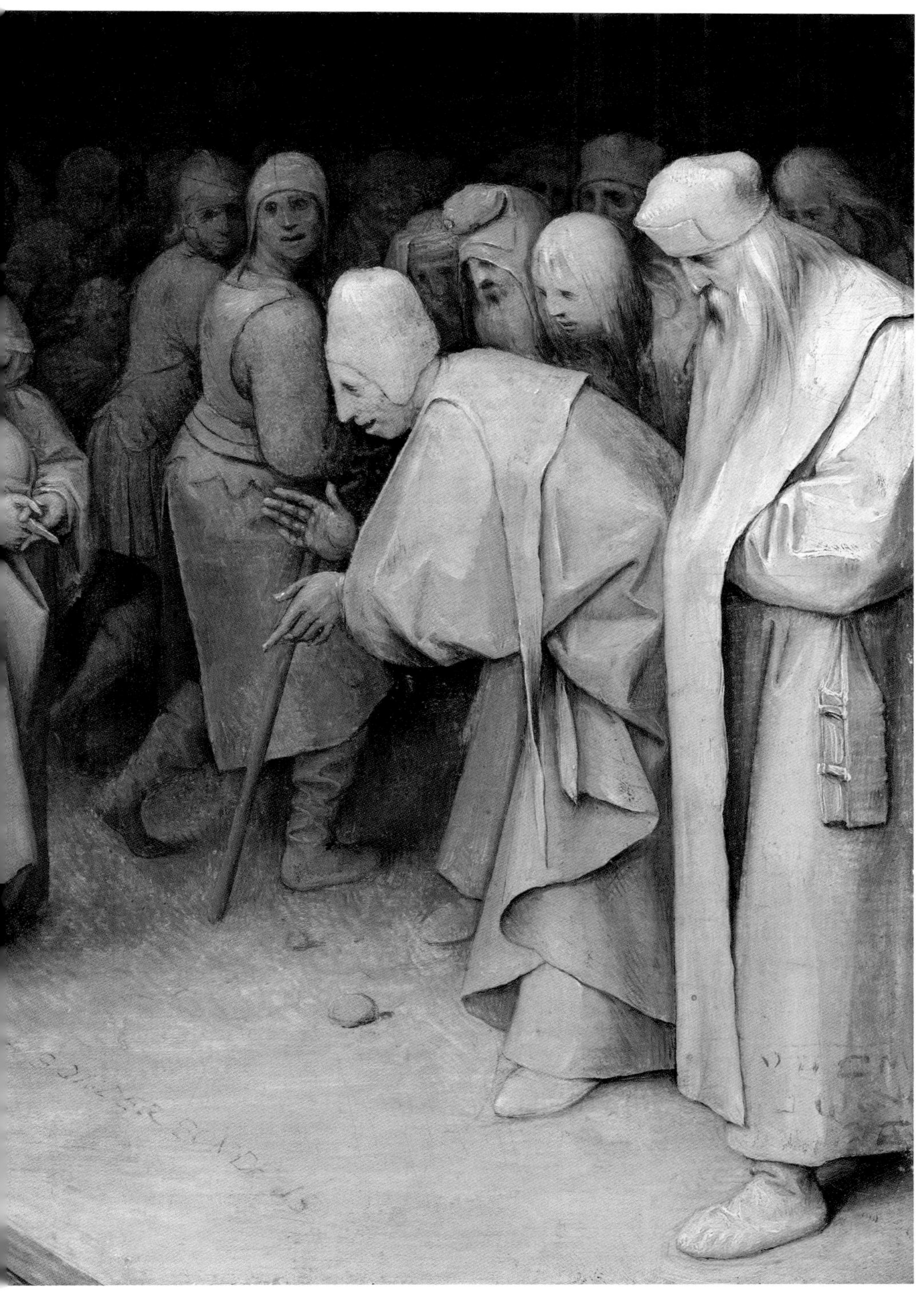

The Three Soldiers, 1568
Grisaille, oil on oak, 20.3 x 17.8 cm (7 ⅞ x 7 ⅛ in.)
New York, The Frick Collection

Pages 246/247
The Death of the Virgin (also: **Dormition of the Virgin**), *c.* 1564
Grisaille, oil on oak, 36.8 x 55.6 cm (14 ½ x 21 ⅞ in.)
Banbury (Warwickshire), Upton House, National Trust

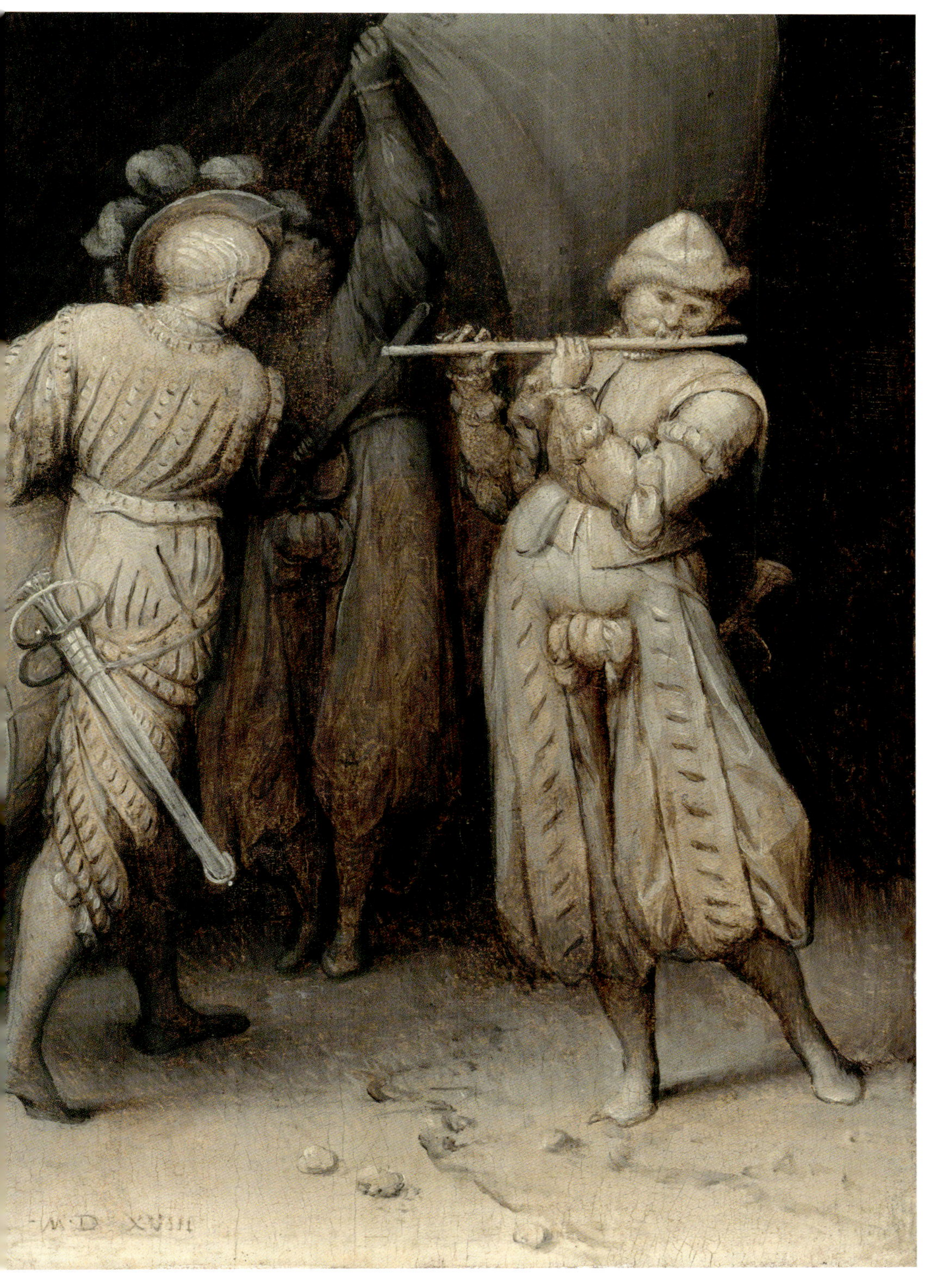
·M·D·XVIII

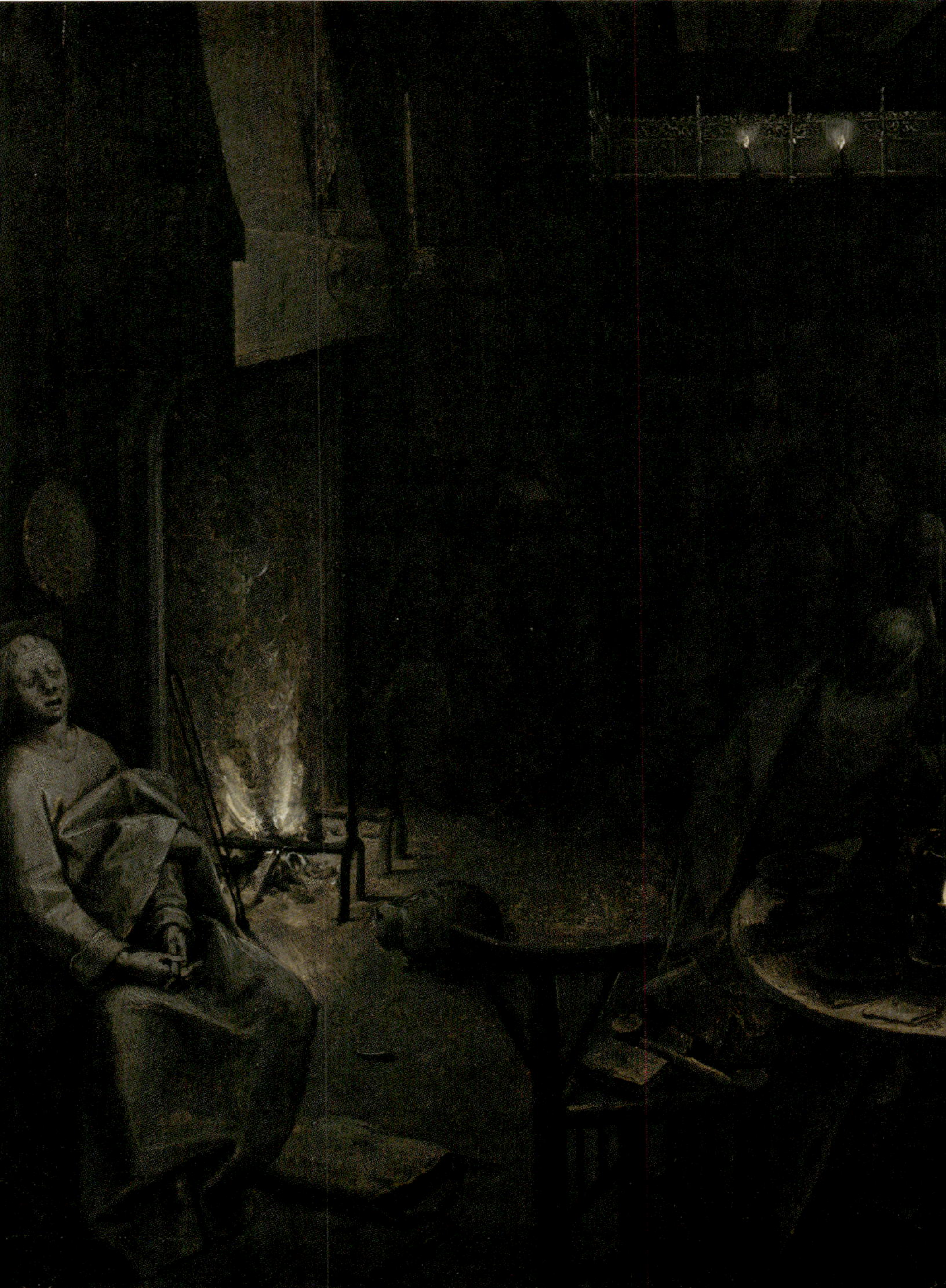

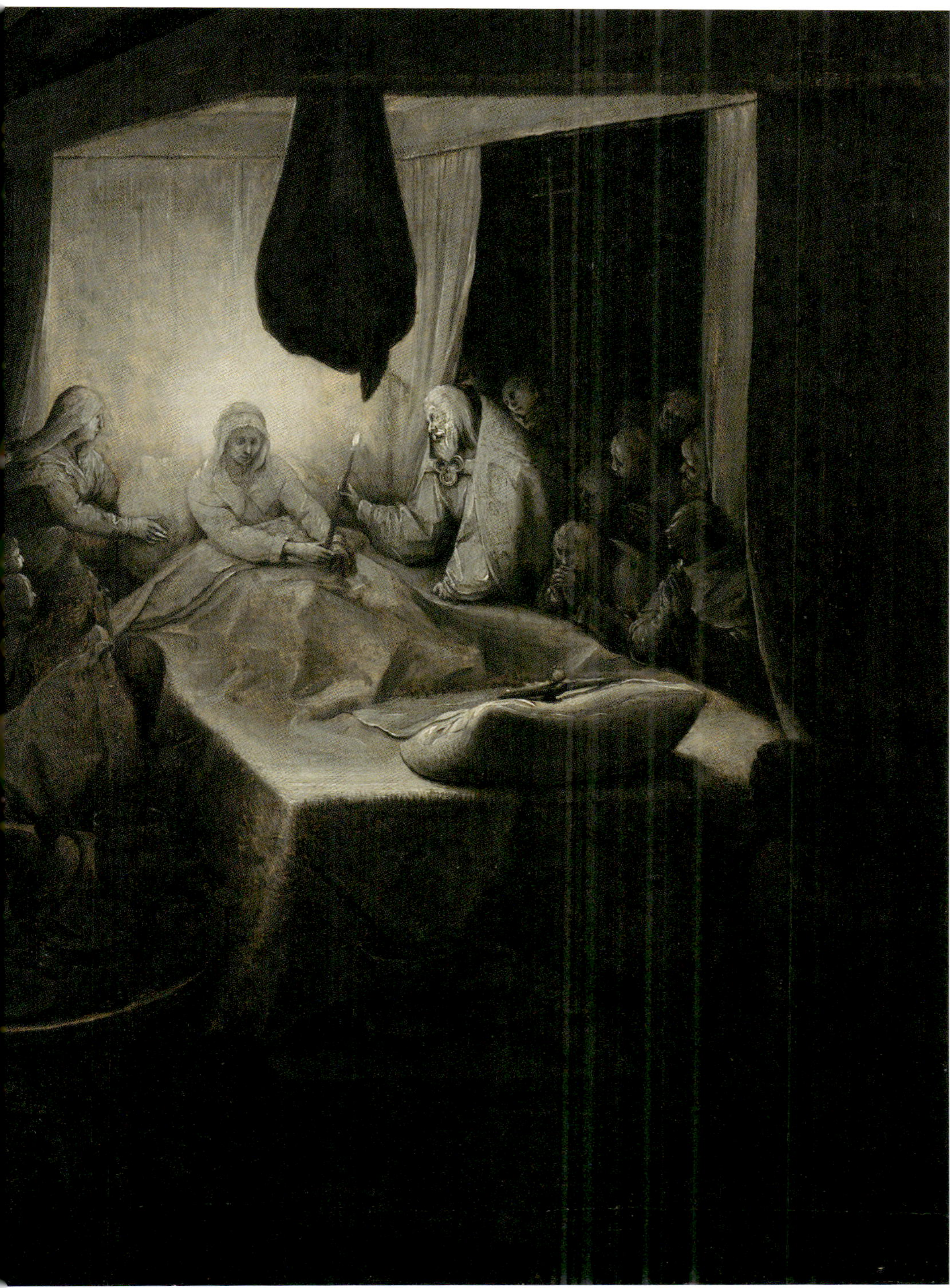

Feasting:
The Peasant
Pictures

*"The kind of painting on which Bruegel concentrated
was scenes from peasant life. He painted peasants
merrymaking, feasting and working, and so people have
come to think of him as one of the Flemish peasants."*
— ERNST GOMBRICH, 1950

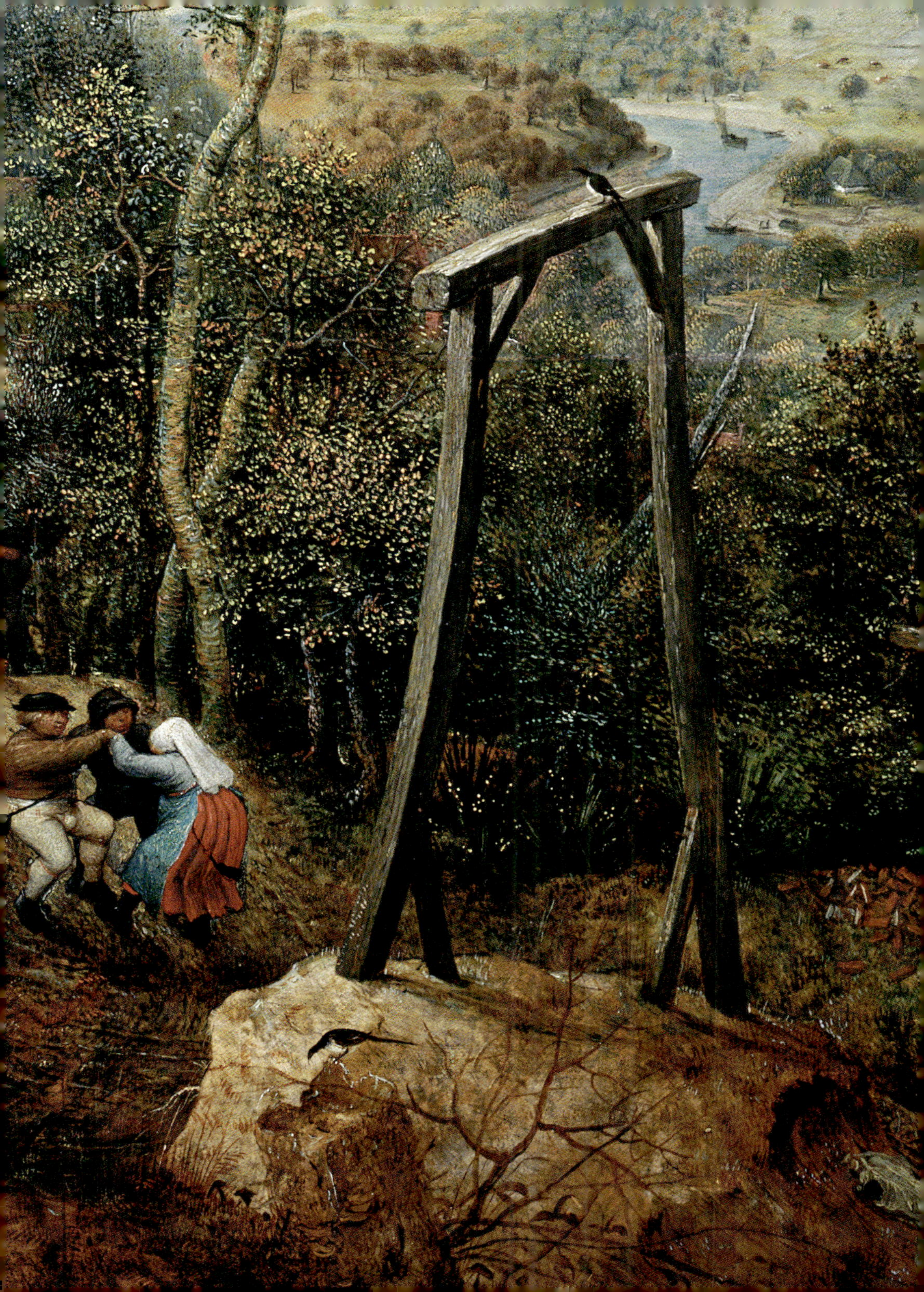

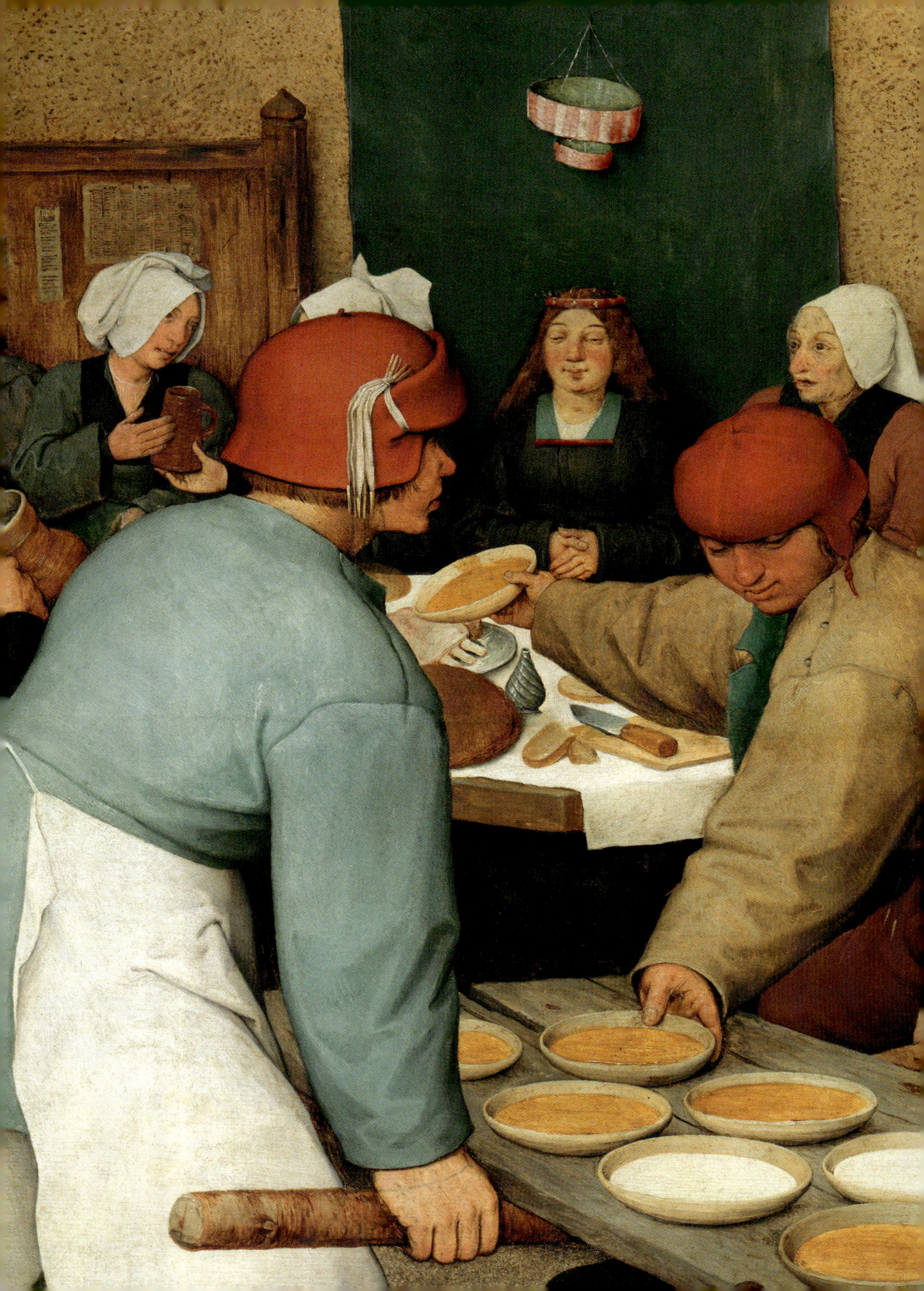

The dancing gallows

Bruegel's *The Magpie on the Gallows* (pp. 272/273, Cat. 37), dated 1568, is one of the most enigmatic of his inventions, featuring a peculiar mixture of the peasant theme and landscape.[149]

We are looking from a high vantage point down into a valley, where we follow the course of a river leading from right to left as far as the horizon. At first our impression is dominated by the enchanting atmosphere of the landscape. Brown, ochre and green tones contrast with the delicate grey and purple nuances of the horizon. For this almost square picture, Bruegel creates the view into the distance by framing his narrative on both sides with trees. This repoussoir also has the task of intensifying the impression of great depth. It is a fine summer's day, and people are enjoying the light and warmth of the evening sun.[150] In the bottom left-hand corner, we see people dancing and making music, Bruegel accentuating them through the colours of their clothes. In the shade of the trees, we detect a man with his hose down, and among the people arriving another man heads urgently into the brushwood to urinate. In the crowd, we also spy a bagpiper with a red, pancake-like face inciting all to dance. We cannot discern the cause of the festivities here. However, none of the people dancing, music-making and gesticulating in abandonment seems to be registering that they are entertaining themselves under a gallows. A magpie is perched on its cross beam, and a second crouches in front on a stone, watching the dancers and their actions (p. 249). To the right of the gallows is a horse's skull, marking the location as a place of butchery. Alongside the trees on the left, in the direction from where the people have come, stand a church, a tavern and the houses of a small town, while our glance passes right of the gallows to a cross and a watermill. The picture is enigmatic; the elements do not add up to a whole, but stand incongruously separate in this panoramic *Weltlandschaft* – "world landscape". At all events, the crane flying high at the left is placed so prominently and majestically in the sky that questions arise as to its significance.

Bruegel's picture was produced in the heyday of the Inquisition, and so attempts have been made to interpret the magpies as a critical reference to this institution. This is justified to a certain degree, if we remember how van Mander characterises the picture.

Page 249
The Magpie on the Gallows (detail), 1568
(see ill. pp. 272/273)

The Peasant Wedding (detail), *c.* 1568
(see ill. pp. 274/275)

He mentions it at the end of his biography of the artist and emphasises its controversial content: "In his will he left his wife a picture with a magpie on the gallows. By the magpie he meant the gossips, whom he dedicated to the gallows."[151] With this episode the biographer alludes to the danger of possible denunciation and quotes the magpie as a symbol of scandalmongering and frivolity. If we keep in mind the danger in which Bruegel's widow found herself through his all too critical motifs, gossips are perhaps not meant here so much as the denunciators who would betray dissenters to the Catholic Inquisition. Do the men at bottom left standing with their backs to the observer, and apparently coming from a different direction from that of the peasants, correspond to the two magpies and provide an explanation? Does the motif of the crane flying away represent a warning to keep one's peace in religious matters? And what significance does the watermill have, which is being trodden by one person at that moment? All this remains ambiguous.

At least we may say that the peasants, instead of quaffing in the tavern or on the square in front of the houses, have gone out to entertain themselves in the shambles. They do not blench before the macabre place riddled with rotting cadavers. They follow nature's call, they are themselves part of the order of creatures subject to becoming and decaying. So they are not capable of looking beyond their physical well-being and hence of recognising the cross below the gallows, but remain captive to a world of physical needs and sensual desires. It is instructive how closely death and pleasure are juxtaposed here. There may be a certain significance in easily visible millwheel; it alludes just as much to the Wheel of Fortune as it does to the ever-recurring Passion interpreted by Franck, and also to *The Procession to Calvary* (Cat. 15), as we saw before. At any event, the horse's skull crops up in both pictures as an attribute of the shambles "Golgotha". It cannot be determined if the picture as a whole might be seen as a warning against denunciation, or about peasants who turn to the gallows and not to the cross, who, to quote the blunt saying, even "shit" on it.

What is striking is the peculiar multi-perspective rendering of the gallows. Bruegel is inventing a paradox here. While the cross beam at the top projects obliquely into the space, the vertical supporting beams seem to be parallel. We cannot observe this gallows framework without its form constantly changing as we look at it. Bruegel studies have asked whether he was indulging here in a trompe l'oeil, wanting to depict a "dancing" gallows. An interesting feature of this ambiguous image is that its shape-changing cannot be stopped. Even after its construction has been understood, its cavorting cannot be "deactivated", so that we are fooled, time and again. Reality as a presence assured by the senses is being denied. The crazy gallows remains in our memory, seeming to mock us again and again, but also the senseless hustle and bustle of the peasants confronted by an inconceivably beautiful world.

The Last Day

The Viennese *Peasant Wedding* (pp. 274/275, Cat. 31) has always been regarded as an exemplary expression of Bruegel's art.[152] Van Mander tells of how the artist, along with his friend, the merchant Hans Franckerl, dressed up as peasants and went to country weddings to study the people there undetected. We are cautious today about the truth of such anecdotes. But of course this caution does not spare us the question of why the biographer mentions Franckert's name – Bruegel could, after all, have gone to the weddings on his own.

An adequate explanation has never been provided for this curious episode in his biography. It wasn't noticed that Bruegel has portrayed Franckert in the *Peasant Wedding* at the far right edge of the picture (p. 255). Van Mander possibly mentioned the episode because he was familiar with the profile portrait of the Nuremberg man from a medal of Jacques Jonghelinck's (1530–1606). So we may presume that Bruegel had a very close relationship to his patron, otherwise he would never have dared portray him in all the carousal of a peasants' wedding.

Admittedly, the literature of the first half of the twentieth century concentrated far less on such suppositions than on Bruegel's robust style in his portrayal. It was thought to demonstrate his closeness to the "folk", genuinely expressed in his peasant pictures. Our response to the *Wedding Meal* or *Peasant Wedding* – it is known by both names – dated around 1568 is at first monopolised by the few figures in the foreground. Even before we detect the actual theme or analyse the many actions, we see two men carrying plates on an unhinged door to the table crowded with the hungry wedding party. The light-blue jacket and white apron of the man walking behind stand out from the dominant yellow-brown tones, thus immediately striking the viewer's eye.

In comparison with the other people, the two plate bearers are shown disproportionately large. Their monumentality accentuates the heaviness of their burden. After this, our eye is caught by the man in the front left corner of the picture; he is filling a jug with ale. A child is seated next to him, wallowing in the memory of the porridge he has just eaten, a piece of bitten-into bread and butter lying on his blue apron. Only after perusing the figures in the foreground do we gradually take note of the persons around the table. This carefully considered address to the observer in accentuating the foreground leads to a perspective effect upon the action. Even before we can turn to the many people present, food and drink is established as the defining context.

The people are seated together crowded elbow-to-elbow around the table. Overall, we find a colourful wedding party assembled here. Behind the bride in black is a greenish-blue cloth, and a crown hangs above her head. In keeping with tradition, she sits still and isolated in the midst of chattering and laughing people.[153] She has her eyes closed and grins in a private reverie – we cannot avoid the strong impression that this is because she's tipsy (p. 250). The red hat adorned with a peacock feather worn by the porridge-slurping child in the foreground is much too big for him. Someone could have pulled it over his head. Since everyone present is wearing some sort of headgear, maybe the one who did this has vanished from the observer's view and is busy doing something that a headdress with a peacock feather would impede.

To the right of the bride are her mother and father, at the left a young woman (obscured by a man's headgear) who is handing her neighbour a tankard. The father of the bride stands out from the other guests because he is the only one sitting on a chair with a backrest, while all the others have taken their places on simple benches, or have improvised with tubs and baskets.

The long bench at the left seems to have been made especially for the occasion – the bark seems fresh and the wood lighter than the bench we can see on the right. For the observer, it is evident that more guests are turning up at this party than have been hosted by the bride's family before. Musicians with bagpipes entertain the party. The strenuous bustle in serving the ale and in handing round the porridge shows that the wedding party is in full swing.

Compared with the traditional chastisement of vice inherent in the peasants' wedding motif, Bruegel's critique is discreet, only visible at second glance. Hence the more riotous drinkers are seated not at the top but at the bottom end of the table, so we see them relatively late. But eventually we note the many ale tankards the men and women are voraciously raising to their mouths. Bruegel's intention is critical in portraying these drinkers, also evident in the fact that their faces are all covered by their raised tankards, seemingly robbing them of their identity. In the literature, the chastisement of vice was emphasised as the most important function of the peasant pictures,[154] with a repertoire of fixed types and actions attached to the genre. In no way is an empathetic portrayal of his own country folk evident in the theme.

The focus here is on intemperance and unchaste behaviour in a whole series of scenes. Everywhere, everyone is "quaffing" and "guzzling". At the far end of the table, a women is handing a tankard to a handsome blonde. The child next to her is hers and shows she is a married woman. It's not clear if her husband is the one on her left being spoken to by another woman, or the one round the table corner placing a tankard to his lips without wasting a look at his surroundings. What is clear is her interest in the man leaning over her to whom she is handing the drink.

The Peasant Wedding (detail), *c.* 1568
(see ill. pp. 274/275)

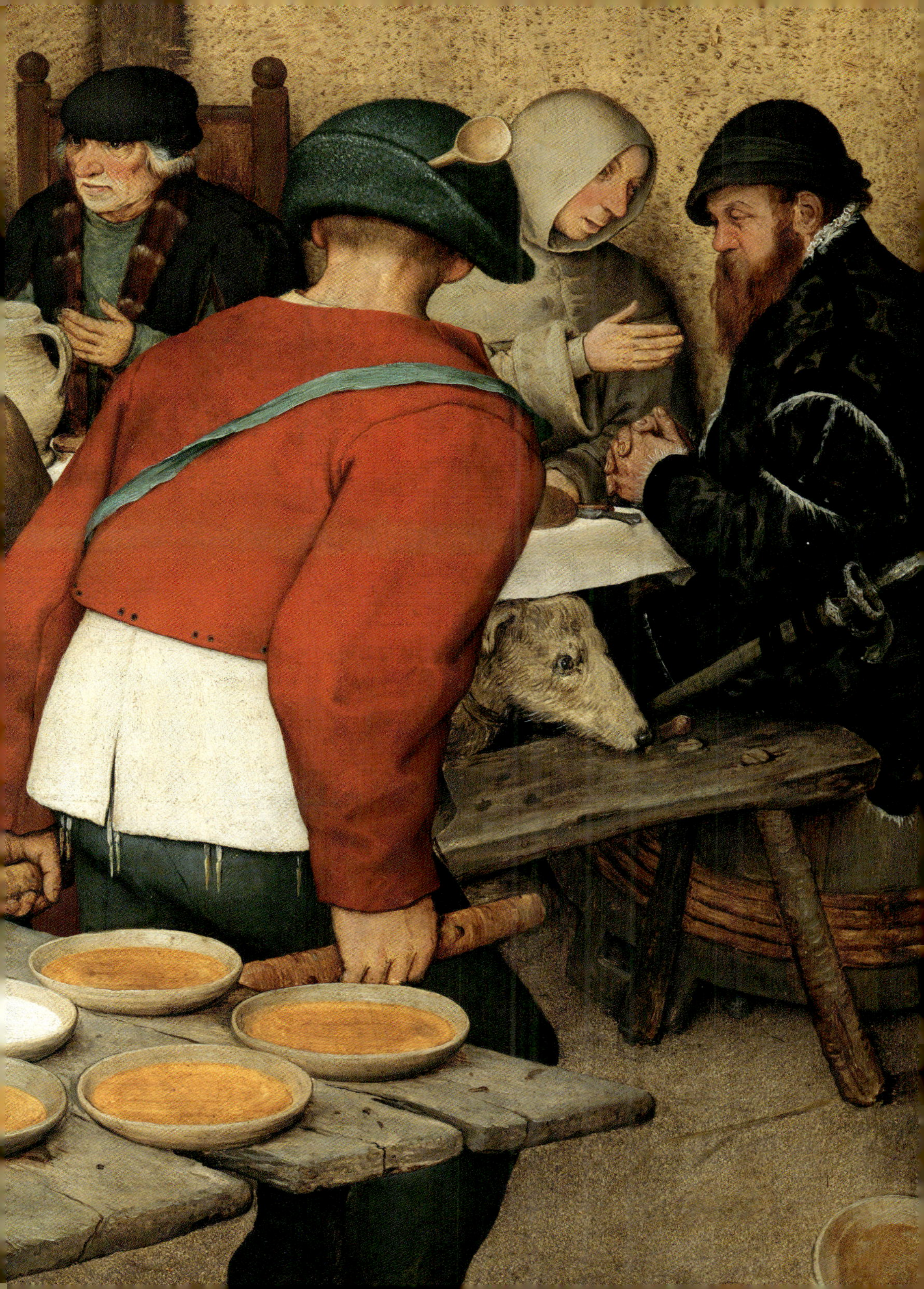

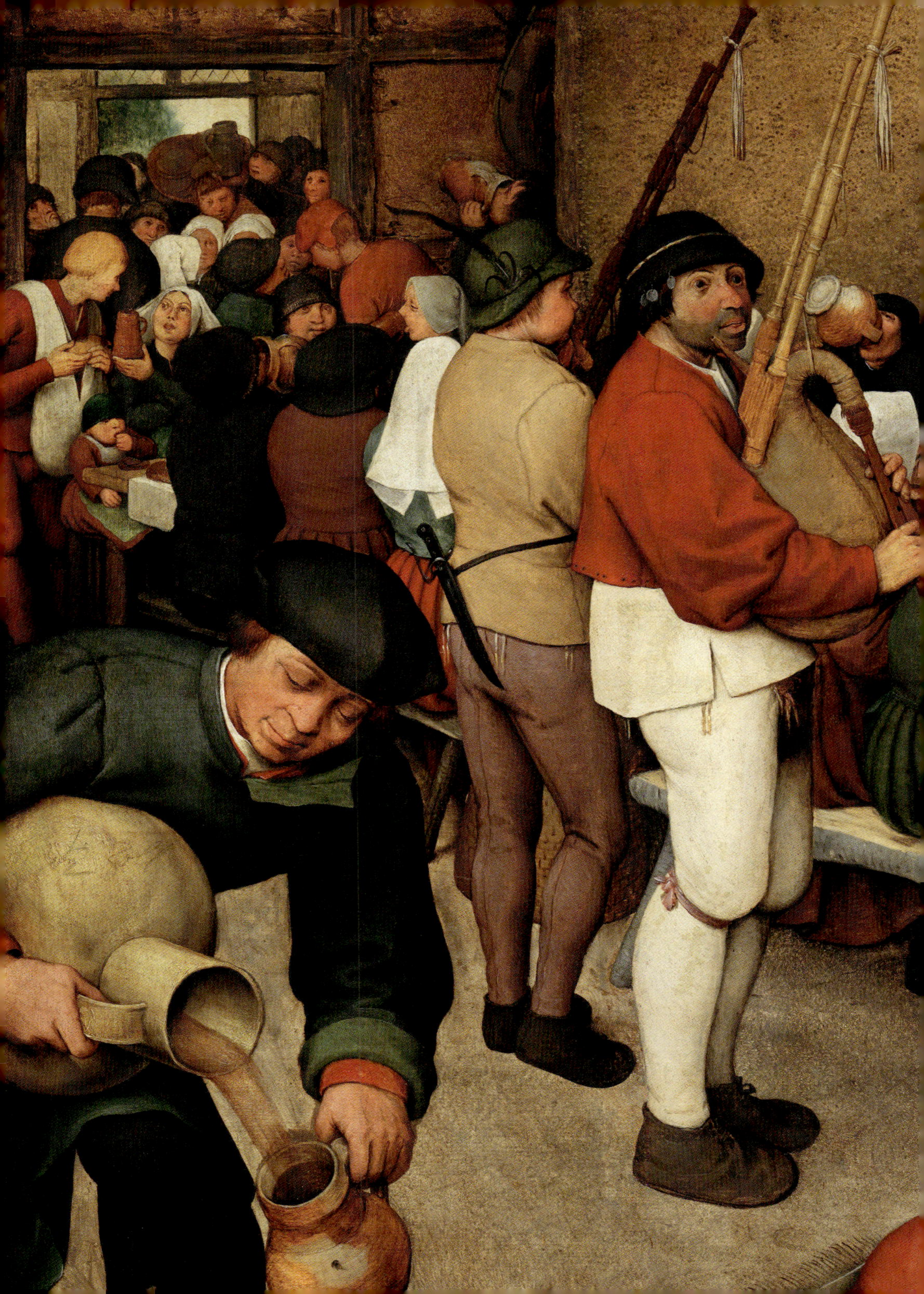

Not only the actions of those present are characteristic of vice; so is the location. The party is taking place in a spacious barn; we can see the straw stacked high behind the party table. Two stout wooden beams are placed between, bearing the weight of the barn roof. The entrance is at the far end of the room, and through it we can detect a timber-framed wall. It is surely no coincidence that Bruegel endeavours to make the straw correspond optically to the rendered walls. Only at second glance does it become clear that the rear wall is not a rendered timber-frame wall, but simply a wall of straw bales.

The barn with its hayloft may be seen as reference to a disreputable location. It is staged figuratively as a place of lust. Thus in the left rear corner we can see a ladder leading up to the straw. A reddish-brown cover is hanging above it on the beam, its colour alluding to love and lust and making the concealed love nest there even more enticing. A pigeon is perched in the barrel hanging on the wall, another hint of the erotic context.

The serving of plates with milk-and-oats porridge on an unhinged door is not a simple undertaking, as is distinctly seen in the foreground scene. The two men make their way forwards tentatively, but their movements do not seem in unison. While the man at the front staunchly steps forward without consideration of the man at the rear, the latter has to counteract the ensuing unsteadiness. The two figures have a third person allotted to them. The man seated at the end of the table takes the porridge dish with his left hand to pass it on to the hungry party with his right hand. Bruegel has indulged in a mischievous joke at the expense of this trio. The door is at the moment covered all over with plates, but an imbalance will soon occur (pp. 250, 255) – the half of the door relieved of porridge plates will be too light and the whole thing will tip over.

In an ironic vein, Bruegel shows a misfortune that will happen without our being able to see it. He lets the future invade the present. No less skilful is the running gag of the man serving ale in the left corner (p. 256) – every time the observer looks over at this figure, he sees the jug has by no means been emptied in the meantime. The ale flows and flows…

The literature has noted that the theme of the wedding in general – above all the motif of the serving man in the foreground at the left – offers an iconographic reference to the Marriage Feast at Cana.[155] This is plausible also because Bruegel has based his composition on a corresponding picture, probably the work of his teacher Pieter Coecke (p. 259). Here, too, there is a similar structure with a table placed obliquely in the room, reinforcing the sense of depth.

The Peasant Wedding (detail), *c.* 1568
(see ill. pp. 274/275)

With the iconographic reference to the Marriage Feast at Cana, Bruegel's *Peasant Wedding* is given an allegorical dimension, first of all *ex negativo*. The biblical narrative alludes to the shortage of wine as a symbol of temperance, which is entirely missing here amongst the carousing peasants. Traditionally, the story of the miraculous increase of wine has an eschatological significance. Jesus responds to his mother with the words "my time is not yet come", only to then transform the water into wine. This tastes much better than the wine set forth for the guests by the bridegroom, thus it offers a fore-taste of the coming of the Messianic kingdom.

Bruegel's allusion to the Marriage Feast at Cana may also be pointing a warning finger towards the Last Judgement.[156] The party indulging itself in so carefree a fashion in pleasures of the flesh would then be an allegory of the sinful world. Especially the child delighting in his porridge is a curious symbol of seduced, oblivious mankind – the peacock feather is a clear sign of this (p. 18).

But it is not only the boozing party that supports such an interpretation; the subtle staging of the event leads us far more along an apocalyptic trail.[157] Merely the supposed fun Bruegel permits himself with the loaded door hints at the precipitous change threatening the wedding. We must only look at the horrified glances of the bagpiper and of the guest at his right, staring at something terrifying at the right, outside the picture space. These looks also become indirectly thematic through the bride's father and the mother, who have noticed the horrified men and are now staring at them as though stunned. Also the guest to the left of the bride spooning up his porridge is staring in fright towards the seated man with a green hat, who is apparently so shocked that he has even put down his tankard.

Only now do we realise how subtly Bruegel is playing with the motif of time. His first concern in his picture is to suggest the continuum of time. Everyone is joining in the revelling, drinking and eating with great gusto. The ale flows like the wine at Cana. But, simultaneously, the artist provides clues that hint at the end of the world and time itself.

Only within this context can we recognise the full sense of the figure in the foreground at the left, since the diversion with the never-ending supply of ale contains a reference to the "measure is not yet full", the "time is not yet come". Together with the walls of straw and wheat stalks lying around, we are reminded of the sentence "the chaff that is separated from the wheat" (Matthew 3: 12), again an allusion to the end of time and the Last Judgement.

Now the question arises regarding the significance, in this context, of the two men at the right edge of the picture. Here, seated at the furthest end of the bench, are a Franciscan friar and an elegant patrician whom we have identified as Hans Franckert (p. 255). Friars and monks could of course join in a peasants wedding; we only have to look at an

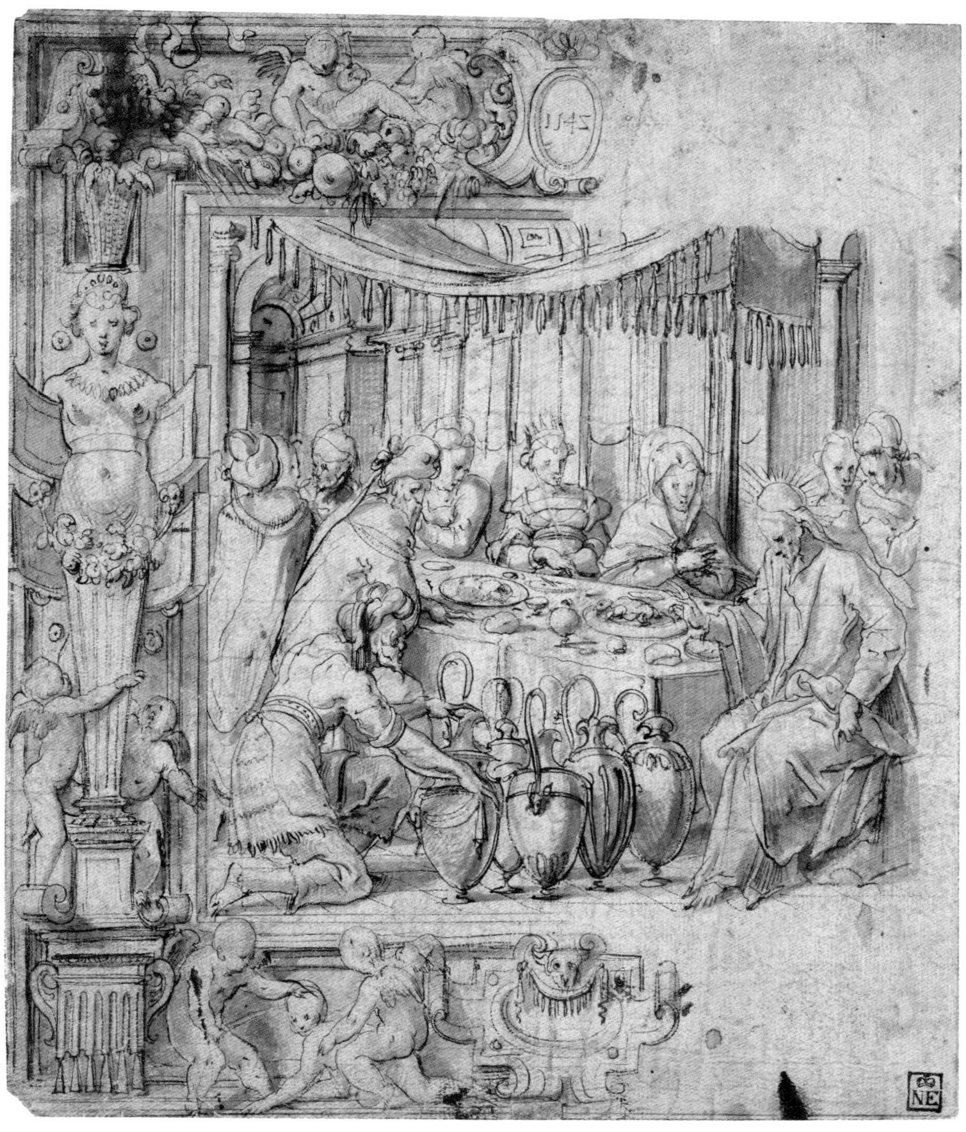

Pieter Coecke van Aelst (?), **Christ at the Marriage Feast at Cana**, 1540s
Drawing ink and black chalk, 29 x 24.4 cm (11 ⅜ x 9 ⅝ in.) Budapest, Szépművészeti Múzeum

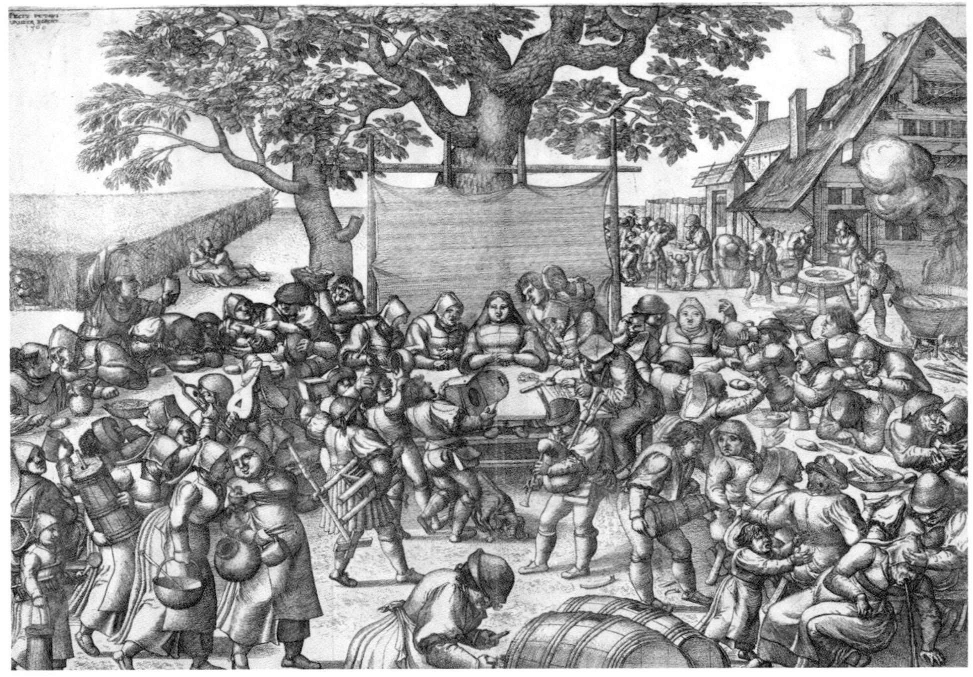

Pieter van der Borcht, **Peasant Wedding**, 1560
Etching, 37 x 51.3 cm (14 ⅝ x 20 ¼ in.). New York, The Metropolitan Museum of Art

engraving by Pieter van der Borcht (p. 260). But they appear to be just as riotous as the other revellers and keep up with the gluttons with no difficulty. Whereas in Bruegel's picture, someone is apparently being shriven. The warning of the friar and the readiness for penance of the man who, with lowered eyelids, is contemplating the state of his soul presents an alternative to the behaviour of the other guests.

Dancing on the brink of the abyss

It seems obvious to see *The Wedding Dance* (pp. 276/277, Cat. 25) and *The Peasant Wedding* as counterparts. They have almost identical formats and are complementary in theme. The dance follows the meal, and so the party has moved outdoors to continue their revelling. We have the impression that the erstwhile mildly smiling bride from the barn has been transformed into a wildly dancing young woman, yet, through her chaplet and her high-flying blond hair, she remains recognisably one and the same person. If we see the pictures as counterparts, we are challenged to set up a connection between them.

So how is the theme of the impending end of the world applicable to such a hedonistic feast? This doesn't seem to make sense, and so all interpreters have rejected a deeper meaning in the picture and have seen the chastisement of vice as the pictorial agenda.[158]

In the foreground on the right, we can make out two bagpipers entertaining the party. Bruegel has succeeded wonderfully in transporting the rhythm of the music onto the dancers' movements. What especially strikes the eye are the codpieces of the men in the foreground, so big that later owners of the picture had them painted over. The dancer on the left is approaching his partner in a particularly ribald way, flaunting the size of his manhood. He supports his hands on his hips and his tight jerkin is stretched across his belly. His partner seems to be joining in the fun and imitates his posture. She excitedly performs rapid tripping steps to the music. The dance is represented here unambiguously as a sexual game.

But we note that the face of the attractive woman dancer is far too small. She is defined through her body. A couple to the right of this scene have even interrupted their dance to kiss. Above the former couple we also discover a passionate embrace. And far distant in the background where improvised grassy banks have been set up we see another couple who are not content simply to dance with each other.

While provocative movements dominate the foreground scene, the people in the centre ground have got together to talk. On the left, a young man in a red jerkin and with a head that is much too small has approached a group made up of father, mother and daughter in order to ask the young woman to dance. She glances shyly to the side, while the parents eye the "cavalier" sceptically. The intemperate drinking, such as we have encountered in *The Peasant Wedding*, plays a relatively small role here. The only comparable drinking elements here are a man pouring ale into jugs, and, opposite, above the bagpiper, a man holding a jug to his mouth. The riotous dancing and its association with sexual attraction form the dominant theme of the picture.

From the technical point of view, Bruegel seems to be intent on representing an extremely large group of people in the most confined space. No fewer than 125 wedding guests can be counted in the picture.[159] We can perceive the persons in isolation, but also as a connected, heaving mass. It is as if Bruegel wanted not only to portray a wedding party, but also a symbol of mankind. The picture, with juxtaposition of colourful and monochrome colours, seems almost to pulsate. The ochre, brown and green tones are placed next to red, white and blue. It is this dynamic carpet of colour that gives the eye no rest.

Once again Bruegel exploits a distinctive method of composition. In *The Wedding Dance*, he allows the picture space front right to fall off so sharply that we fear the figures positioned there at the bottom edge might fall off the picture into an undefined abyss.

The Peasant Dance (detail), *c.* 1568
(see ill. pp. 278/279)

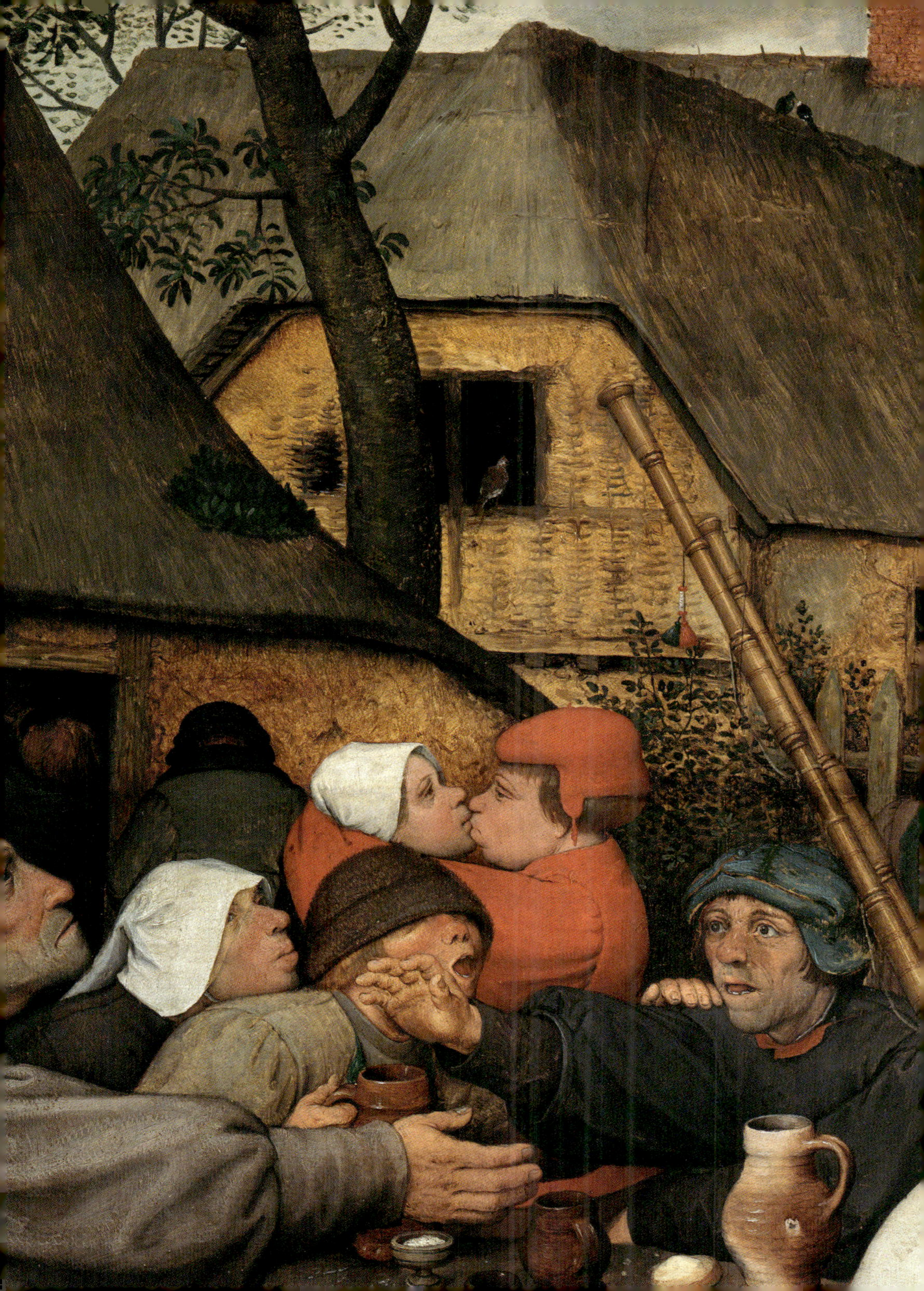

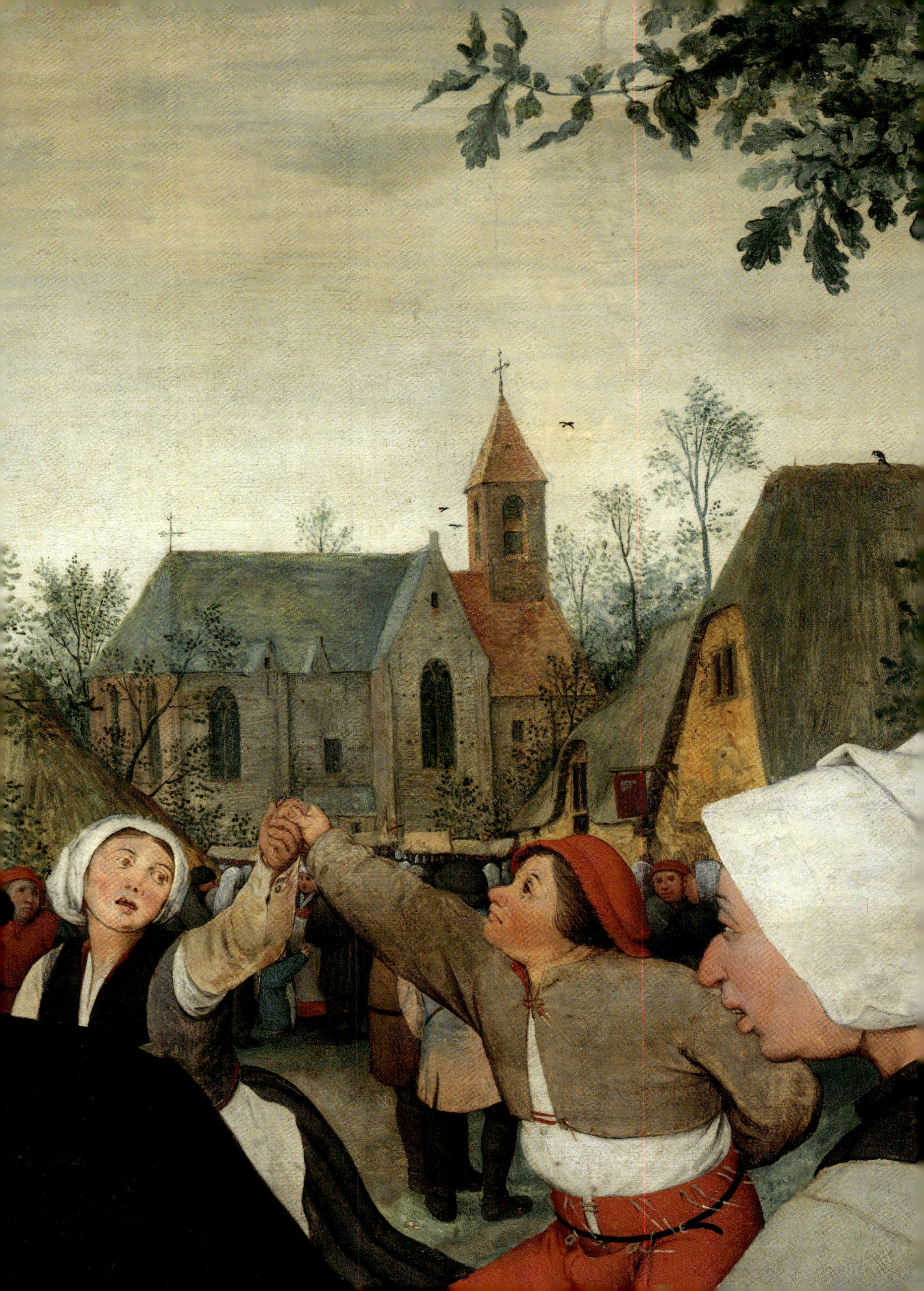

Especially the dancer in a tight white hose flinging his limbs around and chasing his partner with much whooping is in danger of falling into nothingness. At any event, Bruegel is giving us a hint here that the bride is the most important figure in the picture, for our vantage point is on the same horizontal axis as the young woman's face, thus requiring a higher viewpoint. She dances wildly with a partner, whom we can hardly identify as her bridegroom.

Bruegel has had to address a structural problem as a consequence of the steep fall-off of the pictorial space, since it was necessary to include optical counterweights in order to prevent this disturbing moment from disrupting the picture's overall impression. Therefore, he uses a strongly rising pictorial space to generate an immense pull into its depth towards the horizon; this is supported by the rising diagonals left and right. In addition, the raised, entwined arms of the dancers act as signposts towards the depth of the pictorial space. We might mention in this context the enigmatic figure of the darkly attired man in the front corner at the left, who is standing in extreme shadow under a tree. In technical terms, he provides an optical brake: he prevents the wedding party from slipping off the picture, as it were – the ground seems considerably flatter in his immediate vicinity.

We could continue describing scene after scene to illustrate Bruegel's richness of invention. But it has become quite clear that the panel has succeeded in two tasks. Firstly, it responds to the technical demand of diversely portraying an extremely large group of people. Secondly, the artist stages the allegory of oblivious humanity lost in debauchery, who are dancing at the brink of the abyss without being aware of the impending danger.

The picture's narrative is clear. However, the panel can be variously understood, depending on whether we perceive it with or without a connection to *The Peasant Wedding*. The connection between the approaching Apocalypse and the metaphor of the bride as *sponsa Christi* can be understood as an argument critical of the Church, which is not immediately detectable in *The Wedding Dance Outdoors*. The bride has not succeeded in her task; so, as Bruegel sees it, she relates to superficially experienced faith. Bruegel's achievement consists in making us forget the allegorical dimension of the picture by using a visual argument. The prerequisite for understanding the picture is based not only on an awareness of the symbolism of the bride, but also the overall view.

If Bruegel juxtaposes vice with the approaching end of the world in the two pictures, this is in no way new. On the contrary, Sebastian Brant, in his popular *Ship of Fools* (1494), already saw an unmistakeable sign of the approaching end of the world in the increase in

The Peasant Dance (detail), *c.* 1568
(see ill. pp. 278/279)

debauched, immoral behaviour, which he perceived in the times he lived in. And the eschatological mindset plays a central role most particularly in the writings of Sebastian Franck.[160] In his *Geschichtsbibel* (History Bible) and in the early *Vom greulichen Laster der Trunkenheit* (On The Horrible Vice of Drunkenness), both translated into Dutch in Bruegel's time, we find writings on the Apocalypse. Franck sees it as a mystery, its date unknown. At the same time, he describes the oblivious state of the world that will be caught unprepared for this event.

Laughing or crying?

From the technical point of view, Bruegel used various artistic devices for his composition of *The Peasant Dance* (pp. 278/279; Cat. 32). This begins with the positioning of the observer at the height of the couple who are rushing in. Our viewpoint does not tally with the picture's vertical axis, but is shifted into the former direction. We are standing opposite the church tower visible far away in the distance! Despite this, the artist makes the central axis into a sightline, but also accentuates the empty middle ground towards which the couple are heading.

To the left of the table a bagpiper is seated with a table behind him where numerous people have taken their places. Other persons in the middle ground are dancing, watching, or have found their way to the many stands and booths built up for the fair to celebrate the anniversary of the church's consecration. There is significance in the presence of a jester in a yellow-and-red jerkin, who is standing next to a man cantankerously staring at the scene (p. 271). Both remind us of the ancient pair of philosophers Democritus (460/59–371 BC) and Heraclitus (*c.* 520–*c.* 460 BC), who represented opposite philosophies of life and interpreted the world as a reason either to laugh or to cry. At any event, the jester combines in his costume the two colours that apply to practically all the protagonists.

Confronted by this scene, which indeed makes one laugh but is meant to make one sad, a certain ambivalence enters with the aforementioned couple. Bruegel's picture has a double meaning. It is humorous in a ribald way, but distances us simultaneously from the peasants. So it was thought that this view of peasants was that of the townspeople, who prefer to keep their distance.

To portray the motifs of the dancing, music-making and drinking peasants, Bruegel makes use of the tradition of pictures of fairs, reminding us of the prints by the Nuremberg "little masters", but also his contemporary Pieter van der Borcht.[161] However, in contrast to the tradition, Bruegel doesn't opt for an overall picture, but takes a more intensive close-up view, which grants us a precise study of people's faces and behaviour. Bruegel studies have even suspected in this context that the artist transposed the standards of history painting to the peasant genre in order to ennoble it.[162] It has been stated furthermore that Bruegel was most interested in displaying the power of the dance and music. Earlier research particularly emphasised the depiction of vice in the picture and interpreted the panel as a critique of a class, mainly because Bruegel takes every opportunity to portray the ugliness and stupidity of these people.

He achieves this by manipulating the bodies of the protagonists, something we do not immediately note. Thus he gives the impression that the size of the figures in the foreground noticeably diminishes from right to left, which cannot be explained by the laws of perspective. Bruegel uses this trick to make the couple at far right seem even larger and pudgier. Such distortions determine the picture's composition. The bagpiper's legs are too long, his torso too short. The girl to his right seems to be dancing with an even smaller child, thus in turn appearing much too small. This pair, clearly imitating the grown-ups, embody the saying "a chip off the old block", a reference to the incorrigibility of world. Bruegel was also at pains to depict the shoes of the figures in the foreground, all of which are far too big. Ungainly and podgy, the couple barge into the proceedings – a strikingly odd feature is the way Bruegel has depicted the man as though his legs had been attached left for right, and right for left.

The picture dissolves into a variety of more or less amusing scenes, whereby the groups in the foreground draw our attention first. For instance, the bagpiper and the young man with the peacock feather directly next to him are very conspicuously portrayed, the latter characterised as a rake by the feather on his cap.[163] He seems as though he's trying to bribe the musician with a jug of ale and is cajoling him with great urgency. And while many singles have already found a partner, the young man seems to be out of luck. Perhaps he's making a special request for music. Perhaps he's also asking the minstrel to go on playing: because as long as the music is playing, he still has a chance of finding a partner. But his suggestion doesn't seem to get a positive response; the bagpiper turns away, loath to comply.

Let's turn once more to the couple rushing in, who seem to be late in joining the party. They bound towards the festive group with boisterous energy. Bruegel has wittily captured this scene by portraying them half running and half dancing. Their hands are already positioned on their hips. The artist presents both persons in profile, but they make an oddly repulsive impression. He resorts to drastic means when he shows the man's bad teeth and his scurvy complexion. Moreover, the spoon stuck in his cap characterises him as a voracious type (p. 271). The portrayal of the woman is equally negative, with her bulging eyes, thick lips and receding chin. They bound in haste across the picture as if afraid of missing something. This voracity is what best characterises the couple.

As we scrutinise the events and the details become clearer, we notice the many birds perched on roofs and ridges. They are pigeons set as silhouettes in the scene. This always

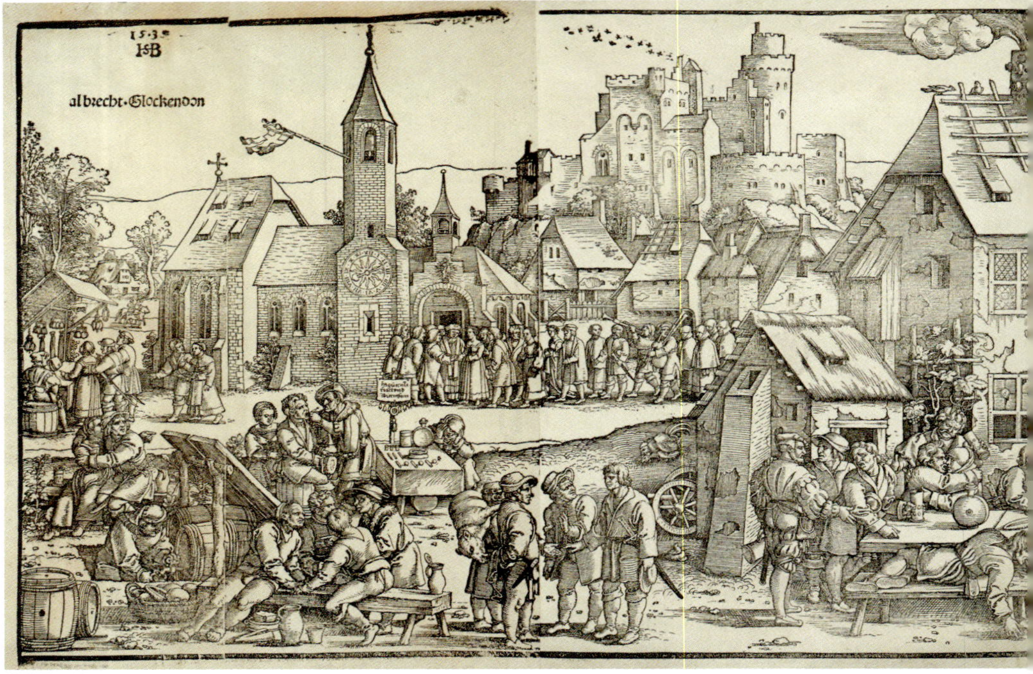

Hans Sebald Beham, **Church Consecration Festival (The Great Fair)**, 1535/39
Woodcut, 36.2 x 114.2 cm (14¼ x 44⅞ in.) Staatliche Museen zu Berlin, Kupferstichkabinett

has a ribald connotation, referring to the Dutch verb "vogelen", to have sexual inter-course, as we saw already in *The Peasant Wedding*.[164] At any event, the presence of the pigeons relate to what is happening inside the building. Like the birds, the motifs of bagpipe and the dance have a cryptic erotic meaning.

However, Bruegel does not stop at merely symbolic allusions; many scenes leave nothing to the imagination. Motifs like the kissing couple at far left (p. 263) and another pair far right in the background are in no way inventions of the Flemish artist, but can be found already in the depictions of fairs by the Beham brothers (pp. 268/269). Looking to the right, we can see another pair on the same horizontal axis; here the woman is about to drag the reluctant "cavalier" into the front garden of the house at the rear. The broken-off handle of a jug conspicuously placed next to the female dancer who is rushing in is a symbol of lost innocence.

That the liberal consumption of ale has its consequences is seen in the motif of the man directly behind the kissing couple at the left, who is urinating uninhibitedly against

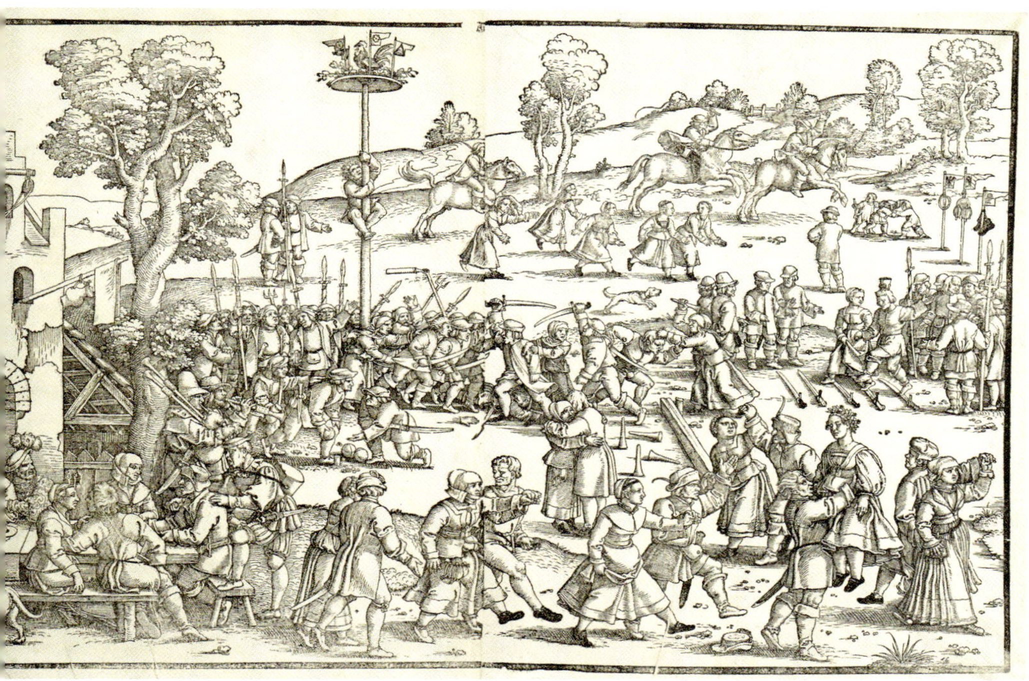

the wall of the house. How the overall festivities will develop becomes clear in the scene at the left (p. 263). Three men and a woman seated at the table are obviously about to fall out. They all seem drunk, are yelling at each other or wildly gesticulating, apparently without any of them knowing why. The woman is trying to appease her husband but is ignored. The fact that his cap has slipped over his eyes also speaks volumes. We can see a man on the left edge of the picture who is pointing towards the couple rushing to join the party, as if he is the jealous husband who already senses impending adultery. This is indicated by the key, characterising the woman as a married mistress of her house.

In this context, it is significant that all the men are armed. Both the bagpiper and the dancer who is rushing in wear short swords, which incidentally were not allowed to all peasants, solely patriarchs with their own households. Vassals and sons are allowed to carry a knife, as we can see on the dancer at the right, who is wearing red hose. The picture indicates clearly that a violent scuffle is about to take place. We may assess this as a commentary on the consequences of intemperate drinking. It is also interesting that the dancer who is rushing in is looking avidly at the happenings round the table, as if he's hoping to join in a brawl. *Gula* (gluttony) is the preliminary to *Ira* (anger). In this scene, one leads unavoidably to the other.

The off-key ballad on unchastity that Bruegel is striking up first sounds out its shrill tones through the theological context of the village fair, when the saints are celebrated to whom the church is dedicated. In this context, it seems no coincidence that the village church in the background occupies a conspicuously position. It may well be dedicated to the Virgin Mary, which we can perhaps assume from the paper picture of the Madonna attached to a tree on the right edge of the picture. A jug of flowers has been placed in veneration under it. The motif of the crossed ears of grain being trodden on by the dancers is also an eloquent detail, as if Bruegel wanted to suggest the true character of the event: the Cross is being trampled upon.

The Peasant Dance (detail), *c.* 1568
(see ill. pp. 278/279)

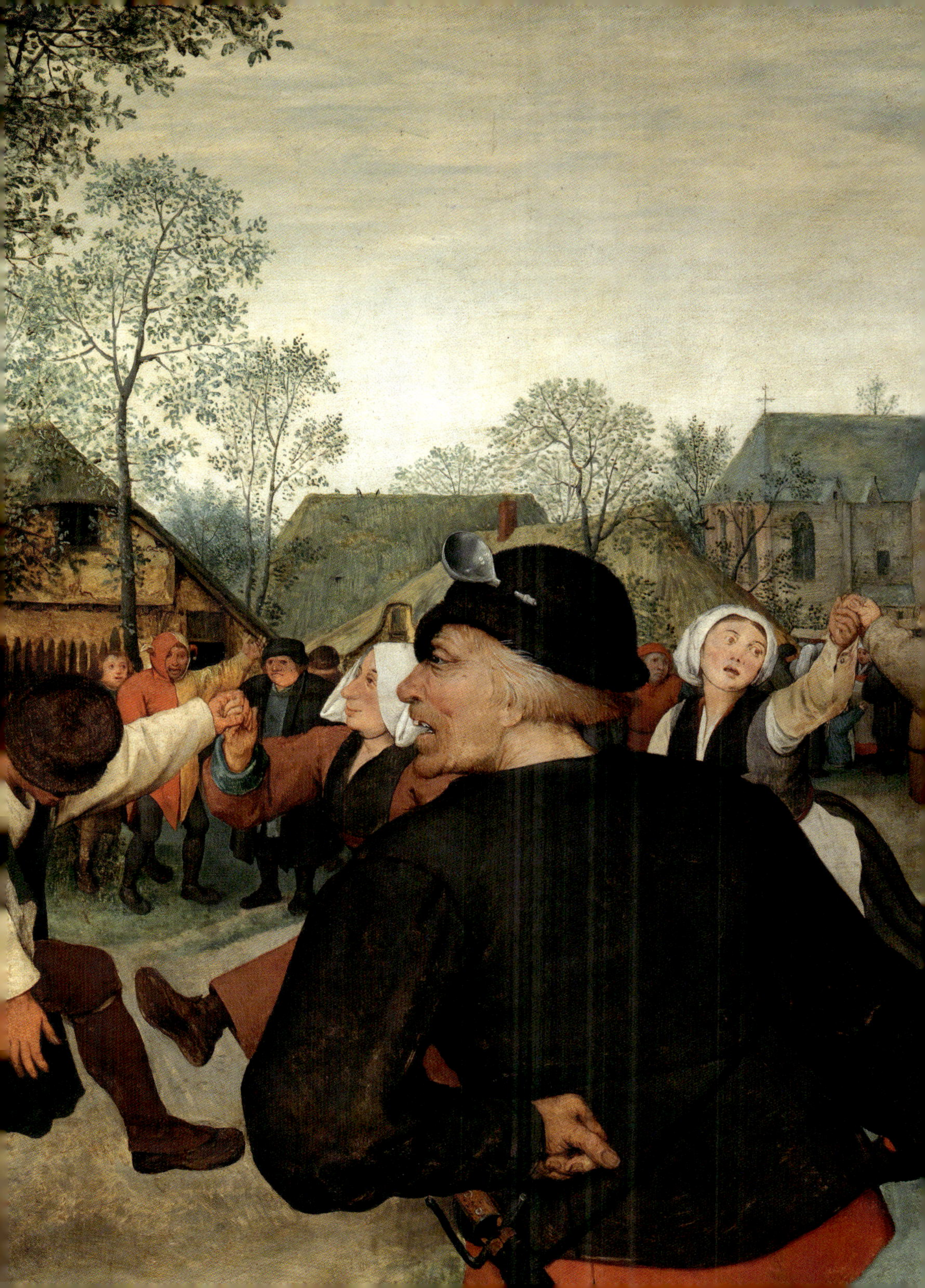

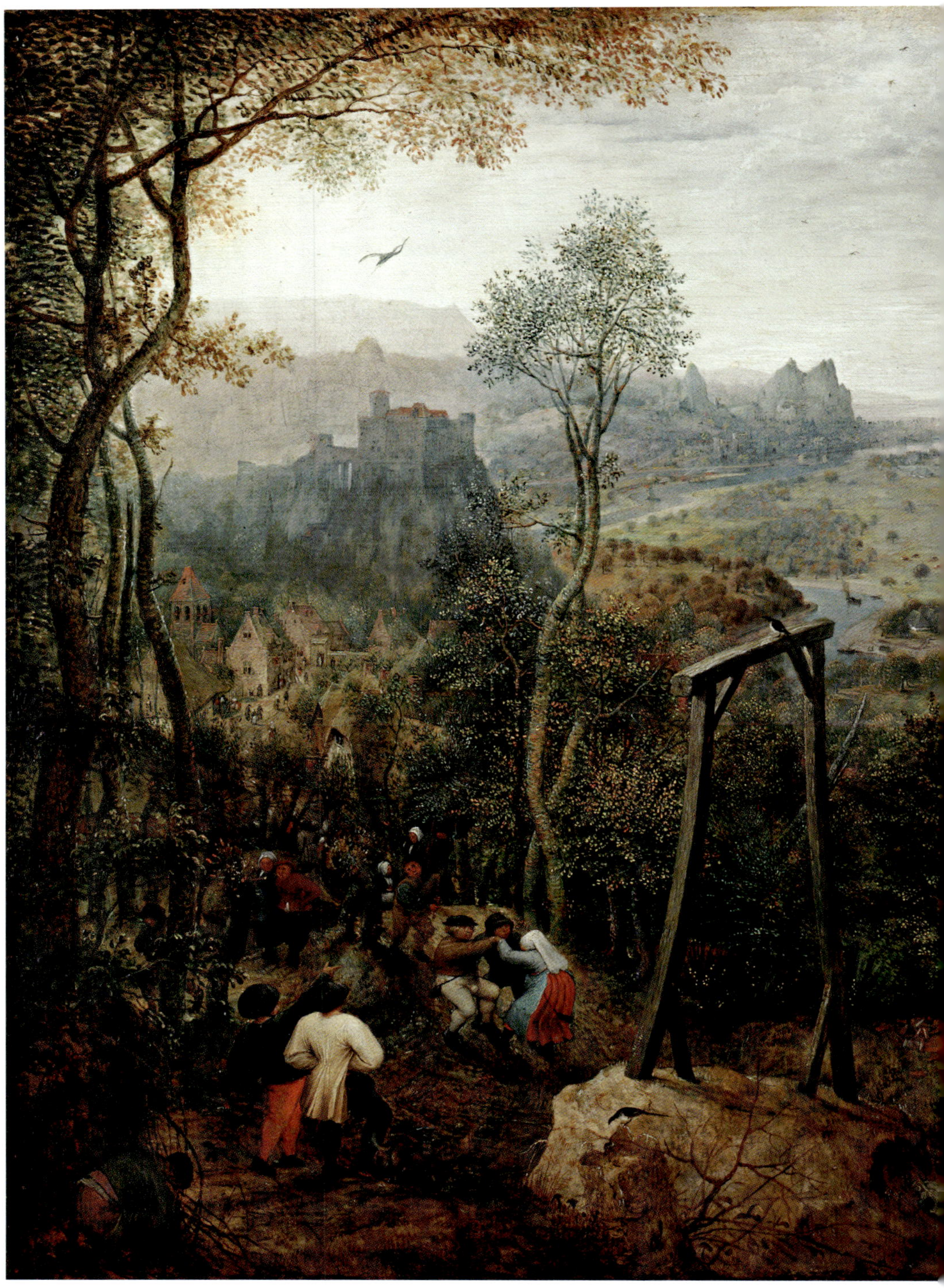

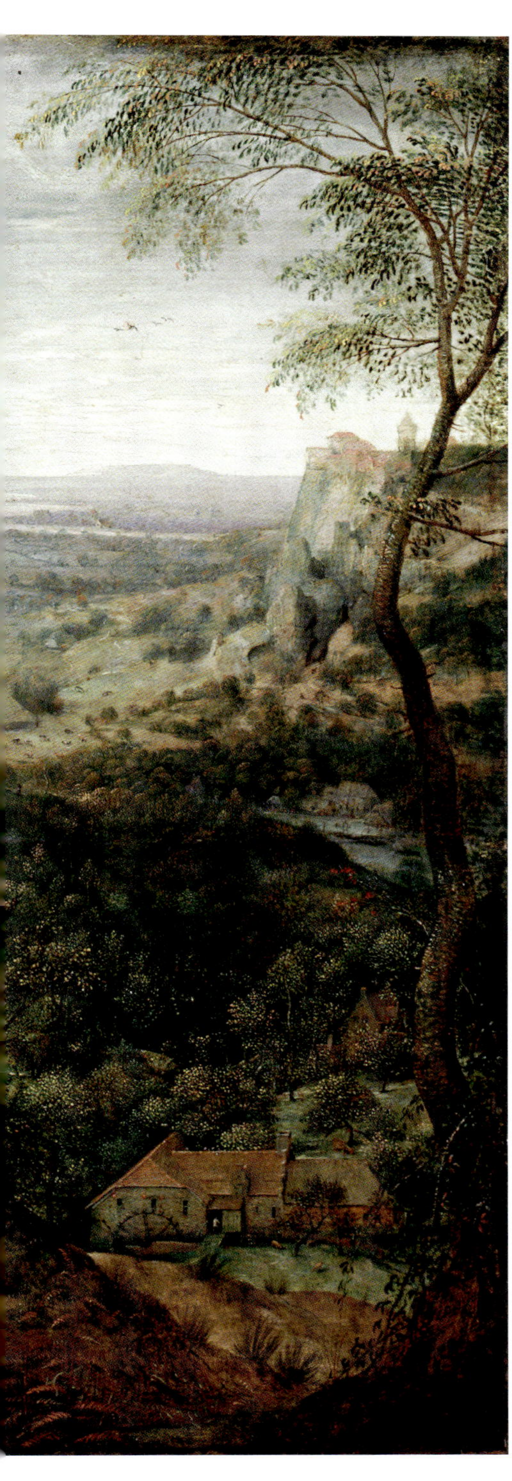

The Magpie on the Gallows, 1568
Oil on wood, 45.9 x 50.8 cm (18 ⅛ x 20 in.)
Darmstadt, Hessisches Landesmuseum

Pages 274/275
The Peasant Wedding, *c.* 1568
Oil on oak, 114 x 164 cm (44 ⅞ x 64 ⅝ in.)
Vienna, Kunsthistorisches Museum,
Gemäldegalerie

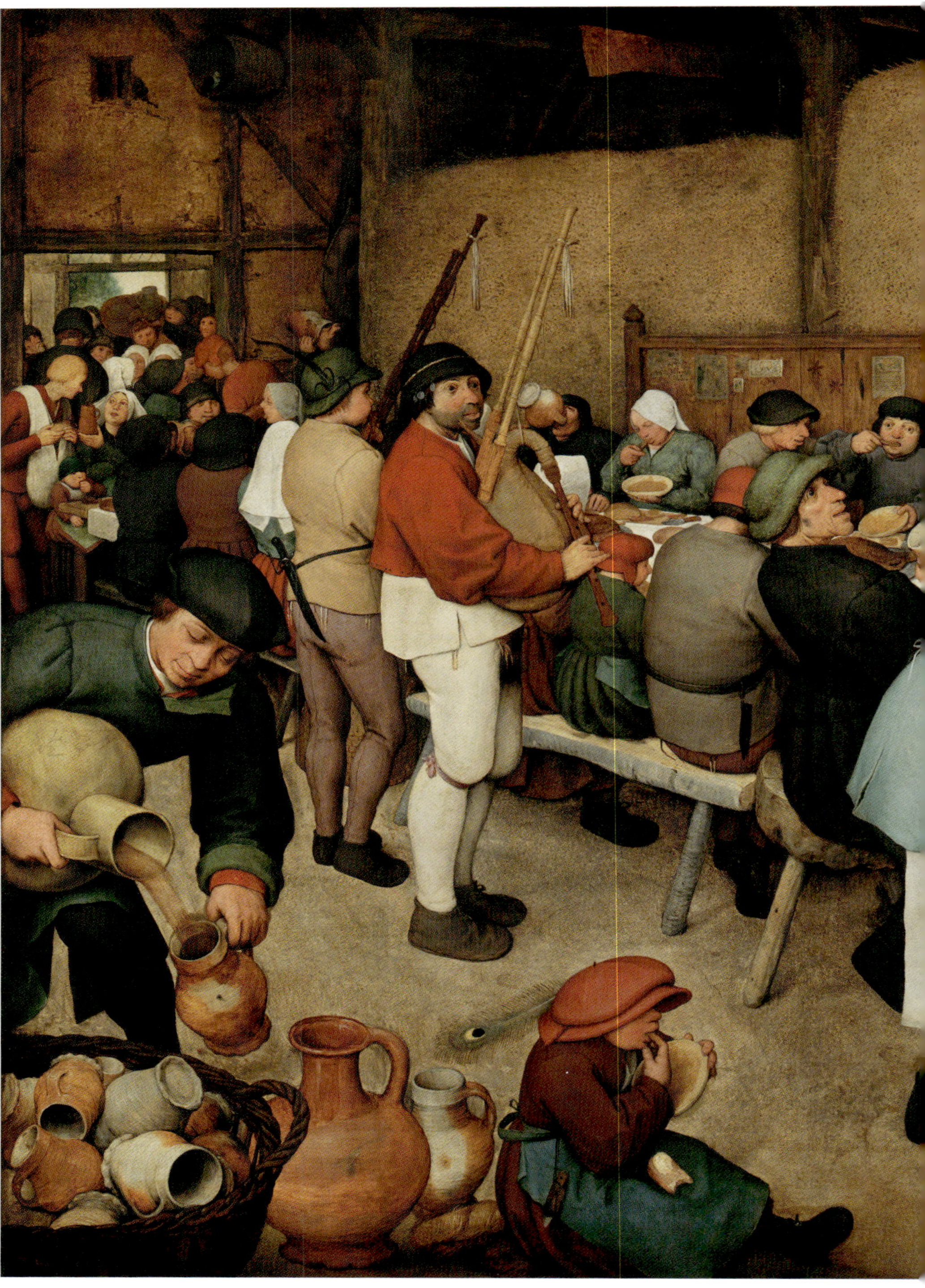

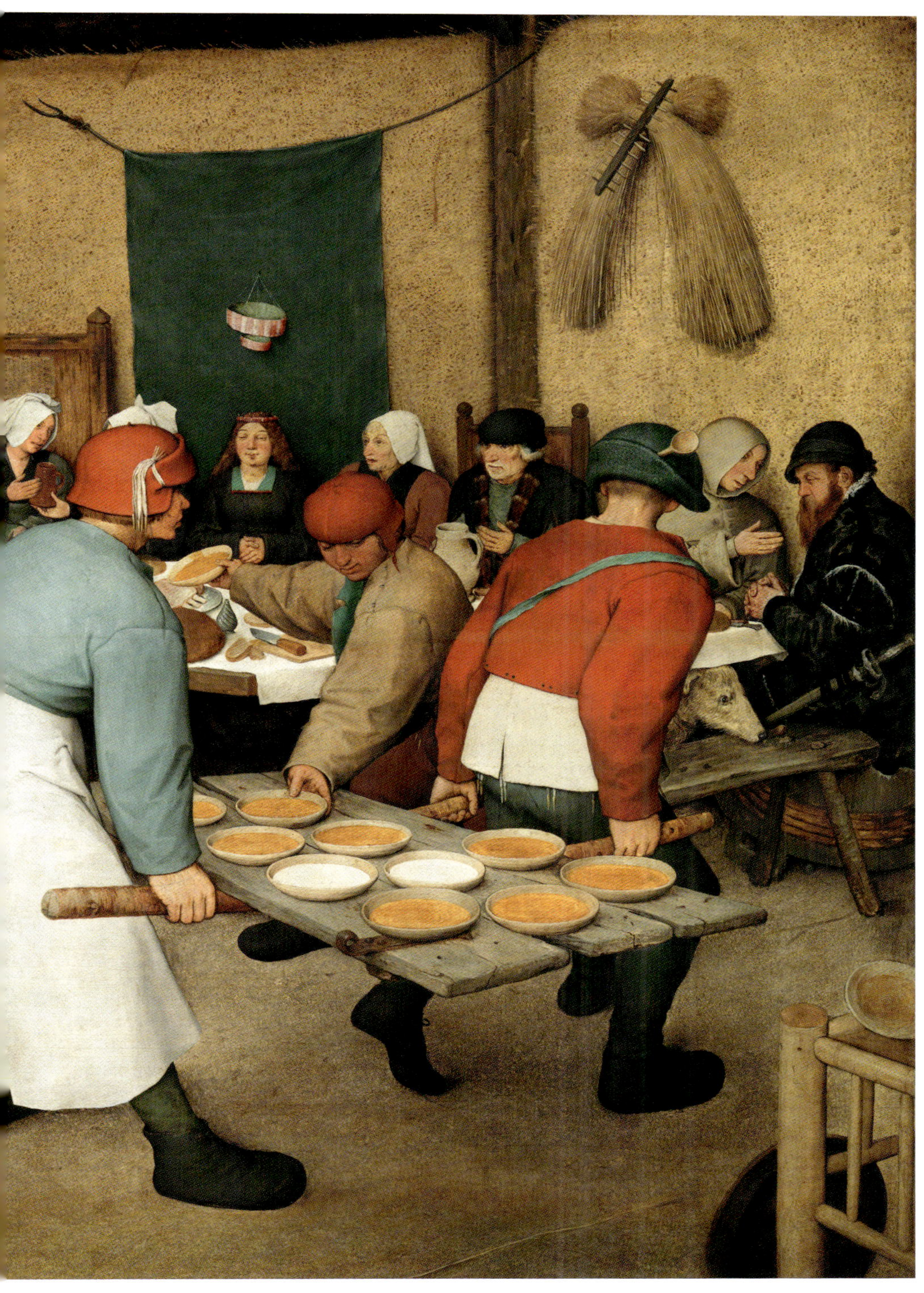

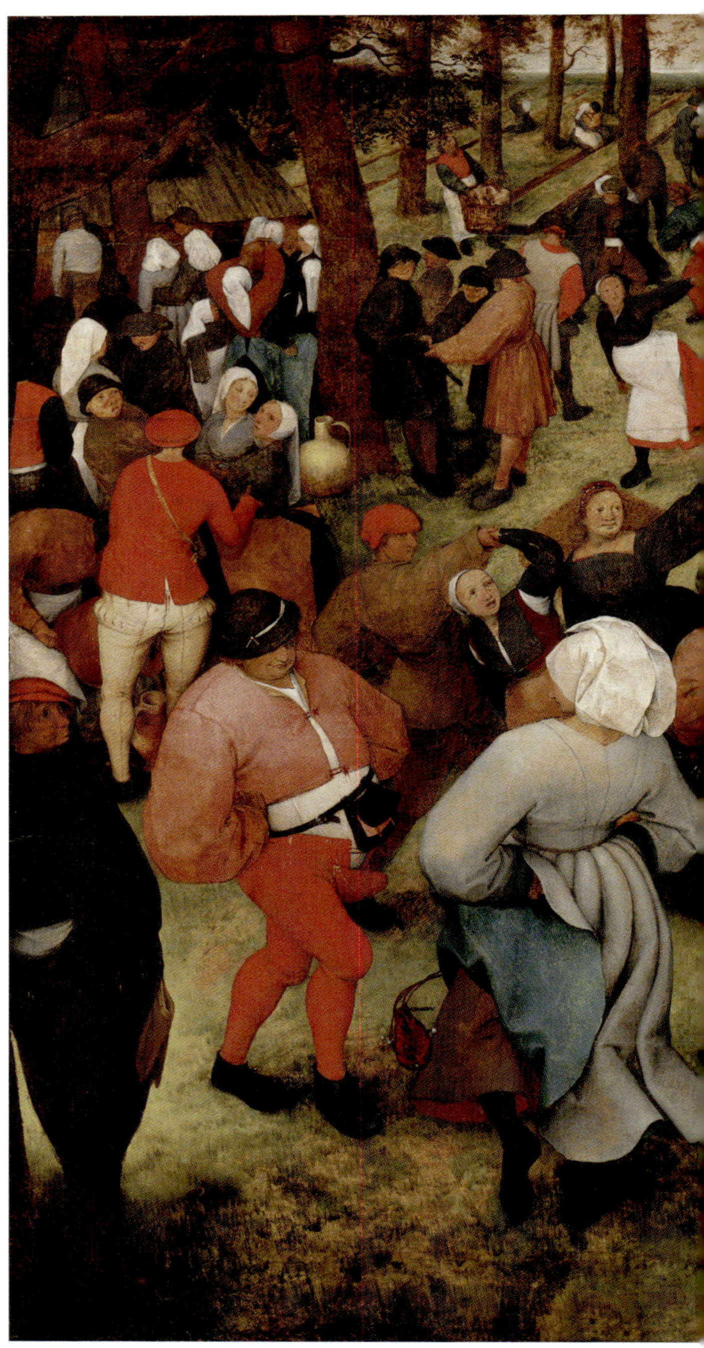

The Wedding Dance, *c.* 1566
Oil on wood, 119.4 x 157.5 cm
(47 ⅛ x 62 ⅛ in.)
Detroit, Michigan,
Institute of Arts

Pages 278/279
The Peasant Dance, *c.* 1568
Oil on oak, 114 x 164 cm
(44 ⅞ x 64 ⅝ in.)
Vienna, Kunsthistorisches
Museum, Gemäldegalerie

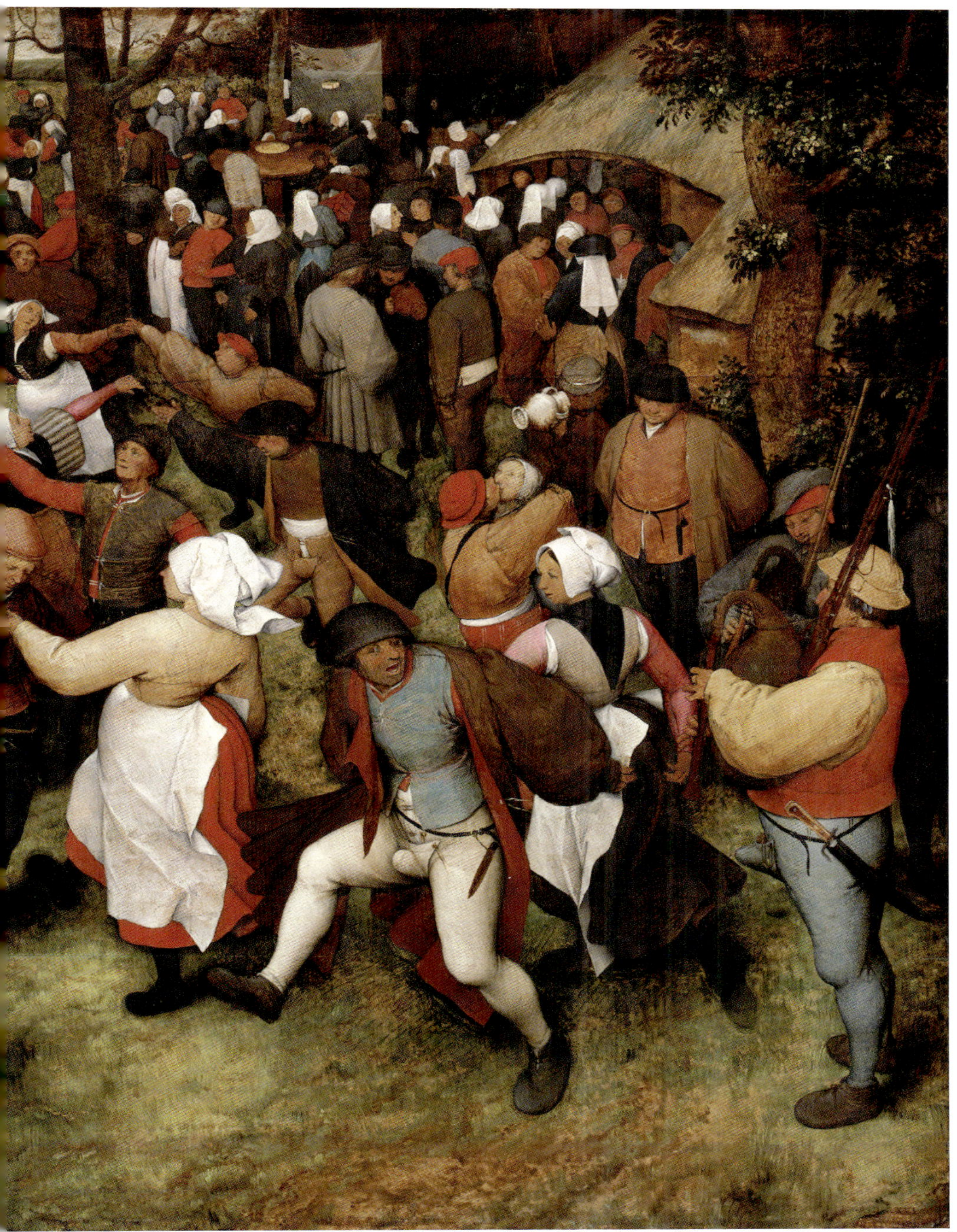

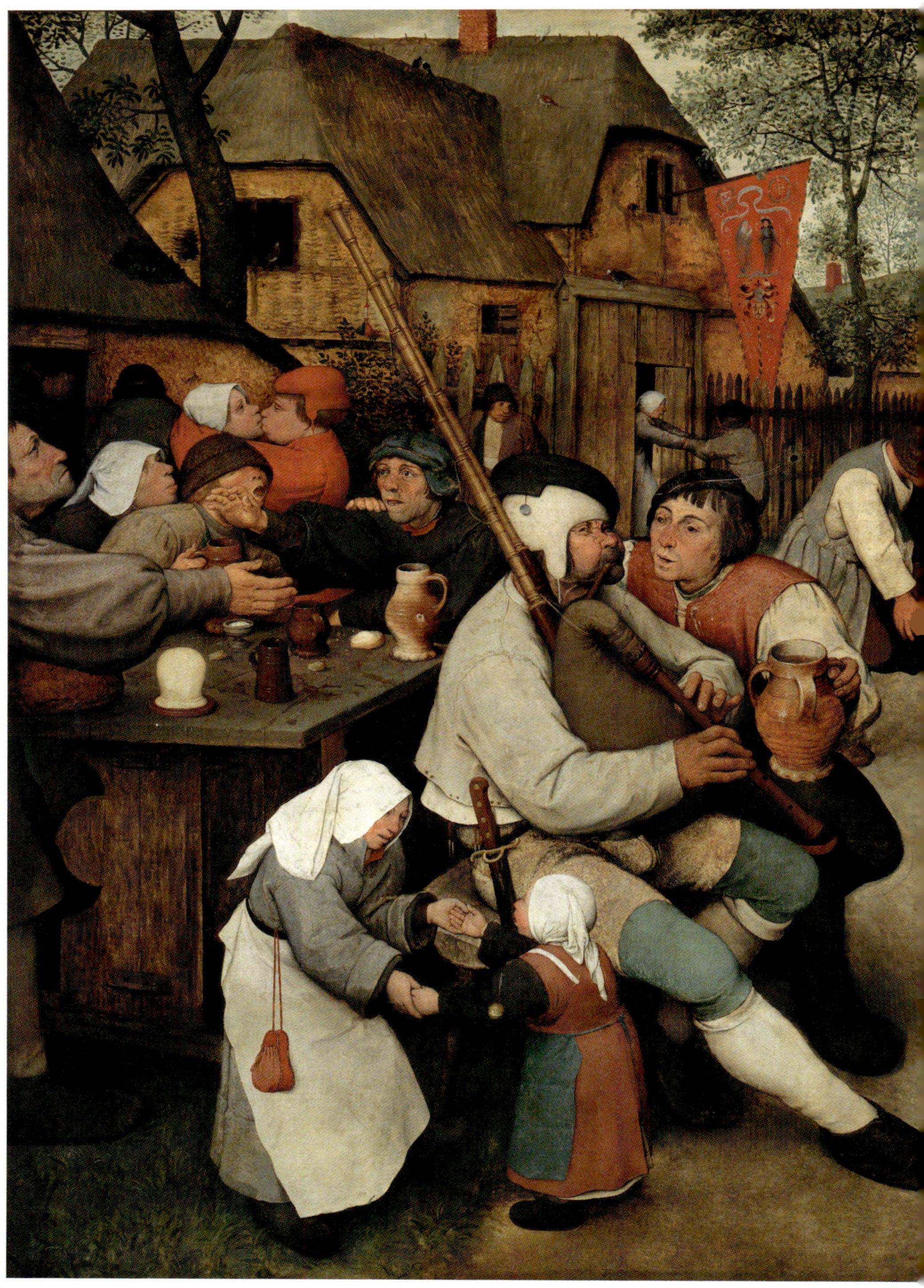

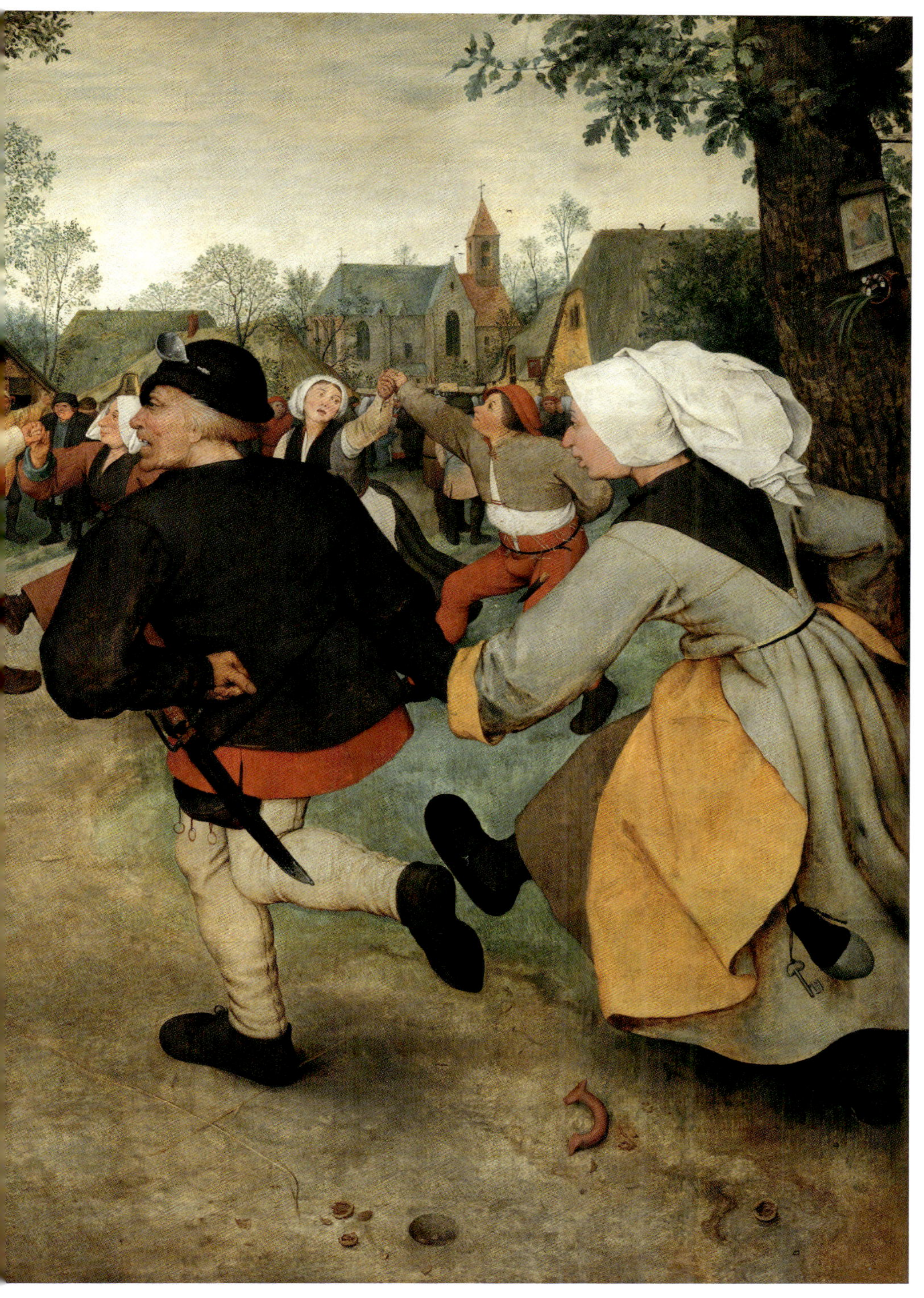

VII.

The Face of the World: Landscapes and Seasons

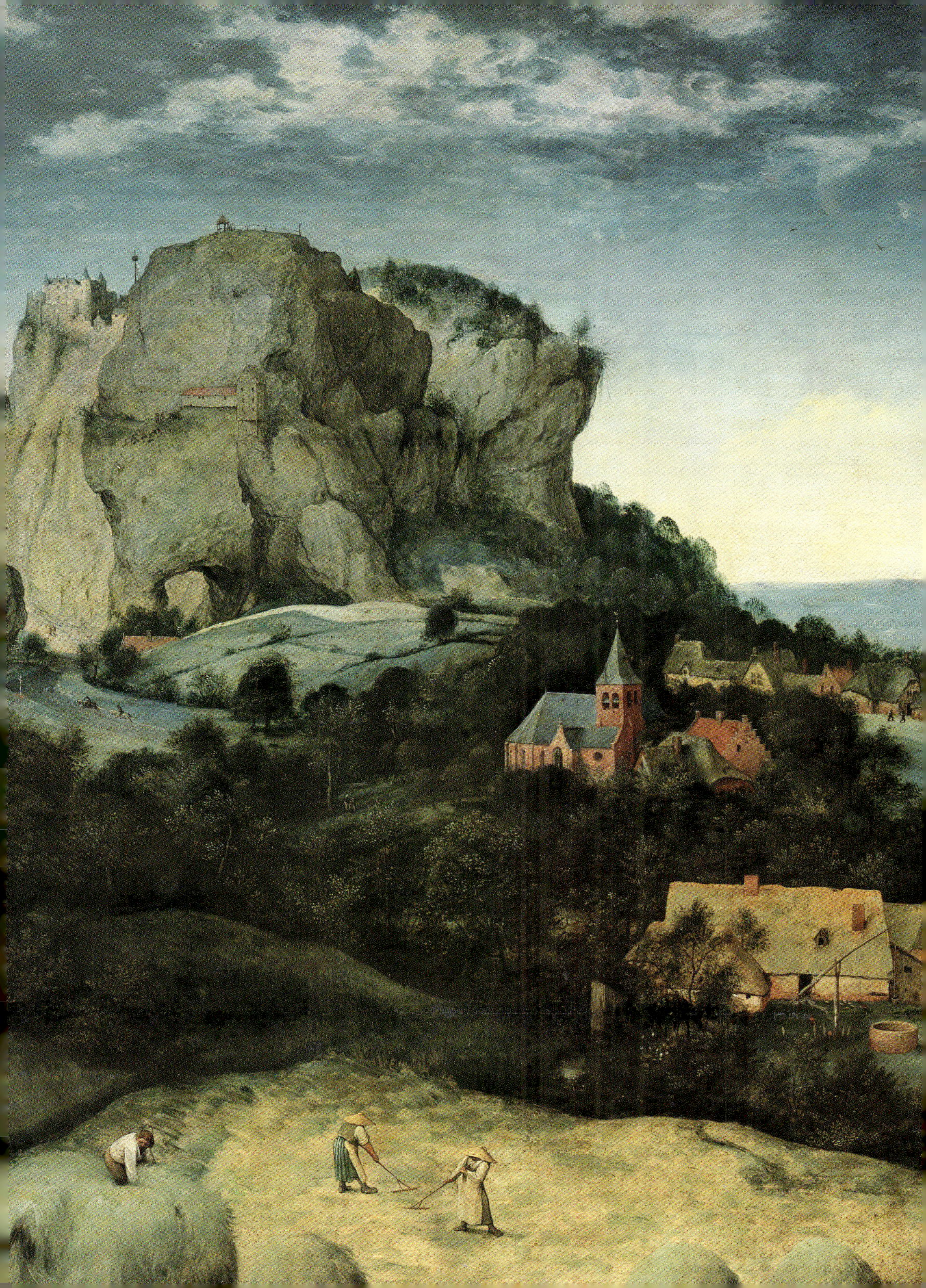

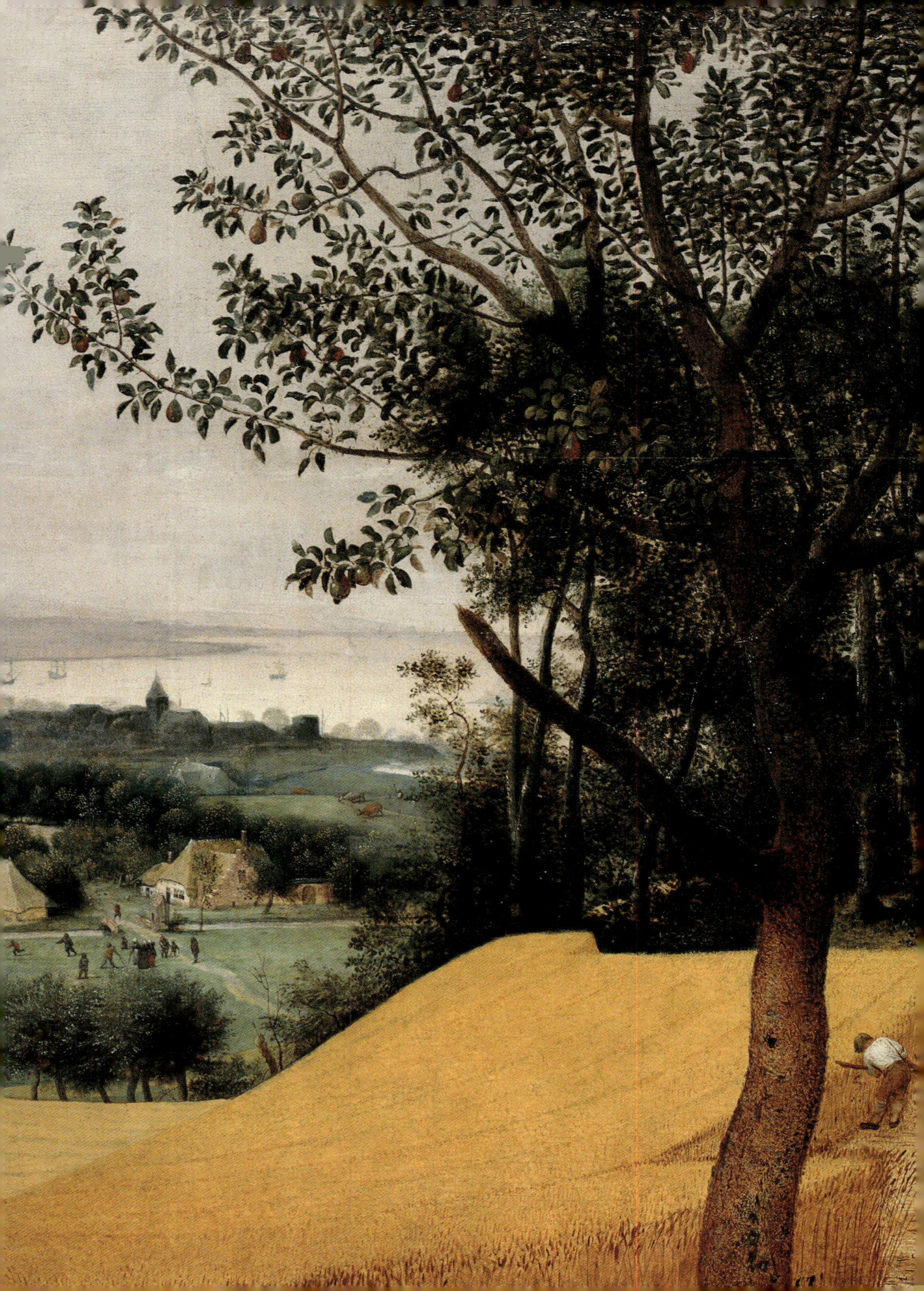

Bruegel's depictions of the seasons form the largest interrelated picture cycle that has come down to us from Bruegel. Five large-format panels show vast landscape panoramas and portray the typical activities of people in the yearly round. It has long been assumed that the cycle comprised six works. For Bruegel did not opt for the classical concept of the four seasons or the twelve months. Each of the pictures, all produced in 1565, represents two months. An inventory informs us that the series was part of Niclaes Jonghelinck's collection; he owned a country villa before the gates of Antwerp and was one of the foremost collectors and art patrons of his day.[165] It's plausible that the cycle originated as a commission. Producing all six panels will have taken up a major part of the year. It is an appealing thought that the artists painted each picture in the corresponding season so as to be able to observe the appropriate atmospheric conditions, though of course there's no proof of this.

The striking feature in all the pictures is Bruegel's ability to observe nature in every detail. The clarity or haziness of the air varies greatly depending on whether it is summer or winter. This is accompanied by a different awareness of depth. Furthermore, the intensity of colours and cloud formation – dependent on the quality of light – changes throughout the year. Bruegel has captured all of this. He doesn't simply show the objects comprising a natural landscape, but also the appearance of the world itself. Today popular titles have become attached to each of the pictures, seeking orientation on a specific event or aesthetic impression. *The Gloomy Day* (pp. 290/291, Cat. 18) shows a blackening sky and a gathering storm. The picture corresponds to the iconography for the months of February and March, revealed in the people in the foreground, busy with the typical activities of pre-spring – cutting osier stakes or celebrating Carnival. They are all alike in their unawareness, devoting themselves to their tasks and ignorant of the threatening storm and floods in the background. There, the first ships are already sinking, and the sea is flooding over the dykes, forcing a cowherd to flee (pp. 294/295).

The Hay Harvest (pp. 296/297, Cat. 19) illustrates in the most glorious colours the abundance of early summer and hay harvesting, the months of June and July. The people's multifaceted tasks are spread across the picture, with the rich harvest being transported to market in overflowing baskets. Bruegel ostensibly allows himself a joke – one of the women labourers striding forth in the foreground suddenly seems to be glancing at the

Pages 281
The Hay Harvest (**June/July**; detail), 1565
(see ill. pp. 296/297)

The Harvesters (**August/September**; detail), 1565
(see ill. pp. 302/303)

observer. Even in all her youthful *joie de vivre* she is threatened with decline and decay, reflected not only in the old woman walking next to her, but also in the reaper at the left edge, towards whom the three women are moving. The man is sharpening his scythe, reminding us that beauty in Bruegel is always linked to transience.

A similar motif is seen in *The Harvesters* (pp. 302/303, Cat. 20), in which a reaper at the left edge is about to hit and break a jug, which he cannot see in the midst of the dense field of corn. But our attention is first drawn to another scene. Although Bruegel leads the eye far into the depths and all the way down to the sea, our eye is primarily caught by the people who are taking a break at the edge of the half-harvested field. Exhausted by their work, they have thrown themselves down in the shade of a tree and now see to their creature comforts. They greatly relish their food; one of the group has even lain down to sleep at the foot of the tree. It is not only the people's activities that convey the atmosphere of late summer, but also the satiated yellow of the wheat and the hazy sky; within the series, the picture represents the months of August and September.

The Return of the Herd (pp. 306/307, Cat 21) in turn shows a group of cowherds driving cattle back through an autumn landscape. The picture impressively captures the mood of the months of October and November. The trees are already bare, and the rich colours of summer have given way to pale brown and yellow tones. The arduous path down a hillside allows the cowherds no time to notice the group in tow behind them, consisting of a rider and several lance-bearers. Steeply towering rocks in the background and the dark clouds brewing up complete the melancholy scene, its darkest motif almost concealed in the middle ground: if we look closely, there, across the river, is a gallows (pp. 308/309).

Finally, *The Hunters in the Snow* (pp. 310/311, Cat. 22), which presents us with an inhospitable winter landscape, represents the months of December and January. We can almost feel the exhaustion of the homecoming hunters, struggling back through deep snow. Deep footprints show how arduous each step must be. The men have bagged little; only one of them has the body of a fox on his shoulders. The hunters' posture tells of disappointment, even the dogs, seem tired as they trot along – one of them seems to be looking at us.

The characterisation evident in all titles demonstrates the wish to individualise the pictures. Countering this, Jonghelinck's inventory simply mentions pictures of the months. Recent research on the series, which has provided interpretative treatments as comprehensive as they are detailed, has revealed an eschatological subtext in the months series.[166] Thus in all the surviving pictures we can discover iconographic hints of the approaching Last Judgement, which is why the secular time embodied in them is likewise to be seen as the end of time. In *The Gloomy Day*, the storm floods, the sinking ships and the white bird against the dark sky reverberate with associations of the biblical deluge.

All these details are markers of the work's eschatological dimension – in the Gospel of St Matthew, the deluge is a typological reference to the end of time, thus the time shortly before Christ's Second Coming for the Last Judgement: "For as in those days that were before the flood [...], so shall also the Coming of the Son of Man be" (Matthew 24: 38–39). In *The Return of the Herd*, the range of motifs revolving around the flood is taken up again when Bruegel paints a rainbow in the vineyard, reminding us of God's covenant at the end of the flood. Bruegel's rainbow is oddly pale; it too points to a relevant exegetic tradition according to which the rainbow has only two colours: a watery one, alluding to the flood, and a fiery one, presaging the Last Judgement. *The Hay Harvest* shows the transience of human life by alluding to the biblical comparison of flesh and grass (Psalm 103: 15). And in the top left corner of *The Hay Harvest*, we see an eclipse of the Sun, which likewise counts as one of the biblical signs of the end of time (Luke 21: 25). Finally, in *The Hunters in the Snow* there is the central motif of the bird trap, which stands not only in general for temptation by the devil, but, especially in the sixteenth century, was an extremely common metaphor of an imminent Last Judgement.

Against this background, Bruegel's choice of the unusual number of pictures can also be explained, in that the series, originally consisting of six panels, allude to the six days of the Creation. Thus the pictures point implicitly to the missing seventh day, the Sabbath, the day of the Lord and simultaneously the Second Coming of Christ on the last day. The point of Bruegel's concept consists in his planning this seventh day as an empty place in the centre of the cycle and ultimately intended for the observer. The latter – in accordance with a mystical tradition – must realise that Christ's Second Coming should not be expected at the end of time, but can take place any time within him, in his soul. The signs of the end of time scattered throughout the pictures would then not be understood literally as a warning of the Last Judgement, but rather as a subtle invitation to cultivate one's own powers of judgement.[167]

The months series takes shape as an epic of almost biblical dimensions in terms of theological concepts about life here and now. In composition, all the pictures are panoramic. The large formats invite viewers to come closer until the scene occupies their whole field of vision, and we step over the imaginary threshold into the inner world of the picture. The structure as panorama creates the conditions for the planned illusionism of the paintings. The cycle comprises a biblical epic in that it presents the order that God imposed upon his creation. The seasons express human nature. Men and women also experience spring, summer, autumn and winter in their lives.

We are confronted directly with the connection of beauty, fertility and transience. In these pictures, the earth nourishes mankind, but can also kill him with its natural forces. The scenes instantaneously evoke this indomitable might of nature. Such ideas presume, however, that we look at the pictures one after the other in order gain an awareness of nature's friendly or hostile character.

One after the other, they stage scenes of nature that are of overwhelming beauty. The eye moves back and forth between the actions and events of the world of mankind in the foreground and the mountains and seas of the background. Bruegel composes his landscapes in such a way that he achieves the maximum in depth. He skilfully uses repoussoirs or, as in *The Return of the Herd*, creates a change of viewpoint: we see the group of animals and people coming from below right and follow them upwards into the depths of the space.

Moreover, all the pictures convey a graphic idea of the distances the people have covered. They frequently appear on the brow of a hill. We see them shortly before they stride down and disappear from our view. Their temporality becomes even more apparent seen against the timeless backdrop of nature. The actual poetry of the cycle evolves out of the tension between the temporal and the timeless. We as observers lapse time and again into the here and now with the people's actions, and then haul ourselves out of it with the view onto the overwhelming panorama. Bruegel also plays with the phenomenon of time in another respect. On one hand, when roaming through the pictures in sequence, we follow the rhythm of the year, which otherwise takes 365 days. On the other, we note the difference between cyclic and linear time. Having arrived at the end, we are at the beginning again. Everything passes, and begins afresh once more.

This beauty of nature is not man-made, and yet it touches us directly. It is a mighty force and has found in Bruegel its foremost interpreter. It has frequently been stated that Bruegel's pictures are aligned to the tradition of the *Weltlandschaften*, "world landscapes". They show cities and villages, rivers and seas, towering mountains with craggy rocks. The artist synthesises impressions of nature into a single picture. To do this, he harks back in a versatile way to motifs of the books of hours and calendar illustrations. Furthermore, the cycle is based on the previous generation of landscape painters. Especially the works of Joachim Patinir (*c.* 1475/80–1524; p. 287) and Herri met de Bles (*c.* 1500/10–1555/60) inspired him in a great variety of ways. These artists were already interested in combining panoramas with figural scenes. But what distinguishes Bruegel from these models and makes him unique is his ability to evoke the "sublime terror" of man in the face of overpowering natural phenomena.

The question thus arises whether Bruegel was familiar with the art theories of late antiquity, namely the text attributed to Pseudo-Longinus, *On the Sublime*. Though written in the 1st century AD, it was first published in 1554 in Greek in Venice and translated into Latin in 1566. The author describes the sublime as something that transfixes us, and defines it as the elemental power of the artist who, with a "well-timed flash of

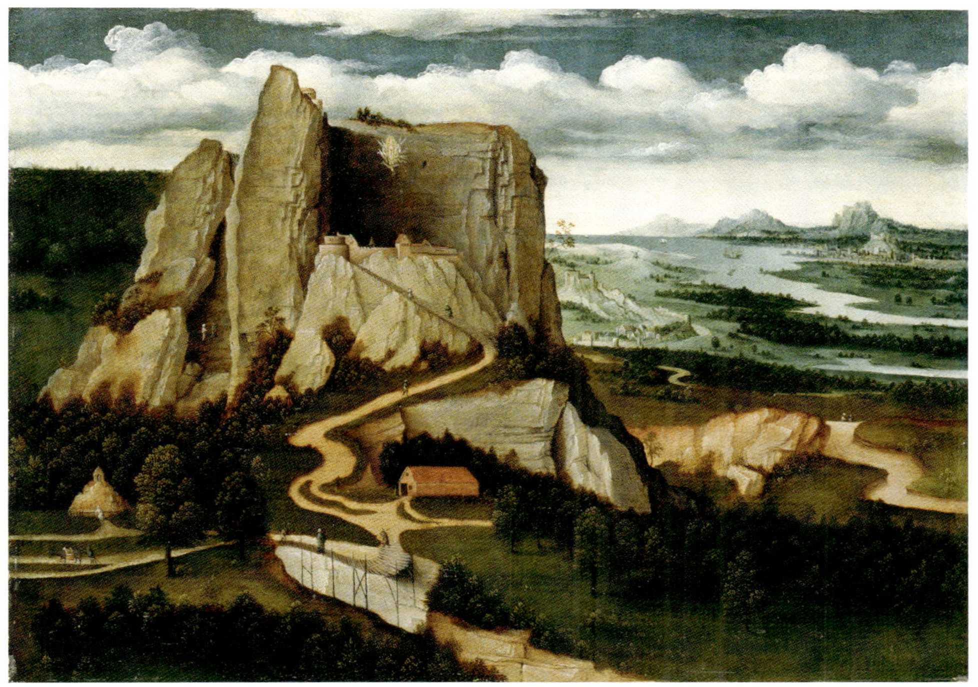

Joachim Patinir, **Landscape with the Ecstasy of St Mary Magdalene**, *c.* 1515–1519
Oil on wood, 26 x 36 cm (10 ¼ x 14 ⅛ in.)
Zurich, Kunsthaus Zürich, Prof. Dr. L. Ruzicka Foundation

sublimity scatters everything before it like a bolt of lightning and reveals the full power of the speaker at a single stroke."[168]

Pseudo-Longinus's text is not comparable with a rhetorical didactic treatise, but simply contains, and comments on, a collection of successful examples of forms of the sublime. The enemy of all that is sublime for Pseudo-Longinus is artificiality. The author does not agree with the idea that a sublime effect is achieved by way of proportionality. On the contrary, he supports the theory that the lowly and the plain are best suited to represent the sublime and so arouse the emotional response of the listener. According to Pseudo-Longinus, art only achieves its goal at all if it seems like nature. Thus he recommends staying close to life and reality. Rhetorical devices are correspondingly most effective therefore when their use remains concealed. "Using pathos", he states, "has a stronger emotional effect when the speaker makes it seem born of the moment, instead of contriving it as a ploy […]."[169] The author also cites examples of the power of language in the Old Testament and is critical of the canon of didactic writings of classical antiquity.

In attempting to understand Bruegel's landscapes, it is interesting to keep in mind Pseudo-Longinus's rhetorical intention in confronting the overwhelming force of nature seen in the rapids and oceans with little streams and burns, or the volcano eruptions of Etna with the light of a candle. And it is instructive to read his introductory words leading up to this comparison: that nature "plants in us an untameable love for everything that is great and more divine than we are".[170]

Bruegel's paintings endeavour to do justice to this "untameable yearning" for "greatness" and "the divine". They show the overwhelming power of nature and yet simultaneously contradict it with the drama of people's daily lives – people who seem oblivious to nature's mighty theatre.

The Hunters in the Snow (Winter; also: **December/January** or **The Return of the Hunters**; detail), 1565
(see ill. pp. 310/311)

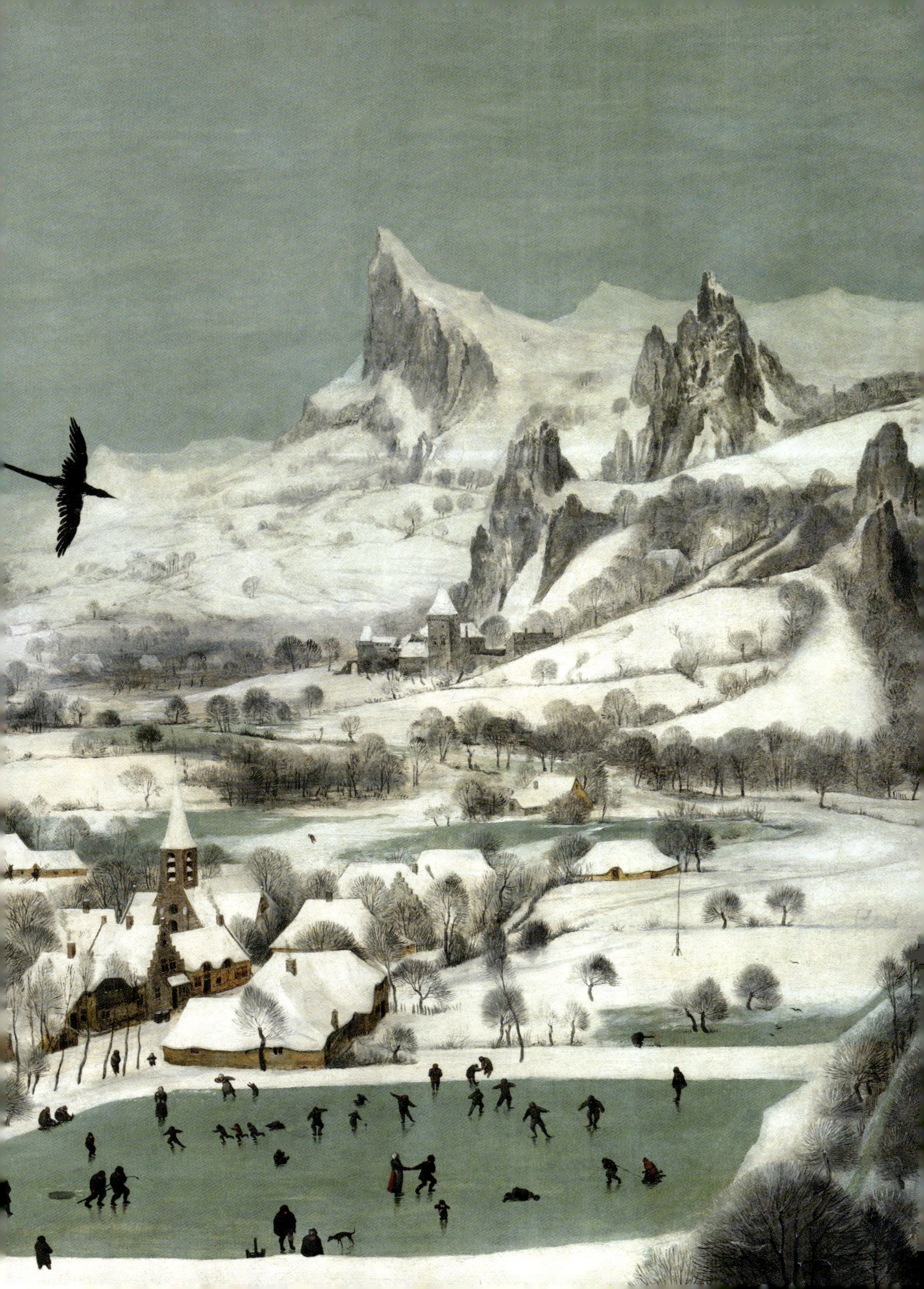

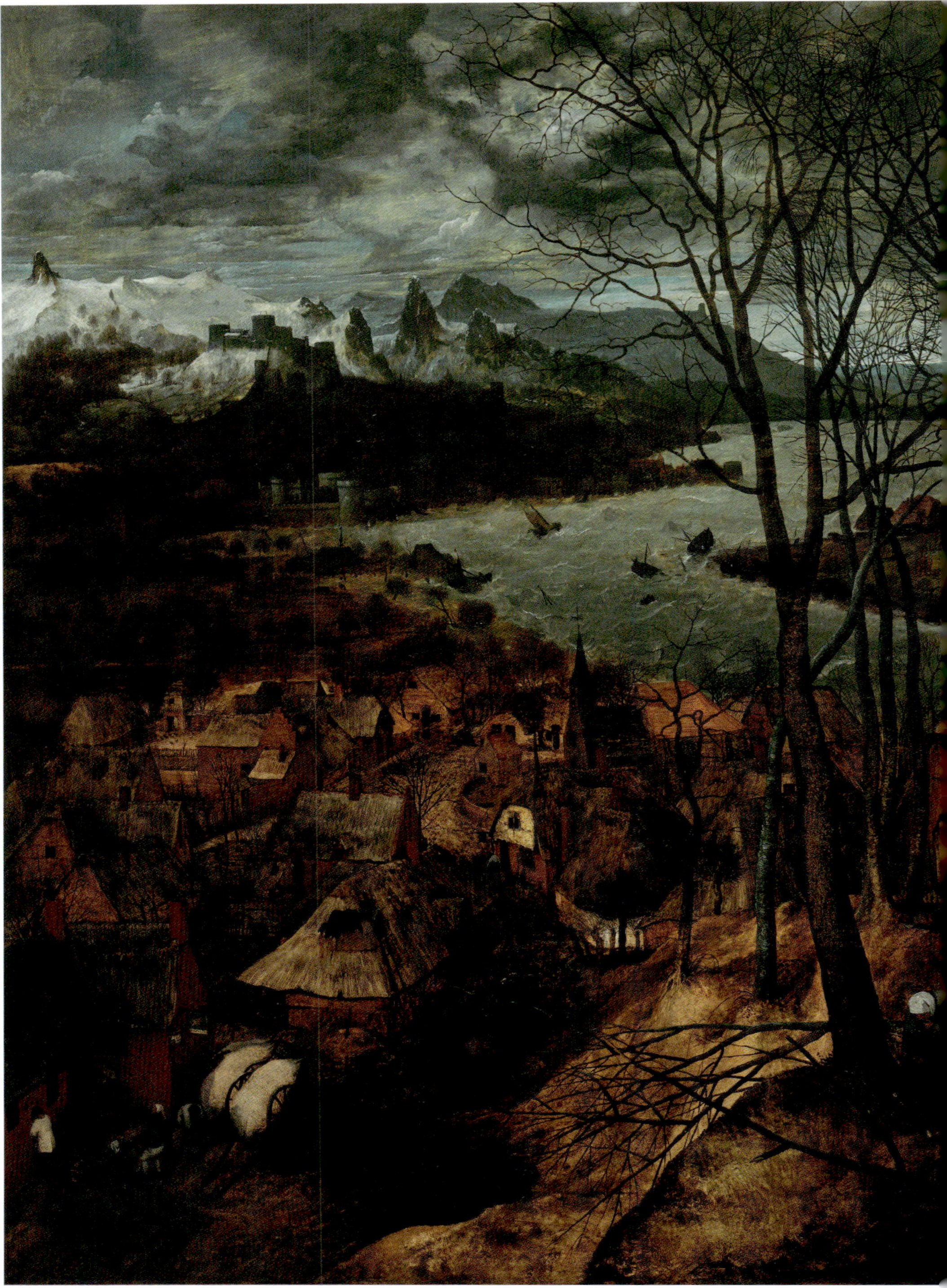

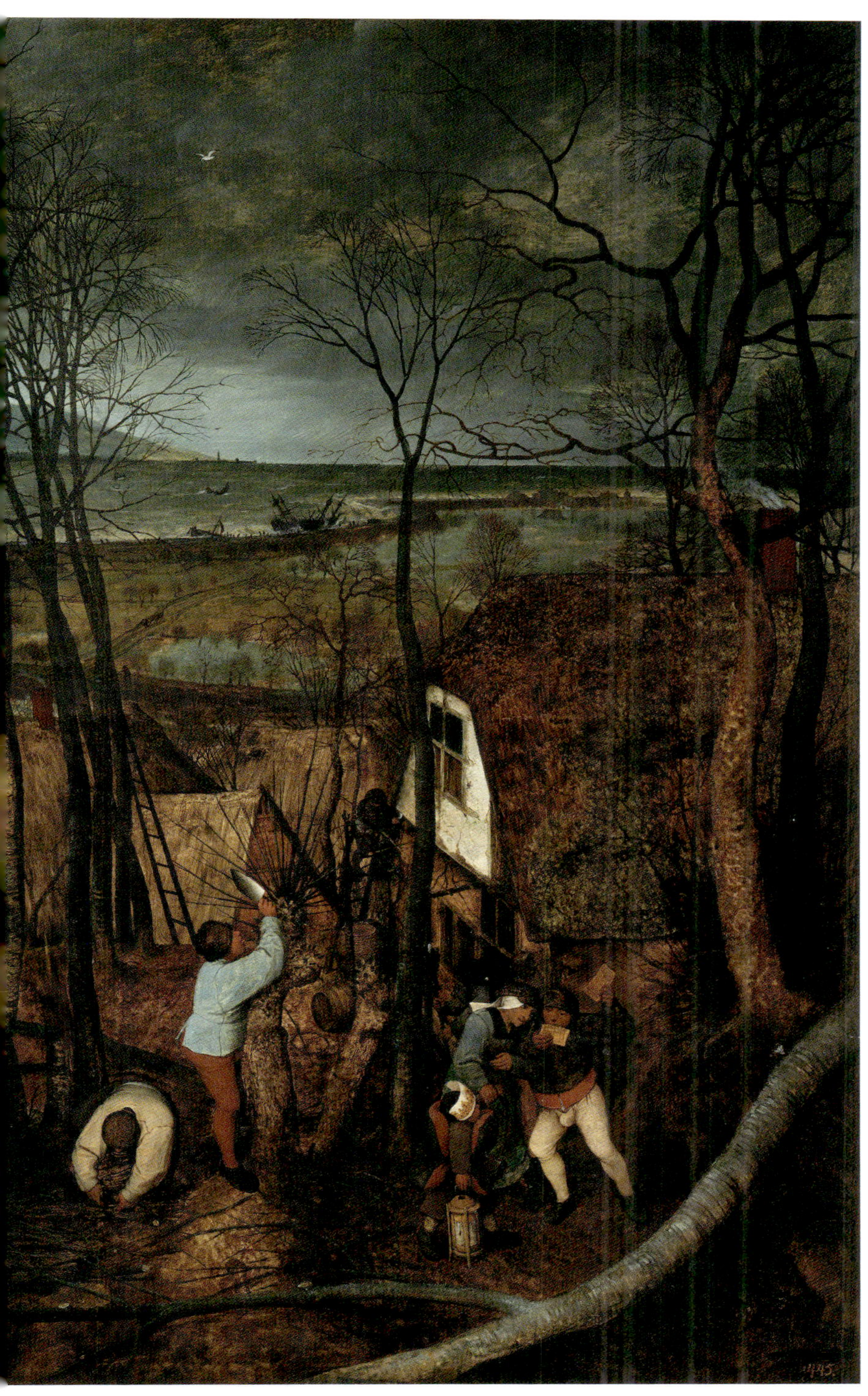

Pages 290/291
The Gloomy Day (February/March), 1565
Oil on oak, 118 x 163 cm (46 ½ x 64 ⅛ in.)
Vienna, Kunsthistorisches Museum, Gemäldegalerie
(details pages 293, 294–295)

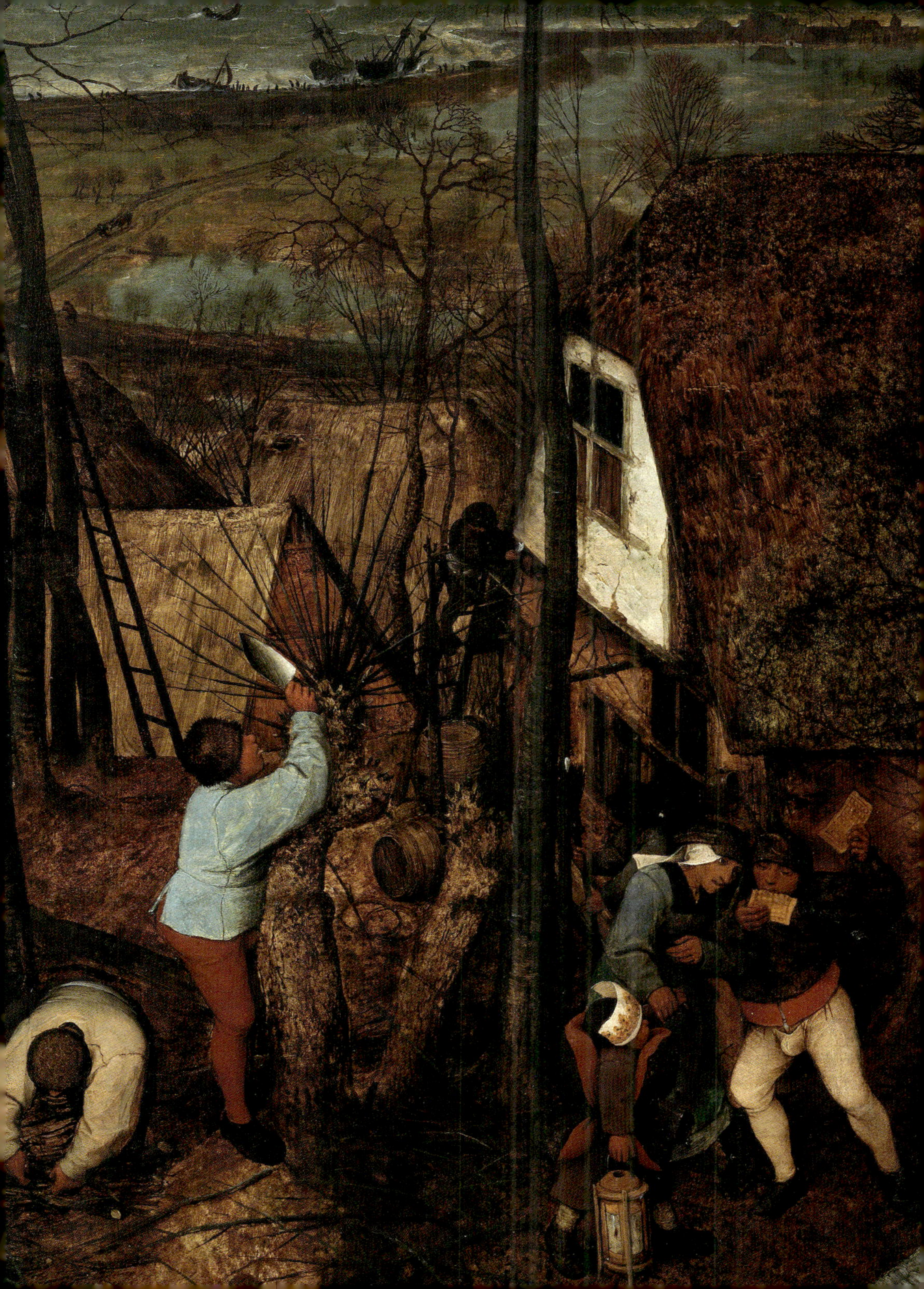

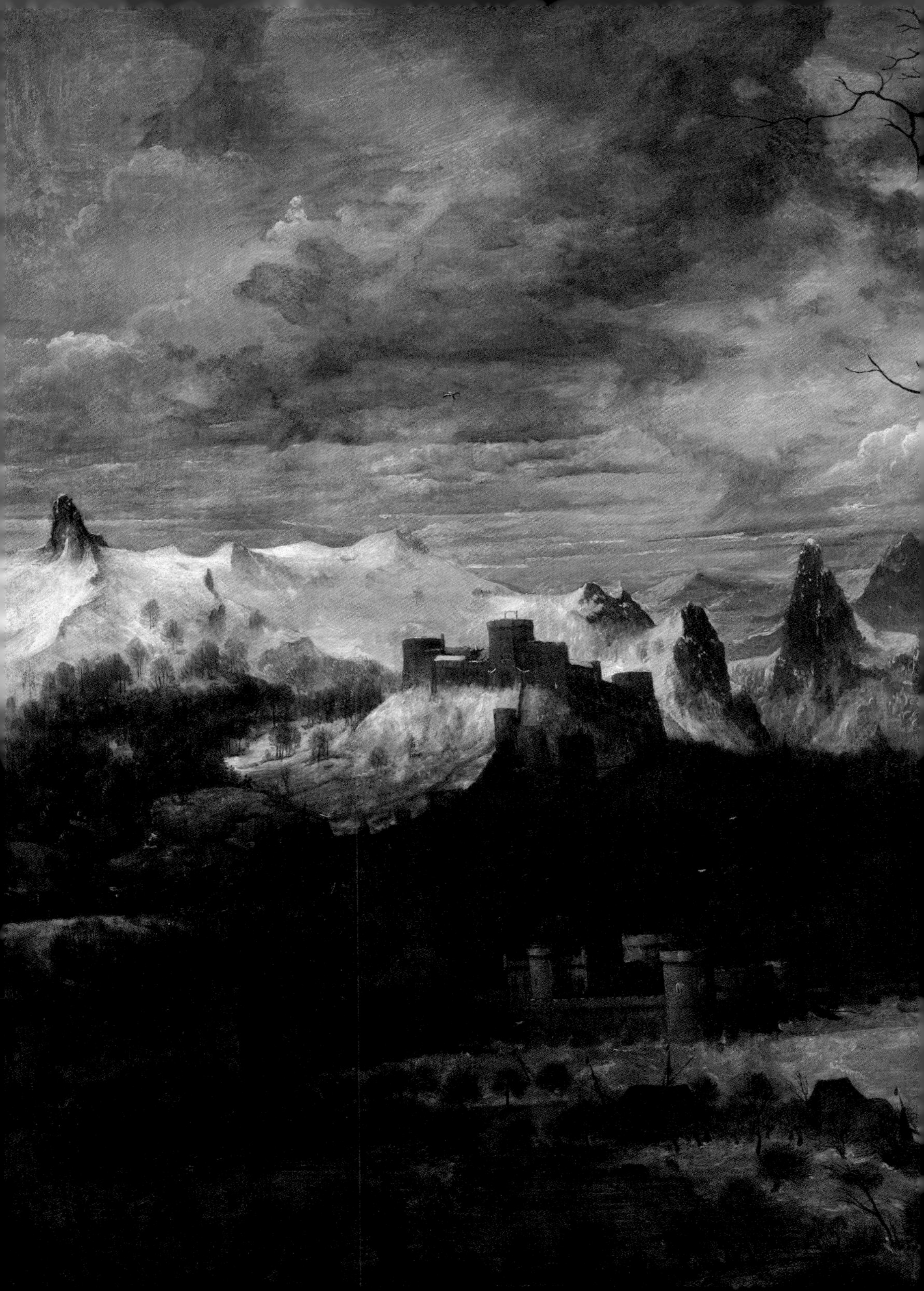

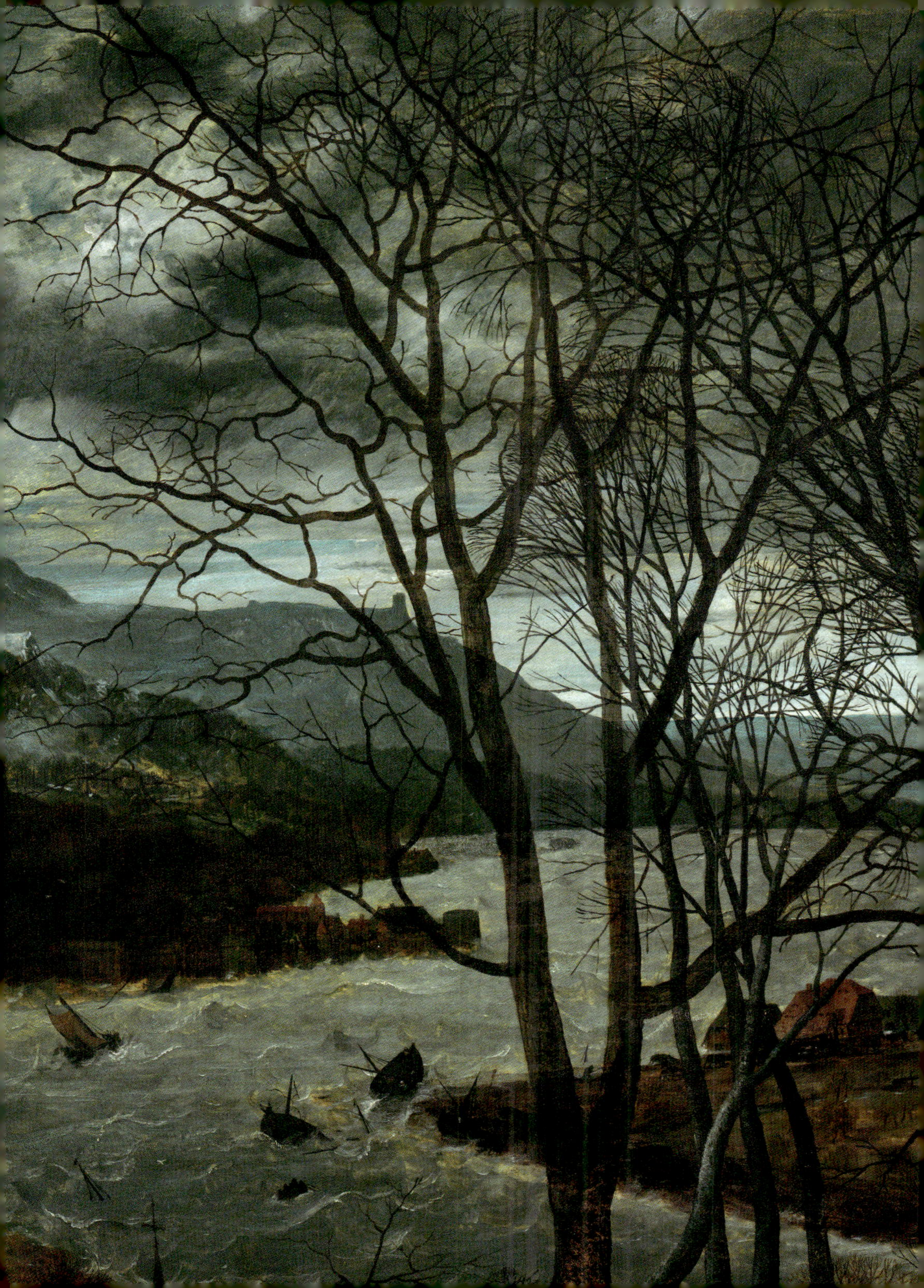

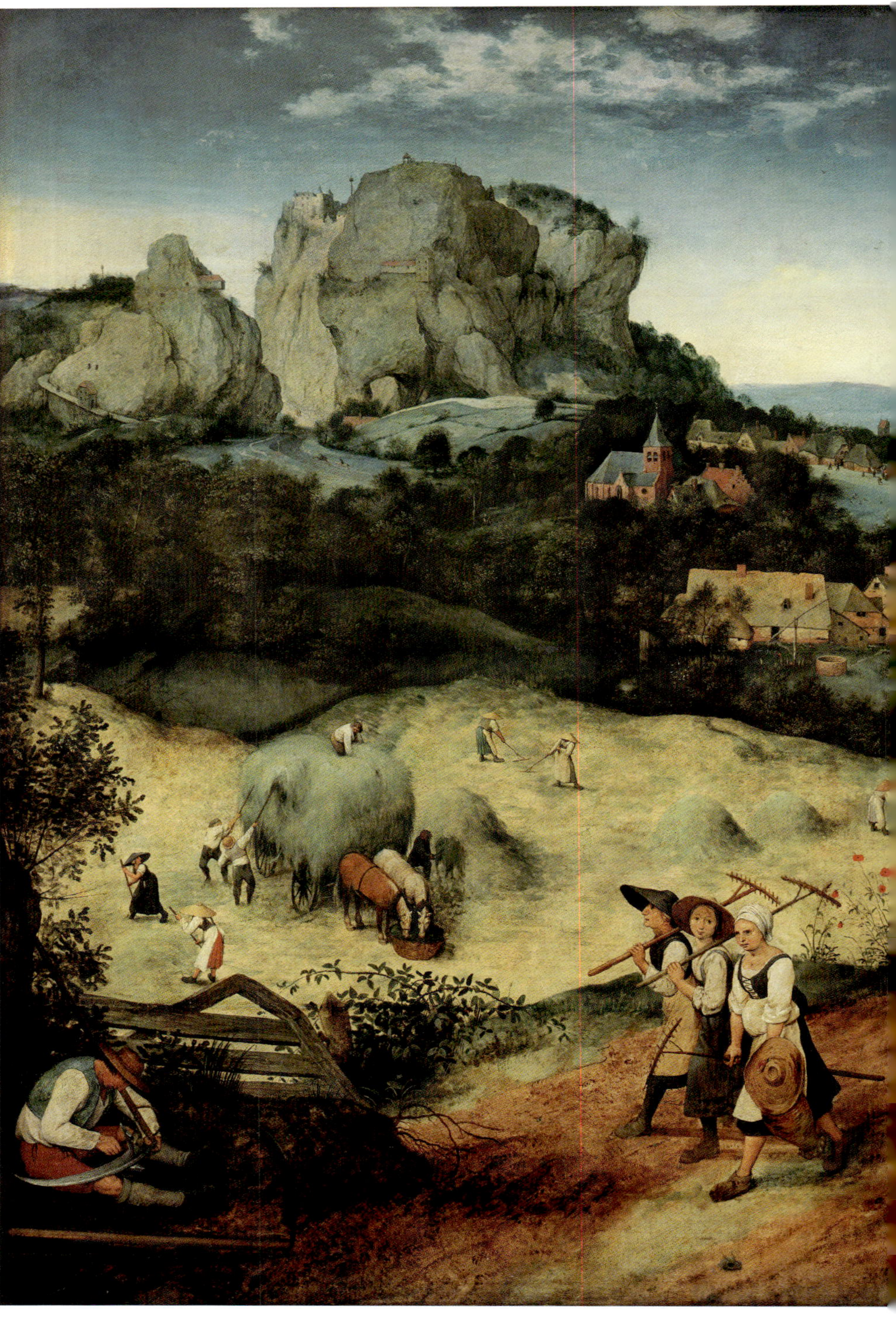

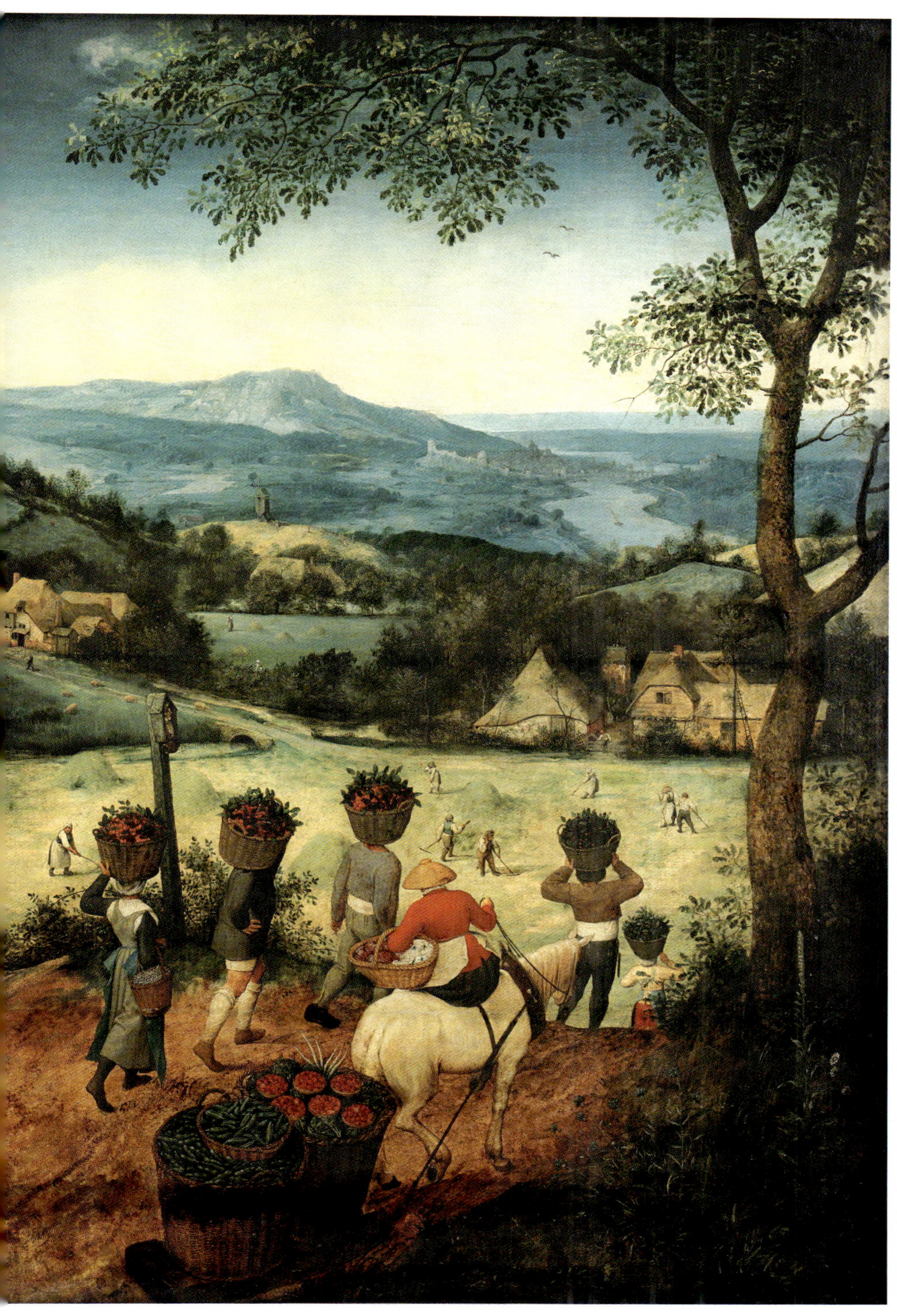

Pages 296/297
The Hay Harvest (June/July), 1565
Oil on wood, 114 x 158 cm (44 ⅞ x 62 ¼ in.). Prague, Palais Lobkowicz
(details pages 299, 300–301)

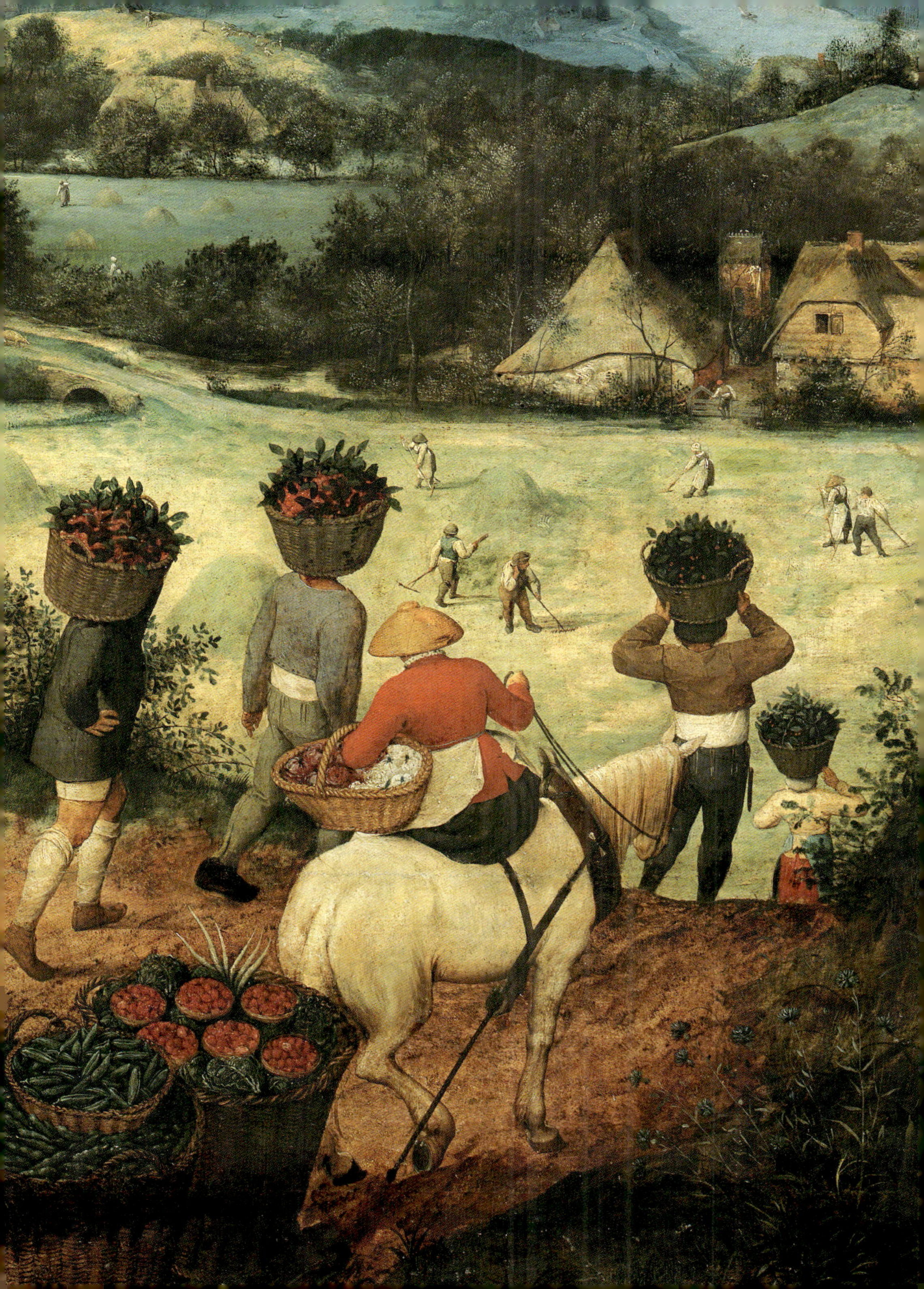

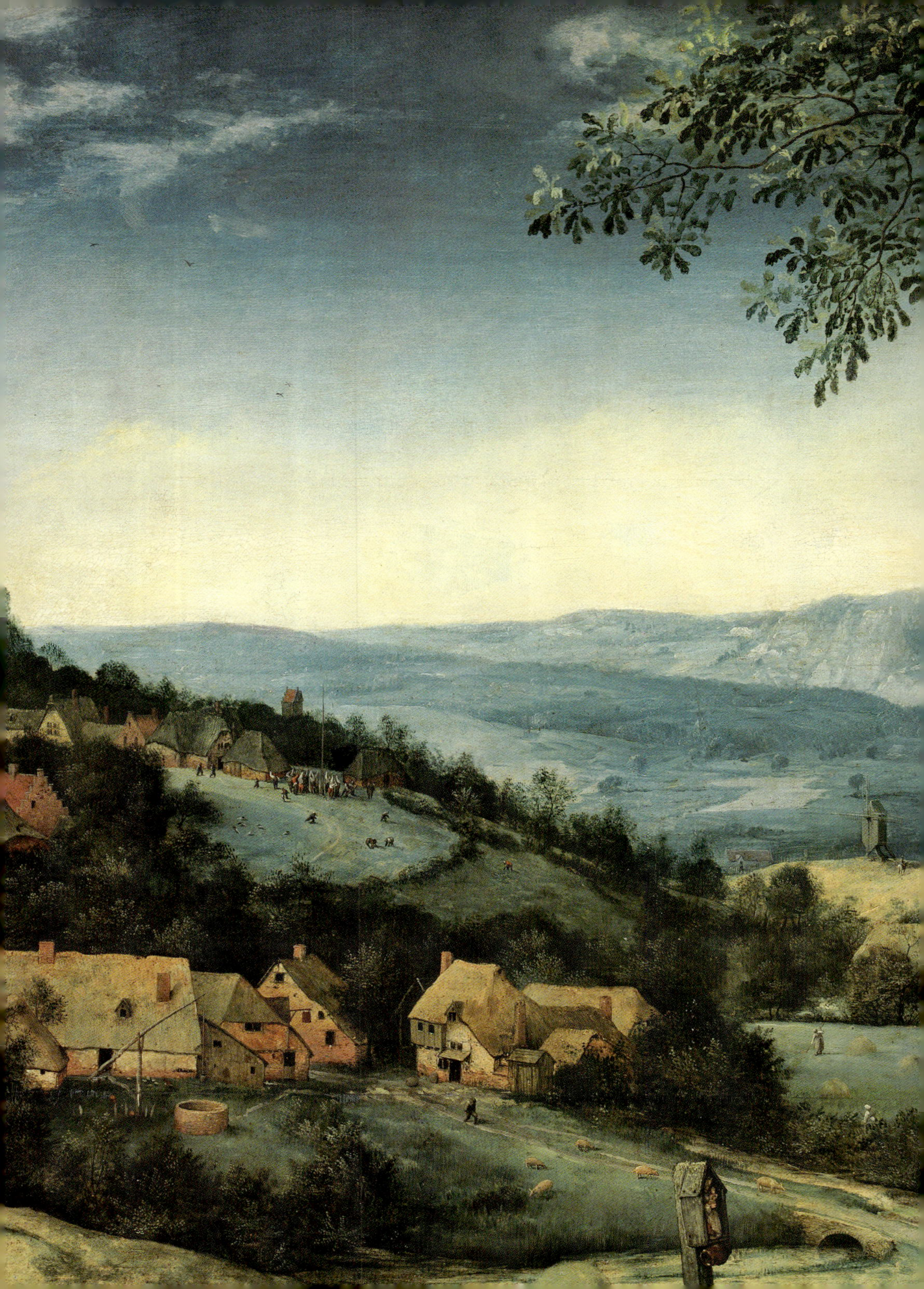

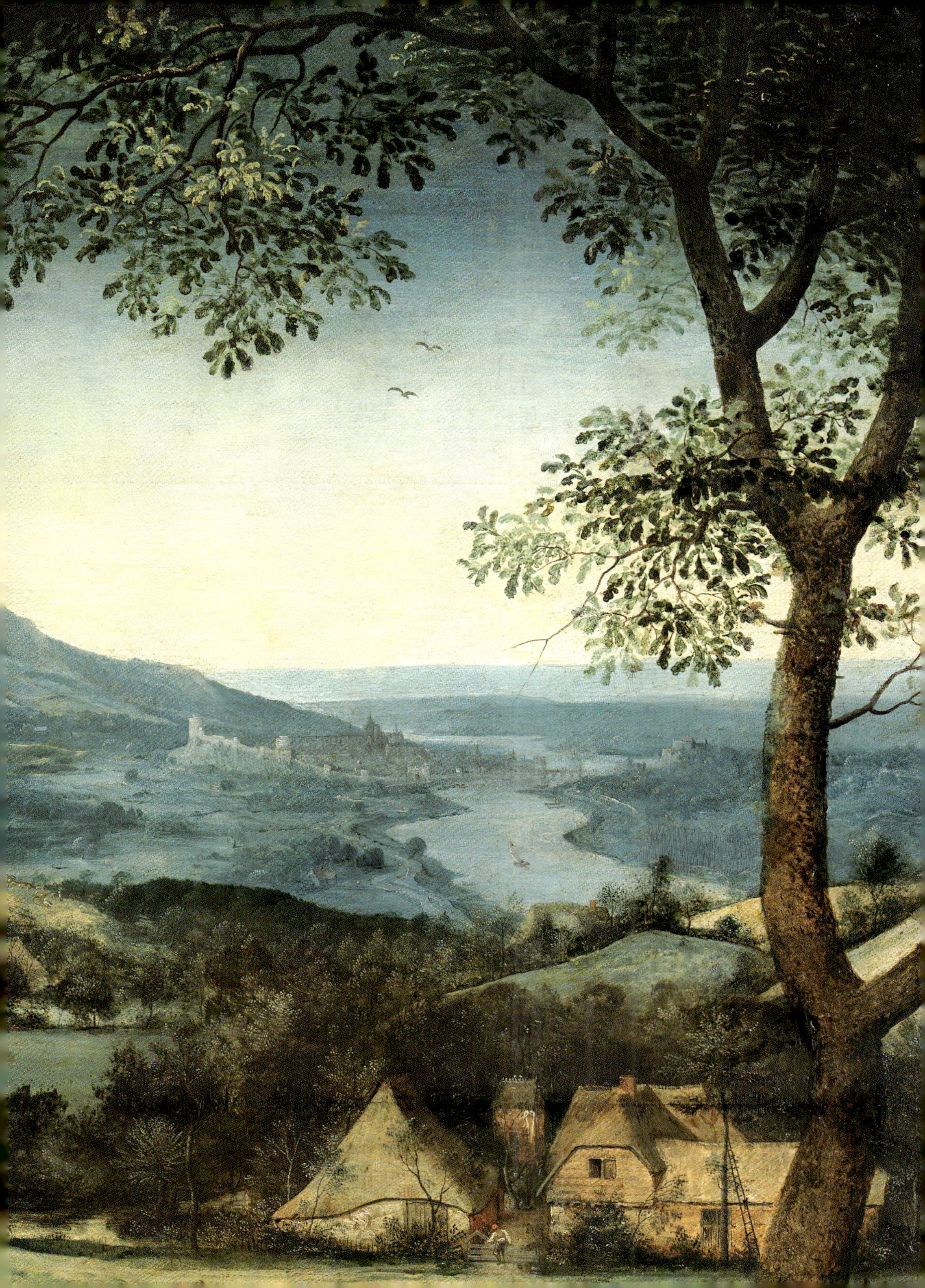

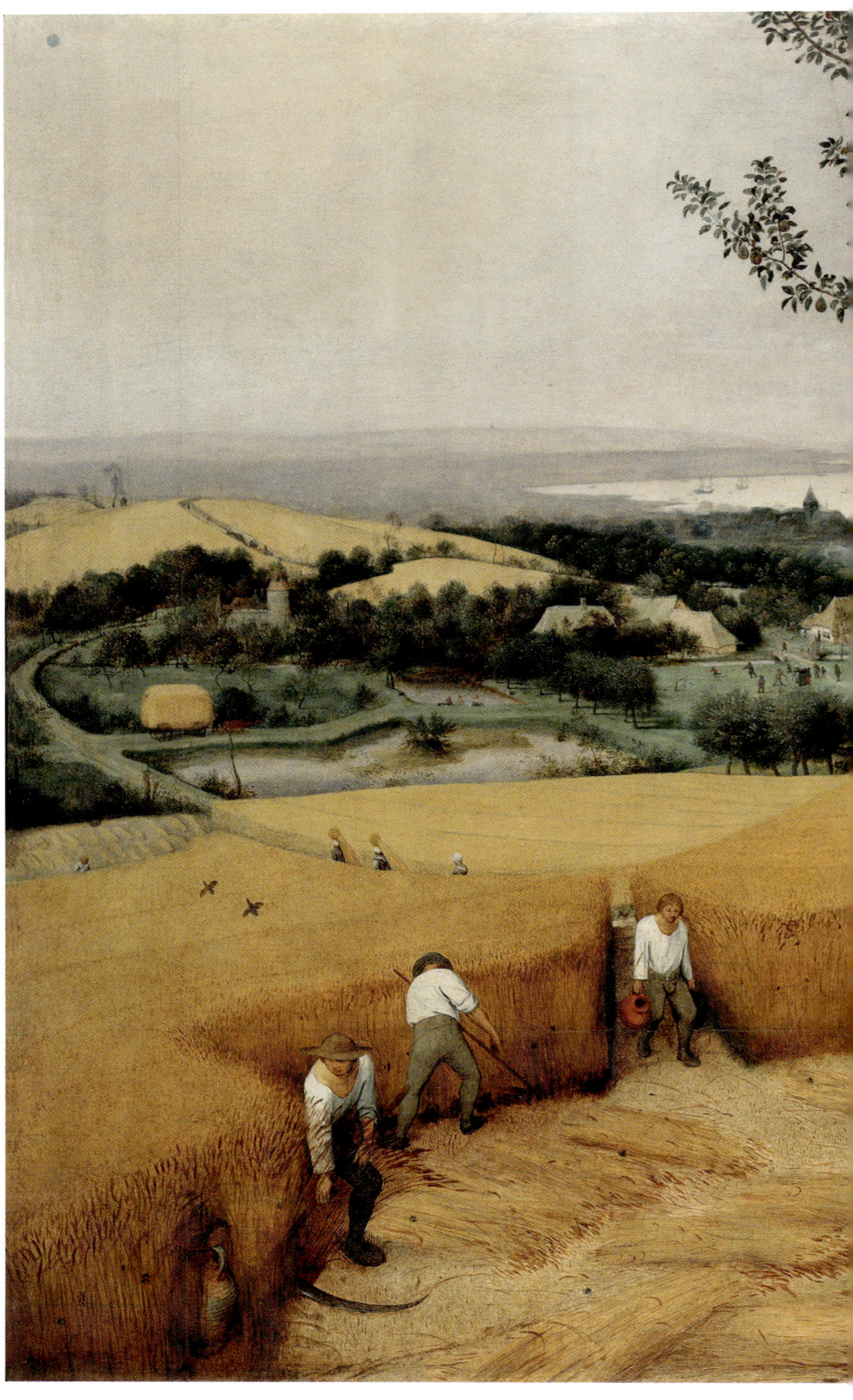

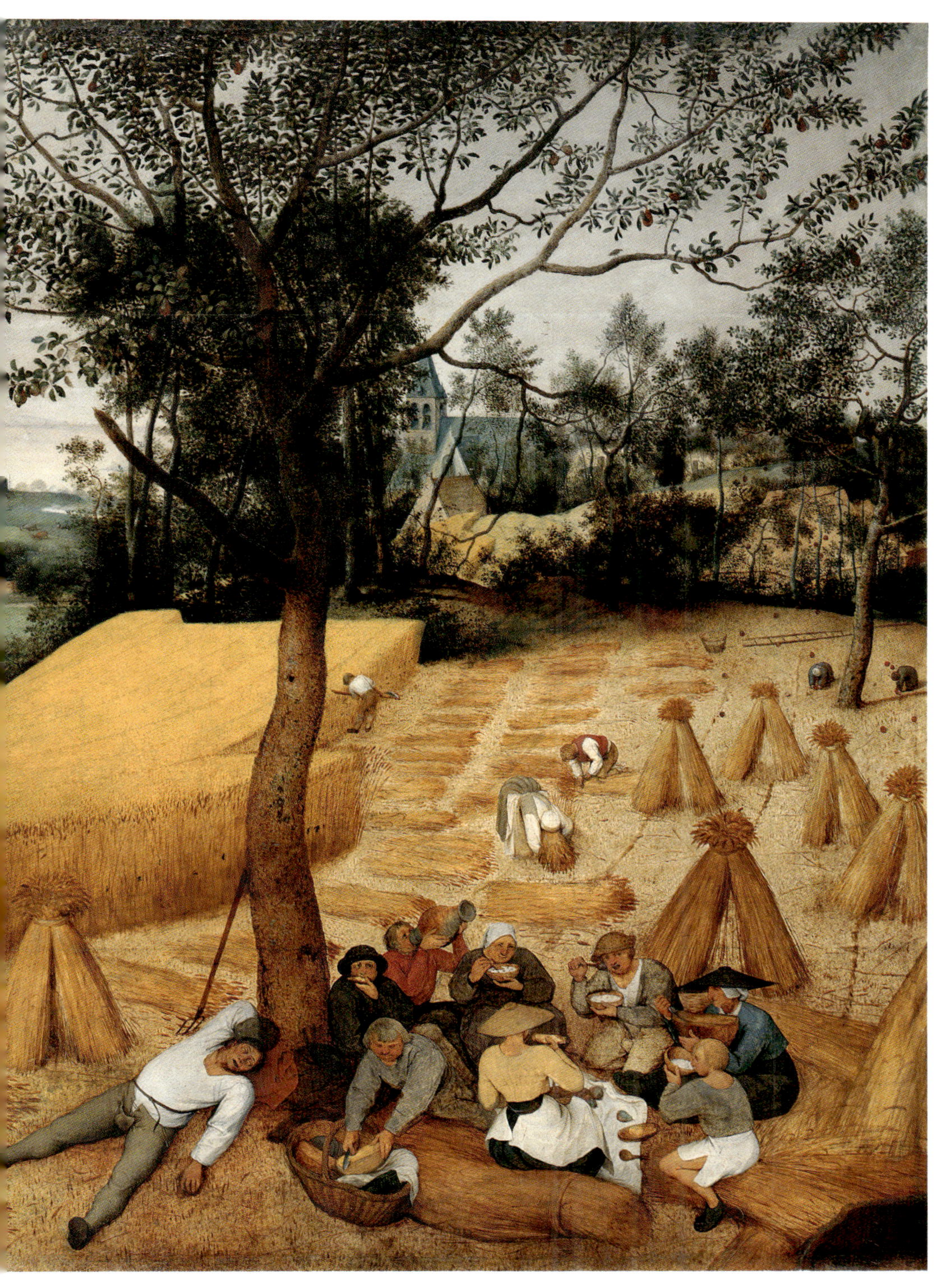

Pages 302/303
The Harvesters (August/September), 1565
Oil on wood, 119 x 162 cm (46 ⅞ x 63 ¾ in.)
New York, The Metropolitan Museum of Art
(detail page 305)

Pages 306/307
The Return of the Herd (**Autumn**, also: **October/November**), 1565
Oil on oak, 117 x 159 cm (46 ⅛ x 62 ⅝ in.)
Vienna, Kunsthistorisches Museum, Gemäldegalerie
(detail pages 308–309)

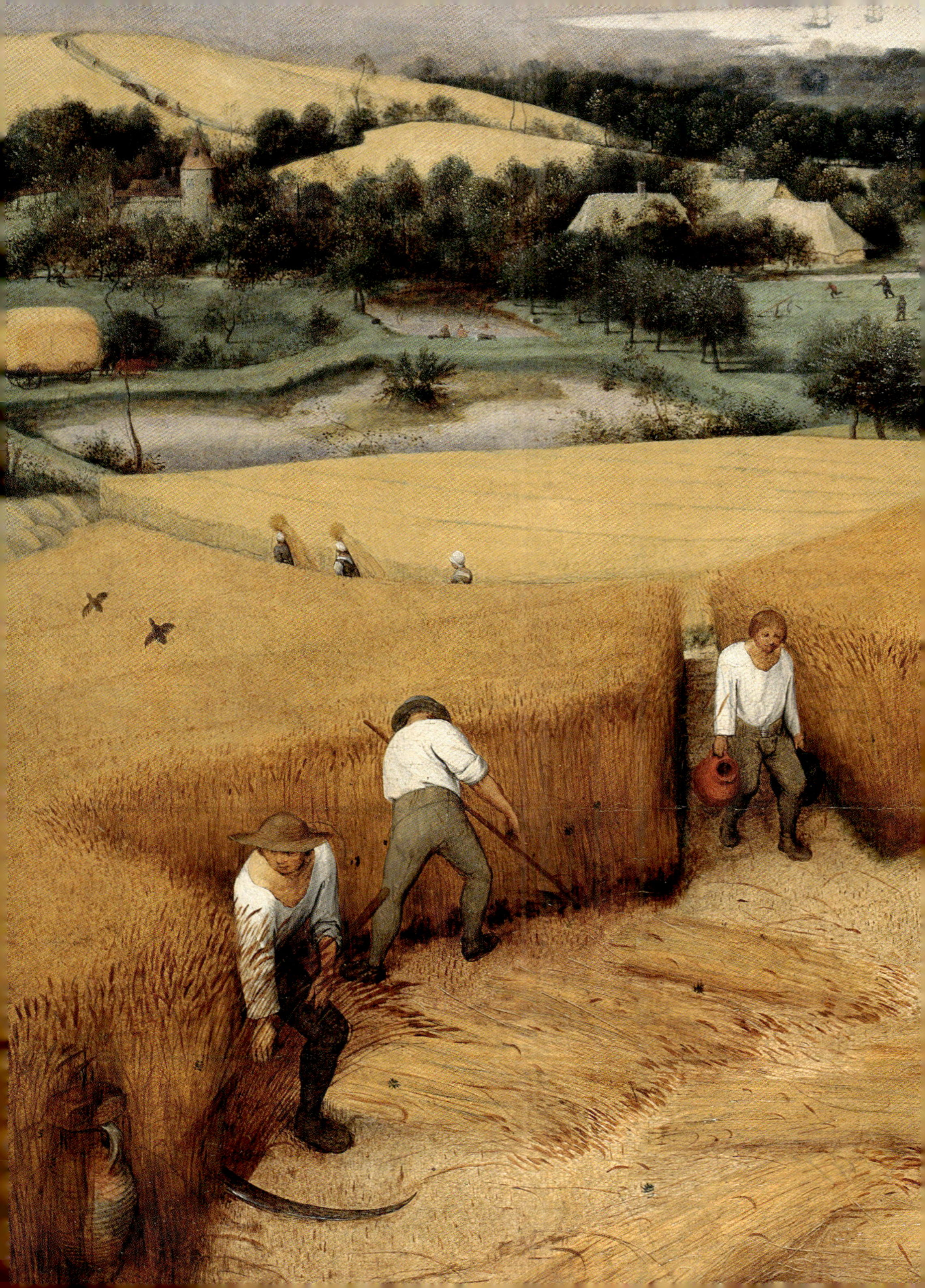

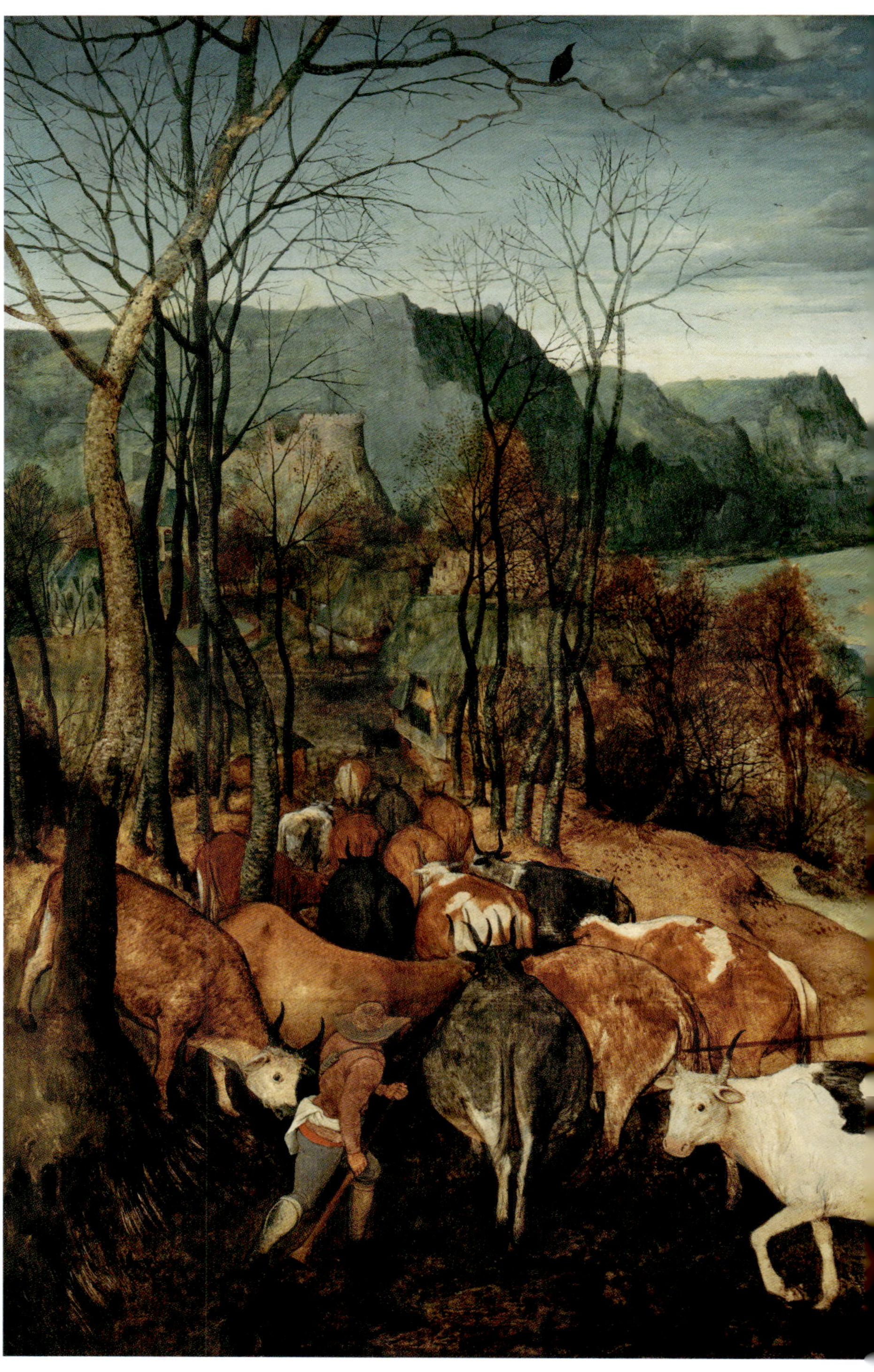

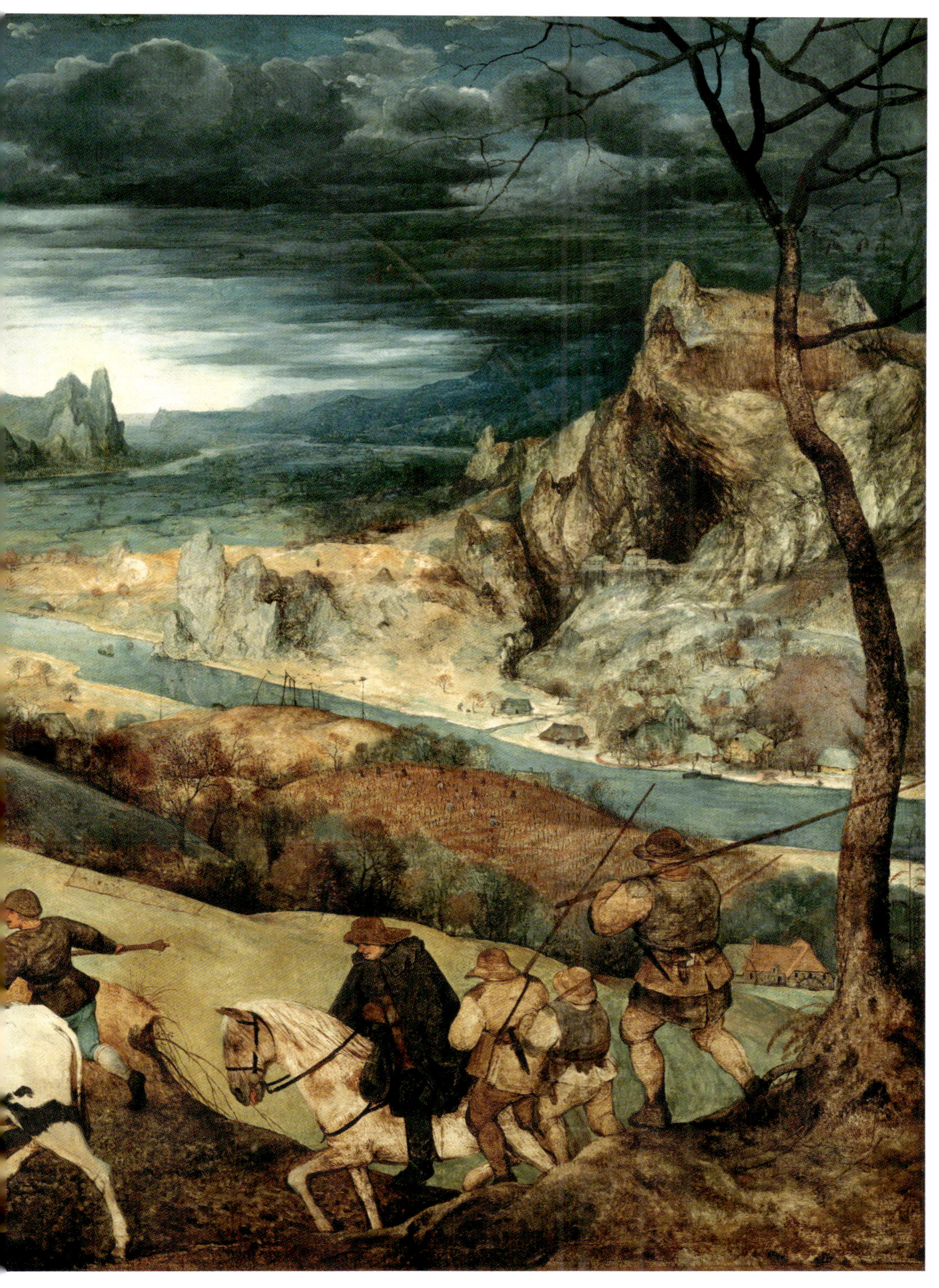

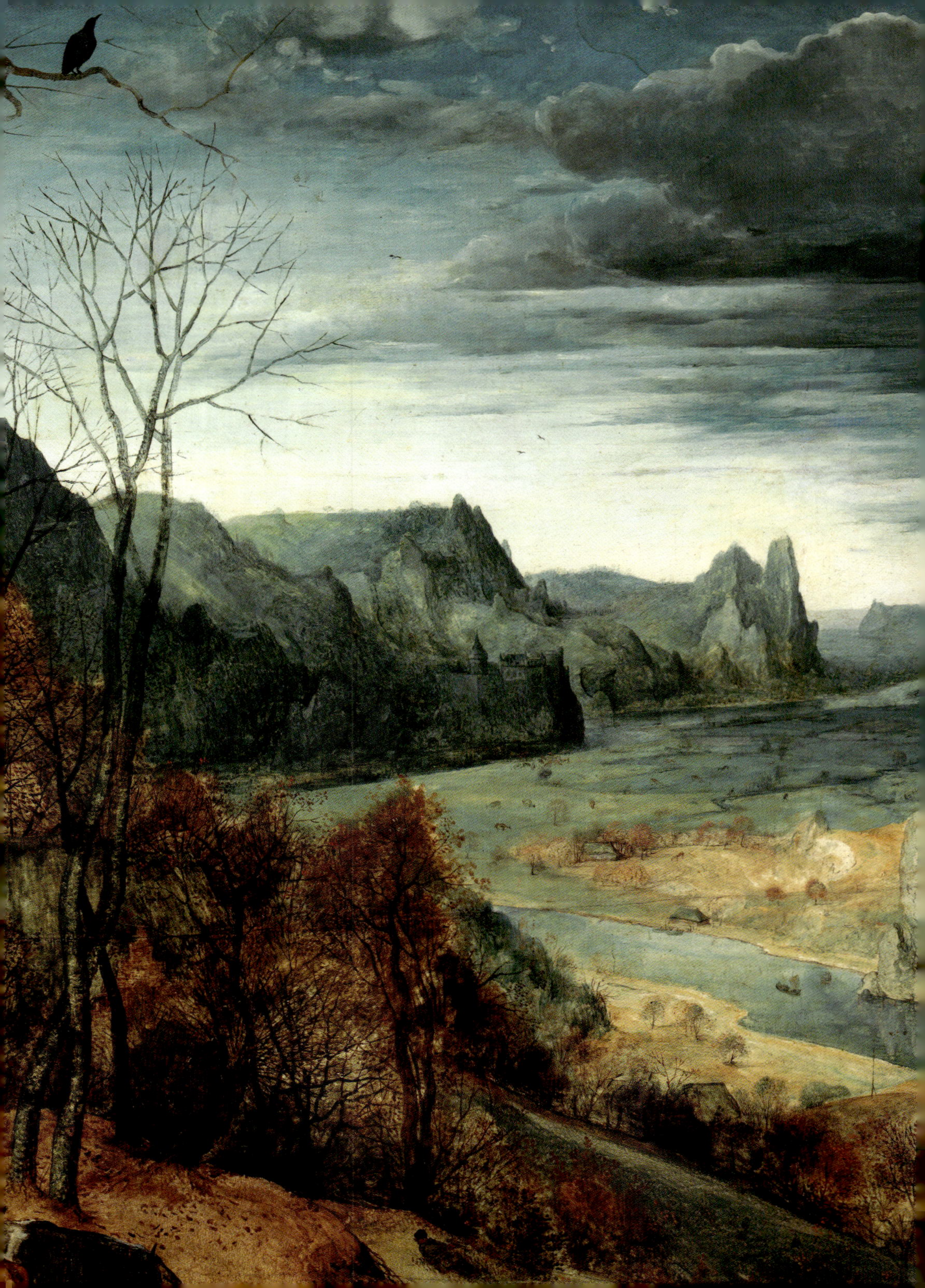

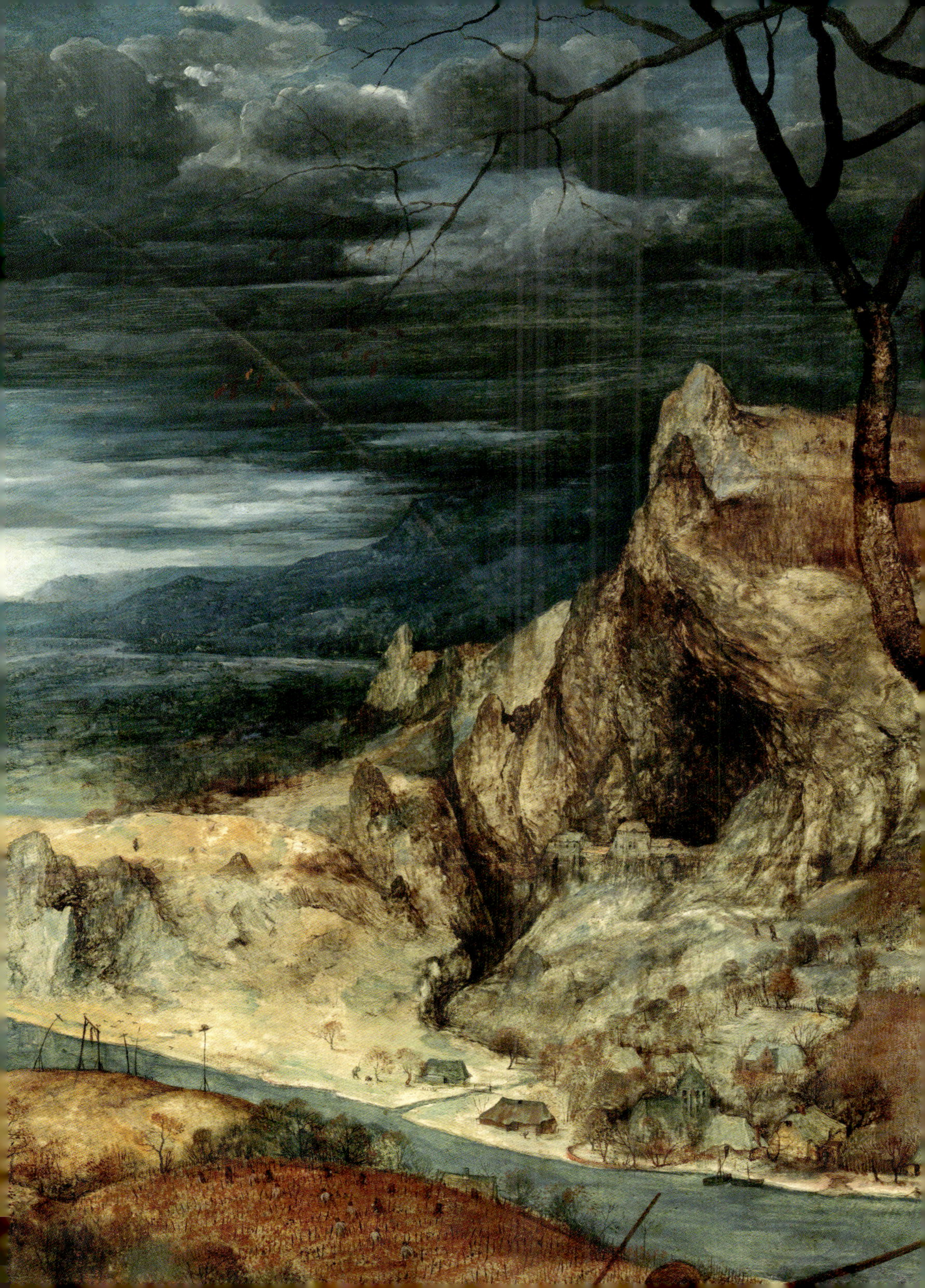

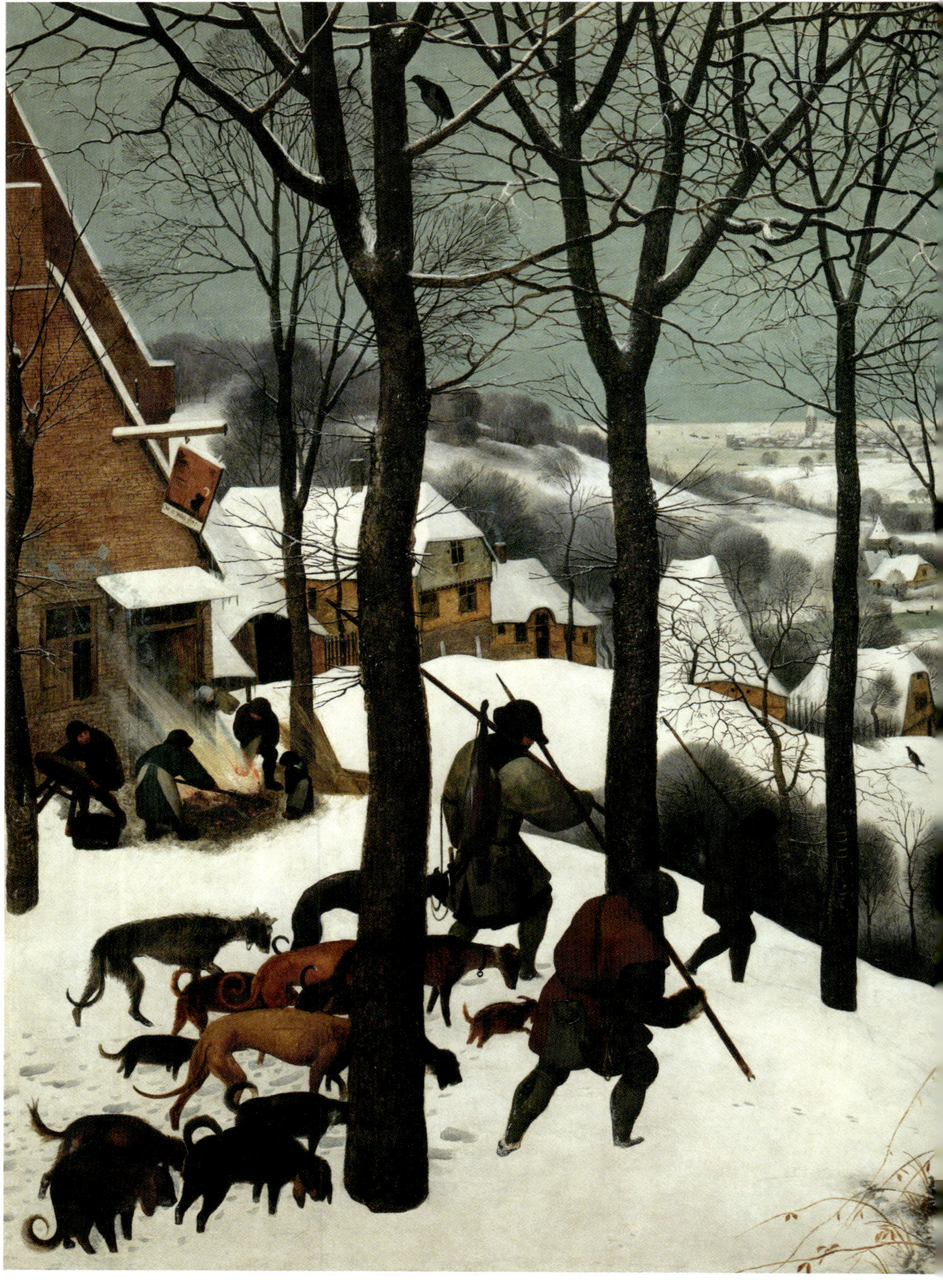

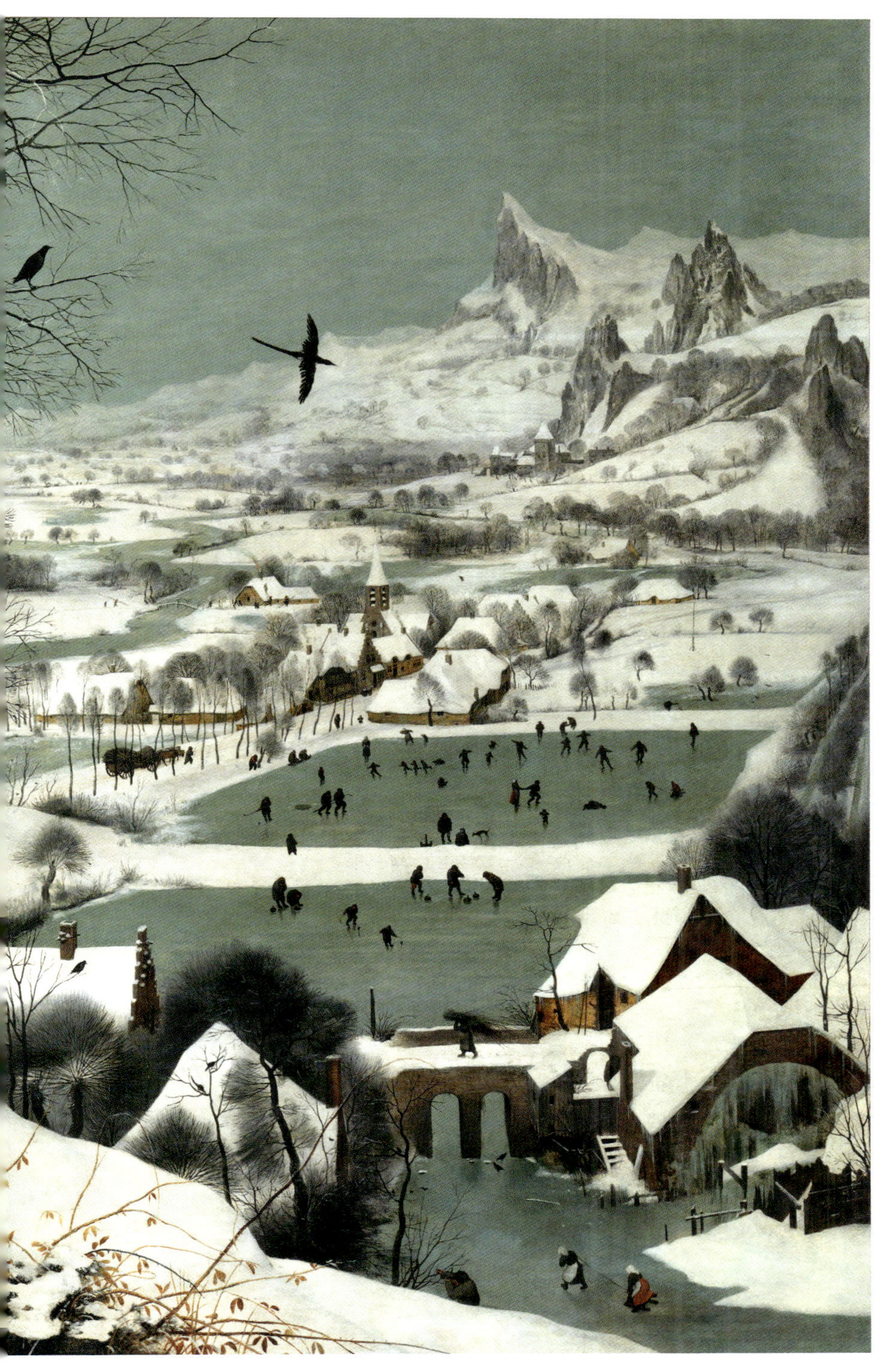

Pages 310/311
The Hunters in the Snow (Winter; also: **December/January**
or **The Return of the Hunters**), 1565
Oil on oak, 117 x 162 cm (46 ⅛ x 63 ¾ in.)
Vienna, Kunsthistorisches Museum, Gemäldegalerie
(detail page 313)

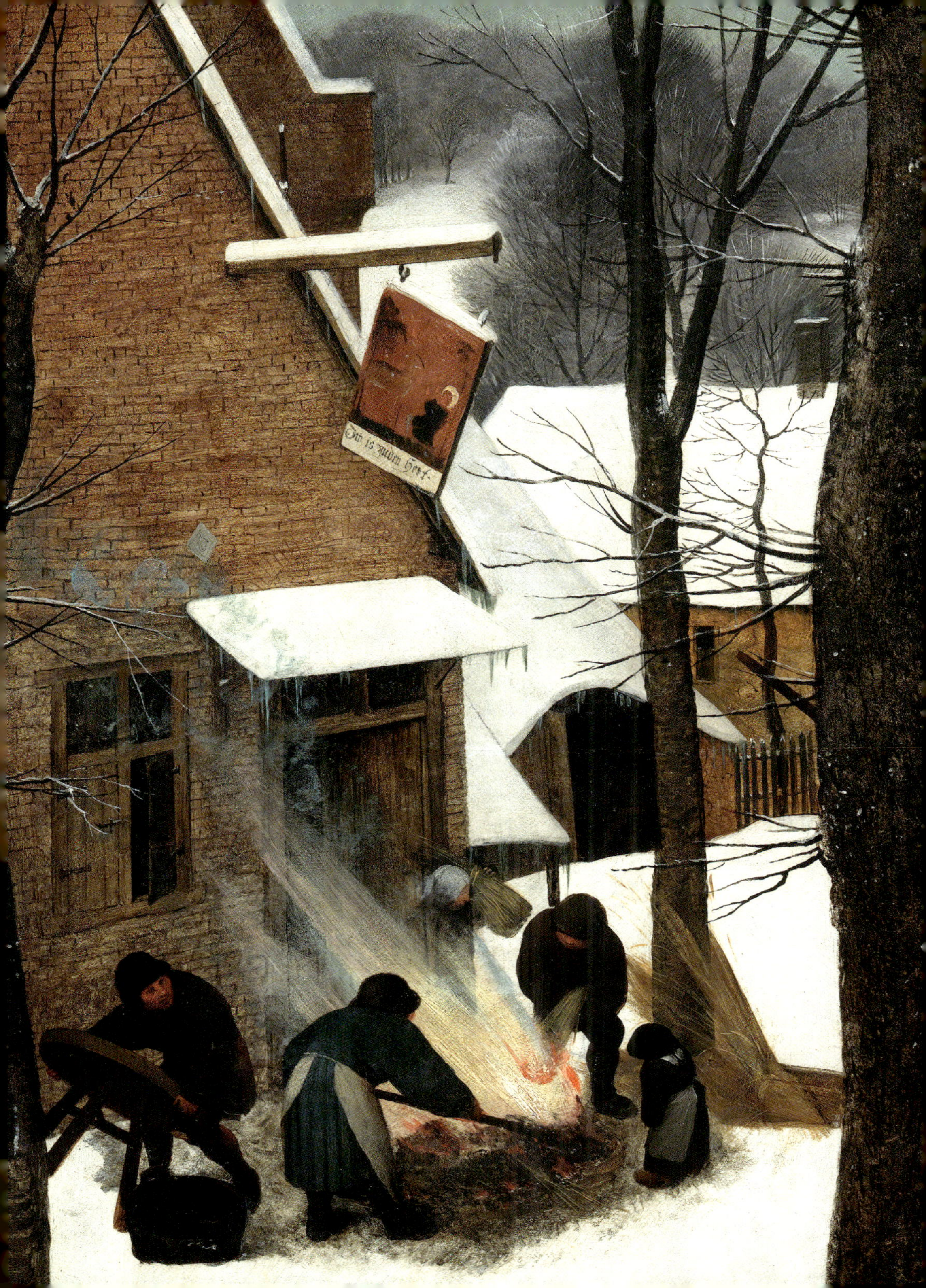
Dit is inden Hert

In Deep Snow:
The Winter Pictures

"What was being enacted between the residents and the soldiers, who were of their ilk, who, as ever, were only carrying out the orders of their superiors, could not be borne, and so, in his permanent gesture of horror, of ice-cold slaughter, it was stamped for ever in the iconic white expanse."

— PETER WEISS ON BRUEGEL'S *THE MASSACRE OF THE INNOCENTS*, 1978

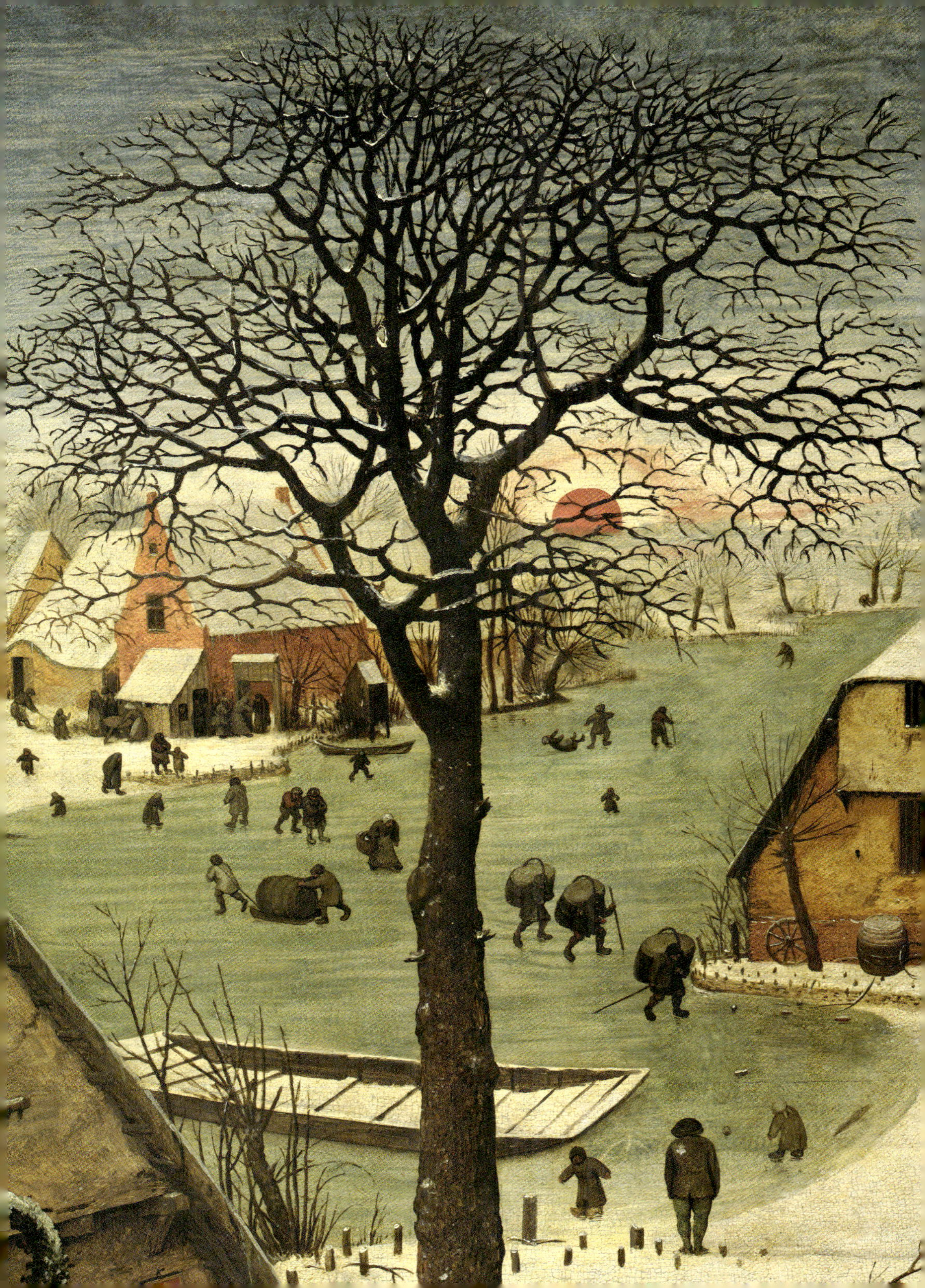

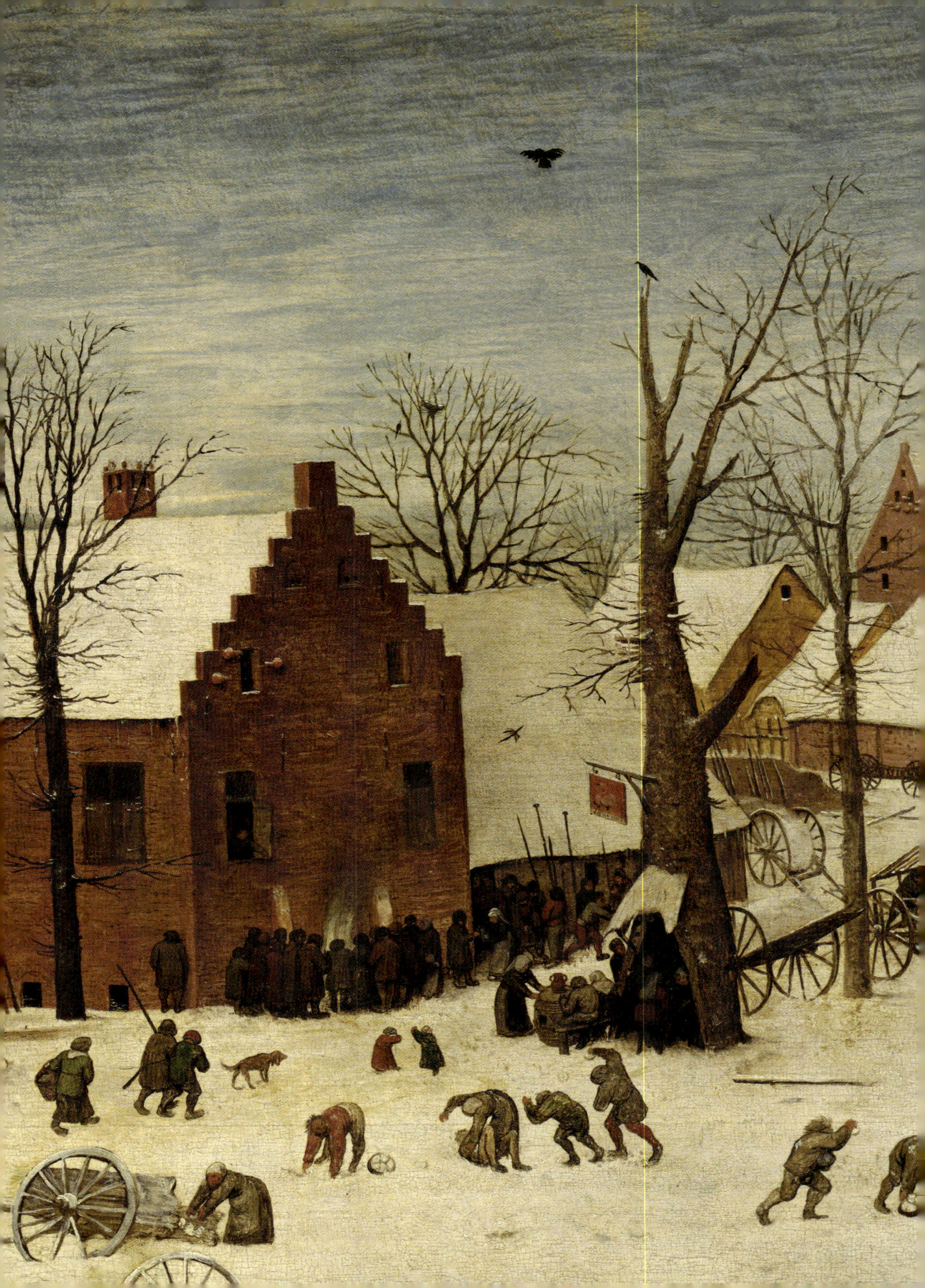

No room at the inn

In *The Hunters in the Snow*, we already encountered Bruegel's impressive ability to represent a winter landscape. The special characteristic of his art lies in the way he conveys the effects of this season on people's lives. So he also uses this backdrop to stage events from the New Testament. This is unusual, because he shifts the biblical narrative into an entirely different context. Such updating and "transferences" may have existed before him, but no artist ever distanced himself so far from the original context as Bruegel.

Numerous genre-type motifs can be found in *The Census at Bethlehem* (pp. 348/349, Cat. 26) that show winter from its best side. Starting at the iced-over river at the right, we see a whole range of seasonal games and activities. Besides the two children swooping along on an ice sledge, we see a lad about to put on his skates, and a girl dragging her little friend along on a stool, while at the top end of the stretch of ice two children play whipping top with their sticks (p. 335). Surveying this exuberant company further, we should mention the two lads in the centre of the picture who have made a slide, while a woman, armed with a broom, tries to cover the slippery surface with snow to save people falling. Meanwhile, above this little group a whole mob is joining in a boisterous snowball fight. One of the children has been thrown onto the ground and is being rubbed with snow (p. 316).

Besides the children we see groups of people everywhere who are busily going about their tasks. It is as though Bruegel wanted to portray the matter-of-fact, industrious present-day of a little Flemish town. The painter uses these genre elements to augment the biblical text. Luke simply reports the bare facts (Luke 2: 1–5): he states what happens, not how. But in contrast to the Bible, the invented ancillary scenes take up so much room in Bruegel's picture that we are in danger of overlooking the two leading protagonists, the Virgin Mary and Joseph. But of course Bruegel shows us enough to prevent any error. The carpenter Joseph is shouldering his saw and leading Mary's donkey, an ox walking next to them. Both animals bring to mind the stable and Christ's birth (p. 331).

The artist's main attention is focused on the inn on the left, housing the tax officials; a crowd of people wait in front. A pig is being butchered in the immediate vicinity of this scene, probably because the innkeeper does not wish to miss any profit promised by the many waiting people. Such a butchery scene is usually part of the iconography of the months, a sign for December. But Bruegel gives it a new meaning. Everything needed for slaughtering an animal can be found in the picture: the axe, to cleave the animal in half, or the straw later needed to singe the bristles from the skin of the pig, as we saw in

Pages 315, 316
The Census at Bethlehem (details), 1566
(see ill. pp. 348/349)

The Hunters in the Snow (Cat. 22). Two children watch the woman catching the pig's flowing blood in a pan. One of the two blows up a pig's bladder, usually used for making sausages. The jugular of a pig is just being opened, the other animal baulks at going to its end and has to be dragged by the ears (p. 322).

We clearly see the Habsburg double eagle on the inn wall, a reference to the sovereign rulers of the Southern Netherlands in Bruegel's time. Moreover, it is obvious to the observer that everyone waiting to be registered has no wish to waste any time getting into the inn – which is already full. And because this place promises warmth and welcome, it will very shortly be heaving with people. When it is the turn of Mary and Joseph, they will have to move into the stable, "because there was no room in the inn", as Luke writes (Luke 2: 7).[171] Joseph is pointing hopefully at the building, but we know his request for accommodation will be in vain. A visual narrative imagination is needed to represent and interpret a scene in this way. For what has just been described is not what can actually be seen, but can only be deduced from the context.

Bruegel's narrative art consists here again in depicting something in such a way that we think we know what happened before and what will happen afterwards. The arrival of Joseph and Mary in Bethlehem, immediately before the birth of the Saviour, finds a parallel in the slaughter scene. The wagon wheel seems to be of special relevance; it is placed – not particularly conspicuously – near the centre of the picture.[172] It has fallen off the cart standing next to it, or has been taken off, and is now lying useless in the snow. At first the wheel might connote the Wheel of Fortune. She steers the fate of the world and shows we are subject to the senseless turning of her wheel – a plausible interpretation, since the castle ruins in the background at the right embody a motif expressing the course of all earthly things (p. 321). The intact church building at the left will also crumble some time or other. The artist thus alludes to the becoming and decaying of all stone churches, in contrast to the invisible Church.

Bruegel's "realism" can be described as the simultaneity of the non-simultaneous. He shapes a divide between form and context. The Bible becomes the trail. It is not a literal, coherent narrative, but an allegory of an unredeemed past that seems to repeat itself eternally – as in the aforementioned words of Franck: "[…] World is always world, and the globe of the world must always roll round, so that what was today will not be tomorrow and come again."[173]

So how is this eternal recurrence manifest in the *Census*? If we hasten ahead of this scene, then following the census we have the Nativity, the Adoration of the Kings and Shepherds, the Slaughter of the Innocents, and the Flight into Egypt. All these stages are forecast visually in the picture. The stable connotes the Nativity and Adoration, Joseph and Mary on the donkey remind us of the Flight into Egypt, the soldiers in the background and the innocently playing children of the Slaughter of the Innocents. Everything is latent and yet seems urgently impelled to become manifest. We should again note the danger threatened by the soldiers visible in the background. The annex of the house is recognisably of stone – in contrast to the inn in the foreground – and is ennobled in addition by the stepped gable. Soldiers are emerging from it, picking up their lances leaning on the house wall (p. 316). Only a few are visible as yet, but we have the impression that far more are inside, soldiers will exit one after the other.

At first glance, none of the figures in the picture seems to have notice the threat to the children. But if we turn to the group of the people who are registering, we notice the scene with mother and child, which conveys a hint of the impending danger. The child is frightened, has become aware of the butchery scene, which in this picture still relates to the animal. Furthermore, the child with the pig's bladder may be interpreted as referring to the idea of the *homo bulla* (man is a bubble), the mortal, transient human being. Yet again, Bruegel's picture is an encounter with the past emerging from the future, and vice versa – that the future has long since taken place in the past. Just as Mary, Joseph and Christ have to flee before the pursuers, so true Christians have to flee the present day and the power of the Habsburgs. Christianity in the present day is as it was in the days of the martyrs.

Biting cold

The Adoration of the Kings is one of the few themes that Bruegel depicted twice, although in different seasons. Comparing the London picture (p. 141, Cat. 17) with the Winterthur *Adoration of the Kings in the Snow* (pp. 336/337, Cat. 14), it is noticeable that Bruegel eschews a close-up view and keeps us at a distance. Thick snowfall has covered everything and distances us even more from the scene.[174] The evocation of winter is so strong that we cannot help wanting to seek shelter. Bruegel is particularly successful in rendering the snow haze veiling the scene. We see the world as if wrapped in cotton wool. Every sound is muffled by the snow, everything seems to slow down. Compared with the other "Bible pictures", this painting has a cabinet format. Moreover, it belongs to the few works by Bruegel with a provenance traceable back to the seventeenth century. In an inventory of 1696, it is described thus: "Un hiver, avec quantité de figures; sur le devant, les trois roys qui adorent Nostre Seigneur; il tombe beaucoup de neige, et un petit enfant se promène sur la glace dans un petit traisneau; vieil Brugel" (A winter landscape with numerous figures; in the foreground the three kings adoring Our Lord; snow is falling, and a small child goes sledging on the ice; Old Brugel).[175]

This description suggests that the depiction of the season is the actual theme of the picture, thus it begins with "A winter landscape" and only afterwards refers to Christian iconography. This description is understandable, because the Adoration scene

The Census at Bethlehem (detail), 1566
(see ill. pp. 348/349)

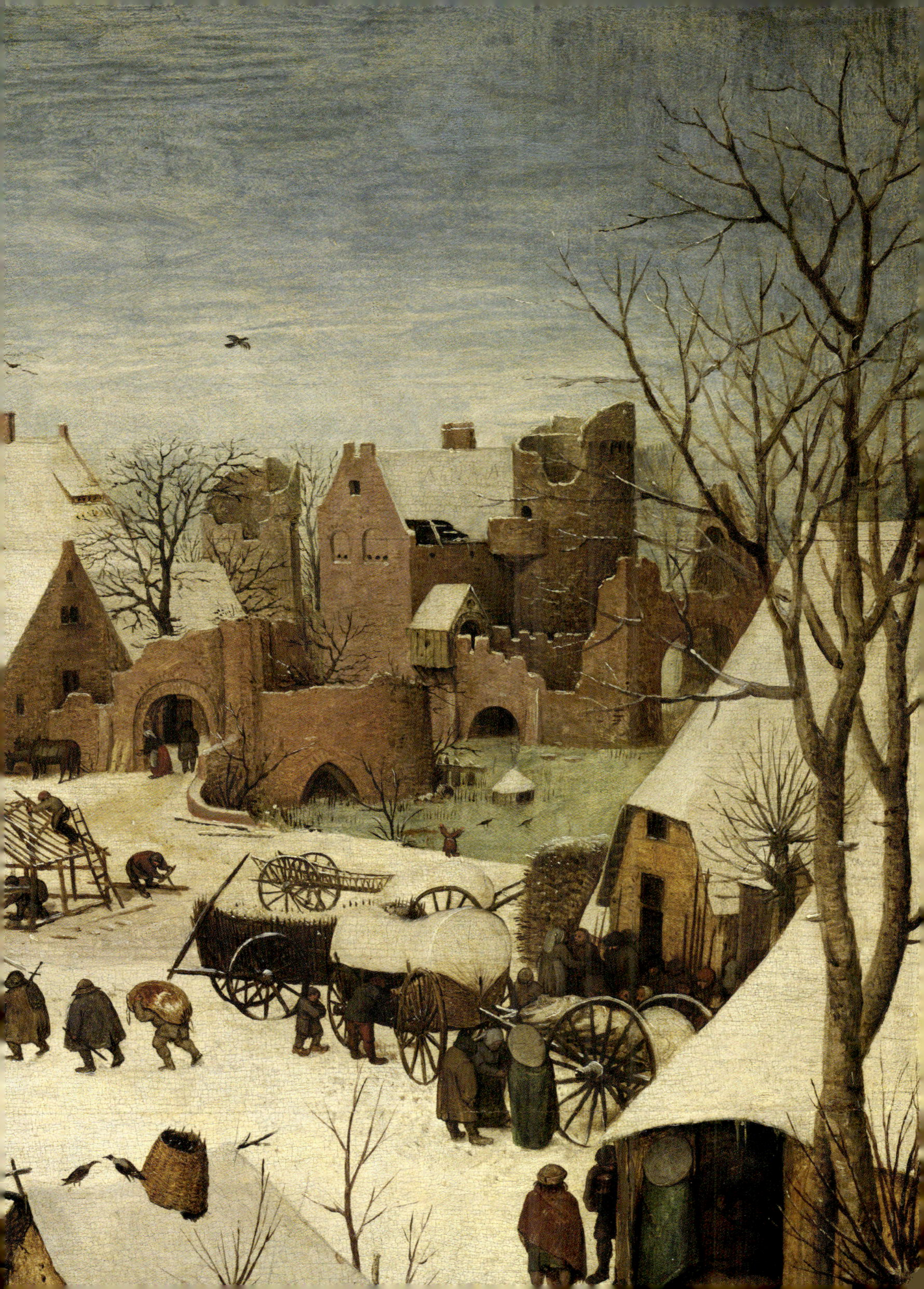

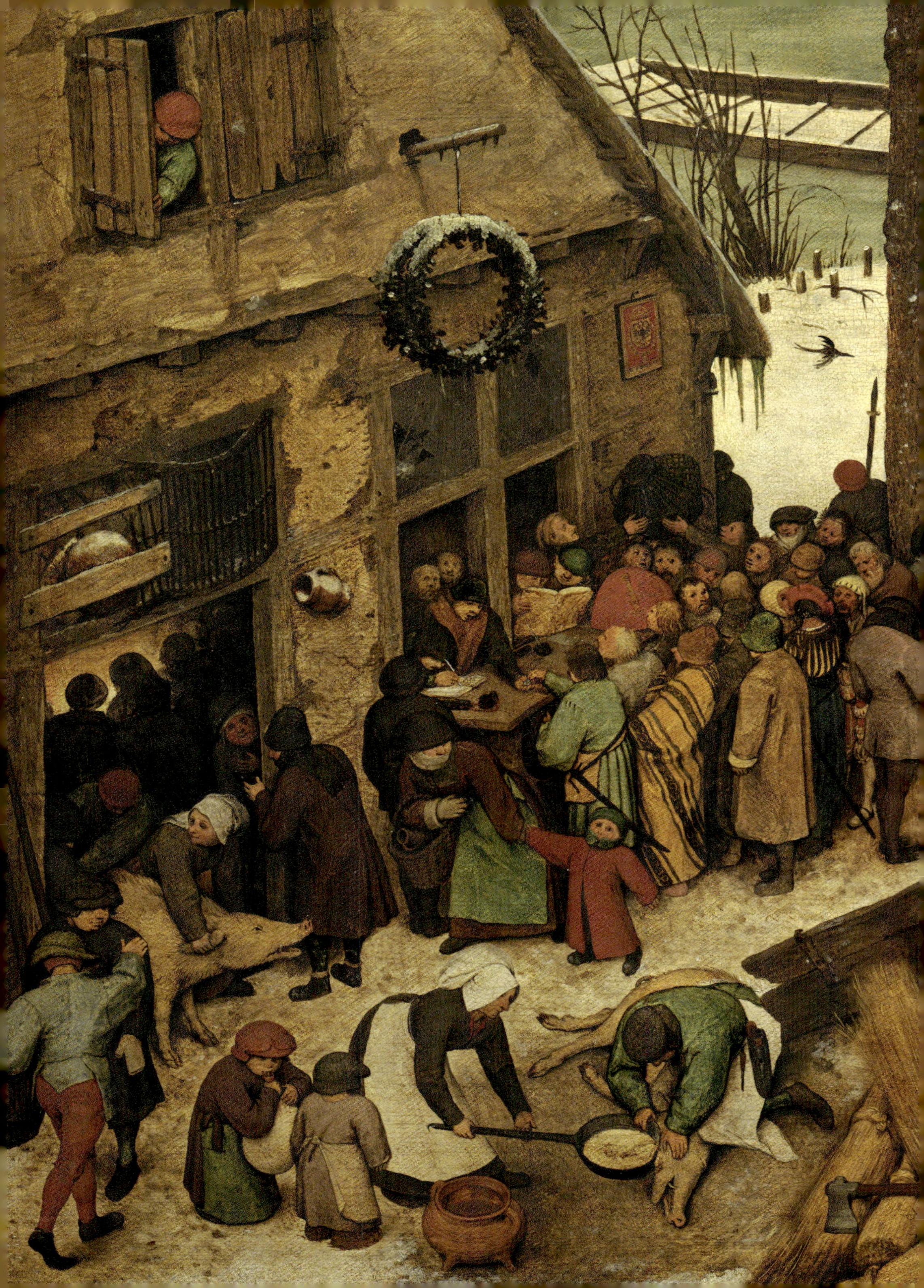

is marginalised to the left edge of the picture. The Virgin Mary with the Christ Child is sheltering behind a wall and barely discernable. The picture's aesthetic achievement consists in Bruegel's skill in convincingly capturing a winter scene. It is probably the first painted snow flurry in the history of panel painting.

Bruegel has scattered thick snowflakes across the entire picture, as if the snow is about to become heavier and form drifts. The sky is leaden and the air hazy with snow, which, since the Sun isn't shining, no longer looks white. Instead, he resorts to the many yellow and ochre tones in the surroundings, creating an overall impression of flatness. The sole spatial accent is created by a diagonal leading from left to right, so to speak against the stream of approaching people. Yet the spatial impression of depth in the picture is minimal.

The village square is backed by a large farmhouse, closing off the view into the farther distance. There is barely space for a narrow passage between the houses to left and right; perhaps we can detect the wheel of a cart and people. Behind this we intimate the towers of a castle (p. 339). Overall it is conspicuous how many correspondences in content there are between the two halves of the picture. The stable at the left, the location for the Adoration of the Kings, corresponds to the improvised inn at the right. A lean-to roof has been set up against the wall of the castle ruins, the entrance covered by a makeshift cloth. A jug hangs on a projecting beam, marking the place as a drinking booth. Directly before it, people make their way to a frozen stream. They have knocked a hole in the ice to get water.

Just near this we see a child skidding carefree over the ice on a sledge. The imprudent child seems to have caught the mother's attention, for she is gesticulating in his direction. The castle ruins, clearly recognisable, close off the picture at the right. A striking feature is the strong beam supporting the building. Inside the ruins, a huge pile of rubble towers up, covered in snow. The gate visible behind the building is also in ruins. The wall is abruptly broken off on the left.

In the stable we find Mary and Joseph and two kneeling kings; a third stands a little to the side with his retinue. The village people are oblivious of the scene, as is particularly noticeable in the woman cutting osier stakes directly next to the Adoration scene. Nor have the two men to the right noticed anything and seem to be heaving a tree trunk out of the ice (pp. 340/341). The picture is defined not by the birth of the Redeemer, but by the cold season and the human activities associated with it. In front of the improvised drinks booth, we see figures on the right busy hauling and unloading wood.

The Census at Bethlehem (detail), 1566
(see ill. pp. 348/349)

Directly under the slanting roof is the light of a fire, likewise on the opposite half of the picture a fire is shown next to the stable with the adoration scene.

Overall, we have the impression that Bruegel is hardly focusing on typical winter pleasures. The cold season is showing its malicious side. It seems as if winter is mercilessly absorbing all the people's energy and attention. Everyone is freezing and rushing to get home. Even the children's games on the ice allow no grounds for enjoyment, only anxiety. Bruegel doesn't make things easy for the observer. Thick snowflakes thwart our perception, but not only the fall of snow, also the wall at Mary's left and the diagonal leading inwards into the picture block our sightlines and continually distract the eye from the core content of the pictorial narrative. No matter how intensively we look, we cannot discern the Christ Child. What key has Bruegel provided so that we can interpret the picture? We must first investigate the scene on the right. The supporting beam is extremely prominent, raising the question as to its meaning. This safety measure was taken to prevent the complete collapse of the building threatened by the heavy snowfall after the roof fell in. The heap of stones inside the ruin indicates that the building is no longer usable. The necessity of a supporting beam, however, shows the force with which the rubble heap is pushing from the inside against the walls.

But the action taken on one side to prevent the collapse is lacking on the other side of the drinking booth. The thin beams bearing the roof are not properly anchored, but project beyond the walls. Bruegel is not without irony in introducing hazards into the scene: the anxious mother terrified her child might break through the frozen water is not aware that she herself is in far greater mortal danger in the shadow of the ruins and their impending collapse. The fire especially gives cause for concern. The smoke rising from under the improvised roof shows that the fire is roaring uninhibitedly. Wood is stacked at the corner of the building, and a man is busy adding to the pile. The heat at any event will eventually cause the collapse of the shaky roof construction. In contrast, the fire under the open sky on the left seems the safer option.

In terms of composition, the vertical axis of the picture is approximately at the height of the bridge. Therefore the adoration in the stable is sited opposite ruins and tavern. Bruegel is apparently shifting the Adoration scene away from the castle building. To accentuate this, he has set the bridge between the two places, a metaphor expressing connection, yet also separation. Traditionally, the ruins stand for the superseding of the Old Covenant, which Bruegel associated with a spiritualistic critique of the ministerial Church; it is, after all, a secular ruin of a castle. The building in the background is also part of this critique. There can be no connection to the old ministerial Church. In his *Paradoxa*, Sebastian Franck describes the transition from the Old to the New Testament as the abolition of ecclesiastical hierarchy, of the rites and sacraments.[176]

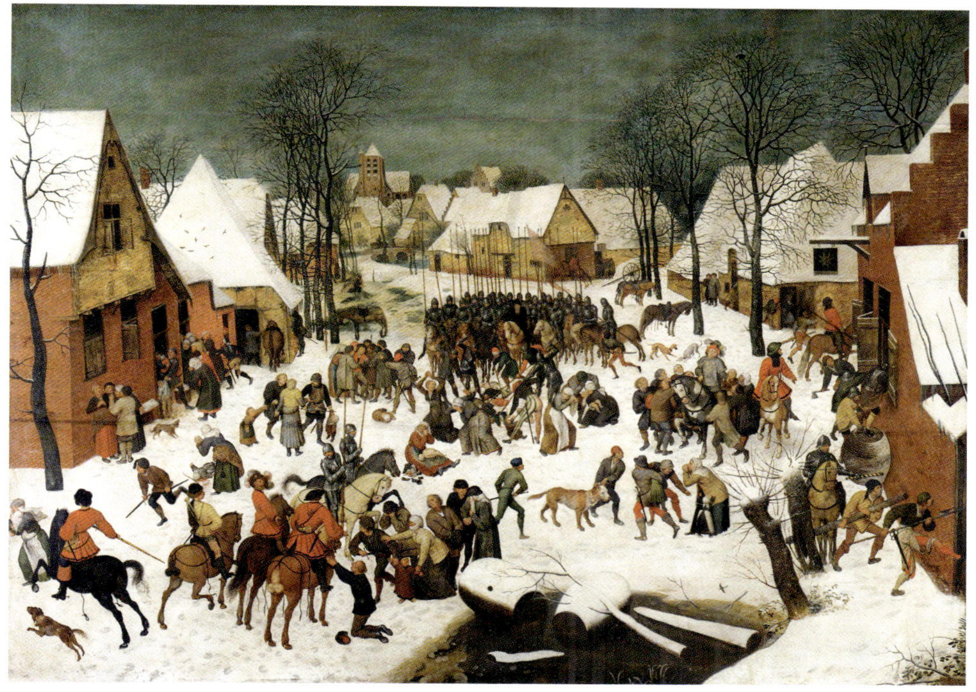

Copy of: Pieter Bruegel the Elder, **The Massacre of the Innocents,**
fourth quarter of 16th century. Oil on oak, 116 x 160 cm (45 ⅔ x 62 ⅞ in.)
Vienna, Kunsthistorisches Museum, Gemäldegalerie

Many of the metaphors used here are familiar to us: the hidden wheel connoting the unredeemed cyclic dynamic of history, and the accompanying allusion with the ruins as symbol of the demise of the ministerial Churches, the ineffability of God, who in this picture is evoked in the absence of the Christ Child. Fitting into the cyclic dynamic of history yet again are the soldiers in the background with their long lances, presaging the Slaughter of the Innocents in Bethlehem, as we already encountered in the *Census*. Thus the child sliding on the ice actually is in great danger, but not the kind of danger imagined by the fearful woman. Bruegel has not presented a coherent past in his picture, but his own ephemeral present, pointing ahead of and prior to the present day.

The Habsburgs in Bethlehem

Bruegel's original *Massacre of the Innocents* (pp. 350/351, Cat. 28) in London is today hardly to be identified as such, since later overpainting has transformed the subject into a Flemish plundering expedition, whereby animals are the main victims of the slaughter.

However, an early copy in Vienna approximates the original composition (p. 325). Here we see how soldiers, with the utmost savagery, are attacking the civilian population. Armed soldiers drag the local children to the man in black, the centre point of the picture, and they are massacred before his eyes. This improvised place of execution is also the actual centre point of the picture's content. The command to kill is issued here, and it is here the soldiers return to carry out the killings.

Many children are already lying dead in the snow, wept over by their mothers. If we compare this with the brief mention in the Bible, we are struck by the freedom Bruegel takes for his composition – Matthew solely reports: "Then Herod, when he saw that he was mocked of the wise men, was exceeding wroth, and sent forth, and slew all the children that were in Bethlehem, and in all the coasts thereof, from two years old and under, according to the time which he had diligently inquired of the wise men" (Matthew 2: 16).

As a rule, the iconography of the Slaughter of the Innocents does not keep to a strict compositional pattern. The number of actors is usually symbolically reduced. But Bruegel has, so to speak, expanded a real, full report out of a short headline. Only the star in the inn sign reminds us of the biblical narrative.

The observer is ushered into the scene with a dramatic *coup de théâtre*. Front left, we see a young woman who is desperately trying to rescue her child. She is pursued by a soldier, his sword already drawn. Not he, however, but the rider on an oddly elegant galloping horse will reach the woman in the next instant and murder the child. How helpless in contrast appears the man directly to the right of this group; he is kneeling down and imploring the two riders to have mercy on the children. He has subserviently taken off his cap – we can just detect the red lining. The two officers are portrayed in all their callous imperiousness, either refusing to look at him, or simply ignoring him (p. 352).

The people are helpless before the soldiers. On the right, we see how a pursuer has crashed his way into a house while a mother, holding her child, is trying to flee through a side door. But a henchman is waiting here, obviously expecting this attempt to flee. On the opposite side we see a most agitated man. If a neighbour was not holding him back, he would probably hurl himself at the murderer's assistant, whose victim lies at his feet. Directly next to this is a scene in which a father tries to exchange his daughter, whom he is indicating vigorously with his arm, for his son, who is being carried off by a soldier.

Time and again we hope that at least one mother manages to escape the murderers, only to realise how hopeless this is. The picture's perspective sets the scene as a great optical prison that is not easy to grasp visually. The buildings on the left and right of the street frame the scene and simultaneously lead into the depth of the closed-off space. The observer confronts the heavily armed mounted lancers as an impenetrable phalanx;

in the middle, the black-armoured leader sits on his horse. But in case a child actually does escape the pursuers, a mounted guard has been positioned as a precaution on the bridge in the background. Above the tethered horse at the left we can see a person who is trying to slip away with a child. The observer knows very well this attempt will fail; even though the way across the bridge seems to offer a chance of escaping the soldiers, the rider is waiting there without mercy. And the houses offer no protection against the soldiers. Front right, dark figures are breaking into a house on the command of their captain, while another group is about to climb through a window, having placed a barrel against the house wall to do so.

A curious detail can be detected in the left half of the picture. A rider is urinating against a house wall, while a servant holds his horse; a scene that at first must seem like a cynical commentary, and that incidentally also appears in *The Census at Bethlehem* (Cat. 26). The earlier literature saw the Flemish folk genre playing a part in such incongruous additions. But this suggestion does not really explain the presence of the urinating soldier. It may be noted after all that the soldier's call of nature has enabled the aforementioned fleeing person in the background at the left to slip away. But already in the next instant this supposedly peace-loving man, subject like everyone to his bodily needs, will be transformed back into a murderer.

Bruegel is evidently trying to portray all the emotional potential of such an event, desperation and profound despondency, incredulity and perplexity. But not only the victims, also the perpetrators are characterised in great diversity. Bruegel shows, for instance, the obduracy of the soldiers who will not be mellowed by the people's pleas and unflinchingly carry on murdering.

In iconographic terms, the artist makes his statement in incidental details. We might look for instance at the white footprints on the ice front right, which betray that someone must have run over this spot. The two barrels lying there are placed so prominently at the picture's edge that they provoke questions as to their significance. An open tap hole reveals that the barrel on the left is empty, whereas the one on the right, which doesn't seem to have an opening, is to be seen as full. Bruegel stresses through the white trail on the iced puddle that all liquids must be frozen. So if the right-hand barrel is really full of liquid it will soon burst.

An emblem exists that can be applied to Bruegel's motif. It shows a barrel in danger of bursting and is contained in the compendium of emblems *Emblemata Moralia Et Aeconomica* of 1627 by Jacob Cats.[177] The picture is a symbol of the brevity of the rule of despotism, and the epigram describes that whatever is closed in too tightly is in danger of bursting open. Even if the emblem was produced considerably later than Bruegel's panel, it might derive from an earlier literary tradition.

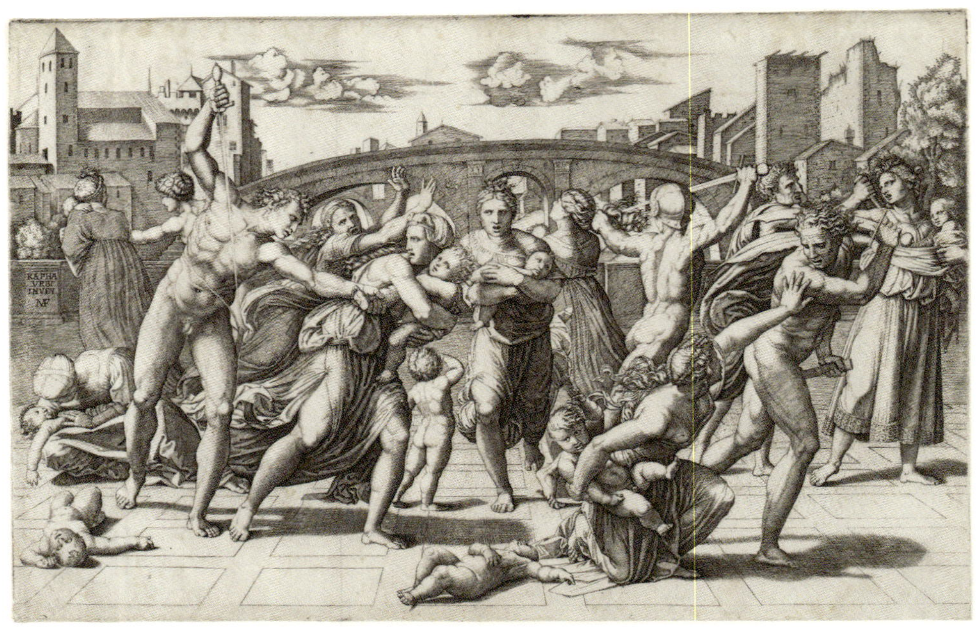

Marcantonio Raimondi after Raphael, **The Massacre of the Innocents**, 1510–1512
Copper engraving, 28.1 x 43 cm (11 ⅛ x 16 ⅞ in.)
New York, The Metropolitan Museum of Art

Nonetheless, the shared horizon of meaning of painting and emblem is clear. While the people are represented by the barrel, the surrounding rings stand for sovereignty. Bruegel might have known this metaphor. Soon the frozen liquid in the barrel will cause it to burst. Accordingly, it is only a question of time before the people rise up against the oppressors and break the bondage of despotism. Bruegel's painting allows us to use the past as a typological foil through which the present can be comprehended. It refers to the rule of the Habsburgs in the Southern Netherlands. The black-clad leader in the centre of the picture is frequently identified with the Duke of Alba.[178] Apart from this, we might note the youthful messenger on the right; several townspeople are crowding round his horse. He is wearing the Habsburg double eagle on his breast, thus an unambiguous marker of contemporary history (p. 355). Moreover, the double eagle is seen on the roof ridge of the house situated on the vertical axis of the picture. The painting is taking sides against brutal despotism.

If we wish to evaluate Bruegel's artistic methods adequately, we might refer to a famous interpretation of the scene with which Bruegel enters into ideal competition.

Marcantonio Raimondi's engraving of *The Massacre of the Innocents* (p. 328) after Raphael is a successful example of the Italian theory of art being put into practice. In his subtle composition, Raphael spans the opposite corners, producing a kind of optical membrane. This is pierced open in the next moment by the woman holding her dead child in her arms and now striding like a fury towards the observer, her mouth open in a scream. Several children lie murdered on the ground. Directly next to the woman in the centre, we see a crying boy who has lost his mother in the melee.

To the right of the vertical centre, a henchman yanks a child up in order to kill it with his sword, forcefully swinging back his sword arm to strike. Raphael uses multiple occasions to depict the momentum of the soldiers' movements and so increase the dynamics of the scene. Especially the pair to the left and right of the fleeing woman in the centre are remarkable as the epitome of this technique. Thus the sword arm of each of the men is about to make a kill or aim, and each torso is in a state of extreme tension, as shown by he musculature. Finally, we must note the architectural framework, its symmetry acting as a foil for the woman in the centre.

In the histories of Raphael and Bruegel, the main concern revolves around the presentation and arousal of the emotions. Both artists treat the observer as an eye witness. Raphael opts for a relatively close-up view. Quite in the spirit of the Italian theory of art, he takes a representative selection of scenes and figures. In contrast, the Flemish artist distances the observer and shows a large-scale pictorial section. It is as if we are looking down from the window of a house, at the height of the opposite roofs. Raphael's strategy of overwhelming energy generates pathos through the composition of the naked, writhing figures and the gestures and facial expressions of the horror-stricken women; Bruegel shows the savagery of the scene unfiltered. His pictorial narrative fragments into multiple individual scenes, giving the picture an episodic structure. Moreover, he integrates seemingly incidental and everyday motifs into his picture. This varies the degree of the emotional tension, establishing a rhythm of calm and agitation. So when we compare the two artists, Michelangelo's depiction of heroic conflict is an aestheticising interpretation of the massacre of the innocents, while Bruegel's version appeals to the viewer's empathy. The perpetrators are not shifted into a diffuse time in the past, but are identifiable as very present. Raphael's pathos is generated in the men through the energy of heroic bodies, in the women through a gestural eloquence such as might be used for the Erinnyes, Greek goddesses of revenge. The Italians used a classical-antique vocabulary of forms aiming at affect through the expressiveness of the form.[179] In contrast, Bruegel appeals to the observer's compassion. In doing so he does not portray gestures of pathos, far more a story worthy of compassion. He confronts the pathos of antiquity with the compassion of Christianity. This combination of agitation and calm once more relates to the treatise

On the Sublime by Pseudo-Longinus. The classical author warns of false pathos arising when the level of agitation in a work keeps to the same intensity; the result is that the effect of the artistic methods necessarily wanes. Thus he advises combining the everyday with the dramatic in order to control the level of intensity. Against this background, therefore, the realistic elements in Bruegel's painting act to avoid hollow pathos just as they intensify true pathos. Through the contrast of lofty and humble pictorial motifs, he endeavours to strengthen their effect.

The Church as trapper

Winter Landscape with Skaters and Bird Trap (pp. 342/343, Cat. 23) is the most commonly copied of Bruegel's pictures, which is no wonder, since it seems to be the very epitome of the winter genre. We see the houses and the church of a small township situated to the left and right of a frozen river, its course gently meandering through the picture. The high vantage point allows the observer a view of the river course through the immediate foreground and middle ground; then it disappears and we can only guess its course as it makes its way to the town in the far distance. The Sun is nowhere to be seen in the picture, but it is obviously late afternoon. Numerous folk have gathered together on the ice, the Sun's warmth of the day is still lingering before dark falls and, more ominously, it grows bitterly cold.

Great fun is being had by all on the ice. Skaters are seen next to people with sticks and bats, playing curling on the ice, others are joining in a race; a mother has even brought her child onto the ice to teach him to skate. At the same height, two children run across the slippery surface tentatively, arms wide outstretched to keep their balance. All are exhilarated at the pleasures of winter. On skates they feel gravity has been over-come, for perhaps no other type of locomotion tempts people to more bravado than skating. But everyone knows – and above all feels on the ice – how quickly pride comes before a fall.

This painting is striking for Bruegel's skill in creating a realistic, atmospheric scene. He has captured yet another facet of winter. The lighting is especially successful. It seems as if the light from the river illuminates not only the ice, but also the entire scene – though admittedly only the snow-covered houses on the left are warmed by this light, the snow on the right side seeming colder. Bruegel achieves this effect by setting a succession from left to right of ochre and gold merging into purple, blue and grey. This skilful colour harmony is conveyed so subtly that it does not immediately strike

The Census at Bethlehem (detail), 1566
(see ill. pp. 348/349)

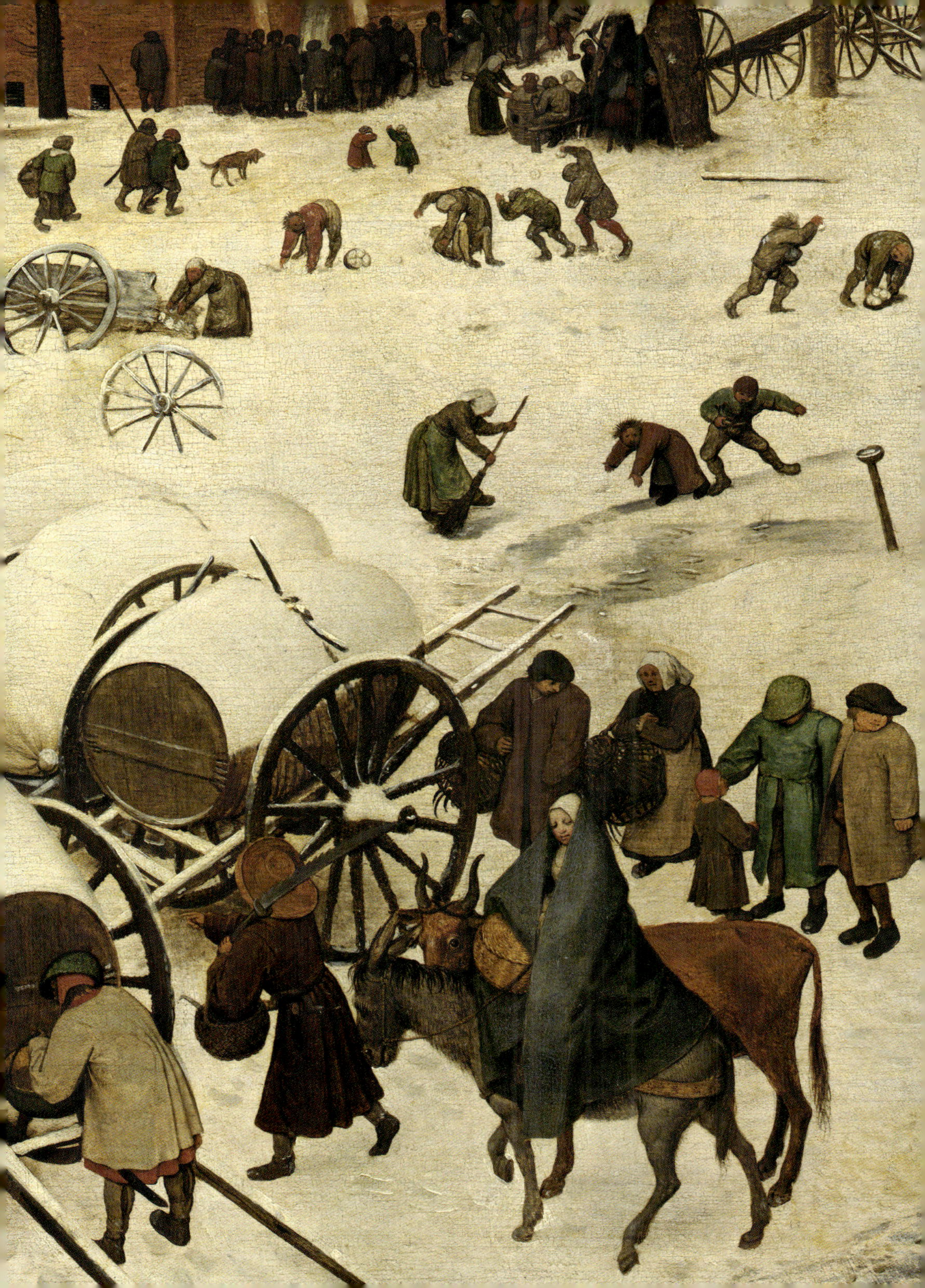

the eye. The colouration of the river stands out from that of the surrounding snow, which is remarkable, for the ice, though the coldest and most inhospitable element in the picture, exercises the most visual appeal. The many people on the frozen water seem to confirm this impression. The sky absorbs the delicate, pale lilac tones of the town silhouette. Bruegel's dramatic achievement is not based on aesthetic self-indulgence. On the contrary, the "optical temptation" cannot be separated from the communication of a specific pictorial content.

When looking for other significant elements, we may notice the scene in the foreground at the right. Birds have surrounded a bird trap, intending to eat the seeds – the bait. Some particularly rash birds are already under the heavy hanging door resting on a small stake. In the bushes and branches directly in front of this scene, we see birds gathering which will soon follow their fellows (p. 345). The literature has pointed out the huge crow in the top right corner, its warning caws re-echoing unheard. This crow represents "a monumental warning" for those birds that are venturing too close to the trap.[180] The literature moreover pointed out the two birds in the foreground, intermediaries between human activities and the scene around the bird trap.

We as observers are challenged to investigate the meaning of this parallel. It might be that the people on the ice are in the same situation as the endangered birds.[181] Oblivious and carefree, they are preoccupied with their pleasures without realising they are in danger. The type of danger is made more precise by the scene with the bird trap. Namely, the trapper, who has hidden himself, is waiting until as many birds as possible venture under the door before he activates the trap. He seems to be watching everything and patiently waiting for the right moment to strike. Without being able to see him, we know that he can be located in the first house at the right, to which the tightly tensed cord fastened to the stake leads. He must have hidden behind the house wall, where an inconspicuous hole acts as a peep hole.

The image of the bird catcher or fowler is of biblical origin and to be understood as a symbol of the Devil.[182] Hence the picture is a warning to the observer against temptation from the Devil. The people on the ice, too, stand for the "slipperiness of human life", as is captioned on an engraving of Bruegel's depicting the typical activities of winter before the gates of Antwerp (p. 333). But doesn't this interpretation keep too much to a general significance? It does not in any way include the most important compositional analogy in the picture. When Bruegel structures a composition's meaning in significant allusions, he hands an active role to the observer in deciphering it. The discovery the observer has to glean relates to the church that is visible in the picture. Namely, from the structural point of view, the people are in the same relationship to the church building as the birds to the house of the bird catcher.[183] This interpretation finds an affirmation in the

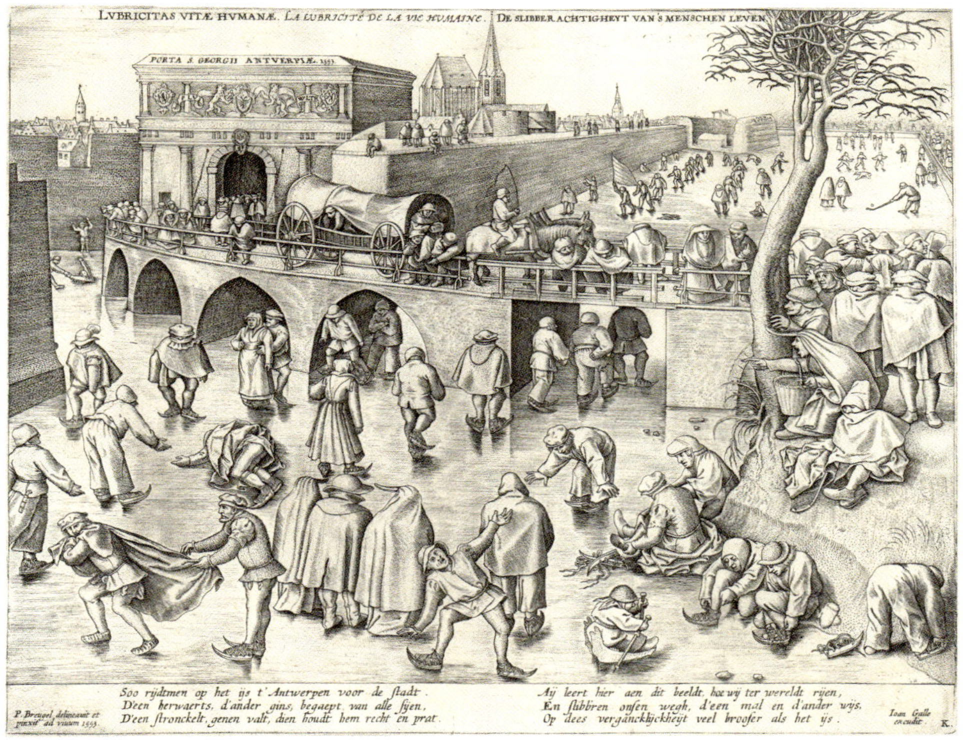

Johannes Galle after Pieter Bruegel the Elder
Skating before the Gate of St George in Antwerp, after 1553
Copper engraving, 23.2 x 29.7 cm (9 ¼ x 11 ¾ in.). Vienna, Albertina

Bible, when we find in Jeremiah: "For among my people are found wicked men, that lie in wait as fowlers, setting snares and traps to catch men. As a net is full of birds, so their houses are full of deceit" (Jeremiah 5: 26–27).

Drawing on the bible quotation, the "houses" refer not only to the bird catcher's house, but also to the Church, which is in a similar relationship to the people on the ice as the bird catcher to the birds. And so it is no coincidence that the number of people more or less corresponds to the number of birds. Accordingly, the picture may be interpreted as a critique of the ministerial Church. Thus it is probably hardly a coincidence that, of all things, a magpie is perched a short way before the church choir – a thieving and also treacherous bird.

The Census at Bethlehem (detail), 1566
(see ill. pp. 348/349)

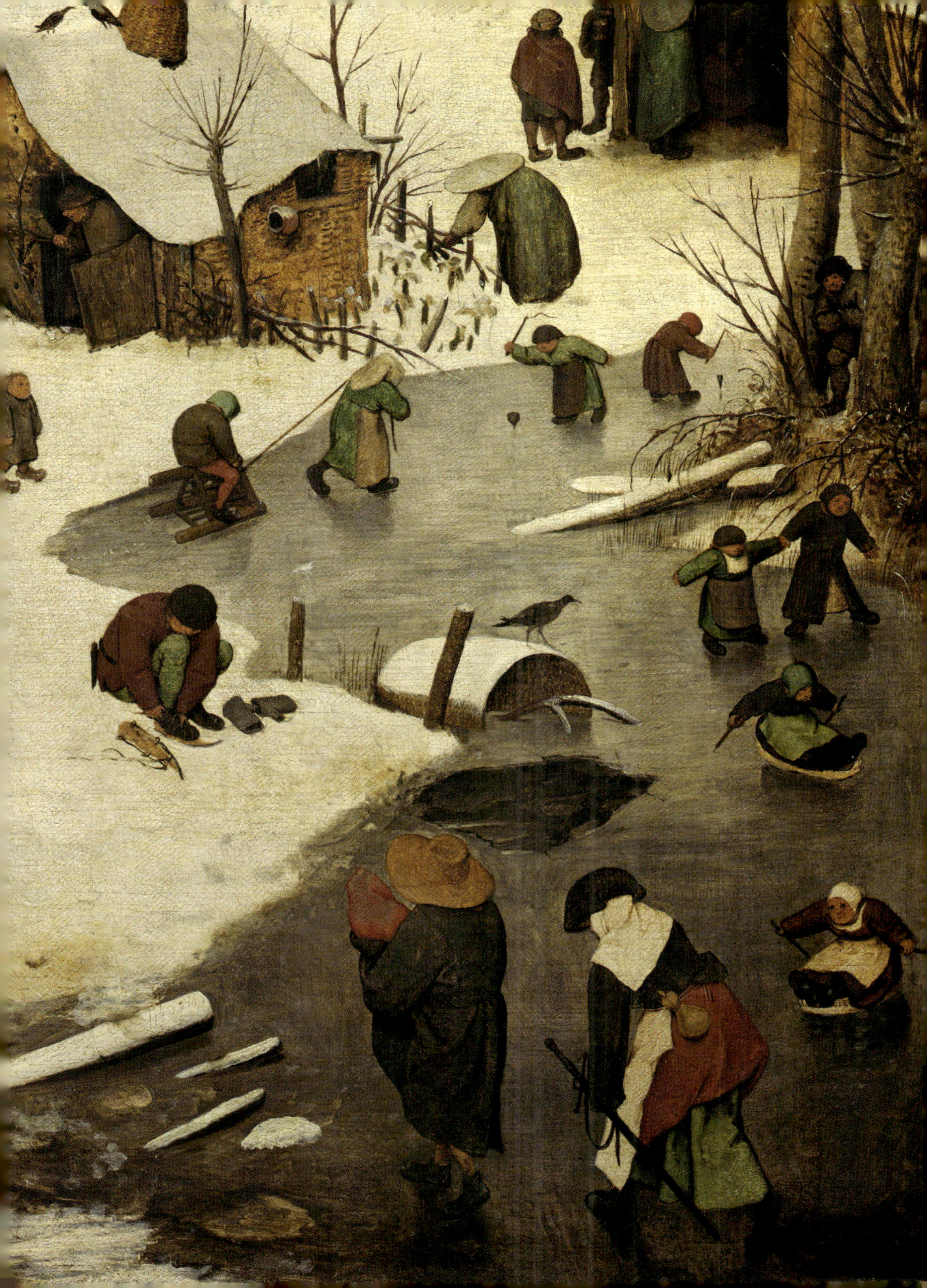

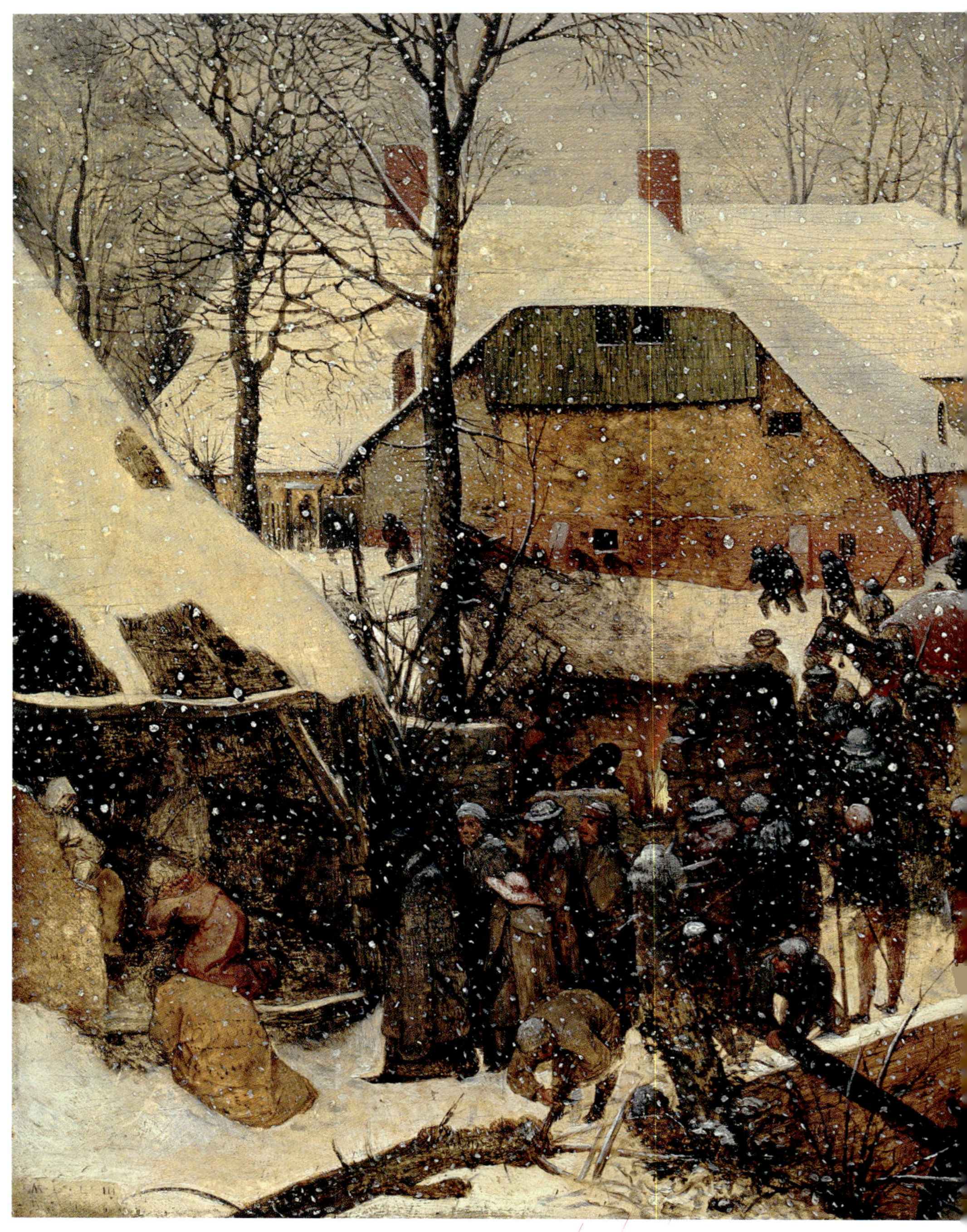

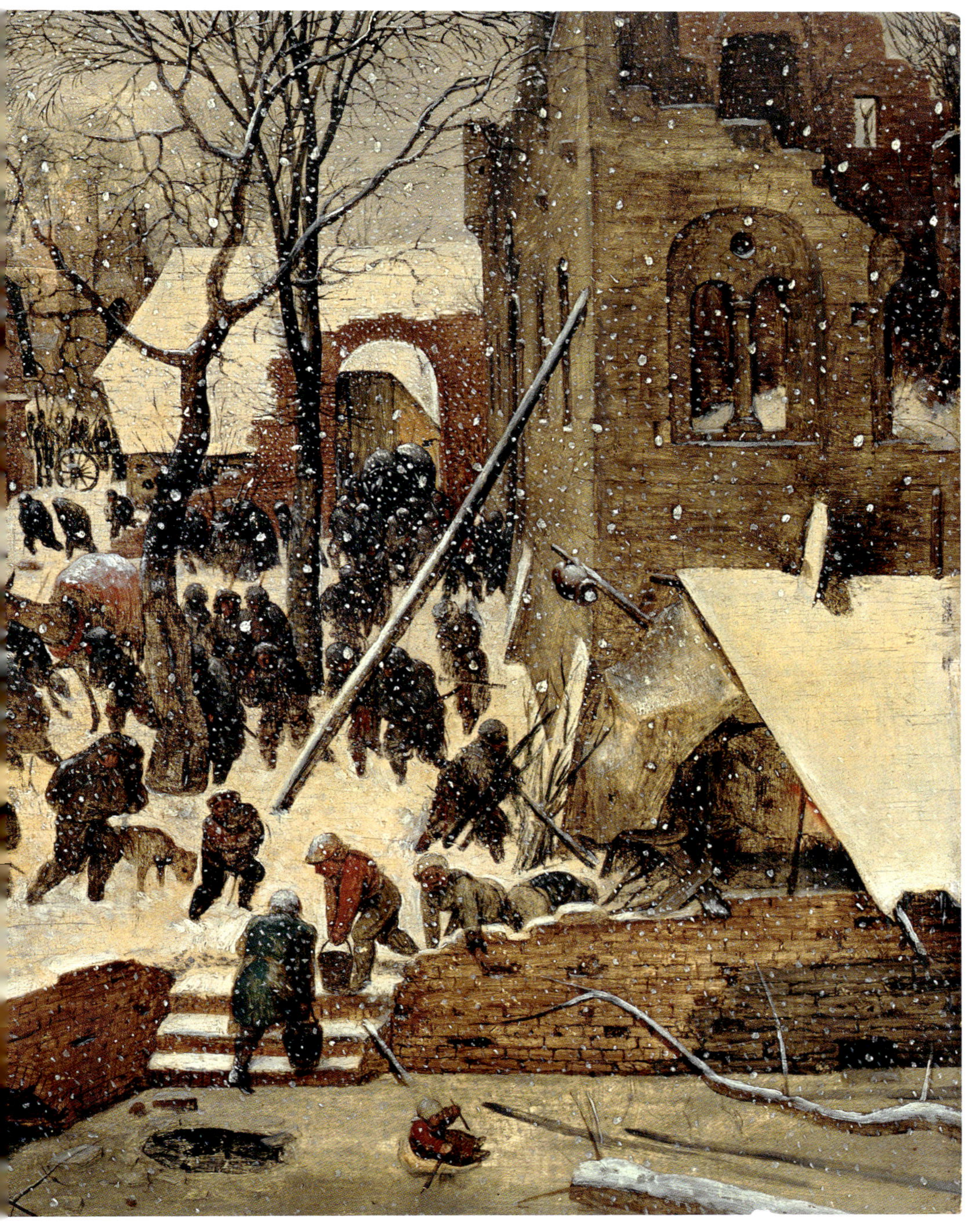

Pages 336/337
The Adoration of the Kings in the Snow, 1563 or 1567
Oil on wood, 35 x 55 cm (13 ¾ x 21 ⅔ in.)
Winterthur, Oskar Reinhart Collection "Am Römerholz"
(details pages 339–341)

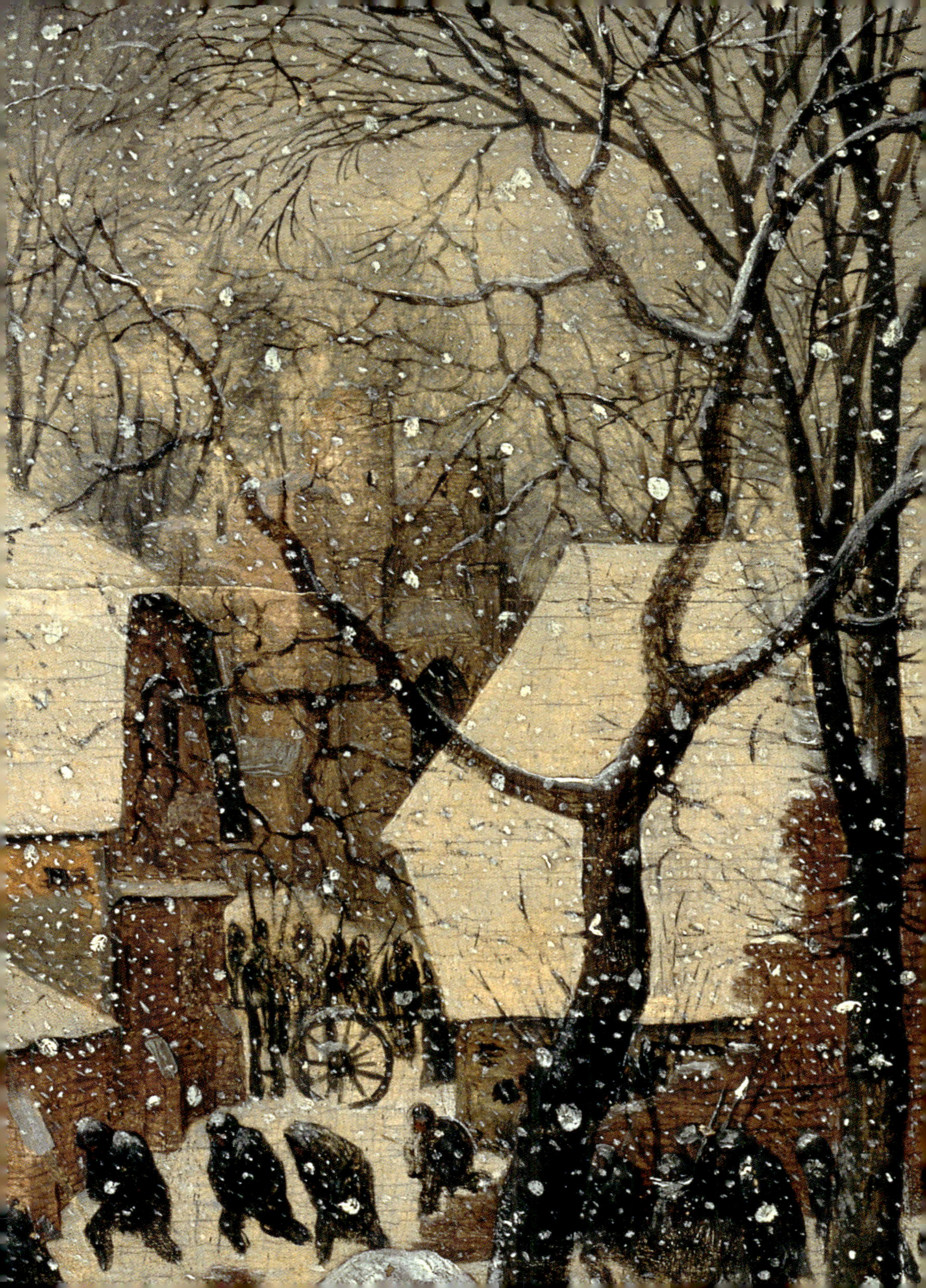

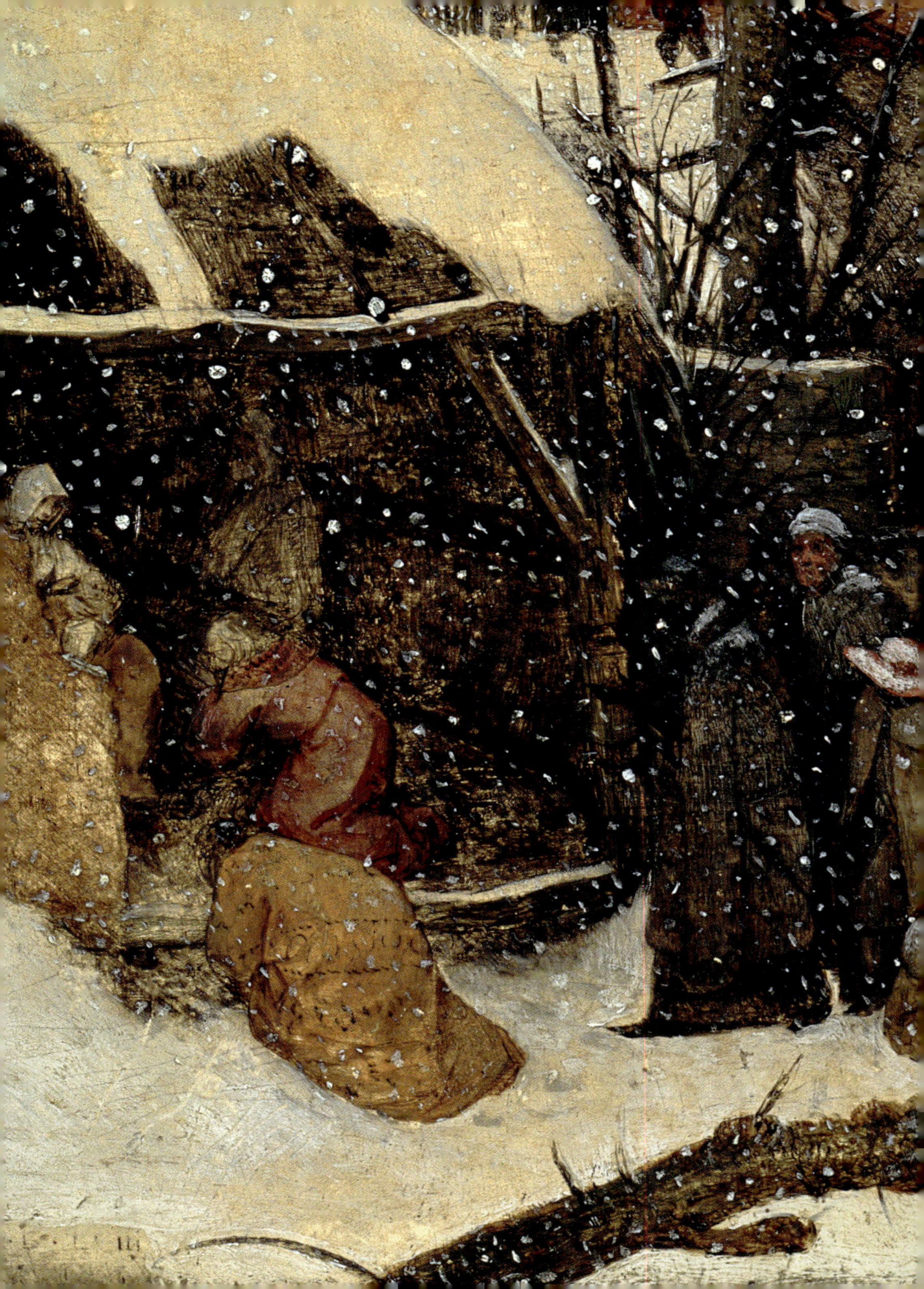

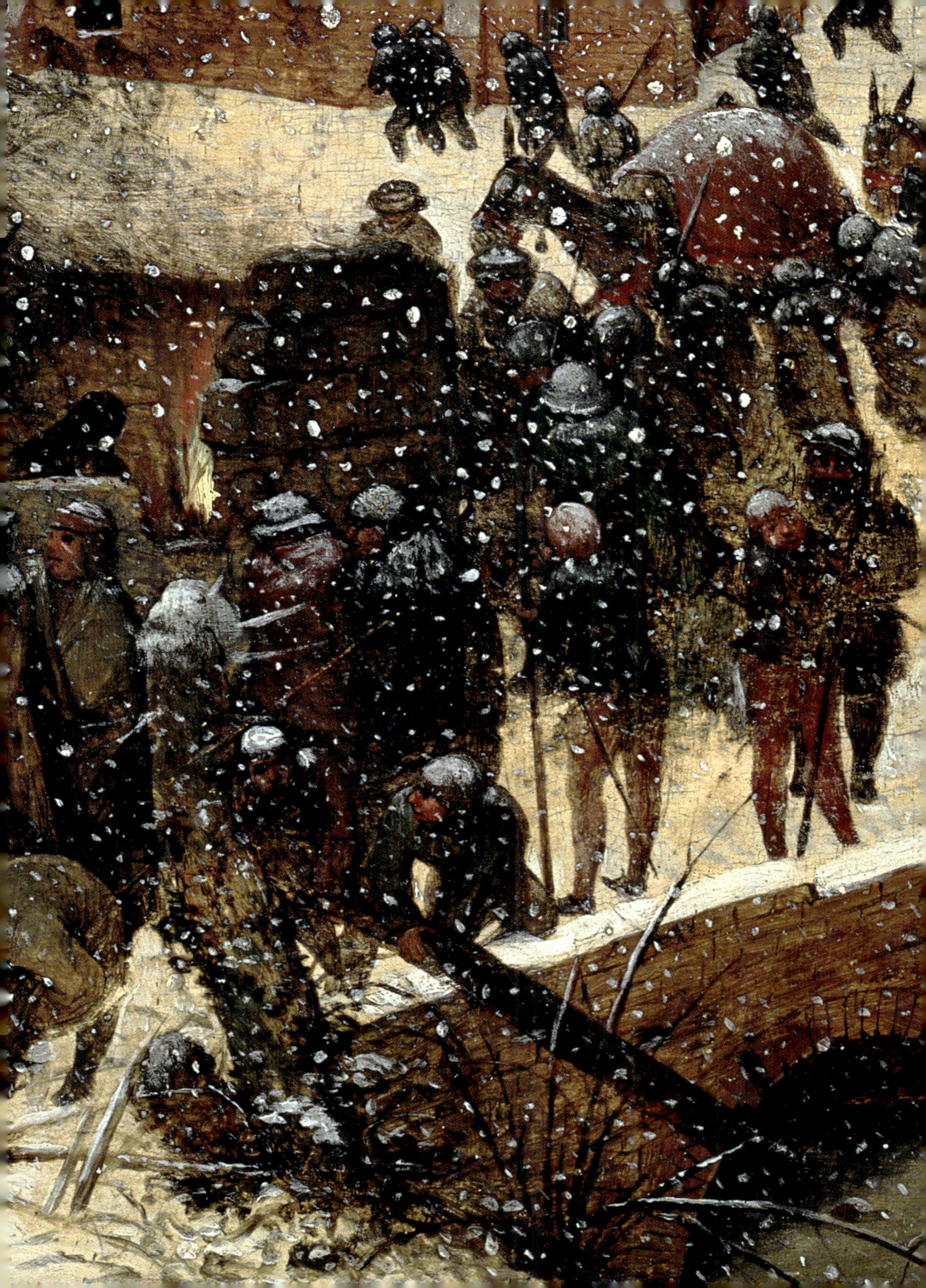

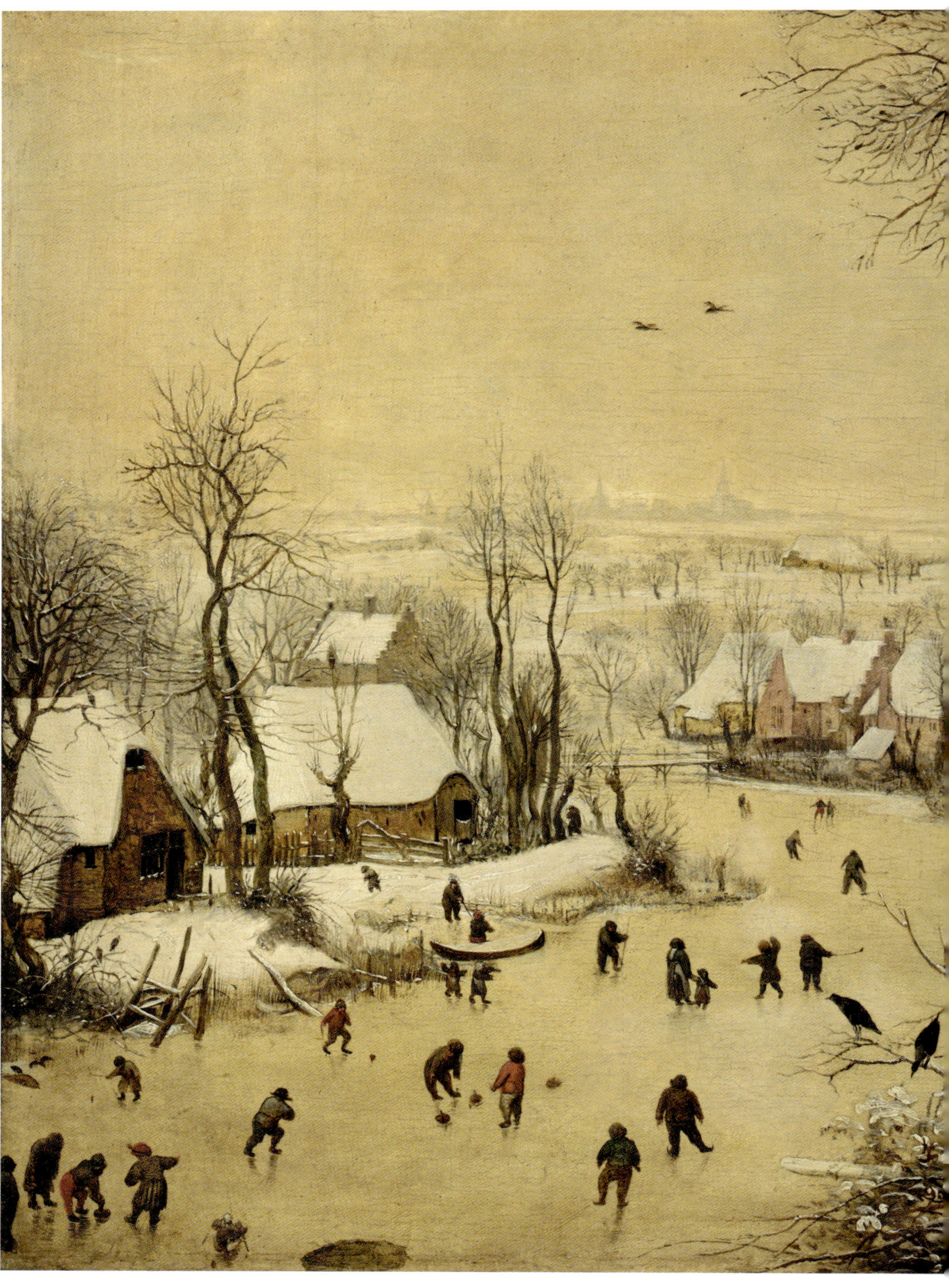

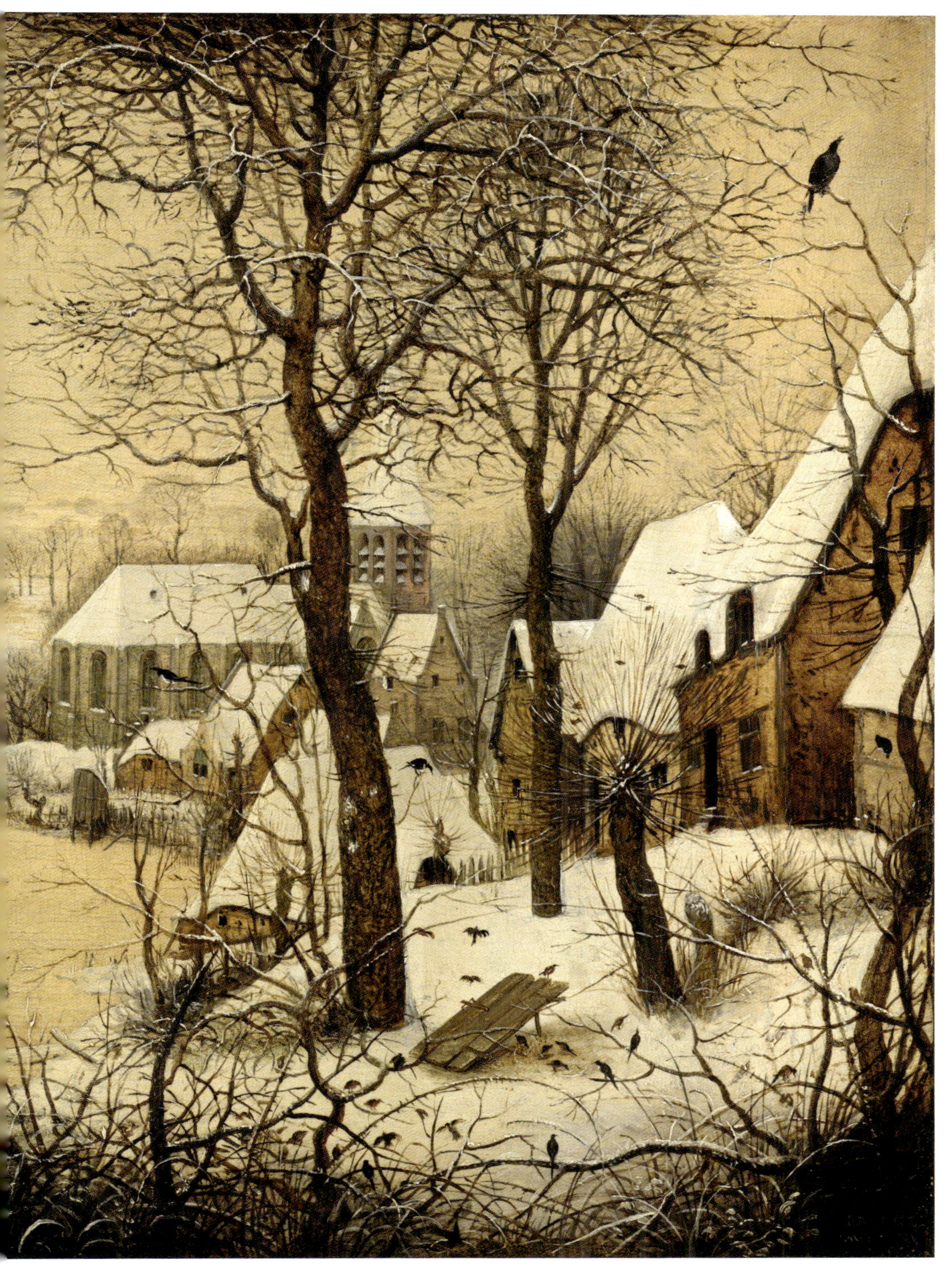

Pages 342/343
Winter Landscape with Skaters and Bird Trap, 1565
Oil on oak, 37 x 55.5 cm (14 ⅝ x 21 ⅞ in.)
Brussels, Musées royaux des Beaux-Arts de Belgique/
Koninklijke Musea voor Schone Kunsten van België
(details pages 345–347)

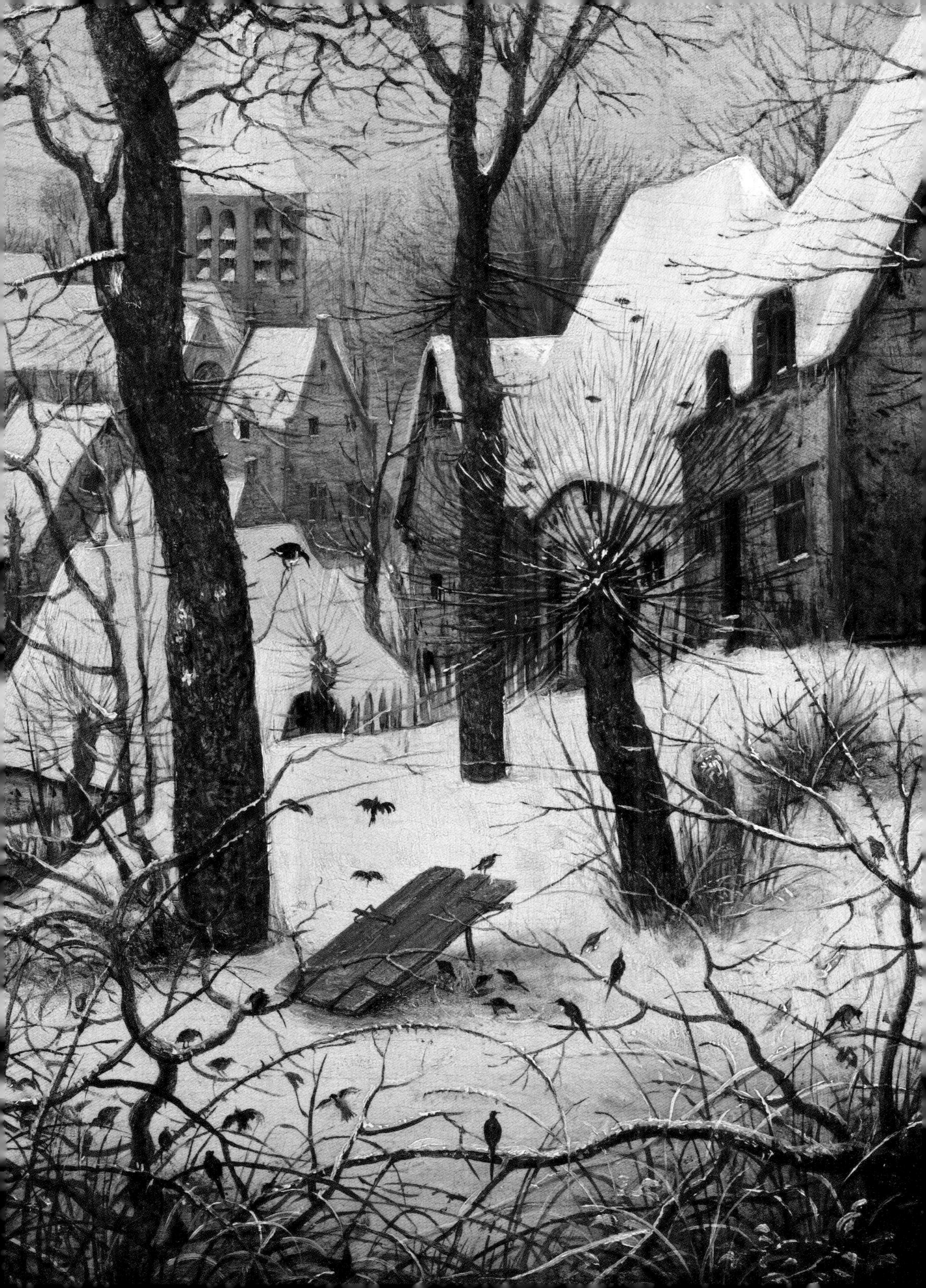

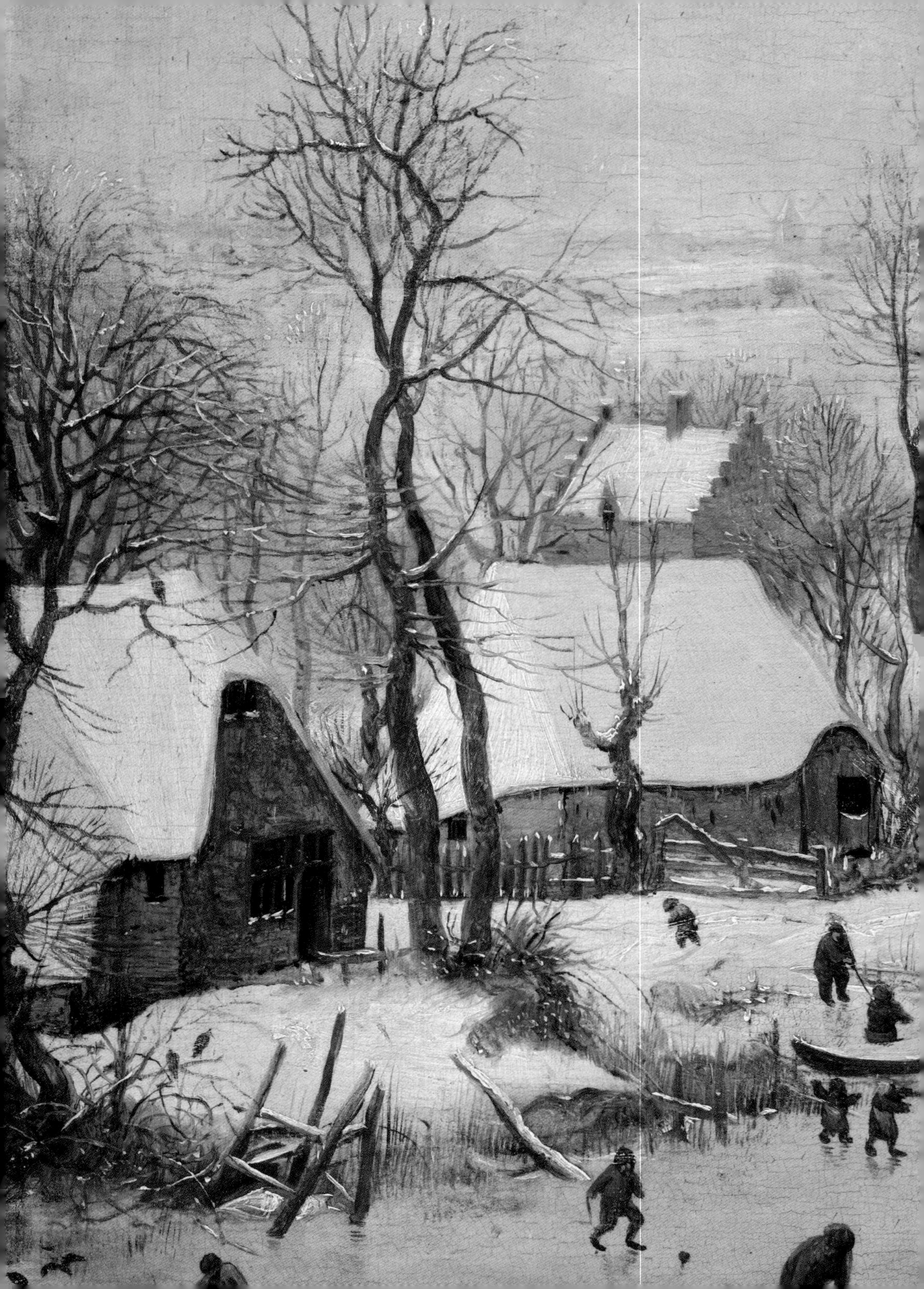

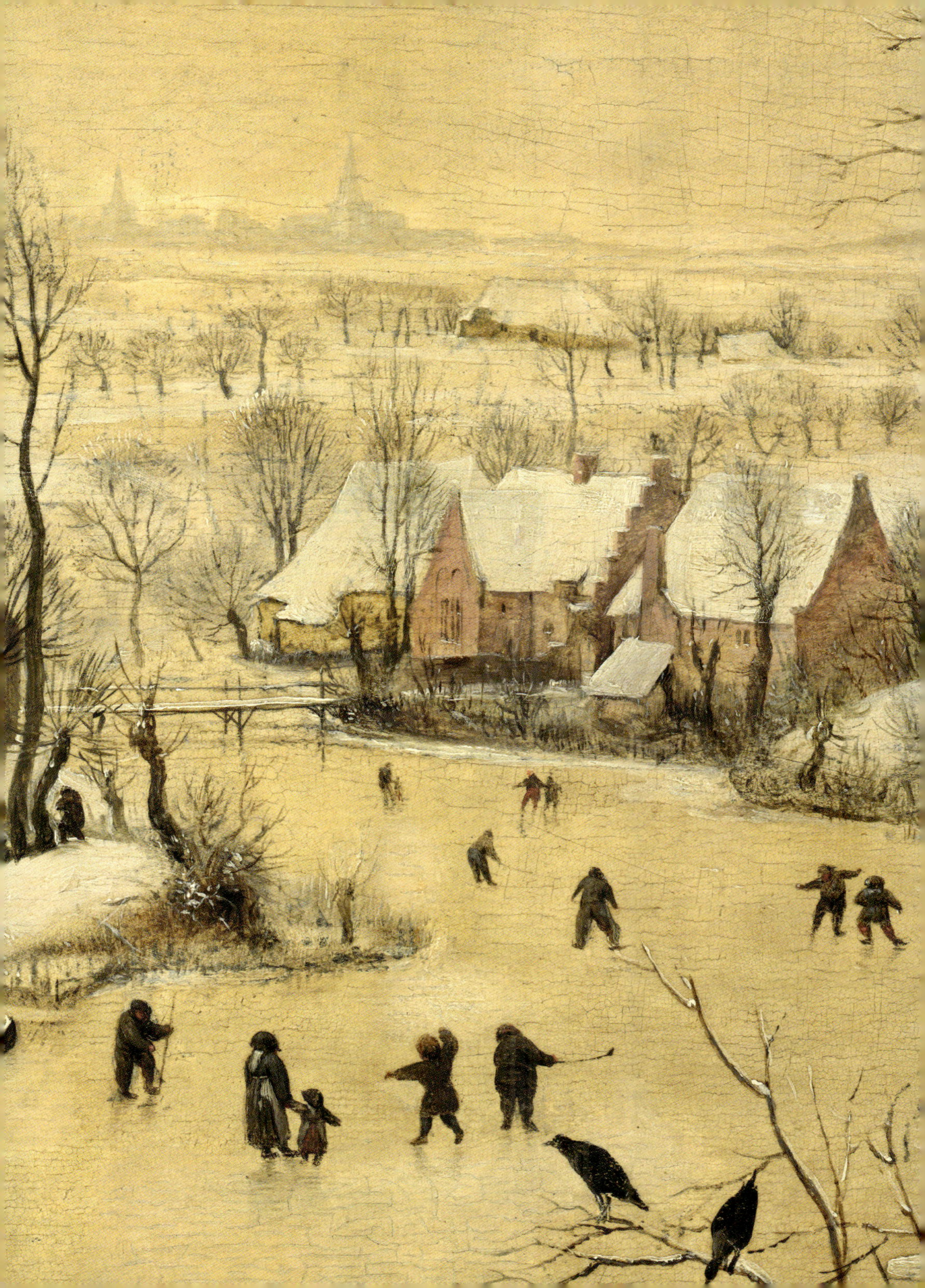

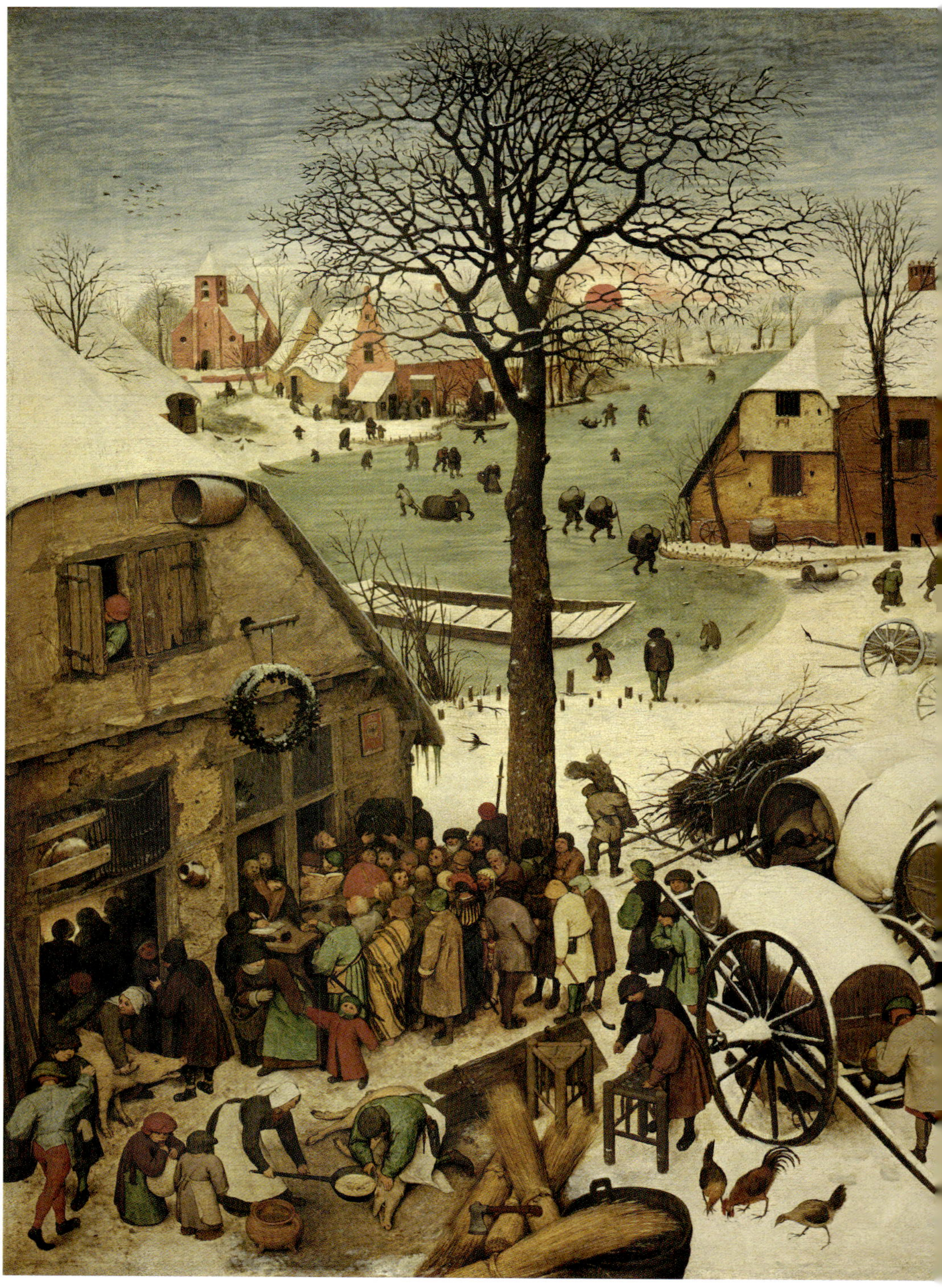

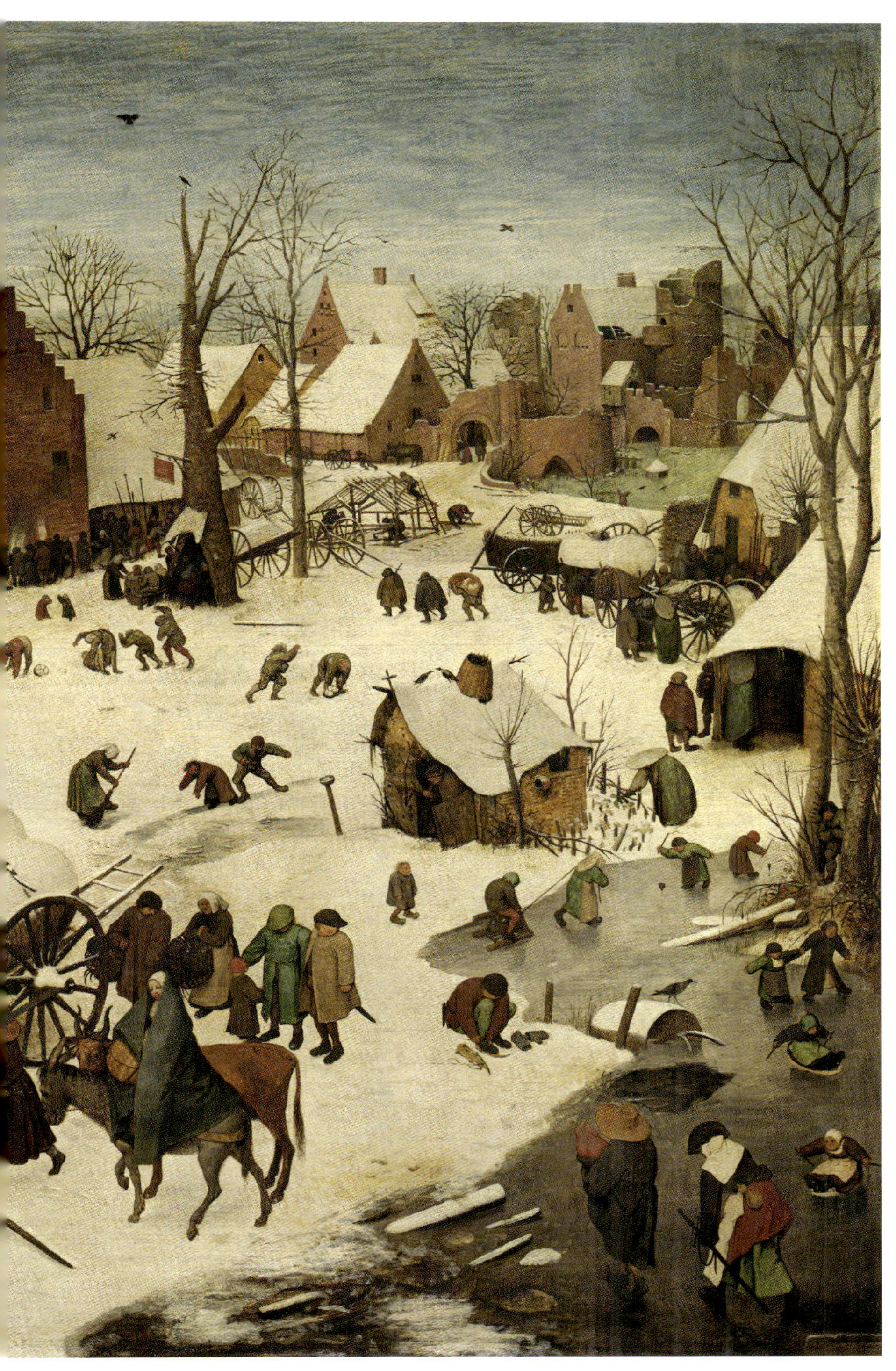

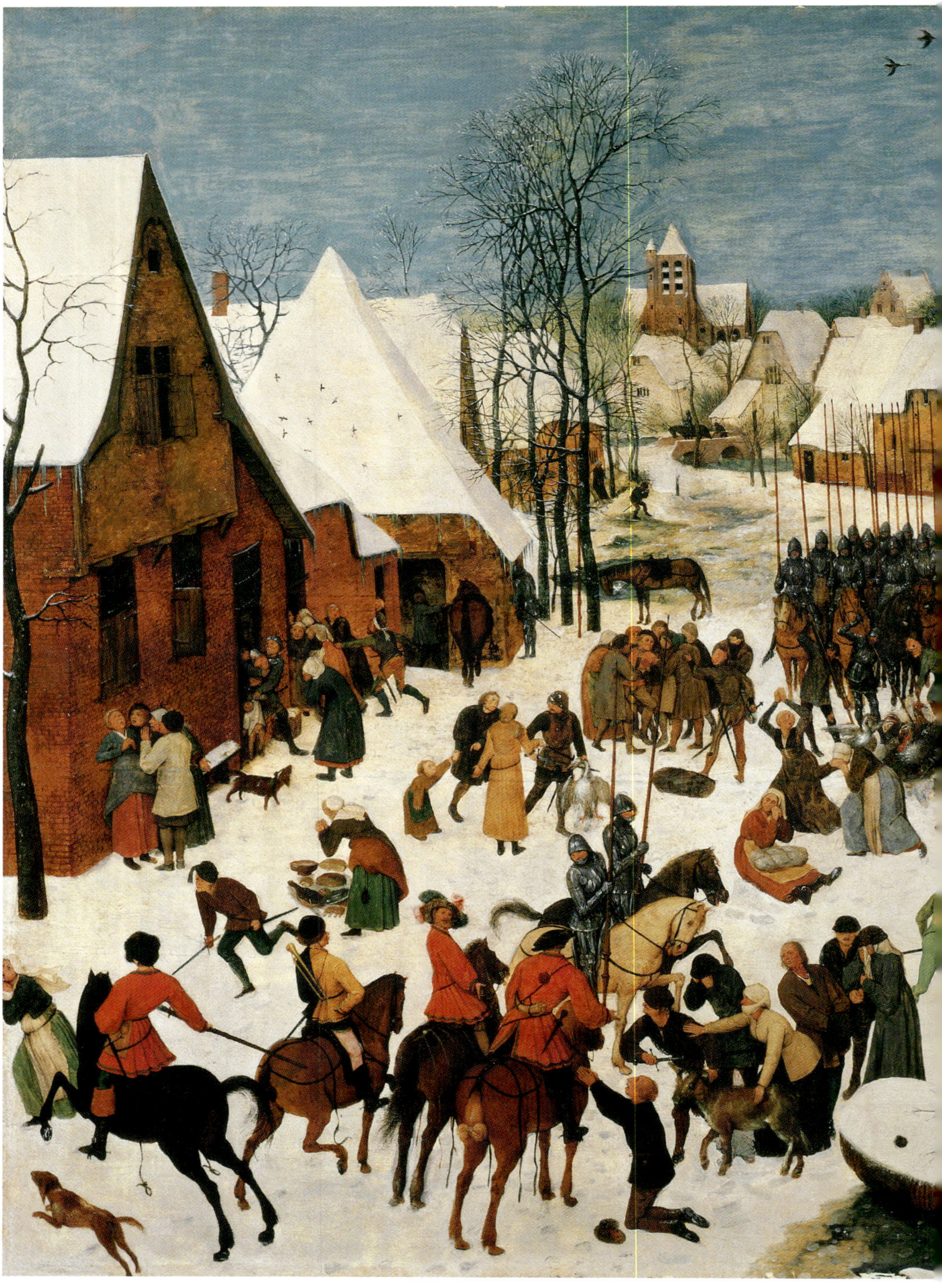

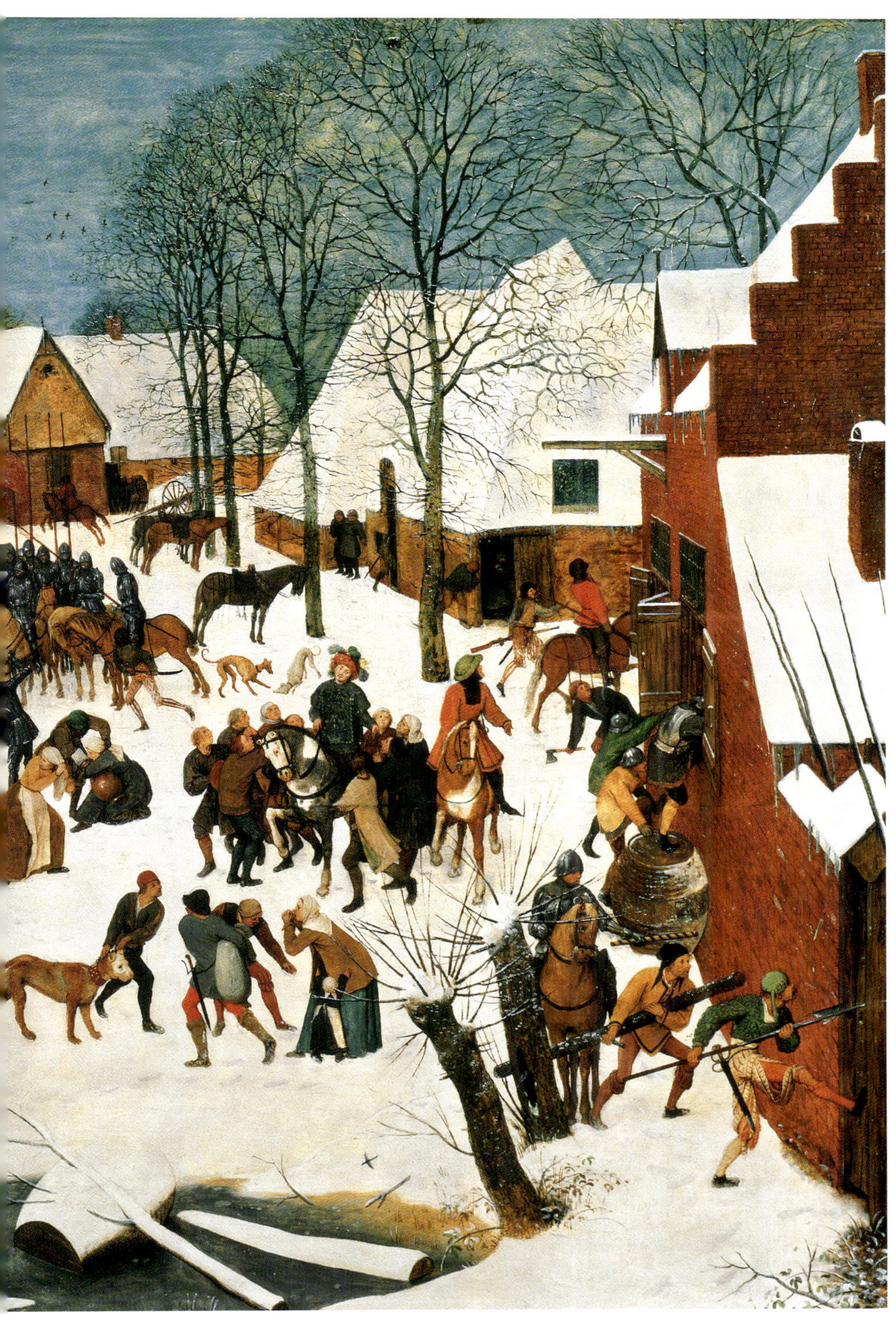

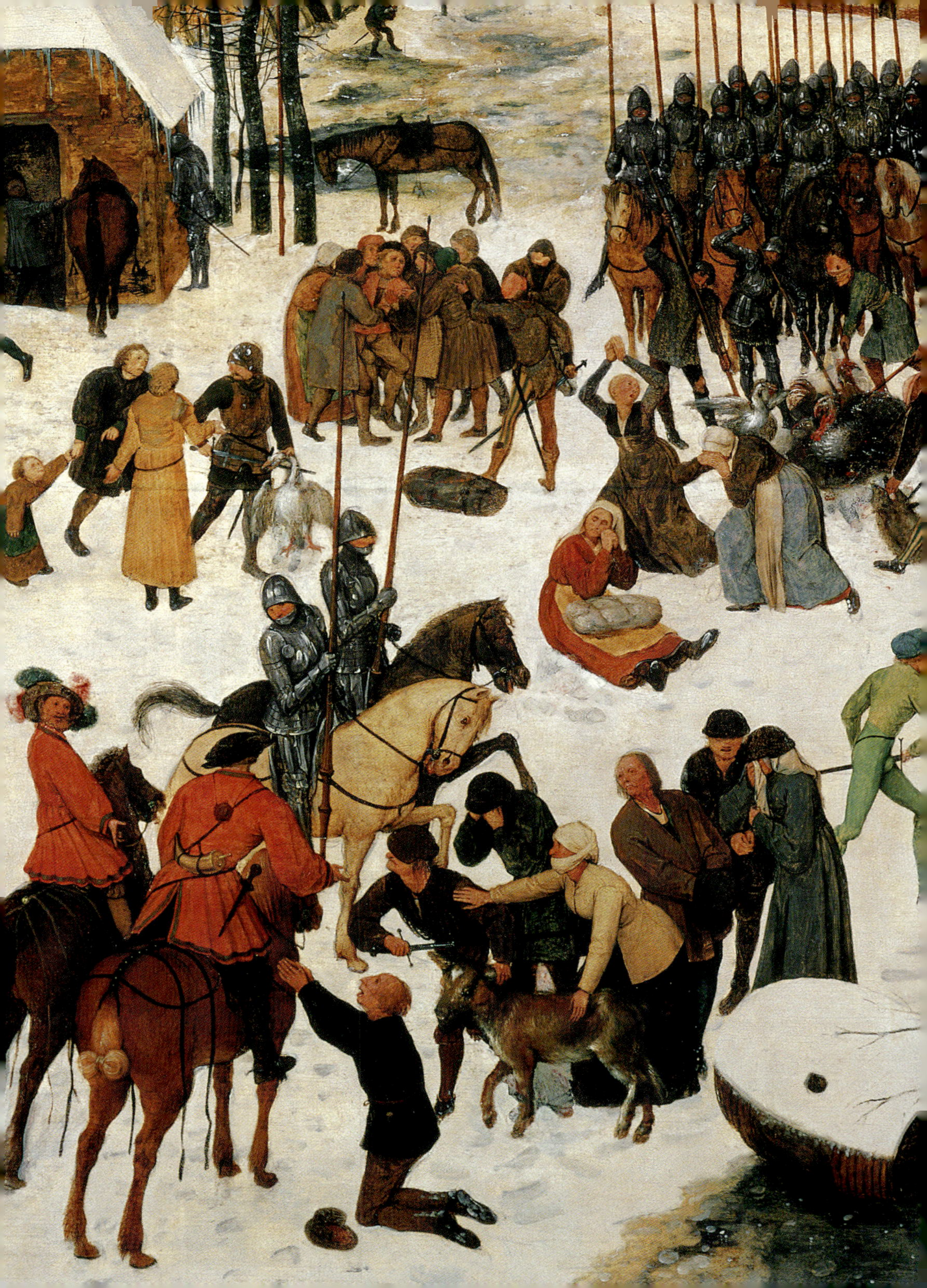

Pages 348/349
The Census at Bethlehem, 1566
Oil on oak, 115.5 x 163.5 cm (45 ½ x 64 ⅜ in.)
Brussels, Musées royaux des Beaux-Arts de Belgique/
Koninklijke Musea voor Schone Kunsten van België

Pages 350/351
The Massacre of the Innocents, *c.* 1565–1567
Oil on oak, 109.2 x 158.1 cm (42 ⅞ x 62 ¼ in.). London, Royal Collection
(details pages 352, 355)

354

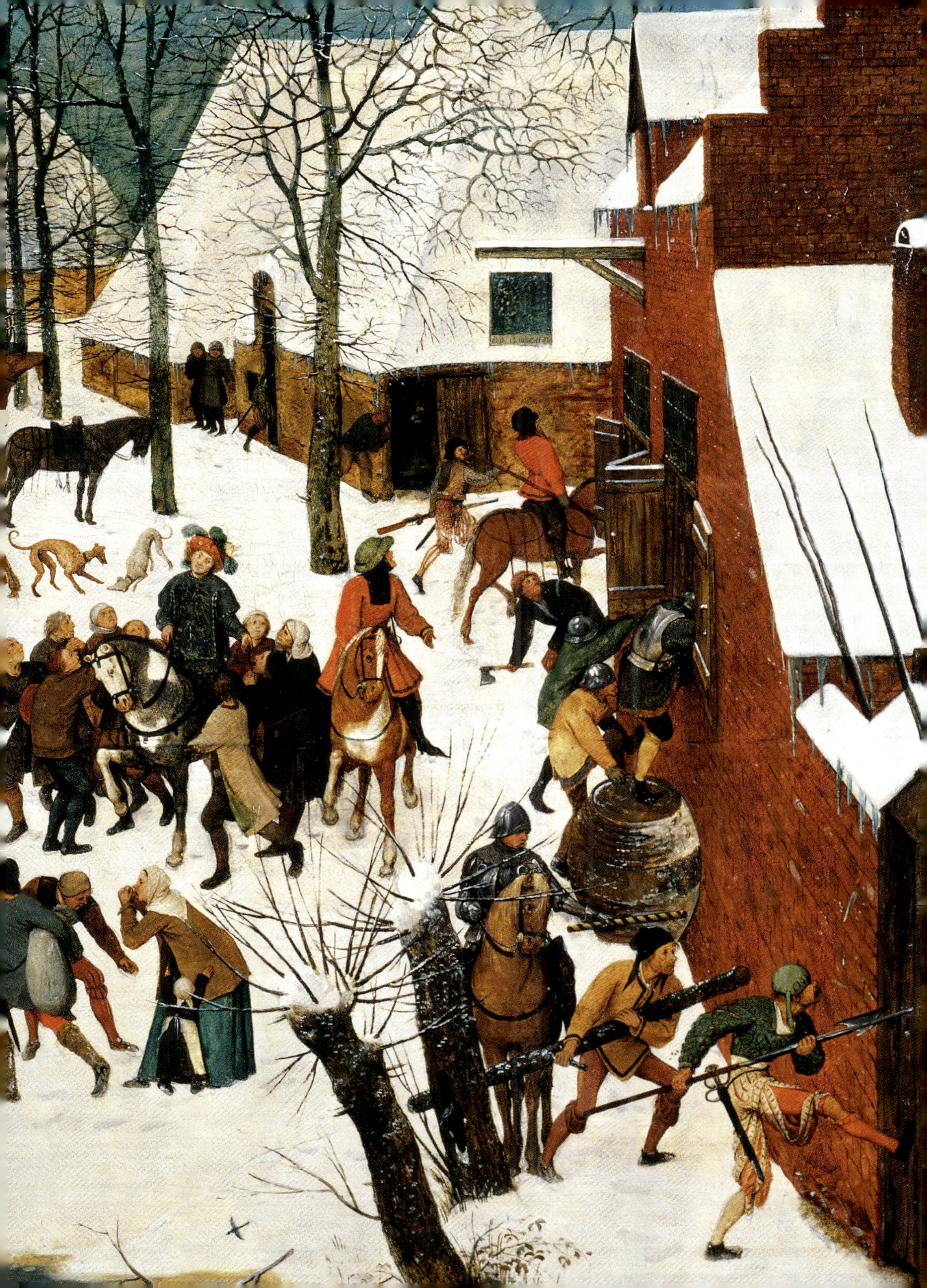

An Aesthetic of Subversion: The Late Works

Eat smaller portions [is] the meaning. If you live in a land where the roofs are made of pies, learn to pace yourself."
— DAVID NICHOLLS ON BRUEGEL'S *THE LAND OF COCKAIGNE*, 2014

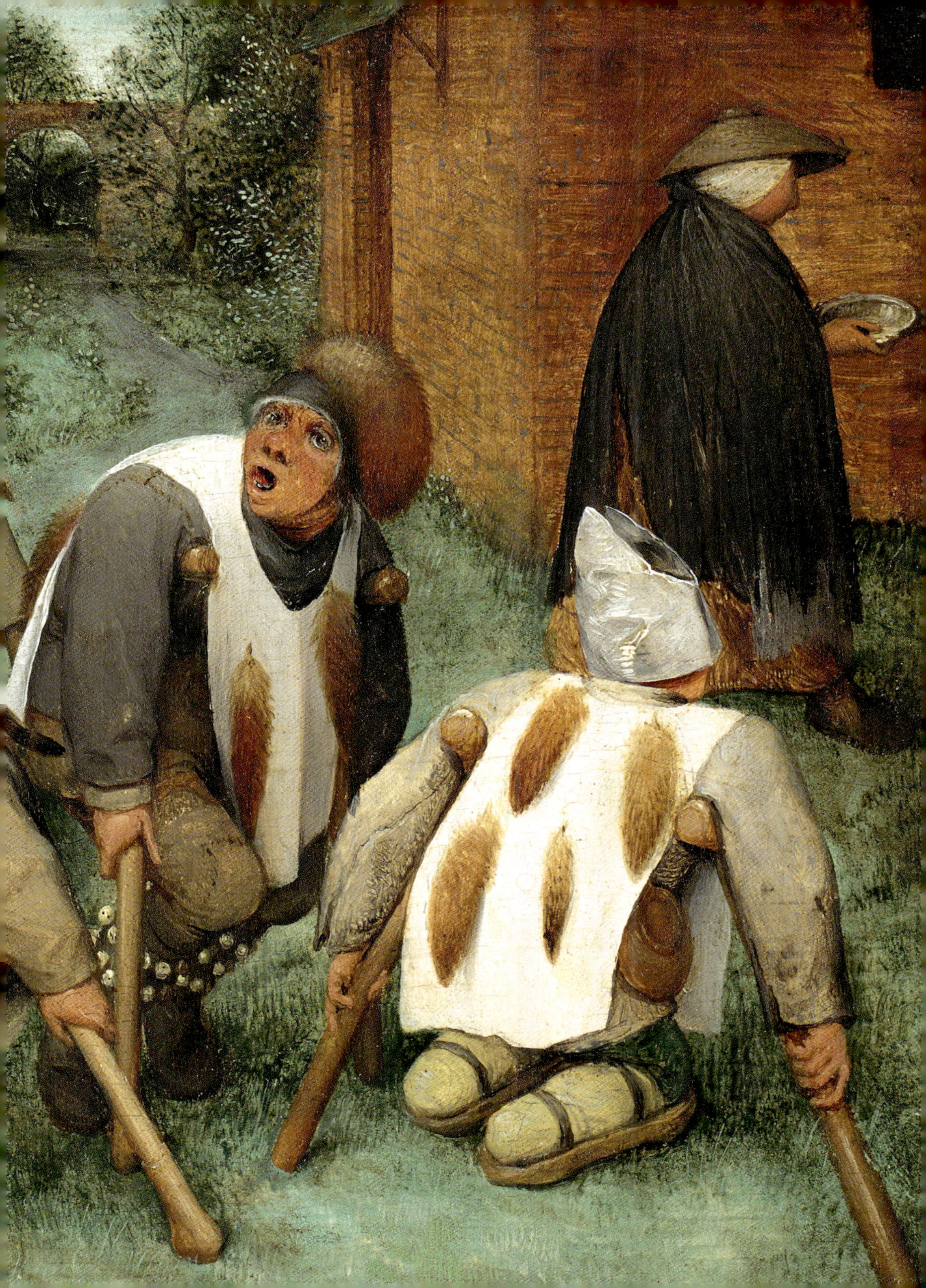

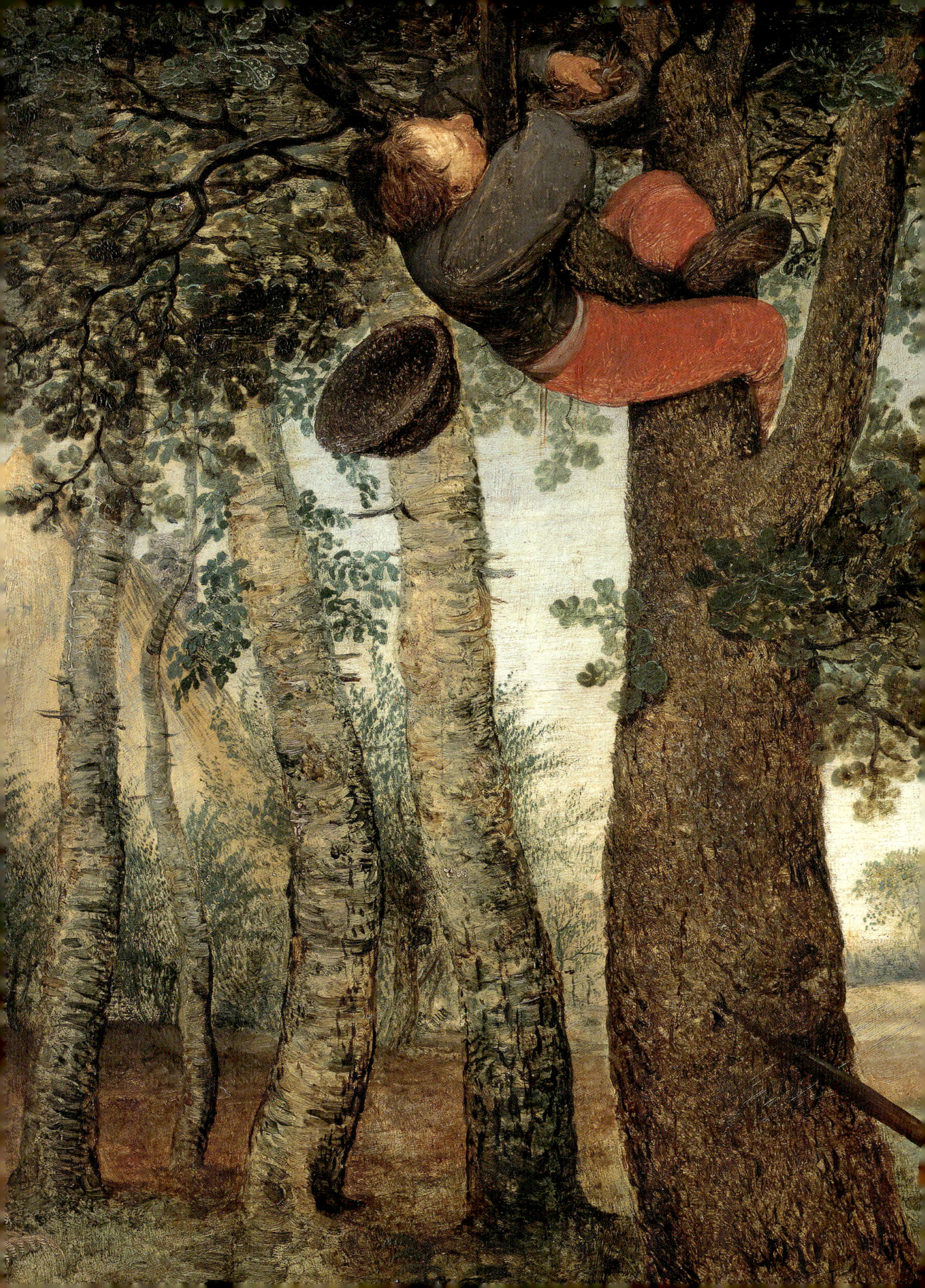

The heretic as seeker after God

Bruegel's *The Beekeepers* (pp. 360/361) is one of the most beautiful and enigmatic drawings of the sixteenth century. It is not difficult to describe the objects in the picture, but to say what it all means is by no means easy. Bruegel has portrayed three beekeepers at work. Two of them are carrying or opening a hive. A third has put his load down – it is not clear whether he has put his hive down, or whether the beekeeper to his right has handed it to him. The beekeepers have been made anonymous by their attire to such a degree that there is something uncanny and disturbing about them. They are wearing thick woollen robes and their hoods are closed with masks of fine, interwoven willow. Their appearance faintly resembles monks' habits. Oddly, neither bees nor receptacles for the honey can be seen in the drawing. Even today the drawing radiates a mysterious, almost surreal aura, mainly owing to the bizarre beekeepers. The man at the left looking towards the observer seems particularly sinister. Indeed, there is something threatening about him, for the impression is given that he has discovered something forbidden and has now been perceived by the perpetrators.

On the right, next to the beekeeper, we see a tree looming up, on which a man is clinging tightly with arms and legs to a branch. We cannot identify exactly what he is up to, since his back is turned to us. We notice he is positioned at the same height as the church tower opposite. The work is signed on the right, in Latin capitals: "BRVEGEL MDLXV [1565]". But some scholars think that the sheet has been cropped on its right side, which caused them to doubt the date, opting for a date around 1566–1568, even around 1568.

Another inscription is added in the bottom left corner, which at first sight has no apparent connection to the content of the scene. It is a saying in Flemish which translates as "He who knows the nest, knows it; but who he robs it, has it". The saying refers to the luck of the bold and can be found everywhere in collections of Flemish proverbs.[184] It praises the *vita activa*, the active life. But why this man in the tree should be superior to the beekeepers, and why Bruegel thought up such a bizarre scene in order to express something so self-evident, remains a puzzle in this interpretation.

The motif of the climber in the drawing is inadequately explained if we link it solely to the Viennese panel *The Nest Thief* (Cat. 33) and define both pictures as praise of the

Page 357
The Cripples (also: **The Beggars**; detail), 1568
(see ill. pp. 400/401)

The Nest Thief (detail), 1568
(see ill. pp. 394/395)

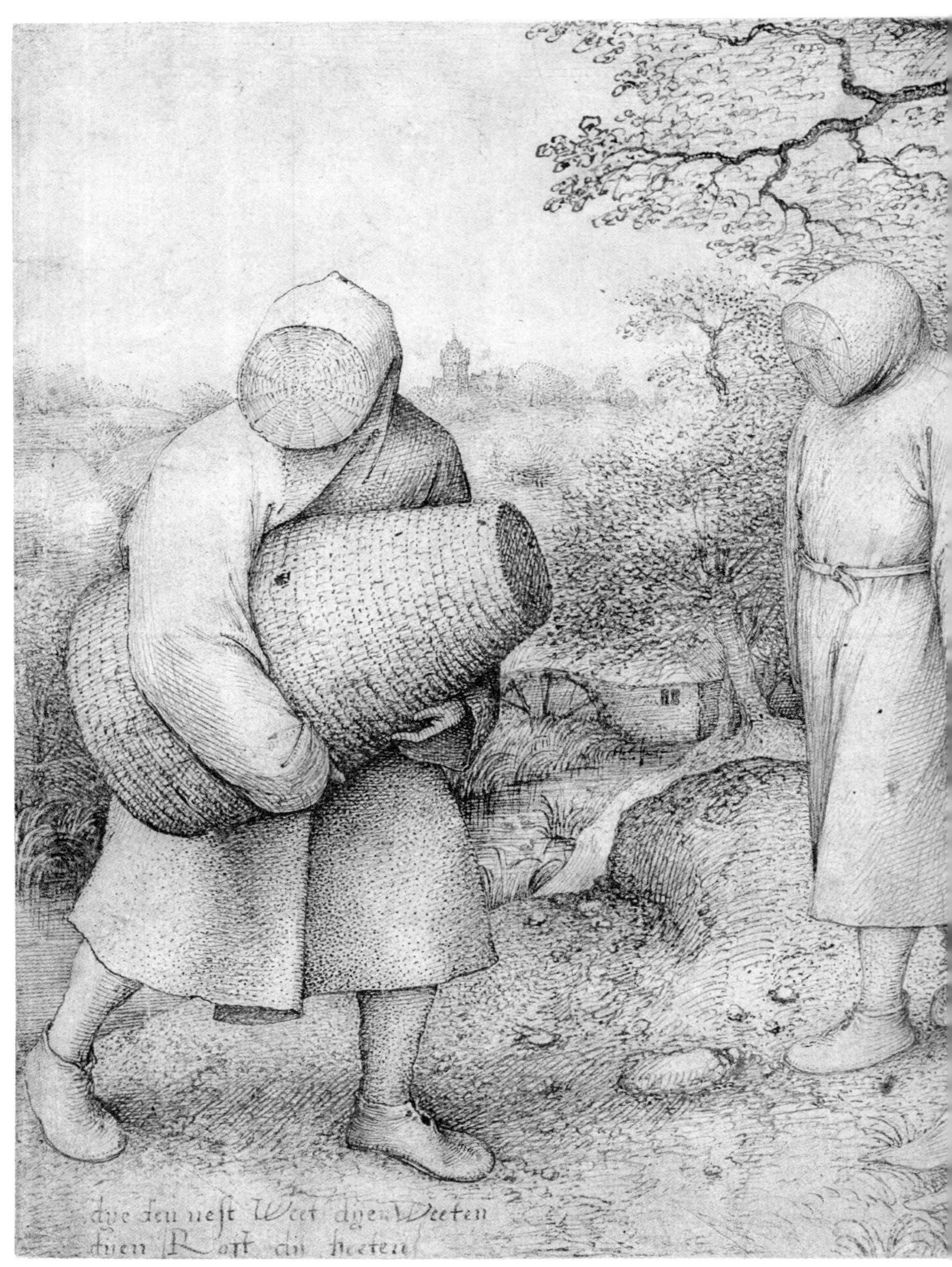
dye den nest Weet dyen weeten
dyen Roft dii heeten

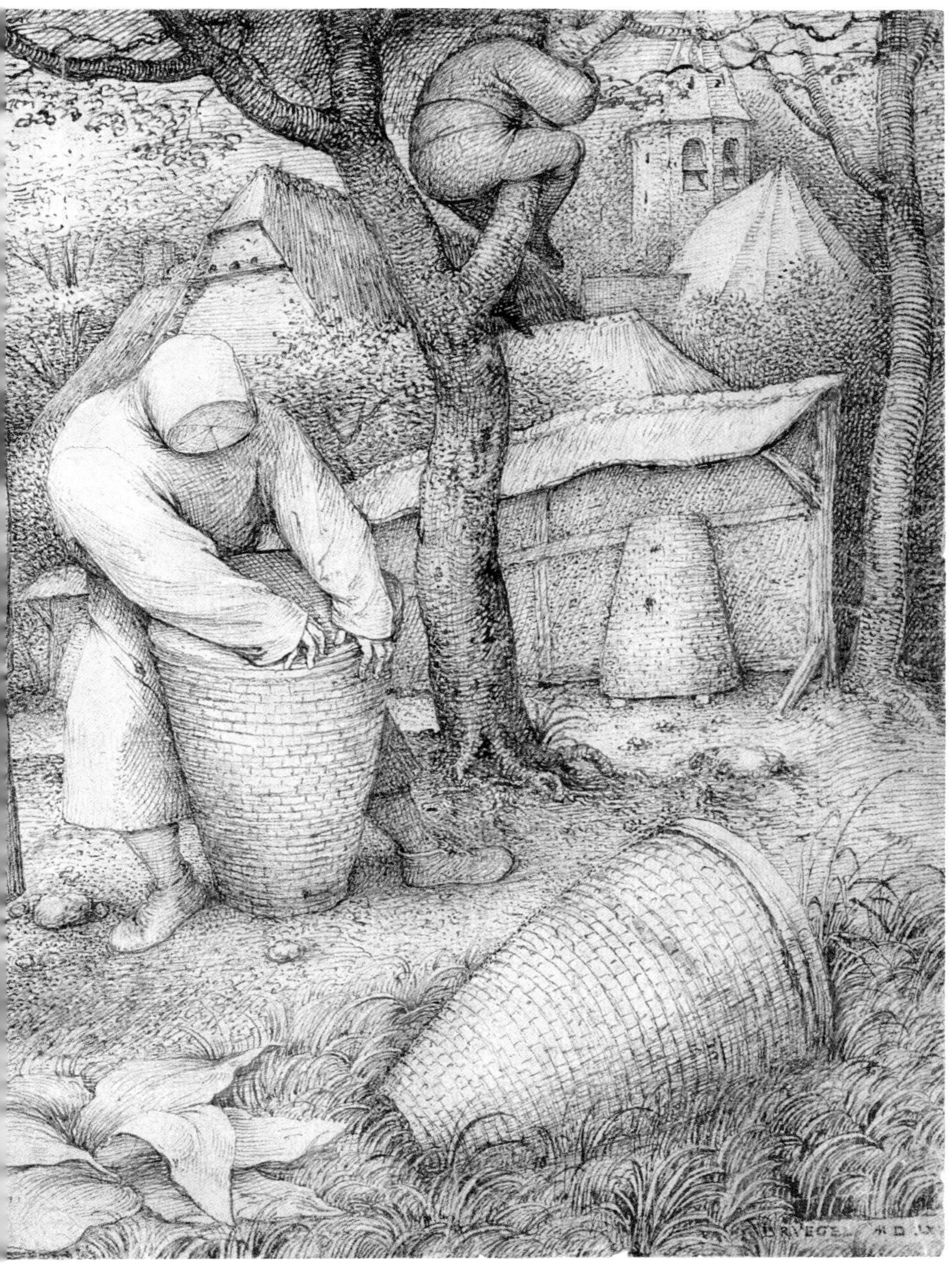

vita activa. In other words, the motif is to be understood as a symbol of heresy, as we find in the 36th chapter of Sebastian Brant's *Ship of Fools* (p. 365). In contrast to Brant, however, Bruegel is not content with this negative sense; he links the symbol of the heretic far more to a figure from the New Testament.

On the way to Jerusalem, Christ passes through Jericho, where he meets the publican, or tax collector, Zacchaeus and goes into his house to complete his conversion. The tax collector is a small man and, like the tree climber in Bruegel's drawing, has to shin up a tree to be able to see Christ. In similar portrayals from the first quarter of the sixteenth century, the tax collector usually sits on a tree at the height of a church located opposite, while Christ and the apostles move past. As a rule, the artists capture the moment when Jesus looks up to address the publican. Finally, a portrayal of Zacchaeus from a collection of printed sermons by Johann Gieler von Kaisersberg (1445–1510) from the early sixteenth century is significant (p. 363), in which the publican acts as a metaphor for the aspiration to know God.

Zacchaeus is seen as the dauntless climber, who ascends to "charity" by way of "faith" and "hope", as we read in the First Letter to the Corinthians. Hans Burgkmair the Elder (1473–1531), who made the woodcut, places the biblical figure of Zacchaeus in a pilgrim's robe to identify him as a seeker after God. Geiler comments that Zacchaeus wanted to see Christ face to face in order to attain true realisation, which is why he had to climb the fig tree. We find a similar interpretation in the commentaries on the New Testament by Erasmus. According to his reading, the tree and the Cross are one, and climbing the tree connotes the Crucifixion. When the tax collector climbs the tree he is lifting himself above those who solely follow the "letter of the law" and indulge in ceremonies and superficialities. The tree climber in Bruegel's drawing must be understood as a positive figure. In superimposing two motif traditions, Bruegel is establishing an intentional ambivalence. Analogous to the figure of the tax collector climbing up the tree to see Chris, we should also identify the nest robber positively as a seeker after God. He doesn't seek his fate with the institutions available to him, but goes his own way.

In contrast, the beekeepers represent something negative through their habit-like attire. Accordingly, they stand for the Catholic Church, which we see in the background represented as a stone building. It is no coincidence that a beehive is located on the vertical axis of the church tower as the traditional symbol of the Church. Moreover, scholars recognised early on that Bruegel, to portray the sinister beekeeper, borrowed from an ancillary figure from the Sistine Chapel, which Michelangelo included in the fresco of *Noah's Thanksgiving Sacrifice*.[185]

If we turn to the flora appearing in the drawing, we find further clues, like the willow in the background directly next to the river. Andreas Alciatus (1492–1550) takes the tree as a theme in his *Emblematum liber*. He refers to the famous passage in the Odyssey where Homer writes of the barrenness of the willow. Homer's verse about the "fruit-blighting willow" is frequently interpreted by the Church Fathers.[186] They relate it to those people who cannot hear the Word of God and thus bear no fruit for Christ's message of salvation.

Much more prominent than the willow in the background, Bruegel has placed another plant in his drawing. In the foreground, we can see the large leaves of a mandrake, which relates to various traditions of symbolism. In the folk tradition, it is credited with all kinds of magical powers. From the Christian perspective, it can be understood positively as an archetypal symbol of man's

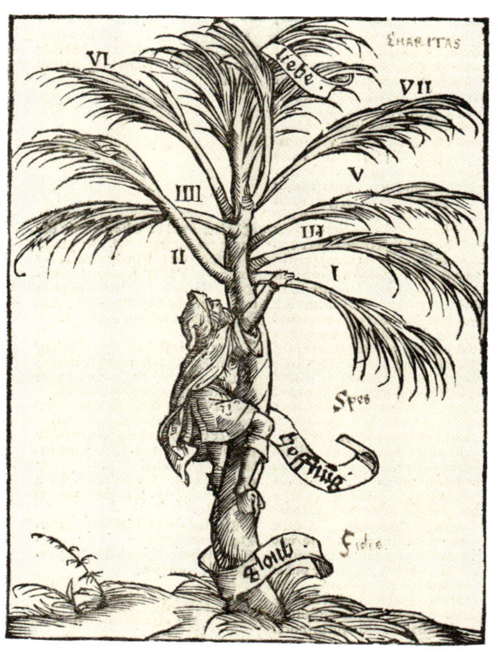

quest to find God. Just as the climber relates to the beekeepers, so the mandrake relates to the willow.[187]

In order to be able to formulate such an apology for heresy, Bruegel has used several ploys. In this context, we must note the basic ambivalence of the proverb added to the drawing as a hermeneutic key. What "nest" are we talking about here? The literature speaks unanimously of a bird's nest and refers time and again to Bruegel's painting *The Nest Thief*. But the drawing is less clear. We are looking merely at the back of a man who has climbed a tree; we cannot see what he is actually doing. And if we combine this with the beekeeper scene on the ground, we must conclude that it has something to do with a bees' "nest". The bees might have left the basket hives and made their own nest in the trees.

Hans Burgkmair the Elder, **Zacchaeus Climbing a Tree to See Christ**, 1508–1510
Illustration for Johann Geiler von Kaisersberg's *Predigen teütsch*
Woodcut, 18.9 x 14.2 cm (7 ½ x 5 ⅝ in.). London, The British Museum

Pages 360/361
The Beekeepers, *c.* 1568
Pen and brown ink, 20.3 x 30.9 cm (7 ⅞ x 12 ⅛ in.)
Staatliche Museen zu Berlin, Kupferstichkabinett

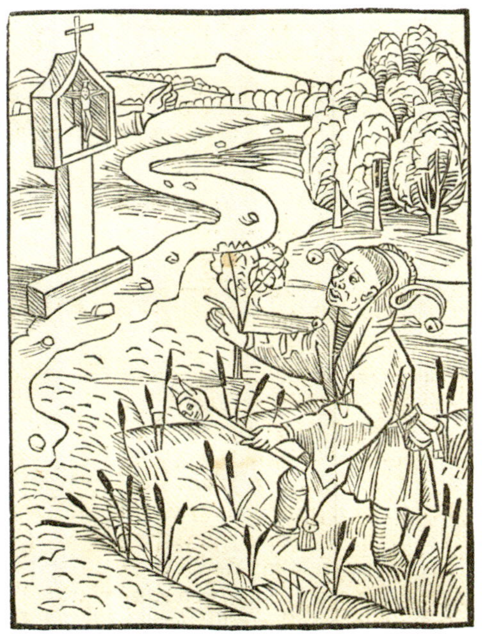

After all that has been said, it is evident that Bruegel's *The Beekeepers* is extremely enigmatic. A heterodox-heretical dimension lurks beneath the surface. The drawing's theme thus proves to be subversive. So the artist has to make sure he conceals the key to the interpretation of his work. Bruegel's hermeneutic strategy consists in setting everything into the picture without addressing it directly. His narrative mode in the drawing never once becomes explicit. Only when the decisive elements are properly linked together do critical ideas about the Church emerge, signalling notions beyond what is depicted. Nevertheless, the artists would always be able to counter any imputation of heresy, thus insuring himself against the Inquisition. If the picture caption mentions the nest, he could have pointed to the nest of wild bees, although the bird's nest of the heretic is meant. Moreover, Bruegel, by superimposing two traditions, construes another ambivalent element with the figure of the man in the tree. With this in mind, it is plausible that this virtuosic sheet might have served as a friendship token within the artist's heterodox circle.

Appearance deceives

Now the time has come to interpret the work of art that is directly linked to *The Beekeepers*. *The Nest Thief* (pp. 394/395, Cat. 33) also features a man who has climbed a tree, and here too we wish to elaborate on the panel's heretical content. Such an interpretative hypothesis seems fallacious at first sight: here we have a well-nourished countryman striding cheerily towards us, pointing behind him; there we discern a young man who has climbed a tree to rob a bird's nest. He has wrapped his legs tightly around a

Albrecht Dürer, **The Fool,** 1494
Illustration for Sebastian Brant's *Ship of Fools*, Chapter 21, "Vom Tadeln und Selbertun"
("Of them that correct other, them self culpable in the same faut"), 1494
Woodcut, 15.5 x 20.8 cm (6 ⅛ x 8 ¼ in.). Schweinfurt, Otto Schäfer Collection

branch in order to reach inside the nest. His action is not without risk, as we see from his cap, which is falling down. He has no free hand to catch it (p. 358).

In the background on the right, we see a farm with thatched roof. A horse is being led into the stable; the farm is indeed a welcoming and friendly sight in the midday Sun; in this part of the picture, the flat landscape seems accessible, while it is closed off on the opposite side by the tree trunks. The artist is cleverly steering our perception of the picture, because even before we know what it is all about, our glance follows the peasant's signalling gesture. He is carrying a drinking horn on his belt, and a stick. We are confronted not by the owner of the farm as by a farmhand or cowherd.

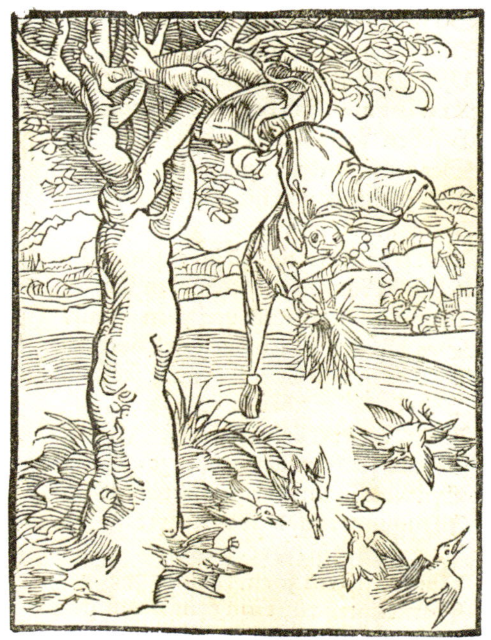

A sack is lying to the right of the peasant figure, probably left on the ground by the nest robber for transporting the stolen eggs afterwards. The sack might have drawn the large figure's attention to the nest robber. But in time it becomes clear that the all-too-self-assured man is just about to stumble and fall head over heels. He would have done better to pay more attention to himself instead of pointing at the nest robber, who is at the moment able to hold onto the branches.

To approach the picture's iconography, we must again refer to Sebastian Brant's *Ship of Fools*.[188] Firstly, the 21st chapter gives us a clue as to the cowherd (p. 364). This refers to a fool who wants to show others the way but will himself end up in a pool. Brant accuses such fools of malice, since they are ready to vilify everyone and are yet not capable of seeing the beam in their own eye. Dürer illustrates this by showing a fool with the crucified Christ on a wayside shrine, while he himself stands in water.

Albrecht Dürer, **The Nest Thief**, 1494
Illustration for Sebastian Brant's *Ship of Fools*, Chapter 36,
"Von Eygenrichtikeit" ("Of Self-righteousness"), 1494
Woodcut, 15.5 x 20.8 cm (6⅛ x 8¼ in.). Schweinfurt, Otto Schäfer Collection

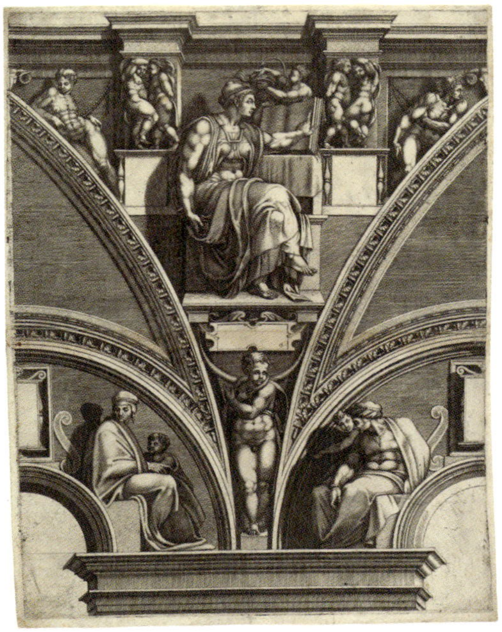

The 36th chapter, too, titled *Von Eygenrichtikeit* – "Of Self-righteousness" – can be related to Bruegel's picture. The illustration in this chapter shows a nest robber/fool who falls out of the treetop to the ground. Birds are lying around, which the careless thief has grabbed from the nest and killed (p. 365). The beginning of the text describes people who have left the right path and not noticed they have gone astray. Already in the first verses the humanist underlines the obstinacy of such people, who think they are so clever. The ninth verse teaches us about the consequences of false stubbornness: "Oft those turn into heretics, they / Who from the path of censure stray; / Who rely alone on their own art / To gain fame and favour, for their part."[189] What began as a critique of foolish behaviour now becomes a charge against heresy, the cause of which is seen as "Eygenrichtikeit" – self-righteousness. The vanishing point of the entire chapter is the image of the "seamless garment of Christ", which we should never try to divide. Heretics on the other hand strive to tear the Church apart.[190]

In the context of the interpretation, we might mention another motif through which the artist gives voice to his anti-Catholic critique. Namely, our cowherd is striding towards us straight out of Michelangelo's fresco for the Sistine Chapel (p. 366).[191] It is surely no coincidence that in his borrowed motif Bruegel is alluding to *the* key work of Catholic orthodoxy. It meanwhile verges on high comedy that out of a noble, resolute figure striding forwards he makes a cloddish cowherd about to stumble into a pond.

Bruegel's painted picture takes its impetus from Brant's chapter. But he turns the humanist's supposed wisdom upside down. His image tempts us at first to agree with Brant and see the cowherd as wise, and the nest robber in danger – until we realise that precisely the opposite is the case. The supposedly flat and harmless path on the right side is veined with channels. The way up into the trees seems more difficult at first, but in the

Giorgio Ghisi after Michelangelo, **The Erythraean Sibyl**, 1570–1575
Copper engraving, 57 x 43.2 cm (22 ½ x 17 ⅛ in.). New York, The Metropolitan Museum of Art

end is less hazardous. Ultimately, the heretic is the wiser, because he does not fall, in contrast to the peasant.

Bruegel succeeds in an unexpected way in updating the famous conceptualisation of the two paths. The primrose path of vice starts broad and seems without danger, while that of virtue is arduous. The painter thus opts for a clever pictorial programme by vividly and evocatively defending heresy as a virtuous path, yet simultaneously obscuring it. Here, too, Bruegel discreetly applies the symbolism of plants. The water lily relates to its counterpart, the blighted willow, which equally tends towards the same fate as the stumbling cowherd. Franck describes the lily in his 234th Paradox: "The Church, a lily among thorns […], will be trampled on until the end."[192]

A false paradise

The Land of Cockaigne (pp. 396/397, Cat. 30), dated 1567, also has an element of parody in its effect.[193] The picture maintains a firm composition; it is arranged in a star formation, with a circular movement around a centre. Bruegel orients his idea on an engraving by Pieter Baltens (*c.* 1527–1584) of around 1560 (p. 369), which he follows in many details. The literary tradition of the land of Cockaigne is, however, much older and goes back to the Middle Ages.[194] Numerous examples demonstrate the popularity of this traditional, folk-based motif of a sensuous and sensual Paradise for good-for-nothings.[195]

Bruegel follows this concept by inventing a bizarre world of earthly pleasures. Its characters surrender to the joys of the palate, which they can enjoy as a gift without having to work for it. Three men are lying on the ground around a central tree, their heads almost touching the trunk. They are arranged like the spokes of a wheel. At the same time, the figures represent a cross section of the estates of society. On the left, we recognise a peasant with threshing flail, on the right a burgher in a fur-lined coat. He has with him a writing set, a book and a manuscript document. Bruegel has also included a soldier in a coat of mail, resting his head on a bolster, his lance and steel gauntlets lying at his feet.

Meanwhile, Bruegel makes the special character of this location quite clear. Hence drinking beakers are hanging on the branches of the tree instead of fruit. The wattle fence on the left is made with sausages, and in the middle ground on the right a roasted pig is running past, a knife stuck in its skin. The cactus in front is made of rounds of flat bread. An original idea is the egg running in the foreground with a spoon stuck in it; despite its short legs, it is nimbly running on its way, a counter-image to the lethargic men. An improvised table is set up around the tree trunk, where we discern other delicacies: roasted chickens, pasties, beakers and jugs, salt and another egg. In the background is an expansive lake; the literary tradition tells us it is of milk and has to be crossed to reach

Cockaigne. Several boats are making their way across. A port city is visible on the horizon, whence the people in the picture may have come.

At the top edge there is another soldier, with helmet and steel gauntlets. He is lying in a kind of lean-to, his arms comfortably resting on a cushion, and staring open-mouthed at the awning-like roof of the house. He is waiting for the pancakes to slip off and fall directly into his mouth. On the opposite side is a man who has eaten his way through a mountain of buckwheat porridge in order to get into Cockaigne. He has pluckily grabbed hold of the branch of a leafless tree to free himself from the porridge. The three men in the centre are lying apathetically stretched out after a prodigious meal. The soldier has fallen asleep, the peasant has rolled his plump body to the side and crossed his legs. Only the burgher is performing a minimal action, opening his mouth to catch a drop dripping out of the upset jug. He gazes catatonically upwards and has placed his arms behind his head, which is not without a certain element of situation comedy. The prodigious sloth of the figures is embodied in their shapelessness.

We owe to Bruegel studies some fundamental interpretations of his painting.[196] They succeeded in showing that the artist is here providing a highly allusive commentary on the political situation in the Netherlands around 1567, cryptically expressing his sympathy for the struggle for liberty against the Habsburgs. For this we must refer to the vernacular sayings of the time. The basis for such an interpretation is seen in the pyramid of the social estates; we realise that the nobility are missing. This is explained when we see the goose as a wordplay on *geuze*, or *geus*, thus as a reference to the group of the high nobility who opposed the Habsburgs during the wars of liberation and identified themselves as *geuze* (beggars), actually a term of abuse.[197] The artist has distributed the products of the land of Cockaigne so evenly across the picture that the roast goose would not have been particularly conspicuous if it had not belonged to the figures centrally arranged around the tree trunk. Easily visible, it lies on a pewter plate, under which a white napkin is spread. If regarded merely as just another delicacy, it wouldn't need any further interpretation. But understanding it as a fourth element completing the order of the estates of the men lying around the tree causes us to investigate further.

In the circular arrangement of the figures, Bruegel is once more alluding to the Wheel of Fortune. This evokes the idea of the folly of this world, which is not guided by reason but senselessly driven round and round in circles by chance and fate – a cycle which finds its correspondence in the round table top. The fallen beaker next to the soldier also hints at the movement of the table attached to the tree. A baleful timelessness characterises this place. The enjoyment of food has been perverted into its opposite. It does not represent a reward, but is the cause of apathy.

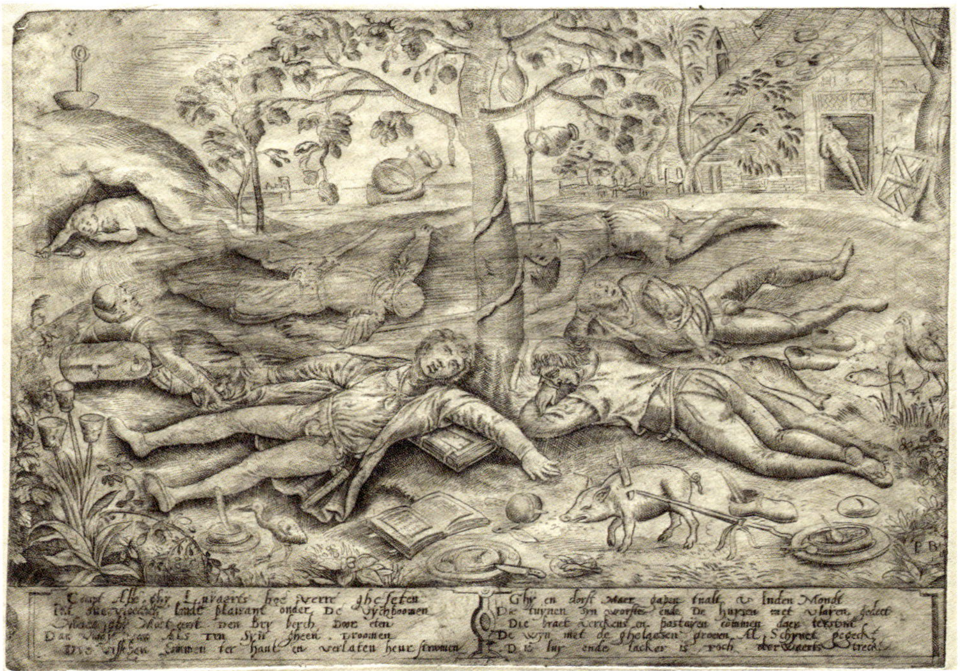

Pieter Baltens, **The Land of Cockaigne**, *c.* 1560
Copper engraving, 31.2 x 22.8 cm (12 ⅜ x 9 in.)
The Cleveland Museum of Art, Gift of FitzRoy Carrington

To reflect this affliction, Bruegel uses a witty allusion. The ancient story of Laocoön and his sons was deemed in the classical theory of art to be the artistic epitome of pain and can be encountered in various forms in many artworks of the time (p. 373). Bruegel makes fun of it by construing the figures of the famous sculpture in a completely incongruous context. The three persons attacked by a serpent are transformed here into three gluttons who have only to fight against the consequences of extreme greed. In the foreground, with outstretched arms, lies the pendant to the father of the ancient group, his mouth open not in a cry of agony, but in order to consume more food more comfortably. The younger – dying – son in the group corresponds to the stretched-out peasant, his lolling legs laxly crossed. Finally, the soldier, who has turned his head towards us and has bent his legs, is the parallel figure to the son on the right, who is looking over his shoulder at his father and has pulled up a leg to avoid the serpent's coils.

Bruegel has manoeuvred an artful arrangement of the figures by making them seem to revolve not only around the tree trunk, but simultaneously around their own axes.

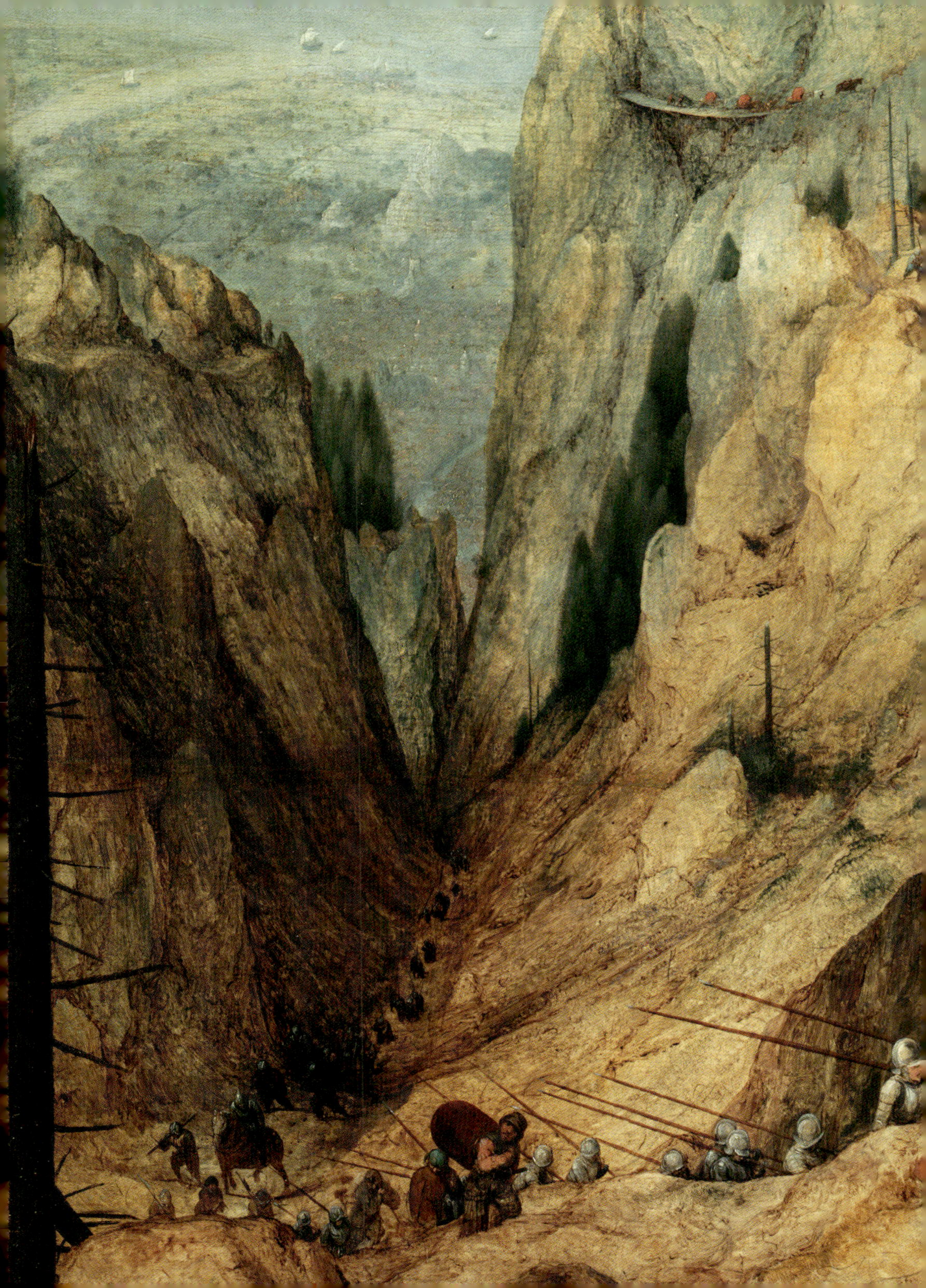

The Conversion of St Paul (detail), 1567
(see ill. pp. 392/393)

He stages a gruesome carousel on which the figures are force-fed, as we can see from the fat shapelessness of the peasant's body. This mischievously caricatures the figural ideal of the superlative physical aura embodied in the father of the ancient group. Bruegel makes the dying priest and his sons into bloated joke figures. It is as if the tragic figure of the priest Laocoön is blown up by Bruegel so that its pathos bursts and fizzles out into ridiculousness.

The tragic as a grimace

The Yawner (Cat. 43) is a curious picture. It is neither dated nor signed and even now has never been unequivocally attributed. It is also a singular work within Bruegel's oeuvre and cannot be assigned to any of the existing work constellations. Only *The Head of an Old Peasant Woman* (p. 398, Cat. 38) offers a comparison – albeit this picture is a fragment. But the unrealistic portrayal of the old woman's facial expression differs fundamentally from that seen in *The Yawner*. The peasant woman reminds us far more of distinctive figure types we know from the graphic works.

The Yawner is usually designated as a character study or the study of a humour or expression, without involving a real interpretation. Stylistically, we can assign it to the period after 1565. An engraved copy by Lucas Vorsterman (1595–1675) tells us that the picture – owned by Rubens in the seventeenth century – was held to be authentic, even though the engraver changed the oval format to a circular one.

The painting is indeed of someone yawning – the pleated nightgown and nightcap lend this reading credence. Bruegel shows the exact moment when the man is overcome by tiredness. His eyelids are screwed up, and his mouth opens quite alarmingly, as happens in the reflex of yawning. We see the man's top incisors and his tongue. The painter has meticulously depicted wrinkles and skin folds forming on the outer edges of the eyes and above the eyebrows. Nonetheless, the facial expression retains a certain ambivalence. Covering the top part of the head, we might interpret the gaping mouth as a cry of pain. So how do we go about understanding the picture? We access its meaning only if we bear in mind the concept of art that the creator of this composition is opposing. With his *Yawner*, Bruegel is making a statement on the theory of art. The key argument here is the mouth, opened as if in a cry, an indispensible motif in a convincing evocation of pain. Pain is an indication of pathos, intended to overwhelm the observer. Accordingly, it is the most important task of history painting, which occupies the highest position in the hierarchy of genres.

In Italian treatises of the time, the portrayal of heroes and extraordinary events, as *istoria*, was defined as the most important task of painting. The pain of the figures is intended to purge the observer's soul through catharsis. Artists like Michelangelo demonstrated their technical mastery with the ability to represent extreme emotions. We only need to glance at a drawing by the Italian artist from the year 1525 with the title *The Damned Soul* (p. 374). It is awe-inspiring and terrible, the mouth opened in a scream, the eyes glaring, the skin around the eyes wrinkled and folded, the veins protruding. Even the damned soul's hair is standing on end. We are meant to have a vicarious experience of the horror that is looming up before the man's eyes and mirrored in his face. It is quite apparent that the artist has expressed the greatest possible terror in this picture. With this showpiece, the virtuoso demonstrates his mastery in overcoming the greatest possible artistic hurdle.

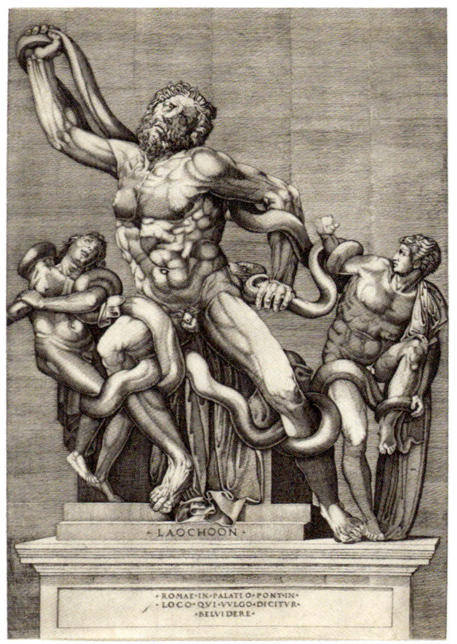

In contrast, Bruegel shows that the detail of a gaping mouth is by no means automatically to be seen as sublime and cathartic. He employs an elevated motif for a humble event and has fun debunking the criterion of purging the observer's soul with the portrayal of terror. His reinterpretation of this artistic practice through the banality of yawning makes the Italian's pathos seem hollow and exposes it to ridicule. For what happens if a facial expression is more ambivalent than it aims to be? And what happens when the terrifying expression does not fit the cause? When the fear of Hell becomes the fear of the dentist? Or when the pain of a foot operation is represented with the same facial expression as the infinite suffering of a martyr? Many genre pictures from Bruegel's time similarly make fun of the criteria set by the Italian theory of art.

And yet the joke is that Bruegel is well able to rival the supposedly serious models in portraying pain. We simply have to change the context and the yawning man would become a damned soul. This involves a dual discovery for the observer. On one hand, it reveals the ambivalence of a facial expression, on the other, the Flemish artist shows he is technically capable of vying with the Italian paragon Michelangelo.

Nicolas Beatrizet after Cornelis Bos, **Laocoön Group**, 1540–1565
Copper engraving, 47.4 x 32.5 cm (18 ⅔ x 12 ¾ in.). New York, The Metropolitan Museum of Art

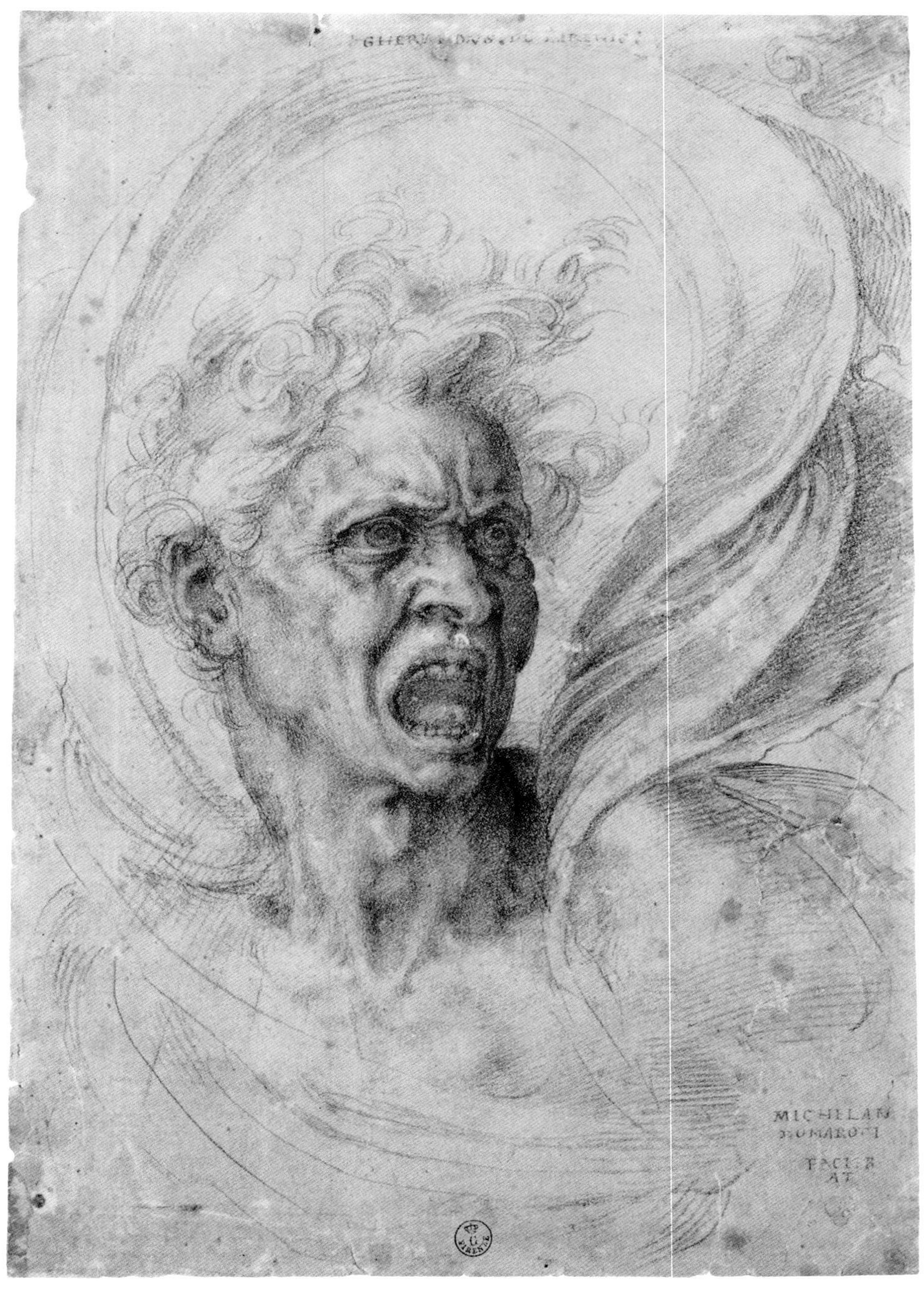

GHERARDVS DE LIBRI
MICHELAN
BONAROTI
FACI B
AT

Downthrow and overthrow

In its power to convey a feeling of dizziness, Bruegel's *The Conversion of St Paul* (pp. 392/393, Cat. 29) of 1567 is an extraordinary picture. We see an army moving upwards from below into a mountain range. It includes infantry and cavalry, almost all accoutred with the weapons and attire of Bruegel's time. He employs a cunning compositional strategy, because when looking at the picture we are forced to make a change of perspective. If we look into the gorge and to the distant coastal landscape, we have to swivel our gaze round to the right in order to be able to continue following the route the soldiers are taking. As so often, Bruegel has marginalised the crucial event. It takes a while until we discern the fallen Paul, the soldier rushing to help him and his horse (p. 378). The army has to pause for a moment; the persons in the foreground at the right turn towards the mishap, and a mounted soldier even points to the figure of Paul on the ground.

The literature has suggested a possible political dimension in the picture – the crossing of the Alps by the Duke of Alba in 1567, who moved his troops across Haute-Savoie, bringing oppression and servitude to the Netherlandish people.[198] The painting is thus associated with the hope that Alba would rethink his strategy – Saul would become Paul, as it were. Other interpretations have generally referred to humanity's fallen state and the need to convert, which Paul experienced in the flesh. At any event, we may also discern an image of hubris here, created by the impression that the soldiers are marching into misfortune, as suggested by the storm brewing in the top right corner (p. 376). Bruegel possibly knew Michelangelo's version of the Fall of Paul, whose concept he contradicts here.

Man seems lost, even ridiculous, in his desire to bring war and destruction. He is in danger of being swallowed up by the mountains. Bruegel has paid most attention in depicting the soldiers' weapons and various uniforms. Slightly left of the vertical axis, we see two marching soldiers, one of whom is bearing on his back a red shield showing a Habsburg eagle (p. 378).

The way out

As yet there has been no satisfactory interpretation of *The Cripples* (*The Beggars*; pp. 400/401, Cat. 36). In format and structure, the painting is comparable to the (pp. 146/147, Cat. 10). It is in fact a self-citation by the artist. In *The Fight between Carnival and Lent* (pp. 76/77, Cat. 4), produced nine years previously, the same scene is already taking place at the side of the Carnival, but without being very noticeable in the teeming melee.

Michelangelo Buonarroti (?), **Ideal Head** *The Damned Soul (Il dannato)*, 1525
Black chalk on grey-toned paper, pen, 29.8 x 20.5 cm (11 ¾ x 8 ⅛ in.)
Florence, Gallerie degli Uffizi, Gabinetto Disegni e Stampe

The Conversion of St Paul (detail), 1567
(see ill. pp. 392/393)

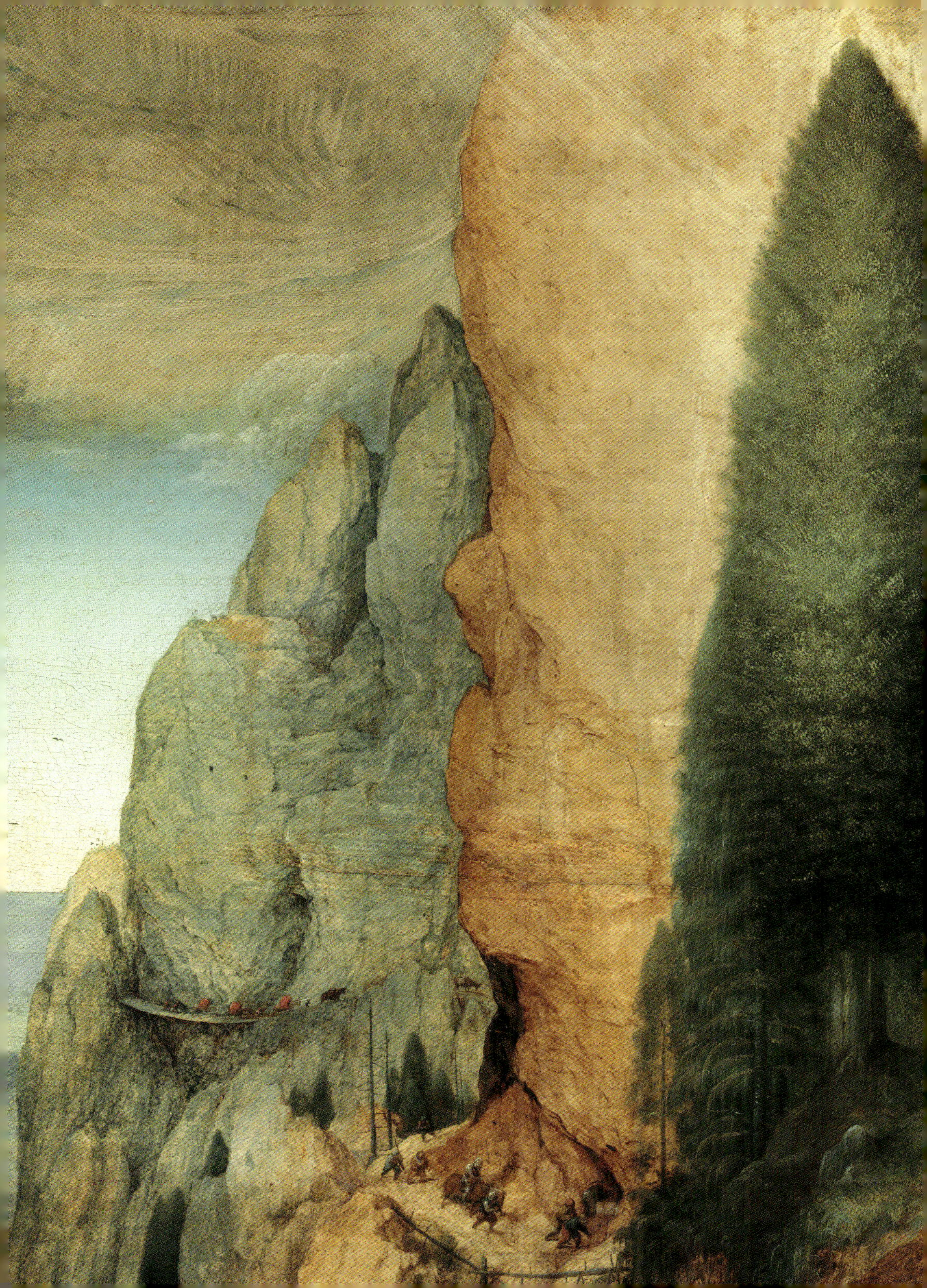

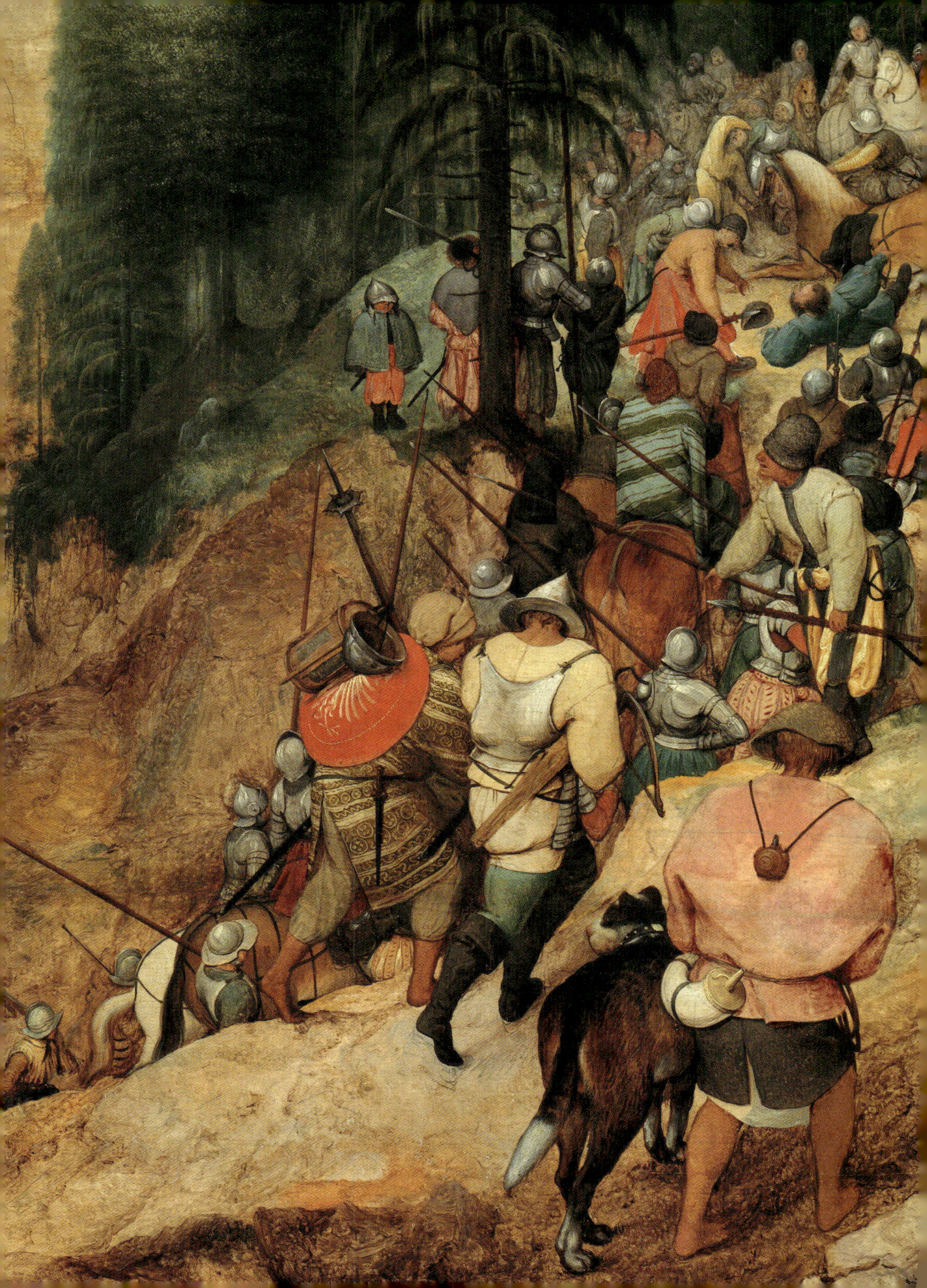

But while there the cripples seem quite agile and are scheming where they could go next, in the small painting they seem apathetic and immobile.

Bruegel does not stress the pitiable state of the figures; he exaggerates their appearance into the truly grotesque. Five maimed men are gathered together in a very confined space, while a poorly dressed woman carrying a plate leaves the scene at the right. The cripples all wear some headgear or other and, with one exception, have foxtails on chest and back. The second from the right seems to have fastened little bells on his calves and appears to be shouting out. It is not clear what's vexing him. The scene is acted out in an interior court-yard surrounded by a brick wall. A path leads to a gate between the two, behind which we discern trees and perhaps a garden. One of cripples, seen from the rear, gazes longingly in this direction. An apt explanation of the different headgear has been made in that they all correspond to the various classes of society.[199] The paper mitre alludes to the clerical estate, the cardboard crown to the nobility, and the helmet to the military, while the hat refers to the burgher and the cap to the peasant classes. Since the foxtail was known as the symbol of the *geuze* (beggars), the nickname of those opposing Habsburg despotism, the five beggars were also understood as symbolising these fighters. Moreover, the fox tail was also seen at the time as a symbol of hypocrisy, so the artist would seem to be rebuffing society as a whole.[200] Finally, Flemish sayings have been quoted that speak of the lie as a cripple.[201]

This is all more or less plausible, but has no relation to the visual structure of the composition, which demands a more precise description in this regard. A starting point is the woman, who in contrast to the cripples is walking away briskly and simultaneously carrying something, while the cripples are forced to use their hands and arms to be able to move at all. Meanwhile it is important to see that Bruegel has placed the viewer in the axis of both the picture and the path, which the perspective has rendered as extremely long, so that the gate seems inaccessibly distant. The picture also suggests that this is the only path open to the cripples.

Another defining factor is the impression of impotence and the fact that the cripples seem unable to communicate with one another; Bruegel has portrayed them as distinctly separate. All look in different directions, not taking any notice of one another. Perhaps we may interpret this as Bruegel's complaint about the lack of unity and the diverging interests of the various social estates, when what mattered was to pull together in the fight for freedom. This idea is supported by the perspective pull towards the gate and the yearning look of one of the maimed beggars. The path, without doubt arduous for the cripples, involves a challenge. It must be followed to attain the direction leading to freedom.

The Conversion of St Paul (detail), 1567
(see ill. pp. 392/393)

The deluding world

The painting the literature has entitled *The Misanthrope* (p. 399, Cat. 34) is signed and dated 1568. It is an exception in many ways, because, along with *The Parable of the Blind* from the same year, it is one of the works that Bruegel painted on canvas and not on wood.[202] Furthermore, it is the only painting that has an explanatory caption. Written in Gothic letters are the words: "Om dat de werelt is soe ongetru, Daer om gha ic in den ru" (Because the world is so false, I wear mourning). Also the square format surrounding a tondo occurs only one single time in Bruegel and relates to panels by Hieronymus Bosch. Whether this inscription was added by Bruegel himself has been doubted, because the script type cannot be documented prior to 1680. An engraved copy of the painting by Jan Wierix supplies no further information to help interpret the picture but does contain the same Flemish text (Müller/Schauerte 2018, Cat. G45). So it is suspected that the picture's inscription was added later and the template for the engraving followed. However, it is improbable that the Italian owner after 1680 had a Flemish inscription added, and since panels by Hieronymus Bosch contain comparable inscriptions, this solution seems highly questionable.

The picture's content is quickly described. A man blanketed in a black cowl is portrayed slightly to the left of centre; he resembles a monk. Only his nose, mouth, beard and folded hands are seen emerging from his cloak. We might identify him as an itinerant preacher. Karl Tolnai has admiringly spoken of the figure possessing "Giottoesque monumentality".[203] With his narrow, clenched and pulled-down lips, the wanderer seems grave, indeed morose. Furthermore, his white beard signals his advanced age and accentuates the venerable aura emanating from his figure. But his eyes remain hidden, and the body's contours are difficult to determine under the cloak.

While the man strides on, a little man – a male personification of the world (Mundus) is stealing his red, heart-shaped money pouch. The little man is stuck in a glass sphere, a conventional symbol that occurs frequently, including in *Netherlandish Proverbs* (Cat. 3). Gnome-like, hunched inside the spherical shape, Mundus has crept up on the man. Even though the latter is striding on, he cannot evade the theft – Mundus is about to grab the purse and cut it off. For a moment, the man's cloak has been lifted by the band fastened there, and we discern that one leg is shorter than the other: this monk limps.

The literature has produced several interpretations of the picture. One of them is the literary figure of the misanthrope, a character from classical antiquity widely known since the Renaissance was widespread.[204] Lucian's satire *Timon the Misanthrope* is a key reference. This "hater of mankind" is a tragic figure. He withdraws from the world – his supposed friends have only exploited him. This identification is questionable, however, since the title *Misanthrope* first appeared in an eighteenth-century inventory. Another inventory of the museum designates the picture as a depiction of heresy.

We shall therefore attempt to decipher the picture. Bruegel employs a clever narrative ruse to characterise the central figure. For, lying on the path just in front of the man, we see star spikes which he evidently has not seen. The next step will make him tread on one. The man fleeing the world cannot escape this world, which has set traps for him ahead and behind. A more relevant comparison than the ancient satire is that of a drawing by Urs Graf the Elder (*c.* 1485–1528) of 1512 (p. 381).[205] Graf shows an itinerant preacher who is holding a cross in one hand and a Rosary in the other, thus signs of faith and veneration. However, behind him is a devil with a wooden leg about to whisper evil things into the ears of the brave champion of God. Graf has conceived an image of hypocrisy. The monk intends evil.

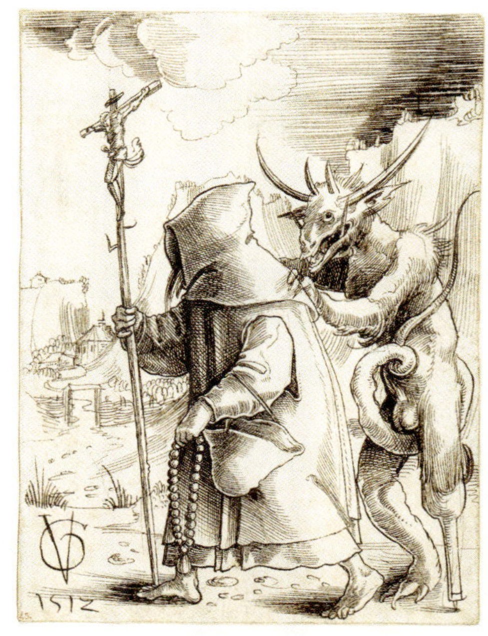

Furthermore, an engraving by Hans Sebald Beham (1500–1550) shows an allegory of Mishap or Adversity (p. 383). The position of the little devil hanging on the woman's skirt recalls the constellation of monk and Mundus in the Bruegel, especially in composition. However, Beham's engraving also needs interpreting, because at first it is not clear how Adversity *(Infortunium)* is involved with the female figure. She is forced by the little demon – who is pulling with the utmost strenuousness on her robe – to progress sideways, crab-fashion, indicated by a conspicuous crab at her feet. At her next step the woman will tread on sharp stones, like our monk on the mantraps. Nor can she protect herself against the hail suddenly falling down on her, since she cannot see it. Bruegel has adopted Beham's engraving not only as inspiration for the structural composition of the central figural group, but also for the dramatic scenario. Both pictures are so arranged that the main figure faces unavoidable misfortune and a baleful prospect, which is visible only to the observer.

Urs Graf the Elder, **Mendicant Monk Guided by the Devil**, 1512
Pen and dark-brown ink, 21.2 x 15.6 cm (8⅓ x 6⅛ in.)
Kunstmuseum Basel, Kupferstichkabinett, Amerbach-Kabinett

If we see Bruegel's monk as a venerable and pious man, this piety is evidently being contradicted by the cutpurse Mundus. The red purse is in striking contrast to the dark robe, a seeming comment on the man's avarice concealed behind outer modesty. Bruegel, too, is thus setting up an allegory of hypocrisy.[206] The monk has no idea that he is being soundly outwitted by the world that he so despises. This is an ingenious ploy on Bruegel's part. The more pious the monk wishes to appear, the more hypocritical he is shown to be.

This contradictory message is expressed through an interplay of word and image. At first, the monk's statement about the false world seems to be commenting on the cutpurse Mundus. Initially, the content of the text seems to be taking shape. The monk's supposed mourning appears justified. But exactly the opposite is the case, since it is being transferred onto an image of avarice and hypocrisy. Even more: by robbing the monk, Mundus is revealing the truth by unmasking the former. The picture's statement – as so often with Bruegel – is formulated as a paradox. The liar brings the truth to light. And may we not apply this to the painting per se? We note that the Mundus motif corresponds to its spherical shape. The spherical world is rendered in the shape of a tondo. This parallel approach to inner and outer form plays on the relation of lying and visual deception that is perforce practised in every illusionistic painting in order to bring truth to light, or to unmask evil.

The painting contains many enigmatic details that can relate as a commentary to the scene in the foreground. The windmill in the background might allude to the hustle and bustle of the world, yet a world in which fortune reigns. Seen pessimistically, this would express the idea that the course of the world will not change. The world is ruled by fraud and deception. The scene with shepherd and sheep alludes to the Bible, which refers to white and black sheep (1 Moses 30: 32). This poses the question of who is culpable, and also whether the monk before us really has anything in common with a good shepherd.

As so often, Bruegel had concealed a motif as a miniature in the background. The middle ground of the painting moves seamlessly into the horizon, where a windmill is set off prominently against the sky. This also accentuates the shepherd's head, which protrudes slightly above the horizon, and attracts our eye to what is happening on the horizon. We can discern a burning house on the right, which incidentally can also be found in the engraving by Wierix. Why has Bruegel miniaturised this dramatic detail? The red of the purse corresponds in colour to that of the fire, reducing the available options for perceiving a connection. Conceivably, we are meant to see an evil-doer in the monk, who is fleeing from the scene of the crime. In this case, the purse is his reward, its blood-red colour becoming increasingly charged with the extra connotation of treachery and the reward given to Judas. But who or what was betrayed here? At any rate, the monk in this context would not merely be on his way somewhere, he would be in flight.

Fauna and flora also seem to comment on this situation. Besides a hollow tree trunk, we see numerous mushrooms, and a heron – according to Pliny's *Natural History*, and the emblematic lore of Bruegel's time, it is a creature as pious as it is silent. The question now arises as to how we can combine all these elements. Apart from all the moral and art-theoretical meanings about the fraudulence of the world and of painting – does the picture also suggest a quite practical level that tells of denunciation and persecution? In this case, the monk's habit would signify that the hypocritical monk has betrayed reformed Christians to the Inquisition. As a seeming "good shepherd", he has investigated the beliefs of these Christians and denounced them. Bruegel's painting is an allegory of deception, but in a concrete historical context.

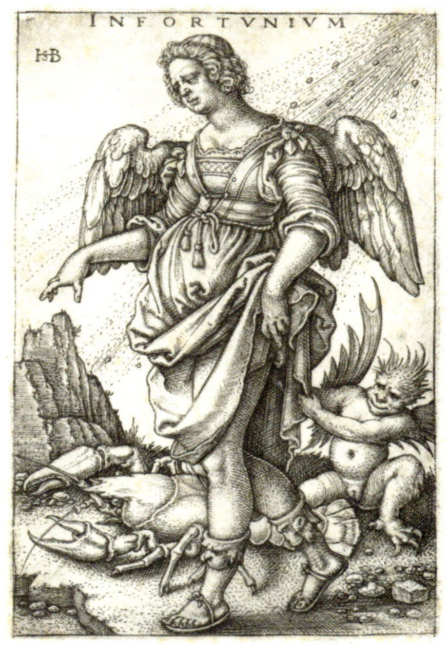

The pious monk reveals himself to be a traitor and beadle of the Catholic Inquisition.

As so often with Bruegel, his picture aims at the reversal of what is happening. If at first we think the man in a dark cowl is an honourable person because of his advanced age and his folded hands, we must in the end recognise him as a brutal villain and deceived deceiver.

The Church leading the blind

Bruegel was more productive than ever in his last years. Between 1565 and 1568 he produced twenty-three paintings, more than half of his total output. There is no doubt that *The Parable of the Blind*, also known as *The Blind Leading the Blind* (pp. 402/403, Cat. 35), of 1568 is one of the summits of his achievement. Six blind men have joined together. Some of them want to make music, while others are going to beg. They are moving in a line one behind the other, each man touching the one ahead with a hand or a stick. While the last man strides on confidently, the first man has already stumbled and fallen into the ditch. The easily visible hurdy-gurdy player is about to plunge into the

Hans Sebald Beham, **Infortunium (Misfortune)**, 1510–1550
Copper engraving, 7.8 x 5.1 cm (3 ⅛ x 2 ⅛ in.). Amsterdam, Rijksmuseum, Rijksprentenkabinet

water with the leader. The blind man at the end of the row also seems to be carrying an instrument under his wide cloak, while the third has a plate fastened to his belt, which might be for collecting alms. The men were probably on the way to the church to perform for the faithful coming out.

The mishap of the blind men's fall takes place in the flat Brabantian countryside. Only gradually do we become aware of the event's location – we are so spellbound by the men's unavoidable fall. Our eye is particularly struck by the late-medieval church building on the right; it was has been identified as the Church of Sint-Anna-Pede near Brussels (p. 405). The steeple reaches to the top of the picture. The late-medieval building forms the centre of the township, its houses, gables and roofs discernable on the left behind the blind men.

While most of the objects in the background overlap, the church can be clearly seen. Moreover, it is accentuated by the picture's construction. Thus we may ask whether the third blind man from the right will be able to pull himself free or land in the water with the stumbling man and the one who is already down. An ingenious perspective intensifies the staging of this dramatic moment, for it takes place at the level of the church. It is the focal point of our perception.

But where do we find ourselves as observers? Are we standing outside or under the group of blind men? There is no clear answer to this question. If we look at the two stumbling men at the right, we are looking downwards; if we look at the rest of the group, we have the impression we are looking upwards. This is a clever ploy by Bruegel, aiming to unsettle the viewer. Without a fixed vantage point, we, too, start to totter with the blind men in the picture. Moreover, it seems that the stumbling blind man with the white cap is looking at us. Bruegel alarmingly questions our habitual idea of seeing and discernment, when we think empty eye sockets are staring at us in recognition.

The Blind Leading the Blind is a masterpiece in representing emotion. If we view the men from left to right, we note they express different psychological stages the sequence of events. Step by step, their insecurity intensifies to sheer horror. The painter employs every means – starting with the large picture format – to treat the genre picture as an *istoria*. This aesthetic ennoblement is contradicted by the picture's humble content. Nor does it seem quite fitting that maimed people are being portrayed, whose disabilities are being paraded, so to speak, front of stage. Bruegel has satisfied all the criteria of the history picture, yet without creating one.

In Bruegel's painting we recognise his endeavour to describe an event as it proceeds. Here we must be aware of Bruegel's aspiration – an immense achievement in terms of technique – to conjure up an impression of acceleration in the picture. Starting with the blind man standing on the balls of his feet and being pulled forward abruptly by the man ahead, he accentuates the instant that suddenly marks an intensification for the stumbling men. The picture represents and enacts not only a brief but also a dramatic moment short-circuited through acceleration.

The theme of the blind leading the blind is mentioned three times in the New Testament. In the Gospel of St Matthew, Jesus calls the Pharisees "the blind leading the blind", leading the people astray so that they fall into the pit. In Luke, the rhetorical question is posed as to whether a blind man can lead another blind man without both falling into the pit. And the Apostle Paul cites the parable in his Letter to the Romans, to emphasise that simply knowing God's commandments is not sufficient for salvation. Since the Renaissance, the parable of the blind leading the blind had circulated widely.

Numerous works can be quoted as sources for Bruegel's version, which is now in Naples. An initial link for the visual arts can be found in Sebastian Brant's *Ship of Fools*. The first verses of the 40th chapter evoke the theme of the blind leading the blind; there is a reference to the daily witnessed fall of fools who are nevertheless not aware it is their own fault. A woodcut after Hans Holbein the Younger (pp. 388/389) can be cited in comparison, which underlines the Basel artist's reformatory intention.[207] On the left, humble Protestant Christians have gathered, following Christ as the "true Light", who points towards the burning candle. Whereas on the right false Catholic dignitaries have assembled, who, despite all authority and ancient erudition, are falling into the pit. This reference to Holbein is important because he addresses the denominational content that was associated during the Reformation with the iconography of the blind leading the blind. Even before Bruegel, the biblical parable was used to denounce the respective other denomination in text and image. Time and again, Luther names the pope as leading the blind. Erasmus and Calvin also use the metaphor of the blind leading the blind as utterly self-evident.

However, before we look for other sources and their meaning for Bruegel, we must refer to copies of the picture, without which we cannot understand it sufficiently. Whoever examines the picture in Naples closely will discover that the upper body of a man is hinted at in front of the church. Inappropriate cleaning caused the top paint layers of the canvas to be strongly abraded, so that several motifs can now be only be guessed at. Not until we compare it with copies of *The Blind Leading the Blind* kept in Paris, Parma and Vaduz can we reconstruct the original stock of motifs. We then note that on the meadow between the church and the blind there is a farmhand with geese and cows; he is resting on his crook and looking towards the blind men. He doesn't notice that one of his cows has wandered off and is about to fall into the ditch. It is leaning over to drink, but too far, and will at any moment stumble in head over heels (p. 406). The fall of the blind men implies a conceptual correspondence to the animal's fall, and moreover offers an analogy to the viewer identifying the faithless shepherd with the stone church. In addition, we notice that all copyists have added features to

The Conversion of St Paul (detail), 1567
(see ill. pp. 392/393)

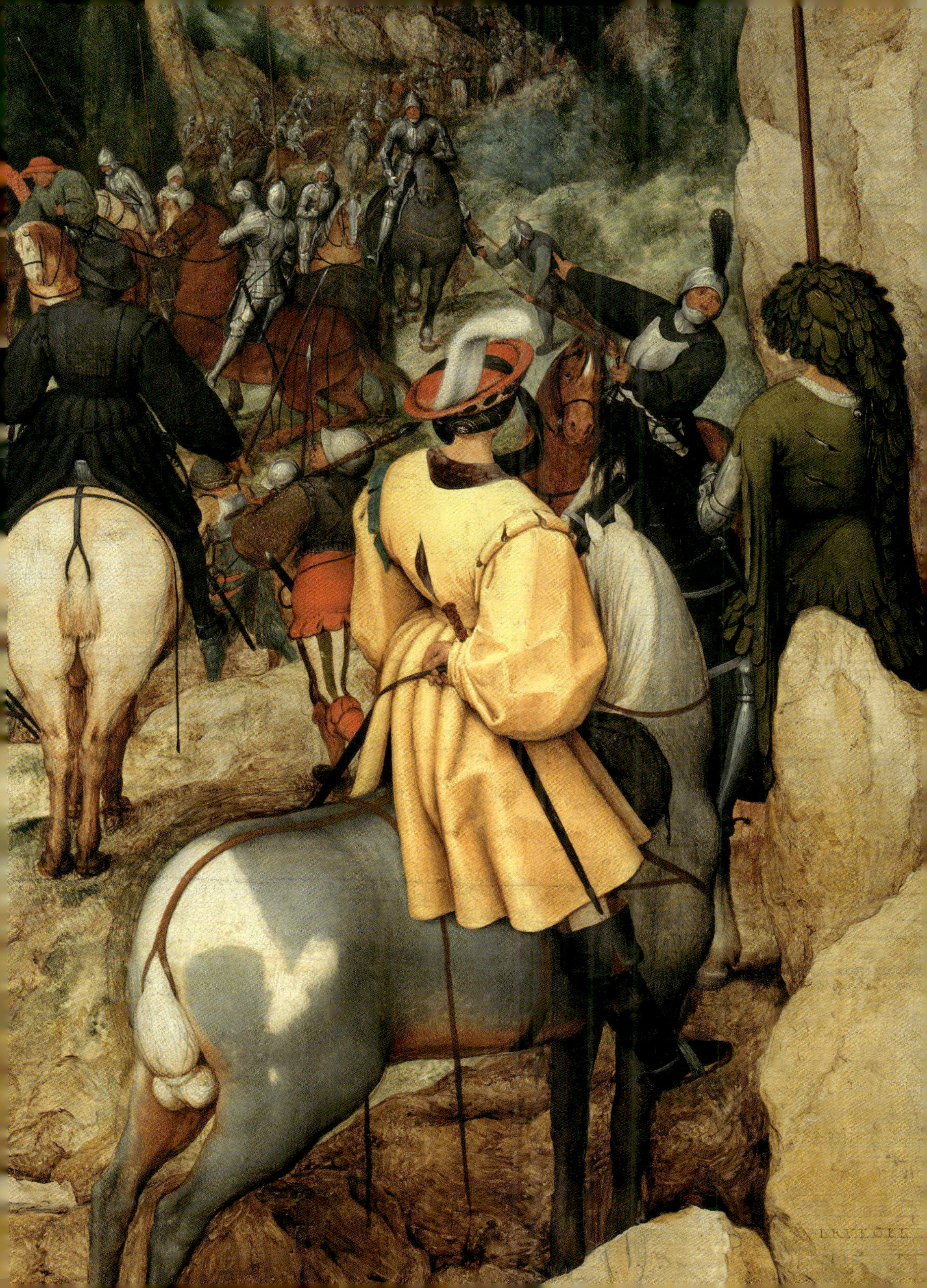

BRVEGEL

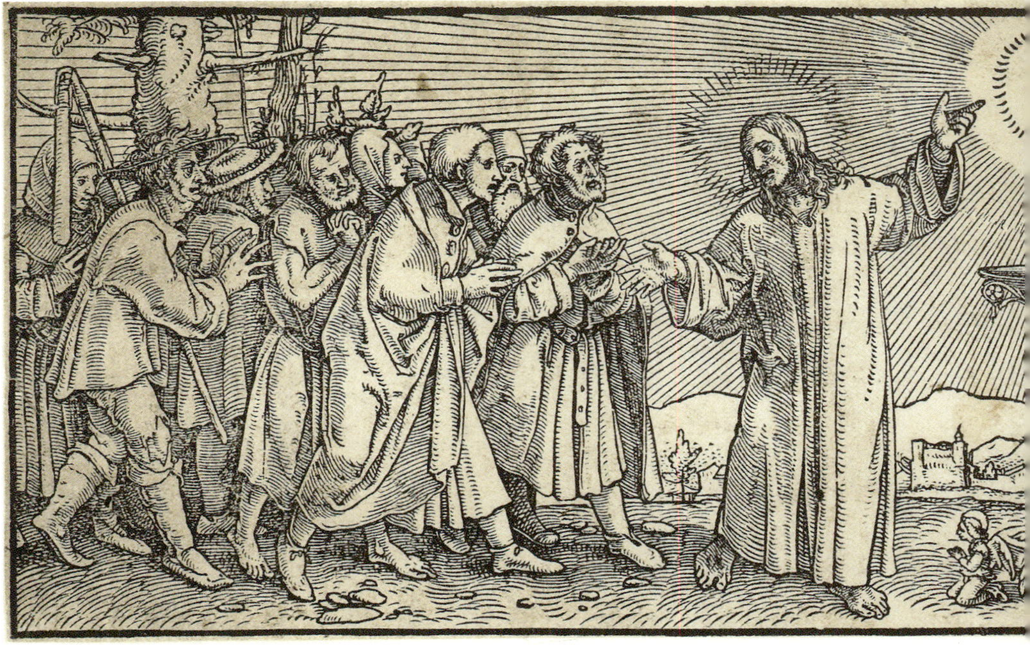

Hans Holbein the Younger, **Christ as the True Light**, 1520–1525
Woodcut, 8.4 x 27.5 cm (3 ¼ x 10 ⅞ in.). London, The British Museum

the picture at the top and the right. The artist provides a hint for the observer by imparting consequential significance to the picture section he has chosen, at least in his depiction of the church. We see the church steeple is cut off at the top – the cross is missing. This is doubtlessly very odd, which is why several interpreters thought the picture might be cut off at the top.

This hypothesis can be rebutted by pointing out that the painting has a black border, usual in a "Tüchlein" picture (cloth).[208] Based on this empirical diagnosis, there can be no question of a later alteration to the picture. And the question is all the more insistent as to why Bruegel opted for this odd gap in the picture, in which the cross is missing from the top of the spire.

A possible explanation can be found in an engraving after Hans Bol of 1561, which was already mentioned in the secondary literature, but did not play any further role in the discussion. It portrays two pilgrims to St James of Compostela, joined by two others – a man carrying a child on his back. In contrast to Holbein, positive and negative examples are juxtaposed in the engraving. In the background we see two men who

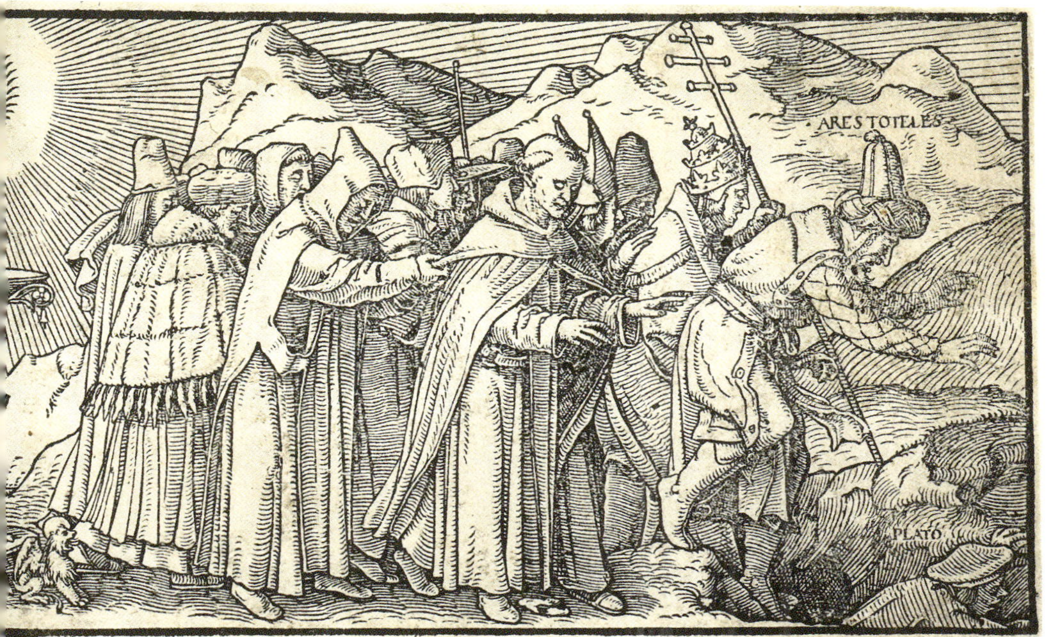

have stopped before a crossroads, point to it, and pray. The dark stone cross is pre-eminent, for it is located on a vertical axis with the church behind it. Moreover, there is a small wayside shrine front left, bearing a cross. Bol makes it clear to the observer that the blind have gone astray and fallen short of the Christian message, while the pious people praying in the background are on the right path to God. The ship also demonstrates that they have found salvation. The church and its symbol of the cross expressly confront the blind. In Bol's iconographic concept, the cross does indeed have the function of manifesting the true faith; its absence signifies error and a straying from the right path.

This very function of the cross as manifesting the true faith cannot be found in the Bruegel. The peculiar picture section forces him to leave out the cross. Far more, he makes the observer seek it. It does not occur as a sign of secure salvation. In Bruegel it is not the sign of orthodoxy with a monopoly of the truth. On the contrary, the cross is merely an item worn by the blind men. The second blind man from the left wears it around his neck. It prevents him neither from going astray nor stumbling.

If the previous insights are correct, must not Bruegel's *The Blind Leading the Blind* be seen as symbolic of the difficulty of seeking God? In his picture it is evidently not sufficient to wear a cross around one's neck. Hans Sedlmayr has with some reason pointed out the opposition of Ecclesia and Synagogue in the context of his interpretation of *The Blind Leading the Blind*.[209] The stone church confronts the errors of the heretics, represented by the blind. In medieval church sculpture, the triumphal cross of the Church is traditionally placed opposite the broken emblem of the Synagogue, whose blindfold, furthermore, symbolised blindness. But Bruegel challenges what appears so compelling and illuminating in the context of this opposition.

Against the background of the blind Synagogue and the idea of erroneous heretical doctrine, it is imperative to refer to Sebastian Franck's chronicle of heresy of 1531, which, translated into Dutch, was included as early as 1558 in the *Chronica, Zeytbuch und geschychtbibel*. In his foreword, the German theologian starts off by saying that the reader must not believe he would really label all those as heretics whom he is about to list in the subsequent text. On the contrary, such a judgement would not reflect that of the author, but that of the pope. One can scarcely formulate more radically than Franck the description of heretics as the true Christians, who are aligned to the tradition that Christ was the first heretic. Simply put, Bruegel's *The Blind Leading the Blind* illustrates this world view. For we do not see an excluding contradiction between Ecclesia and Synagogue rendered in the picture, but a seamless transition. The blind man at the far left still represents a seeker after God in a positive way, while two of the men after him carry rosaries, pointing to the rites of the ministerial Church; their fall is apparently programmed. The Church itself is unmasked as leading the blind.

Against the background of Franck's positive evaluation of heresy, the picture of the blind men appears in a new light. For in the attempt to know God, all men are blind. Seen this way, the blind man's stick is an ambivalent symbol. As long as it acts as a metaphor for knowledge and reflects the latter's main characteristic – its fragmentary nature – it can be judged positively and seen as a radical image of the principle of the ineffability of God. But if people believe it can guarantee the right way and misunderstand it as a reliable pointer in the right direction – as if they can feel their way to God with it – they must fail, as we can easily see.

In terms of the theology of spirit, Bruegel's *The Blind Leading the Blind* deals less with personal error than far more with the demise of the Christian religion through conflicting denominations. It leads the blind astray if it misunderstands itself as an institution endeavouring to establish orthodoxy. The quest for God thus ends up as an externalisation of faith. Bruegel would not be Bruegel if he did not both communicate a message to us, and challenge us to self-discernment. We might have complacently adapted ourselves in a world full of religious errors, believing that this situation will never happen to us. But the picture contains an insight that targets us as observers and discreetly warns us. As described, the top of the church steeple is cut off by the edge of the picture. Yet the very part of the steeple that is missing is visible left of centre on the other side of the hill. We can discern the top point of another church. The painter has thus allowed the missing part of the church steeple to crop up at another spot. The steeple top behind the hill can be seen as the axis of the event in the foreground. It divides up the group of men into those who have already fallen and those who are about to fall. Are we going too far if we wish to see this as a warning to us? We are in the same position as the third blind man: we cannot be sure whether he will fall or not. It would be wrong if we feel superior to the distressed and blinded men in the foreground, when we are also in danger, unawares, of following a leader who is blind.

As we have seen, blindness and the falling of the blind have always been a metaphor in Christianity for the defining the exclusiveness of orthodoxy. In contrast to all other interpretations, my view of *The Blind Leading the Blind* addressed Bruegel's questioning of the excluding opposition of the true Church and heresy. His picture criticises the principle of denunciation and exclusion. Whenever I have thought about orthodoxy and heresy, I have assumed that religious deviance in the time before the Council of Trent (1545–1563) occurred more frequently than the historiography of art has long tried to make us believe, oriented as it has always been on the strict opposition of the denominations.

In conclusion, we might recall the admirable formulation by the Swiss cultural historian Jacob Burckhardt (1818–1897), who once wrote that a successful work of art is like an arrow that shoots through the centuries. Following the historian, it is the privilege of Bruegel's *The Blind Leading the Blind* to give us an idea of what enormous errors accompany history. Anyone looking into the empty eyes of the stumbling blind men will not forget this so easily. For these lifeless eyes show us not only the terror before the fall, but also a shock realisation of one's own culpability.

Pages 392/393
The Conversion of St Paul, 1567
Oil on oak, 108 x 156 cm (42 ½ x 61 ⅜ in.)
Vienna, Kunsthistorisches Museum, Gemäldegalerie

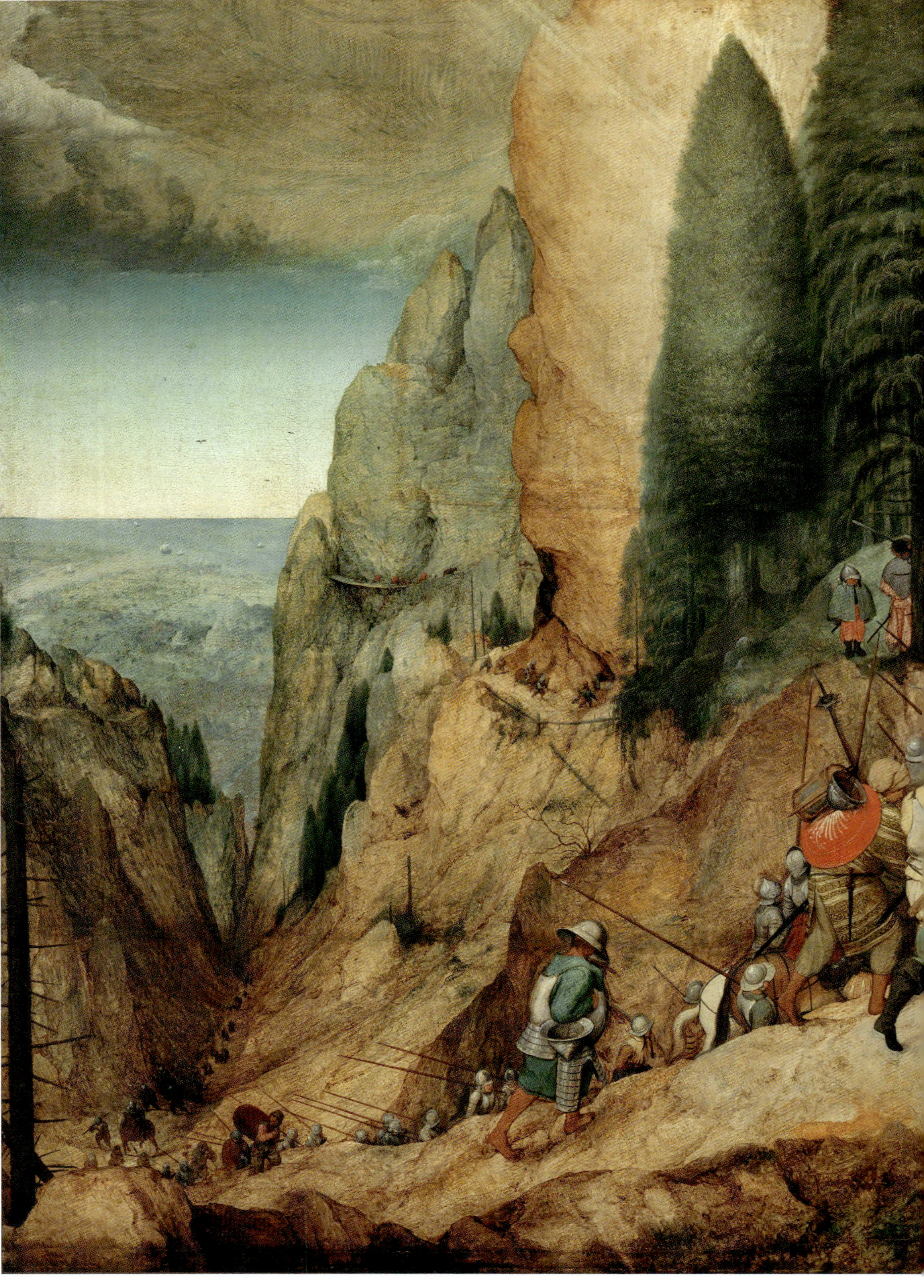

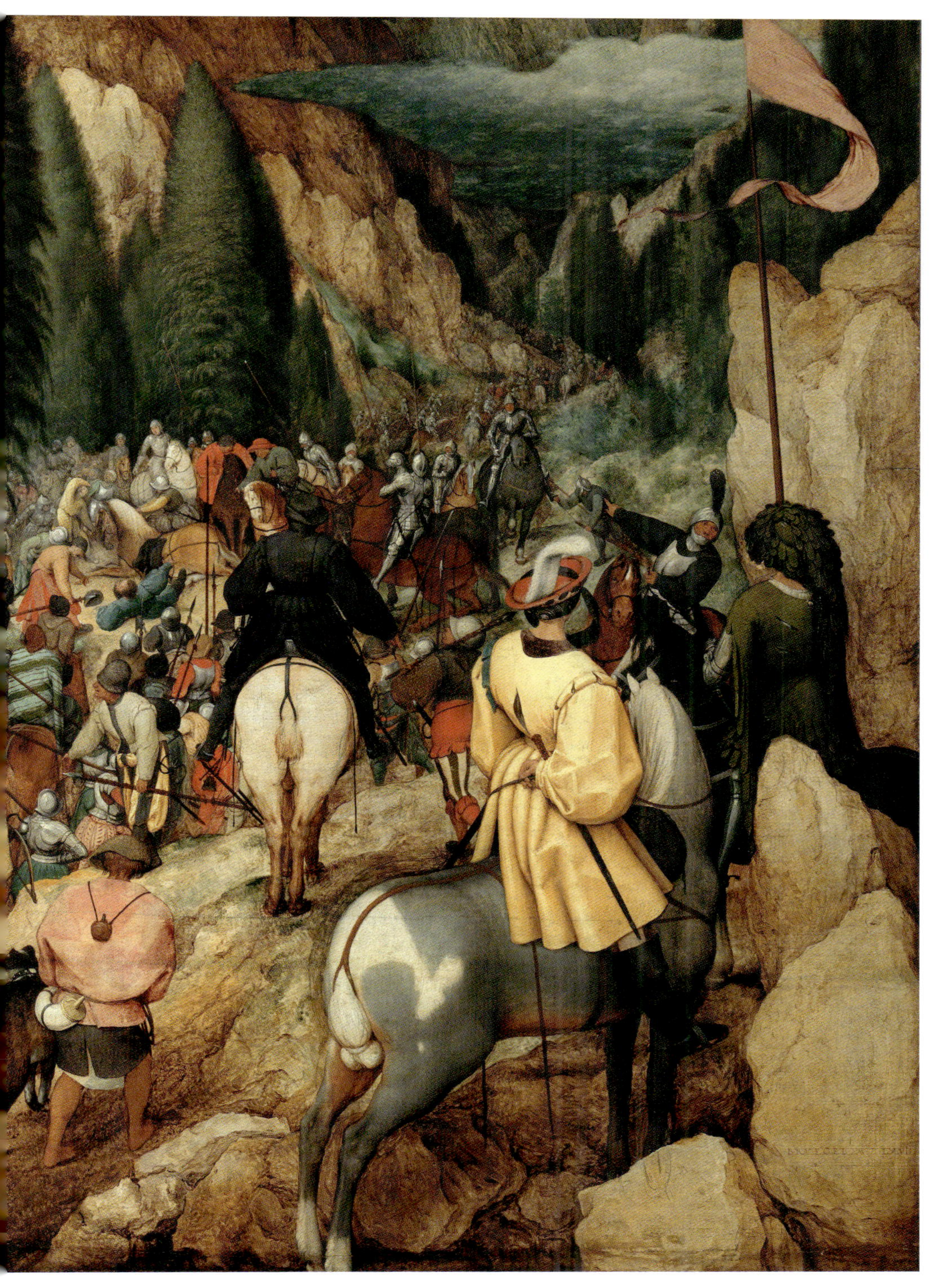

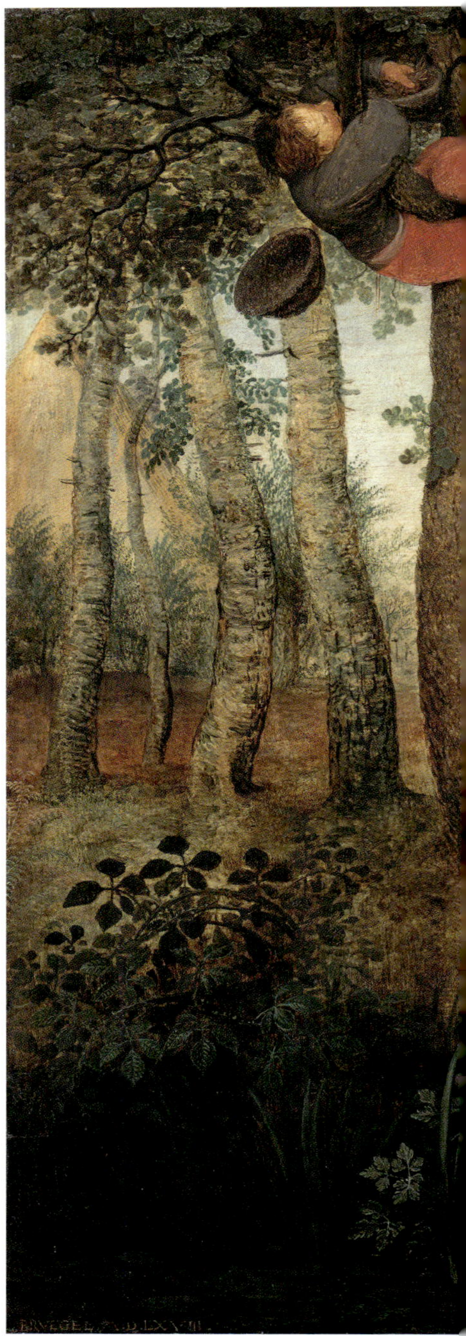

The Nest Thief, 1568
Oil on oak, 59.3 x 68.3 cm (23⅓ x 26⅞ in.)
Vienna, Kunsthistorisches Museum, Gemäldegalerie

Pages 396/397
The Land of Cockaigne, 1567
Oil on oak, 51.5 x 78.3 cm (20¼ x 30⅞ in.)
Munich, Bayerische Staatsgemäldesammlungen,
Alte Pinakothek

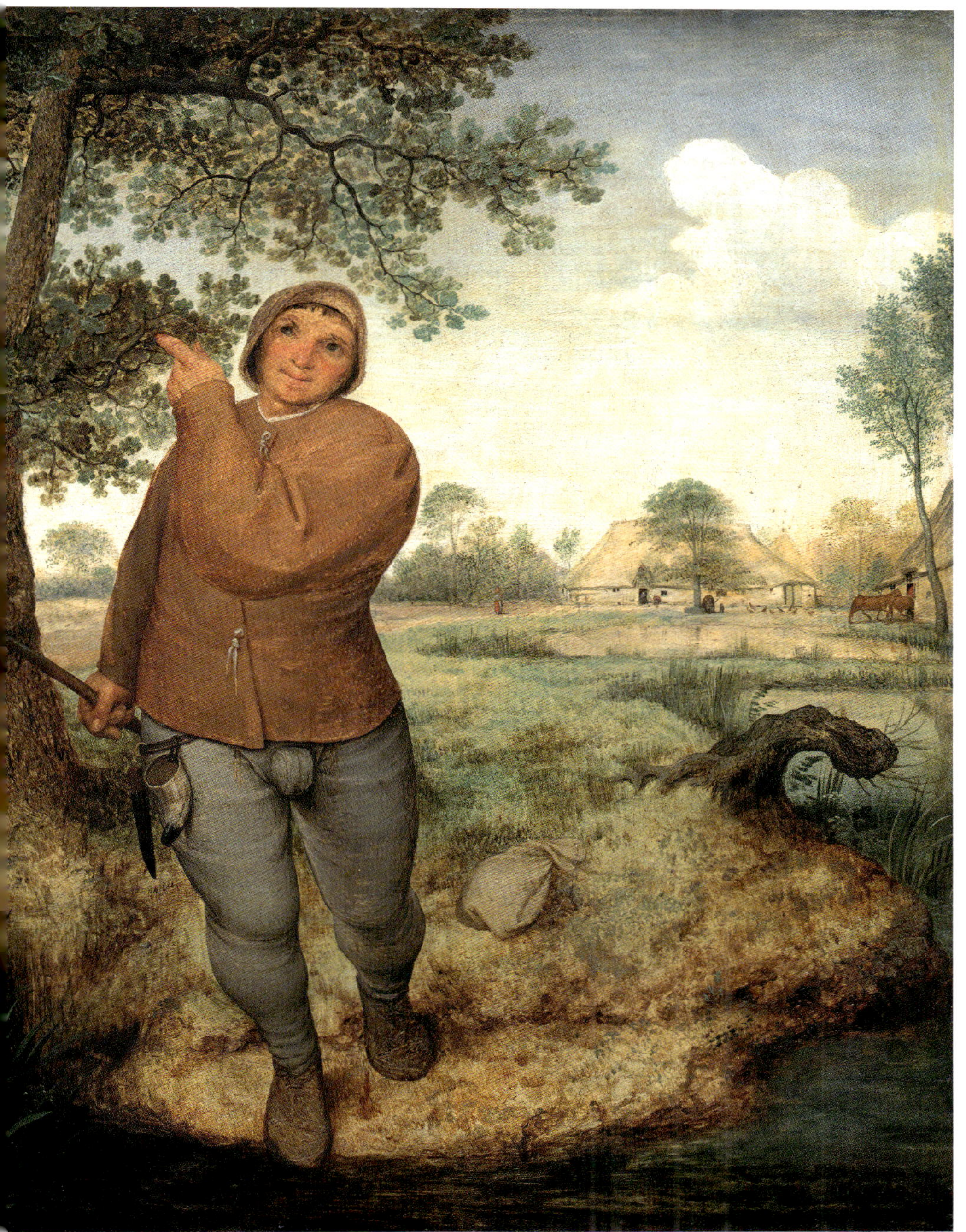

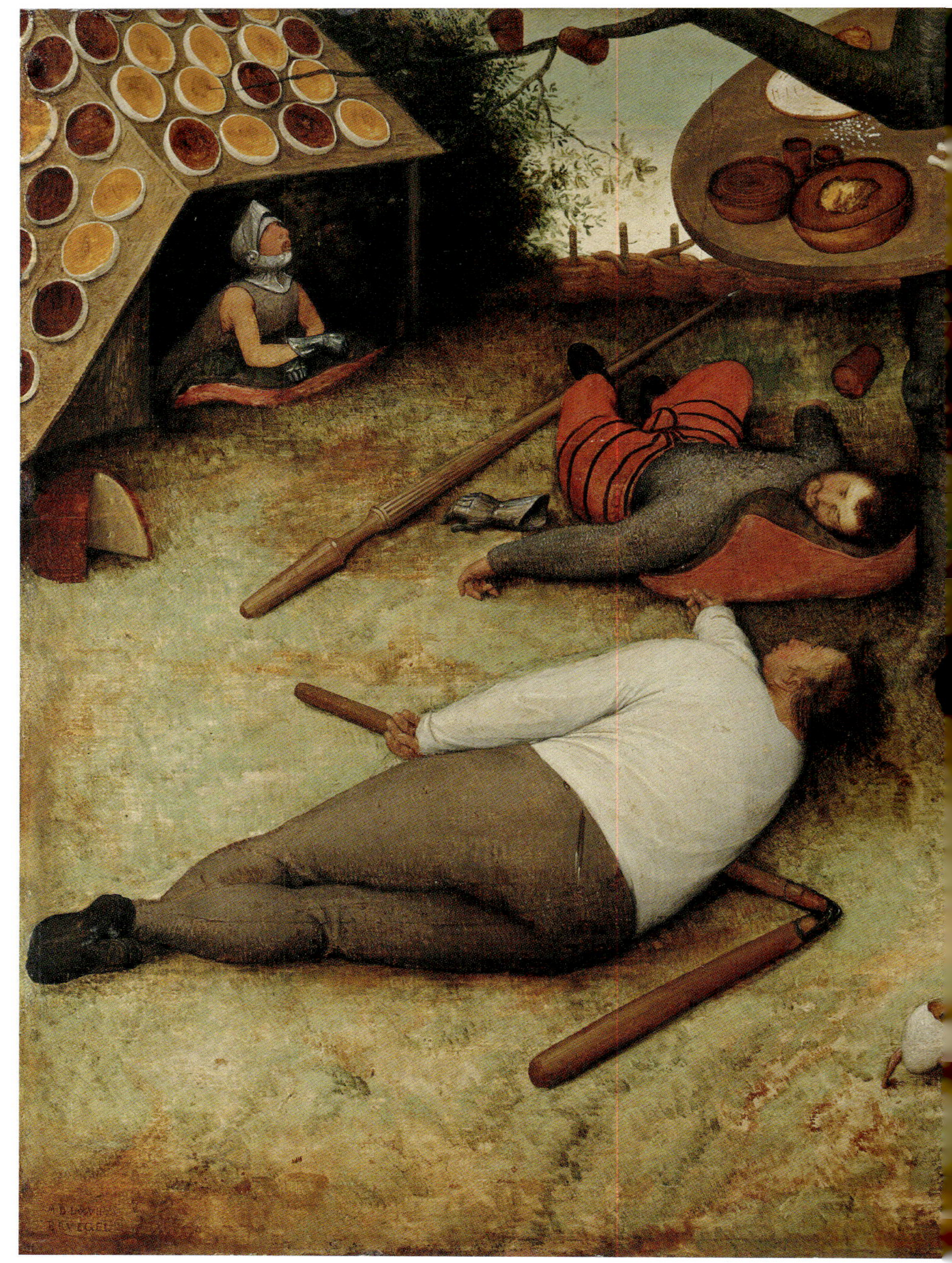

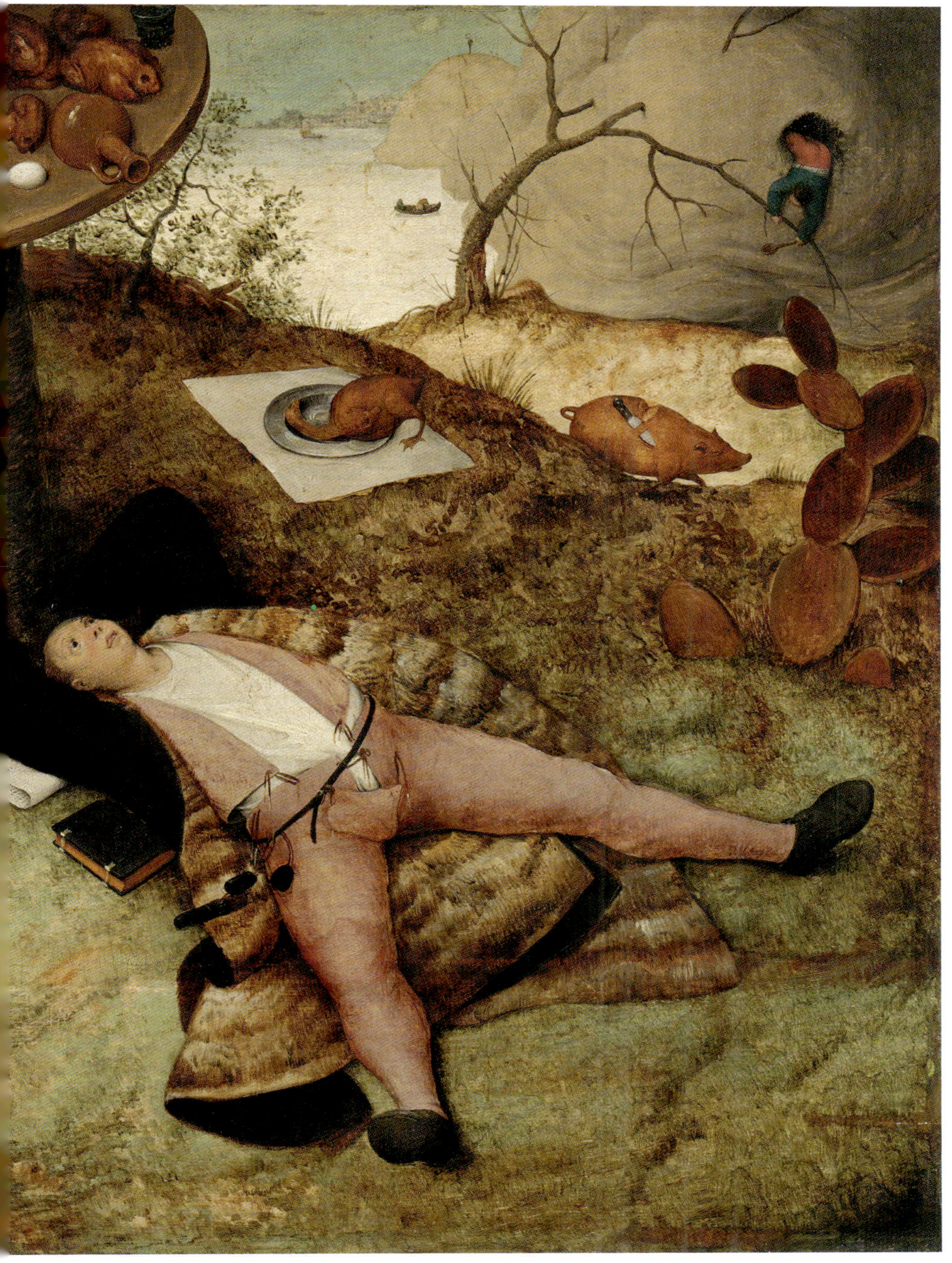

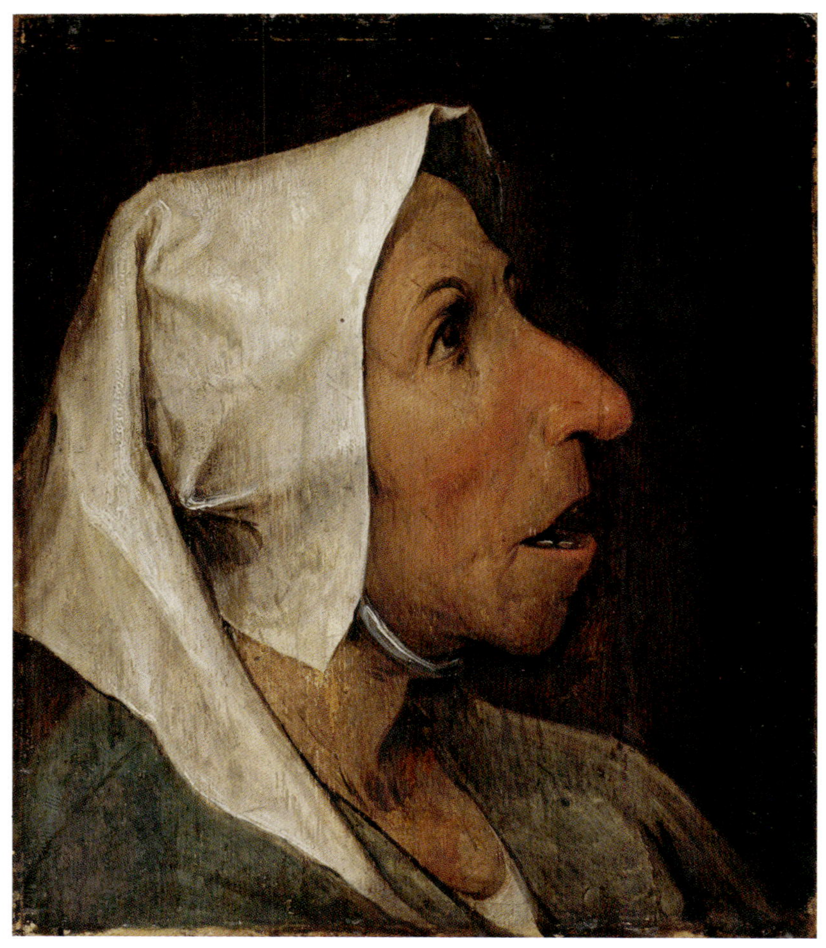

The Head of an Old Peasant Woman, *c.* 1568
Oil on wood, 22 x 18 cm (8⅔ x 7⅛ in.)
Munich, Bayerische Staatsgemäldesammlungen, Alte Pinakothek

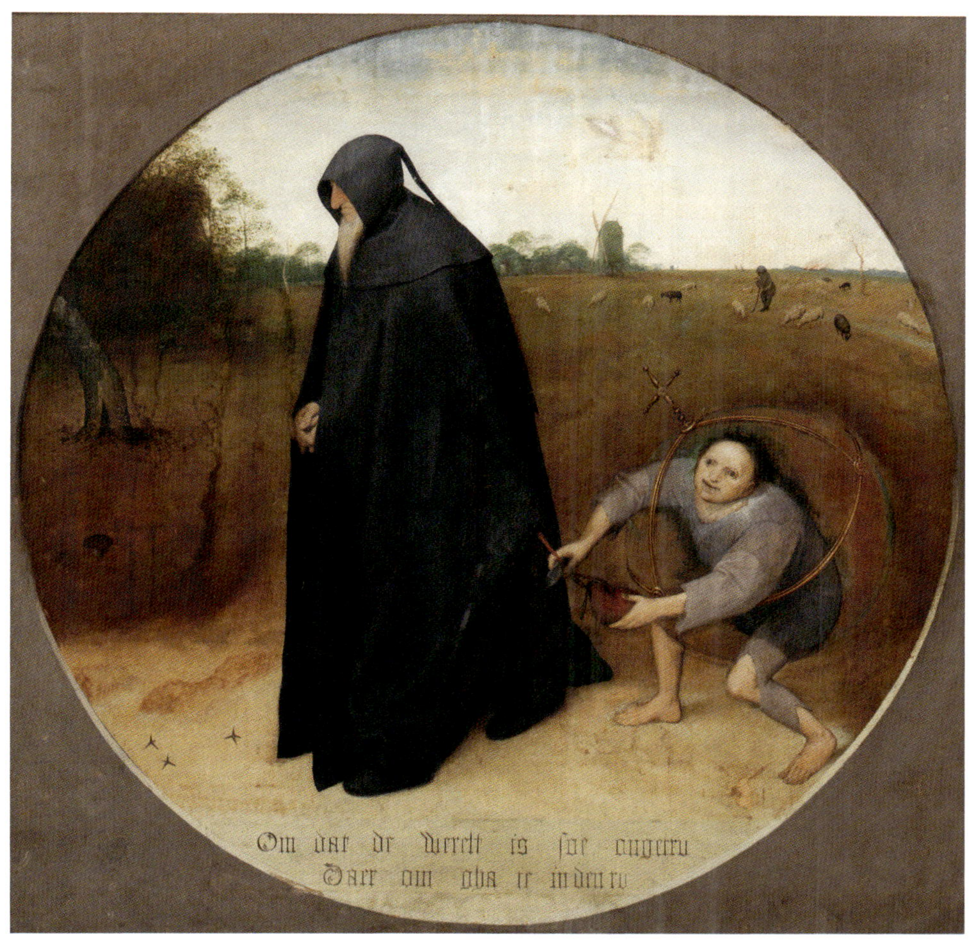

The Misanthrope, 1568
Tempera on canvas, 86 x 85 cm (33 ⅞ x 33 ½ in.)
Naples, Museo di Capodimonte

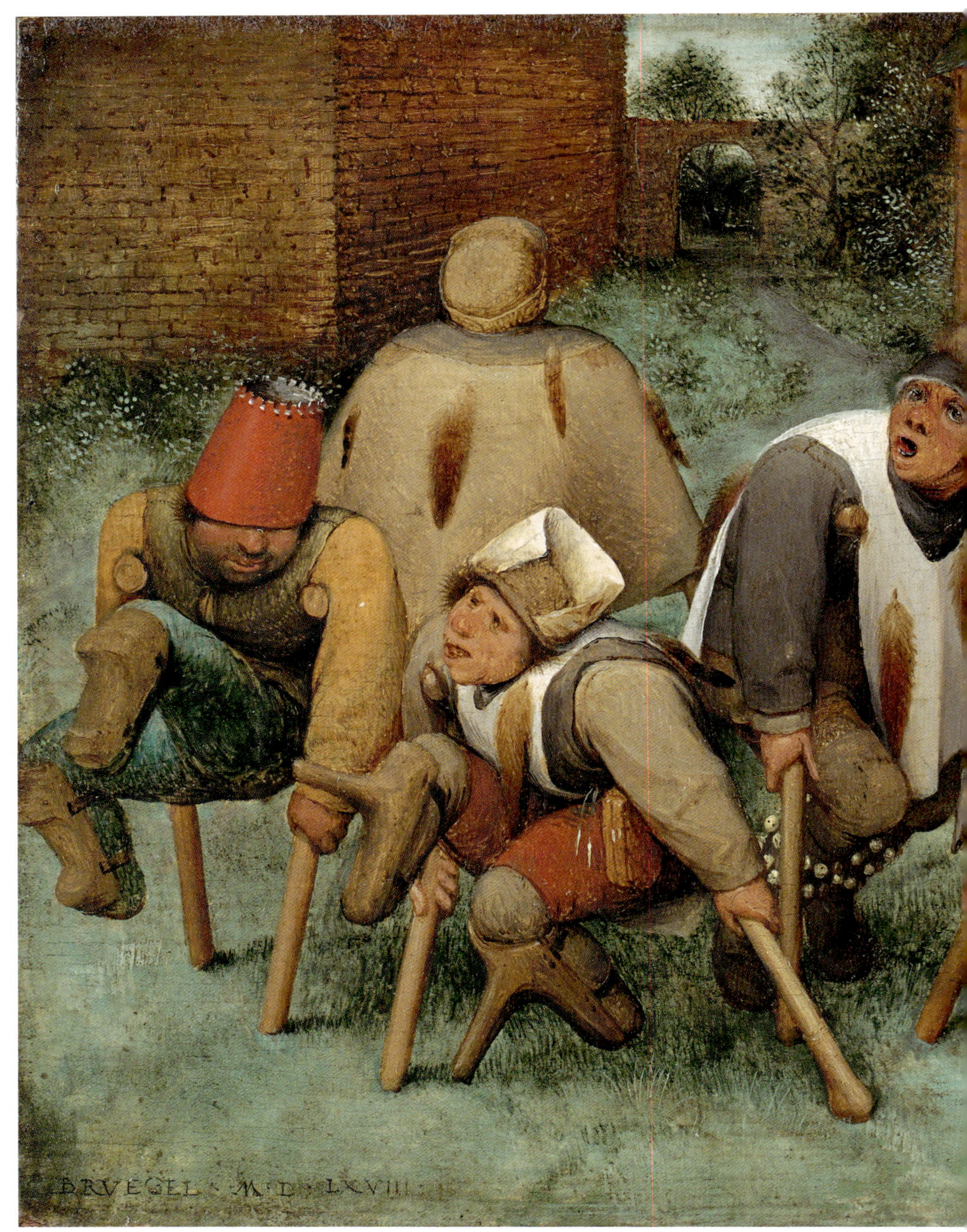

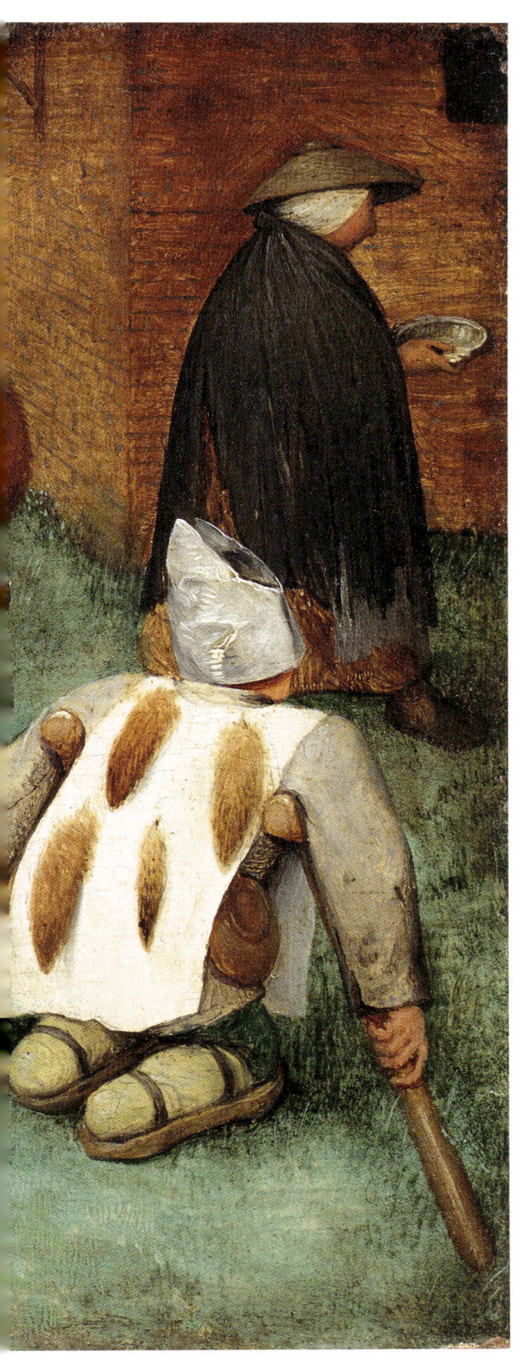

The Cripples (also: **The Beggars**), 1568
Oil on wood, 18.5 x 21.5 cm (7 ¼ x 8 ½ in.)
Paris, Musée du Louvre

Pages 402/403
The Parable of the Blind
(also: **The Blind Leading the Blind**), 1568
Tempera on canvas, 85.5 x 154 cm (33 ⅔ x 60 ⅝ in.)
Naples, Museo di Capodimonte

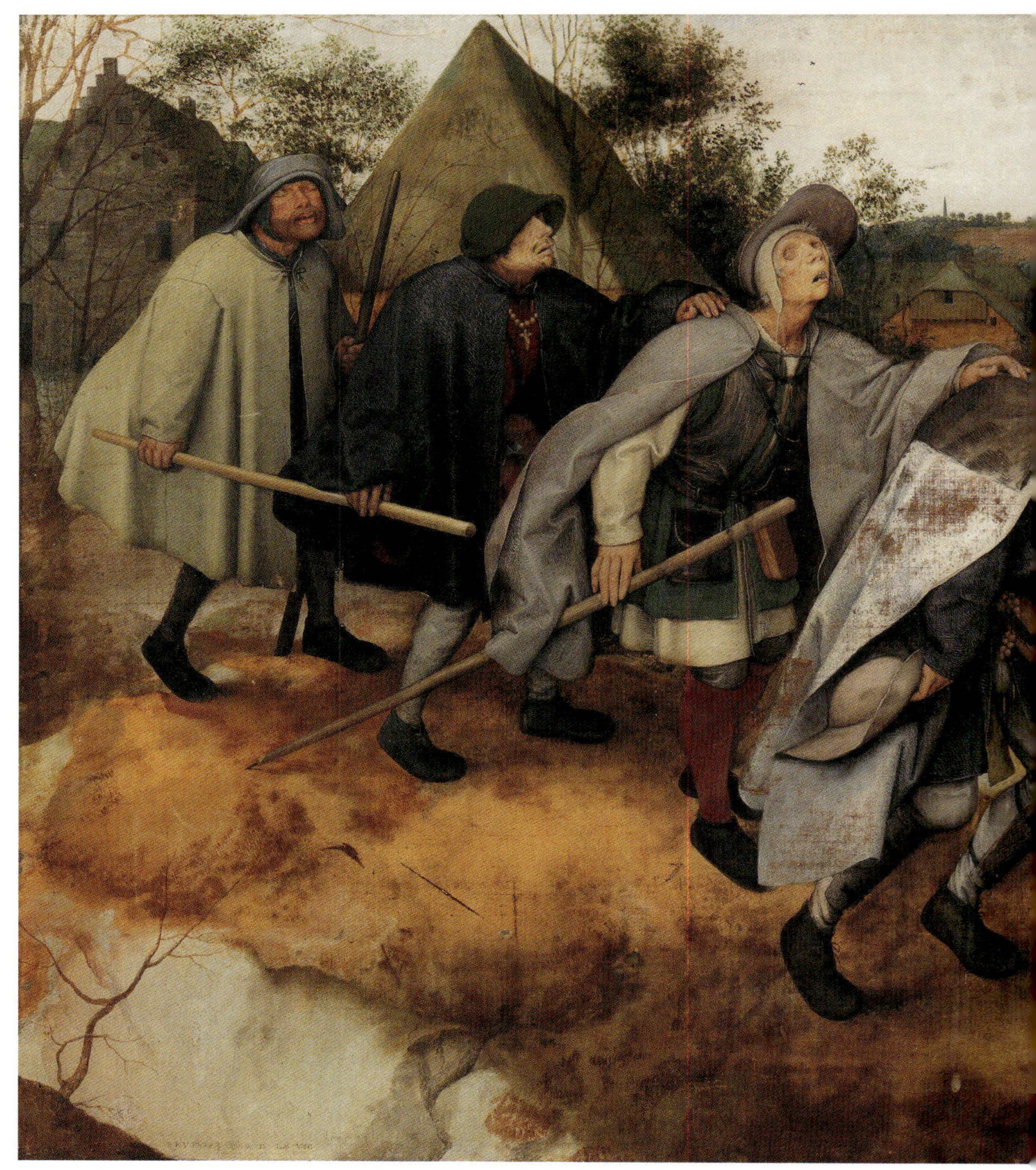

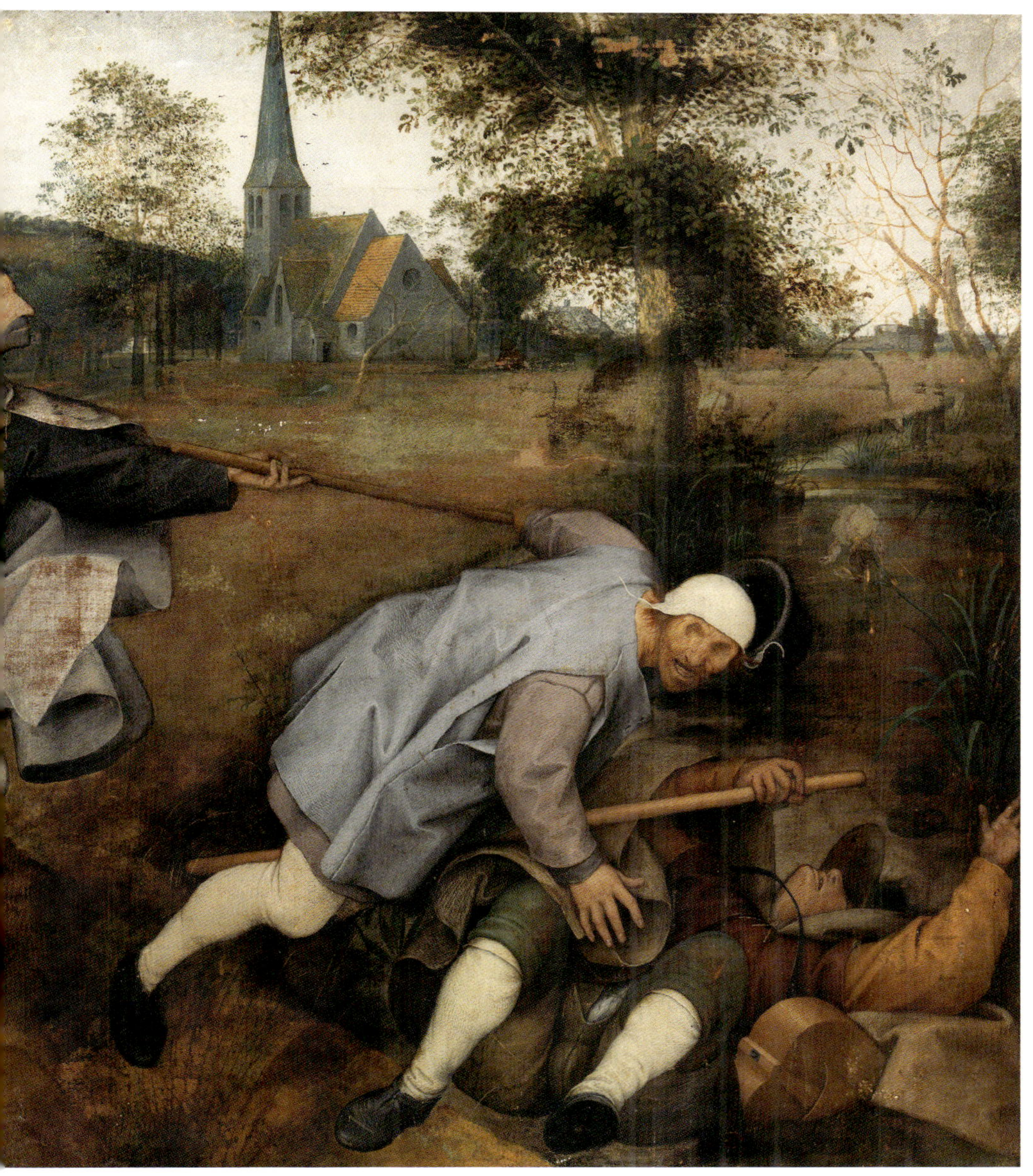

Epilogue

*"Nevertheless, this feeling, time and again, that someone
sees us, someone who stays silent, off-kilter, from above.
So we hold onto one another by the hand once more
and call out: hey, is someone out there looking at us?
But, apart from the sounds of the air and of the earth,
and those we make ourselves (with our hearts, our lungs,
our throats, our mouth), everything is still and quiet
around us."*

— GERT HOFMANN, 1985

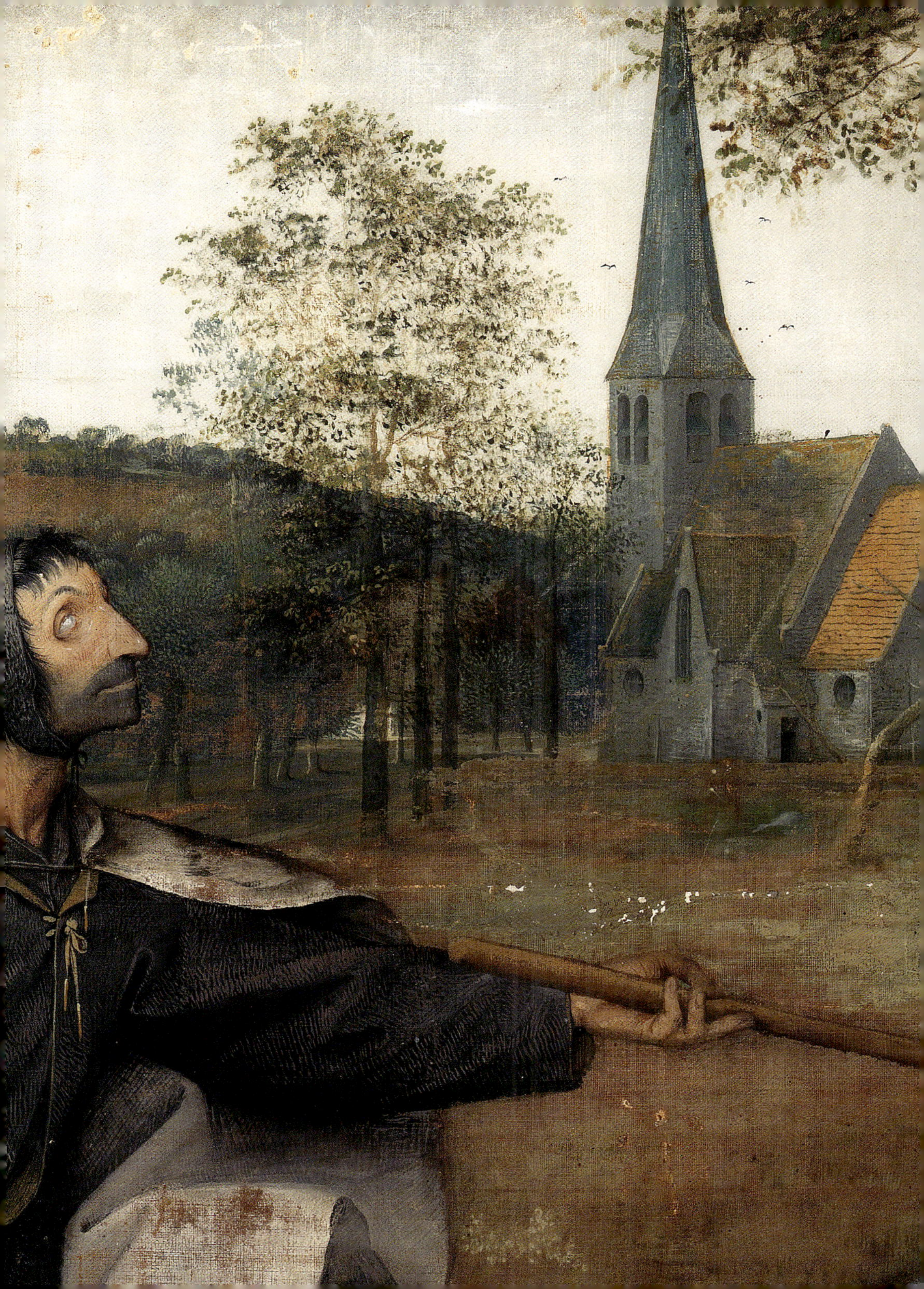

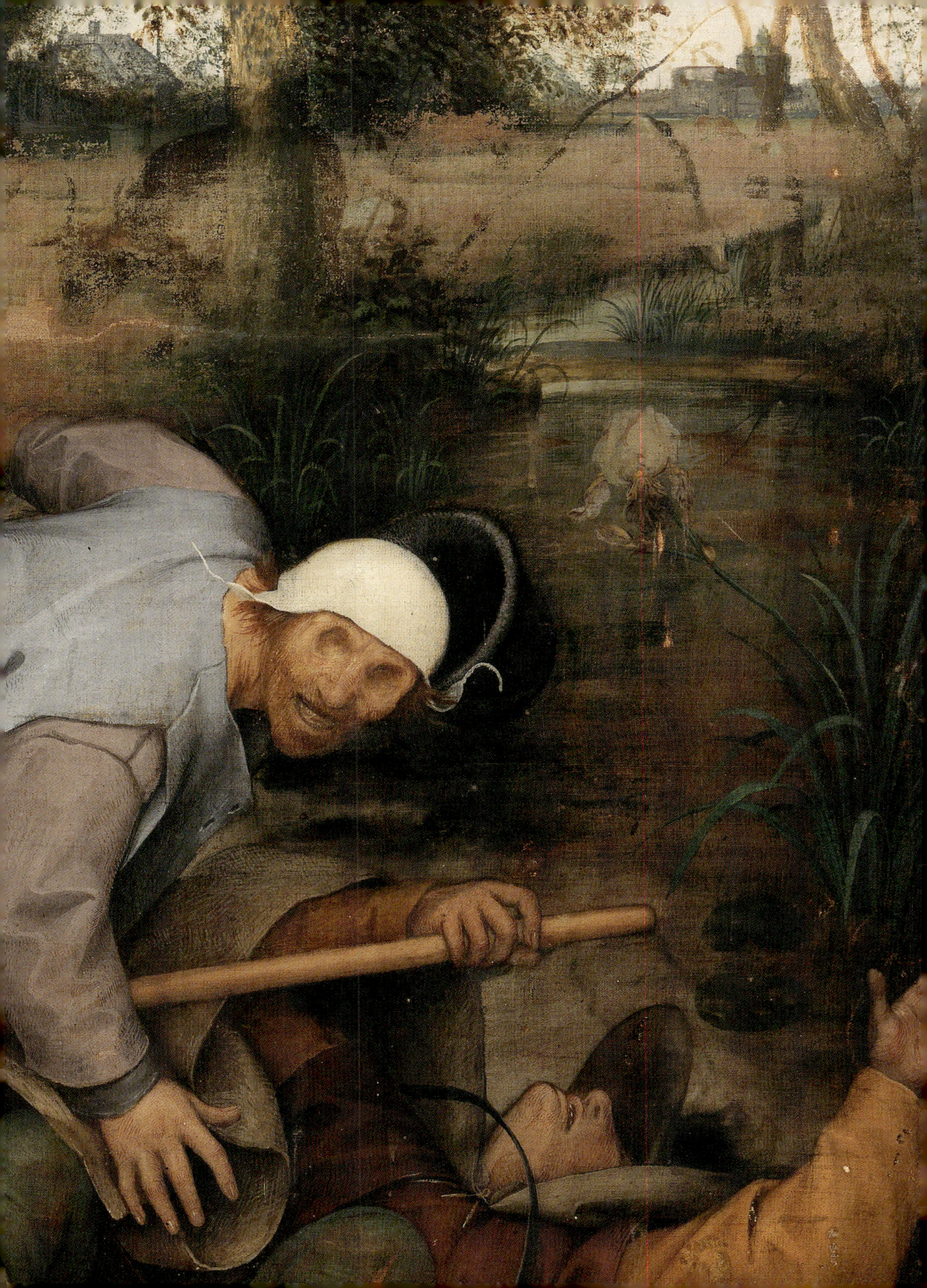

Epilogue

At the beginning, the theory was proposed that Pieter Bruegel the Elder was an enlightener. This may be regarded as a modernistic label enabling us to judge the painter with contemporary criteria. But in an age in which people sought to define their relationship to God, the position in which all denominations, indeed, all religions are valid as equal, seems to be the sole possibility of assigning every individual the same rights. Furthermore, Bruegel fought against the bugbears of religion. He mocked the depictions of Hell of a Hieronymus Bosch by transforming dark demons into clumsy goblins. And he shows, ironically, that a contentious woman is more dangerous than all the devils put together. He lets everyone ascend to heaven on the Last Day, and not just a select few.

The assessment of Bruegel as an enlightener seems justified as well in that his pictures constantly demonstrate to us how Christian faith can switch over into terror. Hence in his biblical picture the artist tells less about the past and far more about the dangers of his own present day. The events described in the New Testament keep recurring over and over again. It is as if the past is encountering us in the present in this unredeemed world of ours, as Sebastian Franck formulated in his *Paradoxa*.

Bruegel's adversaries are the ministerial Churches. He questions sacraments and rituals and warns against the dangers of the secularisation of religion into rigid orthodoxy. He even reinterprets the negative image of the heretic as a positive by seeing him as a seeker after God. And it must have seemed hypocritical to people even of his own time

Pages 405, 406
The Parable of the Blind (also: **The Blind Leading the Blind**; details), 1568
(see ill. pp. 402/403)

when killing took place in Christ's name. Not death but killing is the actual nightmare, as so many of his pictures vehemently demonstrate. In the course of the investigation, references were continually made to the writings and ideas of Sebastian Franck, with our argument that Bruegel was an attentive reader of his. The complexity of his pictures cannot be fathomed without reference to his reaction to the German theologian.

Bruegel's works are subject to the law of reversal. The significant emerges out of the insignificant. This is not discerned at first glance. A Silenian aesthetic exists in his pictures. In this, and in much more, he follows the ideas of Sebastian Franck. The writings of the now forgotten theologian were widely circulated, above all in the circles surrounding Abraham Ortelius, which Bruegel frequented and where he found his patrons. He follows Franck when he takes as his theme the limits of what can be represented, by marginalising or miniaturising important scenes. Moreover, we must draw attention to his sense of visual patterns of argumentation. He manipulates the observer through discontinuous pictorial spaces. Bruegel knows exactly how to trick his public.

In his pictorial aesthetic, too, the Flemish artist opposes an ideological stance towards art. He rejects the dictate imposed by the canon of succession to Raphael and Michelangelo. This escalates in a conflict in which Bruegel is denounced in a lampoon as a painter of fairground puppets because he refuses to follow the model of classical antiquity. Subsequently, he produces a series of works supporting stylistic pluralism. His position might be summarised thus: an artist should follow many models, not always the same ones, and choose his subjects accordingly. Furthermore, it is astonishing how frequently he reacts to already existent pictorial themes from his immediate environment. His panels *The Fight between Carnival and Lent, Netherlandish Proverbs, The Blind Leading the Blind* and *The Land of Cockaigne* etc. owe much to the engravings of his time. He also makes use of motifs from Italian and ancient models, which he is able to transpose into incongruous contexts. In his months series, he raises landscape painting to a new level by endeavouring for the first time to represent the sublime awesomeness of nature in all its destructive power. Bruegel is able to differentiate between beauty and prettiness. The human body for him – in contrast to the Italian Renaissance – has no dignity per se. Beauty remains reserved to nature and its phenomena, the times of the year and of the day, to light and its associated moods – God's creation is beautiful but awesome and beyond understanding.

A further unique feature of his art is his treatment of time. He even conceived an allegory on this theme (pp. 410/411). Like no other artist, he made it his task to represent permanence and ephemerality. In his pictures we can observe the course of time, but also its abrupt transitions from one moment to the next. *The Blind Leading the Blind* shows him devoting a picture especially to the phenomenon of acceleration.

He constructs optical paradoxes when he makes a gallows jig or produces a never-ending flow of beer. Time, as the Church Father St Augustine said, is the phenomenon with which God encrypts his creation. Bruegel is on its trail it in his art. Wheels and circular movements in connection with the Passion of Christ signal for us the motif of recurrence. As regards the events of the Passion, in the course of the narrative he can integrate impending elements and thus allows the future to be present when, in *The Adoration of the Kings in the Snow* and *The Census at Bethlehem,* he shows the henchmen who are later responsible for the massacre of the innocents. Whoever wishes to portray the world is referred to the mystery of time.

But no matter how much we struggle to understand his pictures, something enigmatic remains. We do not know who Pieter Bruegel was. But when we delve into his art, a wilful, indeed courageous, man appears, who throughout all the years never gives up his view of the world, but clings to it resolutely.

Pages 410/411
Philipp Galle after Pieter Bruegel the Elder, **The Triumph of Time**, 1574
Copper engraving, 21.1 x 30.4 cm (8 ⅜ x 12 in.). New York, The Metropolitan Museum of Art

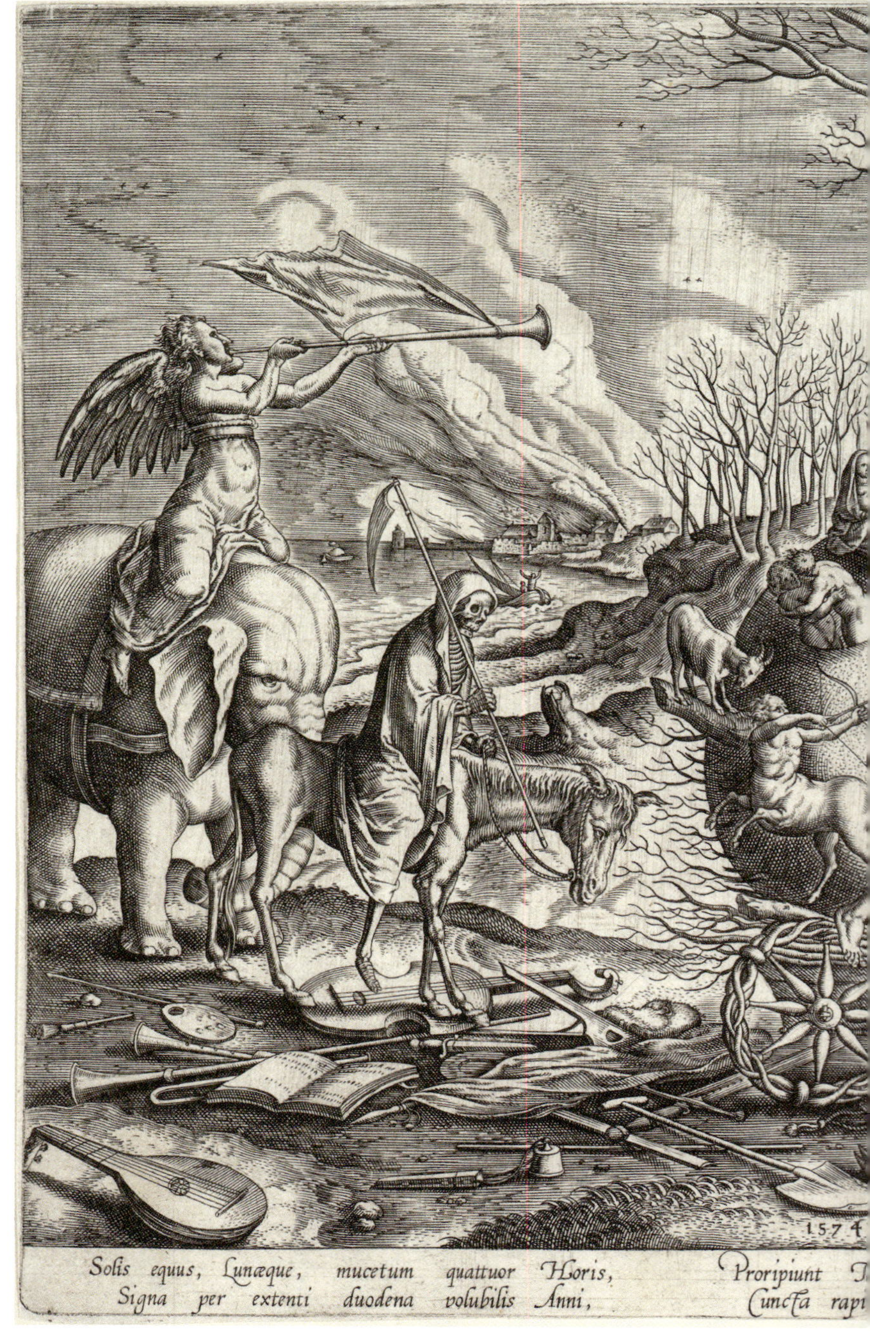
1574
Solis equus, Lunæque, mucetum quattuor Horis,   Proripiunt
Signa per extenti duodena volubilis Anni,   Cuncta rapi

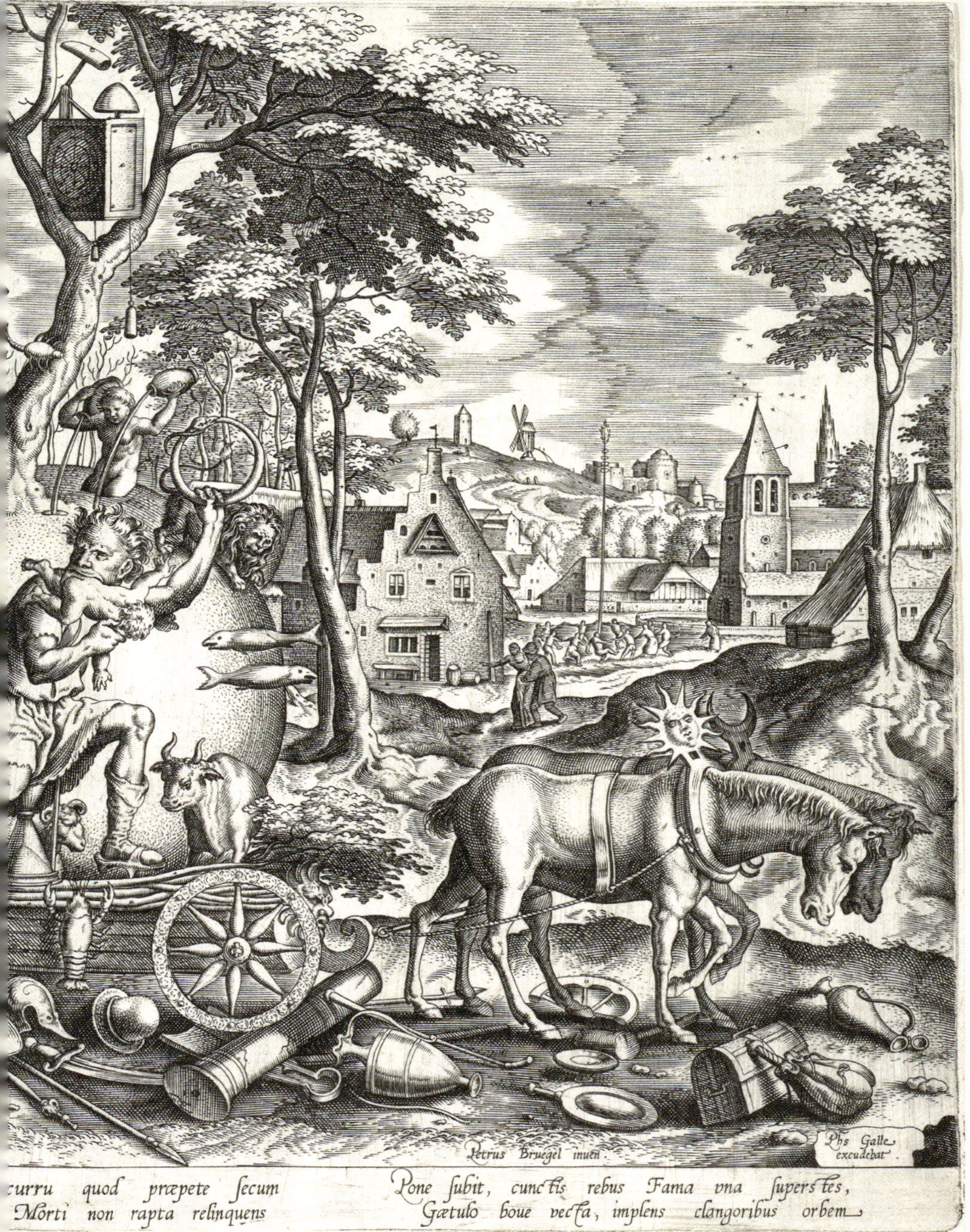

curru quod præpete secum   Pone subit, cunctis rebus Fama vna superstes,
Morti non rapta relinquens   Gætulo boue vecta, implens clangoribus orbem

Catalogue of Paintings

Jürgen Müller

"In Breughel's Icarus, for instance:
how everything turns away
Quite leisurely from the disaster; the ploughman may
Have heard the splash, the forsaken cry,
But for him it was not an important failure [...]"
— W. H. AUDEN, 1939

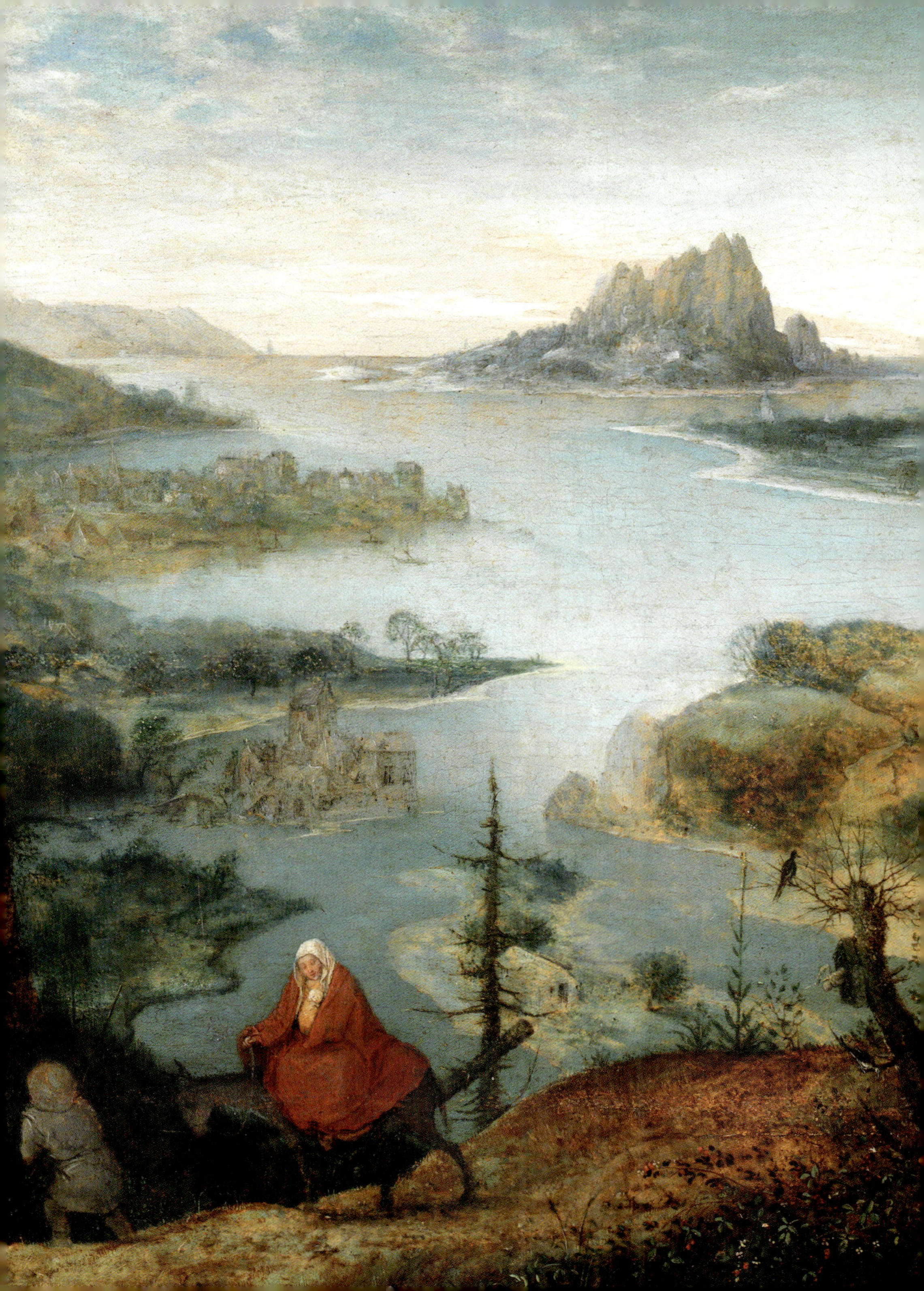

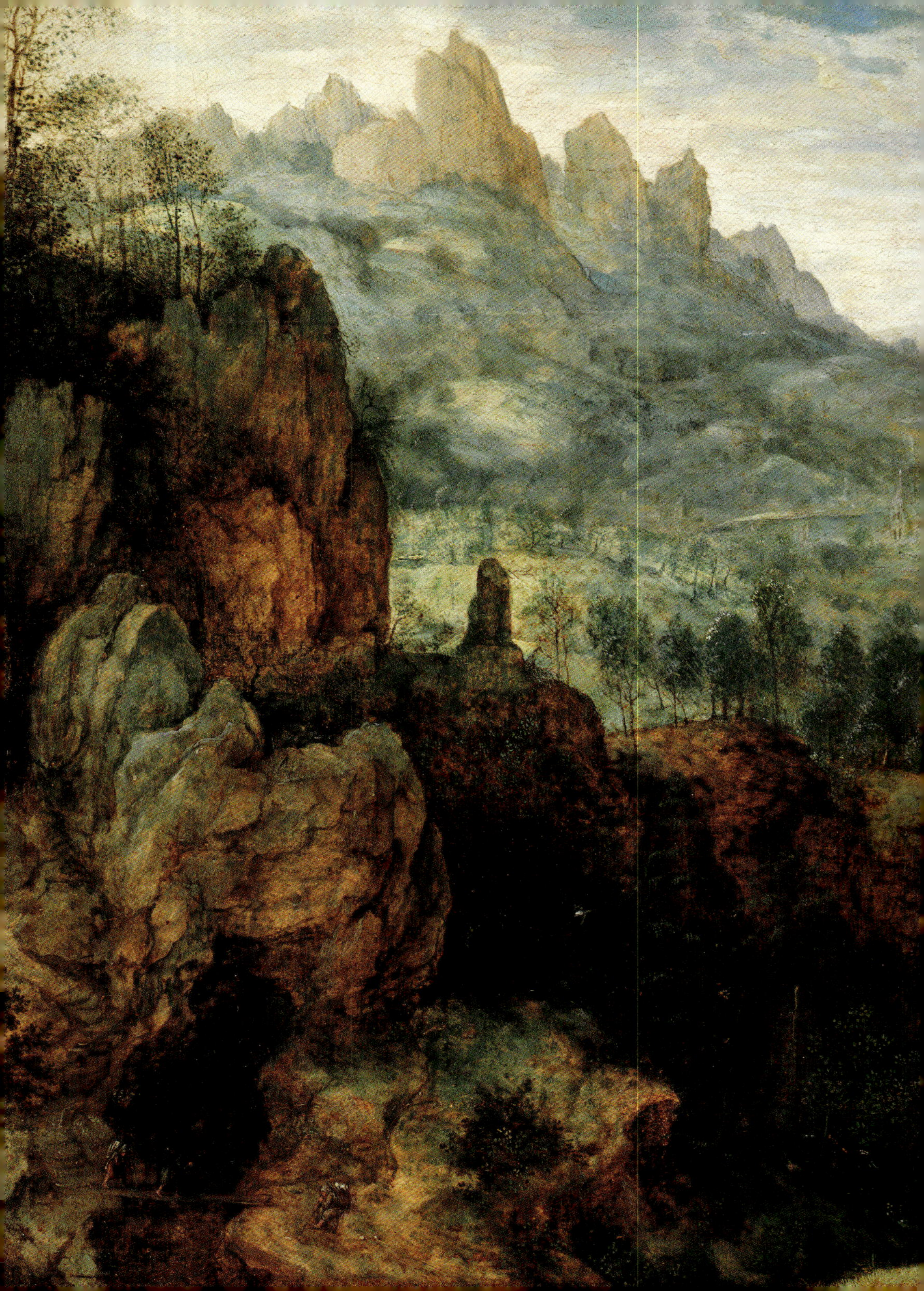

Explanatory Notes on the Paintings Catalogue

The works of Pieter Bruegel the Elder have always attracted great attention. As early as the sixteenth century his fame had already spread across Europe, and important humanists and members of the patrician class can be named as commissioners for many panels. The great majority of pictures entered royal and imperial collections accessible only to a select few. Hence their fame was increased all the more by the copies and variations of the works produced by Bruegel's son, Pieter the Younger. However, what pre-eminently fashioned the artist's public image were the copper engravings made after his drawn designs. Today, the largest interrelated inventory of the Flemish artist's panels is in the Kunsthistorisches Museum in Vienna. So it is self-evident that important investigations started out here, with studies by Gustav Glück, Max Dvořák and Hans Sedlmayr being at the forefront.

Looking at his oeuvre as a whole, it is evident that Bruegel was preoccupied most of all with works of Christian iconography. Only a few panels take the peasantry as their main subject, and these, contrary to the opinion of earlier interpreters, are to be seen as thoroughly critical. Simply on account of its scale, the series of months assumes a special place in the complete works. These originally six panels represent a turning point in landscape painting in that their thematic focus is directed on the elemental dangers of nature – snow, fire and ice, water and storm. It is unusual that besides the many panels in oil and tempera on wood, two works can be found in Bruegel's late work for which he turned to the technique of Tüchlein (cloth) painting. And he experimented not only with paints and supports but also with formats and the relation of figures to picture size. Many of his works handle traditional motifs, which, however, he radically changes. At first, Bruegel's works tended to be seen as a type of folkloric art. This conviction goes back not least to the assessment of Karel van Manders made in 1604, according to which Bruegel himself, the son of simple farmers, had to be a peasant as well. The overcoming of this

Pages 413, 414
Landscape with the Flight into Egypt (details), 1563
(see ill. pp. 44/45)

one-sided interpretation made room for the humanist Bruegel to enter the scene. Karl Tolnai's research in particular motivated investigations of the artist's theological and humanist sources.

The assessment of the works has always provided food for discussion among scholars. We may recall the dispute between Hans Sedlmayr and Karl Tolnai during the 1930s, and in the more recent past the debate between Hessel Miedema and Svetlana Alpers. The defining factor in all the debates surrounding Bruegel was always the question of the limits and possibilities of iconographic interpretation. How critical should we imagine him to have been? How rich in allusions should we judge his visual imagery? Accordingly, scholars have repeatedly discussed the question of the religious identity of Bruegel, whose creative phase coincided with the age of religious wars. The question is how far he himself was affected by the direct consequences, and whether he commented on the ruling contemporary conditions in his pictures. Ever since Tolnai's research, the theologians Sebastian Franck and the humanist Erasmus of Rotterdam have been cited in this context, and David Freedberg has reminded us of the discussion being held at that time about Nicodemism, the movement whereby people merely acted as if they belonged to the Catholic Church.

An important contribution for judging Bruegel is also provided by the investigations of Hans-Joachim Raupp in the early 1980s; by referring to the work of the Beham brothers, he was able to demonstrate how aptly Bruegel's peasant pictures can be localised in tradition. Since then, many individual studies have been published that cannot be dealt with singly here. However, in 1997 a comprehensive bibliography by the author was published on Bruegel, which documents academic studies that have appeared to the present day (in: *Nederlands Kunsthistorisch Jaarboek* 47/1997, pp. 247–271).

Furthermore, important exhibitions have taken place in recent years. Among them, the comprehensive show of Bruegel's drawings in New York and Rotterdam in 2001 takes first place. The most recent exhibition of Bruegel's prints was held in Chemnitz in 2014. The accompanying catalogues yet again contain important bibliographic references. Therefore it will not be difficult even for general readers to inform themselves in depth and detail about Pieter Bruegel the Elder.

River Landscape with a Sower (detail), 1557
(see ill. pp. 42/43)

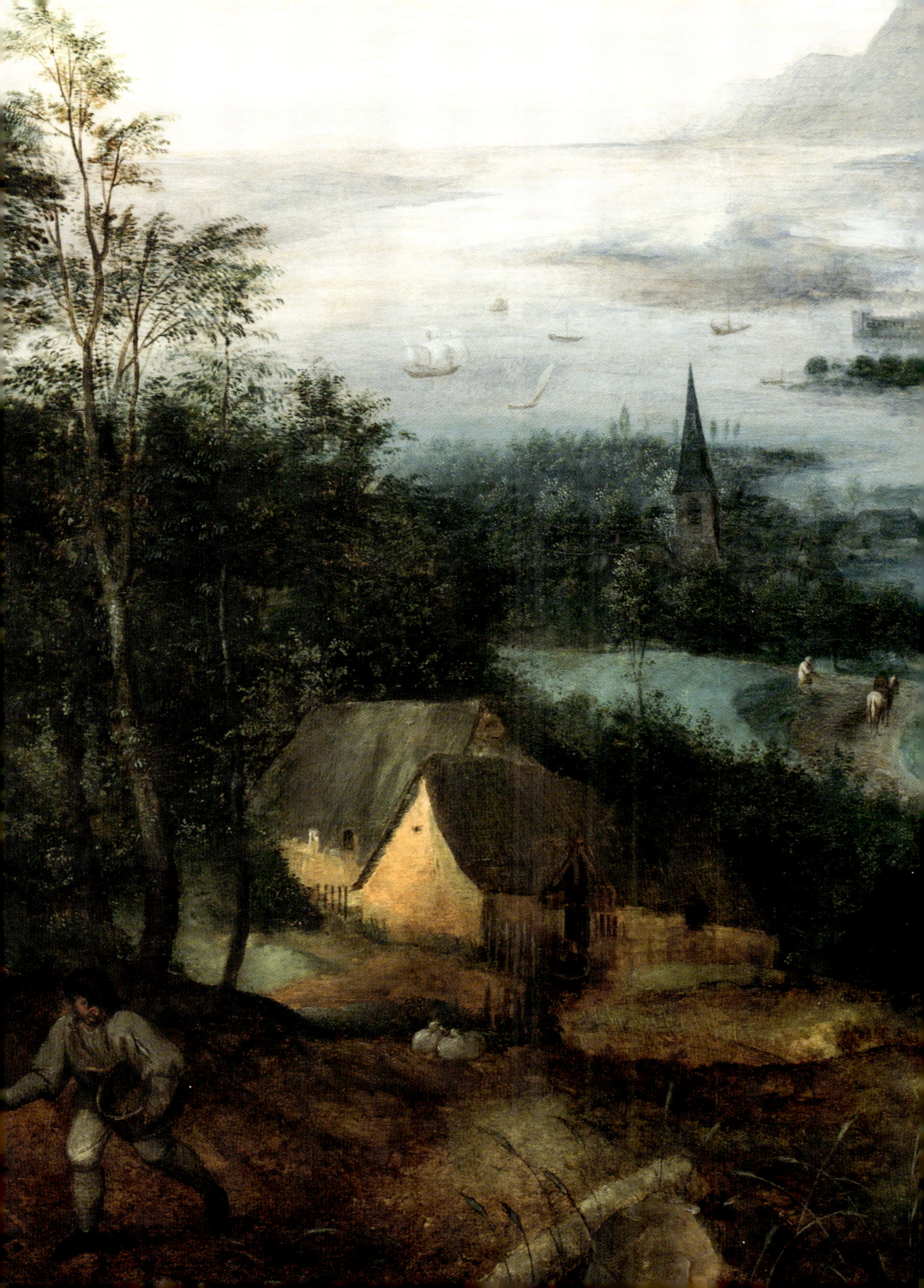

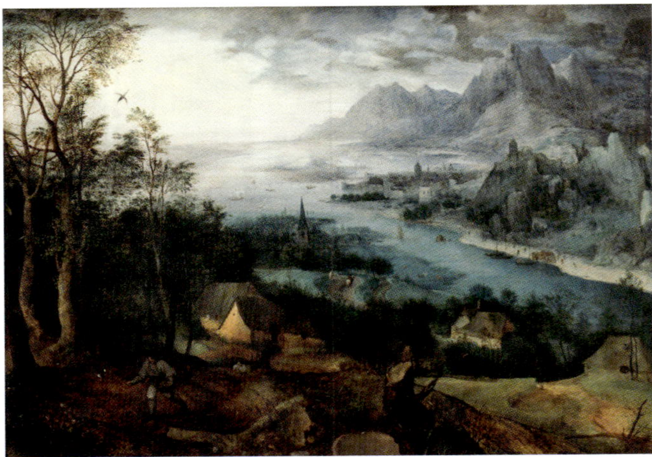

I

I
River Landscape with a Sower, 1557
Oil on wood, 73.7 x 102.9 cm (29 x 40 ⅝ in.),
inscribed b. r.: […]VEGHEL [.] 557
San Diego, California, Timken Museum
of Art, Inv. 1957:002

Based on the date of 1557, *River Landscape with a Sower* has repeatedly been seen as Bruegel's earliest extant painting, though the attribution to the artist must be deemed debatable at the very least. The painterly execution of the sowing peasant and his surroundings is too weak, and in concept the picture is strictly beholden to tradition. The observer's eye roams from an elevated vantage point over a landscape that attains its impression of depth above all from the graduations of colour. The brown of the foreground is distinctly set off from the bluish-green of the river valley in the middle ground. A mountain range kept in blue and grey tones crowns the top right-hand half of the picture, while to the left of this the Sun dips everything lying below it in a yellowish light. Painters like Joachim Patinir (*c.* 1475/80–1524) in the first half of the sixteenth century had already established this triple-ground scheme used here by the artist (p. 287). Similar ploys can also be found in Bruegel's later works, though they are less schematic.

The artist placed the peasant busy at his sowing at the front left edge of the picture. Birds seem to be picking up the cast grain under the adjacent trees. For some scholars, the scene alludes to the Parable of the Sower that Jesus narrated while seated in a boat (Matthew 13: 1–20). And in fact a large crowd of people has gathered to the right, on the opposite bank. However, they are standing in front of an evidently empty boat, which suggests the missing figure was possibly lost during a later restoration.

The panel is signed and dated bottom right. The designation was first found in 1924 during

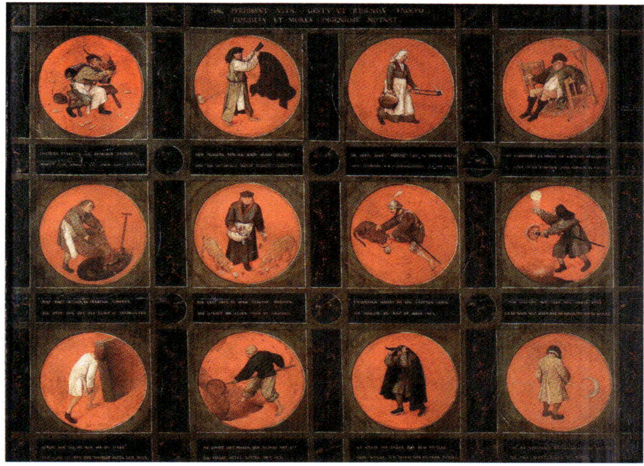

2

restoration work, after the Antwerp collector Fernand Stuyck del Bruyère (1887–1960) had auctioned the picture earlier in the year in Brussels as "Flemish School, 17th Century". The work was taken to the USA immediately before outbreak of the Second World War, then was purchased in 1957 by the Putnam Foundation and since 1965 has been part of the collection of the Timken Museum of Art in San Diego. See also pp. *42/43*.

LITERATURE: Gibson 1977, pp. 42–43; Marijnissen 1988, p. 382; Roberts-Jones 2002, pp. 123–124; Sellink 2012, p. 111.

2

Twelve Proverbs, *c.* 1558–1560
Oil on oak, 74.5 x 98.4 cm (29 ⅜ x 38 ¾ in.), inscribed on last panel, m. l.: 1558
BRVEGHEL
Antwerp, Museum Mayer van den Bergh, Inv. MMB.0046

After Bruegel's death, the critical reception of his work gained a momentum that tells us how famous the artist was already during his lifetime. It is particularly to his son Pieter the Younger (1564–1638) that we owe many copies and works that recombine elements from his father's oeuvre. The twelve square oak panels in their contemporary arrangement are 74.5 x 98.4 cm (29 ⅜ x 38 ¾ in.). Their attribution to Bruegel is controversial, and they were only brought together later. The depictions of the twelve proverbs show numerous parallels to the *Netherlandish Proverbs* in Berlin (Cat. 3), hence it is plausible that an anonymous artist worked on the 1559 "wimmel picture" (a picture teeming with figures and events) after the original or a copy of it. Its weak quality, visible in the figural rendering and in the simplistic additive schema, also makes an attribution to Pieter the Elder seem doubtful. The proverb texts were added later, making the scenes into mere illustrations. Although Bruegel may have frequently reverted to dramatic interpretations of sayings, here the composition and didactic concept are extremely mechanical and untypical of the artist. While in the Berlin panel the teeming confusion motivates our endeavour to make active comparisons between the depicted proverbs, their form and their content, this juxtaposition of image and text shows such a lack of complexity that it dampens any further intellectual challenge. Thus the description of the man concealed under the blue cloak is juxtaposed with a pictorial rendering that totally misses the logical narrative in the Berlin panel.

A signature and vestiges of a date can be found on the bottom right panel, which shows a peasant urinating against the crescent Moon. This caused Hulin de Loo to date it to 1558, only one year prior to the multi-figural "wimmel" pictures, among which the *Netherlandish Proverbs* is found. A first mention still referring to Pieter Bruegel the Elder and naming twelve illustrations is found in the inventory of Nicolas

Cheeus compiled between 1621 and 1623. However, Pieter the Younger is already named for the same pictures in 1663, in the inventory of Cheeus' widow. There are further references to similar compilations, whose signatures in part also indicate the son.

See also pp. *74/75*.

LITERATURE: Van Bastelaer/Loo 1907, pp. 277–279, Gibson 1977, p. 66; Coo 1978, pp. 40–46; Marijnissen 1988, pp. 383–384; Seipel 1998, p. 160; Meadow 2002; Roberts-Jones 2002, pp. 212–213; Sellink 2012, pp. 123–124.

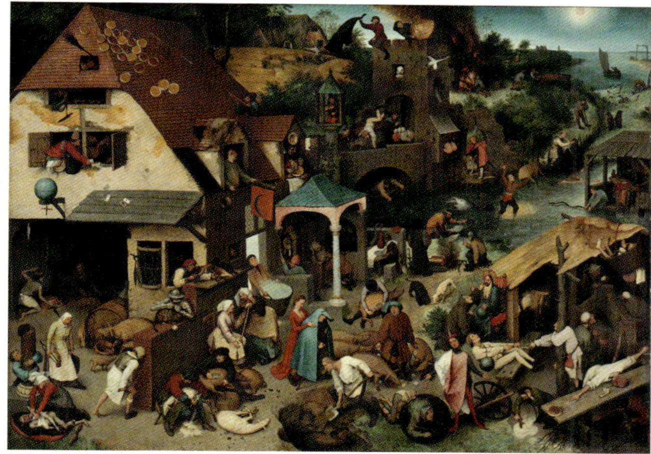

3

3

Netherlandish Proverbs, 1559
Oil on oak, 117 x 163 cm (46 x 64 ¼ in.),
inscribed b. r.: BRVEGEL 1559
Staatliche Museen zu Berlin, Gemäldegalerie,
Inv. 1720

No fewer than 119 proverbs have been discovered
up to now in the picture, which is today in the
Berlin Gallery of Old Masters. Employing a
high horizon and a clear perspective from above,
the artist presents a village landscape in which
nearly a hundred people, animals and objects
jostle together in a multitude of individual
scenes. The architecture structures the way
through the teeming masses. Starting out from
a house dominating the left third of the picture,
the eye roams over a village street, its other side
bordered by a thatched hut. At the upper end
of the path, the landscape opens up on the right
to the expanse of the sea. Top left, other scenes
are enacted along the coastline behind a

half-ruined tower. Most of the depicted actions
are still a puzzle, for instance the old woman
muzzling a devil, a man falling through a straw
basket hung on the roof ridge, or a monk trying
to "tie a flaxen beard to the face of Christ". But
other scenes have retained their significance to
this day, for instance the large fish about to eat
a smaller one.

The popularity of the *Netherlandish Proverbs*
among Bruegel's contemporaries is measured
in the sheer number of preserved reproductions.
Sixteen copies by his son Pieter the Younger
alone have come down to us. Bruegel himself
had possibly already devised the controversial
Antwerp panel of the *Twelve Proverbs* (Cat. 2)
beforehand. The direct model for the composition may have been a 1558 engraving by
Frans Hogenberg (1535–1590); Bruegel's panel
shares with it the steeply ascending pictorial
space and numerous motifs (p. 58). Also, the
eponymous scene in the sheet *De Blau Huicke*
(The Blue Cloak) crops up again here: a woman

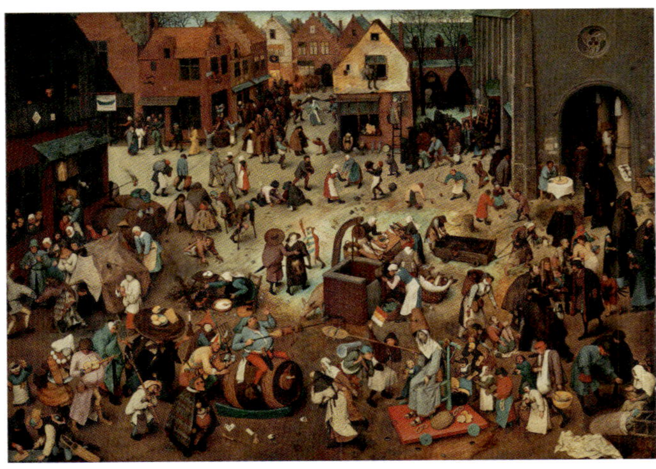

4

places a blue cloak round her husband's shoulders, a sign of her unfaithfulness. Many of the scenes in general allude to moral flaws, and the theme of the topsy-turvy world also crops up repeatedly in the picture. Thus an upside-down orb hangs on the gable of the front house. Moreover, the first mention of the panel in an inventory underlines this aspect: it is listed in 1668 with the title *Le Monde renversé, représenté par plusieurs Proverbes et Moralités* (The world turned upside down, represented by many proverbs and moralities) in the collection of the Antwerp officer for the poor, Pieter Stevens, who owned no fewer than eleven paintings by Bruegel. The panel was still mentioned in the 17th century, but subsequently could not be found until 1913, in an English private collection. With its purchase in 1914 by the Kaiser-Friedrich Museum, the work went to Berlin.
See also pp. 53–55, 58–59, 61, *88/89.*
LITERATURE: Roh 1960; Berlin 1975, p. 69; Gibson 1977, pp. 65–89; Marijnissen 1988,

pp. 133–145; Sullivan 1991, pp. 431–466; Müller 1999, pp. 155–171; Müller 2000, pp. 29–36; Meadow 2002; Roberts-Jones 2002, pp. 202–212; Grosshans 2003; Mieder 2004a/b; Fraenger 2008; Büttner 2012, pp. 197–221; Sellink 2012, pp. 128–129.

4

The Fight between Carnival and Lent, 1559
Oil on oak, 118 x 164.5 cm (46 ½ x 64 ⅞ in.),
inscribed b. l. on a stone:
BRVEGEL (V and E ligature) 1559
Vienna, Kunsthistorisches Museum,
Gemäldegalerie, Inv. GG_1016

The eponymous fight between Carnival and Lent has a compositional structure based on contradictions. The scene is played out on the market place of a Flemish town, the location of the encounter in the immediate foreground of the two protagonists, "Carnival" and "Lent".

They are heading towards each other in a kind of joust. As representatives of the conflict, they are dramatised diametrically opposed to each other. Thus the overweight representative of the Carnival – frequently observed as being a little like Luther – is shown jousting mounted, with humorous symbolism, on a wine barrel. His weapon is a roasting spit, on which he has skewered the head of a suckling pig, a roast chicken, and sausages. His haggard opponent has only a baking shovel as weapon, on which we see a fish, the food of Lent. The figure's other attributes also stand for temperance, contrition and renunciation: the embodiment of Lent wears a penitent's robe and is seated on a church chair. She wears a beehive on her head, while the Carnival prince balances a pasty on his. The personifications in the surroundings show allegories of gluttony and temperance elaborated in numerous individual scenes. In the left half of the picture, Carnival customs are depicted in the vicinity of two inns, while on the right the rituals of Lent are allotted to a church building. The picture clearly has a denominational background and has been frequently interpreted by scholars as an allusion to the contemporary feud between Catholics and Protestants. But even if at first we see good deeds on the right of the picture as indicative of Catholics, on closer inspection we discover all kinds of foolery here as well. The playing children show us that the world consists of nothing but fools, and so it is no coincidence that in the dead centre of the picture a jester carrying a torch lights a couple on their way through the scene. As already mentioned for the *Netherlandish Proverbs* (Cat. 3), a possible model for *The Fight between Carnival and Lent* is an engraving by Frans Hogenberg published in 1558 by Hieronymus Cock (1518–1570; p. 51). In contrast to Hogenberg, who acts with much more reserve in this regard, Bruegel mocks both faiths in his version. The fact that the artist was greatly interested in the theme is demonstrated

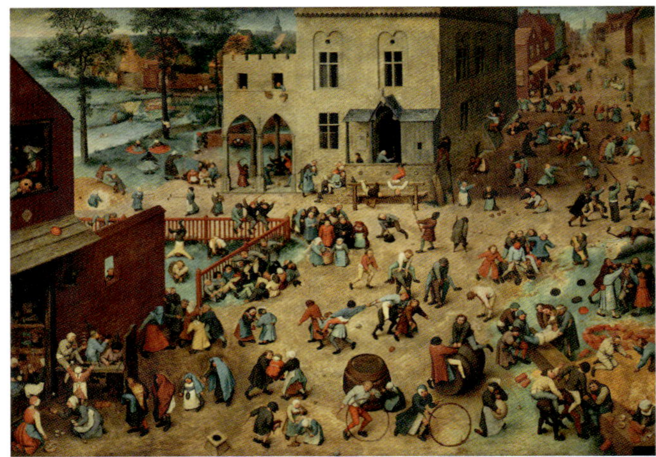

5

by the two later engravings depicting the *Lean Kitchen* and the *Fat Kitchen* (pp. 68/69, 70/71). Since the dimensions of the wooden panel differ little from those of the Berlin *Proverbs*, it has been surmised that the two compendium pictures, each dated 1559, might be pendants. Both compositions have a high-set horizon and the associated steeply ascending pictorial space. The picture was first named by Karel van Mander (1548–1606), but he does not list it among the works owned by Emperor Rudolf II (1552–1612). The latter might have purchased the work in the course of his collecting activities; it was in fact moved in 1748 from the Secular Treasure Chamber of the Habsburgs to their Painting Gallery.
See also pp. 49–53, *76/77*.
Literature: Gibson 1977, pp. 65–89; Demus 1981, pp. 61–68; Marijnissen 1988, pp. 146–157; Härting 1996; Wied 1996; Seipel 1998, pp. 18–31; Kavaler 1999, pp. 111–148; Roberts-Jones 2002, pp. 114–120; Sellink 2012, pp. 130–131; Schneider 2015, pp. 219–230.

5
Children's Games, 1560
Oil on oak, 118 x 161 cm (46 ½ x 63 ½ in.), inscribed b. r. on the block of wood:
BRVEGEL 1560
Vienna, Kunsthistorisches Museum, Gemäldegalerie, Inv. GG_1017

In format, the oak panel of *Children's Games* is not only larger than Bruegel's earlier "wimmel pictures" but also surpasses them in the confusion of the teeming scene. The encyclopaedic rendering of around ninety children's games strikes the observer at first as utter confusion, an impression accentuated by the overall brown tonality of the picture and the small size of the protagonists enacting the scene. Bruegel's picture shows no fewer than 168 boys and 78 girls within urban architecture arranged like flats in a theatre. The horizon was set at the top edge of the picture so that the scene is presented in a steeply ascending pictorial space.

The architectural framework starts from the bottom left edge and goes on to define the composition with a diagonal line, cut in the centre of the picture by a vertically aligned street. This specifies the painting's direction for the observer. Besides clearly identifiable games like leap frog or blindman's buff, it shows children at play imitating rituals from the adult world. These include an implied baptismal procession in the left foreground, also a wedding ceremony taking place at the junction. Like Bruegel's other compendium pictures, *Children's Games* too was read for symbols of the folly and the topsy-turvy world.

Karel von Mander's information on Bruegel already mentions a picture that shows "all kinds of children's games", though the owner is not named. The painting belongs to the works bought in 1594 in Brussels by Archduke Ernst (1553–1595), Rudolf II's younger brother, after the former had been named as Governor of the Spanish Netherlands. According to the notes of his private secretary, Blasius Hütter, he paid 538 guilders for the wooden panel and two other paintings. After Ernst's death in 1595, his collection was taken to Vienna. *Children's Games* was consequently transferred into Rudolf II's Prague collection as part of a batch of at least ten Bruegel paintings.

See also pp. 61–63, 66, *98/99*.

Literature: Gibson 1977, pp. 65–89; Demus 1981, pp. 68–72; Marijnissen 1988, pp. 161–163; Snow 1997; Hills 1998; Seipel 1998, pp. 32–45; Müller 1999, pp. 40–54; Roberts-Jones 2002; pp. 221–226; Orrock 2012, pp. 1–20; Sellink 2012, p. 153.

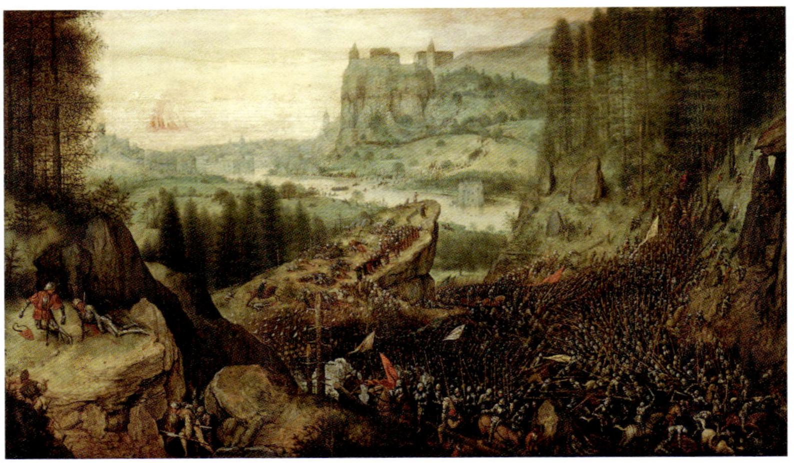

6

6

The Suicide of Saul in the Battle on Gilboa Mountain, 1562

Oil on oak, 33.5 x 55.5 cm (13 ¼ x 21 ⅞ in.), inscribed b. l. between two rocks: SAVL. XXXI. CAPIT.; and: BRVEGEL. M.CCCCC.LXII

Vienna, Kunsthistorisches Museum, Gemäldegalerie, Inv. GG_1011

Considering the imposing battle scene conceived by Bruegel in this composition, he seems to have chosen an extraordinarily small format for it. The oak panel, measuring only 33.5 x 55.5 cm (13 ¼ x 21 ⅞ in.), also refers to the depicted event bottom left next to signature and date. The designation *SAVL. XXXI. CAPIT.* refers to an Old Testament narrative describing Saul's suicide (1 Samuel 31). This occurs on a rocky plateau above the inscription. Saul, the first king of Israel, resolved to put an end to himself and fall on his sword after defeat in the battle against

the Philistines and the death of his three sons. Bruegel shows the moment when the first pursuers reach the scene, and Saul's weapon bearer is about to follow his lord to his death.

The rest of the foreground is not so much dominated by recognisable battle lines as by an impenetrable forest of lances. We see the battle has been decided in the soldiers who seek to withdraw from the scene of battle at the margins of the valley. Parallel to the upward dynamic of the troops climbing up a mountain wall, Bruegel arranged a rocky promontory in the centre of the picture; here, archers are targeting the fleeing army. Behind them we see rows of dead soldiers. The landscape in the background is already suffused with the red of sunset; besides a meticulously drawn urban background and a castle enthroned on a rock, we see another group of soldiers, who have retreated by crossing a nearby river.

In the Vienna gallery, the painting was documented for the first time in the 1783 catalogue

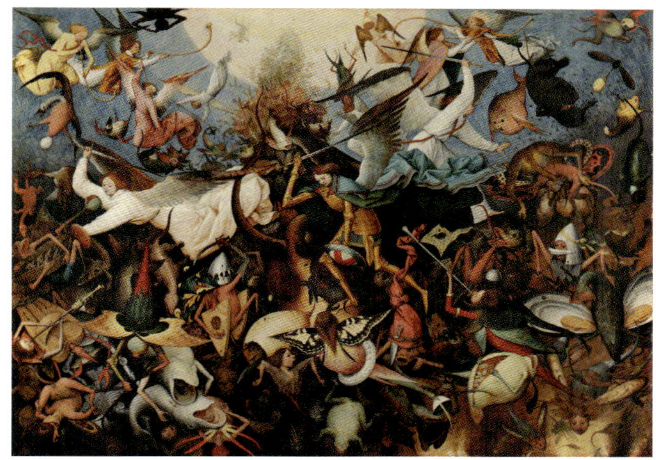

7

of Christian von Mechel (1737–1817). Tolnay already surmised that it might be identical with the picture listed in 1540 in Peter Paul Rubens' (1577–1640) estate inventory as "Battle between Turks and Christians", a misunderstanding that may have been based on the clothing of the centrally placed archers.
See also pp. *148/149*.
Literature: Gibson 1977, pp. 88–90; Demus 1981, pp. 72–76; Marijnissen 1988, pp. 172–179; Gibson 1989, p. 74; Seipel 1998, pp. 46–55; Sellink 2012, p. 173.

7

The Fall of the Rebel Angels, 1562
Oil on oak, 117 x 162 cm (46 x 63⅞ in.), inscribed b.l.: M.D.LXII / BRVEGEL
Brussels, Musées royaux des Beaux-Arts de Belgique/Koninklijke Musea voor Schone Kunsten van België, Inv. 584

Bruegel's *The Fall of the Rebel Angels* has frequently been compared to a picture on the same theme by Frans Floris (1517–1570; p. 189), who worked in Antwerp and Brussels around the same time. But while the Romanist used the subject to present his skill in portraying the male nude and shows the demons' bodies in all conceivable positions and postures, Bruegel opts for interpreting the event in a fantastical manner. The panel dates from 1562 and is marked by extreme confusion; only the Archangel Michael in the dead centre provides a kind of optical focus as the bitter struggles rage about him. A striking feature is Michael's extremely attenuated appearance; the artist portrays him as very slender. This might be a reference to the spiritual identity of the figure, but also a deliberate nod to the Early Netherlandish painting style and its figural ideal. In its multi-figural confusion, the painting holds many surprises for the attentive viewer. As much as the demons are assembled at random out of human heads and animal bodies, nevertheless we find natural forms and figures appearing in great numbers in the picture, as if the artist were presenting a kind of cabinet of curiosities – a *Wunderkammer* – of flora and fauna. The wing feathers, an open mussel, butterfly wings, puffer fish – whatever he depicts, Bruegel fascinates through his precise study of nature. An impressive feature is the river extending from the foreground into the aureole of light in the background. Angels and devils wrestling tirelessly with one another mirror Bruegel's interest in Hieronymus Bosch (*c.* 1450–1516), to whom we owe similar pictorial inventions. But Bruegel's demons are not from Hell; they are portrayed as grotesque natural forms, creatures that are rebelling against Creation. The panel thus impresses not so much through awesome fear as through amazement at the kaleidoscopic diversity of nature's forms.

The Fall of the Rebel Angels came to the Musées royaux after it had been purchased in 1846 from the private collection of Félix Stappaert (1812–1885). The transaction took place under the assumption that Pieter Brueghel the Younger had painted the picture. Soon afterwards, it was ascribed to Hieronymus Bosch. It was not until the date was discovered in 1894, bottom left on the oak panel, that Pieter Bruegel the Elder was finally specified as creator of the work. Although no copies or earlier mentions of the painting have ever been found, scholars have never seriously contested this assessment.

See also pp. 173–174, 182, 185, 188, *210/211*.

LITERATURE: Gibson 1977, pp. 99–101; Marijnissen 1988, pp. 180–186; Roberts-Jones 2002, pp. 104–114; Pawlak 2011b; Sellink 2012, pp. 174–175; Meganck 2014

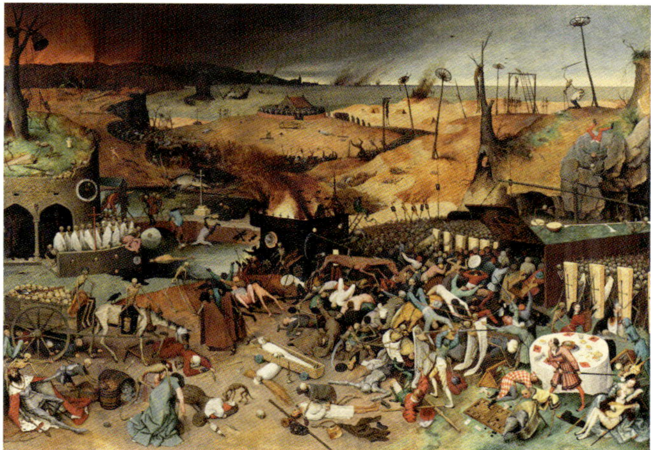

8

8

The Triumph of Death, *c.* 1562
Oil on wood, 117 x 162 cm (46 x 63 ⅞ in.)
Madrid, Museo Nacional del Prado,
Inv. P01393

The Triumph of Death is one of the artist's eeriest pictorial inventions. A small group of people have withdrawn to the right-hand foreground to fight against the mighty army of Death. Their struggle is in vain, as shown by the multitude of people struck down by the all-powerful adversary.
In the tradition of the danse macabre, Bruegel endeavours to portray the classless dimension of the event. At the left edge, we see a dying king, who, though distinguished by all the regalia of power, is mockingly being handed an hourglass by Death. Another skeleton falls upon an earthly treasure, piled up in a bushel. Directly next to this we see a mother lying face down still holding a child her arms, but being sniffed by an emaciated dog. On the right, a nobleman is about to draw his sword to join the fray, while at the far edge a pair of lovers make music together. Bruegel's composition also seems intended to bring together all known religions. Thus a collapsing cleric is being held by a skeleton who, like him, is wearing a cardinal's hat, while on the left next to the table, a man wearing a turban has been struck down. We see a bloated corpse floating in a small stream in the centre ground, while a fleeing young woman is held back by Death. Bruegel's richness of invention knows no limits, and we could go on and on discovering ever more nightmarish scenes. Everything happening in the picture is inevitable; there can be only one winner. The threatening sky intimating impending nightfall also alludes to a gloomy outcome. Death devours everything and everybody. As illustrated here, and not only by those being executed in the background on the gallows and on the wheel, he behaves like

man himself. Death, too, catches human beings with his nets and massacres them in battle.

The panel measures 117 x 162 cm (46 x 63 ⅞ in.) and is not signed. Because of the identical dimensions to *The Fall of the Rebel Angels* (Cat. 7) and stylistic features, a date around 1562 is generally accepted. The attribution to Bruegel has never been seriously questioned, despite the missing signature. Karel van Mander's *Schilder-Boeck* of 1604 contains a description of a painting which depicts all the means directed against death. Gustav Glück rejects this conclusion; it might refer to the *Triumph of Death*, but the mention he cites in an inventory of estate compiled in 1614 in Antwerp cannot be securely identified with the original because of the existence of several copies (Glück 1932, p. 43).

The earliest mention of the painting stems from an inventory compiled in 1774 of the Palacio Real de La Granja de San Ildefonso, which kept the collection of the Spanish queen Isabel de Farnesio (1692–1766). It entered the Prado in 1827.

See also pp. 174–175, 178–179, *196/197*.

LITERATURE: Gibson 1977, pp. 109–119; Marijnissen 1988, pp. 195–200; Gibson 1991, pp. 53–86; Roberts-Jones 2002, pp. 98–104; Pawlak 2011b; Sellink 2012, pp. 176–177.

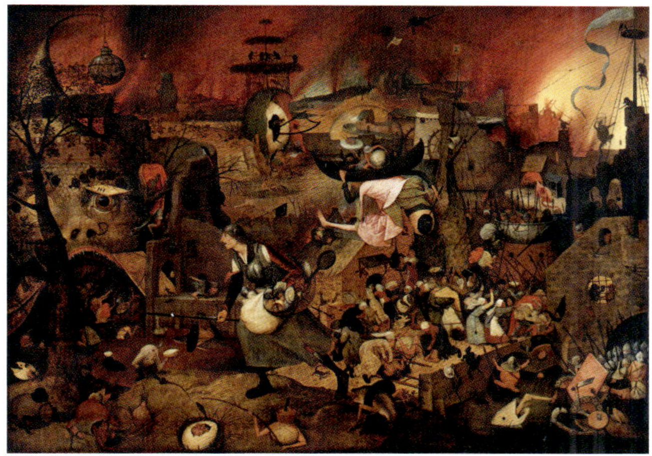

9

9
Dulle Griet (Dull Gret), 1563
Oil on wood, 117.4 x 162 cm (46 ¼ x 63 ⅞
in.), inscribed b. l. (barely legible):
[…] MDLXI[.]
Antwerp, Museum Mayer van den Bergh,
Inv. MMB.0045

With resolute stride an over-sized shrew slashes
her plundering way through the scene. Armed
with cuirass, helmet and gauntlets, she has
collected a booty of bags and baskets full of
silver and gold, and under her arm she carries
a large box. The teeming confusion of human
beings and grotesque creatures makes it difficult
to discern whom she is threatening with her
sword, though we see crowds of armed demons
bursting out of a multitude of openings before
and behind her.

Even though her wide open, staring eyes glare
at a point outside the composition, Dull Gret
seems to be moving towards the fish-like muzzle

of the monster in front of her on the left.
Behind her, a great mob of armed women have
rallied to join the looting and to fight further
monsters. Moreover, there is a remarkable figure
in the centre, similar in dimensions to the main
figure in the foreground. It is a man in women's
clothes seated on a roof ridge trying to balance
a boat filled with demons on his back. Out of
his widely gaping anus he is shovelling great
amounts of money that is being caught in a
basin by one of the enraged women. A second
woman has climbed a ladder so as to be able
to empty the man's wallet, which is hanging
down.

Besides numerous allusions to proverbs and
the topsy-turvy world that can be found in
other pictures by Bruegel, the panel impresses
most through its colouring. This applies especially to the sky, swirling with smoke and
illuminated at the right edge by a spectacular
fire in a burnt-out cityscape. While the infernal
background is mostly composed in red and

yellow, the foreground is dominated by a multitude of brown tones, accentuating the desolation of the scene.

The first interpretation of the content was suggested by Karel van Mander, who spoke of a looting expedition to Hell, the booty of which Dull Gret is dragging with her. Subsequently, however, no other composition by Bruegel has presented scholars with comparable interpretative problems. The last attempt by Pawlak sees the protagonist as a travesty of St Margaret of Antioch and refers to dramaturgical links to Christ's Harrowing of Hell. With recourse to the *Manual of a Christian Knight* by Erasmus of Rotterdam (1466/67/69–1536), the scene in addition seems to be a self-created Hell, out of which there can be no escape for Dull Gret, whose looting expedition is repeated en masse in the background.

At 117.4 x 162 cm (46 ¼ x 63 ⅞ in.), the panel's size differs little from those of *The Fall of the Rebel Angels* and *The Triumph of Death*

(Cat. 7, 8). The closeness to the works that are also stylistically related was affirmed by the restoration in 2018. For instance, the date became visible while cleaning the painting. The work dates from 1563 and was thus produced during Bruegel's time in Brussels.

Karel von Mander presumed in his *Schilder-Boeck* of 1604 that the picture was already owned by Rudolf II at this time. In fact, Count Simon VI of Lippe (1554–1613), the emperor's art agent, seems to have endeavoured to buy the painting before it was sent to the emperor as a gift of Frisian merchants, who had beaten him to the sale.

An inventory of the Imperial Collections drawn up in Prague in 1631 also lists a corresponding work. After the Hradjin was plundered by Swedish troops in 1648 during the Thirty Years' War, the picture entered the collection of Queen Christina (1626–1689), together with *The Massacre of the Innocents* (Cat. 28); she sold it at the latest in 1654. The picture did not appear again until 1894, where it was brought to auction from the private collection of the jeweller Christian Hammer. On the advice of Max Friedländer, the picture was purchased by Fritz Mayer van den Bergh (1858–1901) for only 390 marks.

See also pp. 179, *204/205*.

LITERATURE: Gibson 1977, pp. 102–108; Sullivan 1977; Coo 1978, pp. 33–40; Marijnissen 1988, pp. 187–194; Serebrennikov 1993; Roberts-Jones 2002, pp. 89–97; Gibson 2006, pp. 124–144; Pawlak 2011b; Sellink 2012, pp. 178–179.

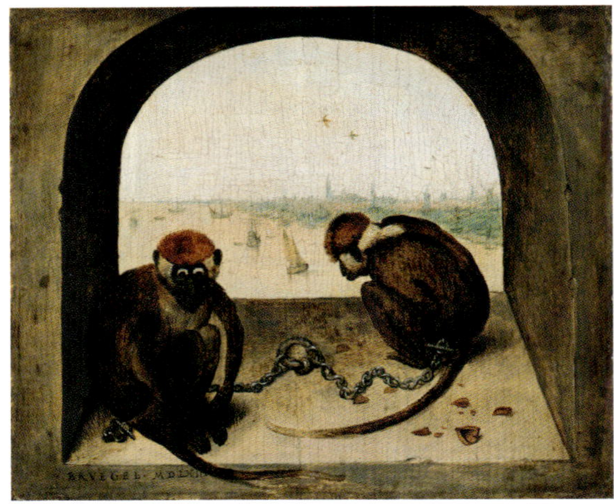

10

10

Two Fettered Apes, 1562
Oil on oak, 20 x 23 cm (7 ⅞ x 9 in.),
inscribed b. l.: BRVEGEL M.D.LXII
Staatliche Museen zu Berlin, Gemäldegalerie,
Inv. 2077

The cabinet format of only 20 x 23 cm (7 ⅞ x 9 in.) suggests a private context in this painting's reception history. Moreover, numerous interpreters have emphasised the composition's immediacy – its content can be summarised in a few words. Two apes are seated on a window sill in a stone window frame. Both animals are fettered by chains on an iron ring fixed in the centre. While the ape on the left fixes the observer with a pitiful look, the head of the monkey on the right is turned away and inclined downwards.

Through the window opening, as if from a great height, we see the sea and a city port in the background, with approaching ships. Two birds, in obvious contrast to the fettered apes, fly freely across the sky. Other details are accentuated through the lighting. Thus the nutshells lying around ignored in the right foreground are distinctly set off from the shadowy window soffit on the left.

A conspicuous feature is the despondency of the animals, with their almost human expression of suffering. Unusual as an autonomous motif in the genre of panel painting, the apes have been interpreted almost without exception as negative. Miserliness, pride, sensual lust, spendthrift waste and quarrelsomeness were considered as the possible key contexts of the scene.

Max Jakob Friedländer, who was then director of the Berlin Gallery of Old Masters, purchased the picture for the museum in 1931. Prior to this it was on offer on the Paris art market, where it had landed from princely Russian ownership. The small panel was entered with ten other works by Bruegel in the estate

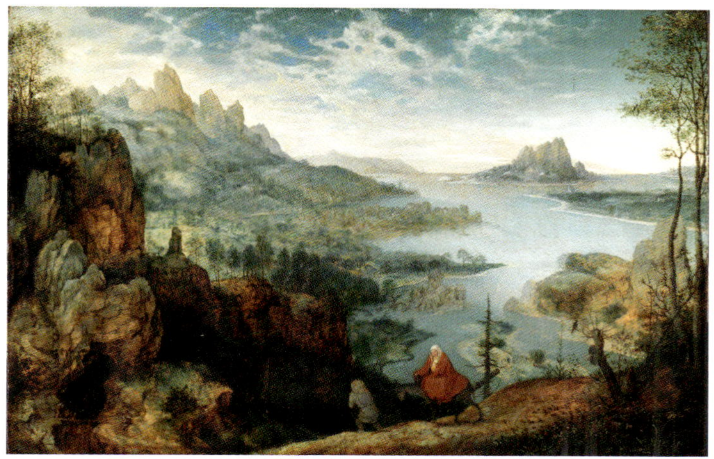

11

inventory, dated 1668, of the Antwerp collector Pieter Stevens. It was described as "La ville d'Anvers avec deux singes" (Glück 1932, p. 46). Although the architecture depicted in the background was unanimously seen by scholars as a veduta of Antwerp, the city silhouette corresponds only in parts to pictures of the great city in contemporary prints.

See also pp. 107–109, *146/147*.

Literature: Berlin 1975, pp. 68–70; Sullivan 1981; Marijnissen 1988, pp. 201–203; Müller 1999, pp. 142–155; Roberts-Jones 2002, pp. 192–193; Sellink 2012, p. 118.

11

Landscape with the Flight into Egypt, 1563
Oil on wood, 37.1 x 55.6 cm (14 ⅝ x 22 in.),
inscribed b. r.: BRVEGEL MDLXIII
London, Courtauld Institute of Art,
Count Antoine Seilern Collection,
Inv. P.1978.PG.47

The small *Landscape with the Flight into Egypt* presents the event described in St Matthew's Gospel (Matthew 2:13) almost en passant at the front edge of the picture. The motif had already enjoyed great popularity in Early Netherlandish painting. The artist places in the foreground the exertion and trials which the travellers have to endure on their long journey. Joseph is descending a steep slope. His faded clothing makes him almost undetectable within the imposing landscape. He is leading the ass bearing his family. The viewer's attention is drawn to Mary. She is wearing a resplendent red cape and holding her child pressed to her body with her left hand. But in the next instant, the Mother of God, seated on the ass, will disappear behind the mountain knoll. Further mountains that the family will have to overcome lie ahead.

This inconspicuous scene is in great contrast to the grandiose landscape perspective. The mountain scenery dominating the left half of the picture is balanced by a plain on the right, through which a broad river flows. Though the picture format is small, Bruegel succeeds in conjuring up a sublime landscape.

The colour gradations of the landscape and likewise the subject are oriented on a painting tradition as established by the artist Joachim Patinir (p. 287). It moreover accords with the early *River Landscape with a Sower* (Cat. 1). As with other landscapes, the rendering of the rocks harks back to Bruegel's impressions during his crossing of the Alps.

The panel is signed and dated on the bottom right edge, though the last two digits of the year are barely legible. It is one of the few works by the artist whose commissioner is known. Bruegel painted the *Landscape with the Flight into Egypt* for the cardinal and art collector Antoine Perrenot de Granvelle (1517–1586). In 1607, the picture was listed in an inventory of the Palais Granvelle in Besançon, before it was bought, possibly by Peter Paul Rubens, whose estate inventory of 1640 contained a picture with the same motif. Further mentions that might refer to the picture point to ownership by the Antwerp senator Pieter Stevens, and after his death in 1668 to its acquisition by the art dealer Diego Duarte (1612–1691). The version in the Courtauld Institute of Art today must have reached England in the early nineteenth century; it was auctioned in 1803 in London.

After several changes of owner, it was purchased in 1939 by Count Antoine Seilern (1901–1978) at the auction of an estate at Christie's. Because he had left his estate in 1978 to the Courtauld, the picture joined the grisaille *Christ and the Woman Taken in Adultery* (Cat. 24) already in the collection, which accordingly now has two works by Bruegel.

See also pp. *44/45*.

LITERATURE: Grossmann 1973, pp. 194–195; Marijnissen 1988, p. 209; Gibson 1989, pp. 66–67; Sellink 2012, p. 186.

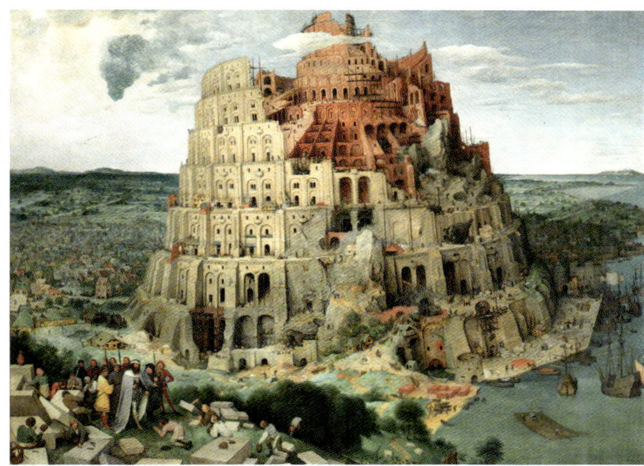

12

12

The Tower of Babel (Vienna version), 1563
Oil on oak, 114 x 155 cm (45 x 61 in.),
inscribed b.l. on a stone block: BRVEGEL.
FE. M.CCCCC.LXIII
Vienna, Kunsthistorisches Museum,
Gemäldegalerie, Inv. GG_1026

Bruegel addressed the problem of monumentality and size in a fair number of his pictures.
His *Tower of Babel* in Vienna is a successful
example, for the building looms up from the
bottom edge of the picture to the clouds border-
ing the picture at the top. Through the consist-
ent contrast of large and small the artist achieves
an evocation of sublimity. The building appears
like a man-made mountain. In the left foreground, we see King Nimrod giving orders to
workers and architects. We are struck by the
general bustle of activity: stones are hewn,
further building materials are transported on
ships and rafts to land, from where cranes heave

heavy loads on high. Like tireless ants, the men
work to finish the building, without noticing
that a grave constructional flaw is taking shape
before their noses. For if we look into the interior of the building we see that the constructed
parts are not aligned centrally to the surrounding walls: disaster will inevitably follow. Re-
gardless of this, Bruegel nevertheless presents
an impressive dramatisation of the building of
the tower described in the Book of Moses
(Genesis 11: 1–9), intensively endeavouring to
convey man's potential and technical mastery
as testified in the imposing building.
This larger version of the two (see Cat. 13) was
first in Niclaes Jonghelinck's (1517–1570) collection, where it can be verified already in 1566
while Bruegel was still alive. The painting came
to the city of Antwerp in the same year as part
of a pledge of sixteen works. Karel van Mander
mentions another larger and yet another smaller
Tower of Babel in 1604 as being owned by Rudolf
II. An inventory entry of 1639 states the work

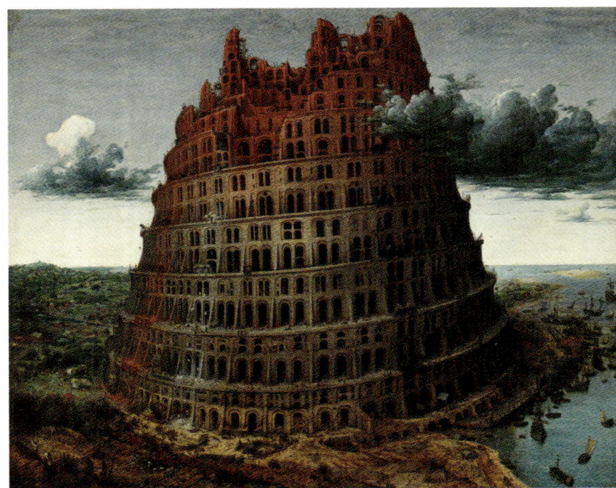

13

originally came into the Imperial Gallery through Archduke Leopold Wilhelm (1614–1662).
See also pp. 123–127, *150/151*.
Literature: Gibson 1977, pp. 93–97; Demus 1981, pp. 76–81; Marijnissen 1988, pp. 210–218; Gibson 1989, pp. 67–68; Seipel 1998, pp. 56–67; Roberts-Jones 2002, pp. 242–251; Sellink 2012, p. 188; Blauensteiner 2014, pp. 173–185.

13

The Tower of Babel (Rotterdam version; also: **The "Small" Tower of Babel**), *c.* 1565
Oil on wood, 59.9 x 74.6 cm
(23 ⅝ x 29 ⅜ in.)
Rotterdam, Museum Boijmans Van Beuningen, Inv. 2443

The Rotterdam version of the Tower of Babel has fewer narrative elements than the Vienna version (Cat. 12). Missing, for example, is the scene with the king; nor is there any visible hint here of the tower's constructional failure. Scholars have always pointed out the closeness of the depicted building to the Colosseum in Rome, from which it adopts the stacked rows of arcading, though it seemingly exaggerates them to great heights. The principle of architectural construction is different from the Vienna version. The tapering, cone-shaped building has a gently ascending surrounding ramp on its outside, providing a continuous ascent from bottom to top. Another interesting feature is the intensity of the artist's thematic focus on the problem of light and shade. While the left side of the building is in the sunshine, the right side lies in the shade of a cloud colliding with the tower and stands out as a dark silhouette against the sky. The rendering of the cloud is impressive, threatening the building as if besieging it. This vividly dramatises the consequences of building the tower, the dark shading of the earthly environment illustrating the prohibited access to the divine sphere. The tower has already reached the sky, as stated in the First Book of Moses (Genesis 11: 4), so that it surpasses the clouds. In both versions, Bruegel succeeds in conveying an impression of the vanity of the building. As technically brilliant as the building might appear, it would take endless time to get from the bottom to the top, suggesting the building's hubris and hypertrophy.

This smaller version of the *Tower of Babel* with a format of 59.9 x 74.6 cm (23 ⅝ x 29 ⅜ in.) arrived at the museum in 1958 as part of the collection of the industrialist and shipping magnate Daniël George van Beuningen (1877–1955). The picture appeared on the Paris art market in 1935 and was purchased by the Amsterdam collector Dr Nicholas Beets. Prior to this, it was probably in Spain, as is supported by a stamp impressed on the rear of the panel with an alliance coat of arms of a Spanish queen and the relevant Latin inscription. Probably the work was intended as a gift of

the Austrian Habsburgs to a Spanish queen, which lends credence to its being the smaller *Tower of Babel* which Karel van Mander described in 1604 as being owned by Rudolf II. See also pp. 127, 131, *164/165*.

LITERATURE: Gibson 1977, pp. 93–97; Marijnissen 1988, pp. 219–222; Gibson 1989, pp. 67–68; Roberts-Jones 2002, pp. 242–251; Sellink 2012, p. 189.

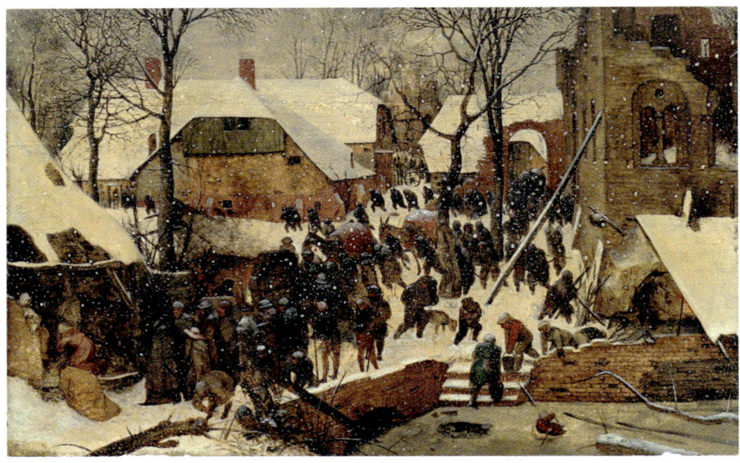

14

14

The Adoration of the Kings in the Sow, 1563 or 1567
Oil on wood, 35 x 55 cm (13 ⅞ x 21 ¾ in.),
inscribed b.l.: M.D.LXIII BRVEGEL
Winterthur, Oskar Reinhart Collection
"Am Römerholz"

Bruegel's *Adoration of the Kings in the Snow* is
a technical showpiece in its portrayal of a great
crowd of people in thick-falling snow. Heavy
flakes are falling, the colour and light creating
a scene dominated by a leaden sky. We do not
discover the Adoration scene at the left edge
until relatively late. It remains unnoticed by
the crowd while they busy themselves with
their everyday winter tasks. At the right edge
we see the ruins of a church, which has to be
supported by a stout beam. The roof is missing,
so a huge mound of snow has piled up inside,
reaching up to the window. Another noticeable
feature is the anonymity of the people in the

picture, some representing the kings' retinue,
others belonging to the village community,
without the groups really being distinguishable
from one another. Finally, there is the stage-like
structure of the picture, which shows us a kind
of marketplace with four bare trees at the sides.
Here we can also detect the loaded pack
animals, undoubtedly allotted to the kings'
entourage. Scholars until now have dealt less
with the striking iconography than with
Bruegel's evocation of atmosphere, his ability
to create such an effect with earthy nuances
of colour.

With a format of 35 x 55 cm (13 ⅞ x 21 ¾ in.),
The Adoration of the Kings in the Snow is not
only one of Bruegel's smallest pictures but also
one of his most copied. There are more than
thirty known examples, most of which stem
from the workshop of his son, Pieter the
Younger. Only *Winter Landscape with Skaters
and Bird Trap* (Cat. 23) enjoyed a similar popularity. The dating is preserved only as a fragment

next to the signature, which is why 1567 has been proposed as the date as well as 1563. The earlier date has become generally accepted because of the infrared analyses of the panel, which makes *The Adoration of the Kings in the Snow* the earliest preserved winter landscape by Bruegel.

There is a number on the back of the panel (No 243) that accords with an entry in the estate inventory of the Cologne banker Eberhard Jabach (1618–1695) from the year 1669 – the earliest mention of the painting. This version must consequently have come into the ownership of the Silesian aristocratic dynasty of Saurma before it was put on sale in 1930 by the Paul Cassirer Gallery in Berlin and purchased by Oskar Reinhart (1885–1965). Prior to this, Reinart had been endeavouring to purchase *The Hay Harvest* (*June/July*; Cat. 19) – now in Prague – from the Lobkowicz Collection.

See also pp. 319, 323–325, *336/337*.

LITERATURE: Gibson 1977, pp. 148–149; Marijnissen 1988, pp. 308–309; Roberts-Jones 2002, pp. 176–177; Reinhard-Felice 2003, pp. 69, 198–200; Sellink 2012, p. 190.

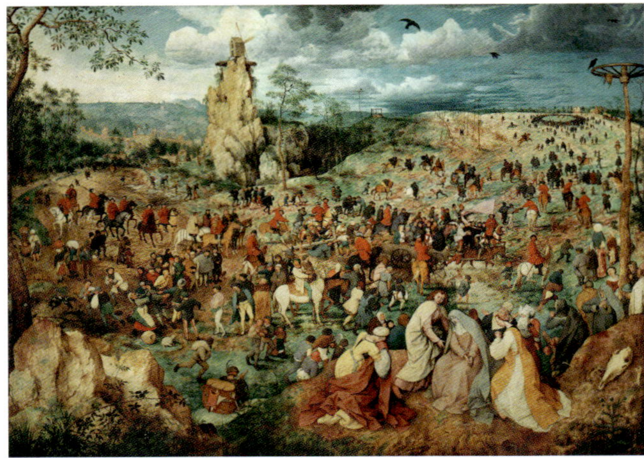

15

15

The Procession to Calvary (Christ Carrying the Cross), 1564
Oil on oak, 124 x 170 cm (48 ⅞ x 67 in.),
inscribed b. r.: BRVEGEL. MD.LXIIII
Vienna, Kunsthistorisches Museum,
Gemäldegalerie, Inv. GG_1025

With a format of 124 x 170 cm (48 ⅞ x 67 in.), *The Procession to Calvary* is not only Bruegel's largest painting; among the "wimmel pictures" with their teeming crowds it is also his most intensive work. Because of the multitude of scenes, the observer sees Christ only at second glance; he has fallen under the cross in the direct centre of picture. The artist thus marginalises the history of salvation. A striking group is that of the Virgin Mary and St John in the right foreground. Over and above this, the panoramic effect must also be remarked on: people and soldiers are underway from the city to the place of execution, while a storm gathers on the horizon, as is stated in the Bible. Emblematic of the whole composition is a hawker in the foreground, shifted slightly out of centre towards the left, for whom everything has turned into an entertaining spectacle. Above the figure we see a steeply ascending rock, on its pointed top a windmill. The function of the needle rock is comparable to that of the wheel hub around which the Passion event is revolving. Scholars have frequently referred to links to Early Netherlandish painting and in particular to Rogier van der Weyden's (1399/1400–1464) *The Descent from the Cross* (p. 121). Also the skull and the vegetation are elements of the iconography of the Passion that can already be found in the Early Netherlandish tradition.

The signed and dated panel was possibly produced as a commission from the Antwerp merchant and art collector Niclaes Jonghelinck; it belonged to his collection in February 1566 along with fifteen other works by Bruegel.

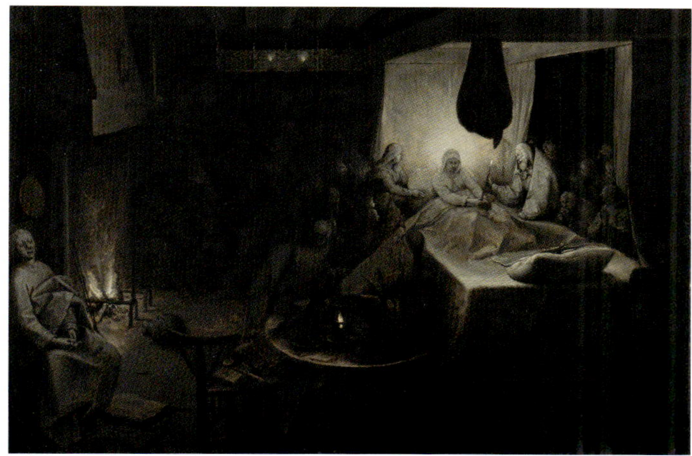

16

In the same year, the collection was transferred as part of a pledge to the ownership of the city. It is probable that the work was purchased in 1594 by Archduke Ernst; his estate documents of 1595 mention a Crucifixion. This is supported by Karel van Mander's statement that a *Procession to Calvary* belonged to Rudolf II's collection as early as 1604. After Ernst's death, the emperor had ordered many pictures from his brother's ownership to be transferred to him in Prague. The picture was mentioned in 1781 in Pressburg/Bratislava, and in 1783 as being in the Gallery in Vienna.

See also pp. 118–121, 123, *142/143*.

LITERATURE: Gibson 1977, pp. 123–133; Demus 1981, pp. 81–86; Marijnissen 1988, pp. 223–232; Falkenburg 1993; Gregory 1997; Meadow 1997a; Seipel 1998, pp. 68–83; Müller 1999, pp. 136–142; Roberts-Jones 2002, pp. 36–44; Sellink 2012, pp. 191–192.

16

The Death of the Virgin
(also: **Dormition of the Virgin**), *c.* 1564
Grisaille, oil on oak, 36.8 x 55.6 cm
(14 ½ x 22 in.), inscribed: BRVEGEL,
date faded and illegible
Banbury (Warwickshire), Upton House,
National Trust, Inv. 446749

The death, or Dormition, of the Virgin Mary is not described in the Bible, but is based on a narrative in the *Legenda aurea* (The Golden Legend, a medieval collection of religious stories). It is of small format – but the largest of the three preserved grisailles by Bruegel – and is signed, but the date is no longer legible.

It is assumed that the painting dates from around 1564, thus close in time to the grisaille likewise devoted to a Christian theme, *Christ and the Woman Taken in Adultery* (Cat. 24). The Death of the Virgin Mary was a frequent motif in Early Netherlandish painting. Here, however, Bruegel bases his picture on the graphic tradition. Furthermore, the small format suggests it was intended as a gesture of friendship, thus a work for a befriended humanist for his personal devotions.

The first owner of the painting – today in Upton House, Banbury – was Abraham Ortelius (1537–1598), who in addition commissioned Philipp Galle (1537–1612) in 1574 to make an engraving of the picture so he could pass the motif around among his friends. Among the latter was Dirck Volkertsz. Coornhert (1522–1590), whose poem of gratitude written in 1578 has been preserved. Several copies, among them a coloured version, are known from Pieter Brueghel the Younger. Later the painting was purchased by Isabella Brant (1591–1626) and entered in the inventory of 1641 compiled after Rubens' death. Rubens himself made a copy of the composition. The work must have subsequently ben taken to England, where it changed owners several times in the first half of the twentieth century, before Walter Samuel, Second Viscount Bearsted (1882–1948), transferred it, together with Upton House, to the National Trust in 1948.

See also pp. 239–240, *245/246*.

Literature: Glück 1930, pp. 284–286; Grossmann 1952, pp. 221–223; Stechow 1974; Gibson 1977, pp. 132–134; Marijnissen 1988, pp. 236–237; Melion 1997; Roberts-Jones 2002, pp. 134–138; Sellink 2012, p. 194.

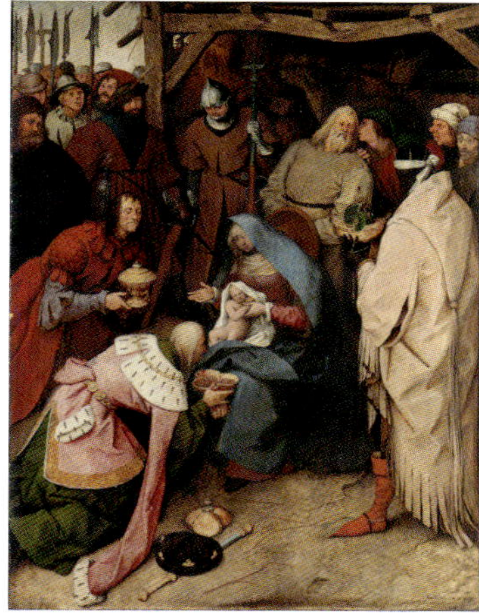

17

17

The Adoration of the Kings, 1564
Oil on wood, 111 x 83.5 cm (43 ¾ x 32 ⅞ in.)
Inscribed b. r.: BRVEGEL M.D.LXIIII
London, The National Gallery, Inv. NG3556

Bruegel's *The Adoration of the Kings* has a singular place in his oeuvre owing to its vertical format. The event is presented in a steeply ascending pictorial space filled with many figures. In the foreground, we see the three kings laying their gifts before the Christ Child, who is seated on a swaddling cloth on his mother's lap. The kings' bodies are attenuated, in keeping with a figural ideal of the Late Middle Ages. This also applies to the Madonna, whose head is very small in relation to her body. Some interpreters have tried to read specific details as intentionally verging on caricature – for instance, the overlong sleeves of the king on the left and his much too large headgear placed on the ground. A noticeable feature is

that the black king at the front on the right is not directing his gaze to the Christ Child but seems immersed in self-contemplation. He is holding an exquisitely decorated vessel in his hands, shaped like a ship known as a cog with a crown set on it. In the background, we see various ancillary figures; the man with the thick spectacles is especially conspicuous at the right edge. The scene immediately next to him, showing a young man whispering into Joseph's ear, is also painted with dramatic impact. Further details we might mention are the armed soldiers, with precisely reproduced hauberks and crossbows. The stable is very dark, but we can pick out the ass and the saddle, placed on a beam, upon which the Virgin Mary rode to Bethlehem.

Archduke Ernst, younger brother of Rudolf II and at the time Governor of the Netherlands, bought a painting in 1594 together with Bruegel's *Children's Games* (Cat. 5) and a painting of the Virgin Mary, of which we know only

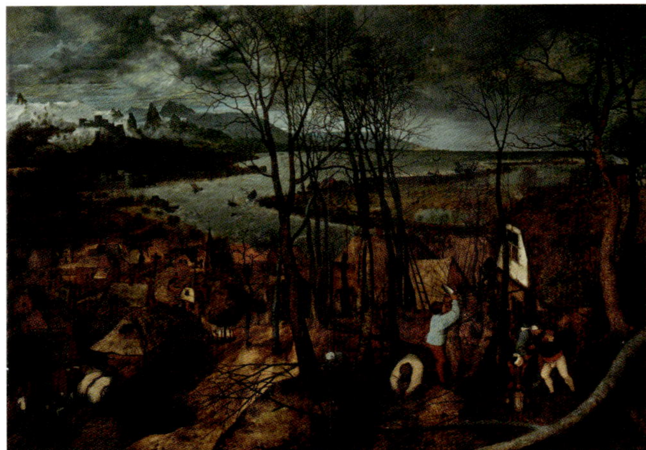

18

the title and the purchase price. Today it is assumed that *The Adoration of the Kings* is identical with the work now in London. It was included in an inventory in 1619 of the Imperial Collection in Vienna, which also named the artist; parts of Ernst's collection were transferred there after his death in 1595. The picture did not appear again until the late nineteenth century, in a private collection in Vienna, and was offered for purchase to the Imperial Gallery, which, however, did not acquire it. In 1920, it came via another collector to London and was taken into the holdings of the National Gallery. See also pp. 112–113, 117–118, *141*.

LITERATURE: Davies 1968, pp. 21–22; Gibson 1977, pp. 133–134; Marijnissen 1988, pp. 233–235; Pinson 1994; Müller 1999, pp. 126–134; Sellink 2012, pp. 196–197.

18
The Gloomy Day (February/March), 1565
Oil on oak, 118 x 163 cm (46 ½ x 64 ¼ in.),
vestiges of signature and date:
[BRVEGEL MDLX]V
Vienna, Kunsthistorisches Museum,
Gemäldegalerie, Inv. GG_1837

The darkness dominating the panel hinders the observer's direct access to the subjects. The storm clouds hang like a shroud portending calamity over the bleak, pre-spring landscape. That Bruegel was in no way painting a night scene here is proven above all by the protagonists arranged on a rise on the right, the colour of their clothing setting them off distinctly from the background. They also provide the clues for placing the event in the context of the series of months (see Cat. 19–22).
For instance, a man in red hose and blue jerkin is cutting willow wands, which are being bundled together by a helper bending down behind

him, while farther left, a third person is gathering faggots – all these are activities belong to
the month of March in the calendar tradition.
People in a group on the right also present a
plausible late-winter scene. A peasant, obscenely
conspicuous through his codpiece, is merrily
eating waffles; his female companion clinging
on to him bends over them avidly. The group
is completed by a child costumed in cushions
and a cowbell. Although the lad is holding a
lantern, it will scarcely brighten up the day for
him since his paper crown has slipped low over
his face. A similar fate is experienced by the
man half hidden by the group, who, though
he has planted a candle on his broom, has his
head stuck in a cooking pot. The scene recalls
a similar group in *The Fight between Carnival
and Lent* (Cat. 4). *The Gloomy Day* has been
interpreted as a representation of the months
of February and March, not least because of
the seasonal classification of the depicted
events.

Common to the revellers and the workers is
their ignorance of the brewing storm. Neither
do they pay any attention to the tree that has
fallen down in the immediate foreground. The
heedless attitude of the dramatis personae
towards the deteriorating weather can also be
seen in the other villagers performing their tasks
at the foot of the hill. Boorish actions and
pleasures are once again juxtaposed to the rural
daily grind. The central, steeply ascending trees
ensure that the foreground scenes are vertically
separated from one another. But in the background of the composition the storm is already
unleashes its full fury. Gales and rain have
caused the river to burst its banks, threatening
to flood the village and the fortress on the left.
On the right, the dykes cannot withstand the
sea, which now surges over the polders, forcing
a cowherd to flee. In the estuary, some ships
are about to capsize and even sink in the face
of the tumultuous floods. The gloomy background scene, as well as the rural activities in the

foreground, have been noted in the literature as having a precedent in an illustration in a book of hours, which anticipates numerous motifs in the picture, but lacks the calamitous intensity of Bruegel's picture. Meanwhile there is a small yet remarkable detail which stands out distinctly because of its colouring. In the space between two trees and above the farmers mowing the meadows we see a white bird flying against an almost black sky. This might well be an allusion to the Flood; a white dove circling above the ark is the attribute that introduces the relevant iconography. Bruegel's painting corroborates this by the suggestion of a church steeple on the horizon on a vertical axis with the bird, establishing a profoundly significant link between these images.

The Gloomy Day belongs to the paintings produced in 1565 for Niclaes Jonghelinck's series of months, which are also documented in Leopold Wilhelm's collection after being presented in 1594 to Archduke Ernst and transferred to Rudolf II. They eventually entered the Gemäldegalerie in Vienna.

See also pp. 283–285, *290/291*.

LITERATURE: Gibson 1977, pp. 146–159; Demus 1981, pp. 94–95; Marijnissen 1988, pp. 252–278; Gibson 1989, pp. 69–74; Seipel 1998, pp. 84–113; Falkenburg 2001; Goldstein 2001; Herold 2002; Roberts-Jones 2002, pp. 152–175; Kaschek 2012; Sellink 2012, pp. 201–211.

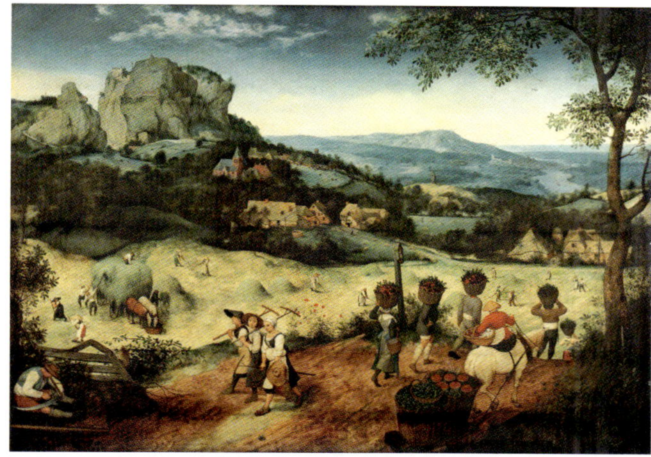

19

19

The Hay Harvest (June/July), 1565
Oil on wood, 114 x 158 cm (45 x 62 ¼ in.),
apocryphal signature removed in 1931, only a
trace remains of the original
Prague, Palais Lobkowicz

If we compare *The Hay Harvest* with the compositional scheme of the other paintings in the months series (Cat. 18, 20–22), what immediately strikes the eye is the conventional interpretation dependant on painting tradition. In design, Bruegel's version of early summer is clearly based on models from the first half of the sixteenth century. This applies especially to the means he uses to create the sense of depth in the landscape through colour nuances. For example, he paints the foreground – which is dominated by land labourers on a road – mainly in brown tones, while the mown meadows of the middle ground shine out in bright yellow. Meanwhile, the settlements and

woodlands situated behind are rendered in glowing and eye-catching green. In this Bruegel painting, too, the right-side landscape merges into the open sea, which in turn touches on the horizon. To the left of this, mountains and rock formations continually elevate the vantage point. Like the plain below, which is intersected by a river valley, the mountains are kept in delicate blue that is mirrored in a clear spring sky interspersed with a few cumulus clouds. It is the only month picture by Bruegel that demonstrates the triple structuring of three landscape levels by means of colour established by Patinir and his successors (p. 287). Nevertheless, earlier works by Bruegel manifest very similar reminiscences (see Cat. 1, 11). The steeply rising rock in the background on the left might be included here, dotted with several practically inaccessible buildings.

The viewer's attention, however, is drawn by the working countryfolk, most of them mowing a meadow and bringing the fruits of their labours home. Thus we see several folk with baskets full of cherries on their heads, while a rider pulls her rich harvest behind her on a sledge. Countrywomen strike with their rakes in the opposite direction, the middle one unashamedly gazing at the viewer. Represented here within the cycle are the months of June and July, as confirmed by several motifs in the picture that were already associated with this period in the calendars of books of hours. This is corroborated not only by the actions of the countryfolk, but also by the archery show in the village centre at the rear.

The Hay Harvest, measuring 114 x 158 cm (45 x 62 ¼ in.), is only a little smaller than the other panels used for the series. The series originally consisted of six pictures and was painted by Bruegel in 1565 for the Antwerp tax official Niclaes Jonghelinck, who commissioned the large-format landscapes for the adornment of his house. Only a year later, however, he was forced to transfer sixteen works by the artist to the city of Antwerp as part of a pledge. Among the paintings, which he was subsequently unable to redeem, were the Vienna *Tower of Babel* (Cat. 12) and also the series of months. In 1594, the city of Antwerp made a gift of the six panels to the nominee Governor Archduke Ernst, which was no doubt the reason they subsequently came into the possession of Rudolf II.

However, the inventory of Archduke Leopold Wilhelm made in 1659 mentions only five works from this series. In 1809, *The Hay Harvest* was acquired by Countess Leopoldine Grassalkowitsch (1776–1864) and passed into the Lobkowicz Collection at Raudnitz Castle in Roudnice nad Labem, where the painting was first documented in 1870. With the German Occupation (1939–1945), the entire Lobkowicz family estate was confiscated and, in the course of the special Linz Commission, the painting was claimed for the planned Führer Museum.

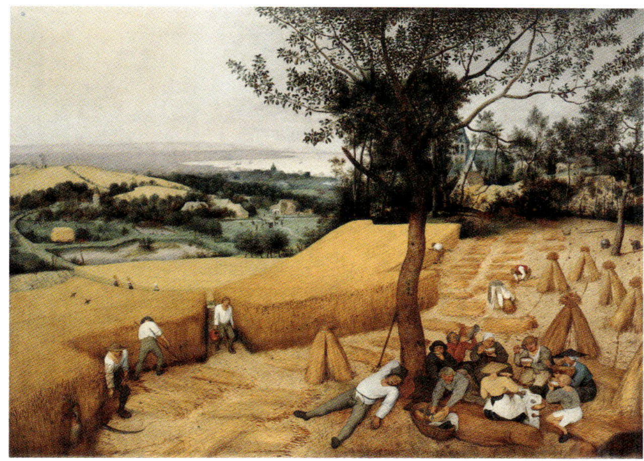

20

After the restitution of the collection in 1945, it was confiscated yet again by the State in 1948, and was hung in the Prague National Gallery. Today the painting is owned once more by the family and is on show in the Palais Lobkowicz in the Prague Castle.

See also pp. 283–285, *296/297*.

Literature: Gibson 1977, pp. 146–159; Demus 1981, pp. 86–94; Marijnissen 1988, pp. 252–278; Gibson 1989, pp. 69–74; Seipel 1998, pp. 84–113; Falkenburg 2001; Goldstein 2001; Herold 2002; Roberts-Jones 2002, pp. 152–175; Kaschek 2012; Sellink 2012, pp. 201–211.

20

The Harvesters (August/September), 1565
Oil on wood, 119 x 162 cm
(46 ⅞ x 63 ⅞ in.),
inscribed b. r.: BRVEGEL / [MD]LXV
New York, The Metropolitan Museum of Art, Rogers Fund, 1919, Inv. 19164

From a slightly elevated vantage point, the viewer's eye roams over a far-flung landscape stretching out beyond a broad cornfield. The high summer harvest is in full swing. In the left lower corner two harvesters with scythes are busy mowing the corn. Bruegel has captured the swinging cut of the sickle with great care, the stalks bending to the side under its impact. In this way, he also draws attention to the jug standing in the field, visible only to the viewer but not to the harvester; he is bound to shatter it in the next instant.

Launching out from this point, the eye roams along the edge and upward in a dynamic diagonal line into the right half of the picture, where another harvester is about to bind the mown crops into sheaves. In the foreground of this scene, other harvesters are resting under a pear tree. Seated on sheaves, they eat their meal out of bowls and baskets; a man steps towards them from out of the field path, carrying more jugs. Behind the resting group, our attention is caught by a large church building seen through the thick stock of trees. Another harvester to the left of the tree has fallen into a deep sleep. His mouth wide open and his legs apart, he has stretched himself out in a pose transferred by Bruegel two years later onto one of the figures in his *Land of Cockaigne* (Cat. 30). Nevertheless, in his obesity and total passivity he can be seen here in *The Harvesters*, too, as a negative embodiment of human vice, not least in the juxtaposition to the hardworking harvesters surrounding him.

While the central tree creates a clear vertical division for the picture, the structural depth is achieved more subtly, especially in comparison with Bruegel's *Hay Harvest* (Cat. 19), which is aligned completely in the tradition of the triple-ground construction. Accordingly, the yellow of the crops dominating the foreground merges into a landscape imbued with green, followed by a hill with another cornfield. In the background, an elongated bay extends under a hazy sky, with unrigged sailing boats and a coastal town. A haywain bulging with crops stands out distinctly on the left in front of the green middle ground. The route of the draught animals seems to be leading towards the nearby village; on closer examination, we see several people before it, gathering for a game. To the left of this, people are bathing in a pond, a motif also associated with the month of August in the Duc de Berry's book of hours.

Like the other paintings in the months series, *The Harvesters* is signed and dated 1565. The designation bottom right was not discovered until 1920, when the picture was cleaned after its purchase by the Metropolitan Museum of Art, and a later addition was removed. After the commissioning patron Niclaes Jonghelinck had had to transfer the series to the city of Antwerp in 1566, the pictures were given to Archduke Ernst in 1594 and went to Rudolf II's collection after the former's death. However, the inventory of his heir, Archduke Leopold

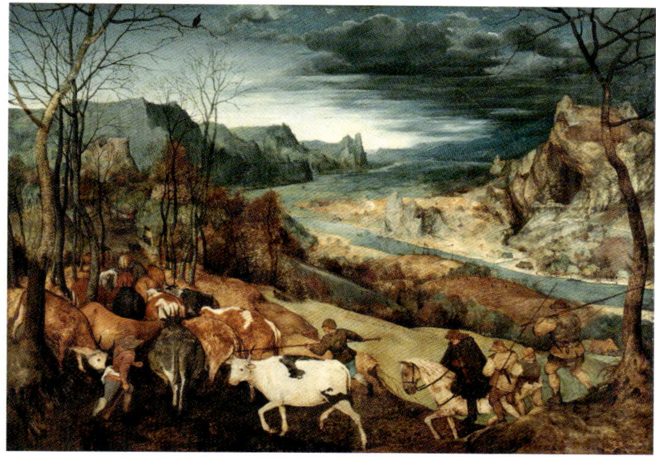

21

Wilhelm, drawn up already in 1659, mentions only five works from this series. But *The Harvesters* is one of those still verified until 1809 in the Imperial Collection, before it was acquired by Antoine-François Andréossy (1761–1828), the French Governor of Vienna, who sold it in Paris in 1816. In 1912, it went to Brussels and was purchased there in 1919 by the New York Metropolitan Museum of Art. See also pp. 284, *302/303*.

LITERATURE: Gibson 1977, pp. 146–159; Demus 1981, pp. 86–94; Marijnissen 1988, pp. 252–278; Gibson 1989, pp. 69–74; New York 1998, pp. 386–391; Seipel 1998, pp. 84–113; Falkenburg 2001; Goldstein 2001; Herold 2002; Roberts-Jones 2002, pp. 152–175; Kaschek 2012; Sellink 2012, pp. 201–211.

21
The Return of the Herd (Autumn; also: October/November), 1565

Oil on oak, 117 x 159 cm (46 x 62 ⅝ in.), traces of a signature b. l. in the corner: (BRVEGE[L])
Vienna, Kunsthistorisches Museum, Gemäldegalerie, Inv. GG_1018

As with the other works in the months series (Cat. 18–20, 22), the action is played out mainly in the foreground, which we view from a slightly elevated vantage point. In this context, *The Return of the Herd* seems particularly hazardous here as a title – the livestock is merely being driven along a narrow section along the front edge of the painting. Behind them the landscape falls steeply into a low-lying river valley in the middle ground. Although the herd's route leads downwards from the mown meadows, the viewer's perspective is directed diagonally upwards towards the hamlet on the left, no doubt the destination of the cowherds. The action points to autumn, as do the colours and the vegetation. The trees through which the cattle are being driven are already bare, the green of the meadows has given way to fallow brown, yellow and ochre tones. Steep rocks loom up on both sides of the river; they are crowned on the right by a threatening bank of cloud, though the clear sky on the left is also dominated by cold blue tones. A place of execution with gibbet and wheels is silhouetted on a rise above the river. In contrast to the previous paintings in the months series, no model possibly referred to by Bruegel is known for this painting.

The herd is followed by a small group of men consisting of a leader on a dappled horse and three lance bearers behind the rider. Arthur Haberland (Haberland 1952, pp. 48–49) related the scene on the right, and with it the picture, to a concrete date: livestock in the Alps is traditionally driven down from the mountain pastures on St Gall's Day, the same day the tithes were collected. It is also plausible that the rider was a hunter with his retinue, as represented in calendar sheets as an embodiment of the month of November.

The Return of the Herd, painted on commission of Niclaes Jonghelinck, was given by the city of Antwerp to the then Governor Archduke Ernst in 1594 as part of the originally six paintings in the series, and became part of his estate in the collection of Rudolf II. The picture was subsequently inherited by Archduke Leopold Wilhelm, thus remaining in Habsburg ownership. An inventory of 1659 names only five of the pictures; then, in 1781, a new cycle was compiled in the Belvedere in Vienna, which contained just one more of the original series besides *The Return of the Herd* and *The Hay Harvest* (Cat. 19). The other parts of the series remaining in Vienna were first mentioned again in 1884, after being discovered in the depot. See also pp. 284–286, *306/307*.

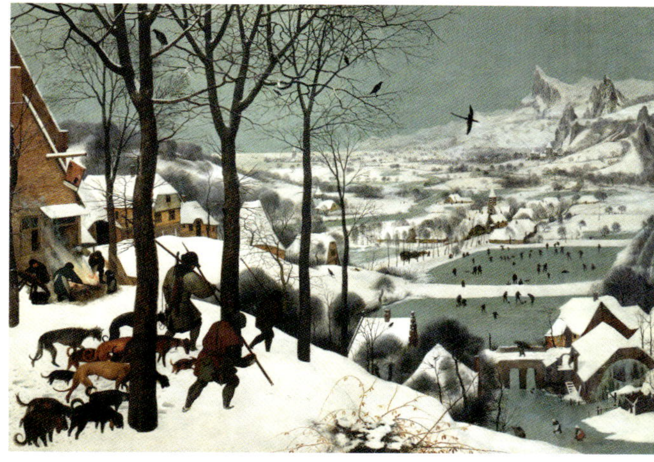

22

LITERATURE: Gibson 1977, pp. 146–159; Demus 1981, pp. 95–99; Marijnissen 1988, pp. 252–278; Gibson 1989, pp. 69–74; Seipel 1998, pp. 84–113; Falkenburg 2001; Goldstein 2001; Herold 2002; Roberts-Jones 2002, pp. 152–175; Kaschek 2012; Sellink 2012, pp. 201–211.

22

The Hunters in the Snow (Winter; also: **December/January**, or **The Return of the Hunters)**, 1565
Oil on oak, 117 x 162 cm (46 x 63⅞ in.), inscribed l. c.: BRVEGEL. M.D.LXV
Vienna, Kunsthistorisches Museum, Gemäldegalerie, Inv. GG_1838

With shouldered lances and lowered heads, the three hunters return to the village through the snow. The yield from the fox hunt preceding their return is frugal; despite their large pack of hounds, they have bagged only a fox. Thus the pack of hounds following them are famished, too, and hanging their heads; one of the dogs seems to have stopped and turned towards us. The view of the men, and with them of the observer, leads from the rise downwards onto a proverbial winter landscape. Snow and ice dominate this world in which mankind stands out only as a dark and teeming hither and thither in front of a backdrop mainly denuded of colour. Besides the white of the snow, the predominant hue is the bluish-green of the murky sky, a colour also used for the iced ponds. The reduced colouring of the world depicted here, in which everything seems to be at peace, is the main factor in enhancing the overall harmonious impression. Numerous interlocking lines in the picture space steer the viewer's attention to the details of the composition. The eye is at first led across the ascending landscape far into the distance, where on the left a river plain is suggested, extending towards the sea, and then on to a steep, craggy mountain range looming up on the right. But the eye is likewise guided from the roof eaves on the left, over the hunters' lances and down the slope, where the villagers frolic in winter pastimes or attend to their everyday tasks – though the latter have come almost to a complete standstill in this water-based culture; even the mill wheel has long been frozen. The most striking attribute of movement is seen in a magpie, seemingly gliding downwards through the scene, its black figure silhouetted as a dark cross in the sky. Another detail placed directly next to the hunters seems to have escaped their attention. Villagers have kindled a fire in front of an inn called "Dit is inden Hert" (This is in the stag) and have fetched a sheaf of straw, a table and a tub in their efforts to defy the icy cold. But how quickly heat thus generated can become hazardous is revealed in the direction in which the flames are licking – a danger seen in the valley, where a chimney is on fire and has to be extinguished.

Despite the impression harmony, if we look at the picture more closely, we clearly see the heedlessness of the protagonists, shown in the borrowing of motifs from *The Ship of Fools* by Sebastian Brant (1457/58–1521). The folk in the valley are literally skating on thin ice and so in danger; this is manifest in a detail set not by chance near the centre. Here Bruegel has placed a bird trap with a bird close to it, which corresponds in size more to the people on the ice than to its fellows in the trap; a similar parallel setting is also seen in Bruegel's small painting *Winter Landscape with Skaters and Bird Trap*, dated the same year (Cat. 23).

The panel is signed and dated on the bottom edge near the bramble bush placed in the centre. Like the other paintings in the series (Cat. 18–21), *The Hunters in the Snow* was produced in 1565 to a commission from Niclaes Jonghelincks. Following its presentation as a gift to Archduke Ernst in 1594, and his death a year later, the series entered the collection

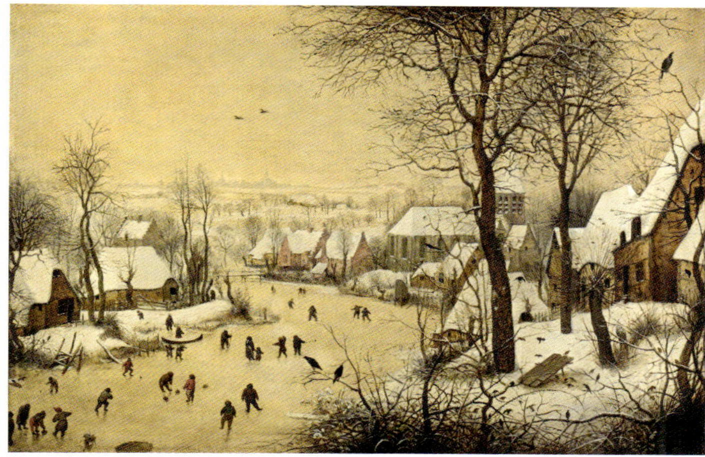

23

of Rudolf II. Only five pictures in the series are listed in an inventory of Archduke Leopold Wilhelm's collection made in 1659. The picture is not mentioned again in the catalogue of the Gemäldegalerie until 1884, accompanied by the note that in the interim it was stored in the depot.

See also pp. 284–285, *310/311*.

Literature: Gibson 1977, pp. 146–159; Demus 1981, pp. 99–103; Marijnissen 1988, pp. 252–278; Gibson 1989, pp. 69–74; Seipel 1998, pp. 84–113; Falkenburg 2001; Goldstein 2001; Herold 2002; Roberts-Jones 2002, pp. 152–175; Kaschek 2012; Sellink 2012, pp. 201–211.

23

Winter Landscape with Skaters and Bird Trap, 1565

Oil on oak, 37 x 55.5 cm (14 ⅝ x 21 ⅞ in.), inscribed b. r.: BRVEGEL / M.D.LXV

Brussels, Musées royaux des Beaux-Arts de Belgique/Koninklijke Musea voor Schone Kunsten van België, Inv. 8724

Winter Landscape with Skaters and Bird Trap dates to 1565 and thus to the same year as the series of month (Cat. 18–22). In contrast to the large-format paintings, this depiction of a winter's day belongs to the group of pictures in which Bruegel adopted a cabinet form: the painting, today in Brussels, is only 37 x 55.5 cm (14 ⅝ x 21 ⅞ in.). And yet it is one of the artist's most frequently copied works. No fewer than 127 copies are known, which tells of the high estimation the picture already enjoyed around 1600. A particularly outstanding feature is the colouring, capturing a sunny winter's day with people having fun on the ice. Here we can question the significance of the striking fact that Bruegel has made the birds and the people the same size. Surely the birds are not the only creatures to be threatened by the trap; are the people not in danger, too, skating on thin ice? We might see the bird top right in this context: its portrayal is remarkable for its size, and it seems to be crying out a warning. The Bible frequently compares the human soul to a bird and the devil to a bird catcher, which opens up the possibility of a Christian interpretation. At first we see the exuberant frolics of the folk on the ice and their delight at the unhampered movement, only then to discover the bird trap and impending danger.

Because so many copies of this painting were made, it is difficult to track the original to the first collection to which it belonged. It is probably documented in 1687 as "Een wintertge van den ouden Brueghel" (A winter scene by Brueghel the elder) in the inventory of an Amsterdam art dealer. It was not rediscovered until 1927, by Friedländer and Lambotte; the painting was shown in the same year in an exhibition in London. At first still part of Dr Delporte's private collection, the picture is now on loan in the Musées royaux des Beaux-Arts de Belgique.

See also pp. 330, 332–333, *342/343*.

Literature: Gibson 1977, p. 148; Marijnissen 1988, pp. 279–282; Maastricht/Brussels 2002, pp. 160–172; Roberts-Jones 2002, pp. 44–48; Kaschek 2011, pp. 13–18; Sellink 2012, pp. 212–213.

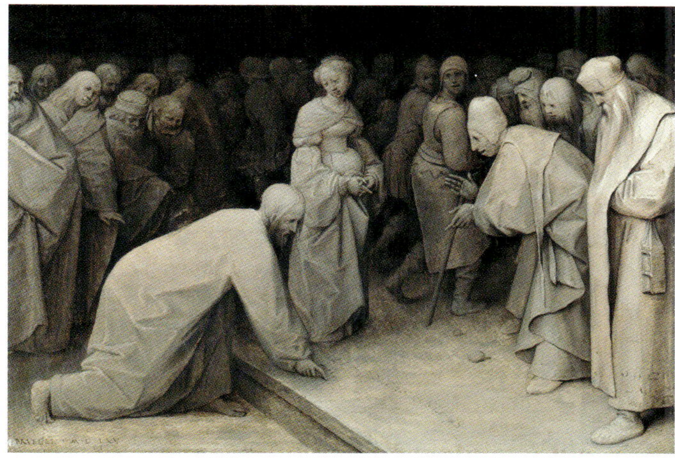

24

24
Christ and the Woman Taken in Adultery, 1565
Grisaille, oil on wood, 24.1 x 34.4 cm
(9 ½ x 13 ⅝ in.), inscribed b. l.:
BRVEGEL.M.D.LXV, Flemish inscription
in centre (near the hand): DIE SONDER
SONDE IS / DIE [St John 8: 7]
London, Courtauld Institute of Art, Count
Antoine Seilern Collection, Inv. P.1978.PG.48

The biblical source for the subject of this painting is to be found in the Gospel of St John, verses 8: 3–11. The theme had been highly topical since the Reformation, as it addresses the issue of an old and a new religion. The picture reflects this visually to a certain extent in that the rabbinic scholars are placed on the right, confronting the kneeling figure of Christ. Bruegel has attached pseudo-Hebrew letters to the bottom hem of the priest's robe. He has cunningly staged the action to culminate in a

dramatic moment. Signature and date are clearly legible on the bottom left half of the picture and correspond to the characteristic stylistic peculiarities of Bruegel after 1558. Corresponding to this moment, Jesus has written in the foreground "Let him who is without sin, […]", which can easily be completed by the observer with the missing "[…] cast the first stone". The grisaille was thought lost until rediscovered in 1952. The composition was known until then in many copies and a copper engraving of the same size made in 1579 by Pieter Perret (1555–1639; p. 230). The compass traces on the edges of the original suggest that the painting served as direct template for reproduction. After Bruegel's death, the work at first remained in the family. His son Jan (1568–1625) placed it at the disposal of Cardinal Federico Borromeo (1564–1631), who had previously endeavoured in vain to acquire an original by Bruegel; the Cardinal had a copy made of the grisaille. Subsequently, the work went back to the family;

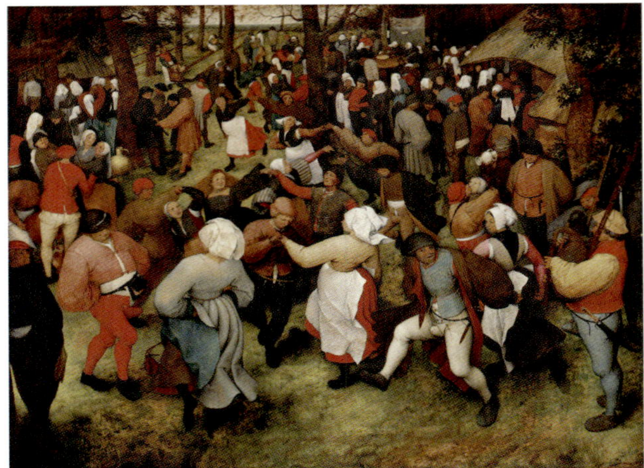

25

further ownership is not clear until 1952, when it was put up for auction by anonymous owners at Christie's. In this way the grisaille entered the collection of Count Antoine Seilern und Aspang, who had already purchased Bruegel's *Landscape with the Flight into Egypt* in 1939 (Cat. 11). Both works in his estate were transferred in 1978 into the ownership of the London Courtauld Institute of Art. The grisaille was stolen from there in 1982 and was not recovered until ten years later, at a renewed attempt to auction it at Christie's.

See also pp. 230–231, 233–236, *242/243*.

LITERATURE: Grossmann 1952; Grossmann 1961; Gibson 1977, pp. 134–139; Marijnissen 1988, pp. 288–289; Roberts-Jones 2002, pp. 138–139; Sellink 2012, p. 214; Melion 2014, pp. 1–41.

25
The Wedding Dance, *c.* 1566
Oil on wood, 119.4 x 157.5 cm (47 x 62 in.), dated b.l.: M.D.LXVI.
Detroit, Michigan, Institute of Arts,
Inv. 30374

The painting shows a crowd of women and men caught up in an energetic dance. At the front edge on the right, we see two bagpipers beating out the rhythm for the party. Perhaps we can also identify the bride among the dancing couples in the girl with her hair down and wearing a wreath. It is of course impossible to decide whether her older partner might be her father. On the same horizontal level we can discern a couple kissing lustily, and directly above them a man doing justice to a large tankard of beer. There is a barn on the right and to its left a table, at which two elderly women are seated. Behind them we see a sheet hanging up, the bridal crown in its centre. The place between the two women – which should be reserved for the bride – is empty. This makes it all the more plausible that she is among the dancers. The dance in turn has a distinctly erotic dimension, demonstrated in the ostentatious codpiece of the musician on the right and the thick-lipped man in red hose on the left, whose jerkin is almost bursting over his belly. He is thrusting his arms to the side and moving, as challenging as he is provocative, towards the young, dancing girl. An amusing detail is seen in the couple on the right. The man steps ahead and from behind pulls his pretty partner with his right hand while he touches her behind with his left hand. Alcohol is playing a role in enhancing the participants' mood, as we see in the many drinking vessels discernible among the crowd.

In order to do justice to the large number of revellers in his portrayal, Bruegel has created a picture space that ascends continuously from the front to the back. He intensifies the impression of a dense throng even more by placing the horizon directly underneath the top edge of the picture and moreover depicts a tree on the right as a margin for the scene. The picture aims to capture the heaving hither and thither of the protagonists. Even observers find themselves in medias res, their eye given no respite, one couple after another crop up unceasingly to be followed and studied.

Besides all the dancing, Bruegel also depicts lively conversations between men and women, their heads close together. In addition, we can discern couples who have already absented themselves from the wedding company, and men who have to relieve themselves and urinate against house walls. Bruegel borrowed many of the motifs from early German graphic works on the subject of peasant life, developed by artists like the Nuremberg Beham brothers (pp. 268/269).

With its size of 119.4 x 157.5 cm (47 x 62 in.), the dimensions of the panel diverges very

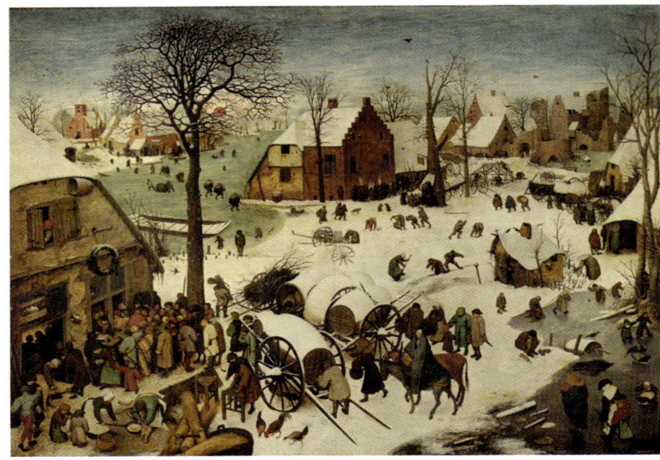

26

little from those of the Vienna peasant feasts of a later date. The painting was first purchased in 1930 on the London art market; prior to this it was in an English private collection. Thus the composition was known solely through several preserved copies until the late attribution of this version to Bruegel.

See also pp. 260–261, 265–266, *184/185*.
Literature: Scheyer 1965; Gibson 1977, pp. 159–162; Marijnissen 1988, pp. 293–295; Gibson 1991, pp. 11–52; Roberts-Jones 2002, pp. 256–260; Silver 2006, pp. 117–119; Sellink 2012, pp. 228–229.

26

The Census at Bethlehem, 1566
Oil on oak, 115.5 x 163.5 cm (45 ½ x 64 ⅜ in.), inscribed b. r.: BRVEGEL / 1566
Brussels, Musées royaux des Beaux-Arts de Belgique/Koninklijke Musea voor Schone Kunsten van België, Inv. 3637

We are looking at the centre of a Flemish town, its inn placed conspicuously in the left third of the picture. A great throng of people have gathered in front of the building, waiting to be registered for the census. Bruegel has here aspired to capture everyday life in winter characteristic of such a community. We see children playing, romping in a snowball fight or sliding on small sledges across the frozen pond. Behind the crown of a leafless tree the ruddy-glowing Sun is just setting on the horizon. It will soon be dark and bitter cold. Shifted slightly to the right of centre we see Joseph, a saw on his shoulder and leading an ass on which Mary riding. They have arrived in Bethlehem unnoticed by the crowd. The inn is full; this is suggested by a man in the upper part of the building who is about to close the shutters to keep out the intensifying cold.

It is interesting how Bruegel manages not only to enrich the biblical story with genre-type elements, but uses them as illustration of part of the story. The observer is challenged to go beyond the capturing of a moment and to look for the stable where Mary and Joseph will spend the night and the Christ Child will come into the world.

The picture was originally in the collection of the family of Van Colen Bouchot. The family are recorded as being in Antwerp from 1542, so a commission for the work is at least plausible. The picture came to the museum in 1902 through an auction of the Edmond Huybrecht estate.

See also pp. 317–319, *348/349*.

LITERATURE: Gibson 1977, pp. 144–145; Marijnissen 1988, pp. 296–303; Maastricht/ Brussels 2002, pp. 134–148; Roberts-Jones 2002, pp. 180–187; Sellink 2012, pp. 230–231; Bell 2015, pp. 259–263.

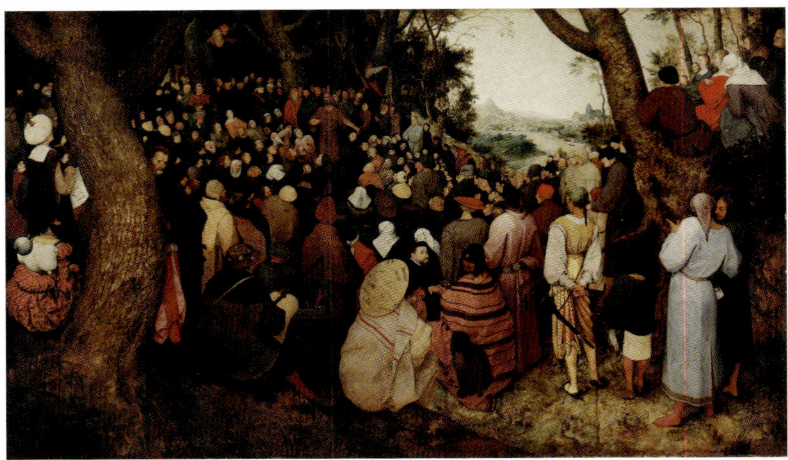

27

27

The Sermon of St John the Baptist, 1566
Oil on oak, 95 x 160.5 cm (37 ½ x 63 ¼ in.),
inscribed b. r.: BRVEGEL M.D.LXVI
Budapest, Szépművészeti Múzeum,
Inv. No. 51.2829

In his *Sermon of St John the Baptist* of 1566,
Bruegel again remains true to his favourite
device of shifting the key scene into the
background and therefore simultaneously
miniaturising it. St John, preaching, is in the
middle of the great throng of people and only
perceptible on closer study. He is shifted
slightly to the left of the vertical axis. Bruegel
has conceived not only a democratic sermon
here, whereby at all estates and classes are
present, but also one that seems to address all
religions. So our attention is drawn to the
Ottoman Turk in a turban standing at the left
edge, likewise the Catholic pilgrim of St James
of Compostella seated next to a mighty tree

trunk, or the Chinese man in the middle. Next
to him, a Mongolian is about to read the palm
of a burgher in patrician garb crouching before
him. Deaf to the words of St John, he seems
more interested in the prediction of his future.
At the far right edge we detect two monks,
one of them pointing his finger in John's
direction.

Bruegel has endeavoured to capture multiple
reactions to the apostle's words, whether ostentatious rejection manifested in the form of arms
folded across the chest, or attentive listening.
Moreover, it seems that some people have been
led to this remote place out of sheer curiosity.
Bruegel portrays grandparents, parents and
their children, armed men, rich and poor, the
whole world seems to be attending the sermon.
In the background on the right we see the
course of a river and detect the Baptism of
Christ in miniature form as frequently interpreted already in Early Netherlandish painting.
Particularly successful in execution is the motif

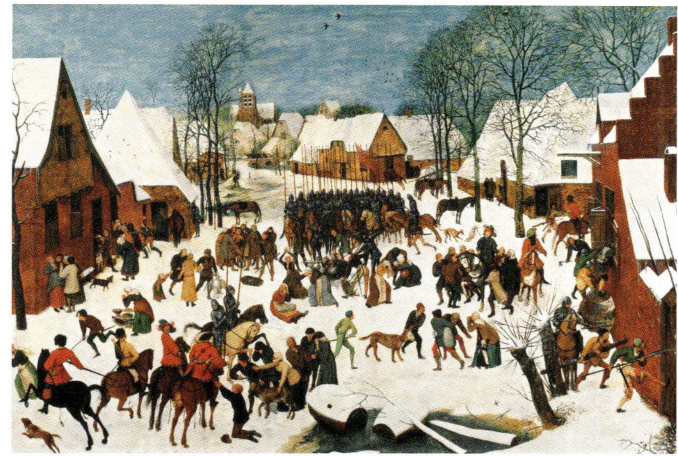

28

of a mighty tree trunk on the left, its bark reproduced with meticulously observed precision. A landsknecht (mercenary) stands here gazing in the direction of the observer, as though just noticing his arrival.

The earliest mention of the picture is in an estate inventory compiled between 1633 and 1650 after the death of Isabella Clara Eugenia of Spain (1566–1633), Governor of the Spanish Netherlands. Subsequently, the work came into the ownership of the noble dynasty of Batthányi and then entered the museum in Budapest. See also pp. 132–136, 138, *166/167*.

Literature: Gibson 1977, p. 144; Marijnissen 1988, pp. 304–307; Roberts-Jones 2002, pp. 251–255; Marijnissen 2003; Sellink 2012, pp. 232–233; Bell 2015, pp. 256–263.

28

The Massacre of the Innocents, *c.* 1565–1567
Oil on oak, 109.2 x 158.1 cm (43 x 62 ¼ in.)
London, Royal Collection, Inv. 405787

Karel van Mander gives us a very precise description of the painting in 1604 in his *Schilder-Boeck*. It testifies to the brutality of Bruegel's original version of the slaughter of the Bethlehem infants described in the Gospel of St Matthew (2: 16). He tells of a mother who begs a herald for the life of her child, but he obeys the king's decree and shows no mercy. In the present version of the painting, this occurrence can only be guessed at. The location is a recognisably Flemish village landscape in winter, presented in a wide-ranging overview taking up two-thirds of the picture space. In front of the blue sky, major looting seems to be occurring. Emerging from a dense throng of Spanish soldiers in the middle of village green, Wallonian soldiers and Flemish infantrymen are about to break down doors, rob people and slaughter animals. But all these motifs were overpaintings made later, masking the actual subject intended by Bruegel. This can be imagined only by comparing it with later copies, fourteen alone by Pieter Brueghel the Younger. His best version in Vienna was long thought to be the original (p. 325). On it we can see the scenes described by van Mander, in which parents beg soldiers for the life of their children, infants are slaughtered, and mothers mourn their dead bodies. The oak panel measures 109.2 x 158.1 cm (43 x 62¼ in.) today, but it has been cropped at the bottom edge, which explains the lost signature. Originally the picture must have had a similar size to the *Census at Bethlehem* (Cat. 26), dated 1566, and a similar dating is plausible. Karel van Mander already conjectured that the painting was in Rudolf II's ownership. A *dorfblinderung* – "village plundering" – by Bruegel is mentioned in the Prague Treasure Chamber and Art Cabinet in 1621 and 1647/48. Consequent to the looting

of the Prague collection in 1648, the work arrived in Sweden, where it is named in 1652 in the collection of Queen Christina. After her abdication and during a trip to Rome in 1654, Christina left parts of her art treasures in Brussels and Antwerp, among them *The Massacre of the Innocents*. In 1656, it was first purchased by William Frizell, who re-sold it in 1660 to the exiled English King Charles II (1630–1685). Two years later the picture was documented in the Palace of Whitehall in London, where it stayed during the reign of James II (1633–1701, r. 1685–1688/89). It was stored in Hampton Court during the reign of Queen Anne (1665–1714, r. 1702–1714), in Somerset House in 1714, and then probably in Kensington; after a sojourn in Windsor, the picture went back to Hampton Court in 1901.

See also pp. 325–330, *350/351*.

LITERATURE: Gibson 1977, pp. 140–144; Marijnissen 1988, pp. 283–287; Roberts-Jones 2002, pp. 128–134; Sellink 2012, pp. 234–235.

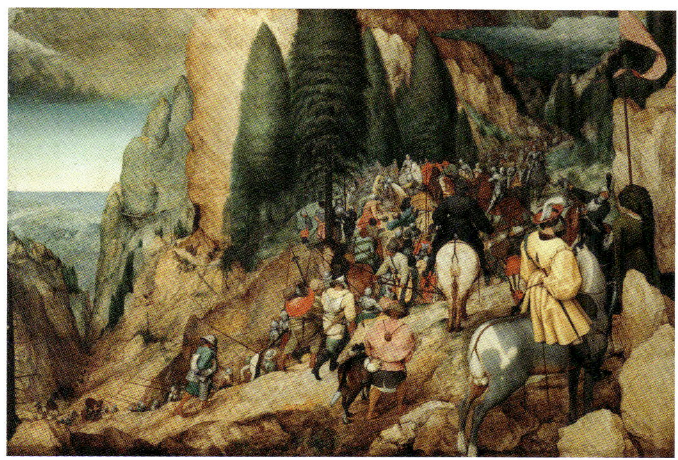

29

29

The Conversion of St Paul, 1567
Oil on oak, 108 x 156 cm (42 ⅝ x 61 ½ in.),
inscribed b. r. on the rock: BRVEGEL.
M.D.LXVII
Vienna, Kunsthistorisches Museum,
Gemäldegalerie, Inv. GG_3690

In a long column on a narrow path, a large
army winds its way up a high and imposing
mountain range. The steeply towering rocks
dominate practically the whole of the picture
space; the peaks tower far beyond the top of
the picture. This applies as well to the top of a
larch tree growing out of the immediate centre
of the picture, dividing the composition vertically into two halves. Only the left half of the
picture grants us a view onto the area from
which the soldiers are unerringly climbing.
Behind a radiantly illuminated green landscape,
we see the sea with sailing ships. The blue
sky above is crowned with clouds, which

seem baulked by the steep mountain ridges.
Meanwhile, the right half of the picture is
defined by a dense and uncoordinated throng
of commanders, riders and infantry. The path
taken by the military procession follows a diagonal through the picture space towards a
constantly narrowing passage until it comes to
a point in the top right-hand corner. In this
way, Bruegel stages an ingenious mise-en-scène
that can be read as a "whence – whither" scenario. We look as it were into the gorge and
turn our eyes in order to look ahead. Scarcely
any light falls into the rocky gorge which the
soldiers are approaching; it is interspersed with
low hanging clouds.
Confronted by this imposingly staged natural
backdrop, the eponymous event of the conversion of St Paul is given a secondary role. To the
right of the larch, and thus slightly off centre,
we see, at the height of the horizon, that a horse
has fallen. Its rider is also lying on the ground,
his back to the viewer. The fall must have just

happened – the man thrown off the horse has just slid his foot out of the stirrup of the slipped saddle and his arm is still grabbing at the reins. Two men are about to rush over to help him, while others ask anxiously how the fall could have happened. Only the faces of the few figures distributed in the background reveal what has occurred. They are staring at the garish beams of light shooting down between the trees onto the horse and the fallen man. They must have dazzled the rider beforehand – this is perceptible in the gesture of the man who is standing in front of the horse and holding his hand before his eyes so as not to be temporarily blinded, like Saul.

On account of its date, 1567, the picture has frequently been related to political events of the day. This is made especially plausible by the group of people in the foreground on the right and most notably by the rider dressed in black. He has his back turned to the observer, but seems quite aware of the scene happening around Paul. This scene has been interpreted by identifying Fernando Álvarez de Toledo Duke of Alba (1507–1582) with the man in black; he had been appointed Governor of the Spanish Netherlands in 1567 and had crossed the Alps on his way northwards.

The painting is one of the works by Bruegel purchased by Archduke Ernst in 1594 after being appointed Governor. The purchase price recorded for *The Conversion of St Paul* was 320 guilders. After Ernst's death, the picture was transferred to Rudolf II's collection, as mentioned by Karel van Mander. Further inventories from the years 1718 and 1737 likewise refer to the painting, which first entered the Imperial Collection in Vienna from Prague in 1876.

See also pp. 372–373, *392/393*.

Literature: Gibson 1977, pp. 180–182; Demus 1981, pp. 104–107; Marijnissen 1988, pp. 310–315; Seipel 1998, pp. 114–121; Roberts-Jones 2002, pp. 140–143; Sellink 2012, pp. 239–240.

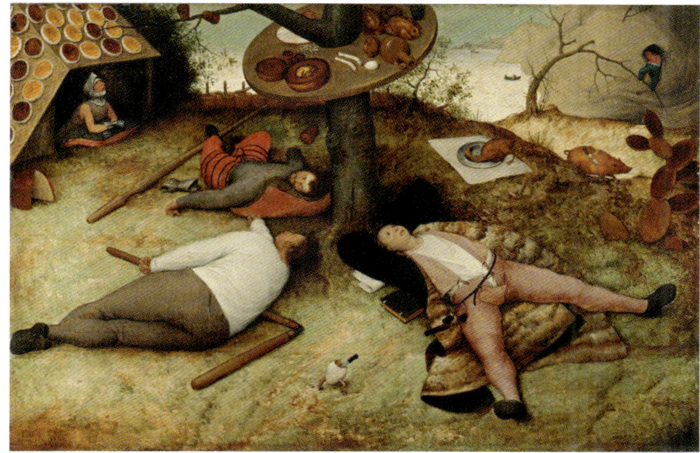

30

30
The Land of Cockaigne, 1567
Oil on oak, 51.5 x 78.3 cm (20 ⅜ x 30 ⅞ in.),
inscribed b. l.: M.DLXVII / BRVEGEL
Munich, Bayerische Staatsgemälde-
sammlungen, Alte Pinakothek, Inv. 8940

Cockaigne is imagined as a caricature of Paradise, where people succumb to all conceivable
culinary delights, enjoyed as a gift without their
doing anything in return. The theme enjoyed
a certain popularity after the Reformation;
Bruegel's rendering shows a curious world of
earthly pleasures as had been described already
in a Dutch poem from the year 1546. In the
Land of Cockaigne, animals run around already
roasted and pancakes grow on rooftops. Access
is granted solely to those who have eaten their
way through a huge pile of buckwheat porridge
beforehand, a task the man at top right has
just managed to perform. But the scene is
dominated by the three male figures in the

foreground, who are lying like wheel spokes
under a centrally placed tree. They are characterised through their clothing and attributes
as representatives of different social classes,
but they are all alike in having helped themselves to the treats scattered around Cockaigne – manifest in their ponderous and
bloated bodies. Only the gourmand in the
foreground on the right – identified as a humanist by his books and writing materials –
manages to imbibe just one drop more from
the jug being tipped over his head. Meanwhile,
knight and peasant have long fallen asleep
over their respective attributes, a lance and a
threshing flail. The impression of total passivity is reinforced by a scene in the background on the left, where another soldier is
gaping open-mouthed at the low-hanging roof
of a house as though waiting for the pancakes
lying there to drop straight into his mouth.
The harmonious composition is remarkable
for its restrained use of colour. Only the

soldier's red hose and cloak set an accent in a landscape otherwise defined by brown, green and ochre hues.

The identification of Cockaigne as a negative symbol of idleness and sloth can be found in a copper engraving of around 1560 by Pieter Baltens (*c.* 1527–1584). Its interpretation already contains a moral message; we see people of different social classes placed around a tree trunk. Bruegel follows this, but places the heads of the protagonists nearer to the tree trunk, reinforcing the impression of a turning wheel – a ploy he uses to allude to the Wheel of Fortune and the unpredictability of human fate. Furthermore, a political interpretation of the painting has repeatedly been conjectured; its date of production, 1567, coincided with the entry of the Duke of Alba into Brussels, who was to introduced repressive measures against the uprisings in the Southern Netherlands. The work is first mentioned in 1621 in an inventory of Rudolf II – the painting belonged to his

Prague collection. In 1648, during the Thirty Years' War, Sweden plundered the Prague Gallery, and as a result the panel went to Sweden. *The Land of Cockaigne* was acquired for the Alte Pinakothek in 1917 at the auction of R. Kaufmann's collection.

See also pp. 367–369, 372, *392/393*.

LITERATURE: Gibson 1977, pp. 178–180; Marijnissen 1988, pp. 333–337; Frank 1991; Roberts-Jones 2002, pp. 238–241; Sellink 2012, p. 242.

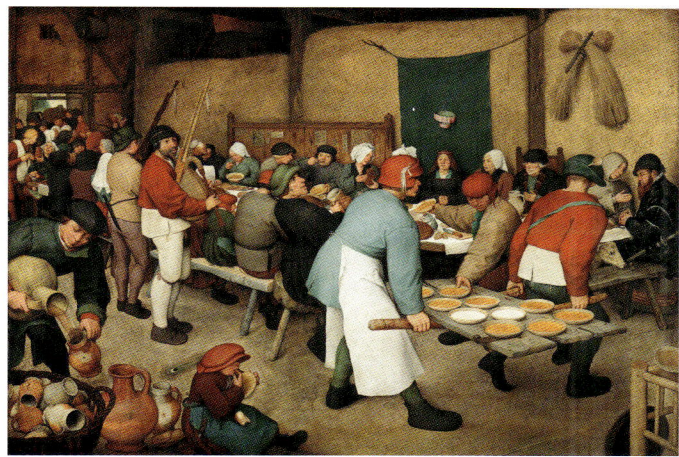

31

31

The Peasant Wedding, *c.* 1568
Oil on oak, 114 x 164 cm (45 x 64 ⅝ in.)
(cut at bottom, then patched with a
5 cm piece)
Vienna, Kunsthistorisches Museum,
Gemäldegalerie, Inv. GG_1027

In a high interior extending diagonally into the picture's depth a festive society has gathered at a long table to celebrate a wedding. Musicians keep the crowded throng at the table entertained, while a constant stream of new guests enters through the door on the left – we have the feeling that the free space in the foreground will soon be filled with people. The party is obviously located in a village – seen not only in the boorish appearance of the characters who are waiting on; at second glance it becomes clear that the wall in the background consists of pressed bales of straw – the party is being held in the barn. The bride is seated at the table in contemplative mood and with her hands clasped together; she stands out clearly under a greenish-blue cloth fastened to the wall.

In keeping with tradition, the bridal crown is hung over her head. The artist has a different treatment for the groom – he cannot be identified with certainty – whereas he pays special attention to the portrayal of the over-proportioned persons in the foreground. Two men are bringing an unhinged door serving as a large tray carrying an array of dishes; these are handed round by the guest at the head of the table. A child has sat down at the front, oblivious to all else as he eats his gruel. Meanwhile, the man conspicuously positioned at the left edge is in charge of filling the ale tankards. In the literature on *The Peasant Wedding*, there are frequent references to his function and its possible iconographic allusion to the Wedding Feast at Cana (p. 259).

Archduke Ernst purchased the picture in 1594, the year he was appointed Governor of the

Spanish Netherlands. The notes of his private secretary Blasius Hütter reveal the purchase price as 160 guilders. The painting went to Vienna with Ernst's estate and accordingly to Rudolf II's court in Prague. It was described in 1659 in Archduke Leopold Wilhelm's inventory and later inherited by Leopold I (1640–1705); it thus re-entered imperial ownership and was eventually transferred into the Viennese collection.

The missing signature and date might have been due to the fact that the bottom edge of the panel has been cropped. A piece measuring around 5 cm was patched on later, possibly in order to restore the original format.

See also pp. 253–254, 257–258, 260, *274/275*.

LITERATURE: Gibson 1977, pp. 161–166; Demus 1981, pp. 110–115; Marijnissen 1988, pp. 316–326; Gibson 1991; Weismann 1992; Seipel 1998; pp. 128–137; Roberts-Jones 2002, pp. 264–271; Majzels 2003; Müller 2005; Sellink 2012, pp. 244–245.

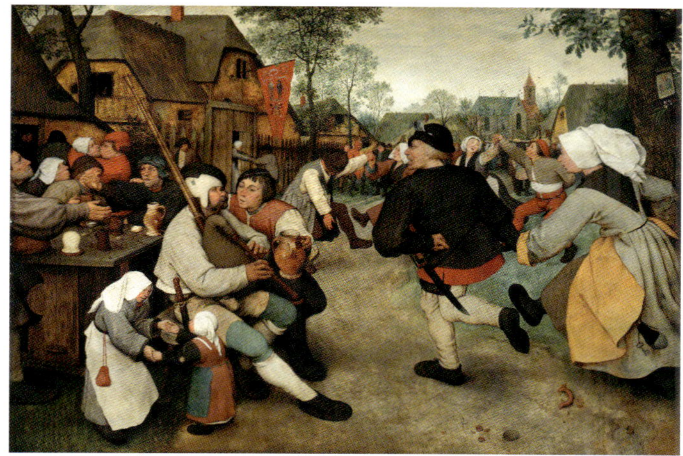

32

32

The Peasant Dance, *c.* 1568
Oil on oak, 114 x 164 cm (45 x 64⅝ in.),
inscribed b. r.: BRVEGEL
Vienna, Kunsthistorisches Museum,
Gemäldegalerie, Inv. GG_1059

The peasant party has gathered to dance before the backdrop of a village street. In the foreground on the right, we see a couple just rushing in to join the revellers. The observer follows the event from the same height as these two peasants. Together with the seated bagpiper and the drinker next to him, they are the largest figures in the composition. This can hardly be based on perspective, but far more on the fact that the figures arranged round about are rendered as unusually small, above all the pair of children dancing in front of the musician. By having the viewer follow the sightline of the peasants rushing in to dance, Bruegel draws attention to a quarrel that is threatening to erupt at the table in front of the inn. The man sitting at the head of the table is reaching back with his hand, apparently aiming his blow at the man opposite, whose body is only partially shown at the left edge. The blow misses him however and hits the peasant at his right, whose cap has already slipped down over his eyes. Other episodes in the wild revelry are illustrated in the background. A peasant relieves himself directly next to the house door, while a podgy couple lustily embrace and kiss in front him. In the next house, a woman tries to pull a man into the house with her. Bruegel has placed a great number of birds on the thatched roof, probably to point to the context of the scene – the Dutch verb "vogelen" was a vulgar expression at the time for sexual intercourse.

The most recent literature is unanimous in seeing the portrayal as a condemnation of peasant behaviour dominated by dance and drinking. The interrelated actions present lust and quarrelling as the result of intemperance, which is moreover quite the opposite of the actual reason for the feast; taking place on the church's consecration day, the village fair is dedicated to some saint or other, the patron of the church. The fact that the church is visible in the background is no coincidence, while the roofs of stands and booths are only hinted at. But while two aloof figures – a surly-looking gentleman in a long cloak and a merry jester – comment on the events in the foreground, all participants ignore the image of the Virgin at the right edge. The panel is signed bottom right and, basing arguments on common measurements and the related subject, is thought possibly to have been produced as a pendant to *The Peasant Wedding* (Cat. 31). Both panels lack a date. Before the picture was transferred from the secular treasure chamber to the Imperial Collection, two mentions of it are found in Vienna inventories of the years 1612–1619, which refer to a peasant social gathering with music.

See also pp. 266–270, *278/279*.
LITERATURE: Gibson 1977, pp. 161–166; Demus 1981, pp. 115–118; Marijnissen 1988, pp. 327–332; Gibson 1991; Seipel 1998, pp. 138–147; Kavaler 1999, pp. 184–211; Roberts-Jones 2002, pp. 271–278; Sellink 2012, pp. 246–247.

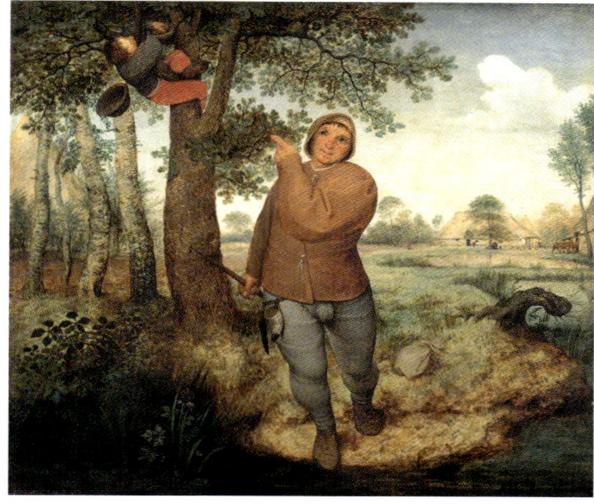

33

33
The Nest Thief, 1568
Oil on oak, 59.3 x 68.3 cm (23 ⅜ x 27 in.)
(cropped on the right and along the bottom),
inscribed b.l. (in gold paint): BRVEGEL
M.D.LXVIII
Vienna, Kunsthistorisches Museum,
Gemäldegalerie, Inv. GG_1020

The Nest Thief fits into Bruegel's late painting
oeuvre, which is characterised by a simplified
composition and simultaneously reduced yet
monumentalised actors. The pictured event is
almost entirely limited to the actions of the
eponymous figure, the attention focusing first
on the protagonist striding through the centre.
Featured rather as cowherd than farmer with
his cow horn, knife and stick, he points out to
the observer the scene in the middle ground:
a young nest thief has climbed an oak to rob
the nest there. The instantaneousness of the
scene is accentuated all the more by the falling

hat. An expansive late-summer landscape
stretches out in the right-hand half of the
picture; the literature has continually drawn
attention to its serenity. In front of the horizon
placed almost in the picture centre, horses are
being led into their stable next to a farm. The
roof of another house is implied at the left edge;
but it remains almost completely concealed by
the trunks of a birch wood. This and the positioning of the protagonists produce a clear
division within the composition: each person
is allotted to one side of the picture.
With Hulin de Loo, an interpretation has
become established that connects the picture to
the *Beekeepers* drawing (pp. 360/361) and the
proverb accompanying it: "Dije den nest Weet,
dije Weeten dijen Roft, dij heeten" (He who
knows the nest, knows it; he who robs it, has it;
van Bastelaer/Loo 1907, pp. 299–300). According
to this and to Kjell Boström, the virtuous but
unsuccessful man in the foreground is contrasted
with the successful thief, an expression of

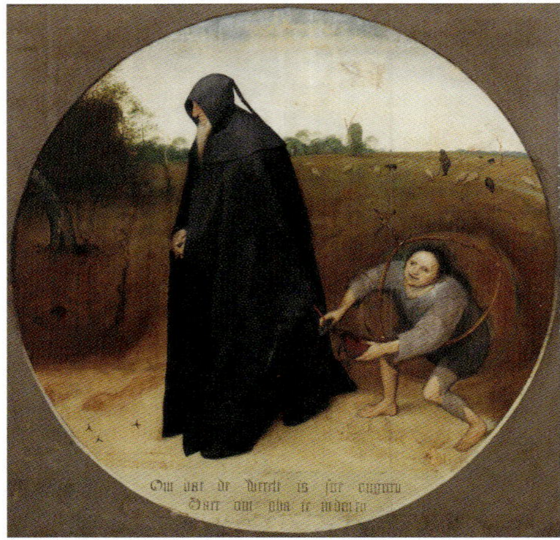

34

Bruegel's pessimistic view of the world (Boström 1949, pp. 77–89). Rodolfo Milla-Villena was the first to link the protagonists in the painting to motifs in Sebastian Brant's *Ship of Fools* (pp. 364, 365), which gives a negative connotation to the role of the peasant pointing at the thief (Milla-Villena 1980, pp. 188–201). He is the one who will fall into the pond on taking his next step, a movement seemingly signalled by the shape of the willow at the right edge.

The description of a composition that might fit the painting can be found in Leopold Wilhelm's 1659 inventory: "A landscape in oil on wood, in which a peasant brandishes a stick in his left hand, threatening a lad on a tree robbing a nest. Original by Bruegel." Because of the minor deviations, Glück however tended to think it was a copy and saw a first reliable mention of the original in Mechel's directory of the Vienna painting collection of 1783 (Glück 1932, p. 61).

See also pp. 364–367, *394/395*.

LITERATURE: Gibson 1977, pp. 192–193; Demus 1981, pp. 107–110; Marijnissen 1988, pp. 348–353; Vinken 1997; Seipel 1998, pp. 122–127; Kavaler 1999, pp. 249–254; Müller 1999, pp. 82–89; Roberts-Jones 2002, pp. 188–191; Sellink 2012, pp. 248–249.

34

The Misanthrope, 1568
Tempera on canvas, 86 x 85 cm
(33 ⅞ x 33 ½ in.), inscribed b. r. on the painted frame: BRVEGEL 1568, inscription on bottom edge: Om dat de werelt is soe ongetru, Daer om gha ic in den ru.
Naples, Museo di Capodimonte, Inv. Q16

Entitled in the literature *The Misanthrope*, this painting is in many ways unusual in Bruegel's oeuvre. Not only is it the only work in tondo format, it is also the only one with an explanatory caption. The text on the bottom edge written in black letter, or fraktur – "Om dat de werelt is soe ongetru, Daer om gha ic in den ru" – means: "Because the world is faithless it therefore wears mourning." Since the letters in fraktur deviate from Bruegel's characteristic style, the genuineness of the inscription was doubted by Jedlicka (Jedlicka 1938, p. 356). However, it can validly be proven to be contemporary and the very same year was transposed by Jan Wierix (1549–c. 1618) into the engraving. The quotation is borne of pessimism and can furthermore be applied to an action that is borne of pessimism.

In front of the background of a Dutch landscape characterised by a windmill and grazing sheep, an old man in black walks down a sloping path. The protagonist is placed slightly left of centre; because of his robe we see little of his body. Only his folded hands and parts of his morose face and a long chin beard can be seen emerging from his cowl. The lower third of the picture on the right is dominated by a figure following the old man. The body of the grotesque little man clothed in rags is stuck in an orb; solely his arms and legs protrude from it. Representing the world and its corruption, the figure has pulled the man's money pouch out of his robe and is about to cut it off with a knife; meanwhile he fixes the observer with his glance.

Together with *The Parable of the Blind* dated the same year (Cat. 35), this is the only work securely attributed to Bruegel that was painted on canvas and not on wood. It must have arrived in Italy very soon after its creation, since it was in Parma until 1611 in the collection of Count Giovanni Battista Masi (1574/75– 1612). In 1611, after Masi had been accused of conspiring against Ranuccio I Farnese (1569– 1622), both paintings were confiscated and transferred from the Palazzo Masi into the Farnese collection. The collection was scattered when the noble dynasty died out after the death of Antonio Farnese in 1731. The two paintings

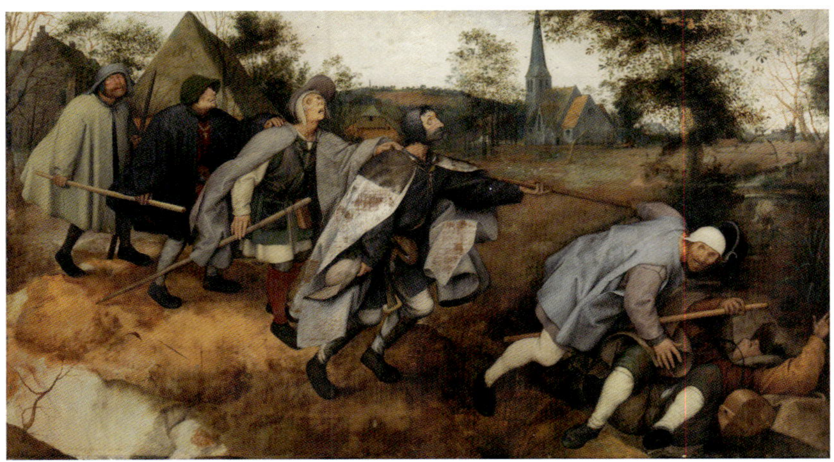

35

by Bruegel came to Naples in 1734 with Charles VII, later King Charles III of Spain (1716–1788). His summer palace, built from 1738 on and now the Museo di Capodimonte, is the painting's present home.

See also pp. 380–383, *399*.

LITERATURE: Gibson 1977, pp. 188–189; Marijnissen 1988, pp. 360–364; Roberts-Jones 2003, pp. 236–237; Richardson 2011a, pp. 151–152; Sellink 2012, pp. 250–251.

35

The Parable of the Blind (also: **The Blind Leading the Blind**), 1568
Tempera on canvas, 85.5 x 154 cm
(33 ¾ x 60 ¾ in.), inscribed b. l. BRVEGEL
M.D.LX.VIII
Naples, Museo di Capodimonte, Inv. 84490

The six blind men in Bruegel's painting dated 1568 are leading one another through the world.

Supporting themselves with their hands on the shoulder of the man ahead, or grasping sticks, they seek a direction, even though their leader has fallen. The second blind man is about to stumble over the one in front, while the others in the retinue unerringly continue their progress. Like links in a chain in an implied downward movement, the men are led from left to right through the picture space and inexorably towards the culmination of their falling down together. This inevitability is accentuated by a diagonal line created by the composition.

The interpretation of the picture has always included the conspicuously positioned church in the background. Hans Sedlmayr saw the men as blind people who had turned away from the Church (Sedlmayr 1962). Carl Gustaf Stridbeck, however, emphasised the anti-clerical tenor of the picture and argued for a negative interpretation of the Church (Stridbeck 1956, p. 262): just as Jesus used parables against the

Pharisees, so Bruegel criticised the institution of the Church and its priests.

The theme of the blind leading the blind can be found three times in the New Testament. In the Gospel of St Matthew (15: 14), Jesus calls the Pharisees the "blind leading the blind", leading the people astray so that both fall into the pit. In St Luke, Jesus poses a rhetorical question by asking if a blind man can lead another blind man without both falling into the pit; the mote in a neighbour's eye is not the one to be cast out, but the beam in one's own (6: 39–41). Finally, the Apostle Paul cites the image of the blind man leading the blind in his Epistle to the Romans (2: 19), emphasising that simply knowing God's commandments is not sufficient for salvation. Subsequently, this forceful image of the blind leading the blind became widely circulated as a proverb. Thus it is no coincidence that one scene in Bruegel's famous proverbs picture (Cat. 3) alludes to this biblical metaphor.

The Parable of the Blind is one of the two works by Bruegel that was not painted on wood, but on canvas, with glue being used as binder for the paints. The second exception, *The Misanthrope* (Cat. 34), was painted in the same year and shares a common provenance with *The Parable of the Blind*. In the early seventeenth century, the two works were owned by Count Giovanni Battista Masi in Parma. After the collection was confiscated in 1611, they were transferred to the Farnese collection. From there they travelled to Naples in 1734, where they are in the Museo di Capodimonte.

See also pp. 383–385, 388–391, *402/403*.

LITERATURE: Sedlmayr 1962; Gibson 1977, pp. 185–189; Marijnissen 1988, pp. 365–369; Roberts-Jones 2002, pp. 56–62; Sellink 2012, pp. 252–253; Müller 2014c.

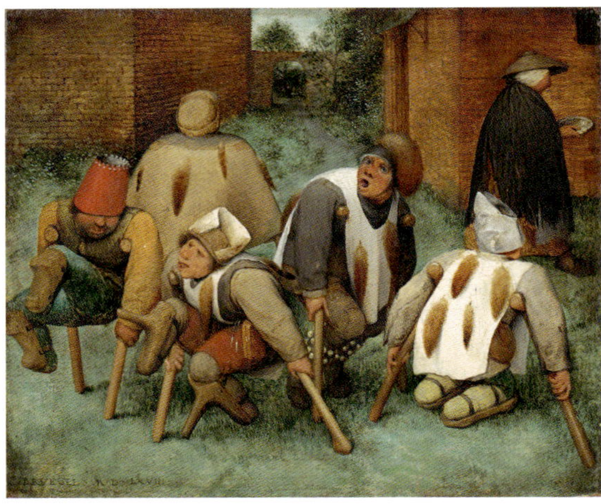

36

36
The Cripples (also: **The Beggars**), 1568
Oil on wood, 18.5 x 21.5 cm (7 ⅜ x 8 ½ in.),
inscribed b. l.: BRVEGEL. M.D. LXVIII
Paris, Musée du Louvre, Inv. R.F. 730

The small panel *The Cripples* occupies a special place within Bruegel's complete works. The format intensifies the impression that the five cripples are crowded in the most confined space and are straining in all directions to get away from one another. They are beggars, as indicated by a person retreating in the background; she is holding a bowl in her hands for collecting or sharing out alms. It is not clear whether the men have met in order to beg in what is implied as a small courtyard.

Bruegel's great determination to show the men's afflictions is a conspicuous feature of the picture. The same applies to their aids for locomotion. Nevertheless, the two figures front left give the impression that they're dancing or wanting to swing out of the picture on their crutches.

The theme of begging had a negative connotation since the Reformation and was similarly portrayed by many artists. Bruegel uses a complicated trick here. The distinctly rising picture space heads in central perspective towards a stone gate in the background, creating a strong magnetic pull into the picture. We come unpleasantly close to the beggars, an impression reinforced all the more through the confined picture space.

The men's objective remains indeterminate. Only the beggar whom we can half detect from his back view seems to be looking through the gate into the outside world. What awaits him there is uncertain, owing to the vegetation that is no more than hinted at. Another noticeable feature is the colour accentuation of certain details within the composition, otherwise generally kept in brown and green tones. One instance of this is the robust red of the left-hand beggar's headgear, formed like a crown, also the fox tails attached to the men's attire, standing out against the white fabric of their tabards. This applies as well – but the other way round – to the white headgear of the beggar on the right, which, placed in front of a dark background, recalls a mitre. Bruegel had already designed a similar collection of beggars nine years previously in *The Fight between Carnival and Lent* (Cat. 4). It almost seems as if he had isolated the group from this composition and transferred it to another context. The narrative background remains enigmatic. Scholars have seen *The Cripples* in terms of the political developments of those years, but also as an allegory pillorying hypocrisy. The fox tails provide an important attribute for identifying the context; they were frequently represented in the earlier composition and deemed to be an emblem of jesters and fools. The date of 1568 assigns *The Cripples* to Bruegel's late work, in which we find more compositions that bring

the observer closer to the action, meanwhile reducing the number of protagonists.

The panel is today in Paris; it is one of Bruegel's smallest paintings measuring 18.5 x 21.5 cm (7 ⅜ x 8 ½ in.) and signed at the bottom edge on the left. Several inscriptions were also found on the back, among them two couplets praising the artist. It is the sole work by the artist in the Louvre, where it arrived in 1892 as a gift of the art historian Paul Mantz. The picture's provenance cannot be reconstructed securely until this date; in fact, possible early mentions are mutually contradictory. Gustav Glück follows a clue in an inventory dating 1642 and points to a similar picture in the Antwerp collection of Herman de Neyt (1588–1642), which was then documented in 1673 as being owned by a Peter Wouters. According to Georges Hulin de Loo, the painting might have left Prague in 1648 for Stockholm, where it was verified as being in the collection of Queen Christina of Sweden in 1652 – without naming the artist.

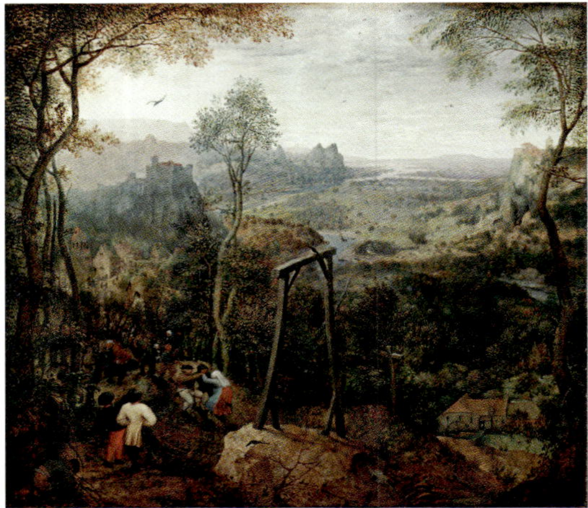

37

An initial naming in 1607 suggests the picture was sold through the Amsterdam Chamber of Orphans.

See also pp. 375, 379, *400/401*.

Literature: Van Bastelaer/Loo 1907, pp. 293; Gibson 1977, pp. 182–185; Marijnissen 1988, pp. 354–358; Roberts-Jones 2002, pp. 230–231; Sellink 2012, pp. 254.

37

The Magpie on the Gallows, 1568
Oil on wood, 45.9 x 50.8 cm (18 x 20 in.), inscribed b. r.: BRVEGEL 1568
Darmstadt, Hessisches Landesmuseum, Inv. GK 165

The action of Bruegel's *The Magpie on the Gallows* is played out in front of a scrupulously fanned out landscape. Its effect of depth, based on the skilful use of colour to achieve a sense of perspective, can be singled out as extraordi-

narily successful. Between the towering trees and rocks, in part crowned by fortifications, the observer's bird's eye view is led across a plain stretching into the far distance, following a wide river that eventually flows into the open sea on the horizon. Besides a village perceptible left of centre, the fertile settlement of the landscape is suggested by the scattered houses and castles, the farmlands and the ships returning on the water.

Several inhabitants of the region are climbing up the hill to the gallows, which is placed centrally in the foreground. The figures, accentuated by colour, stand out conspicuously against the tonally harmonised landscape. They are peasants thronging up in great numbers from the nearby village, moving – some dancing – to the music of a bagpiper. They are awaited by two men, one of whom has raised his arm in greeting; the other rests his hands on his hips while apparently stamping jauntily with his foot in time to the music. Like the dog wagging its tail next to him, they have turned their backs to the observer. This applies as well to another actor who is discovered only on closer examination of the far left in the foreground. He has bared his rear to defecate in the corner, significantly exactly opposite the artist's signature bottom right. The depicted scenes illustrate that the behaviour of the approaching people hardly accords with the location. None of the dancing peasants pays any attention to the place of execution; only the musician seems to look across at the gallows, which is totally distorted in perspective. Its construction is peculiar, in fact physically impossible: the cross beam is aligned differently to the two supporting beams. We have the impression that Bruegel wanted to set up an optical paradox. The eponymous magpie has settled on the crossbeam of the gallows. Starting with Karel van Mander's assessment that Bruegel is referring through the magpie to the gossips he would have loved to have seen on the gal-

lows, many different interpretations have been suggested, on one hand relating the picture indirectly to the terror regime of the Duke of Alba, on the other to contemporary sayings. The puzzling attributes scattered around the place of execution have spawned even more interpretations. A second magpie has settled on a tree stump directly in front of the left-hand post. To the right of this on the ground is the skull of a horse, such as we see in Bruegel's *Procession to Calvary* (Cat. 15). Above this at the height of the gallows is a hollowed-out cross, a burning candle placed within, while red bricks lie scattered on the ground. Down below in the valley a water mill, in exposed position, is doing its work.

The painting is one of Bruegel's smaller works in its practically rectangular format of 45.9 x 50.8 cm (18 x 20 in.); together with a painting by Joachim Patinir, it was acquired in 1865 from the Heidelberg painter Georg Wilhelm Issel (1785–1870). According to van Mander, Bruegel

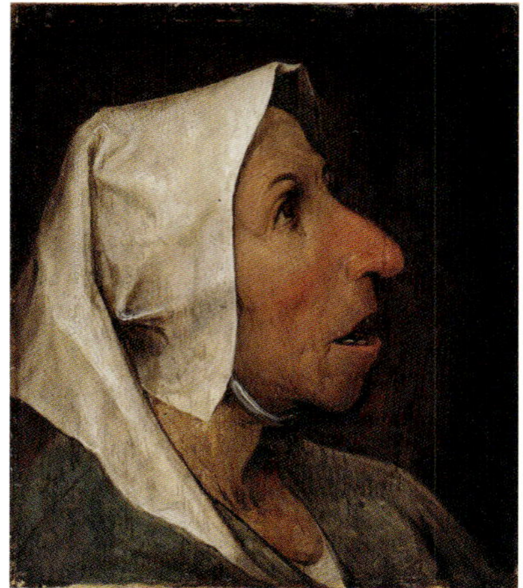

38

originally left the work to his wife. The panel is one of the last works by the artist, as seen in the date of 1568.

See also pp. 251–252, *272/273*.

LITERATURE: Gibson 1977, pp. 193–195; Marijnissen 1988, pp. 370–375; Gibson 1989, p. 75; Kavaler 1999, pp. 217–233; Roberts-Jones 2002, pp. 177–179; Ludwig 2012; Sellink 2012, pp. 255–256.

38

The Head of an Old Peasant Woman,
c. 1568
Oil on wood, 22 x 18 cm (8 ¾ x 7 in.)
Munich, Bayerische Staatsgemäldesammlungen, Alte Pinakothek, Inv. 7057

The Head of an Old Peasant Woman, today in Munich, is an exception within the artist's oeuvre. Disputes continue as to whether the work is original. That an identification was at all possible was based on the characteristic portrayal of the old woman, for which we can easily find examples in Bruegel's printed graphics (Müller/Schauerte 2018, Cat. G33, 35, 36, 56). Hence it may be a pasticcio, an imitation by one of Bruegel's sons, who based his interpretation on trenchant portrayals by his father. Conspicuous in Bruegel's portrayal is the overlong nose and open mouth, giving the face in profile a slight tendency to caricature. Another curious feature is the upward glance, the confined picture space not allowing us to see why the figure is looking up. It might be a study of emotions – but we cannot be sure – aiming to show a surprised facial expression with open mouth. It seems more plausible to see it as a fragment.

As earlier inventories verify, Bruegel painted a certain number of comparable *tronies* (studies of exaggerated facial expressions). Two head studies by the artist were found among Rubens' papers. However, *The Head of an Old Peasant*

Woman is the only preserved work which all interpreters, with the exception of Tolnay, acknowledge as being by Bruegel's hand. As it is a study, it is no wonder that it is neither signed nor dated. The date 1563/64 suggested by Friedländer and Gibson was countered by Sellink, who pointed out the stylistic closeness to Bruegel's late work and preferred a date of 1568. The picture was first named in 1804; the work was in Schloss Neuburg an der Donau at that time. From there it was transferred in 1868 to Schliessheim. After being kept in Nuremberg in the interim, it has been in Munich since 1912.

See also pp. 372–373, *398*.

Literature: Gibson 1977, p. 121; Marijnissen 1988, pp. 346–347; Roberts-Jones 2002, pp. 279–280; Gibson 2006, pp. 57–59; Sellink 2012, p. 257.

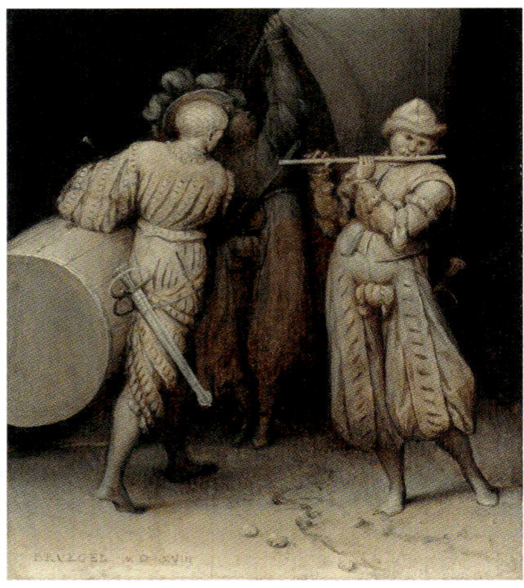

39

39
The Three Soldiers, 1568
Grisaille, oil on oak, 20.3 x 17.8 cm
(8 x 7 in.), inscribed b. l.: BRVEGEL
M.D. [L] XVIII
New York, The Frick Collection,
Inv. 65.1.163

The Three Soldiers, which arrived in the Frick
Collection in New York in 1965, is the only
one of Bruegel's three preserved grisailles to
have a profane theme. We see a flute player, a
drummer and a flag-waving soldier. Bruegel
portrays them in elegant postures and conspicuously close to the observer. Their height
corresponds almost to the full height of the
small panel, while the composition is limited
to portraying the three actors and their characterisation. In contrast to *The Death of the
Virgin* (Cat. 16) and *Christ and the Woman
Taken in Adultery* (Cat. 24), the picture is
composed in vertical format, unusual for

Bruegel. Measuring only 20.3 x 17.8 cm (8 x
7 in.), it is the smallest and also – since generally read to be dated 1568 – the last work within
the grisaille group.

The painting was first noted in an inventory
dated 1639 of the collection of the English King
Charles I (1600–1649), which moreover names
Endymion Porter (1587–1649) as its previous
owner. According to a mark burned into the
back of the panel, it must already have been in
royal ownership before the future king ascended
the throne in 1625. After being mentioned in
the collection of James II and last in 1714 in
the Royal Collection in Somerset House, the
picture was not recorded again until 1900, in
an English private collection, before it was
purchased by an antique dealer and auctioned
at Christie's in 1964.

See also pp. 238–239, *244/245*.

LITERATURE: Munhall 1966; Gibson 1977,
p. 134; Sellink 2012, p. 260.

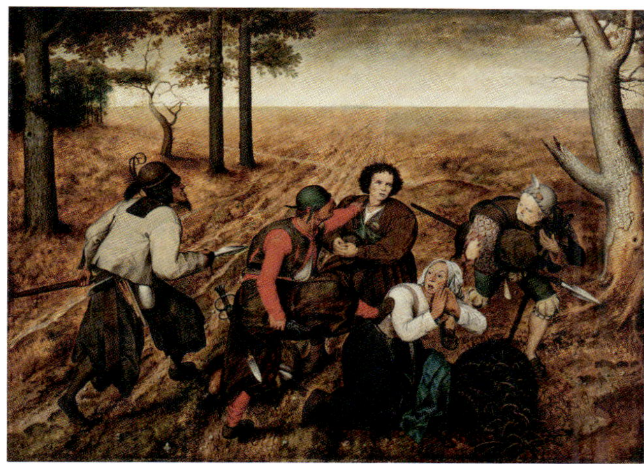

40

40
Pieter Bruegel the Elder and Workshop
The Attack, 1567
Oil on wood, 96 x 128 cm (37 ⅞ x 50 ½ in.),
inscribed b. r.: M.D.LX VII BRVEGEL
Stockholms Universitets Konstsamling,
Inv. 17

The Attack had long been attributed to Pieter
Brueghel the Younger. However, restorations
have shown that another signature is preserved
in the bottom right-hand corner under the
signature P. Bruegel/1630, indicating a possible
date of 1567 for the painting's creation and
revealing the name Pieter Bruegel the Elder
in writing that was typical of him at that time.
But an attribution to the father is still a matter
of dispute. Dendrochronological analyses
(Weibull 1999, p. 98) date the picture to
the time after 1567, and we might ask who
would have been interested in adding a signature of the father underneath that of the son.

This lends credence to the panel's possible
authenticity.
Within the context of the complete works,
we might be reminded of Bruegel's interpretation of *The Unfaithful Shepherd* (Cat. 41),
which shows a similarly extreme perspective
construction. The scene in the foreground of
an ambush is set against a continuously receding picture space reaching to the horizon.
Three marauding soldiers are threatening a
peasant couple with spears and pistols in order
to rob them of their belongings. The soldiers'
attire is motley and shabby; they are not so
much troopers as highwaymen, out for loot.
The artist has precisely depicted the men's
weapons and caricatured the robber at front
centre by placing his headgear far down over
his eyes. The wailing of the couple is in vain –
we see the mercenary going for the woman in
full fury. She has her eyes wide open in fright
and is probably about to fall to the ground,
where her basket lies, tipped over. Her husband

witnesses the scene but cannot intervene because the central robber has grabbed him by the collar.

The portrayal of the peasant couple is interesting in iconographical terms as well, for it is noticeable that the young man recalls portrayals of St John the Baptist (Stridbeck 1956) in Early Netherlandish versions of the Deposition from the Cross, while the woman with her wide-open eyes resembles figures from the Passion iconography. A further marauding soldier is hidden behind the trees on the left; he is scanning the path at the horizon, keeping a look out for new victims.

Yet again Bruegel works with the effects of extreme miniaturisation. The horizon shows townships – suggested by church steeples – as well as a rider and a horse and cart approaching the town. Farther away, we see on the left behind the trees a flock of sheep with a shepherd, evoking the similar motif of *The Unfaithful Shepherd*.

The overall impression of the picture is that of a study in perspective. The layout of the paths and furrows greatly accentuates the narrowing perspective and adds extra visual impact to the depth of the picture space. The trees on the left and right framing the action act as repoussoir, making the spatial perspective seem even vaster. In addition, the artist uses local colours in the foreground, which serve the same purpose. It is as if he had made use of an optical instrument to achieve this effect.

Glück mentions the composition in several versions, and it is no longer possible to determine whether the example Constantin Huygens (1596–1687) saw at Diego Duarte's establishment in 1676 is the original (Glück 1932, p. 76).

Literature: Stridbeck 1956, p. 284, Karling 1976; Raupp 1986, p. 231; Gibson 1991, p. 44; Seipel 1998, p. 159; Weibull 1999; Ertz 1988/2000, pp. 775–786; Silver 2011, no. 312; Sellink 2012, p. 276.

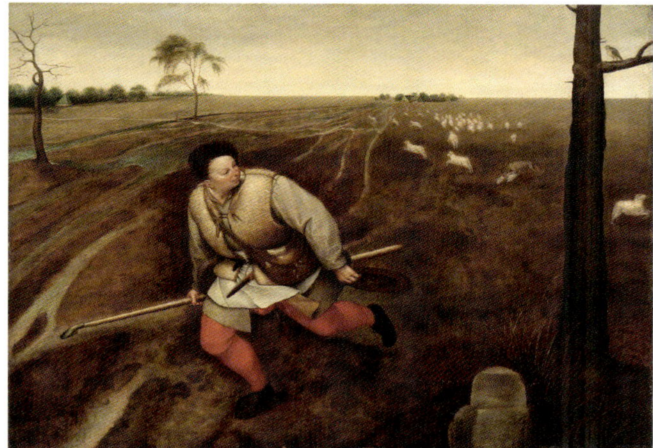

41

41
After Pieter Bruegel the Elder
The Unfaithful Shepherd, *c.* 1575–1600
Oil on wood, 61.6 x 86.7 cm (24⅜ x 34¼ in.)
Philadelphia Museum of Art, John G.
Johnson Collection, Inv. 419

The panel, now in Philadelphia, is one of the late works in which the artist is preoccupied with sophisticated optical experiments. It is generally seen as a copy after a lost original. With the biblical parable of the Good Shepherd (John 10: 1–18) – against which the fleeing shepherd is juxtaposed as a negative figure (John 10: 12–13) – the work does not contain any especially unconventional iconography, but focuses on an interesting problem of artistic representation: the spherical form of the Earth. The artist transposes the narrative to a flat, Flemish landscape. The figure of the fleeing shepherd is placed directly at the front edge. He is wearing a sheepskin waistcoat and a cap to protect himself against the wind. He holds his shepherd's crook in his right hand and a hat in his left. An unusual feature in the composition is the relationship of running figure and the space. He is taking to his heels with wide strides, but glances back in fear at the wolf, which, however, has already found another victim. It has killed several sheep and is about to claim another. The remaining flock is scattering in all directions.

In the reduction to a single, large-format figure, the picture corresponds to Bruegel's late style, in which all other picture elements are subordinate to the main figure. The motif of the fleeing shepherd was correctly identified as based on a work by Raphael (1483–1520) from the Stanze in the Vatican (Stridbeck 1956). Scholars (Jedlicka 1938) have also noted the curious rendering of the landscape and wondered whether it was Bruegel's artistic intention to visualise the curve of the Earth's surface. They point out that all the lines and paths are drawn as arcs and form curves running to a specific point in the background.

In addition, no other picture had ever shown the Earth's surface as part of a huge sphere as convincingly as this. They also note the opposing movements: the shepherd running away as fast he can in the direction of the observer, and that of the Earth, turning in the opposite direction. They accentuate the dizzying image that Bruegel has attempted to paint here, something actually beyond painting's scope: the movement of the globe in space. The landscape appears as if seen from an express train. Within this context, we may refer to the engraving *Temperantia* from the Virtues series of 1559/60 (pp. 192/193). Here we see two astronomers in the background, measuring the distance between the Moon and the Earth. The two of them apparently haven't noticed that the Earth moves around its own axis. The vengeance of the inanimate object will soon cause the fall of the geometrician, who is making a great effort to hang on.

We have to consider in general the disturbance resulting from the new view of the world. The compass orientations depend on a person's location. We sail eastwards and arrive in the west. People are constantly walking over the surface of a sphere, never able to reach its absolute centre. When perceiving a landscape, we see the horizon receding perpetually, giving us no indication that the Earth is curved. If the Earth is a moving globe we can no longer – putting it naively – trust our perception. We walk across a planet that is moving without our noticing it. Likewise, we walk across a curved surface which generally seems flat to us. We do not need to say that from now on the straight line for a painter will be struggling incessantly with the parabola; central perspective turns out to be a system that we can apply to cultural forms – houses or other buildings – but not to the curved surface of the Earth. Or can we? This problem is particularly relevant for a geographer who wishes to calculate the Earth's surface precisely in order to produce a two-dimensional map from a convex surface, as Gerhard Mercator (1512–1594) did in Bruegel's time.

The inventory of the Prague Art and Treasure Chamber made in 1621 makes no specific mention of the picture of a shepherd, while in 1718 a "running messenger" is mentioned, apparently executed in watercolours. The provenance of the panel now in Philadelphia can be traced back to 1899. It was auctioned in Rome in that year and purchased by the museum in Paris shortly afterwards (Glück 1932, p. 64).

Literature: Scott 1994, p. 39; Ertz 1988/2000, vol. 1, no. A 125, pp. 147–150, 210; Silver 2011, no. 254.

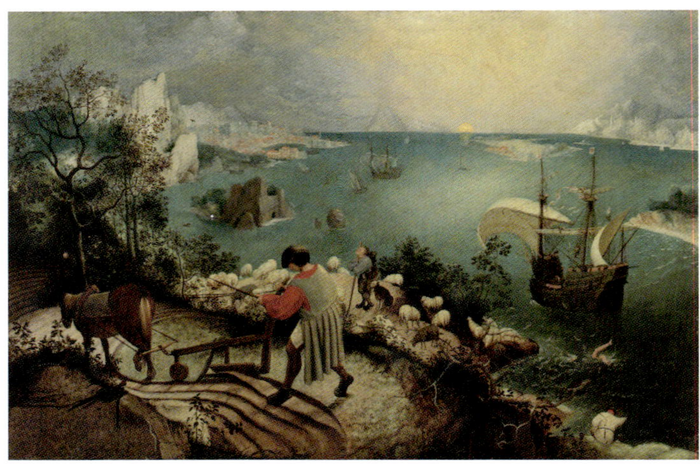

42a

42a
After Pieter Bruegel the Elder
Landscape with the Fall of Icarus
Oil on canvas, 73.5 x 112 cm (29 x 44 in.)
Brussels, Musées royaux des Beaux-Arts de
Belgique/Koninklijke Musea voor Schone
Kunsten van België, Inv. 4030

42b
After Pieter Bruegel the Elder
Landscape with the Fall of Icarus,
c. 1590–1595
Oil on wood, 63 x 90 cm (24 ⅞ x 35 ½ in.)
Brussels, Museum David and
Alice van Buuren

The Icarus myth is associated in the early
modern age with the idea of hubris, of man's
desire to overstep the bounds set by God. This
is experienced by the son of Daedalus, flying
higher and higher until his wings come too
close to the Sun. Its heat melts the wax between

the individual feathers so that Icarus falls to his
death. Bruegel has represented this moment in
an enigmatic form. Only at second glance do
we see the legs of the youth who has just fallen
out of the sky and is about to sink into the sea
in the right-hand corner of the picture. Far
more trenchant for the composition is the scene
in the foreground: a farmer concentrated on
ploughing a field. His baldric is lying in the
foreground, localising the event in the "Iron
Age" which according to Ovid (43 BC –AD 17)
was dominated by brute violence (Wyss 1990).
Frequent models have been named for interpreting the figure (Vöhringer 2002), which
suggest that Bruegel was familiar with the
artistic tradition. Yet neither the farmer nor the
shepherd beyond him, not even the angler,
before whose very eyes the fall is happening,
pay any attention at all to the incident. Instead,
Bruegel gives another hint about the mytho-
logical background by placing a partridge
underneath Icarus. The bird alludes to Perdix,

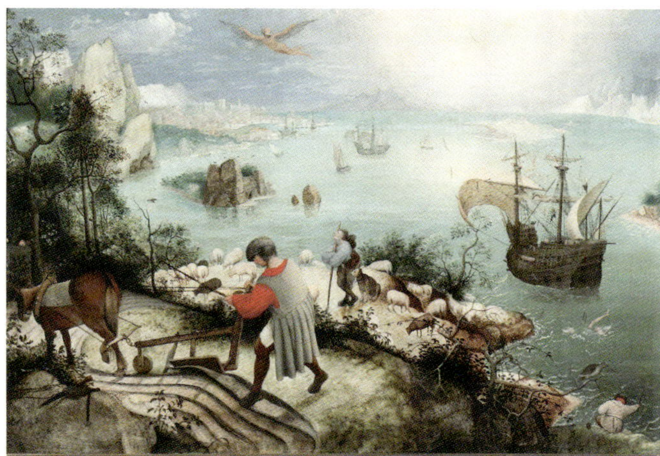

42b

the former pupil of Daedalus, as narrated by Ovid in the *Metamorphoses*. He was once thrown off the Acropolis by his master, but Athene rescued him and changed him into a partridge. Because of its fear of heights, ever since then the bird has flown close to the ground and is thus witness on its branch to the tragic moment. Icarus, the symbol of hubris, is juxtaposed to the embodiment of a man who knows his limits.

In the background, Bruegel unfolds a panorama, letting the eye roam across the sea to the high horizon with the setting Sun. If we consider that Icarus came too near to the Sun when at its zenith, we have an idea of how long the fall must have lasted. In addition, Bruegel manages to create the impression of a convex surface, alluding to the spherical shape of the Earth. In all of this, Bruegel matches the level of scientific knowledge of the time and simultaneously supplies a sceptical allegory of progress; he has positioned a warship above

Icarus as he falls into the water, its cannons easily visible for the observer. It was possible to cross the oceans in ships like this. But this constellation can be read as a very critical symbol of the era's technological potential, particularly as the only person who seems to be taking notice of Icarus falling into the water is a sailor climbing the rigging. Moreover, the picture repeatedly alludes to possible references to contemporary political events.

An inventory of Rudolf II's collection in Prague made in 1612 already mentions a picture of "Daedalus and Icarus" by Pieter Bruegel, although it is not certain if the listed work was the original, believed lost today, or one of the later copies. Both surviving versions are in Brussels today; the larger and superior version in execution was purchased by the Musées royaux on the London art market in 1912. Ludwig Baldass judged it was a Bruegel original made in 1558 (Baldass 1918, p. 152); subsequently, Glück and Tolnay, too, both dated the work to the 1550s. Edouard Michel (Michel 1931, pp. 71–73), pointing out painterly weaknesses, rejected attribution to Bruegel, and even Jedlicka would not recognise either of the versions as an original. Recent analyses showed that the earliest canvas remnants of the picture – which has been remounted many times – were not made before 1600. However, early arguments stated that the work might have originally been painted on wood and transferred later. On top of this, the picture's condition hinders a final decision about authorship. The last verdict argued for a date around 1560 (Silver 2011, p. 131). Because of the closeness to the engraving after Bruegel of 1561, the *Naval Battle in the Straits of Messina* (Müller/ Schauerte 2018, Cat. G19), a corresponding date would seem probable.

A second, smaller version of *The Fall of Icarus*, somewhat inferior in execution, was ascribed to Pieter Bruegel's son, Jan. The main difference is seen in a flying figure of Daedalus, with the shepherd looking up at him. This version painted on wood is today in the Museum van Buuren.

See also pp. 22–23.

LITERATURE: Gibson 1977, pp. 38–40; Marijnissen 1988, pp. 378–379; Gibson 1989, p. 60; Wyss 1990; Allart 1996; Van Strydonck 1998; Roberts-Jones 2002, pp. 287–290; Vöhringer 2002; Kockaert 2003; De Vries 2003; Kilinski 2004; Roberts-Jones 2006; Sellink 2011, p. 271; Silver 2011, no. 110.

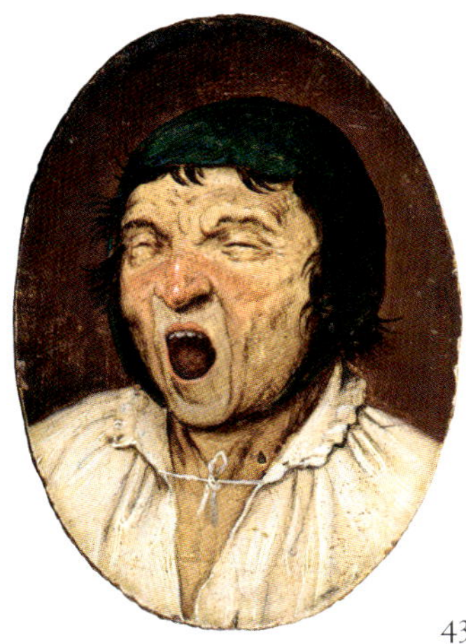

43

43
After Pieter Bruegel the Elder
The Yawner, after 1616
Oil on oak, 12.6 x 9.2 cm (5 x 3⅝ in.),
traces of a signature m. r.: P.
Brussels, Musées royaux des Beaux-Arts de
Belgique/Koninklijke Musea voor Schone
Kunsten van België, Inv. 6509

The oak panel, only 12.6 x 9.2 cm (5 x 3⅝ in.)
in size, shows a yawning man wearing a shirt
closed at the neck and a cap, hinting it is
bedtime. Bruegel has precisely captured the facial
expression of yawning: the closed eyes, the wide-
open mouth and the musculature tensed in reflex,
causing wrinkles around the bridge of the nose.
The open mouth gives us a view of the man's
tongue and the top row of teeth. Bruegel has
meticulously observed all details of the involun-
tary, reflexive process of yawning.
The oil painting has presented scholars with
almost insurmountable puzzles. The authorship
of Pieter Bruegel the Elder is disputed, even
after Walter Gibson most recently ventured an
attribution based on the relationship between
the head of the yawning man and the peasant
woman in Munich (Cat. 38). Moreover, *The
Yawner* is reproduced in an anonymous seven-
teenth-century engraving naming Pieter Bruegel
as artist of the motif. First of all we have to
investigate the question of the picture's original
format. Do we have here a fragment from a
larger context, which was added around the
oval, decorative frame and the marbled wooden
panel? At any rate, it seems insufficient to see
it as a head study, for which there are no real
counterparts in the rest of the artist's oeuvre.
Nor is Walter Gibson's reference to *The Head
of an Old Peasant Woman* convincing, because
the subject's face is all too schematic and almost
a caricature.
One context that is conceivable for interpreting
the picture is provided by studies of the emotions,
which were formulated in the Italian theory of

River Landscape with a Sower (detail), 1557
(see ill. pp. 42/43)

art from the first half of the fifteenth century as a challenge to artists. History painting demanded as a central task the appropriate portrayal of extreme affects such as pain and rage. The open mouth and formation of wrinkles were of special significance in representing intense feelings and their facial expression. If we see the work in this context, we have to conclude that Bruegel is making fun of this artistic position: he shows that all the criteria regarded as exemplary in this context for the facial expression of the Laocoön are also applicable to such a profane situation as yawning.

There might be some justification for this interpretation, that of high art being transformed into low, since many artists around 1560 were producing genre pictures that similarly make fun of the expressions of pain and fear.

A picture corresponding to the present work is already listed in Rubens' estate inventory, though there it is described as round. The Brussels miniature, convincingly attributed by Gustav Glück and lately also by Klaus Ertz to Pieter Brueghel the Younger, first arrived in the Belgian capital in 1949 from the New York art market. Prior to this, it was auctioned in 1907 in Amsterdam by the collector Artur Meier. See also pp. 372–373.

LITERATURE: Ertz 1998, no. 123; Gibson 2006, pp. 57–59.

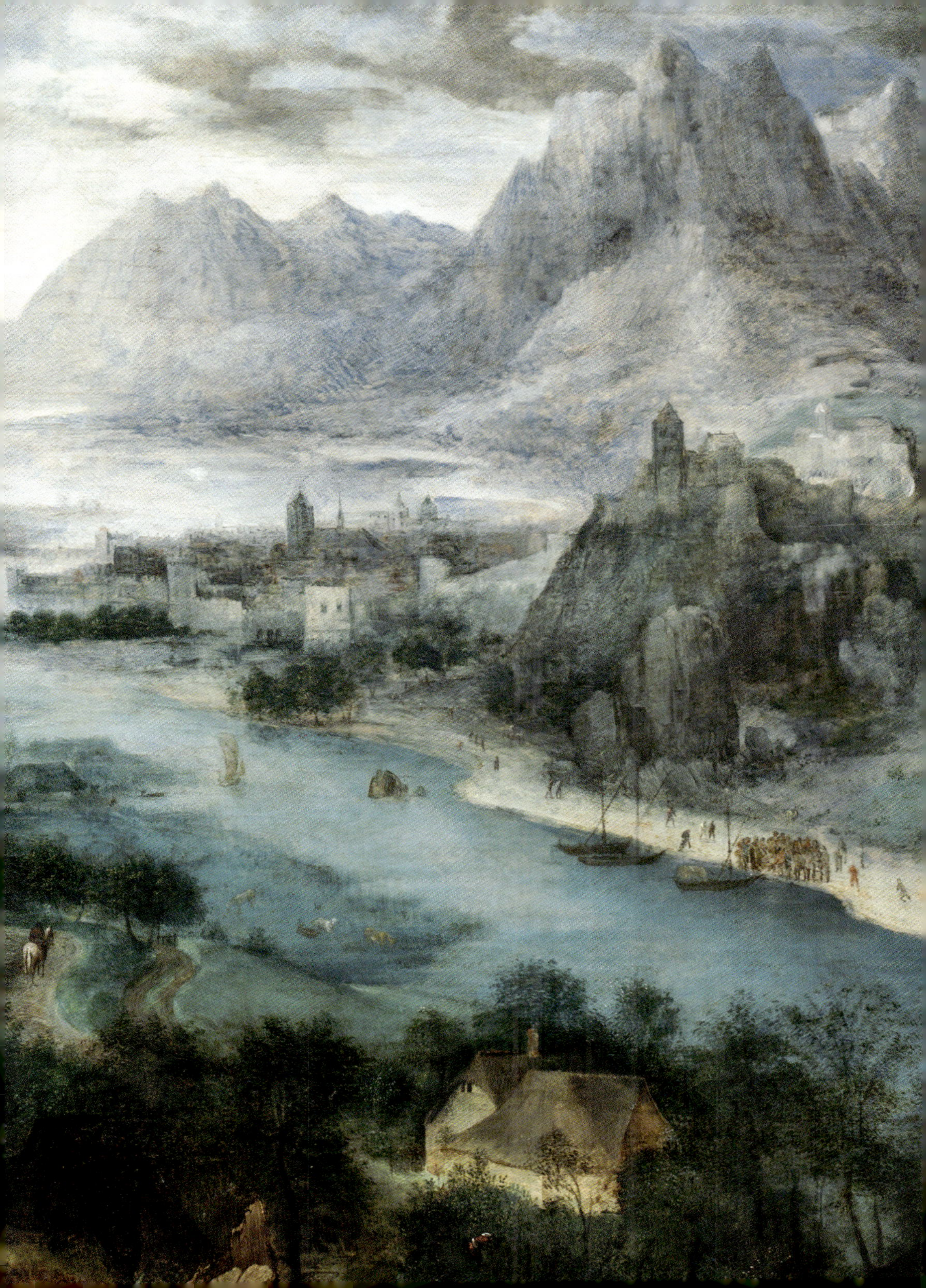

Notes

1 Bedaux/van Gool 1974
2 Müller 1993
3 Müller 2009
4 Gibson 2006
5 Sullivan 1994, pp. 5–69
6 Gibson 1977
7 Stridbeck 1956; Kavaler 1999
8 Warncke 1987, p. 248
9 I'm making a link here with earlier interpretations. Müller 1999
10 Müller 1997
11 Mander 1991, p. 154
12 Ibid., p. 152
13 Ibid., p. 154
14 Ibid., p. 156
15 Ibid., p. 155
16 Kaschek 2001; Kaschek 2014
17 Van Mander 1916, p. 207
18 Bernsmeier 1986
19 Schauerte 2014; Mössinger/ Müller 2014, pp. 144–145
20 Wyss 1988, pp. 233–237
21 Kaschek 2012, pp. 303–346
22 A rendition of the archival material relating to Bruegel is in Marijnissen 2003, pp. 11–16.
23 Tolnai 1925; Tolnai 1934; Tolnay 1935
24 Pawlak 2011a
25 Marijnissen 2003, p. 11
26 We owe to Kaschek 2012 the best overview on the patron Jonghelinck and the humanist circles in which Bruegel moved.
27 Banz 2000; Kaschek 2012
28 Büttner 2000b
29 Marijnissen 2003, p. 12
30 Ibid.
31 Roettig 2001
32 Pawlak 2011a
33 Freedberg 1989, pp. 53–65; Müller 1999, pp. 19–30
34 Ortelius 1969

35 Weismann 2015
36 Mout 1981
37 Stridbeck 1956
38 Freedberg 1989; Müller 1999
39 Fast 1962, pp. 217–233
40 Müller 2014c
41 Zagorin 2003
42 Philips 1811, pp. 542–558
43 Harris 2004, pp. 124–128
44 Becker 1928
45 Langer 1993
46 Augustijn/Parmentier 1993
47 Balke 1987; Marnef 1996
48 On the uprising in the Netherlands, see Geyl 1966.
49 Mössinger/Müller 2014, no. 33
50 Bainton 1972
51 Erasmus 1995a, pp. 371–373
52 Hayden-Roy 1990
53 Müller 1999, pp. 36–37
54 Könneker 1991
55 Bietenholz 2009
56 D'Ascia 1991
57 Erasmus 1995c, p. 129
58 Auerbach 1988, pp. 25–31
59 Müller 1999
60 Auerbach 1988
61 Mander 1991, pp. 155–156
62 Canuteson 1989/90
63 Härting 1997
64 Fraenger 2008
65 Grauls 1957
66 For identification of all proverbs, see Marijnissen 2003, pp. 134–144; most recently: Grosshans 2003
67 Sullivan 1991, p. 461
68 Bauer 1993
69 Franck 1995, p. 5
70 Stridbeck 1956, Müller 1999
71 Marijnissen 2003, pp. 161–162
72 Hindman 1981, pp. 470–474

73 Grossmann 1966, p. 193; Stridbeck 1956, pp. 185–186
74 Vanden Branden 1982
75 Stridbeck 1956, pp. 186–187
76 Vanden Branden 1982, p. 506
77 Hindman 1981, p. 452
78 Ibid., p. 453
79 Müller 1999, p. 49
80 Fast 1962, pp. 219–220
81 Müller 1999, pp. 90–125
82 Franck 1995, p. 154
83 Müller 1999, pp. 97–104
84 Lebègue 1973
85 Tolnay 1935; Stridbeck 1956; Müller 1999
86 Franck 1995, p. 21
87 Lebeer 1969, pp. 77–81
88 Calman 1960, p. 91
89 Mössinger/Müller 2014, no. 50
90 Klein 1963, p. 158
91 Sullivan 1981, pp. 114–126
92 Rahner 1964, pp. 272–304, 659–664
93 Janson 1952, pp. 154–156
94 Franck 1995, p. 153
95 Stechow 1969, p. 88
96 Dvořák 1941; Stridbeck 1956, p. 244
97 Marijnissen 2003, pp. 336–337
98 Pinson 1994
99 Franck 1995, p. 181
100 Falkenburg 1993, p. 18
101 Stechow 1974, p. 86
102 Erasmus 1995a, p. 199
103 Müller 1999, pp. 139–140
104 Gibson 1977, pp. 129–130
105 Erasmus 1995a, pp. 197–205
106 Weismann 1992b, p. 23
107 Franck 1995, pp. 171–172
108 Marijnissen 2003, p. 210–222
109 Snow 1983, p. 46
110 Mansbach 1982
111 Hayden-Roy 1990
112 Franck 1995, p. 3

113 Klamt 1979
114 Marijnissen 2003, p. 222
115 Ibid., 2003, pp. 304–305
116 With thanks to the kind information from my friend Jörg Gödecke.
117 Pokorny 2009, pp. 597–601
118 Jedlicka 1938, p. 273
119 Cited in Fast 1962, pp. 221–222
120 Lebeer 1969, no. 39
121 Recently by Pawlak 2011b, p. 87
122 Tolnay 1935, p. 68, n. 70
123 Pawlak 2011b, pp. 89–142
124 Kaschek 2007, pp. 45–46
125 Gibson 1977, pp. 102–104
126 Harbison 1976
127 Pawlak 2011b, pp. 27–43
128 Meganck 2014, pp. 66–107
129 Pawlak 2011b, pp. 78–83
130 Meganck 2014
131 Kaschek 2012, pp. 55–69
132 Kaschek 2009
133 Ibid.
134 Kaschek 2009, pp. 176–177
135 Muylle 1984
136 Marijnissen 2003, p. 188
137 Grossmann 1961
138 Preimesberger 1991
139 Pliny the Elder, *Naturalis historia* XXXV, 50
140 Quintilian, *Institutio oratoria* XII, 10, 4
141 Pliny the Elder, *Naturalis historia* XXXVI, 67–68
142 Stridbeck 1956, pp. 263–265
143 Grossmann 1952, p. 225
144 Stridbeck 1956, pp. 271–272
145 Irle 1997
146 Silver 2011, p. 385
147 *Legenda aurea* 1979, pp. 583–609
148 Melion 1997, pp. 14–45
149 Ludwig 2012
150 Marijnissen 2003, pp. 371–373
151 Van Mander 1991, p. 156
152 Sullivan 1994, pp. 108–115
153 Raupp 1986, pp. 283–287
154 Ibid., pp. 50–59
155 Ibid., p. 283
156 Weismann 1992a
157 Ibid.
158 Silver 2011, pp. 336–342
159 Scheyer 1965
160 Wagner 2007; Kaschek 2012
161 Stridbeck 1956, p. 216
162 Raupp 1986
163 Grossmann 1966, p. 202
164 De Jongh 1968/69
165 Buchanan 1990
166 Kaschek 2012
167 Ibid.
168 Longinus 1988, p. 7
169 Ibid., p. 57
170 Longinus 1988, p. 87
171 Silver 2011, p. 274
172 Mann 1984, pp. 198–207
173 Franck 1995, p. 171–172
174 Marijnissen 2003, p. 308
175 Quoted in Glück 1932, p. 58
176 Franck 1995, pp. 123–150
177 Emblemata 1996, pp. 270–271
178 Ferber 1966
179 Michels 1988
180 Stechow 1974, p. 107
181 Kaschek 2012, pp. 275–284
182 Bauer 1984, pp. 145–150
183 Kaschek 2012, pp. 15–17
184 Boström 1949, pp. 77–79
185 Tolnay 1952, p. 77
186 Rahner 1992, p. 267
187 Ibid., p. 228
188 Milla-Villena 1980, pp. 188–195
189 Brant 2012, pp. 130–131
190 Ibid., p. 132
191 Stridbeck 1956, p. 285
192 Franck 1995, p. 347
193 Müller 2011a
194 Marijnissen 2003, p. 333–334
195 Silver 2011, pp. 365–366
196 Frank 1991
197 Ibid., pp. 312–315
198 Glück 1932, pp. 59
199 Tolnay 1935, p. 48
200 Stridbeck 1956, p. 213
201 Marijnissen 2003, p. 356
202 Ibid., p. 360
203 Tolnay 1935, p. 46
204 Sullivan 1992, pp. 143–162
205 Würtenberger 1957, p. 145
206 Tolnay 1935, p. 47
207 Trudzinski 1984, pp. 63–116
208 Marijnissen 2003, p. 365
209 Sedlmayr 1962, p. 17

Bibliography

Domenique Allart: "La chute d'Icare des Musées royaux des Beaux-Arts de Belgique à Bruxelles", in: *Art & Fact* 15/1996, pp. 104–107.

Erich Auerbach: *Literatursprache und Publikum in der lateinischen Spätantike und im Mittelalter*, Bern 1958.

Erich Auerbach: *Mimesis. Dargestellte Wirklichkeit in der abendländischen Literatur*, Bern/Stuttgart ⁸1988.

Cornelis Augustijn/Theo Parmentier: "Sebastian Franck in den nördlichen Niederlanden 1550–1600", in: *Sebastian Franck (1499–1542)*, ed. by Jan-Dirk Müller, Wiesbaden 1993 (= Wolfenbütteler Forschungen 56), pp. 303–318.

Roland H. Bainton: *Erasmus. Reformer zwischen den Fronten*, translated by Elisabeth Langerbeck, Göttingen 1972.

Ludwig von Baldass: "Die niederländische Landschaftsmalerei von Patinir bis Bruegel", in: *Jahrbuch der Kunsthistorischen Sammlungen des Allerhöchsten Kaiserhauses* 34/1918, pp. 111–157.

W. Balke: "De invloed van de Anabaptisten te Antwerpen", in: *Bijdragen tot de geschiedenis* 70/1987, pp. 39–60.

Claudia Banz: *Höfisches Mäzenatentum in Brüssel. Kardinal Antoine Perrenot de Granvelle (1517–1586) und die Erzherzöge Albrecht (1559–1621) und Isabella (1566–1633)*, Berlin 2000 (= Berliner Schriften zur Kunst 12).

George Bauer/Linda Bauer: "The Winter Landscape with Skaters and Bird Trap by Pieter Bruegel the Elder", in: *The Art Bulletin* 66/1984, pp. 145–150.

Matthias Bauer: *Im Fuchsbau der Geschichten. Anatomie des Schelmenromans*, Stuttgart/Weimar 1993.

Bruno Becker: "Nederlandsche vertalingen van Sebastiaan Franck's geschriften", in: *Nederlands Archief voor Kerkgschiedenis* 21/1928, pp. 149–160.

Jan Baptist Bedaux/Alexander van Gool: "Bruegel's Birthyear. Motive of an Ars/Natura Transmutation", in: *Simiolus* 7/1974, pp. 133–156.

Peter Bell: "Alltägliches im Ereignis – Fremdes im Eigenen. Zigeunergenre bei Burgkmair, van Leyden und Bruegel", in: Birgit Ulrike Münch/Jürgen Müller (eds.): *Peiraikos' Erben. Die Genese der Genremalerei bis 1550*, Wiesbaden 2015 (= Trierer Beiträge zu den Historischen Kulturwissenschaften 14), pp. 247–264.

Pieter Bruegel d. Ä. als Zeichner. Herkunft und Nachfolge, exh. cat. Kupferstichkabinett, Staatliche Museen zu Berlin, ed. Hans Mielke/Konrad Renger (and others), Berlin 1975.

Uta Bernsmeier: *Die Nova Reperta des Jan van der Straet. Ein Beitrag zur Problemgeschichte der Entdeckungen und Erfindungen im 16. Jahrhundert*, Hamburg 1986 (= Dissertation Hamburg University 1984).

Peter G. Bietenholz: *Encounters with a Radical Erasmus. Erasmus' Works as a Source of Radical Thought in Early Modern Europe*, London 2009.

Björn Blauensteiner: "'Wer bauen will, der schlag erst an, was ihn der Bau wohl kosten kann'. Sebastian Brant, Frans Floris und der Wiener 'Turmbau zu Babel' von Pieter Bruegel d. Ä.", in: *Frühneuzeit-Info* 25/2014, no. 1/2, pp. 173–185.

Kjell Boström: "Das Sprichwort vom Vogelnest", in: *Konsthistorisk Tidskrift* 19/1949, pp. 77–89.

Sebastian Brant: *Das Narrenschiff*, ed. Hans-Joachim Mähl, translated by H. A. Junghans, Stuttgart 2012 (¹1962).

Iain Buchanan: "The Collection of Niclaes Jongelinck: II. The 'Months' by Pieter Bruegel the Elder", in: *The Burlington Magazine* 132/1990, pp. 541–550.

Nils Büttner: "'Quid siculas sequeris per mille pericula terras?'. Ein Beitrag zur Biographie Pieter Bruegels d. Ä. und zur Kulturgeschichte der niederländischen Italienreise", in: *Marburger Jahrbuch für Kunstwissenschaft* 27/2000, pp. 209–242.

Nils Büttner: "Chorographia quid? Oder: warum man Sprichwörter und Kinderspiele malt", in: Natalia Filatkina/Birgit Ulrike Münch/Ane Kleine-Engel (eds): *Formelhaftigkeit in Text und Bild*, Wiesbaden 2012 (= Trierer Bei-träge zu den Historischen Kulturwissenschaften 2), pp. 197–222.

Gerta Calman: "The picture of Nobody", in: *Journal of the Warburg and Courtauld Institutes* 23/1960, pp. 60–104.

John A. Canuteson: "The imagery of the Passion and of carnality in the Battle between Carnival and Lent by Pieter Bruegel the Elder",

in: *Studies in Iconography*
13/1989/90, pp. 191–221.

Jozef de Coo: *Museum Mayer van den Bergh*. Museum catalogue, vol. 1: *Schilderijen, verluchte handschriften, tekeningen*, Antwerp ³1978.

Luca d'Ascia: *Erasmo e l'Umanesimo romano*, Florence 1991.

Martin Davies: *National Gallery Catalogues: Early Netherlandish School*, London ³1968.

Klaus Demus: *Flämische Malerei von Jan Van Eyck bis Pieter Bruegel d. Ä.*, Katalog der Gemäldegalerie, Kunsthistorisches Museum, Vienna 1981.

Max Dvořák: *Die Gemälde Pieter Bruegels des Älteren*, with an introduction by Max Dvořák, Vienna 1941 (¹1921).

Emblemata. Handbuch zur Sinnbildkunst des XVI. und XVII. Jahrhunderts, ed. Arthur Henkel/Albrecht Schöne, Stuttgart/Weimar 1996.

Erasmus von Rotterdam: *Epistola ad Paulum Volzium = Brief an Paul Volz. Enchiridion militis christiani = Handbüchlein eines christlichen Streiters*, in: ibid.: *Ausgewählte Schriften*, 8 vols., Latin/German, ed. Werner Welzig, vol. 1, Darmstadt 1995.

Erasmus von Rotterdam: *Der Ciceronianer oder der beste Stil, ein Dialog*, in: ibid.: *Ausgewählte Schriften*, 8 vols., Latin/German, ed. Werner Welzig, vol. 7, Darmstadt 1995.

Klaus Ertz: *Pieter Brueghel der Jüngere (1564–1637/1638). Die Gemälde mit kritischem Œuvrekatalog*, 2 vols., Lingen 1988/2000.

Reindert Leonard Falkenburg: "Pieter Bruegels Kruisdraging.

Een proeve van 'close-reading'", in: *Oud-Holland* 107/1993, pp. 17–33.

Reindert Leonard Falkenburg: "Pieter Bruegel's Series of the Seasons. On the perception of Divine order", in: Joost van der Auwera (ed.): *Liber amicorum Raphaël de Smedt*, Louvain 2001, pp. 253–276.

Heinold Fast (ed.): *Der linke Flügel der Reformation. Glaubenszeugnisse der Täufer, Spiritualisten, Schwärmer und Antitrinitarier*, Bremen 1962.

Stanley Ferber: "Pieter Bruegel and the Duke of Alva", in: *Renaissance News* 9/1966, pp. 205–219.

Wilhelm Fraenger: *Das Bild der "Niederländischen Sprichwörter". Pieter Bruegels verkehrte Welt*, Amsterdam 2008.

Sebastian Franck: *Paradoxa*, ed. Siegfried Wollgast, Berlin ²1995.

Ross H. Frank: "An Interpretation of 'Land of Cockaigne' (1567) by Pieter Bruegel the Elder", in: *The Sixteenth Century Journal* 22/1991, no. 2, pp. 299–329.

David Freedberg: *Allusion and Topicality in the Work of Pieter Bruegel: The Implications of a Forgotten Polemic*, in: *The Prints of Pieter Bruegel the Elder*, exh. cat. Bridgestone Museum of Art, Tokyo 1989, pp. 53–65.

Pieter Geyl: *The Revolt of the Netherlands, 1555–1609*, New York 1966.

Walter S. Gibson: *Bruegel*, London 1977.

Walter S. Gibson: *Mirror of the Earth: The World Landscape in Sixteenth-Century Flemish Painting*, Princeton 1989.

Walter S. Gibson: *Pieter Bruegel the Elder. Two studies*, Lawrence 1991 (= The Franklin D. Murphy lectures 11).

Walter S. Gibson: *Pieter Bruegel and the Art of Laughter*, Berkeley (etc.) 2006.

Gustav Glück: "A newly discovered painting by Brueghel the Elder", in: *The Burlington Magazine* 56/1930, pp. 284–286.

Gustav Glück: *Bruegels Gemälde*, Vienna 1932.

Claudia Goldstein: "Artifacts of Domestic Life. Bruegel's Paintings in the Flemish Home", in: *Nederlands Kunsthistorisch Jaarboek* 51/2000 (2001), pp. 172–193.

Jan Grauls: *Volkstaal en Volksleven in het werk van Pieter Bruegel*, Antwerp 1957.

Joseph F. Gregory: "Toward the Contextualization of Pieter Bruegel's Procession to Calvary. Constructing the Beholder from within the Eyckian Tradition", in: *Nederlands Kunsthistorisch Jaarboek* 47/1996 (1997), pp. 206–221.

Rainald Grosshans: *Pieter Bruegel d. Ä. Die niederländischen Sprichwörter*, Berlin 2003.

Fritz Grossmann: "Bruegel's 'Woman Taken in Adultery' and other grisailles", in: *The Burlington Magazine* 94/1952, pp. 218–229.

Fritz Grossmann: "Brueghels Verhältnis zu Raffael und zur Raffael-Nachfolge", in: Martin Gosebruch (ed.): *Festschrift Kurt Badt zum siebzigsten Geburtstage. Beiträge aus Kunst- und Geistesgeschichte*, Berlin 1961, pp. 135–143.

Fritz Grossmann: *Bruegel. Die Gemälde*, Cologne ²1966.

Fritz Grossmann: *Bruegel: Complete edition of the paintings*, London 1973.

Craig Harbison: *The Last Judgement in Sixteenth Century Northern Europe: A Study of the Relation between Art and the Reformation*, New York 1976.

Jason Harris: "The Religious Position of Abraham Ortelius", in: Arie-Jan Gelderblom/Jan L. de Jong/Marc van Vaeck (eds): *The Low Countries as a Crossroads of Religious Beliefs*, Leyden 2004, pp. 89–140.

Ursula Alice Härting: "'Werke der Barmherzigkeit'. Zu einem Gemälde Pieter Brueghels II. im Deutschen Brotmuseum Ulm", in: *Nederlands Kunsthistorisch Jaarboek* 47/1996 (1997), pp. 106–123.

Priscilla Hayden-Roy: "Hermeneutica gloriae vs. hermeneutica crucis: Sebastian Franck and Martin Luther on the Clarity of Scripture", in: *Archiv für Reformationsgeschichte* 81/1990, pp. 50–68.

Inge Herold: *Pieter Bruegel der Ältere. Die Jahreszeiten*, Munich (etc.) 2002.

Jeanette Hills: *Das Kinderspiel von Pieter Bruegel d. Ä. (1560). Eine volkskundliche Untersuchung*, Vienna 1998.

Klaus Irle: *Der Ruhm der Bienen. Das Nachahmungsprinzip der italienischen Malerei von Raffael bis Rubens*, Münster 1997.

Horst Woldemar Janson: *Apes and Ape Lore in the Middle Ages and the Renaissance*, London 1952 (= Studies of the Warburg Institute 20).

Gotthard Jedlicka: *Pieter Bruegel*, Zurich 1938.

Eddy de Jongh: "Erotica in vogelperspectief. De dubbelzinnigheid van een reeks zeventiende-eeuwse genrevoorstellingen", in: *Simiolus* 3/1968/69, no. 1, pp. 22–74.

Sten Karling: "The Attack by Pieter Bruegel the Elder in the Collection of the Stockholm University", in: *Konsthistorisk tidskrift* 45/1976, no. 1–4, pp. 1–18.

Bertram Kaschek: "Gottes Werk und Bruegels Beitrag. Zur Deutung der Landschaftsgraphik Pieter Bruegels d. Ä.", in: *Bruegel invenit. Das druckgraphische Werk, Hamburger Kunsthalle*, ed. by Jürgen Müller/Uwe M. Schneede, Hamburg 2001, pp. 31–37.

Bertram Kaschek: "Bruegel in Prag. Anmerkungen zur Rezeption Pieter Bruegels d. Ä. um 1600", in: *Rudolphina* 7/2007, pp. 44–58.

Bertram Kaschek: "'Weder römisch, noch antik?' Pieter Bruegels 'Verleumdung des Apelles' in neuer Deutung", in: Gernot Kamecke (ed.): *Antike als Konzept: Lesarten in Kunst, Literatur und Politik*, Berlin 2009, pp. 167–179.

Bertram Kaschek: *Weltzeit und Endzeit. Die "Monatsbilder" Pieter Bruegels d. Ä.*, Munich 2012.

Bertram Kaschek: "Landschaft als theatrum. Zum graphischen Frühwerk Pieter Bruegels d. Ä.", in: Mössinger/Müller 2014, pp. 47–59.

Ethan Matt Kavaler: *Pieter Bruegel: Parables of Order and Enterprise*, Cambridge, UK (etc.) 1999.

Karl Kilinski: "Bruegel on Icarus: Inversions of the Fall", in: *Zeitschrift für Kunstgeschichte* 67/2004, pp. 91–114.

Johann-Christian Klamt: "Anmerkungen zu Pieter Bruegels Babel-Darstellungen", in: Otto von Simson/Matthias Winner (eds): *Pieter Bruegel und seine Welt*, Berlin 1979, pp. 43–49.

Arthur Klein: *Graphic Worlds of Peter Bruegel the Elder*, New York 1963.

Léopold Kockaert: "La Chute d'Icare au Laboratoire", in: *Nuances* 31/2003, pp. 19–21.

Barbara Könneker: *Satire im 16. Jahrhundert. Epoche –Werke – Wirkung*, Munich 1991.

Otto Langer: "Inneres Wort und inwohnender Christus. Zum mystischen Spiritualismus Sebastian Francks und seinen Implikationen", in: *Sebastian Franck (1499–1542)*, ed. Jan-Dirk Müller, Wiesbaden 1993 (= Wolfenbütteler Forschungen 56), pp. 55–69.

Louis Lebeer: *Beredeneerde catalogus van de prenten naar Pieter Bruegel de Oude*, Brussels 1969.

Raymond Lebègue: "Rabelais, the last of the French Erasmisans", in: *Rabelais*, ed. August Buck, Darmstadt 1973 (= Wege der Forschung 284), pp. 136–166.

Die Legenda aurea des Jacobus de Voragine, translated by Richard Benz, Heidelberg ⁹1979.

Longinus: *Vom Erhabenen*. Greek and German, translated and ed. by Otto Schönberger, Stuttgart 1988.

Heidrun Ludwig: "Pieter Bruegels Elster auf dem Galgen. Forschungsgeschichte und Bibliographie", in: *Kunst in Hessen und am Mittelrhein* 7/2012, pp. 49–65.

Brueghel Enterprises, exh. cat. Bonnefantenmuseum, Maastricht/Musées royaux des Beaux-Arts de Belgique, Brussels, ed. Peter van den Brink, Ghent/Amsterdam 2001.

Claudine Majzels: "'The man with the three feet' in Pieter Bruegel the Elder's Peasant Wedding", in: *Racar* 27/2003, no. 1/2, pp. 46–58.

Karel van Mander: *Das Lehrgedicht des Karel van Mander*. Text, translation and commentary with an appendix by Rudolf Hoecker, The Hague 1916 (= Quellenstudien zur holländischen Kunstgeschichte 8).

Carel van Mander: *Das Leben der niederländischen und deutschen Maler (von 1400 bis ca. 1615)*, translated by Hanns Floerke, Worms 1991.

Heinz Herbert Mann: "Überlegungen zum Thema 'Zeit' bei Pieter Bruegel d. Ä.", in: Christian W. Thomsen/Hans Holländer (eds): *Augenblick und Zeitpunkt. Studien zur Zeitstruktur und Zeitmetaphorik in Kunst und Wissenschaft*, Darmstadt 1984, pp. 198–207.

Stephen A. Mansbach: "Pieter Bruegel's Tower of Babel", in: *Zeitschrift für Kunstgeschichte* 45/1982, pp. 43–56.

Roger H. Marijnissen: *Bruegel. Tout l'œuvre peint et dessiné*, Antwerp 1988.

Roger H. Marijnissen: *Bruegel. Das vollständige Werk*, Cologne 2003.

Roger H. Marijnissen/Max Seidel: *Pieter Bruegel*, Stuttgart 1969.

Guido Marnef: *Antwerp in the Age of Reformation. Underground Protestantism in a Commercial Metropolis, 1550–1577*, Baltimore/London 1996.

Mark A. Meadow: "Bruegel's 'Procession to Calvary'. Aemulatio and the Space of Vernacular Style", in: *Nederlands Kunsthistorisch Jaarboek* 47/1996 (1997), pp. 181–205.

Mark A. Meadow: *Pieter Bruegel the Elder's Netherlandish Proverbs and the Practice of Rhetoric*, Zwolle 2002 (= Studies in Netherlandish Art and Cultural History 4).

Tine Meganck: *Pieter Bruegel the Elder, Fall of the rebel angels. Art, Knowledge and Politics on the Eve of the Dutch Revolt*, Milan 2014 (= Les cahiers des Musées royaux des Beaux-Arts de Belgique 16).

Walter S. Melion: "'Ego enim quasi obdormivi'. Salvation and Blessed Sleep in Philip Galle's Death of the Virgin after Pieter Bruegel", in: *Nederlands Kunsthistorisch Jaarboek* 47/1996 (1997), pp. 14–53.

Édouard Michel: *Bruegel*, Paris 1931.

Norbert Michels: *Bewegung zwischen Ethos und Pathos. Zur Wirkungsästhetik italienischer Kunsttheorie des 15. und 16. Jahrhunderts*, Münster 1988 (= Kunstgeschichte, Form und Interesse 11).

Wolfgang Mieder (ed.): *The Netherlandish Proverbs: An International Symposium on the Pieter Brueg(h)els*, Burlington 2004.

Wolfgang Mieder: "'One Picture that's Worth More than a Thousand Words'. Pieter Bruegel the Elder's Netherlandish Proverbs, Past and Present", in: ibid. (ed.): *Netherlandish Proverbs*, Burlington 2004.

Rodolfo Milla-Villena: "Deux moralités de Pieter Breugel l'Ancien à l'époque de la montée du calvinisme aux Pays-Bas", in: *Bulletin de l'Association d'étude sur l'humanisme, la réforme et la renaissance* 11/1980, no. 2, pp. 188–201.

Ingrid Mössinger/Jürgen Müller (eds.): *Pieter Bruegel d. Ä. und das Theater der Welt*, exh. cat. Kunstsammlungen Chemnitz, Berlin 2014.

Nicolette Mout: "The Family of Love (Huis der Liefde) and the Dutch Revolt", in: A. C. Duke/C. A. Tamse: *Britain and the Netherlands*, vol. 8: *Church and State since the Reformation*, The Hague 1981, pp. 76–93.

Jürgen Müller: "'Pieter der Drollige' oder der Mythos vom Bauern-Bruegel", in: Klaus Ertz (ed.): *Pieter Breughel der Jüngere, Jan Brueghel der Ältere. Flämische Malerei um 1600*, Lingen 1997, pp. 42–53.

Jürgen Müller: *Das Paradox als Bildform. Studien zur Ikonologie Pieter Bruegels d. Ä.*, Munich 1999.

Jürgen Müller: "Gefangene der Wörtlichkeit. Das Rätsel von Pieter Bruegels 'Sprichwörtern'", in: *Kunsthistorische Arbeitsblätter* 12/2000, pp. 29–36.

Jürgen Müller: "Bild und Zeit. Überlegungen zur Zeitgestalt von Pieter Bruegels 'Bauern-hochzeitsmahl'", in: Götz Pochat/Brigitte Werner (eds): *Erzählte Zeit und Gedächtnis. Narrative Strukturen und das Problem der Sinnstiftung im Denkmal*, Graz 2005 (= Kunsthistorisches Jahrbuch Graz 29/30), pp. 72–81.

Jürgen Müller: "Spuren im Schnee. Anmerkungen zu zwei 'Winter-bildern' Pieter Bruegels d. Ä.", in: Kirsten Kramer/Jens Baumgarten (eds): *Visualisierung und visueller Transfer*, Würzburg 2009.

Jürgen Müller: "Ein anderer Laokoon. Die Geburt ästhetischer Subversion aus dem Geist der Reformation", in: Beate Kellner (and others; eds): *Erzählen und Episteme. Literatur im 16. Jahrhundert*, Berlin (etc.)

2011, pp. 389–414 and ill. pp. 436–455.

Jürgen Müller: "Of churches, heretics, and other guides of the blind. *The Fall of the Blind Leading the Blind* by Pieter Bruegel the Elder and the esthetics of subversion", in: Walter S. Melion/ James Clifton/Michel Weemans (eds): *Imago exegetica. Visual images as exegetical instruments, 1400–1700*, Leiden (etc.) 2014, pp. 737–790.

Jürgen Müller/Thomas Schauerte: *Pieter Bruegel. The Complete Works*, Cologne 2018.

Edgar Munhall: "The Frick's Brueghel", in: *Apollo* 83/1966, p. 393.

Jan Muylle: "Pieter Bruegel en de kunsttheorie. Een interpretatie van de tekeningen 'De Schilder voor zijn Ezel': ideëel zelfportret en artistiek credo", in: *Jaarboek van her Koninklijk Museum voor Schone Künsten Antwerpen* 1984, pp. 189–202.

From Van Eyck to Bruegel: Early Netherlandish Painting in The Metropolitan Museum of Art, exh. cat. The Metropolitan Museum of Art, New York, ed. Maryan W. Ainswirth/Keith Christiansen, New York 1998.

Amy Orrock: "Homo ludens. Pieter Bruegel's Children Games and the Humanist Educators", in: *Journal of Historians of Netherlandish Art* 4/2012, no. 2, pp. 1–20.

Abraham Ortelius. Album Amicorum, ed. Jean Puraye, Amsterdam 1969.

Anna Pawlak: "Künstlerruhm und Konfession. Das Grabmal Pieter Bruegels d. Ä. in der Notre Dame de la Chapelle in Brüssel", in: Birgit Ulrike Münch/Markwart Herzog/Andreas Tacke (eds): *Künstlergrabmäler. Genese*

– *Typologie – Intention – Metamorphose*, Petersburg 2011, pp. 80–96.

Anna Pawlak: *Trilogie der Gottessuche. Pieter Bruegels d. Ä. "Sturz der gefallenen Engel", "Triumph des Todes" und "Dulle Griet"*, Berlin 2011.

Dirk Philips: *Enchirdion: oder Handbüchlein von der Christlichen lehre und religion zum dienst von allen liebhabern der Wahreit (durch die Gnade Gottes) aus der Heiligen Schrift gemacht, mit einem schönen und fasslichen register*, Lancaster, PA, 1811.

Yona Pinson: "Bruegel's 1564 Adoration. Hidden meanings of evil in the figure of the old king", in: *Artibus et historiae* 30/1994, pp. 109–127.

Cajus Plinius Secundus the Elder: *Naturkunde. Naturalis Historiae*, Latin/German, ed. and translated by Roderich König in cooperation with Gerhard Winkler, 37 vols., Darmstadt 1973–1993.

Erwin Pokorny: "The Gypsies and their impact on fifteenth-century Western European iconography", in: *Crossing Cultures. Conflict – Migration – Convergence. Proceedings of the 32nd International Congress in the History of Art*, ed. by Jaynie Anderson, Melbourne 2009, pp. 579–601.

Rudolf Preimesberger: "Zu Jan van Eycks Diptychon der Sammlung Thyssen-Bornemisza", in: *Zeitschrift für Kunstgeschichte* 60/1991, pp. 459–489.

Hugo Rahner: *Symbole der Kirche. Die Ekklesiologie der Väter*, Salzburg 1964.

Hugo Rahner: *Griechische Mythen in christlicher Deutung*, Freiburg/ Basel/Vienna 1992.

Hans-Joachim Raupp: *Bauernsatiren. Entstehung und Entwick-*

lung des bäuerlichen Genres in der deutschen und niederländischen Kunst, ca. 1470–1570, Niederzier 1986.

Mariantonia Reinhard-Felice (ed.): *Sammlung Oskar Reinhart "Am Römerholz" Winterthur.* Catalogue raisonné, Basel 2003

Todd M. Richardson: *Pieter Bruegel the Elder: Art Discourse in the Sixteenth Century Netherlands*, Farnham 2011.

Philippe Roberts-Jones/Françoise Roberts Jones: *Pieter Bruegel*, New York 2002.

Philippe Roberts-Jones: "Bruegel invenit. La Chute d'Icare: mise au point et controverse", in: *Bulletin de la Classe des Beaux-Arts/Académie Royale de Belgique* 17/2006, no. 1/6, pp. 179–189.

Franz Roh: *Pieter Bruegel d. Ä. Die niederländischen Sprichwörter*, Stuttgart 1960.

Petra Roettig: "'Bruegel invenit' – 'Cock excudit'. Pieter Bruegel d. Ä. und sein Verleger Hieronymus Cock", in: *Bruegel invenit. Das druckgraphische Werk, Hamburger Kunsthalle*, ed. by Jürgen Müller/Uwe M. Schneede, Hamburg 2001, pp. 22–30.

Thomas Schauerte: "Schiffe", in: Mössinger/Müller 2014, pp. 253–281.

Ernst Scheyer: "'The Wedding Dance' by Pieter Bruegel the Elder in the Detroit Institute of Arts, its relation and derivations", in: *The art quarterly* (Detroit) 28/1965, no. 3, pp. 167–193.

Norbert Schneider: *Von Bosch zu Bruegel. Niederländische Malerei im Zeitalter von Humanismus und Reformation*, Berlin/Münster 2015 (= Karlsruher Schriften zur Kunstgeschichte 10).

Curtis R. Scott: *Paintings from Europe and the Americas in the Philadelphia Museum of Art:*

A concise catalogue, Philadelphia 1994.

Hans Sedlmayr: "Pieter Bruegel. Der Sturz der Blinden", in: *Hefte des Kunsthistorischen Seminars der Universität München 7/8*, 1962, pp. 5–22.

Wilfried Seipel (ed.): *Pieter Bruegel the Elder at the Kunsthistorisches Museum in Vienna*, Milan 1998.

Manfred Sellink: *Bruegel, het volledige werk. Schilderijen, tekeningen, prenten*, Ghent 2011.

Manfred Sellink: *Pieter Bruegel ongezien! De verborgen Antwerpse collecties*, Louvain 2012.

Larry Silver: *Peasant Scenes and Landscapes. The rise of Pictorial Genres in the Antwerp Art Market*, Philadelphia 2006.

Larry Silver: *Pieter Bruegel*, New York/London 2011.

Edward A. Snow: *Bruegel Inside. The Play of Images in Children's Games*, New York 1997.

Wolfgang Stechow: *Pieter Bruegel the Elder*, New York 1969.

Wolfgang Stechow: *Pieter Bruegel*, Cologne 1974.

Carl Gustav Stridbeck: *Bruegelstudien. Untersuchungen zu den ikonologischen Problemen bei Pieter Bruegel d. Ä. sowie dessen Beziehungen zum niederländischen Romanismus*, Stockholm 1956.

Margaret A. Sullivan: "Pieter Bruegel the Elder's Two Monkeys: A new interpretation", in: *The Art Bulletin 63/1981*, pp. 114–126.

Margaret Sullivan: "Bruegel's Proverbs: Art and Audience in the Northern Renaissance", in: *The Art Bulletin 73/1991*, no. 3, pp. 431–466.

Margaret A. Sullivan: "Bruegel's Misanthrope: Renaissance Art For A Humanist Audience", in: *Artibus et Historiae 26/1992*, XIII, pp. 143–162.

Margaret A. Sullivan: *Bruegel's Peasants: Art and Audience in the Northern Renaissance*, New York 1994.

Karl von Tolnai: *Die Zeichnungen Pieter Bruegels*, Munich 1925.

Karl von Tolnai: "Studien zu den Gemälden P. Bruegels d. Ä.", in: *Jahrbuch der Kunsthistorischen Sammlungen in Wien*, N. F. 8/1934, pp. 105–136.

Charles de Tolnay: *Pierre Bruegel L'Ancien*, 2 vols., Brussels 1935.

Charles de Tolnay: *Die Zeichnungen Pieter Bruegels*, Zurich ²1952.

Meinolf Trudzinski: "Von Holbein zu Brueghel. 'Christus vera lux, philosophi et papa in foveam cadentes'", in: *Niederdeutsche Beiträge zur Kunstgeschichte 23/1984*, pp. 63–116.

René van Bastelaer/G. Hulin de Loo: *Pieter Bruegel l'ancien, son œuvre et son temps*, Brussels 1907.

Jean-Pierre Vanden Branden: "Les jeux d'enfants de Pierre Bruegel", in: *Les Jeux à la Renaissance. Études réunies par Philippe Ariès et J.-C. Margolin*, Paris 1982, pp. 499–524.

Mark van Strydonck (and others): "Radiocarbon Dating of Canvas Paintings: Two Case Studies", in: *Studies in Conservation 43/1998*, pp. 209–214.

Pierre Vinken: "Pieter Bruegels Nestrover en de mens die de dood tegemoet treedt", in: *Nederlands Kunsthistorisch Jaarboek 47/1996 (1997)*, pp. 54–79.

Christian Vöhringer: *Pieter Bruegels d. Ä. Landschaft mit pflügendem Bauern und Ikarussturz. Mythenkritik und Kalendermotiv im 16. Jahrhundert*, Munich 2002.

Lyckle de Vries: "Bruegel's 'Fall of Icarus'. Ovid or Solomon?", in: *Simiolus 30/2003*, no. 1/2, pp. 4–18.

Andreas Wagner: *Das Falsche der Religionen bei Sebastian Franck. Zur gesellschaftlichen Bedeutung des Spiritualismus der radikalen Reformation*, Berlin 2007.

Carsten-Peter Warncke: *Sprechende Bilder – sichtbare Worte. Das Bildverständnis in der Frühen Neuzeit*, Wiesbaden 1987 (= Wolfenbütteler Forschungen 33).

Nina Weibull: "The Assault. A Bruegel Painting in the Stockholm University Collection of Paintings", in: *Proceedings/Estonian Academy of Arts 6/1999*, pp. 94–102.

Annabella Weismann: "Was hört und sieht der Dudelsackpfeifer auf der Bauernhochzeit? Bemerkungen über ein allzu bekanntes Gemälde von Pieter Bruegel", in: Dietmar Kamper/ Christoph Wulf (eds): *Schweigen. Unterbrechung und Grenze der menschlichen Wirklichkeit*, Berlin 1992 (= Historische Anthropologie vol. 18.), pp. 225–245.

Annabella Weismann: *Golgatha. Vergangenheit mit Jetztzeit geladen*, Kampen 1992, p. 23.

Annabella Weismann: *Pieter Bruegel d. Ä.*, Reinbek bei Hamburg 2015.

Franzsepp Würtenberger: *Pieter Bruegel d. Ä. und die deutsche Kunst*, Wiesbaden 1957.

Beat Wyss: "Der Dolch am linken Bildrand. Zur Interpretation von Pieter Bruegels Landschaft mit dem Sturz des Ikarus", in: *Zeitschrift für Kunstgeschichte 51/1988*, pp. 222–242.

Beat Wyss: *Pieter Bruegel. Landschaft mit Ikarussturz. Ein Vexierbild des humanistischen Pessimismus*, Frankfurt am Main 1990.

Perez Zagorin: "Looking for Pieter Bruegel", in: *Journal of the History of Ideas 64/2003*, pp. 73–96.

Index

Index of Works by Pieter Bruegel the Elder

Copper Engravings

Drawings

Photo credits

The following abbreviations below stand for: t. = top,
t. l. = top left, t. r. = top right, b. = bottom, b. l. = bottom
left, b. r. = bottom right.

Agenzia Fotografica Scala, Florence: pp. 125, 233
Albertina, Vienna: pp. 15, 186–187, 227, 333
Archive of the publisher, the authors or collectors:
pp. 106
Bayerische Staatsbibliothek, Munich: pp. 113, 364, 365
bpk | Bayerische Staatsgemäldesammlungen: pp. 396–
397, 398, 469, 484
bpk | Gemäldegalerie, Staatliche Museen Berlin:
pp. 146–147, 434
bpk | Gemäldegalerie, Staatliche Museen Berlin |
Foto: Luciano Romano: pp. 88–90, 93–94, 96–97,
421
bpk | Kupferstichkabinett, SMB | Dietmar Katz:
pp. 91, 268–269, 360–361
bpk | The Metropolitan Museum of Art: pp. 260, 282,
302–303, 305, 451
The Cleveland Museum of Art: p. 369
Detroit Institute of Arts, USA / City of Detroit
Purchase / Bridgeman Images: pp. 276–277, 460
The Frick Collection, New York: pp. 232, 241, 244–
245, 486
Hessisches Landesmuseum Darmstadt: pp. 249, 272–
273, 482
Koninklijke Bibliotheek van België, Prentenkabinet:
pp. 180–181
Koninklijk Museum voor Schone Kunsten, Antwerp,
Belgium / © Lukas – Art in Flanders VZW /
Bridgeman Images: p. 189
© 2015 Kunsthaus Zurich: p. 287
Kunsthalle Bremen, Kupferstichkabinett: pp. 55
Kunsthistorisches Museum, Vienna: pp. 325, 426
Kunsthistorisches Museum, Vienna, Foto: Luciano
Romano: pp. 1–5, 18, 47, 48, 57, 60, 73, 76–77,
79–86, 98–99, 101, 130, 137, 139, 142–143, 145, 150–151,
153–156, 158–161, 162–163, 250, 255, 256, 263–264, 271,
274–275, 278–279, 289–291, 293, 294–295, 306–311,
313, 358, 370, 377–378, 387, 392–393, 394–395, 422,
424, 437, 442, 446, 453, 455, 467, 471, 473, 475, 512,
front cover
Kunstmuseum Basel, Kupferstichkabinett,
Amerbach-Kabinett: p. 381
The Lobkowicz Collections, Czech Republic: pp. 281,
297–298, 299, 300–301, 449, back cover

© The Metropolitan Museum of Art, New York:
pp. 22, 28–29, 32, 176–177, 190–191, 192–193, 328,
366, 373, 410–411
© Musée du Louvre, Dist. RMN-Grand Palais /
Gérard Blot: pp. 357, 400–401, 480;
Museo del Prado © Photo MNP/Scala, Florence:
pp. 121, 116, 171–172, 183–184, 194–202, 237, 429
Museo di Capodimonte, photo: Luciano Romano:
pp. 399, 402–403, 405–406, 476, 478
© Museum Boijmans Van Beuningen, Rotterdam:
pp. 64–65, 103–104, 115, 122, 129, 164–165, 438
Museum David and Alice van Buuren, Brussels:
p. 495
© Museum Mayer van den Bergh, Antwerp: pp. 6, 8,
13, 74–75, 204–206, 209, 419, 431
The National Gallery, London: pp. 117, 141, 445
Niedersächsische Staats- und Universitätsbibliothek,
Göttingen: p. 17
Philadelphia Museum of Art, Sammlung John G.
Johnson: p. 489
The Putnam Foundation, Timken Museum of Art,
San Diego, USA / Bridgeman Images: pp. 42–43,
417–418
© Rijksmuseum, Amsterdam: pp. 24, 27, 34, 51, 58,
68–71, 109, 126, 133, 134, 136, 230, 235, 238, 383
Royal Collection Trust / © Her Majesty Queen
Elizabeth II 2018: pp. 350–352, 355, 465
© Royal Museums of Fine Arts of Belgium, Brussels /
image by Google: pp. 210–211, 212–219, 315–316, 321,
322, 331, 335, 342–343, 345–349, 427, 457, 462
© Royal Museums of Fine Arts of Belgium, Brussels:
pp. 492, 495
Oskar Reinhart Collection "Am Römerholz",
Winterthur: pp. 336–337, 339–340, 440
The Samuel Courtauld Trust, The Courtauld Gallery,
London: pp. 44–45, 212–222, 229, 242–243, 413–414,
435, 459
Soprintendenza Speciale per il Patrimonio Storico,
Artistico ed Etnoantropologico e per il Polo Museale
della città di Firenze, Gabinetto Fotografico: pp. 374
Stockholms Universitets Konstsamling: p. 487
Szépművészeti Múzeum, Budapest: pp. 19, 166–167,
169, 259, 464
© The Trustees of the British Museum. All rights
reserved: pp. 25, 37, 41, 224–225, 363, 388–389
Upton House © National Trust / Ruth Bubb:
pp. 246–247, 443

Acknowledgements

The publisher wishes to thank the museums, archives and institutions named in the illustration captions and photo sources for their friendly support of the publication. Numerous curators and collectors, likewise photographers and photographic agencies, have made a decisive contribution to the success of this project through their personal endeavours; we take the opportunity to thank them here by name: Iain Calderwood (The British Museum, London), Penelope Currier (The Frick Collection, New York), Louisa Dare (The Courtauld Institute of Art, London), Michel Draguet (Royal Museums of Fine Arts of Belgium, Brussels), Helmy Frank (Museum Boijmans Van Beuningen, Rotterdam), Sarah Goble (National Turst, Swindon), Ilse Jung (Kunsthistorisches Museum, Vienna), Ingrid Kastel (Grafische Sammlung Albertina, Vienna), Achim Kathan (Bridgeman Images, Berlin), Florence Le Bègue (Oskar Reinhart Collection, Winterthur), Katja Lehmann (Scala Picture Library, Florence), Franz Pichhorner (Kunsthistorisches Museum, Vienna), Virginie Rodriguez (Royal Museums of Fine Arts of Belgium, Brussels), Petr Slouka (The Lobkowicz Collections), Maria Stein (Staatliche Museen zu Berlin – Gemäldegalerie), Stephan Weppelmann (Kunsthistorisches Museum, Vienna), Astrid Winde (bpk, Berlin), Julie Zeftel (The Metropolitan Museum, New York). In particular our great thanks go to the photographer Luciano Romano (Grafiluce, Naples) for the superb photo campaign. We also wish to thank the lithographer Guiseppe Brisotto (Fotolito Brisotto, Tezze di Piave) for the excellent cooperation.

EACH AND EVERY TASCHEN BOOK PLANTS A SEED!

Project Management: Petra Lamers-Schütze, Cologne
Translation: Abigail Prohaska, Henndorf am Wallersee

Printed in Bosnia-Herzegovina
ISBN 978–3–8365–8096–0

Front cover and page 512
The Hunters in the Snow (Winter; also: **December/January**, or **The Return of the Hunters**; details), 1565
Oil on oak, 117 x 162 cm (46 ⅛ x 63 ¾ in.)
Vienna, Kunsthistorisches Museum, Gemäldegalerie

Back cover
The Hay Harvest (June/July; detail), 1565
Oil on wood, 114 x 158 cm (45 x 62 in.)
Prague, Palais Lobkowicz

Pages 1–5
The Procession to Calvary
(Christ Carrying the Cross; details), 1564
(see ill. pp. 142/143)

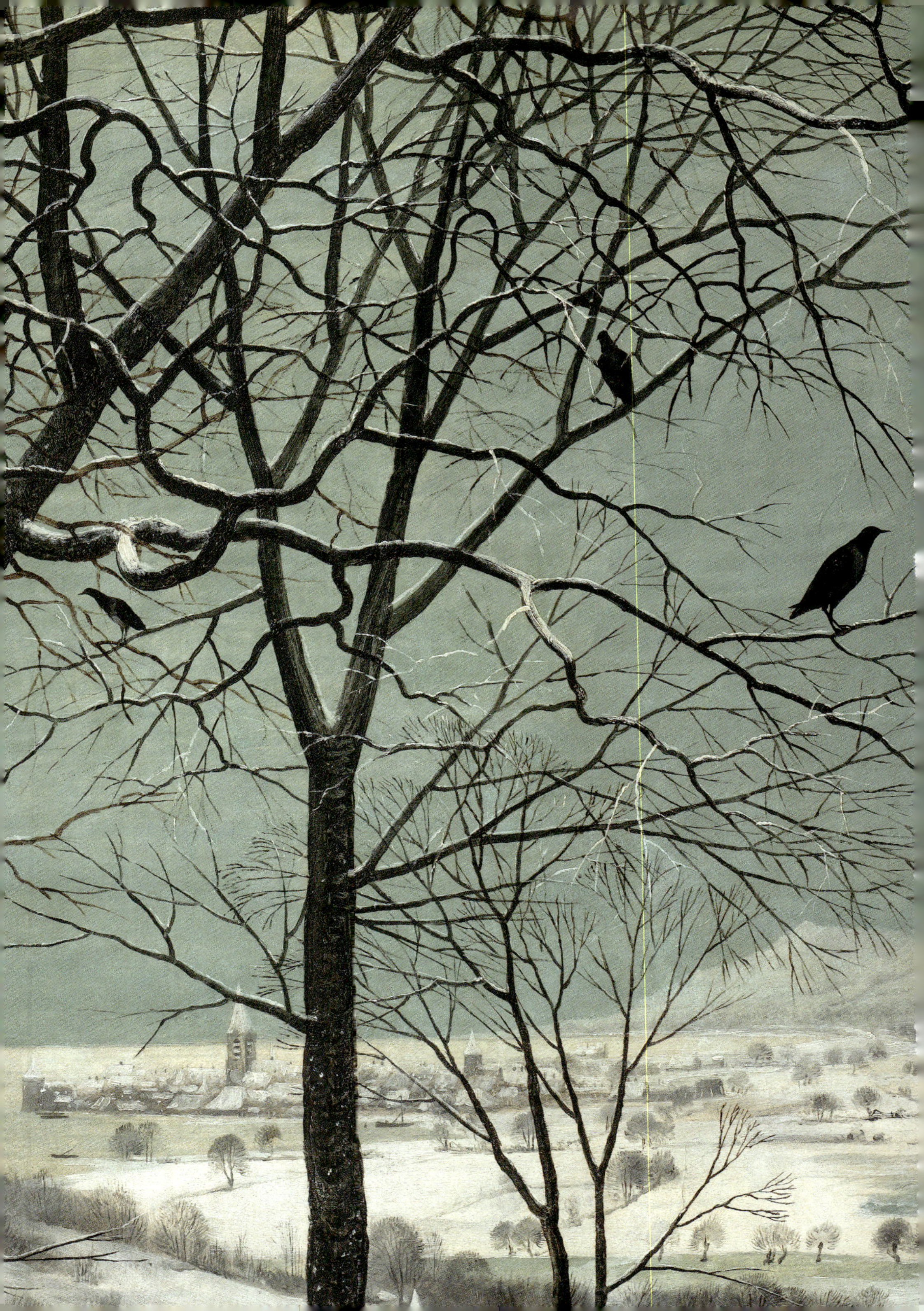